문법 10회

독해 10회

청취 5회

내 점수를 빠르고 확실하게 올려주니까!

3

내 예상 점수를
빠르고 정확하게 알려주는
무료 자동 채점 및 성적 분석 서비스

4

명쾌한 정·오답 해설로
내 점수를 확실하게 올려주는
약점 보완 해설집

해커스 지텔프 LEVEL 2 실전모의고사 독해 10회

200% 활용법

무료 지텔프 기출 단어암기장 (PDF)

해커스인강(HackersIngang.com) 접속 ▶
상단 메뉴의 [G-TELP → MP3/자료 → 무료 MP3/자료] 클릭 ▶
본 교재의 [지텔프 기출 단어암기장] 클릭하여 이용하기

[무료 MP3/자료]
바로가기 ▶

무료 자동 채점 및 성적 분석 서비스

교재 내 수록되어 있는 모의고사의 채점 및 성적 분석 서비스를 제공합니다.

[무료 자동 채점 및 성적 분석 서비스]
바로 이용하기 ▶

G-TELP 무료 학습 콘텐츠

지텔프 정답
실시간 확인

지텔프 단기 고득점
비법강의

해커스 지텔프
무료 모의고사

매일 지텔프
문법 풀기

이용방법 **해커스영어**(Hackers.co.kr) 접속 ▶ **[공무원/지텔프]** 메뉴 클릭하여 이용하기

* QR코드로 [해커스영어] 바로가기 ▶

해커스 지텔프 LEVEL 2 실전모의고사 독해 10회

문제집

실전모의고사 + 정답 한눈에 보기

(OMR 답안지 수록)

해커스 어학연구소

해커스 지텔프 LEVEL 2 실전모의고사 독해 10회

문제집

실전모의고사 + 정답 한눈에 보기

(OMR 답안지 수록)

해커스 어학연구소

실전완성

문제집

READING AND VOCABULARY SECTION

DIRECTIONS:

There are four passages in the Reading and Vocabulary Section. Comprehension and vocabulary questions follow each passage. Select the best answer from the four choices provided for each question. Then, fill in the correct circle on your answer sheet.

Read the following example passage and question.

Example:

Brenda Kenwood was born in Detroit. After finishing university in Los Angeles, she settled in San Francisco.

Where was Brenda Kenwood born?

(a) San Francisco
(b) Los Angeles
(c) London
(d) Detroit

As the correct answer is (d), the circle for this answer has been filled in.

ⓐ ⓑ ⓒ ●

TURN THE PAGE TO BEGIN
THE READING AND VOCABULARY SECTION

자동 채점 및 성적 분석 서비스 ▶

권장 시간: 40분

시작: ____ 시 ____ 분 ~ 종료: ____ 시 ____ 분

정답·해석·해설 p.126

***PART 1.** Read the biography article below and answer the questions. The two underlined words are for vocabulary questions.*

HANS ZIMMER

Hans Zimmer is a German music producer and composer known for scoring the soundtracks for over 150 Hollywood films. He is considered to have redefined modern film music by combining electronic music with traditional orchestra works to create new pieces.

Hans Florian Zimmer was born on September 12, 1957, in Frankfurt, Germany. He became interested in music at an early age and began taking piano lessons at only three years old. However, he quit after two weeks because he disliked the discipline of formal classes. The death of his father when he was six <u>prompted</u> Zimmer to turn to music to deal with his grief, and the same year, he decided to become a composer after falling in love with *Once Upon a Time in the West*, a blockbuster Western film directed by Sergio Leone. He focused so much of his attention on learning music on his own that he rarely did his schoolwork and was ultimately expelled from eight schools.

Zimmer's musical career began in the late 1970s when he moved to the UK and started playing music with bands and writing advertising jingles. He then cofounded a recording studio with the English film composer Stanley Myers in the 1980s. They created music for several acclaimed films, including *Moonlighting* and *My Beautiful Laundrette*.

His first true break came when Hollywood director Barry Levinson approached him. Levinson's wife had told him about a soundtrack CD that she had enjoyed. Interested, Levinson listened to the soundtrack himself before getting in touch with Zimmer, who had composed it. Levinson hired Zimmer to write the score for his 1988 film *Rain Man*, much of which featured songs performed on an electronic keyboard and steel drums. It also included pan pipes and female gospel vocals, making the soundtrack charming, unique, and ultimately unforgettable for its sense of style.

Zimmer's music had become a Hollywood staple by the early 1990s. However, it wasn't until the 1994 Disney film *The Lion King* that Zimmer enjoyed his biggest commercial success. *The Lion King* soundtrack won numerous awards including Zimmer's first Academy Award for Best Original Score. To this day, Zimmer is regarded as one of the <u>leading</u> film music composers of all time, and his signature style and talent are highly sought after by directors.

53. What is Hans Zimmer famous for?

(a) being a producer of popular Hollywood films
(b) hosting an electronic music festival
(c) conducting the Hollywood Orchestra
(d) creating a large amount of film music

54. Which is true about Hans Zimmer's childhood?

(a) He could not afford piano lessons.
(b) He received high grades in music classes.
(c) He could play multiple musical instruments.
(d) He was not suited to formal education.

55. When did Zimmer first become interested in being a composer?

(a) after being expelled from a number of schools
(b) after watching a popular movie
(c) when he was studying with Sergio Leone
(d) when he was taking care of his father

56. According to the article, what made Barry Levinson contact Zimmer?

(a) a prior working relationship with Stanley Myers
(b) a success of Zimmer's collaboration with Hollywood filmmakers
(c) a recommendation made by his spouse
(d) a soundtrack in his favorite film

57. What can most likely be said about *The Lion King*?

(a) It became the first animated film to win musical honors.
(b) It is the only Disney film that Zimmer has worked on.
(c) It brought Zimmer recognition from the public.
(d) It was nominated for more awards than it won.

58. In the context of the passage, <u>prompted</u> means __________.

(a) assisted
(b) motivated
(c) reminded
(d) persuaded

59. In the context of the passage, <u>leading</u> means __________.

(a) original
(b) famous
(c) best
(d) latest

PART 2. *Read the magazine article below and answer the questions. The two underlined words are for vocabulary questions.*

MILLENNIALS AND GENERATION Z EMBRACE SUSTAINABILITY

Studies have found that the younger generations—Millennials and Generation Z—are more socially and environmentally conscious than their older counterparts. This is particularly true when it comes to consumer behavior, with many actively forcing corporations to adopt sustainable practices.

Just like previous generations, the attitudes of Millennials and Generation Z have been profoundly influenced by major events occurring during their lifetime. For Millennials, it was the Great Recession of 2008. This event resulted from financial institutions engaging in high-risk, socially irresponsible lending practices. It made many people question whether the procedures of banks and lending institutions were ethical, especially since taking out high-interest student loans became necessary for a large number of Millennials.

For Generation Z, who not only grew up in the aftermath of the recession but watched as the pandemic shut down world economies, just how fragile the planet is was made very clear. As factories ceased production, and the smog lifted over the world's most polluted cities, people began to realize the extent to which the planet is being damaged. This inspired more intense environmental awareness.

This consciousness has been spread across the Internet. Social media influencers who support sustainability have shared their values with the digitally connected generations. This encouraged young people to pay closer attention to issues like plastic and deforestation as well as to the brands they buy and the foods they eat. Given that influencers are today's trendsetters and many have millions of followers, being like them has become fashionable.

Platforms like Twitter also give regular people the power to publicly support companies that make an effort to be sustainable and condemn those that fail in this regard. When companies neglect sustainability, the news spreads quickly on social media, and young people work together to boycott the brand until changes are made. For example, thousands of students are currently boycotting the financial institution Barclays to pressure it into ceasing its funding of fossil fuels. If this trend continues, then Millennials and Generation Z, who make up the largest share of the global population, will continue to dictate corporate practices and make the world a more sustainable place.

60. What did researchers find out about the younger generations?

(a) that they are more aware of their consumerism
(b) that they pay more attention to sustainability
(c) that they care more about their social status
(d) that they are more influenced by corporations

61. According to the article, which best describes Millennials?

(a) They are able to borrow money at better rates than their parents.
(b) They do not make high-risk investments.
(c) They do not trust banking institutions.
(d) They have similar attitudes to previous generations.

62. How did ideas about sustainability become widespread online?

(a) by popular figures spreading their beliefs
(b) by influencers sharing posts amongst themselves
(c) by media outlets publishing more news on the Internet
(d) by social media users creating sustainable products

63. What do young people do when a company does not practice sustainability?

(a) petition for an investigation into the brand
(b) protest outside of the company's physical location
(c) make frequent posts complaining about its customers
(d) unite to withdraw their support for the company

64. According to the passage, what will most likely result from the younger generations' vast population?

(a) Businesses will be forced to change for the better.
(b) The number of products sold globally will increase.
(c) The purchasing power of future generations will suffer.
(d) Businesses will have to improve their online presence.

65. In the context of the passage, <u>fragile</u> means __________.

(a) breakable
(b) light
(c) delicate
(d) subtle

66. In the context of the passage, <u>condemn</u> means __________.

(a) punish
(b) criticize
(c) convict
(d) restrain

PART 3. *Read the encyclopedia article below and answer the questions. The two underlined words are for vocabulary questions.*

SLOTHS

Sloths are tree-dwelling mammals that are native to Central and South America. Until about 11,000 years ago, several species of sloths existed in North America, but these became extinct shortly after human hunters migrated to the continent.

The word *sloth* means "laziness" in English, and sloths were given this name for their inactivity. Sloths spend about 90 percent of each day absolutely <u>motionless</u>, using their sharp claws to hang from tree branches. When they do move through the trees, they go very slowly from branch to branch, averaging no more than four meters per minute. If they descend to the ground, their speed drops to less than two meters per minute. This is because their legs are so weak that they have to drag their bodies with their powerful arms.

Scientists speculate that one reason for their slow movement is the food they eat. Sloths primarily consume leaves that do not provide many nutrients. Fortunately, their sedentary lifestyle results in little energy expenditure on physical activity. In addition, sloths have an extremely slow metabolic rate, so they do not use much energy for basic bodily functions like breathing and body temperature regulation.

The sluggishness of sloths is an advantage when it comes to surviving in an environment with many predators. As every movement sloths make—from turning their heads to blinking their eyes—is incredibly slow, other animals have difficulty in spotting them. Furthermore, because sloths need very little energy to survive, they are able to wait a long time before getting something to eat if predators are nearby.

Another survival skill is the sloths' ability to hide due to the algae and fungi on their bodies. The sloths' hairs are the perfect habitat for these microorganisms to grow. These turn the sloths' fur green so that they can blend in with the surrounding trees. As an added bonus, they also mask the sloths' scent, making them harder for predators to detect.

Overall, sloths are resilient creatures that are well <u>adapted</u> to their environment. If the rainforests they inhabit are protected, sloths will continue to thrive long into the future.

67. Why most likely are sloths no longer present in North America?

(a) because they migrated to another continent
(b) because they were replaced by invasive animals
(c) because they experienced a lack of food
(d) because they were wiped out by people

68. How do sloths travel along the ground?

(a) by swinging from the lower branches
(b) by supporting their weight with their claws
(c) by using their arms to pull their bodies
(d) by grasping tree trunks to remain upright

69. What is a reason sloths can live on nutrient-deficient food?

(a) They maintain a low body temperature.
(b) They spend little energy on their movements.
(c) They consume extremely large quantities of food.
(d) They slow their metabolism while sleeping.

70. According to the passage, how are sloths able to avoid predators?

(a) by staying away from predators' territory
(b) by spotting dangerous animals from a distance
(c) by waiting an extended period to eat
(d) by going a long time without blinking

71. Which is not true about the algae and fungi on sloths?

(a) They expose the sloths' bodies.
(b) They grow on the sloths' fur.
(c) They change the sloths' color.
(d) They disguise the sloths' smells.

72. In the context of the passage, <u>motionless</u> means __________.

(a) mindless
(b) restless
(c) silent
(d) stationary

73. In the context of the passage, <u>adapted</u> means __________.

(a) suited
(b) adopted
(c) tamed
(d) established

PART 4. *Read the business letter below and answer the questions. The two underlined words are for vocabulary questions.*

Martin Giles
Manager
Flavor City

Dear Mr. Giles:

I am writing to inform you about the inferior food and service my family received at your restaurant on Christmas Eve.

We've been eating at Flavor City for years and were excited to spend this special occasion there. One of the main reasons we come back so often is because of the kids' menu, which has long featured healthy, gourmet food. So imagine our surprise when we found that the children's spaghetti Bolognese had been switched out for unhealthy, frozen chicken tenders.

I was relieved to see that the beloved starter was still available: the crab cakes. But that joy was short-lived. As I bit into one, I noticed that it tasted off. I asked the waiter if the dish was fresh, and he replied impolitely, "I don't know. The crab comes from a can." Besides being disappointed with the lack of fresh ingredients used in the appetizer, I also believe the response from the waiter—I didn't catch his name—to be unprofessional.

Considering the menu changes and the overall diminished quality, my partner and I, as well as several other acquaintances I've spoken to about this matter, are skeptical about visiting Flavor City again.

I understand that Flavor City was recently sold and is now under new management, but I had hoped that it would retain some of the same charms that made it not only a personal favorite but one of the best eateries in town.

Respectfully,

Alice Reed

74. Why did Alice Reed write a letter to Martin Giles?

(a) to place an order for Christmas Eve
(b) to explain the changes in a restaurant's service
(c) to protest the opening of a business
(d) to complain about a dining experience

75. Based on the letter, why did Reed visit Flavor City regularly?

(a) because of the frequent updates to the kid's menu
(b) because they had large portions of spaghetti Bolognese
(c) because they provided nutritious meal options for kids
(d) because of the available seating on special occasions

76. What happened to the spaghetti Bolognese on the children's menu?

(a) It seemed to include the wrong ingredients.
(b) It was served after the other courses.
(c) It cost more than the frozen chicken strips.
(d) It was replaced by a less healthy alternative.

77. How did a staff member react to Reed's question about a dish?

(a) by offering complimentary crab cakes
(b) by apologizing for the slow service
(c) by answering in a rude manner
(d) by saying that the customer was incorrect

78. What probably occurred at Flavor City recently?

(a) It changed its previous operation policy.
(b) It was named as the best place in town.
(c) It diminished the managers at the restaurant.
(d) It moved to a new location in the city.

79. In the context of the passage, <u>beloved</u> means __________.

(a) lovable
(b) familiar
(c) precious
(d) popular

80. In the context of the passage, <u>skeptical</u> means __________.

(a) pessimistic
(b) doubtful
(c) indecisive
(d) afraid

정답·해석·해설 p.126

자동 채점 및 성적 분석 서비스 ▶

02회 실전모의고사

자동 채점 및 성적 분석 서비스 ▶

권장 시간: 40분　시작: ___ 시 ___ 분 ~ 종료: ___ 시 ___ 분

정답·해석·해설 p.144

***PART 1.** Read the biography article below and answer the questions. The two underlined words are for vocabulary questions.*

FRIEDRICH FRÖBEL

Friedrich Fröbel was a German educator and reformer best remembered for creating the concept of kindergarten. It was an educational approach recognizing that young children learn most effectively while interacting with their peers as they play, sing, and explore.

Friedrich Fröbel was born on April 21, 1782, in Oberweissbach, Germany to Johann Fröbel and Jacobine Friederike. He was raised by his father and a stepmother after his mother died when he was nine months old. They were inattentive to his needs, so he moved in with his maternal uncle in Stadtilm at 10 years old. In school, his primary areas of interest were plants and nature, and he became a forestry apprentice at 15.

After his apprenticeship, Fröbel attended university and later found work as a land surveyor. It wasn't until he accepted a teaching position at a school in Frankfurt that he realized his true calling. The school was run by Anton Gruener and modeled on the philosophies of Swiss educator Johann Pestalozzi, who was an advocate for the poor and believed that everyone had a right to an education. In 1808, Fröbel went to Switzerland to study under Pestalozzi, who taught him that early childhood was crucial to human development.

With his new knowledge in hand, Fröbel returned to Germany in 1816 and founded the Universal German Educational Institute. This school flourished and became a large community. He also wrote about early childhood education, asserting that every child is born with a God-given force and that externalizing this force is necessary for growth. In 1837, he opened an institute for young children that he named Kindergarten, which means "garden of children." It was here that he developed the educational toys he called "Fröbel Gifts." These were objects such as cubes, spheres, and rings designed to encourage children's exploration of the world through play.

Fröbel's philosophy for teaching young learners led more kindergartens to open throughout Germany. However, in 1851, the minister of education Karl von Raumer banned all kindergartens because he believed they undermined the traditional notion that play was a form of idleness. Kindergartens were eventually allowed to reopen in 1860, eight years after Fröbel's death. Once the kindergartens opened again, they quickly spread throughout Europe, and today, they are a standard part of children's education globally.

53. How did Fröbel think children learn best?

(a) by working independently of a teacher
(b) by participating in various activities with friends
(c) by being involved in the creation of artistic works
(d) by observing peers in an academic setting

54. Why did Fröbel go to live with his maternal uncle?

(a) because he was neglected by his parents
(b) so he could attend a school in Stadtilm
(c) so he could accept a position as a forester
(d) because he wanted to find out more about his mother

55. Based on the article, what did Fröbel do when he was in Switzerland?

(a) He studied education under Gruener at a local university.
(b) He advocated for the rights of people living in poverty.
(c) He developed new teaching methods with Pestalozzi.
(d) He learned about the importance of childhood in development.

56. What did Fröbel contribute to early childhood education in Germany?

(a) kindergartens modeled after institutes in other countries
(b) books about the importance of religion in schools
(c) playthings to aid in the education of young learners
(d) language classes for a complete education

57. What can probably be said about Fröbel's later life?

(a) He failed to get his books published because of Karl von Raumer.
(b) He never got to see the reestablishment of kindergartens.
(c) He used kindergartens to spread unconventional theories.
(d) He personally helped establish kindergartens in Europe.

58. In the context of the passage, <u>flourished</u> means ________.

(a) thrived
(b) swelled
(c) glowed
(d) resurrected

59. In the context of the passage, <u>notion</u> means ________.

(a) principle
(b) fact
(c) idea
(d) faith

PART 2. *Read the magazine article below and answer the questions. The two underlined words are for vocabulary questions.*

EVER GIVEN BLOCKAGE DISRUPTS GLOBAL SUPPLY CHAIN

In March 2021, the 400-meter-long, 200,000-ton container ship *Ever Given* became wedged in the Suez Canal, blocking all traffic and causing a global supply chain crisis. The vessel was stuck for six days and is estimated to have prevented $9.6 billion in trade.

Located in Egypt, the Suez Canal is <u>vital</u> to trade between Europe and Asia. It is 193 kilometers long and, despite an expansion having been completed in 2015, it is less than 300 meters wide. This means that it is a single-lane waterway in many parts, and convoys of ships must take turns traveling through the canal.

On the day of the incident, March 23, *Ever Given* was caught in a sandstorm, and strong winds caused it to turn sideways and go aground in the banks of the canal. As a consequence, three hundred sixty-nine ships were blocked on either side. Since up to $3 billion in cargo passes through the canal daily, there were immediate concerns about the effect the obstruction would have on global trade. While many ships docked in nearby areas or remained in place, some shipping companies opted to divert their ships around the Cape of Good Hope in South Africa, a route that can set shipping schedules back by two weeks or longer.

In the immediate wake of *Ever Given* getting stuck, Egyptian, Dutch, and Italian rescue teams worked to free the ship. The first step was to lighten the vessel, so fuel and nine tons of ballast water were drained from the tanks. At the time, *Ever Given* was carrying 18,000 shipping containers, but removing them would have been time-consuming and could have damaged the ship. Meanwhile, approximately 20,000 tons of sand and silt were dug out, and tugboats worked to pull the ship free. Finally, in the early hours of March 29, it was dislodged. Cargo traffic <u>resumed</u> a few hours later.

The incident exposed just how fragile the global supply chain actually is and how much of an effect a single accident could have. It also revealed how necessary it is to improve existing infrastructure. The Egyptian government has since announced plans to widen the narrowest parts of the canal by a further 40 meters.

60. What is the article all about?

(a) a shipping disaster that caused long-term environmental disruption
(b) a method of handling an emergency involving the supply chain
(c) a construction failure of the world's largest supply chain
(d) an incident that temporarily impacted global trade

61. Based on the article, why did *Ever Given* run aground in the Suez Canal?

(a) because it exceeded weight limits for ships on the canal
(b) because it went off course due to extreme weather conditions
(c) because it was obstructed by hundreds of other ships
(d) because it was accidentally steered sideways by the ship's crew

62. Why most likely did some shipping companies send their ships on a different route?

(a) They were directed to deliver goods to South Africa.
(b) They expected the canal to be closed for more than two weeks.
(c) They hoped to make their deliveries ahead of schedule.
(d) They were given extra time to transport their goods.

63. How was weight removed from *Ever Given*?

(a) through unloading all the cargo
(b) through damaging a section of the ship
(c) through emptying a significant amount of liquid
(d) through evacuating the on-board personnel

64. What is the government of Egypt expected to do in the near future?

(a) It will restrict the size of cargo ships allowed on the canal.
(b) It will launch an investigation into the steering mechanism error.
(c) It will expand the waterway in several specific locations.
(d) It will decrease the overall amount of traffic in the canal.

65. In the context of the passage, vital means __________.

(a) essential
(b) standard
(c) decisive
(d) public

66. In the context of the passage, resumed means __________.

(a) arrived
(b) attained
(c) reunited
(d) continued

PART 3. *Read the encyclopedia article below and answer the questions. The two underlined words are for vocabulary questions.*

MINECRAFT

Minecraft is a critically acclaimed video game developed by the Swedish company Mojang Studios. With over 238 million copies sold, *Minecraft* currently holds the record of being the best-selling computer game of all time.

The programmer who created *Minecraft*, Markus Persson, worked on the prototype in his spare time while employed at a software company. In 2009, he released the initial version of *Minecraft*. The game attracted so much attention that Persson quit his job the following year to form his own business, Mojang Studios. Over the next five years, *Minecraft* achieved great success due to its innovative gameplay.

Minecraft is a sandbox game, meaning that there are no set goals or victory conditions. In addition, starting a new game <u>triggers</u> the creation of a generated 3D world—one that is randomized based on a computer algorithm unlike any other. This gives players a great deal of freedom. There is no right way to play *Minecraft*, which encourages the use of imagination and creativity.

As the name suggests, one of *Minecraft*'s core gameplay elements is the need to "mine" materials, such as stones, wood, and plants, to "craft" items like tools, clothing, and buildings. Another key aspect is exploration. Scattered throughout each world are villages, temples, and other landmarks, many of which contain rare items that are difficult to locate elsewhere. Players can also fight monsters, such as zombies and giant spiders, although this option can be turned off by parents to make the game suitable for young children.

The flexibility of *Minecraft* has led many experts to consider it a valuable educational tool. It is commonly used by teachers to provide students with simulated experiences that they might otherwise miss out on. In addition, the British Museum is now recruiting volunteers to construct its entire building in a *Minecraft* world so that students everywhere can explore its exhibits.

Minecraft will likely continue to attract new users because it is constantly being released on new platforms. It is now <u>available</u> on computers, smartphones, and consoles, and a version of the game for virtual-reality devices is currently in development.

67. What is *Minecraft*?

(a) an effective computer sales strategy
(b) a record-breaking electronic device
(c) a digital entertainment product
(d) a successful video game developer

68. Why did Markus Persson leave his position in 2010?

(a) He wanted to study programming at university.
(b) He started to run his own software company.
(c) He planned to create a popular video game.
(d) He managed to join an established game studio.

69. What is probably a benefit of generating a *Minecraft* world?

(a) experiencing a unique playing environment
(b) keeping gameplay exciting with randomized goals
(c) sharing common locations with other users
(d) meeting players from all around the planet

70. Based on the article, how can parents make *Minecraft* appropriate for younger kids?

(a) by increasing the crafting speed
(b) by reducing the exploration area
(c) by changing an item's rarity
(d) by disabling a game feature

71. What is the British Museum planning to do for students?

(a) develop an educational version of a program
(b) have a copy of a facility built for virtual tours
(c) include *Minecraft* items in a physical exhibit
(d) hire teachers to show them around a building

72. In the context of the passage, triggers means ________.

(a) frightens
(b) admits
(c) shoots
(d) provokes

73. In the context of the passage, available means ________.

(a) affordable
(b) exchangeable
(c) accessible
(d) traceable

PART 4. *Read the business letter below and answer the questions. The two underlined words are for vocabulary questions.*

Dave Berry
Lead Contractor
Peak Construction

Dear Mr. Berry:

I am writing in regards to the inconvenience caused by the ongoing construction in front of the Pelican Apartments. I received your contact information from an on-site worker named Robert Walsh. He suggested I get in touch with you so that my concerns could be addressed properly.

The issue I would like to bring to your attention is the parking obstruction. It occurs outside regular working hours, as defined by the signs posted at the site. They say that construction will only last from 8 a.m. to 6 p.m., Monday through Friday.

For the last week, I've had to park several blocks away when I get home from work at 6:30 p.m. because all the parking spots on my apartment's street are taken up by Peak Construction work vehicles. Not only is parking far away bothersome, but also it is perilous. My fellow neighbors and I are concerned that our cars may be damaged or stolen if left overnight in dark, unfamiliar areas.

I believe it would be more appropriate if your crew finished their work and vacated the premises by the agreed time. Of course, I understand that the work will sometimes run late. Therefore, I am asking that all work vehicles be moved to another street by 6 p.m. so that residents can park in front of the apartment building.

If this issue is not resolved promptly, I will have no other choice but to inform the Building Department of this violation. You can contact me with your desired course of action by e-mail at sjackson@fastmail.com or by phone at 354-555-0172.

Respectfully,

Sophia Jackson

Sophia Jackson
Unit 903

74. What is the main purpose of the letter?

(a) to file a lawsuit against an on-site worker
(b) to notify neighbors of the ongoing construction
(c) to raise a complaint about a local disturbance
(d) to ask for the parking lot's contact information

75. How was Ms. Jackson able to obtain Mr. Berry's contact details?

(a) by asking a neighbor at the Pelican Apartments
(b) by writing to the construction company
(c) by visiting the contractor's office
(d) by talking with a member of his staff

76. What is Ms. Jackson's concern about parking far from the apartment?

(a) Resident automobiles are not allowed to park there.
(b) The area might be too congested to park cars.
(c) Resident automobiles may not be safe.
(d) The area is known for criminal activity.

77. What is Ms. Jackson asking Mr. Berry to do about the parking obstruction?

(a) prohibit the workers from parking on the apartment's street
(b) have the construction team leave by the appointed time
(c) report to the residents currently on the premises
(d) finish the project near the apartment building

78. What will most likely happen if the parking problem is not solved soon?

(a) Ms. Jackson will start coming home at an earlier time.
(b) Ms. Jackson will no longer directly deal with the company.
(c) The work vehicles will be moved to undesirable areas.
(d) The Building Department will contact Ms. Jackson in person.

79. In the context of the passage, regular means __________.

(a) normal
(b) rational
(c) exact
(d) steady

80. In the context of the passage, resolved means __________.

(a) promised
(b) approved
(c) settled
(d) received

정답·해석·해설 p.144

자동 채점 및 성적 분석 서비스 ▶

자동 채점 및 성적 분석 서비스 ▶

권장 시간: 40분 시작: ___ 시 ___ 분 ~ 종료: ___ 시 ___ 분

정답·해석·해설 p.162

***PART 1.** Read the biography article below and answer the questions. The two underlined words are for vocabulary questions.*

JOHN DAVISON ROCKEFELLER

John Davison Rockefeller was an oil tycoon famous for being the wealthiest person in modern history. His net worth in 1937 was over 1.5 percent of the total GDP of the United States at the time.

Rockefeller was born on July 8, 1839, in New York. His father was a salesman who was often away from home due to his involvement in dishonest get-rich-quick schemes. By contrast, his mother had strong moral principles and believed in saving money. At 16, following her lead, Rockefeller began working long hours as a bookkeeper. It was at this job that he first learned how to run a business and negotiate. As he grew into a hard worker and became more disciplined, he began distancing himself from his father.

After learning all he could from the bookkeeping job, Rockefeller founded his first business, a food company called Clark & Rockefeller, with his partner Maurice B. Clark in 1859. It was extremely successful and only prospered more when the Civil War broke out as the demand for food <u>soared</u>. Although Rockefeller did not join the army, he donated money to the Union, supporting Abraham Lincoln and his anti-slavery platform. At the end of the war, he got out of the food business and set his sights on what was then a rising commercial industry: oil.

Shortly thereafter, Rockefeller and Clark built an oil refinery. With the help of several other partners and Rockefeller's shrewd business sense, it thrived. Over the next several years, Rockefeller expanded the business, which later became Standard Oil in 1870. Through Standard Oil, Rockefeller was able to buy out competing companies, and by 1882, he had gained control of nearly 90 percent of the US oil market. However, Standard Oil engaged in monopolistic practices and was eventually broken up into 34 smaller companies. As Rockefeller remained the primary shareholder of all these companies, the dissolution of Standard Oil was to his benefit since the profits from the multiple enterprises were much greater than those of Standard Oil alone.

Rockefeller retired from Standard Oil in 1897 and devoted his attention to charity. Through the Rockefeller Foundation, he donated more than $550 million to educational, religious, and scientific establishments with <u>exceeding</u> generosity. He died on May 23, 1937, at the age of 97, and to this day, he is viewed both as a charitable man and as an insatiable enterpriser.

53. What is John Davison Rockefeller mostly known for?

(a) establishing the first successful US oil company
(b) creating laws for the modern American oil industry
(c) being the first tycoon in the state of New York
(d) having the largest fortune in recent history

54. What most likely caused Rockefeller to grow apart from his father?

(a) his book reading habit during his teenage years
(b) his mother's advice to be an honest person
(c) his developing appreciation for working hard
(d) his father's frequent absences due to his unstable job

55. When did Rockefeller leave his first business?

(a) when Maurice B. Clark came to him with a business idea
(b) before he gave a financial contribution to the Union Army
(c) while he served in the army on the side of Abraham Lincoln
(d) when the Civil War eventually came to a conclusion

56. According to the article, which is not true about Rockefeller's oil business?

(a) It flourished with the assistance of a number of associates.
(b) It caused Rockefeller financial distress when it was dissolved.
(c) It pursued anticompetitive business activities.
(d) It controlled the majority of the American oil industry.

57. How did Rockefeller spend the time during his retirement?

(a) by donating money to certain organizations
(b) by boosting the size of his wealth through oil investments
(c) by returning to school to further his education
(d) by sharing his business methods with other establishments

58. In the context of the passage, <u>soared</u> means ________.

(a) changed
(b) soaked
(c) increased
(d) spread

59. In the context of the passage, <u>exceeding</u> means ________.

(a) touching
(b) admiring
(c) surpassing
(d) stunning

PART 2. *Read the magazine article below and answer the questions. The two underlined words are for vocabulary questions.*

THE CHANGING FACE OF MURAL ART

Murals are large-scale paintings made directly on walls or other flat surfaces. They are found all over the world and are considered the earliest type of art. The most ancient murals were discovered inside caves and date back at least 40,000 years to the Upper Paleolithic era, when the most <u>common</u> scenes to be depicted were inspired by everyday activities such as hunting and gathering.

Throughout history, the purpose of murals has varied depending on the culture and the period. Murals portraying the deceased have been found in ancient Egyptian tombs, while murals from the Baroque Period in Europe usually illustrated scenes from the Bible and mythology. These were most often painted on the ceilings of churches or in the homes of affluent patrons. Frequently, the work of artists of this period was not only required to be beautiful but also to symbolize the status and wealth of their clients. Artists sometimes accomplished this by painting their patrons as characters in the mural.

In the late 1960s, inspired by the earlier Mexican Mural movement <u>led</u> by Diego Rivera, David Alfaro Siqueiros, and José Clemente Orozco, murals began making their way to the exterior of buildings in America. These artworks were often used to make political or cultural statements about inner-city life. Commissioned murals of the period were usually painted using the fresco method, which involves applying water-soluble paints to wet plaster carefully prepared in advance of the artwork. However, most of the art that ended up on public buildings at the time was done without permission and was carried out quickly, causing some to see murals in cities as a form of gang-related vandalism, now referred to as "graffiti."

As time progressed and street art evolved, people began to view it not just as the damaging of public property, but as a cultural representation of modern life. Consequently, programs gradually emerged that gave urban muralists opportunities to showcase their art legally, and today, mural art is part of mainstream culture. Many major cities are seeking out gifted muralists to create unique work that engages residents and visitors and beautifies formerly run-down neighborhoods. In addition, numerous top brands are also employing them to work on promotional campaigns that command attention and leave a mark.

60. What is probably true about individuals during the Upper Paleolithic era?

(a) They migrated all over the world while hunting and gathering.
(b) They painted the earliest known cave murals.
(c) They created murals mostly based on their imaginations.
(d) They lived in caves covered in art for 40,000 years.

61. How did Baroque era muralists signify the prominence of their clients?

(a) by painting on ceilings to suggest their elevated status
(b) by artistically depicting the most influential biblical stories
(c) by using their patrons as models for their work
(d) by creating some of the most expensive work to date

62. What can probably be said about the majority of late 1960s murals in America?

(a) They paid respects to figures involved in Mexican Muralism.
(b) They were always created by artists using the fresco method.
(c) They often had to be covered with commissioned murals.
(d) They were usually painted on the outside walls of buildings.

63. Why were some graffiti artists given a chance to paint legally?

(a) because they volunteered to paint over acts of vandalism
(b) because there was a shift in how their artwork was interpreted
(c) because they began to change their style to showcase their talent
(d) because there were changes made to property laws

64. According to the article, why are major cities looking for talented muralists?

(a) to create unique artwork for private residences
(b) to inspire creativity in residents
(c) to attract sponsorship deals from big brands
(d) to improve the look of once-neglected areas

65. In the context of the passage, <u>common</u> means ________.

(a) banal
(b) shared
(c) ordinary
(d) exemplary

66. In the context of the passage, <u>led</u> means ________.

(a) planned
(b) headed
(c) begun
(d) spurred

***PART 3.** Read the encyclopedia article below and answer the questions. The two underlined words are for vocabulary questions.*

ALCATRAZ PRISON

Alcatraz prison was a maximum-security facility located on Alcatraz Island. This island is a remote rocky outcrop near the mouth of San Francisco Bay in California, which earned it the nickname "The Rock." The name of the island is derived from the word *alcatraces*, which is the Spanish name for the gannet birds that reside on its shores.

Alcatraz was first acquired by the US government during the Mexican-American War, which lasted from 1846 to 1848. It was originally envisioned as a defensive outpost to guard against future invasions, and it was further fortified to meet that purpose. However, by 1865, it had found use as a temporary detention center for rebellious soldiers. In 1907, it was officially designated as a military prison.

In 1933, the US Department of Justice acquired the facility and modernized it to serve as a federal prison for civilians. It was believed that the island's isolation made the prison inescapable, so it was used for the new wave of criminals that had arisen during Prohibition—the period from 1920 to 1933 when alcohol was illegal in the US. Alcatraz gained a reputation for being a prison of last resort, where those who had caused problems at other penal institutions could be sent.

Although Alcatraz had the capacity to hold 450 convicts in total, fewer than 250 inhabited it at one time, most of them living in sparsely furnished cells. Some of its most notorious inmates included the Chicago mobster Al Capone and convicted murderer Robert Stroud, also known as the "Birdman of Alcatraz."

While several of its inmates attempted to escape, none are known to have been successful. In one famous incident in 1962, three escapees managed to get past the prison walls and, using a simple raft, set off from the island's shores. However, what happened next remains a mystery. Their story is popularized in the Clint Eastwood film, *Escape from Alcatraz*.

Eventually, with the upkeep proving to be too expensive, Alcatraz was shut down in 1963. The prison and its grounds became part of the newly formed Golden Gate National Recreation Area in 1972, and today Alcatraz is one of San Francisco's most popular tourist destinations.

67. Where did Alcatraz Island get the nickname "The Rock"?

(a) from its geographic features
(b) from its security system
(c) from the dense population of its prison
(d) from its location near a rocky shore

68. According to the passage, why was Alcatraz initially built?

(a) to keep the country's worst criminals
(b) to detain soldiers who rebelled
(c) to protect against hostile forces
(d) to train new military personnel

69. How did Alcatraz gain its reputation as one of the ultimate prisons?

(a) by keeping prisoners isolated from each other
(b) by successfully rehabilitating some criminals
(c) by housing difficult inmates from other prisons
(d) by including many modern security features

70. What can be inferred about the prisoners depicted in *Escape from Alcatraz*?

(a) They managed to board a passing sea vessel.
(b) They were not recaptured by the authorities.
(c) They returned to the prison due to rough waters.
(d) They were not able to scale the prison's walls.

71. What led to the closure of Alcatraz?

(a) a national crime reduction
(b) a recreation facility opening
(c) excessive tourist complaints
(d) high maintenance costs

72. In the context of the passage, <u>inhabited</u> means _________.

(a) inhibited
(b) relocated
(c) occupied
(d) entered

73. In the context of the passage, <u>incident</u> means _________.

(a) disorder
(b) crisis
(c) example
(d) occasion

***PART 4.** Read the business letter below and answer the questions. The two underlined words are for vocabulary questions.*

Ms. Alyssa Benoit
Recruitment Manager
Alimentary Concepts
701 Whitelock Boulevard
Tallahassee, FL 21217

Dear Ms. Benoit,

I am writing to express an interest in the position of development chef. Alimentary Concepts is a company I have long admired for its leadership in the industry and the many restaurants that it operates.

I am confident that I can make valuable contributions to your firm. Throughout my career, I have maintained a passion for food. I have a particular interest in finding creative ways to combine ingredients, which is why I was selected to be a judge on the hit TV show *Cooking with Fire*.

I have had many opportunities to broaden my skills and experience. After earning a degree in food science from Bayfront University, I worked in the kitchens of various notable chefs, including Alton Flynn, learning to make food to the highest standards. In addition, I was with Celadon Cruises for 12 years. While on board, we had to produce food on a large scale and simultaneously cater to different tastes and food safety guidelines. Most recently, I was a partner in a food truck business called Nourishing Fusion but gave up my stake to move with my family here to Florida.

Now, I am seeking employment with Alimentary Concepts, where I want to devote the rest of my career. I am certain I can meet the job's demands for designing cost-effective recipes and menus, staying aware of the latest food and restaurant trends, and adhering to precise specifications.

My résumé is enclosed for your review. I look forward to interviewing online as per the instructions in your advertisement in *Restaurant Outlook* magazine.

Sincerely,

Kenneth Chen

Kenneth Chen

74. Why did Kenneth Chen write to Alyssa Benoit?

(a) to voice appreciation for a local chef's food
(b) to apply for employment in the culinary field
(c) to get in touch with the leader of a business
(d) to offer restaurant operations consultant services

75. What did Chen learn when he worked on a cruise?

(a) the skill of producing food in large volumes
(b) the safety measures of ocean liners
(c) the business strategies of famous restaurants
(d) the value of an educational food background

76. Why did Chen surrender his share in the food truck business?

(a) because he got into an argument with his partner
(b) because he failed to popularize fusion food in Florida
(c) because he recently moved to a new location
(d) because he wanted to start a solo business

77. What is one of the requirements for the development chef?

(a) creating a list of unique recipes
(b) interviewing chefs at competing restaurants
(c) meeting arbitrary regulations
(d) developing affordable food items

78. According to the letter, how did Chen probably become aware of the job opening?

(a) He read through a colleague's referral.
(b) He checked an online job board.
(c) He found it in an industry publication.
(d) He was informed at a culinary job fair.

79. In the context of the passage, particular means _________.

(a) great
(b) specific
(c) profound
(d) relevant

80. In the context of the passage, tastes means _________.

(a) likings
(b) cravings
(c) savors
(d) traits

정답·해석·해설 p.162

***PART 1.** Read the biography article below and answer the questions. The two underlined words are for vocabulary questions.*

DAFFY DUCK

Daffy Duck is one of the main characters of two animated series, *Looney Tunes* and *Merrie Melodies*. Produced by Warner Bros., both series had half-hour-long episodes and involved talking cartoon animals in comedic situations. On account of the significant impact both shows had on American pop culture, Daffy Duck has been called one of the greatest cartoon characters of all time.

Daffy Duck was created by animators Bob Clampett and Tex Avery. The character was first introduced to audiences in 1937's *Porky's Duck Hunt* as a black-feathered duck with a ring of white feathers around his neck. He was intended to be a secondary character hunted by the main character Porky Pig, but he quickly became a fan favorite due to his assertive, combative, and unrestrained personality. Hopping around wildly as he yelled "Woo-hoo," Daffy Duck left an impression on <u>juvenile</u> viewers, who were unused to seeing characters behave this way.

One of Daffy Duck's most characteristic features is his lisp—a speech defect resulting in the letters "s" and "z" being pronounced like "th"—but this was hardly apparent in the early cartoons he appeared in. There is some debate about the origin of the lisp. The most commonly told story is that it was based on the voice of the studio's founder, Leon Schlesinger, who actually had a lisp. However, Mel Blanc, who portrayed Daffy Duck for 52 years, said the lisp was simply something he thought a long-billed duck would have. In any case, as Daffy Duck's personality became more defined, the lisp would become <u>markedly</u> pronounced and used for comedic effect.

Daffy Duck starred in about 130 short films, with his popularity peaking in the 1950s and 1960s when he was paired with his friend and occasional rival Bugs Bunny. Following the end of *Looney Tunes* in 1969, Daffy Duck would make appearances in various cartoon compilations released by Warner Bros., and was used in major films such as the 1988 Disney movie *Who Framed Roger Rabbit*. More recently, in 2021, he appeared in *Space Jam: A New Legacy* and was voiced by Eric Bauza. Although Daffy Duck appears far less frequently than in the past, he lives on in the memories of generations of children who grew up watching his antics.

53. Why is Daffy Duck such a celebrated animated personality?

(a) He is credited with being the first talking cartoon character.
(b) He influenced the development of half-hour-long TV shows.
(c) He was part of culturally important TV programs.
(d) He helped Warner Bros. become a successful company.

54. What made Daffy Duck more beloved than originally anticipated?

(a) his strange manner of speaking
(b) his out-of-control behavior
(c) his funny catchphrase
(d) his startling appearance

55. What can probably be said about Daffy Duck's characteristics?

(a) His appearance evolved a lot over the years.
(b) His pronunciation was meant to mimic Porky Pig's.
(c) He was initially unpopular with viewers.
(d) He did not have a distinct lisp in *Porky's Duck Hunt*.

56. According to Mel Blanc, why most likely did Daffy Duck speak with a lisp?

(a) because a long bill would cause the speech impediment
(b) because he used his natural voice when playing Daffy Duck
(c) because the animators wanted to make Daffy Duck hard to understand
(d) because the size of Daffy Duck's bill increased over time

57. When did Daffy Duck reach the height of his popularity?

(a) when he began appearing in full-length films
(b) when *Looney Tunes* was taken off the air
(c) when he appeared with Bugs Bunny
(d) when Eric Bauza began providing his voice

58. In the context of the passage, juvenile means ________.

(a) mature
(b) young
(c) chief
(d) childish

59. In the context of the passage, markedly means ________.

(a) delicately
(b) unbelievably
(c) discreetly
(d) noticeably

PART 2. *Read the magazine article below and answer the questions. The two underlined words are for vocabulary questions.*

HAVING SOMEONE TO LISTEN TO MAY PREVENT COGNITIVE DECLINE

A recent study published in *JAMA Network Open* suggests that having a strong social support system composed of people who listen to us helps keep the brain in good condition and protect it against age-related cognitive decline.

The study, led by Dr. Joel Salinas, involved more than 2,000 participants with an average age of 63, all of whom were surveyed on how they viewed the availability of emotional support in their life. This included factors such as whether they had love and affection, contact with friends and family, good listeners around them, and access to advice.

Following the survey, the participants underwent MRI scans to gauge their total brain volume. This was done to determine their cognitive resilience, which is the ability of the brain to act as a buffer against disease and remain healthy with age. It was found that participants with fewer people in their lives who listened to them when they needed to talk had a lower brain volume and lower cognitive capabilities. In fact, the brains of these individuals appeared to be four years older than those of individuals with friends or relatives who listened to them.

This ultimately suggests that feeling acknowledged as we get older can improve our cognitive resilience and help slow down or prevent Alzheimer's disease and other types of cognitive impairment. The researchers theorize that this could be because it is stimulating to talk to another person and that stimulation boosts neuroplasticity. A boost to neuroplasticity establishes new pathways among the nerve cells in the brain, making it easier for the brain to continue functioning well as time passes.

Given that cognitive decline associated with aging lowers the quality of all aspects of life, the findings of the study are important because they imply that people can address their cognitive resilience before it is too late. By finding someone to listen to us, we may be able to provide our brain with the protection needed to live a fulfilling life into old age.

60. What did the study find out about cognitive decline?

(a) that it damages a person's ability to hear
(b) that it can be averted with social ties
(c) that it normally inflicts sociable individuals
(d) that it can be slowed by listening more to others

61. What were the participants in the study not asked about?

(a) whether they had communication with loved ones
(b) whether there were people who cared about them
(c) whether they were willing to take advice from others
(d) whether there were people who listened to them

62. Why did the researchers measure the brain volume of the participants?

(a) to determine the ability of their brains to resist disease
(b) to identify the condition of their memories
(c) to see the impact of brain volume on the aging process
(d) to correlate the size of the brain to an individual's intelligence

63. In what way does an increase in neuroplasticity benefit the brain?

(a) by stimulating the brain to have a deeper level of thought
(b) by increasing the speed of responses to nerve stimulation
(c) by creating additional nerve paths in the brain
(d) by allowing the brain to follow nerve pathways faster

64. Which of the following do the findings of the study ultimately reveal?

(a) People should pursue a fulfilling life.
(b) People can take action to help themselves.
(c) Cognitive decline cannot be significantly slowed.
(d) Cognitive decline does not necessarily mean a low quality of life.

65. In the context of the passage, <u>included</u> means __________.

(a) affected
(b) added
(c) integrated
(d) comprised

66. In the context of the passage, <u>address</u> means __________.

(a) handle
(b) enhance
(c) identify
(d) cure

PART 3. *Read the encyclopedia article below and answer the questions. The two underlined words are for vocabulary questions.*

FONDUE

Fondue, the national dish of Switzerland, is made by heating up cheese, oil, or chocolate in a particular type of pot used specifically to prepare the dish. It is a communal comfort food that provides a relaxed dining experience for friends and family members. People choose what foods they want—usually bread, fruit, vegetables, or cured meats—and dip them in the melted sauce.

The dish takes its name from the French word *fondre*, meaning "to melt," as it originated in the French-speaking region of Switzerland. This name was initially used for a combination of scrambled eggs and cheese, but it was applied <u>exclusively</u> to the modern dish featuring cheese and bread by the end of the 19th century. Although there are many theories about fondue's origin, the most probable explanation is that the Swiss had to make old bread soft enough to eat.

The earliest fondue recipe was published in 1875, and the preparation process has not changed significantly since then. A combination of cheese, wine, and garlic is heated over a portable stove at the center of the dining table. The temperature has to be managed carefully to ensure that the cheese does not burn. Once the ingredients are blended, the sauce must be stirred continuously to prevent it from sticking to the pan. Bread is then dipped into the sauce before being eaten.

There are many different types of fondue. The most notable is chocolate fondue, created in the 1960s by the Swiss chef, Konrad Egli. He operated a popular restaurant Chalet Suisse in Manhattan and was approached by the company that produces Toblerone chocolate to develop a dessert featuring its product. Egli's response was to serve heated chocolate with fruit and nuts, and he finally debuted his chocolate fondue to his customers on July 4th, 1964.

Although fondue remains associated with the Swiss, it is now popular around the world. As the <u>simple</u> dish is very versatile in terms of what it can be made with, it is likely to remain an international favorite for years to come.

67. According to the article, what will Swiss people probably avoid doing?

(a) sharing a meal from a common dish
(b) eating fondue with family members
(c) offering many different food options
(d) using a random pan to warm up fondue

68. What was likely the origin of fondue?

(a) the demand to make more varieties of bread
(b) the preference of the Swiss for French cooking
(c) the increase in the supply of cheese
(d) the need to consume stale food

69. Which is not true about the process of making fondue?

(a) It has been essentially unchanged over time.
(b) The ingredients are heated separately.
(c) The temperature must be regulated.
(d) It was first recorded in 1875.

70. Why did Chef Konrad Egli decide to serve chocolate fondue?

(a) because he faced competition from a restaurant
(b) because he wanted to update an ancient dish
(c) because he received a request from a producer
(d) because he employed a new dessert maker

71. Which has contributed to the global popularity of fondue?

(a) its long-term connection to Swiss culture
(b) its inclusion of high-quality food items
(c) its adaptability with regard to ingredients
(d) its promotion by international companies

72. In the context of the passage, exclusively means __________.

(a) solely
(b) totally
(c) certainly
(d) readily

73. In the context of the passage, simple means __________.

(a) quick
(b) humble
(c) casual
(d) natural

***PART 4.** Read the business letter below and answer the questions. The two underlined words are for vocabulary questions.*

Ms. Dana Murphy
Nature's Greenhouse
22 Main Street
Worcester, Massachusetts

Dear Ms. Murphy,

I'm contacting you about your request to order one of our products. I see that you are interested in our 1-liter orchid pots for your flower business. While we are very glad that you chose us as one of your suppliers, I regret to inform you that this particular product is currently not available at our store here in Worcester.

We will be talking to our warehouse in Maryland to restock this product as soon as possible. Usually, we can get nursery pots shipped to us in two to three business days. However, as you know, spring is the most hectic time of year in our industry, and this time frame is not feasible at the moment. I estimate we can get them within a week. If this works for you, we will process your order and bill you when it is ready. I'll let you know if it takes longer than I <u>anticipated</u>.

Also, please send us your retail certificate. As we are a wholesale distributor, we can only sell to those who are licensed for retail sales. Once we <u>verify</u> this, we will enter your information into our database so that you do not have to provide it in the future. If you are not a retailer, I do know a company that sells to wholesalers.

Should you have any questions or concerns, or if you need to make changes to your order, don't hesitate to contact me personally. You can reach me at 555-764-3115 or at Jwallace@nsupplies.com. Thank you for considering us, and we look forward to adding you as a customer!

Sincerely,

Jimmy Wallace

Jimmy Wallace
Sales Representative
Nursery Supplies Inc.

74. Why did Jimmy Wallace write to Dana Murphy?

(a) to invite her to try one of their products
(b) to inform her of their new store location
(c) to let her know the status of a product
(d) to give her directions to their warehouse in Maryland

75. Why will a delivery not be possible in the usual time frame?

(a) because the company's warehouse is located in another state
(b) because the company's delivery truck is currently unavailable
(c) because the company's prices do not include fast shipping
(d) because the company's busy season is underway

76. What does Mr. Wallace ask Ms. Murphy to provide?

(a) an authorization for conducting retail sales
(b) an updated billing address for her business
(c) the exact number of orchid pots she needs
(d) the notification she received for her order

77. According to Mr. Wallace, what most likely will happen if Ms. Murphy is not a retailer?

(a) She will be recommended a different supplier.
(b) She will be put in a database for the record.
(c) She will lose the wholesale discount on her purchase.
(d) She will receive advice on setting up a retail business.

78. How can Dana Murphy update her order?

(a) by emailing customer service
(b) by contacting Mr. Wallace directly
(c) by filling out an online form
(d) by calling the shipping representative personally

79. In the context of the passage, anticipated means ________.

(a) understood
(b) contemplated
(c) evaluated
(d) expected

80. In the context of the passage, verify means ________.

(a) acknowledge
(b) justify
(c) confirm
(d) arrange

정답·해석·해설 p.181

자동 채점 및 성적 분석 서비스 ▶

자동 채점 및 성적 분석 서비스 ▶

권장 시간: 40분 시작: ____ 시 ____ 분 ~ 종료: ____ 시 ____ 분

정답·해석·해설 p.199

***PART 1.** Read the biography article below and answer the questions. The two underlined words are for vocabulary questions.*

LOUIS DAGUERRE

Louis Daguerre was an accomplished French artist, photographer, and theatre designer. He is best remembered for his invention of the daguerreotype, a process used for mechanically producing an image that was more efficient than prior photographic innovations.

Daguerre was born on November 18, 1787, in Cormeilles-en-Parisis, France, to a middle-class family. Due to the start of the French Revolution in 1789, a violent period of social and political change, Daguerre's formal education was frequently interrupted. However, his parents were committed to fostering his artistic talent, so they sent him to become an apprentice to Pierre Prévost, the first French panorama painter, when he was 13.

He later moved to Paris in 1804, where he painted theatrical scenery and gained distinction for his work. There, he partnered with painter Charles Marie Bouton to invent the diorama theatre, a three-dimensional visual spectacle that has been called the forerunner of cinema. While he initially saw success with diorama theatres, by the 1830s, Daguerre had begun to reconsider his involvement with them. The novelty was subsiding for audiences, and a cholera outbreak in the city was negatively affecting ticket sales. Furthermore, since dioramas were costly to produce, Daguerre faced considerable financial problems.

Complicating matters was that Bouton, who had produced half the paintings for the dioramas, had abandoned the partnership. As each diorama featured two realistic paintings measuring 70 feet wide and 45 feet high, Daguerre lacked time to do all the work himself. This prompted him to become interested in utilizing photography to replace his former partner.

Therefore, he got to know Joseph Nicéphore Niépce, who had produced the world's first photograph through a technique known as the heliographic process. With his help, Daguerre achieved his principal goal of refining the photography technique in 1835, when he discovered that an image could be produced by exposing iodized silver plates to light and then developing it using mercury fumes. He called his process the daguerreotype and presented it to the Académie des Sciences in 1839 where it found instantaneous success because it was faster than other photographic processes and less expensive.

Daguerre agreed to make the daguerreotype public and received a pension from France in return. Throughout the decade that followed, millions of daguerreotypes were produced worldwide. Daguerre spent the remainder of his life painting dioramas and died in 1851.

53. How is Louis Daguerre best remembered?

(a) as the first French photographer
(b) as an inventor of the mass-produced camera
(c) as a creator of a new photographic technique
(d) as an interior designer with a long career

54. According to the article, how did the French Revolution affect Daguerre?

(a) It prevented him from receiving a consistent education.
(b) It forced him to leave home to work when he was 13.
(c) It spoiled his plans to formally study art at university.
(d) It sparked his interest in the changes occurring in France.

55. Which was not a cause that made Daguerre rethink diorama theatres?

(a) the decrease in public interest
(b) the spread of a disease
(c) the invention of cinema
(d) the high production cost

56. Why most likely did Daguerre want to use photographs in the dioramas?

(a) because they would attract larger audiences
(b) because they looked far more realistic
(c) because they took much less time to produce
(d) because they were cheaper than paintings

57. When did Daguerre accomplish his main objective?

(a) when he presented the daguerreotype to an academy
(b) when he produced the first heliographic photograph
(c) when he began working for the inventor Nicéphore Niépce
(d) when he found a quicker process for developing a picture

58. In the context of the passage, <u>distinction</u> means ________.

(a) attainment
(b) attention
(c) acceptance
(d) reputation

59. In the context of the passage, <u>instantaneous</u> means ________.

(a) expeditious
(b) temporary
(c) immediate
(d) straight

PART 2. *Read the magazine article below and answer the questions. The two underlined words are for vocabulary questions.*

AN EXPERIMENT SHOWS PEOPLE FEEL LESS RESPONSIBLE AS PART OF A GROUP

The famous Smoky Room experiment of 1968 found that people are more likely to react to an emergency when they are alone than in a group. This phenomenon is known as "diffusion of responsibility" and suggests that people's responses are influenced by those around them.

American social psychologists John M. Darley and Bibb Latané theorized that people look to others in a <u>potential</u> emergency to determine whether the situation is critical. They were inspired by the highly publicized death of Kitty Genovese, who was murdered in front of her apartment building in March 1964 as 38 neighbors watched from their windows and did nothing to help. The researchers posited that the neighbors had been aware that a crime was taking place but failed to act because each assumed that others in the crowd had already called for law enforcement.

To test their theory, Darley and Latané had three different groups of participants fill out a personal survey in a room. They wanted to see how each group would react when the room began to fill with smoke. The participants were made up of volunteers who did not expect the room would be full of smoke and actors who were instructed to behave like nothing was wrong. The experiment found that the smoke was reported mostly when a volunteer was left in the room alone and that volunteers grouped with actors usually tried to <u>disregard</u> the smoke since the actors did not react to it.

It is believed that there are several reasons why diffusion of responsibility occurs, including fear of rejection when offering one's help and simply being too self-conscious to assume a leadership position. The most prevalent cause, however, is the notion that taking action won't make a difference in a situation. For instance, in a life-threatening emergency, some people do nothing because they are not doctors and do not wish to get in the way of any medical professional who might be present.

Ultimately, the results of the experiment suggest just how much of an effect social pressure has on people. They offer an explanation for why information about criminal activity is sometimes not provided to authorities and serve as an important reminder that it is not always wise to simply follow the crowd.

60. What did the researchers find out about people in an emergency?

(a) that they take actions mostly to save themselves
(b) that the presence of others affects their reactions
(c) that they feel pressured to be socially responsible
(d) that the onlookers do not get involved without an incentive

61. Which best describes Kitty Genovese's neighbors?

(a) They were uninterested in helping their neighbors.
(b) They did not perceive the illegal act.
(c) They expected police to come to stop the attack.
(d) They were careless with their own safety.

62. What were participants in the experiment required to do?

(a) write a report about any unusual occurrences
(b) discuss the reactions of other participants
(c) complete a questionnaire about themselves
(d) try to locate the source of smoke

63. Why most likely would individuals not help someone facing a medical crisis?

(a) because they are afraid of contracting a deadly disease
(b) because their assistance could be overlooked
(c) because there may be more qualified people around
(d) because they lack the necessary leadership skills

64. Based on the article, what did the results of the study provide?

(a) suggestions on how to communicate in group settings
(b) reminders that the rate of crime is declining
(c) information on how authorities respond to illegal acts
(d) reasons crimes are not reported by witnesses

65. In the context of the passage, potential means _________.

(a) capable
(b) promising
(c) possible
(d) plausible

66. In the context of the passage, disregard means _________.

(a) ignore
(b) deny
(c) distract
(d) forget

PART 3. *Read the encyclopedia article below and answer the questions. The two underlined words are for vocabulary questions.*

OKTOBERFEST

Oktoberfest, an event featuring beer and a traveling carnival, is the world's largest folk festival. It is held every autumn in Munich, Germany from mid-September to the first week of October, with millions of people attending to feast on beer and sausages.

The festival began in October 1810, when Crown Prince Ludwig of Bavaria was married to Princess Theresa of Munich. To celebrate the wedding, the prince's subjects were invited to attend the festivities which were held on the fields in front of the city gates. The fields were named *Theresienwiese*, which means "Theresa's Meadow," in honor of the Crown Princess. A shortened version of this name, *d'Wiesn*, is what locals call Oktoberfest today.

In the following years, the event was repeated and games, plays, and rides were added, requiring large amounts of space and making the festival resemble a modern fair. However, by the late 1800s, those responsible for Oktoberfest limited the area dedicated to other activities, devoting it instead to beer tents. Over time, Oktoberfest <u>evolved</u> into a hybridized form of beer festival and carnival, known as a *Volksfest* in German.

Beer remains the focus of the modern version of the festival. Participants today consume roughly seven to eight million liters of specialty brews created by six Munich beer-makers, which have a higher alcohol content than typical German beers. The event doesn't kick off until the mayor taps the first keg of the festival and drinks one of these beers.

Oktoberfest also highlights other aspects of Bavarian culture, such as the traditional dress, called the *dirndl*, and traditional foods like the pretzel. Because of this, many German people view Oktoberfest as an important part of their national identity. Furthermore, Oktoberfest <u>reveals</u> German culture to a significant number of outsiders, with international guests arriving from all over the world. As a result of this high turnout, the festival brings more than one billion euros to Munich in revenue annually.

The Oktoberfest celebration has become one of the most well-known parts of German culture, and countries around the world now take part by hosting their own versions of the festival.

67. Based on the article, what was the original purpose of Oktoberfest?

(a) celebrating the accession of Prince Ludwig
(b) commemorating the wedding of a royal couple
(c) promoting German beer-making innovations
(d) attracting visitors to the Kingdom of Bavaria

68. Why most likely did the Oktoberfest organizers reduce the number of activities?

(a) to limit injuries from drunken guests
(b) to allocate more of the budget to brewing beer
(c) to enable a longer period of celebration during the event
(d) to make more room for drinking venues

69. According to the article, what can be said about the beers at Oktoberfest?

(a) They come with hybridized forms of modern beer.
(b) They contain more alcohol than ordinary beer.
(c) They are now the most common beers in Germany.
(d) They are all served from kegs tapped by the mayor.

70. Which of the following statements is incorrect about Oktoberfest?

(a) It puts a spotlight on various aspects of Bavarian culture.
(b) It features traditional clothing and food items.
(c) It draws a large number of tourists from abroad.
(d) It costs Munich over one billion euros to put on.

71. Based on the article, what is a result of Oktoberfest getting more popular?

(a) an increase in Germany's expenditures
(b) the improvement of Munich's tourism facilities
(c) a decline in Germans traveling abroad
(d) the rise of similar events in other regions

72. In the context of the passage, <u>evolved</u> means __________.

(a) extended
(b) stimulated
(c) developed
(d) moved

73. In the context of the passage, <u>reveals</u> means __________.

(a) shows
(b) declares
(c) uncovers
(d) explains

PART 4. *Read the business letter below and answer the questions. The two underlined words are for vocabulary questions.*

To: Pamburns@pearlliterary.com
From: Hankdalton@brightonwriters.com

Dear Pam Burns,

We, the Brighton Writers Club, are pleased to invite you to come and speak at our forthcoming Fiction and Publishing Workshop. This one-day event will be held at the Midtown Convention Center on August 20.

The workshop starts at 9 a.m., and we would like to offer you our keynote speaking slot at 11 a.m. During our spring workshop, you gave one of our most <u>instrumental</u> talks. Your story of how you transitioned from working as a chef to starting your career in the publishing world inspired many of our guests.

For this event, we ask that you detail how you begin getting one of your clients a book deal with a major publishing house. We're sure our attendees including aspiring writers, established authors, students, hobbyists, and other agents like yourself will be keenly interested to learn about the whole picture of this process.

Your prepared remarks need only to be 15 minutes long. You may notice that the time allotment is five minutes shorter than <u>previous</u> engagements. We made this change in order to allow time for a question and answer session with the audience.

We very much hope you will be able to participate in our workshop and impart your knowledge and experience. To respond, please send me an email at Hankdalton@brightonwriters.com. Once your attendance has been confirmed, I will be in contact in regards to taking care of transportation, accommodation, or any other logistical issues you may have.

Sincerely,
Hank Dalton

74. Why did Hank Dalton write an email to Pam Burns?

(a) to ask about her forthcoming work of fiction
(b) to invite her to appear at a seminar
(c) to send her a one-day pass to the convention
(d) to inform her about the benefits of the club

75. What happened at the spring workshop?

(a) The opening speech lasted two hours.
(b) The keynote lecture started at 9 a.m.
(c) Pam Burns spoke about changing professions.
(d) Pam Burns talked about the world of food.

76. What is probably true about Burns's job?

(a) She is an established fiction writer.
(b) She still has a career as a chef.
(c) She helps authors publish books.
(d) She runs her own company.

77. According to Hank Dalton, who will listen to Pam Burns's speech?

(a) those who manage a publishing company
(b) those who teach students in a literature department
(c) those who enjoy writing stories for fun
(d) those who specialize in the performing arts

78. What will Hank Dalton do if Ms. Burns decides to come?

(a) make a lodging reservation
(b) share his experience about past workshop issues
(c) give her email address to a transportation service
(d) verify the attendance figures

79. In the context of the passage, <u>instrumental</u> means __________.

(a) symbolic
(b) influential
(c) dominant
(d) agreeable

80. In the context of the passage, <u>previous</u> means __________.

(a) ensuing
(b) due
(c) following
(d) earlier

정답·해석·해설 p.199

자동 채점 및 성적 분석 서비스 ▶

자동 채점 및 성적 분석 서비스 ▶

권장 시간: 40분 시작: ___ 시 ___ 분 ~ 종료: ___ 시 ___ 분

정답·해석·해설 p.217

PART 1. *Read the biography article below and answer the questions. The two underlined words are for vocabulary questions.*

KATHERINE JOHNSON

Katherine Johnson was an American mathematician whose work played a vital role in America's first voyages into space. She is best known for helping to break down racial and gender barriers as one of the first African-American women to work at NASA.

Katherine Johnson was born on August 26, 1918, in West Virginia as the youngest child of parents Joshua Coleman and Joylette Lowe. She exhibited a strong <u>aptitude</u> for mathematics from a very young age. In fact, by the time she was 10, she had completed the eighth grade, the highest level of education available to African Americans in her town. Not wanting to limit her potential, her family moved 120 miles away to another county, where she attended high school. Johnson completed high school at 14 and enrolled in West Virginia State College, graduating with degrees in Mathematics and French at the age of 18.

Johnson worked as a teacher until 1952 when she learned that the National Advisory Committee for Aeronautics (NACA) was hiring African-American women with math experience to serve as "computers" in a <u>segregated</u> office. These human computers were required to complete time-consuming calculations for engineers, who would use them to create aircraft for national defense. She began working in 1953 at the NACA with other African-American women. Unlike the other computers, Johnson was assertive and asked questions. After only two weeks on the job, she conducted a review of an engineer's calculations and caught a mistake. Impressed with this display of knowledge in analytical geometry, Johnson's boss reassigned her to work closely with the engineers, all of whom were white men.

Johnson quickly gained the respect of the engineers and was entrusted with increasingly important tasks. She worked on calculating the path Alan Shepard took when he became the first American to travel to space. She also helped send John Glenn into orbit around Earth in 1962, and this was the first time an American astronaut accomplished this feat. At this point, NACA had been renamed NASA and was using electronic computers for calculations, but Glenn refused to fly until Johnson checked the figures herself.

Johnson retired from NASA in 1986, with numerous achievements to her name, including mapping the moon's surface and helping the Apollo 13 astronauts return to Earth. Johnson died on February 24, 2020, at age 101, having devoted her twilight years to encouraging students to follow their dreams of studying science, technology, engineering, and mathematics.

53. What is Katherine Johnson most famous for?

(a) being the first African-American woman astronaut
(b) demanding the employment of women at NASA
(c) aiding in eliminating discrimination at NASA
(d) using a computer on the first space voyage

54. What could have prevented Johnson from getting an education?

(a) the family's move to an out-of-state town
(b) the lack of higher education for African Americans
(c) the high cost of receiving a university education
(d) the discrimination against female students

55. Why did Johnson's boss give her a new job?

(a) because the office became integrated
(b) because she earned an engineering degree
(c) because NACA stopped using human computers
(d) because she pointed out a mathematical error

56. Why most likely did Glenn need Johnson's confirmation for his flight?

(a) He had no experience using electronic computers.
(b) He trusted her more than electronic computers.
(c) The electronic computers could not calculate the orbit.
(d) The computers made a dangerous miscalculation before.

57. How did Johnson spend the final years of her life?

(a) by studying the moon's surface
(b) by inspiring students to pursue their ambitions
(c) by teaching technology at a college
(d) by completing calculations for Apollo 13 engineers

58. In the context of the passage, <u>aptitude</u> means ________.

(a) talent
(b) vigor
(c) passion
(d) attitude

59. In the context of the passage, <u>segregated</u> means ________.

(a) confined
(b) classified
(c) dedicated
(d) differentiated

PART 2. *Read the magazine article below and answer the questions. The two underlined words are for vocabulary questions.*

RESEARCH FINDS A CLOSE LINK BETWEEN FACIAL EXPRESSIONS AND EMOTION

Numerous studies have led many scientists to theorize that facial expressions do more than represent emotions. Known as the facial feedback hypothesis, this concept suggests the physical act of making a facial expression can provide feedback to the brain and influence our state of mind.

The facial feedback hypothesis stems from Charles Darwin's observation that the experience of emotions is more intense when emotions are expressed freely and less intense when repressed. This idea was later developed by William James, who suggested that if we did not make facial expressions, we would not have emotions. Since then, extensive research has been done on the facial feedback hypothesis, with the most notable study being conducted by researchers Fritz Strack, Leonard Martin, and Sabine Stepper in 1988.

In this study, participants were asked to observe humorous cartoons, either while holding a pen between their lips or teeth. The participants who held a pen between their teeth reported that the cartoons were funny more often than those who held a pen between their lips. The researchers concluded this was because holding something between one's teeth forces the mouth into a smile. The physical act of smiling, therefore, can convince people that they are experiencing happiness.

A 2009 study involving Botox, a drug used to prevent sagging skin, also supports the hypothesis. Using fMRI, a technique that measures brain activity, researcher Andreas Hennenlotter had participants react to situations meant to induce anger before and after receiving a Botox treatment. Following the Botox treatments, participants were unable to frown naturally due to the facial paralysis resulting from the drug. He found the areas of their brains involved in processing emotions were no longer being activated with as much intensity as before. This shows the inability to physically express emotions changes how the brain responds to stimuli.

The most discussed implication of the facial feedback hypothesis is that, since the brain responds to smiling by releasing chemicals that actually make a person feel happier, even fake smiling may help elevate mood. Another suggestion is that cognitive processes are influenced by smiling because physically altering one's facial expressions can affect the volume and temperature of blood flow to the brain.

60. What does the article say about the facial feedback hypothesis?

(a) that physically expressing an emotion generates that emotion
(b) that expressions do not always indicate feelings
(c) that we can understand others through their facial expressions
(d) that different brain regions are responsible for different emotions

61. What did Charles Darwin discover about emotional experiences?

(a) People cannot feel any emotions without them.
(b) They force people to feel more positive emotions.
(c) People are inclined to suppress intense negative feelings.
(d) They are enhanced when emotions are not inhibited.

62. Why most likely were some participants not able to enjoy the cartoons as much?

(a) because they were unfamiliar with watching cartoons
(b) because they were incapable of making a happy face
(c) because they reported feeling unhappier than usual
(d) because they could not see their facial expression

63. Which can be said about Hennenlotter's research?

(a) It involved situations prompting the same emotion.
(b) Participants were able to move their faces normally.
(c) Participants' brain activity remained consistent.
(d) It relied on the use of a mental health treatment.

64. According to the facial feedback hypothesis, how does the act of smiling have an effect on the brain?

(a) by adding more intellectual processes
(b) by altering its total volume
(c) by changing features of blood flow
(d) by reducing the intensity of chemicals

65. In the context of the passage, extensive means __________.

(a) contemplative
(b) comprehensive
(c) consequential
(d) experimental

66. In the context of the passage, induce means __________.

(a) deepen
(b) influence
(c) guide
(d) cause

PART 3. *Read the encyclopedia article below and answer the questions. The two underlined words are for vocabulary questions.*

METAVERSE

The metaverse is a highly immersive virtual world in which cutting-edge technologies enable people to interact whenever and however they like.

The term comes from *meta*, meaning "beyond", and universe, and was introduced by science-fiction author Neal Stephenson in his 1992 novel, *Snow Crash*. In Stephenson's fictional metaverse, human avatars interact inside a 3D virtual world that is clearly distinct from the physical one. As envisioned today, however, the metaverse will link the virtual and physical worlds through the Internet so that they are closely intertwined.

The metaverse is <u>considered</u> to be the next step in the Internet's natural evolution. Whereas the Internet's current social and mobile innovations provide rich content and functionality, the metaverse aims to utilize the newest technologies like artificial intelligence and virtual-reality headsets to create a more deeply engaging version of today's Internet. This will allow people to seamlessly interact across different virtual platforms for work, entertainment, and more, giving people the ability to perform Internet-enabled activities in a more cohesive way.

Some have compared metaverse to living within the Internet rather than viewing it from the outside. And while the metaverse as a whole does not presently exist, many parts of it already do. Examples include streaming technologies that permit large groups of people to hold live chats online, video games with complex rule-based systems and virtual economies, and software-based robots that help people do their jobs in finance, medicine, customer service, and more.

For the metaverse to become widespread, however, three key challenges must be overcome. First, Internet access will have to be persistent, or available everywhere at all times, requiring wider adoption of wireless network technologies. Second, the metaverse must allow users to work across multiple platforms and devices with minimal trouble. Finally, issues like security and privacy should be solved.

Because of these and other obstacles, the metaverse is unlikely to be monopolized by a single company. Rather, it will demand that competing firms combine their <u>efforts</u>. And if these firms should succeed, together they will create a powerful platform that will integrate people's digital and physical worlds.

67. What was Stephenson's idea of a metaverse?

(a) a video game where people choose their avatars
(b) a digital world separate from the real one
(c) an online space where money can be exchanged
(d) an electronic device installed in a laboratory

68. How can the existing Internet be converted into the metaverse?

(a) by exploiting current mobile networks
(b) by taking advantage of social media
(c) by centralizing the processing of data
(d) by using the latest tech advancements

69. Based on the passage, which of the following is true about the metaverse today?

(a) It requires robots to monitor streaming technologies.
(b) It draws people closer physically than before.
(c) It depends on technologies that are not yet available.
(d) It exists as smaller pieces of a whole.

70. What is one difficulty that the developers of the metaverse have to address?

(a) making it easier to use across various devices
(b) enabling persistent updates on Internet networks
(c) lowering the price of metaverse hardware products
(d) providing guidance to unfamiliar new users

71. Why most likely will companies not hold monopolies in the metaverse?

(a) to relieve excessive competition
(b) to avoid the risks of the metaverse market failing
(c) to bring about a merged reality collectively
(d) to deploy marketing strategies for the metaverse

72. In the context of the passage, <u>considered</u> means ________.

(a) spotlighted
(b) assumed
(c) regarded
(d) valued

73. In the context of the passage, <u>efforts</u> means ________.

(a) purposes
(b) endeavors
(c) duties
(d) benefits

PART 4. *Read the business letter below and answer the questions. The two underlined words are for vocabulary questions.*

Mr. Robert Meyers
849 Springer Drive
Rochester, NY 15074

Dear Mr. Meyers,

We are delighted to offer you the position of staff photographer at Moment Magazine.

Out of all the candidates, you made the strongest impression during the interview process. Our hiring managers were struck by your confidence, experience, and knowledge, all of which will be major assets going forward in this role.

In addition, the photography project you shared with us as a required work sample not only <u>showcased</u> your skill but also summed up the mission of our monthly magazine. As you know, we aim to capture moments of extraordinary individuals accomplishing great feats despite difficult challenges.

For this position, Moment Magazine is providing a full-time, one-year contract starting on November 1 at our downtown office. Standard work hours of 9 a.m. to 6 p.m., Monday through Friday, will apply. The staff photographer works under the editor-in-chief, with whom you had your final interview.

As for compensation, you will be paid a yearly salary of 50,000 dollars, with payments made once every two weeks via direct deposit. Also, as an employee at Moment Magazine, you will be eligible for health and dental insurance, and an employer-matching retirement plan.

Should you accept this <u>offer</u>, we would like to ask that you respond to this email as soon as possible. We are intent on completing job training before October 17 at the latest. Please feel free to reach me by phone at 508-555-7122 with any questions you may have.

Congratulations! We are looking forward to having you join the team.

Sincerely,

Mary Wilson

Mary Wilson
Hiring Director
Moment Magazine

74. Why did Mary Wilson write a letter to Robert Meyers?

(a) to extend an employment opportunity at a magazine
(b) to list the qualities of a good photographer
(c) to inform him about an available writer position
(d) to explain the interview process in detail

75. How can Robert Meyers most likely be described?

(a) He is the only applicant for the photographer role.
(b) He is not confident about getting the job.
(c) He is competent enough as a photographer.
(d) He is an experienced interviewer.

76. According to Ms. Wilson, what is the goal of Moment Magazine?

(a) to give motivation to accomplished individuals
(b) to document people's everyday problems
(c) to capture readers going through difficult moments
(d) to share stories of remarkable achievements

77. Which is not true about the photographer role at the company?

(a) It will last until October next year.
(b) It will oversee the editor-in-chief.
(c) Its schedule consists of normal weekday hours.
(d) Its duties will be performed at the downtown office.

78. Why is Ms. Wilson asking Mr. Meyers for an immediate reply?

(a) because she wants to finish career training by a certain date
(b) because she will temporarily close the office at the month's end
(c) because she needs a photographer for the company's latest project
(d) because she will have to start contacting photography subjects

79. In the context of the passage, showcased means __________.

(a) boasted
(b) assessed
(c) demonstrated
(d) guaranteed

80. In the context of the passage, offer means __________.

(a) inquiry
(b) proposal
(c) decision
(d) deal

정답·해석·해설 p.217

자동 채점 및 성적 분석 서비스 ▶

정답·해석·해설 p.236

PART 1. *Read the biography article below and answer the questions. The two underlined words are for vocabulary questions.*

GRETA THUNBERG

Greta Thunberg is a Swedish environmental activist who is leading millions of young people to demand climate change action. She is famous for publicly challenging world leaders even at a young age and she became the first teenager chosen to be *Time* magazine's Person of the Year since that tradition started in 1927.

Greta Thunberg was born on January 3, 2003, in Stockholm, Sweden. Her father, Svante Thunberg, is an actor, and her mother, Malena Ernman, is an international opera singer. Greta Thunberg first learned about climate change when she was eight years old. She did not understand why so little was being done about it and fell into a deep depression. She began asking her family to reduce their environmental impact by becoming vegan and giving up air travel. When they complied with her demands, her mother even sacrificing her career, Thunberg felt hopeful that she could make a real difference.

Greta Thunberg's climate change activism began in August 2018. That was when she started missing school to spend her days outside the Swedish Parliament holding up a sign reading "School Strike for Climate." She was reportedly inspired by teenagers in the United States who refused to go to school as a result of <u>mounting</u> gun violence. Turning to social media helped Thunberg spread her message. By October, she was participating in demonstrations across Europe. Two months later, an estimated 20,000 students in over 270 cities were skipping school on Fridays to join her campaign, which brought the world's attention to how strongly young people want to effect change.

Thunberg has gained considerable notice for her many speaking engagements, with her appearance at the 2018 United Nations Climate Change Conference making her known around the world. Thunberg, who was 15 at the time, joined <u>iconic</u> figures like the Dalai Lama, former US Vice President Al Gore, and British naturalist Sir David Attenborough in urging world leaders to reduce emissions.

For her contributions to raising awareness of climate issues, Thunberg received three consecutive Nobel Peace Prize nominations from 2019 to 2021 and was named one of the 10 most valuable people of 2019 by *Nature*, a world-renowned scientific journal. The following year, a Nathan Grossman documentary about her life called *I Am Greta* was shown at the Venice Film Festival. Clearly, her activism has made her a global leader in the cause.

53. What is Greta Thunberg best known for?

(a) challenging conventional ideas about activists
(b) logging the effects of global warming
(c) being the youngest environmental leader in Sweden
(d) questioning influential people as a youth

54. Why most likely did Greta Thunberg's mother give up her career?

(a) because she wanted to support her daughter
(b) because she decided to pursue her dream of acting
(c) because she found it hard to manage childcare
(d) because she chose to go on an international trip

55. What prompted Greta Thunberg to hold the "School Strike for Climate"?

(a) the school's lack of commitment to climate change action
(b) the demonstrations by young people throughout Europe
(c) a protest by other youths concerned about a social issue
(d) a post on social media about how students can be campaigners

56. According to the article, how did Greta Thunberg gain widespread attention?

(a) by presenting at a conference on the environment
(b) by meeting the US President at the White House
(c) by engaging in an American publicity campaign
(d) by having a meeting with noted naturalists

57. What did Greta Thunberg accomplish in 2019?

(a) She received her third Nobel Peace Prize nomination.
(b) She was honored by a publication for her achievements.
(c) She spoke about her activism at the Venice Film Festival.
(d) She won an award for making a film about her life.

58. In the context of the passage, <u>mounting</u> means ________.

(a) alarming
(b) rising
(c) emerging
(d) loading

59. In the context of the passage, <u>iconic</u> means ________.

(a) heroic
(b) brand-new
(c) well-known
(d) photogenic

PART 2. *Read the magazine article below and answer the questions. The two underlined words are for vocabulary questions.*

SCIENTISTS CREATE A SHIRT THAT MONITORS THE HEART

Scientists at Rice University have developed a "smart" shirt embedded with carbon nanotube fibers that can monitor a person's heart rate. Carbon nanotubes (CNTs) are carbon-based elements that have a diameter measured in nanometers, a unit equal to one billionth of a meter. Fibers made from them are soft, flexible, and as conductive as metal wire. The research center Carbon Hub introduced them in 2013, and since then, their potential uses in various fields have been explored.

One of the initial challenges of using CNT fibers as thread was that they are too fine for a sewing machine. To create a thread they could use, the researchers first wove together three bundles of seven fibers each and then put them together, making them as thick as regular thread. They were unable to do this by hand, so they had to specially order the construction of a machine to help them. The machine was similar to a larger version of a device used to make ropes for model ships.

The result was fibers that could be sewn into a shirt. As long as the shirt is worn very close to the chest, it is able to monitor the wearer's heart rate. At the same time, it provides a continual electrocardiogram (ECG), a test that measures and records a person's heart rhythm and electrical activity. In fact, so far, the shirt has given slightly more accurate ECGs than machines typically used for this purpose. According to researcher Lauren Taylor, the team will use denser patches of the fibers in later versions of the shirt so that even more of them touch the skin directly.

The fibers in the smart shirt also serve as electrodes. They allow electronics such as Bluetooth transmitters to be connected so they can relay information to devices that help keep track of data. Fibers made of CNTs may be beneficial for other implementations as well. They have been found to be more effective at dispersing energy than Kevlar, the material used in bulletproof vests. This means that they could be used to create more defensive military uniforms in the future.

60. What is the article mainly about?

(a) the development of versatile thread
(b) the invention of clothing containing CNTs
(c) the thermal properties of CNTs
(d) the establishment of a process for making clothes

61. What was the early problem with utilizing CNT fibers?

(a) There was no perfect method for producing CNTs.
(b) There were not enough fibers available.
(c) They were too rigid to be woven.
(d) They were far thinner than typical fabric thread.

62. How did the researchers obtain thread for their work?

(a) by employing a specially created device
(b) by putting regular thread into three bundles
(c) by stitching fibers together using a sewing machine
(d) by having a model ship maker do the weaving work

63. Why most likely will compact fibers be included in forthcoming shirts?

(a) to allow for the creation of larger garments
(b) to facilitate the use of electronic devices
(c) to further improve future ECG results
(d) to make wireless connections possible

64. Based on the article, why might future military uniforms be comprised of CNT fibers?

(a) because they enable the military to track personnel
(b) because they afford intelligence information
(c) because they provide soldiers with more protection
(d) because they result in clothing weighing less

65. In the context of the passage, embedded means ________.

(a) covered
(b) engraved
(c) fit
(d) set

66. In the context of the passage, records means ________.

(a) depicts
(b) documents
(c) catalogs
(d) remembers

PART 3. *Read the encyclopedia article below and answer the questions. The two underlined words are for vocabulary questions.*

JOHN HENRY EFFECT

The John Henry effect is a cognitive bias that can be exhibited by participants in an experiment. It occurs when the members of one group think that they need to outperform those of another group, thereby invalidating the experiment.

This phenomenon takes its name from John Henry, an American steel driver who worked for a railway company building a tunnel. According to the legend, the company began using a steam-powered device to drill holes for explosives, claiming that it could surpass human workers. This hurt Henry's pride because he believed his abilities were being unfairly questioned, so he offered to race the machine using only his hammer and spike. Henry won, but in doing so, he exerted such a great effort that he died.

A similar competitive instinct can affect an experiment that includes a control group, whose members do not receive the experimental treatment, and a treatment group. When people perceive that they are in the control group and feel other participants possess an unfair advantage, they may put in additional effort to prove their worth. This will distort the data and lead to inaccurate results.

The John Henry Effect is particularly common in studies related to the workplace, as participants are naturally motivated to avoid being rated negatively. For example, when an accounting company considers adopting a new software program to minimize errors, it may decide to test its effectiveness first. To do this, management would divide workers into one group that uses the current application and another that uses the new one. In order for this experiment to succeed, the only variable should be the type of software used. However, if the members of the control group do their tasks twice as fast as usual to overcome the perceived disadvantage, it would be impossible for the company to accurately compare the two programs.

The most effective way to prevent the John Henry effect from occurring is to make certain that experiment participants do not know which group they belong to. If this is not possible, ensuring that the groups cannot observe each other's progress can reduce the impact of this effect on the results of the study.

67. What is the John Henry effect?

(a) a method of selecting group members
(b) a prejudiced view of experiment results
(c) a preconception that negatively affects a study
(d) a mental disorder that limits performance

68. Why did John Henry challenge the machine?

(a) because his company tried to motivate its staff
(b) because he felt an insult to his pride
(c) because his co-workers were being unfairly treated
(d) because he wanted to try new equipment

69. Based on the article, which of the following is not true about the members of a control group?

(a) They are unable to receive the treatment that is being tested.
(b) They have a significant advantage over other participants.
(c) They may purposely adjust their behavior during an experiment.
(d) They might cause the collection of erroneous information.

70. Which is probably a factor that could make the accounting company's experiment unreliable?

(a) The purpose of the tasks is unclear.
(b) The duration of the test is too long.
(c) The sizes of the groups are varied.
(d) The number of variables is too large.

71. What can researchers do to avoid the occurrence of the John Henry effect?

(a) ensure that observers are impartial
(b) provide participants with more information
(c) ban communication between the groups
(d) limit the scope of the results

72. In the context of the passage, claiming means __________.

(a) asserting
(b) complaining
(c) requesting
(d) opposing

73. In the context of the passage, minimize means __________.

(a) demean
(b) lessen
(c) remove
(d) downsize

PART 4. *Read the business letter below and answer the questions. The two underlined words are for vocabulary questions.*

Natalie Holmes
Marketing Manager
Rasputin Technologies

Greetings! I'm reaching out in regard to the Technology Development Conference your company will host at the Civic Auditorium on October 17. We have successfully accommodated hundreds of events at this venue before, and we would like to offer our unique catering services to you.

Cool Catering provides the tastiest selection of finger foods in the state. Each one of our bite-sized dishes is prepared by a professionally trained chef, so the quality is guaranteed. In addition to the outstanding flavor, our style of cuisine is perfect for the vibe of a conference, as attendees can conveniently enjoy the finger foods while walking and without the need for special cutlery.

Our three menu options make it easy to choose the <u>right</u> variety of dishes that will appeal to all of your guests.

Basic: Preset cold dishes
Dish: 4 finger foods
Price: $10 per person

Standard: Select three hot options and three cold options
Dish: 6 finger foods, 20 dishes to choose from
Price: $17 per person

Deluxe: Full selection available
Dish: 8 finger foods, 28 dishes* to choose from (**includes seasonal seafood options*)
Price: $22 per person

Each menu serves one portion of each dish for the number of guests specified in the order. To provide a meal's worth of food, we recommend six to eight servings per person. On the day of the event, our team will deliver the food on visually-pleasing plates and <u>arrange</u> chafing dishes to keep hot items warm during service. If you have any questions, please feel free to contact me at 402-444-0508.

Best Regards,
Ed Bowen
Outreach Coordinator
Cool Catering

74. Why did Ed Bowen write to Natalie Holmes?

(a) to detail success stories from past events
(b) to propose food services for a convention
(c) to invite a company to a tech conference
(d) to offer an upgrade to an event venue

75. How does Cool Catering ensure the quality of its food?

(a) by employing skilled culinary experts
(b) by getting feedback from food critics
(c) by using the freshest ingredients in the state
(d) by exclusively serving tasty finger foods

76. According to Mr. Bowen, why are Cool Catering's dishes suitable for conferences?

(a) because they vary depending on the needs of the event
(b) because they come with convenient cutlery
(c) because they help provide a professional vibe
(d) because they can be eaten on the move

77. What can Ms. Holmes request if she orders the highest-priced menu option?

(a) seasonal desserts
(b) larger portions
(c) more beverage options
(d) seafood dishes

78. Why most likely would Ms. Holmes choose to order six to eight portions per guest?

(a) to get a discount on an order
(b) to qualify for free delivery
(c) to ensure everyone gets enough food
(d) to prepare for a number of unexpected guests

79. In the context of the passage, <u>right</u> means __________.

(a) genuine
(b) accurate
(c) proper
(d) pleasant

80. In the context of the passage, <u>arrange</u> means __________.

(a) adjust
(b) give
(c) decorate
(d) organize

정답·해석·해설 p.236

자동 채점 및 성적 분석 서비스 ▶

정답·해석·해설 p.254

***PART 1.** Read the biography article below and answer the questions. The two underlined words are for vocabulary questions.*

LI NA

Li Na is a Chinese former professional tennis player known for being the first Asian to win a Grand Slam tournament. She is considered the driving force behind an explosion of the sport's popularity in China.

Li Na was born on February 26, 1982, in Hubei, China. Her father, Li Shengpeng, was a professional badminton player. Inspired by her dad, Li began playing badminton at six years old. However, two years later, Li accepted her coach's suggestion and started to play tennis. Li sharpened her tennis skills, and when her father died in 1996, she decided that playing the sport could be a means of supporting her mother. Li joined China's National Tennis Team and became a professional player at age 16. Although she saw tremendous success initially, Li chose to take a break from tennis in 2002 to fulfill her dream of studying journalism at university.

When Li returned to the sport in 2004, she managed to resurrect her career, climbing up the ranks and winning several cash prizes. Up until this point, she had remained part of the Chinese Tennis Association, which took 65 percent of her winnings. Li was critical of this practice and participated in a program called "Fly Solo" in 2008. Under "Fly Solo," Li only had to contribute eight percent of her winnings to the Chinese Tennis Association. However, she had to hire her own coaches and pay for all training and touring costs herself.

Her triumphant performance at the 2010 Australian Open marked a crucial moment for her, and more success followed in 2011 when her worldwide ranking leaped to No. 4 with her first Grand Slam singles win at the French Open. This win was historic since Li was the first Asian tennis player, either male or female, to win a Grand Slam singles event. This prompted her popularity to grow considerably throughout China, and people began to see her as an icon. Her celebrity status was cemented when she won her second Grand Slam singles title in 2014.

Li retired in September 2014 due to a knee injury but her legacy has no doubt lived on. Li has plans to found her own tennis academy for young athletes, although she is still looking for the right location and wants to make sure she partners with a school that provides a comprehensive education.

53. When did Li Na begin to play tennis?

(a) when her father introduced her to the sport
(b) when it started to get popular in China
(c) when her instructor suggested it to her
(d) when it became more lucrative

54. Why did Li take a break from tennis at the beginning of her career?

(a) because she could not play professionally at the time
(b) because she wanted to receive higher education
(c) because she felt a need to get away from journalists
(d) because she was grieving the death of her father

55. Based on the passage, what is probably a benefit of the Chinese Tennis Association?

(a) protecting winnings from bad investments
(b) finding companies to offer athletes sponsorships
(c) creating events for players to participate in
(d) paying the training expenses for its players

56. Which of the following did not happen to Li from 2010 onward?

(a) She competed in the Australian Open.
(b) She was named the world's top tennis player.
(c) She won two Grand Slam singles titles.
(d) She grew increasingly famous in her home country.

57. How does Li plan to influence the next generation of tennis players?

(a) by partnering with former professional players
(b) by traveling to locations to discuss her career
(c) by developing sports injury prevention steps
(d) by opening a comprehensive tennis school

58. In the context of the passage, <u>resurrect</u> means __________.

(a) retain
(b) save
(c) restore
(d) construct

59. In the context of the passage, <u>cemented</u> means __________.

(a) established
(b) earned
(c) clarified
(d) defended

PART 2. *Read the magazine article below and answer the questions. The two underlined words are for vocabulary questions.*

THE AMAZON WAS MORE INHABITED THAN BELIEVED

Archaeologists have discovered numerous Pre-Columbian earthworks in the Amazon. In the past, they believed that Pre-Columbian civilizations were concentrated only in rich floodplains. However, the new findings show that there were also significant populations in areas of mixed grassland and forest.

The earthworks cover a massive area in modern-day Bolivia and Brazil. Some have geometric patterns that are square, circular, or hexagonal. These patterned earthworks, which are formed by the careful arrangement of materials on the ground, are known as geoglyphs. The researchers consider these to have been ceremonial centers because they have found evidence of ritualistic sacrifices but no objects suggesting actual human habitation. However, near the geoglyphs were villages located in rings on large mounds, <u>deliberately</u> kept above the level of seasonal floods.

In some areas, there were large settlements connected by causeways—the equivalent of modern roadways. These communities were reinforced for protection and surrounded by one or more channels. In this sense, they were clearly constructed for long-term occupation and represent primitive, low-density urban populations. According to the researchers, these populations were not migratory and had hierarchical social classes. Furthermore, they had frequent interactions both at the community and regional levels.

Researchers used satellite imagery and other remote sensing technology to spot potential settlements and sent out teams to investigate the sites. In total, they found 81 previously unrecorded sites, which helped fill in large gaps in the archaeological record. The areas they discovered span an interconnected space of 1,800 kilometers from east to west.

The researchers then entered data into a computer model to <u>estimate</u> the population size. After revising the results for differences in population density, they determined that there were 1,087,150 residents. This number dwarfs the census data recorded by the Jesuit missionaries who conducted population surveys after the arrival of Columbus. This can probably be explained by the devastation European diseases, such as smallpox, brought to the native population.

Although the distances covered by the settlements were enormous, they were found in similar terrains and climates. The alternating wet and dry seasons produced sparse forests, which made it easier to clear existing trees. This sheds new light on the environmental impact of Pre-Columbian communities as scientists now believe that it was far greater than was previously presumed.

60. What did the study find out about the Amazon before Columbus?

(a) that its floodplains were popular settlements
(b) that it was actually occupied quite extensively
(c) that its population density transformed the landscape
(d) that it had a major effect on future civilizations

61. Why do the researchers believe that the geoglyphs were used for rituals?

(a) The geoglyphs feature patterns that reflect worship.
(b) The researchers uncovered proof of ancient rites.
(c) The geoglyphs are located in the center of the civilization.
(d) The researchers found objects suggesting habitation.

62. According to the article, what was a characteristic of the people in large settlements?

(a) a habit of migrating to new locations with the seasons
(b) a common conflict between different social classes
(c) a tendency to mix with people from other communities
(d) a lack of knowledge about channel construction

63. Why most likely did the Jesuits document low population numbers?

(a) because the surveys were conducted in a limited area
(b) because the methods used in the census were flawed
(c) because most of the native people refused to participate
(d) because many natives had died from exotic diseases

64. What can be concluded about Pre-Columbian people based on the geographical feature?

(a) They had difficulty cutting down the forests.
(b) They adapted to life in dissimilar surroundings.
(c) They grew different crops depending on the season.
(d) They altered the environment more than thought.

65. In the context of the passage, deliberately means ________.

(a) willingly
(b) systematically
(c) intentionally
(d) accidentally

66. In the context of the passage, estimate means ________.

(a) calculate
(b) solve
(c) imagine
(d) assume

***PART 3.** Read the encyclopedia article below and answer the questions. The two underlined words are for vocabulary questions.*

HARPSICHORD

The harpsichord is a keyboard instrument that is closely associated with the Renaissance and Baroque periods. Most music historians consider it to be a predecessor of the modern piano, which it strongly resembles.

The earliest known reference to the harpsichord was made in 1397, and this instrument was widely used throughout Europe from the early 16th century until the end of the 18th century. Many prominent composers, such as Bach and Vivaldi, created musical pieces <u>specifically</u> for it. The design of the harpsichord played an important role in its early popularity. The other keyboard instrument commonly used during this period—the pipe organ—cannot be moved without great difficulty due to its size and complexity. In contrast, the harpsichord is convenient to transport. Furthermore, it is less expensive to make and easier to clean and repair.

Harpsichords rely on a relatively simple mechanism to generate sound. A harpsichord key functions like a lever. When the musician presses down on the front of a key, the back of it rises. This motion pushes a narrow wooden board called a jack upwards as well. As the jack ascends, it quickly pulls and releases a string, producing a musical note in a manner similar to that of a guitar string being plucked.

The primary disadvantage of the harpsichord is that a musician cannot change the volume or length of a note. Regardless of how hard or how quickly a key is struck, the action of plucking a string results in a sound of the same volume and duration each time. It was this limitation that eventually caused the harpsichord to be superseded by the piano. This newer instrument includes hammers that strike the strings with different speeds and intensities depending on how the musician presses the keys.

Although the harpsichord had lost its popularity among musicians by the end of the 18th century, it has experienced a limited revival in modern times. It was played by early pop groups, such as the Beatles, and featured in the celebrated 2015 musical *Hamilton*. However, it remains a <u>niche</u> instrument used mainly in performances of historical pieces, rather than in popular modern compositions.

67. Based on the article, how do academics view the harpsichord?

(a) as superior to modern instruments
(b) as being based on the designs of the first piano
(c) as better suited for Baroque than Renaissance music
(d) as the early form of a contemporary instrument

68. Which is not a benefit of the harpsichord over the pipe organ?

(a) its more complex design
(b) its greater mobility
(c) its cheaper production cost
(d) its simpler maintenance

69. What is the function of the jack?

(a) to press a key
(b) to lift a board
(c) to activate a lever
(d) to pluck a string

70. Why most likely did musicians switch from the harpsichord to the piano?

(a) because the harpsichord's music is produced at a very low volume
(b) because the harpsichord's player cannot alter the qualities of notes
(c) because the harpsichord's keyboard is difficult to operate
(d) because the harpsichord's hammers generate inconsistent sounds

71. What can be inferred about the recent renewal of interest in the harpsichord?

(a) It is unlikely to be widespread.
(b) It was revived by historical performances.
(c) It will probably be limited to pop music.
(d) It resulted from a famous musical.

72. In the context of the passage, <u>specifically</u> means ________.

(a) essentially
(b) particularly
(c) absolutely
(d) partially

73. In the context of the passage, <u>niche</u> means ________.

(a) suitable
(b) sophisticated
(c) specialized
(d) marginal

PART 4. *Read the business letter below and answer the questions. The two underlined words are for vocabulary questions.*

Mr. Ralph Henderson
Marketing Director
Corporate Headquarters

Dear Mr. Henderson,

Welcome back! While you were on vacation, we announced the implementation of the Total Management System (TMS), which will go into full effect on July 12. Not only will the TMS make the company more efficient but it will simplify many processes for managers and team members alike.

The TMS is a paperless system that holds employee payroll information, attendance record, and emergency contact numbers in one convenient place. In addition, this system can be used to easily request days off and schedule meetings, without the inconvenience of tracking down a coworker to choose a time or place.

To access the TMS, first set up your account and password with this link (www.startTMS.com). Before the system is fully implemented, explore the system and get familiar with the attendance and vacation request features, which will be most frequently used.

To ease the transition, we will email a user manual to each team member. The manual will cover the system's basic functions, and will also detail how to handle less common situations like bereavement leave, employee complaints, and resignations. Please note that while the TMS can be used on a mobile device, accounts must be set up on a PC.

Finally, we ask that you join the other department heads for an educational session this Friday at 10 a.m. in the main conference room. This training will last until lunchtime and will equip you with the knowledge to cope with any TMS inquiry you may receive. If you can't attend the group session, contact me by email at jstewartHR@littlefoot.org and we can arrange a private meeting, preferably before July 12.

Thank you in advance for your cooperation.

Sincerely,

Julie Stewart
Julie Stewart
HR General Manager
Littlefoot Shoes

74. What is the main purpose of Julie Stewart's letter?

(a) to celebrate the productivity of the company
(b) to introduce a new organizational tool
(c) to share employee contact information
(d) to launch a system to reduce paper waste

75. How does the new system assist workers at Littlefoot Shoes?

(a) It reports emergency situations automatically.
(b) It simplifies the ordering process.
(c) It offers them more opportunities for days off.
(d) It allows them to organize meetings more simply.

76. What does Ms. Stewart suggest workers do prior to using the system?

(a) follow the TMS link to a manager's account
(b) monitor the time in the attendance function
(c) take a look at the common features
(d) delete the default password

77. Which TMS feature will be used less frequently?

(a) requesting holiday leave
(b) maintaining attendance records
(c) registering worker dissatisfaction
(d) tracking staff payroll hours

78. Why most likely did Ms. Stewart mention her contact information in the letter?

(a) so Mr. Henderson can schedule a potential individual training
(b) so Mr. Henderson can ask department heads about the system
(c) to share the schedule for the group session
(d) to get the lunch orders of the training participants

79. In the context of the passage, <u>announced</u> means ________.

(a) authorized
(b) declared
(c) discussed
(d) divulged

80. In the context of the passage, <u>equip</u> means ________.

(a) provide
(b) position
(c) award
(d) entreat

정답·해석·해설 p.254

자동 채점 및 성적 분석 서비스 ▶

09회 실전모의고사

자동 채점 및 성적 분석 서비스 ▶

권장 시간: 40분 시작: ___ 시 ___ 분 ~ 종료: ___ 시 ___ 분

정답·해석·해설 p.273

***PART 1.** Read the biography article below and answer the questions. The two underlined words are for vocabulary questions.*

ALFRED HITCHCOCK

Alfred Hitchcock, known as the "Master of Suspense," was a prolific British movie director who became one of the most influential and widely studied filmmakers in cinema history.

Alfred Joseph Hitchcock was born on August 13, 1899, in Leytonstone, England. He grew up in a strict household under the watchful eyes of a devoted mother and an oppressive father. As a youth, Hitchcock spent a lot of time alone and learned to entertain himself. He was creative, and to satisfy his impulses, he later studied art at university. In 1920, he found an entry-level job designing title cards for silent films, which introduced him to moviemaking.

In 1925, Hitchcock made his directorial debut with *The Pleasure Garden*, a silent drama film. However, as it was unlike the movies for which he is now admired, film enthusiasts acknowledge the 1927 thriller *The Lodger: A Story of the London Fog* as his first real work. By the time Hitchcock concluded his first talking film, *Blackmail*, in 1929, he had a wealth of experience in visual storytelling and every aspect of production.

Over the next decade, Hitchcock developed his craft, producing mainly suspenseful thrillers. Following the international releases of *The Man Who Knew Too Much* and *The 39 Steps*, he drew the attention of noted film producer David O. Selznick, who invited him to Hollywood.

During this time, Hitchcock popularized a plot device known as the "MacGuffin," an element that is indispensable to the beginning of a film's plot and the motivation of the protagonist but meaningless to the overall story. A famous example of a MacGuffin is the money the character Marion Crane steals at the start of the movie *Psycho*, which is the reason she finds herself at the Bates Motel, the story's setting. However, this fortune soon becomes insignificant when Crane gets murdered and the money sinks to the bottom of a swamp.

Hitchcock directed over 50 feature films in total. He remains a familiar face to this day thanks to his enjoyment of making cameos in his films, a habit that endeared him to fans. Near the end of his life, Hitchcock was working on the script for a film called *The Short Night*, but it was never filmed. He died of kidney failure on April 29, 1980, at his home in Los Angeles.

53. How did Hitchcock first become exposed to moviemaking?

(a) by majoring in film studies in college
(b) by watching movies with his parents
(c) by taking a small job in the film industry
(d) by studying art with a well-known director

54. Why most likely is Hitchcock's 1927 thriller considered to be his first film?

(a) because it was his first talking film
(b) because it showed his esteemed style
(c) because it received much international praise
(d) because it garnered him a fan base

55. Based on the article, what made Hitchcock move to Hollywood?

(a) attention from an industry figure
(b) the release of American horror films
(c) the slow pace of the traditional film industry
(d) rejection from movie critics in England

56. What can be said about the money stolen by a character in *Psycho*?

(a) It was Hitchcock's first known use of a MacGuffin.
(b) It had little to do with the actual plot of the film.
(c) It proved its importance at the end of the movie.
(d) It was mentioned often by characters throughout the film.

57. What has caused people to be familiar with Hitchcock's image?

(a) his work on the screenplay for *The Short Night*
(b) his many interactions with loyal fans
(c) his brief appearances in his own movies
(d) his habit of spending time out in Los Angeles

58. In the context of the passage, satisfy means ________.

(a) amuse
(b) fulfill
(c) match
(d) verify

59. In the context of the passage, craft means ________.

(a) skill
(b) scheme
(c) enthusiasm
(d) bottom

PART 2. *Read the magazine article below and answer the questions. The two underlined words are for vocabulary questions.*

ANIMALS ARE ADAPTING BECAUSE OF CLIMATE CHANGE

A new study in *Trends in Ecology & Evolution* suggests that some animals are physically adapting in response to climate change. This makes it clear that global warming is not just a problem for humans to navigate.

Just like humans, warm-blooded animals must maintain their body temperature within a specific range in order to survive. In warm climates, they must disperse the heat to keep from overheating. Birds do this through their bare beaks and legs, while in mammals, this process occurs primarily through their ears or tails. These body parts are vital for thermoregulation, or the ability to regulate body temperature, because they tend not to be insulated with feathers or fur.

According to the study, these body parts are growing larger as climates are getting increasingly warmer. For instance, the beak size of some Australian parrots has increased as much as 10 percent since 1871, and a slight increase in the tail length of field mice has also been reported. While the documented changes have been <u>negligible</u> so far, one of the researchers, Sara Ryding of Deakin University, says that such growth is worrying because it is happening at a much faster rate than what would normally occur through evolution. She believes that the size of the body parts regulating temperature could only continue to increase in correlation with the changing climate and that, in the future, many animals may look very different than they currently do.

At this point, it is known that animals are adapting in an attempt to survive, but whether they actually will remains to be seen. Apart from <u>affecting</u> how they look, these adaptations could alter them in ways that somehow endanger them or have ecological consequences. For example, it is possible that having a larger beak could change how and what birds are able to eat. Further research is still needed to determine exactly which animals have faced repercussions so far, and the researchers intend to start this investigation by using a 3D scanner to examine various bird specimens from the past century.

60. According to the article, how are some animals responding to climate change?

(a) by improving their natural navigational abilities
(b) by searching for new home environments
(c) by approaching areas where humans reside
(d) by undergoing changes to their bodies

61. What do birds do to control their body temperature?

(a) puff out their feathers regularly
(b) release heat through featherless parts
(c) travel to regions with cooler climates
(d) disperse excess warmth through their tails

62. Why does Ryding suggest that the documented changes are a concern?

(a) because they have been considerable so far
(b) because they may create serious disadvantages for some species
(c) because they imply that climate change is inevitable
(d) because they are occurring more rapidly than what is natural

63. What does Sara Ryding believe about the connection between climate and the size of certain body parts?

(a) that it will impact the appearance of animals
(b) that it will only be evident in bird species going forward
(c) that it will eventually shrink some body parts
(d) that it could be reversed with temperature drops

64. Why most likely do researchers want to study old bird specimens?

(a) to determine what their eating habits were
(b) to see which birds have changed physically over time
(c) to discover the factors that resulted in their death
(d) to confirm some previous findings on bird physiology

65. In the context of the passage, <u>negligible</u> means ________.

(a) careless
(b) meager
(c) irresponsible
(d) unimportant

66. In the context of the passage, <u>affecting</u> means ________.

(a) influencing
(b) transferring
(c) simulating
(d) reforming

PART 3. *Read the encyclopedia article below and answer the questions. The two underlined words are for vocabulary questions.*

ARCHERY

Archery is the practice of shooting an arrow from a bow. It was ubiquitous throughout much of human history and made its Olympic debut as a sport in 1900.

The earliest evidence of archery is a collection of bone and stone arrowheads discovered at Sibudu Cave in South Africa. These artifacts are approximately 70,000 years old and depict that the bow and arrow was used for hunting over an extended time period. The first known instance of its employment as a weapon occurred at a site in Kenya, where a human skull from around 10,000 years ago was found with the remains of a stone-tipped arrow in it.

Archery came to play a vital role in medieval warfare because the bows of that era were capable of regularly punching through the metal protective gear soldiers wore. In much of Asia, the military preferred the composite bow, a short bow constructed using layers of bone and wood. The combination of materials gave it great strength despite its small size. In contrast, Western Europeans used a single piece of wood, usually yew or ash, to create a bow that was powerful because of its great length.

By the 16th century, however, the use of archery by the military declined dramatically due to the introduction of guns. Nevertheless, it continued to be practiced as a hobby by a small number of enthusiasts. In the late 18th century, archery underwent a revival among the nobility. Many archery societies were formed, and membership in these was viewed as an indicator of high social status because people from the middle and lower classes were generally excluded.

In modern times, archery has been reborn as a competitive sport, and it has been featured in every Summer Olympics since 1972. Olympic archery is performed exclusively with the compound bow. It utilizes mechanical parts such as a pulley to increase arrow velocity and a sophisticated sight to improve accuracy. However, the inclusion of these components can pose a problem, as they cause it to weigh much more than other types of bow.

67. What was the original use for archery?

(a) a tool for pursuing prey
(b) a way to defend against enemies
(c) a means to damage tough armor
(d) a symbol for displaying wealth

68. Why is the site in Kenya considered the place where archery was first used as a weapon?

(a) It was home to an ancient group of warriors.
(b) It had a large collection of bows and arrows.
(c) It was filled with the remains of many skulls.
(d) It had evidence of a human dying by an arrow.

69. Based on the passage, why was archery commonly used in medieval military conflicts?

(a) because it had a greatly increased range
(b) because it was made from strong metals
(c) because it had a compact design
(d) because it was able to pierce armor

70. Which of the following is probably true about the 18th-century archery societies?

(a) They were available to all classes.
(b) They had aristocratic members.
(c) They were restored by the military.
(d) They held frequent public competitions.

71. What makes the bow for Olympic archery different from other types of bows?

(a) its quick loading of arrows
(b) its frequent need for repairs
(c) its relatively greater weight
(d) its expensive electric parts

72. In the context of the passage, ubiquitous means _________.

(a) existing
(b) continuous
(c) widespread
(d) fashionable

73. In the context of the passage, featured means _________.

(a) presented
(b) treated
(c) favored
(d) described

PART 4. *Read the business letter below and answer the questions. The two underlined words are for vocabulary questions.*

John White
Hiring Manager
Easy Learning

Dear Mr. White,

It is my immense pleasure to endorse Shawn Gardner for employment at Easy Learning. For the last 10 years, I have worked with him as the education team manager at Tier Leap, an early childhood education company. In his position as senior content developer, Shawn was responsible for the creation of the company's curriculum, learning products, toys, and award-winning textbooks.

As long as I have known him, Shawn has always exhibited tremendous professionalism, routinely going above and beyond the scope of his duties. His tasks were completed on time and to a high level without exception. He also maintained strong relationships with his peers, who frequently turned to him for advice when they needed a fresh perspective on a project or idea.

Ultimately, his strengths lie in his creativity, attention to detail, and writing ability. Because of these skills, he was chosen as the lead scriptwriter for Tier Leap's TV series. Thanks in part to Shawn's dedication and craftsmanship, the program currently airs in 10 countries across three continents. It continues to provide thousands of children around the world with access to entertaining and informative content.

I am confident Shawn will be a great asset to your company. I sincerely hope that you give his candidacy favorable consideration. If you need any further information, please do not hesitate to email me at nclark@Tierone.com or call me at 818-555-0172. My office hours are from 9 a.m. to 4:30 p.m.

Sincerely,

Nicole Clark

Nicole Clark
Manager
Education Team
Tier Leap

74. What is the main purpose of Nicole Clark's letter?

(a) to publicize newly released children's books
(b) to recommend a colleague for a position
(c) to give an endorsement for learning tools
(d) to offer a work contract to a recent interviewee

75. What did Shawn Gardner do as a content developer at Tier Leap?

(a) He was in charge of hiring education team members.
(b) He won content creator awards.
(c) He defined early childhood learning theories.
(d) He produced Tier Leap's syllabus.

76. What was one reason why Shawn was picked to write the TV series scripts?

(a) because he came up with the show's concept
(b) because of his acting experience
(c) because of his strong imagination
(d) because he knows television trends

77. How does Nicole Clark regard Tier Leap's TV series?

(a) as a program teaching children to write
(b) as an academic show for international viewers
(c) as an educational product for all ages
(d) as a talk show for the national audience

78. Based on the letter, how can Mr. White get more information about Shawn Gardner?

(a) by contacting educational TV broadcasts
(b) by writing an email to Shawn Gardner
(c) by calling Nicole Clark during work hours
(d) by stopping by the Tier Leap company

79. In the context of the passage, completed means ________.

(a) performed
(b) finished
(c) submitted
(d) stopped

80. In the context of the passage, candidacy means ________.

(a) expertise
(b) election
(c) admission
(d) application

정답·해석·해설 p.273

자동 채점 및 성적 분석 서비스 ▶

PART 1. *Read the biography article below and answer the questions. The two underlined words are for vocabulary questions.*

FRIDA KAHLO

Frida Kahlo was a Mexican painter best known for her colorful and imaginative self-portraits. Her portraits explore themes of pain, identity, and gender while also incorporating Mexican history.

Frida Kahlo was born on July 6, 1907, in Coyoacán, Mexico. Her father Guillermo Kahlo, a photographer, was of German descent, and her mother Matilde Calderón y González was of mixed European and Indigenous heritage. Kahlo routinely assisted her father in his studio, where she developed an eye for detail. While she took drawing classes in her youth, her interest was in science. So in 1922, she enrolled in the National Preparatory School to study medicine.

Kahlo would have become a doctor had it not been for a near-fatal bus accident in 1925. Confined to bed for months, she turned to painting self-portraits to pass the time. After she recovered, she met Diego Rivera, a renowned muralist who encouraged her to keep painting, and they started a relationship.

In August of 1929, they got married. As both of them were artists, they were often competitive with each other, with Kahlo sometimes feeling overshadowed by her husband. Rivera's numerous extramarital affairs and Kahlo's multiple miscarriages complicated matters further.

During their relationship, Kahlo created many pieces that conveyed her grief. Her 1932 painting *Henry Ford Hospital* represented her miscarriage, while *The Two Fridas*, finished in 1939 during their divorce, depicted two versions of Kahlo sitting hand in hand: the woman Rivera fell in love with and the one he left with a broken heart. The following year, she completed *Self-Portrait with Cropped Hair*. This piece showed her sitting on a chair in men's clothing, having cut off her long hair, which Rivera had loved. Soon after, in *Self-Portrait with Thorn Necklace and Hummingbird*, she painted herself with thorns around her neck to render her anguish.

The final years of her life were dedicated to campaigning for peace and promoting political causes. Kahlo died on July 13, 1954, never having received recognition outside of Mexico. In fact, it was not until the 1970s, when academics commenced publishing books about her, that international interest in her began to develop.

53. What is Frida Kahlo most famous for?

(a) her use of natural materials
(b) her ideas about imagination
(c) her strong Mexican identity
(d) her artistic depictions of herself

54. When did Kahlo develop her keen eye?

(a) when she attended university to study medicine
(b) when she studied different drawing techniques
(c) when she helped out at her father's workplace
(d) when she discovered her passion for science

55. What can most likely be said about Kahlo and Rivera's marriage?

(a) It ended because of Kahlo's affair.
(b) It made them less competitive with one another.
(c) It faced many difficulties that made it hard to sustain.
(d) It complicated Rivera's artistic identity.

56. Based on the passage, which characterizes Kahlo's artworks in the 1930s?

(a) They depict interpretations of her personality.
(b) They portray her feelings of emotional distress.
(c) They represent the slow passage of time.
(d) They show the changes in her appearance.

57. How did Kahlo live out her final years?

(a) by releasing art books internationally
(b) by participating in political activism
(c) by developing other Mexican painters
(d) by devoting herself to medical care

58. In the context of the passage, <u>interest</u> means _________.

(a) curiosity
(b) novelty
(c) preference
(d) confidence

59. In the context of the passage, <u>conveyed</u> means _________.

(a) transported
(b) conquered
(c) dispatched
(d) expressed

PART 2. *Read the magazine article below and answer the questions. The two underlined words are for vocabulary questions.*

MEDITATION MAY HELP SHARPEN YOUR FOCUS

A recent study led by Jeff Lin, a psychologist at Michigan State University, has found that meditation may reduce the number of mistakes that people make. The findings of the study suggest that this is because meditation enhances brain function, changing how we detect and respond to errors.

The study focused on open monitoring meditation, also known as choiceless awareness meditation. Unlike other forms of meditation, which can center on a single thing, such as one's breathing, a sound, or simply an object in the room, open monitoring meditation requires practitioners to sit quietly and pay careful attention to everything that is going on in their mind and body. The goal is to cultivate awareness of thoughts and physical sensations as they arise because it is believed that acknowledging them helps people transform bad cognitive and emotional habits over time.

The researchers recruited more than 200 participants with no prior meditation experience for the study. They were connected to an electroencephalography (EEG) machine, which measures electrical activity in the brain, and guided through a 20-minute choiceless awareness meditation session. They were then asked to complete a computerized test designed to distract them and assess their concentration.

Through the use of the EEG, the scientists discovered that a specific neural signal linked to conscious error recognition was stronger in the meditators than in the participants of the control group. The meditators essentially demonstrated a greater ability to identify the mistakes they made on the test shortly after making them. Although the group of meditators did not outperform the control group on the actual test, Lin believes their relatively fast awareness of slipups indicates meditation's influence on brain performance.

Though meditation and mindfulness have become increasingly popular in recent years, Lin's research team is one of the few to study the effect these practices have on the brain and its functions. They intend to conduct further research to see if lasting behavioral changes can occur as a result of the influence of meditation on brain activity.

60. What did the study find out about meditation's effect?

(a) that it may boost the brain's information processing speed
(b) that it could improve people's accuracy
(c) that it might alter how a person's brain reacts to changes
(d) that it can release chemicals to enhance intelligence

61. How does open monitoring meditation differ from other forms of meditation?

(a) It requires meditators to emit a soft noise.
(b) It makes people pay attention to a single activity.
(c) It includes acknowledging bad habits.
(d) It involves focusing on the full state of oneself.

62. How did the researchers attempt to measure the participants' ability to concentrate?

(a) by checking them for cognitive disorders with an EEG
(b) by distracting them during the meditation session
(c) by asking them to engage in a test for 20 minutes
(d) by having them take a deliberately diverting exam

63. Why most likely did the meditators in the study notice their mistakes promptly?

(a) They made a conscious effort to be as accurate as possible.
(b) They realized that they were being distracted.
(c) They benefited from a more intense cognitive function.
(d) They had higher test results than the other participants.

64. What is the goal of Lin's future research on meditation?

(a) to verify the influence of various meditation types
(b) to test the effectiveness of meditation as a therapy
(c) to determine the long-term observable impact of meditation
(d) to define meditation's connection with attentiveness

65. In the context of the passage, <u>transform</u> means __________.

(a) transmit
(b) change
(c) preserve
(d) transcribe

66. In the context of the passage, <u>identify</u> means __________.

(a) recognize
(b) analyze
(c) comprehend
(d) resolve

PART 3. *Read the encyclopedia article below and answer the questions. The two underlined words are for vocabulary questions.*

BAOBABS

Baobabs are a group of nine different species of trees native to Madagascar, mainland Africa, and Australia. Found in arid regions, baobabs play a vital ecological role in the ecosystems they inhabit. Studies have shown that a baobab tree maintains soil humidity and prevents erosion, allowing nearby plants to grow more easily.

Baobabs have an extremely long life span, with the record-holding tree being 2,450 years old when it died in 2011. This makes baobabs some of the oldest-known flowering plants on the planet. Also, baobabs can reach an immense size because they continue to grow throughout their life. One of the largest known individual trees is the Sunland Baobab, which is located in South Africa. It has a height of 22 meters and a trunk diameter of just over 10 meters.

Baobabs utilize a unique method of growth. Similar to the way that other trees sprout new branches, baobabs grow additional stems. These stems join with one another, merging into a ring around the center of the tree, creating a chamber that enables the tree to hold large amounts of water. The baobab is capable of storing up to 120,000 liters of water, which is crucial to surviving periods of drought.

The fruit produced by these trees is extremely dense in nutrients and can remain edible for up to three years after being harvested. It is rich in fiber and vitamin C, and it contains the largest amount of antioxidants of any fruit. Additionally, the seeds can be a source of vegetable oil for many people, and the oil they produce stimulates collagen growth, leading to it being frequently used in cosmetic products, particularly moisturizers.

Unfortunately, baobab trees throughout the world have been dying off, with many of the largest and longest-lived trees expiring since 2005. Scientists are currently unsure why this is happening as the dead trees showed no signs of disease. Researchers hypothesize that the mass death of these trees is related to the rise in global temperatures.

67. What makes the baobab tree ecologically important?

(a) its tendency to provide extensive shade
(b) its effect on moisture removal
(c) its ability to replace eroded soil
(d) its benefit on other vegetation

68. Based on the article, how do baobab trees become extremely large?

(a) by bearing numerous seasonal flowers
(b) by maintaining a lifelong pattern of growth
(c) by utilizing the nutrients in dead trees
(d) by growing rare blossoms at great heights

69. Why do baobab trees most likely produce extra stems?

(a) to cope with exceptionally dry periods
(b) to support the weight of the branches
(c) to protect the surrounding trees
(d) to survive infestation by pests

70. What is the oil from baobab seeds used for?

(a) producing a range of vitamin C tablets
(b) creating fiber supplements for daily use
(c) making products to relieve dry skin
(d) developing various antioxidant pills

71. Which is not true about the mass die-off of baobab trees?

(a) It involves trees that seemed to be healthy.
(b) It is possibly related to the global warming trend.
(c) It was restrained by scientific intervention.
(d) It also affected some of the oldest specimens.

72. In the context of the passage, merging means __________.

(a) turning
(b) twisting
(c) weaving
(d) blending

73. In the context of the passage, rich means __________.

(a) valuable
(b) plentiful
(c) affluent
(d) greasy

PART 4. *Read the business letter below and answer the questions. The two underlined words are for vocabulary questions.*

Ryan Evans
Principal
Parkside High School

Dear Mr. Evans:

Thanks to your participation in our past events, we at The Giving Tree Food Bank could help feed those in need. With this year's holiday season approaching, we are once again wholeheartedly asking for your further support in our Winter Food Drive.

As you already know, many of the families in our community often don't have enough to eat, especially at the end of the year. But with your help, the Winter Food Drive can ensure that everyone will have plenty of food to have a safe and happy holiday season. We're confident this event will be a success because last year we received a record number of donations, in large part due to the generous contributions made by the parents, students, and faculty of Parkside High School.

As in past years, donations can be left at our facility located at 436 Pepper Avenue. Perishable items must be delivered between our operating hours of 10 a.m. and 4 p.m. so that the food can be properly stored in our refrigerator. All other items can be donated at any time by simply depositing them in the secure "Giving Boxes" located outside our facility. You can donate any nonperishable food, but please note that dented cans cannot be accepted because they could contain harmful bacteria.

If you have any questions or need more information about the drive, please do not hesitate to directly reach out to our operations director, Jack Thomas, by phone at (402) 555-1017 or by email at operations@givingtree.org.

Once again, we thank you for your continued generosity.

Respectfully,
Elle Richards
Outreach Manager
The Giving Tree Food Bank

74. Why did Elle Richards write the principal a letter?

(a) to send warm wishes for the holiday season
(b) to offer food supplies for a school event
(c) to explain how a charity program works
(d) to make a request for charitable contributions

75. What happened during the previous Winter Food Drive?

(a) The school community gave an unprecedented amount of aid.
(b) The school provided a place to hold the event.
(c) Parkside citizens were unable to claim food donations.
(d) Parkside High School teachers were ineligible to participate.

76. Based on the letter, when can perishable items be donated?

(a) before 10 a.m. on school days
(b) at night in the "Giving Boxes"
(c) during food bank business hours
(d) anytime during the food drive

77. What will most likely happen when the canned foods are donated?

(a) They will be disinfected to prevent the spread of bacteria.
(b) They will be closely inspected for any damage.
(c) They will gradually be transferred to the refrigerator.
(d) They will be distributed outside the cafeteria.

78. What does Ms. Richards recommend that Mr. Evans do to learn more about the campaign?

(a) send an email to the outreach manager
(b) get in touch with the head of operations
(c) sign up for an online mailing list
(d) visit the office of Jack Thomas

79. In the context of the passage, wholeheartedly means __________.

(a) gladly
(b) faithfully
(c) hopefully
(d) sincerely

80. In the context of the passage, depositing means __________.

(a) dropping
(b) collecting
(c) hoarding
(d) banking

정답·해석·해설 p.292

자동 채점 및 성적 분석 서비스 ▶

정답 한눈에 보기

01회

53 (d) 54 (d) 55 (b) 56 (c) 57 (c) 58 (b)
59 (c) 60 (b) 61 (c) 62 (a) 63 (d) 64 (a)
65 (c) 66 (b) 67 (d) 68 (c) 69 (b) 70 (c)
71 (a) 72 (d) 73 (a) 74 (d) 75 (c) 76 (d)
77 (c) 78 (a) 79 (d) 80 (b)

02회

53 (b) 54 (a) 55 (d) 56 (c) 57 (b) 58 (a)
59 (c) 60 (d) 61 (b) 62 (b) 63 (c) 64 (c)
65 (a) 66 (d) 67 (c) 68 (b) 69 (a) 70 (d)
71 (b) 72 (d) 73 (c) 74 (c) 75 (d) 76 (c)
77 (b) 78 (b) 79 (a) 80 (c)

03회

53 (d) 54 (c) 55 (d) 56 (b) 57 (a) 58 (c)
59 (c) 60 (b) 61 (c) 62 (d) 63 (b) 64 (d)
65 (c) 66 (b) 67 (a) 68 (c) 69 (c) 70 (b)
71 (d) 72 (c) 73 (d) 74 (b) 75 (a) 76 (c)
77 (d) 78 (c) 79 (b) 80 (a)

04회

53 (c) 54 (b) 55 (d) 56 (a) 57 (c) 58 (b)
59 (d) 60 (b) 61 (c) 62 (a) 63 (c) 64 (b)
65 (d) 66 (a) 67 (d) 68 (d) 69 (b) 70 (c)
71 (c) 72 (a) 73 (b) 74 (c) 75 (d) 76 (a)
77 (a) 78 (b) 79 (d) 80 (c)

05회

53 (c) 54 (a) 55 (c) 56 (c) 57 (d) 58 (d)
59 (c) 60 (b) 61 (c) 62 (c) 63 (c) 64 (d)
65 (c) 66 (a) 67 (b) 68 (d) 69 (b) 70 (d)
71 (d) 72 (c) 73 (a) 74 (b) 75 (c) 76 (c)
77 (c) 78 (a) 79 (b) 80 (d)

06회

53 (c) 54 (b) 55 (d) 56 (b) 57 (b) 58 (a)
59 (d) 60 (a) 61 (d) 62 (b) 63 (a) 64 (c)
65 (b) 66 (d) 67 (b) 68 (d) 69 (d) 70 (a)
71 (c) 72 (c) 73 (b) 74 (a) 75 (c) 76 (d)
77 (b) 78 (a) 79 (c) 80 (b)

07회

53 (d) 54 (a) 55 (c) 56 (a) 57 (b) 58 (b)
59 (c) 60 (b) 61 (d) 62 (a) 63 (c) 64 (c)
65 (d) 66 (b) 67 (c) 68 (b) 69 (b) 70 (d)
71 (c) 72 (a) 73 (b) 74 (b) 75 (a) 76 (d)
77 (d) 78 (c) 79 (c) 80 (d)

08회

53 (c) 54 (b) 55 (d) 56 (b) 57 (d) 58 (c)
59 (a) 60 (b) 61 (b) 62 (c) 63 (d) 64 (d)
65 (c) 66 (a) 67 (d) 68 (a) 69 (d) 70 (b)
71 (a) 72 (b) 73 (c) 74 (b) 75 (d) 76 (c)
77 (c) 78 (a) 79 (b) 80 (a)

09회

53 (c) 54 (b) 55 (a) 56 (b) 57 (c) 58 (b)
59 (a) 60 (d) 61 (b) 62 (d) 63 (a) 64 (b)
65 (d) 66 (a) 67 (a) 68 (d) 69 (d) 70 (b)
71 (c) 72 (c) 73 (a) 74 (b) 75 (d) 76 (c)
77 (b) 78 (c) 79 (b) 80 (d)

10회

53 (d) 54 (c) 55 (c) 56 (b) 57 (b) 58 (a)
59 (d) 60 (b) 61 (d) 62 (d) 63 (c) 64 (c)
65 (b) 66 (a) 67 (d) 68 (b) 69 (a) 70 (c)
71 (c) 72 (d) 73 (b) 74 (d) 75 (a) 76 (c)
77 (b) 78 (b) 79 (d) 80 (a)

ANSWER SHEET

※ TEST DATE

MO.		DAY		YEAR			

감독 확인	

성 명	

등급	① ② ③ ④ ⑤

성	초 성	㉠ ㉡ ㉢ ㉣ ㉤ ㉥ ㉦ ㉧ ㉨ ㉩ ㉪ ㉫ ㉬ ㉭
	중 성	ㅏ ㅑ ㅓ ㅕ ㅗ ㅛ ㅜ ㅠ ㅡ ㅣ ㅔ ㅐ ㅖ ㅒ ㅘ ㅚ ㅢ ㅝ ㅟ ㅙ
	종 성	㉠ ㉡ ㉢ ㉣ ㉤ ㉥ ㉦ ㉧ ㉨ ㉩ ㉪ ㉫ ㉬ ㉭ ㄲ ㄸ ㅃ ㅆ ㅉ
명	초 성	㉠ ㉡ ㉢ ㉣ ㉤ ㉥ ㉦ ㉧ ㉨ ㉩ ㉪ ㉫ ㉬ ㉭
	중 성	ㅏ ㅑ ㅓ ㅕ ㅗ ㅛ ㅜ ㅠ ㅡ ㅣ ㅔ ㅐ ㅖ ㅒ ㅘ ㅚ ㅢ ㅝ ㅟ ㅙ
	종 성	㉠ ㉡ ㉢ ㉣ ㉤ ㉥ ㉦ ㉧ ㉨ ㉩ ㉪ ㉫ ㉬ ㉭ ㄲ ㄸ ㅃ ㅆ ㅉ
	초 성	㉠ ㉡ ㉢ ㉣ ㉤ ㉥ ㉦ ㉧ ㉨ ㉩ ㉪ ㉫ ㉬ ㉭
	중 성	ㅏ ㅑ ㅓ ㅕ ㅗ ㅛ ㅜ ㅠ ㅡ ㅣ ㅔ ㅐ ㅖ ㅒ ㅘ ㅚ ㅢ ㅝ ㅟ ㅙ
	종 성	㉠ ㉡ ㉢ ㉣ ㉤ ㉥ ㉦ ㉧ ㉨ ㉩ ㉪ ㉫ ㉬ ㉭ ㄲ ㄸ ㅃ ㅆ ㅉ
란	초 성	㉠ ㉡ ㉢ ㉣ ㉤ ㉥ ㉦ ㉧ ㉨ ㉩ ㉪ ㉫ ㉬ ㉭
	중 성	ㅏ ㅑ ㅓ ㅕ ㅗ ㅛ ㅜ ㅠ ㅡ ㅣ ㅔ ㅐ ㅖ ㅒ ㅘ ㅚ ㅢ ㅝ ㅟ ㅙ
	종 성	㉠ ㉡ ㉢ ㉣ ㉤ ㉥ ㉦ ㉧ ㉨ ㉩ ㉪ ㉫ ㉬ ㉭ ㄲ ㄸ ㅃ ㅆ ㅉ

수 험 번 호														
		–					–							
⓪	⓪		⓪	⓪	⓪	⓪		⓪	⓪	⓪	⓪	⓪	⓪	⓪
①	①		①	①	①	①		①	①	①	①	①	①	①
②	②		②	②	②	②		②	②	②	②	②	②	②
③	③		③	③	③	③		③	③	③	③	③	③	③
④	④	–	④	④	④	④	–	④	④	④	④	④	④	④
⑤	⑤		⑤	⑤	⑤	⑤		⑤	⑤	⑤	⑤	⑤	⑤	⑤
⑥	⑥		⑥	⑥	⑥	⑥		⑥	⑥	⑥	⑥	⑥	⑥	⑥
⑦	⑦		⑦	⑦	⑦	⑦		⑦	⑦	⑦	⑦	⑦	⑦	⑦
⑧	⑧		⑧	⑧	⑧	⑧		⑧	⑧	⑧	⑧	⑧	⑧	⑧
⑨	⑨		⑨	⑨	⑨	⑨		⑨	⑨	⑨	⑨	⑨	⑨	⑨

1) Code 1.

	⓪ ① ② ③ ④ ⑤ ⑥ ⑦ ⑧ ⑨
	⓪ ① ② ③ ④ ⑤ ⑥ ⑦ ⑧ ⑨
	⓪ ① ② ③ ④ ⑤ ⑥ ⑦ ⑧ ⑨

2) Code 2.

	⓪ ① ② ③ ④ ⑤ ⑥ ⑦ ⑧ ⑨
	⓪ ① ② ③ ④ ⑤ ⑥ ⑦ ⑧ ⑨
	⓪ ① ② ③ ④ ⑤ ⑥ ⑦ ⑧ ⑨

3) Code 3.

	⓪ ① ② ③ ④ ⑤ ⑥ ⑦ ⑧ ⑨
	⓪ ① ② ③ ④ ⑤ ⑥ ⑦ ⑧ ⑨
	⓪ ① ② ③ ④ ⑤ ⑥ ⑦ ⑧ ⑨

주민등록번호 앞자리							고 유 번 호						
⓪	⓪	⓪	⓪	⓪	⓪		⓪	⓪	⓪	⓪	⓪	⓪	⓪
①	①	①	①	①	①		①	①	①	①	①	①	①
②	②	②	②	②	②		②	②	②	②	②	②	②
③	③	③	③	③	③		③	③	③	③	③	③	③
④	④	④	④	④	④	–	④	④	④	④	④	④	④
⑤	⑤	⑤	⑤	⑤	⑤		⑤	⑤	⑤	⑤	⑤	⑤	⑤
⑥	⑥	⑥	⑥	⑥	⑥		⑥	⑥	⑥	⑥	⑥	⑥	⑥
⑦	⑦	⑦	⑦	⑦	⑦		⑦	⑦	⑦	⑦	⑦	⑦	⑦
⑧	⑧	⑧	⑧	⑧	⑧		⑧	⑧	⑧	⑧	⑧	⑧	⑧
⑨	⑨	⑨	⑨	⑨	⑨		⑨	⑨	⑨	⑨	⑨	⑨	⑨

문항	답 란	문항	답 란	문항	답 란	문항	답 란	문항	답 란
1	ⓐ ⓑ ⓒ ⓓ	21	ⓐ ⓑ ⓒ ⓓ	41	ⓐ ⓑ ⓒ ⓓ	61	ⓐ ⓑ ⓒ ⓓ	81	ⓐ ⓑ ⓒ ⓓ
2	ⓐ ⓑ ⓒ ⓓ	22	ⓐ ⓑ ⓒ ⓓ	42	ⓐ ⓑ ⓒ ⓓ	62	ⓐ ⓑ ⓒ ⓓ	82	ⓐ ⓑ ⓒ ⓓ
3	ⓐ ⓑ ⓒ ⓓ	23	ⓐ ⓑ ⓒ ⓓ	43	ⓐ ⓑ ⓒ ⓓ	63	ⓐ ⓑ ⓒ ⓓ	83	ⓐ ⓑ ⓒ ⓓ
4	ⓐ ⓑ ⓒ ⓓ	24	ⓐ ⓑ ⓒ ⓓ	44	ⓐ ⓑ ⓒ ⓓ	64	ⓐ ⓑ ⓒ ⓓ	84	ⓐ ⓑ ⓒ ⓓ
5	ⓐ ⓑ ⓒ ⓓ	25	ⓐ ⓑ ⓒ ⓓ	45	ⓐ ⓑ ⓒ ⓓ	65	ⓐ ⓑ ⓒ ⓓ	85	ⓐ ⓑ ⓒ ⓓ
6	ⓐ ⓑ ⓒ ⓓ	26	ⓐ ⓑ ⓒ ⓓ	46	ⓐ ⓑ ⓒ ⓓ	66	ⓐ ⓑ ⓒ ⓓ	86	ⓐ ⓑ ⓒ ⓓ
7	ⓐ ⓑ ⓒ ⓓ	27	ⓐ ⓑ ⓒ ⓓ	47	ⓐ ⓑ ⓒ ⓓ	67	ⓐ ⓑ ⓒ ⓓ	87	ⓐ ⓑ ⓒ ⓓ
8	ⓐ ⓑ ⓒ ⓓ	28	ⓐ ⓑ ⓒ ⓓ	48	ⓐ ⓑ ⓒ ⓓ	68	ⓐ ⓑ ⓒ ⓓ	88	ⓐ ⓑ ⓒ ⓓ
9	ⓐ ⓑ ⓒ ⓓ	29	ⓐ ⓑ ⓒ ⓓ	49	ⓐ ⓑ ⓒ ⓓ	69	ⓐ ⓑ ⓒ ⓓ	89	ⓐ ⓑ ⓒ ⓓ
10	ⓐ ⓑ ⓒ ⓓ	30	ⓐ ⓑ ⓒ ⓓ	50	ⓐ ⓑ ⓒ ⓓ	70	ⓐ ⓑ ⓒ ⓓ	90	ⓐ ⓑ ⓒ ⓓ
11	ⓐ ⓑ ⓒ ⓓ	31	ⓐ ⓑ ⓒ ⓓ	51	ⓐ ⓑ ⓒ ⓓ	71	ⓐ ⓑ ⓒ ⓓ		
12	ⓐ ⓑ ⓒ ⓓ	32	ⓐ ⓑ ⓒ ⓓ	52	ⓐ ⓑ ⓒ ⓓ	72	ⓐ ⓑ ⓒ ⓓ		
13	ⓐ ⓑ ⓒ ⓓ	33	ⓐ ⓑ ⓒ ⓓ	53	ⓐ ⓑ ⓒ ⓓ	73	ⓐ ⓑ ⓒ ⓓ		
14	ⓐ ⓑ ⓒ ⓓ	34	ⓐ ⓑ ⓒ ⓓ	54	ⓐ ⓑ ⓒ ⓓ	74	ⓐ ⓑ ⓒ ⓓ		
15	ⓐ ⓑ ⓒ ⓓ	35	ⓐ ⓑ ⓒ ⓓ	55	ⓐ ⓑ ⓒ ⓓ	75	ⓐ ⓑ ⓒ ⓓ		
16	ⓐ ⓑ ⓒ ⓓ	36	ⓐ ⓑ ⓒ ⓓ	56	ⓐ ⓑ ⓒ ⓓ	76	ⓐ ⓑ ⓒ ⓓ		
17	ⓐ ⓑ ⓒ ⓓ	37	ⓐ ⓑ ⓒ ⓓ	57	ⓐ ⓑ ⓒ ⓓ	77	ⓐ ⓑ ⓒ ⓓ		
18	ⓐ ⓑ ⓒ ⓓ	38	ⓐ ⓑ ⓒ ⓓ	58	ⓐ ⓑ ⓒ ⓓ	78	ⓐ ⓑ ⓒ ⓓ		
19	ⓐ ⓑ ⓒ ⓓ	39	ⓐ ⓑ ⓒ ⓓ	59	ⓐ ⓑ ⓒ ⓓ	79	ⓐ ⓑ ⓒ ⓓ		
20	ⓐ ⓑ ⓒ ⓓ	40	ⓐ ⓑ ⓒ ⓓ	60	ⓐ ⓑ ⓒ ⓓ	80	ⓐ ⓑ ⓒ ⓓ		

password

⓪	⓪	⓪	⓪
①	①	①	①
②	②	②	②
③	③	③	③
④	④	④	④
⑤	⑤	⑤	⑤
⑥	⑥	⑥	⑥
⑦	⑦	⑦	⑦
⑧	⑧	⑧	⑧
⑨	⑨	⑨	⑨

ANSWER SHEET

※ TEST DATE

MO.		DAY		YEAR			

감독관 확인	

성 명	

등급	① ② ③ ④ ⑤

성명란		
	초 성	ㄱ ㄴ ㄷ ㄹ ㅁ ㅂ ㅅ ㅇ ㅈ ㅊ ㅋ ㅌ ㅍ ㅎ
	중 성	ㅏ ㅑ ㅓ ㅕ ㅗ ㅛ ㅜ ㅠ ㅡ ㅣ ㅔ ㅐ ㅖ ㅒ ㅘ ㅚ ㅢ ㅝ ㅟ ㅙ
	종 성	ㄱ ㄴ ㄷ ㄹ ㅁ ㅂ ㅅ ㅇ ㅈ ㅊ ㅋ ㅌ ㅍ ㅎ ㄲ ㄸ ㅃ ㅆ ㅉ
	초 성	ㄱ ㄴ ㄷ ㄹ ㅁ ㅂ ㅅ ㅇ ㅈ ㅊ ㅋ ㅌ ㅍ ㅎ
	중 성	ㅏ ㅑ ㅓ ㅕ ㅗ ㅛ ㅜ ㅠ ㅡ ㅣ ㅔ ㅐ ㅖ ㅒ ㅘ ㅚ ㅢ ㅝ ㅟ ㅙ
	종 성	ㄱ ㄴ ㄷ ㄹ ㅁ ㅂ ㅅ ㅇ ㅈ ㅊ ㅋ ㅌ ㅍ ㅎ ㄲ ㄸ ㅃ ㅆ ㅉ
	초 성	ㄱ ㄴ ㄷ ㄹ ㅁ ㅂ ㅅ ㅇ ㅈ ㅊ ㅋ ㅌ ㅍ ㅎ
	중 성	ㅏ ㅑ ㅓ ㅕ ㅗ ㅛ ㅜ ㅠ ㅡ ㅣ ㅔ ㅐ ㅖ ㅒ ㅘ ㅚ ㅢ ㅝ ㅟ ㅙ
	종 성	ㄱ ㄴ ㄷ ㄹ ㅁ ㅂ ㅅ ㅇ ㅈ ㅊ ㅋ ㅌ ㅍ ㅎ ㄲ ㄸ ㅃ ㅆ ㅉ
	초 성	ㄱ ㄴ ㄷ ㄹ ㅁ ㅂ ㅅ ㅇ ㅈ ㅊ ㅋ ㅌ ㅍ ㅎ
	중 성	ㅏ ㅑ ㅓ ㅕ ㅗ ㅛ ㅜ ㅠ ㅡ ㅣ ㅔ ㅐ ㅖ ㅒ ㅘ ㅚ ㅢ ㅝ ㅟ ㅙ
	종 성	ㄱ ㄴ ㄷ ㄹ ㅁ ㅂ ㅅ ㅇ ㅈ ㅊ ㅋ ㅌ ㅍ ㅎ ㄲ ㄸ ㅃ ㅆ ㅉ

수 험 번 호														
		–					–							
⓪	⓪		⓪	⓪	⓪	⓪		⓪	⓪	⓪	⓪	⓪	⓪	⓪
①	①		①	①	①	①		①	①	①	①	①	①	①
②	②		②	②	②	②		②	②	②	②	②	②	②
③	③		③	③	③	③		③	③	③	③	③	③	③
④	④	–	④	④	④	④	–	④	④	④	④	④	④	④
⑤	⑤		⑤	⑤	⑤	⑤		⑤	⑤	⑤	⑤	⑤	⑤	⑤
⑥	⑥		⑥	⑥	⑥	⑥		⑥	⑥	⑥	⑥	⑥	⑥	⑥
⑦	⑦		⑦	⑦	⑦	⑦		⑦	⑦	⑦	⑦	⑦	⑦	⑦
⑧	⑧		⑧	⑧	⑧	⑧		⑧	⑧	⑧	⑧	⑧	⑧	⑧
⑨	⑨		⑨	⑨	⑨	⑨		⑨	⑨	⑨	⑨	⑨	⑨	⑨

1) Code 1.

	⓪ ① ② ③ ④ ⑤ ⑥ ⑦ ⑧ ⑨
	⓪ ① ② ③ ④ ⑤ ⑥ ⑦ ⑧ ⑨
	⓪ ① ② ③ ④ ⑤ ⑥ ⑦ ⑧ ⑨

2) Code 2.

	⓪ ① ② ③ ④ ⑤ ⑥ ⑦ ⑧ ⑨
	⓪ ① ② ③ ④ ⑤ ⑥ ⑦ ⑧ ⑨
	⓪ ① ② ③ ④ ⑤ ⑥ ⑦ ⑧ ⑨

3) Code 3.

	⓪ ① ② ③ ④ ⑤ ⑥ ⑦ ⑧ ⑨
	⓪ ① ② ③ ④ ⑤ ⑥ ⑦ ⑧ ⑨
	⓪ ① ② ③ ④ ⑤ ⑥ ⑦ ⑧ ⑨

주민등록번호 앞자리							고 유 번 호						
⓪	⓪	⓪	⓪	⓪	⓪		⓪	⓪	⓪	⓪	⓪	⓪	⓪
①	①	①	①	①	①		①	①	①	①	①	①	①
②	②	②	②	②	②		②	②	②	②	②	②	②
③	③	③	③	③	③		③	③	③	③	③	③	③
④	④	④	④	④	④	–	④	④	④	④	④	④	④
⑤	⑤	⑤	⑤	⑤	⑤		⑤	⑤	⑤	⑤	⑤	⑤	⑤
⑥	⑥	⑥	⑥	⑥	⑥		⑥	⑥	⑥	⑥	⑥	⑥	⑥
⑦	⑦	⑦	⑦	⑦	⑦		⑦	⑦	⑦	⑦	⑦	⑦	⑦
⑧	⑧	⑧	⑧	⑧	⑧		⑧	⑧	⑧	⑧	⑧	⑧	⑧
⑨	⑨	⑨	⑨	⑨	⑨		⑨	⑨	⑨	⑨	⑨	⑨	⑨

문항	답 란	문항	답 란	문항	답 란	문항	답 란	문항	답 란
1	ⓐ ⓑ ⓒ ⓓ	21	ⓐ ⓑ ⓒ ⓓ	41	ⓐ ⓑ ⓒ ⓓ	61	ⓐ ⓑ ⓒ ⓓ	81	ⓐ ⓑ ⓒ ⓓ
2	ⓐ ⓑ ⓒ ⓓ	22	ⓐ ⓑ ⓒ ⓓ	42	ⓐ ⓑ ⓒ ⓓ	62	ⓐ ⓑ ⓒ ⓓ	82	ⓐ ⓑ ⓒ ⓓ
3	ⓐ ⓑ ⓒ ⓓ	23	ⓐ ⓑ ⓒ ⓓ	43	ⓐ ⓑ ⓒ ⓓ	63	ⓐ ⓑ ⓒ ⓓ	83	ⓐ ⓑ ⓒ ⓓ
4	ⓐ ⓑ ⓒ ⓓ	24	ⓐ ⓑ ⓒ ⓓ	44	ⓐ ⓑ ⓒ ⓓ	64	ⓐ ⓑ ⓒ ⓓ	84	ⓐ ⓑ ⓒ ⓓ
5	ⓐ ⓑ ⓒ ⓓ	25	ⓐ ⓑ ⓒ ⓓ	45	ⓐ ⓑ ⓒ ⓓ	65	ⓐ ⓑ ⓒ ⓓ	85	ⓐ ⓑ ⓒ ⓓ
6	ⓐ ⓑ ⓒ ⓓ	26	ⓐ ⓑ ⓒ ⓓ	46	ⓐ ⓑ ⓒ ⓓ	66	ⓐ ⓑ ⓒ ⓓ	86	ⓐ ⓑ ⓒ ⓓ
7	ⓐ ⓑ ⓒ ⓓ	27	ⓐ ⓑ ⓒ ⓓ	47	ⓐ ⓑ ⓒ ⓓ	67	ⓐ ⓑ ⓒ ⓓ	87	ⓐ ⓑ ⓒ ⓓ
8	ⓐ ⓑ ⓒ ⓓ	28	ⓐ ⓑ ⓒ ⓓ	48	ⓐ ⓑ ⓒ ⓓ	68	ⓐ ⓑ ⓒ ⓓ	88	ⓐ ⓑ ⓒ ⓓ
9	ⓐ ⓑ ⓒ ⓓ	29	ⓐ ⓑ ⓒ ⓓ	49	ⓐ ⓑ ⓒ ⓓ	69	ⓐ ⓑ ⓒ ⓓ	89	ⓐ ⓑ ⓒ ⓓ
10	ⓐ ⓑ ⓒ ⓓ	30	ⓐ ⓑ ⓒ ⓓ	50	ⓐ ⓑ ⓒ ⓓ	70	ⓐ ⓑ ⓒ ⓓ	90	ⓐ ⓑ ⓒ ⓓ
11	ⓐ ⓑ ⓒ ⓓ	31	ⓐ ⓑ ⓒ ⓓ	51	ⓐ ⓑ ⓒ ⓓ	71	ⓐ ⓑ ⓒ ⓓ		
12	ⓐ ⓑ ⓒ ⓓ	32	ⓐ ⓑ ⓒ ⓓ	52	ⓐ ⓑ ⓒ ⓓ	72	ⓐ ⓑ ⓒ ⓓ		
13	ⓐ ⓑ ⓒ ⓓ	33	ⓐ ⓑ ⓒ ⓓ	53	ⓐ ⓑ ⓒ ⓓ	73	ⓐ ⓑ ⓒ ⓓ		
14	ⓐ ⓑ ⓒ ⓓ	34	ⓐ ⓑ ⓒ ⓓ	54	ⓐ ⓑ ⓒ ⓓ	74	ⓐ ⓑ ⓒ ⓓ		
15	ⓐ ⓑ ⓒ ⓓ	35	ⓐ ⓑ ⓒ ⓓ	55	ⓐ ⓑ ⓒ ⓓ	75	ⓐ ⓑ ⓒ ⓓ		
16	ⓐ ⓑ ⓒ ⓓ	36	ⓐ ⓑ ⓒ ⓓ	56	ⓐ ⓑ ⓒ ⓓ	76	ⓐ ⓑ ⓒ ⓓ		
17	ⓐ ⓑ ⓒ ⓓ	37	ⓐ ⓑ ⓒ ⓓ	57	ⓐ ⓑ ⓒ ⓓ	77	ⓐ ⓑ ⓒ ⓓ		
18	ⓐ ⓑ ⓒ ⓓ	38	ⓐ ⓑ ⓒ ⓓ	58	ⓐ ⓑ ⓒ ⓓ	78	ⓐ ⓑ ⓒ ⓓ		
19	ⓐ ⓑ ⓒ ⓓ	39	ⓐ ⓑ ⓒ ⓓ	59	ⓐ ⓑ ⓒ ⓓ	79	ⓐ ⓑ ⓒ ⓓ		
20	ⓐ ⓑ ⓒ ⓓ	40	ⓐ ⓑ ⓒ ⓓ	60	ⓐ ⓑ ⓒ ⓓ	80	ⓐ ⓑ ⓒ ⓓ		

password

⓪	⓪	⓪	⓪
①	①	①	①
②	②	②	②
③	③	③	③
④	④	④	④
⑤	⑤	⑤	⑤
⑥	⑥	⑥	⑥
⑦	⑦	⑦	⑦
⑧	⑧	⑧	⑧
⑨	⑨	⑨	⑨

ANSWER SHEET

※ TEST DATE	MO.	DAY	YEAR

성 명		등급	① ② ③ ④ ⑤	감독 확인	

성명란		
성	초 성	㉠ ㉡ ㉢ ㉣ ㉤ ㉥ ㉦ ㉧ ㉨ ㉩ ㉪ ㉫ ㉬ ㉭
	중 성	ㅏ ㅑ ㅓ ㅕ ㅗ ㅛ ㅜ ㅠ ㅡ ㅣ ㅔ ㅐ ㅖ ㅒ ㅘ ㅚ ㅢ ㅝ ㅟ ㅙ
	종 성	㉠ ㉡ ㉢ ㉣ ㉤ ㉥ ㉦ ㉧ ㉨ ㉩ ㉪ ㉫ ㉬ ㉭ ㄲ ㄸ ㅃ ㅆ ㅉ
명	초 성	㉠ ㉡ ㉢ ㉣ ㉤ ㉥ ㉦ ㉧ ㉨ ㉩ ㉪ ㉫ ㉬ ㉭
	중 성	ㅏ ㅑ ㅓ ㅕ ㅗ ㅛ ㅜ ㅠ ㅡ ㅣ ㅔ ㅐ ㅖ ㅒ ㅘ ㅚ ㅢ ㅝ ㅟ ㅙ
	종 성	㉠ ㉡ ㉢ ㉣ ㉤ ㉥ ㉦ ㉧ ㉨ ㉩ ㉪ ㉫ ㉬ ㉭ ㄲ ㄸ ㅃ ㅆ ㅉ
	초 성	㉠ ㉡ ㉢ ㉣ ㉤ ㉥ ㉦ ㉧ ㉨ ㉩ ㉪ ㉫ ㉬ ㉭
	중 성	ㅏ ㅑ ㅓ ㅕ ㅗ ㅛ ㅜ ㅠ ㅡ ㅣ ㅔ ㅐ ㅖ ㅒ ㅘ ㅚ ㅢ ㅝ ㅟ ㅙ
	종 성	㉠ ㉡ ㉢ ㉣ ㉤ ㉥ ㉦ ㉧ ㉨ ㉩ ㉪ ㉫ ㉬ ㉭ ㄲ ㄸ ㅃ ㅆ ㅉ
란	초 성	㉠ ㉡ ㉢ ㉣ ㉤ ㉥ ㉦ ㉧ ㉨ ㉩ ㉪ ㉫ ㉬ ㉭
	중 성	ㅏ ㅑ ㅓ ㅕ ㅗ ㅛ ㅜ ㅠ ㅡ ㅣ ㅔ ㅐ ㅖ ㅒ ㅘ ㅚ ㅢ ㅝ ㅟ ㅙ
	종 성	㉠ ㉡ ㉢ ㉣ ㉤ ㉥ ㉦ ㉧ ㉨ ㉩ ㉪ ㉫ ㉬ ㉭ ㄲ ㄸ ㅃ ㅆ ㅉ

수 험 번 호															
		–					–							
⓪	⓪		⓪	⓪	⓪	⓪		⓪	⓪	⓪	⓪	⓪	⓪	⓪
①	①		①	①	①	①		①	①	①	①	①	①	①
②	②		②	②	②	②		②	②	②	②	②	②	②
③	③		③	③	③	③		③	③	③	③	③	③	③
④	④	–	④	④	④	④	–	④	④	④	④	④	④	④
⑤	⑤		⑤	⑤	⑤	⑤		⑤	⑤	⑤	⑤	⑤	⑤	⑤
⑥	⑥		⑥	⑥	⑥	⑥		⑥	⑥	⑥	⑥	⑥	⑥	⑥
⑦	⑦		⑦	⑦	⑦	⑦		⑦	⑦	⑦	⑦	⑦	⑦	⑦
⑧	⑧		⑧	⑧	⑧	⑧		⑧	⑧	⑧	⑧	⑧	⑧	⑧
⑨	⑨		⑨	⑨	⑨	⑨		⑨	⑨	⑨	⑨	⑨	⑨	⑨

1) Code 1.

	⓪ ① ② ③ ④ ⑤ ⑥ ⑦ ⑧ ⑨
	⓪ ① ② ③ ④ ⑤ ⑥ ⑦ ⑧ ⑨
	⓪ ① ② ③ ④ ⑤ ⑥ ⑦ ⑧ ⑨

2) Code 2.

	⓪ ① ② ③ ④ ⑤ ⑥ ⑦ ⑧ ⑨
	⓪ ① ② ③ ④ ⑤ ⑥ ⑦ ⑧ ⑨
	⓪ ① ② ③ ④ ⑤ ⑥ ⑦ ⑧ ⑨

3) Code 3.

	⓪ ① ② ③ ④ ⑤ ⑥ ⑦ ⑧ ⑨
	⓪ ① ② ③ ④ ⑤ ⑥ ⑦ ⑧ ⑨
	⓪ ① ② ③ ④ ⑤ ⑥ ⑦ ⑧ ⑨

주민등록번호 앞자리							고 유 번 호						
⓪	⓪	⓪	⓪	⓪	⓪		⓪	⓪	⓪	⓪	⓪	⓪	⓪
①	①	①	①	①	①		①	①	①	①	①	①	①
②	②	②	②	②	②		②	②	②	②	②	②	②
③	③	③	③	③	③		③	③	③	③	③	③	③
④	④	④	④	④	④	–	④	④	④	④	④	④	④
⑤	⑤	⑤	⑤	⑤	⑤		⑤	⑤	⑤	⑤	⑤	⑤	⑤
⑥	⑥	⑥	⑥	⑥	⑥		⑥	⑥	⑥	⑥	⑥	⑥	⑥
⑦	⑦	⑦	⑦	⑦	⑦		⑦	⑦	⑦	⑦	⑦	⑦	⑦
⑧	⑧	⑧	⑧	⑧	⑧		⑧	⑧	⑧	⑧	⑧	⑧	⑧
⑨	⑨	⑨	⑨	⑨	⑨		⑨	⑨	⑨	⑨	⑨	⑨	⑨

문항	답 란	문항	답 란	문항	답 란	문항	답 란	문항	답 란
1	ⓐ ⓑ ⓒ ⓓ	21	ⓐ ⓑ ⓒ ⓓ	41	ⓐ ⓑ ⓒ ⓓ	61	ⓐ ⓑ ⓒ ⓓ	81	ⓐ ⓑ ⓒ ⓓ
2	ⓐ ⓑ ⓒ ⓓ	22	ⓐ ⓑ ⓒ ⓓ	42	ⓐ ⓑ ⓒ ⓓ	62	ⓐ ⓑ ⓒ ⓓ	82	ⓐ ⓑ ⓒ ⓓ
3	ⓐ ⓑ ⓒ ⓓ	23	ⓐ ⓑ ⓒ ⓓ	43	ⓐ ⓑ ⓒ ⓓ	63	ⓐ ⓑ ⓒ ⓓ	83	ⓐ ⓑ ⓒ ⓓ
4	ⓐ ⓑ ⓒ ⓓ	24	ⓐ ⓑ ⓒ ⓓ	44	ⓐ ⓑ ⓒ ⓓ	64	ⓐ ⓑ ⓒ ⓓ	84	ⓐ ⓑ ⓒ ⓓ
5	ⓐ ⓑ ⓒ ⓓ	25	ⓐ ⓑ ⓒ ⓓ	45	ⓐ ⓑ ⓒ ⓓ	65	ⓐ ⓑ ⓒ ⓓ	85	ⓐ ⓑ ⓒ ⓓ
6	ⓐ ⓑ ⓒ ⓓ	26	ⓐ ⓑ ⓒ ⓓ	46	ⓐ ⓑ ⓒ ⓓ	66	ⓐ ⓑ ⓒ ⓓ	86	ⓐ ⓑ ⓒ ⓓ
7	ⓐ ⓑ ⓒ ⓓ	27	ⓐ ⓑ ⓒ ⓓ	47	ⓐ ⓑ ⓒ ⓓ	67	ⓐ ⓑ ⓒ ⓓ	87	ⓐ ⓑ ⓒ ⓓ
8	ⓐ ⓑ ⓒ ⓓ	28	ⓐ ⓑ ⓒ ⓓ	48	ⓐ ⓑ ⓒ ⓓ	68	ⓐ ⓑ ⓒ ⓓ	88	ⓐ ⓑ ⓒ ⓓ
9	ⓐ ⓑ ⓒ ⓓ	29	ⓐ ⓑ ⓒ ⓓ	49	ⓐ ⓑ ⓒ ⓓ	69	ⓐ ⓑ ⓒ ⓓ	89	ⓐ ⓑ ⓒ ⓓ
10	ⓐ ⓑ ⓒ ⓓ	30	ⓐ ⓑ ⓒ ⓓ	50	ⓐ ⓑ ⓒ ⓓ	70	ⓐ ⓑ ⓒ ⓓ	90	ⓐ ⓑ ⓒ ⓓ
11	ⓐ ⓑ ⓒ ⓓ	31	ⓐ ⓑ ⓒ ⓓ	51	ⓐ ⓑ ⓒ ⓓ	71	ⓐ ⓑ ⓒ ⓓ		
12	ⓐ ⓑ ⓒ ⓓ	32	ⓐ ⓑ ⓒ ⓓ	52	ⓐ ⓑ ⓒ ⓓ	72	ⓐ ⓑ ⓒ ⓓ		
13	ⓐ ⓑ ⓒ ⓓ	33	ⓐ ⓑ ⓒ ⓓ	53	ⓐ ⓑ ⓒ ⓓ	73	ⓐ ⓑ ⓒ ⓓ		
14	ⓐ ⓑ ⓒ ⓓ	34	ⓐ ⓑ ⓒ ⓓ	54	ⓐ ⓑ ⓒ ⓓ	74	ⓐ ⓑ ⓒ ⓓ		
15	ⓐ ⓑ ⓒ ⓓ	35	ⓐ ⓑ ⓒ ⓓ	55	ⓐ ⓑ ⓒ ⓓ	75	ⓐ ⓑ ⓒ ⓓ		
16	ⓐ ⓑ ⓒ ⓓ	36	ⓐ ⓑ ⓒ ⓓ	56	ⓐ ⓑ ⓒ ⓓ	76	ⓐ ⓑ ⓒ ⓓ		
17	ⓐ ⓑ ⓒ ⓓ	37	ⓐ ⓑ ⓒ ⓓ	57	ⓐ ⓑ ⓒ ⓓ	77	ⓐ ⓑ ⓒ ⓓ		
18	ⓐ ⓑ ⓒ ⓓ	38	ⓐ ⓑ ⓒ ⓓ	58	ⓐ ⓑ ⓒ ⓓ	78	ⓐ ⓑ ⓒ ⓓ		
19	ⓐ ⓑ ⓒ ⓓ	39	ⓐ ⓑ ⓒ ⓓ	59	ⓐ ⓑ ⓒ ⓓ	79	ⓐ ⓑ ⓒ ⓓ		
20	ⓐ ⓑ ⓒ ⓓ	40	ⓐ ⓑ ⓒ ⓓ	60	ⓐ ⓑ ⓒ ⓓ	80	ⓐ ⓑ ⓒ ⓓ		

password

⓪	⓪	⓪	⓪
①	①	①	①
②	②	②	②
③	③	③	③
④	④	④	④
⑤	⑤	⑤	⑤
⑥	⑥	⑥	⑥
⑦	⑦	⑦	⑦
⑧	⑧	⑧	⑧
⑨	⑨	⑨	⑨

ANSWER SHEET

※ TEST DATE	MO.	DAY	YEAR

감독관 확인	

성 명		등급	① ② ③ ④ ⑤

성명란		
성	초 성	㉠ ㉡ ㉢ ㉣ ㉤ ㉥ ㉦ ㉧ ㉨ ㉩ ㉪ ㉫ ㉬ ㉭
	중 성	ㅏ ㅑ ㅓ ㅕ ㅗ ㅛ ㅜ ㅠ ㅡ ㅣ ㅔ ㅐ ㅖ ㅒ ㅘ ㅚ ㅢ ㅝ ㅟ ㅙ
	종 성	㉠ ㉡ ㉢ ㉣ ㉤ ㉥ ㉦ ㉧ ㉨ ㉩ ㉪ ㉫ ㉬ ㉭ ㄲ ㄸ ㅃ ㅆ ㅉ
명	초 성	㉠ ㉡ ㉢ ㉣ ㉤ ㉥ ㉦ ㉧ ㉨ ㉩ ㉪ ㉫ ㉬ ㉭
	중 성	ㅏ ㅑ ㅓ ㅕ ㅗ ㅛ ㅜ ㅠ ㅡ ㅣ ㅔ ㅐ ㅖ ㅒ ㅘ ㅚ ㅢ ㅝ ㅟ ㅙ
	종 성	㉠ ㉡ ㉢ ㉣ ㉤ ㉥ ㉦ ㉧ ㉨ ㉩ ㉪ ㉫ ㉬ ㉭ ㄲ ㄸ ㅃ ㅆ ㅉ
	초 성	㉠ ㉡ ㉢ ㉣ ㉤ ㉥ ㉦ ㉧ ㉨ ㉩ ㉪ ㉫ ㉬ ㉭
	중 성	ㅏ ㅑ ㅓ ㅕ ㅗ ㅛ ㅜ ㅠ ㅡ ㅣ ㅔ ㅐ ㅖ ㅒ ㅘ ㅚ ㅢ ㅝ ㅟ ㅙ
	종 성	㉠ ㉡ ㉢ ㉣ ㉤ ㉥ ㉦ ㉧ ㉨ ㉩ ㉪ ㉫ ㉬ ㉭ ㄲ ㄸ ㅃ ㅆ ㅉ
란	초 성	㉠ ㉡ ㉢ ㉣ ㉤ ㉥ ㉦ ㉧ ㉨ ㉩ ㉪ ㉫ ㉬ ㉭
	중 성	ㅏ ㅑ ㅓ ㅕ ㅗ ㅛ ㅜ ㅠ ㅡ ㅣ ㅔ ㅐ ㅖ ㅒ ㅘ ㅚ ㅢ ㅝ ㅟ ㅙ
	종 성	㉠ ㉡ ㉢ ㉣ ㉤ ㉥ ㉦ ㉧ ㉨ ㉩ ㉪ ㉫ ㉬ ㉭ ㄲ ㄸ ㅃ ㅆ ㅉ

수 험 번 호

		–					–							
⓪	⓪		⓪	⓪	⓪	⓪		⓪	⓪	⓪	⓪	⓪	⓪	⓪
①	①		①	①	①	①		①	①	①	①	①	①	①
②	②		②	②	②	②		②	②	②	②	②	②	②
③	③		③	③	③	③		③	③	③	③	③	③	③
④	④	–	④	④	④	④	–	④	④	④	④	④	④	④
⑤	⑤		⑤	⑤	⑤	⑤		⑤	⑤	⑤	⑤	⑤	⑤	⑤
⑥	⑥		⑥	⑥	⑥	⑥		⑥	⑥	⑥	⑥	⑥	⑥	⑥
⑦	⑦		⑦	⑦	⑦	⑦		⑦	⑦	⑦	⑦	⑦	⑦	⑦
⑧	⑧		⑧	⑧	⑧	⑧		⑧	⑧	⑧	⑧	⑧	⑧	⑧
⑨	⑨		⑨	⑨	⑨	⑨		⑨	⑨	⑨	⑨	⑨	⑨	⑨

1) Code 1.

	⓪ ① ② ③ ④ ⑤ ⑥ ⑦ ⑧ ⑨
	⓪ ① ② ③ ④ ⑤ ⑥ ⑦ ⑧ ⑨
	⓪ ① ② ③ ④ ⑤ ⑥ ⑦ ⑧ ⑨

2) Code 2.

	⓪ ① ② ③ ④ ⑤ ⑥ ⑦ ⑧ ⑨
	⓪ ① ② ③ ④ ⑤ ⑥ ⑦ ⑧ ⑨
	⓪ ① ② ③ ④ ⑤ ⑥ ⑦ ⑧ ⑨

3) Code 3.

	⓪ ① ② ③ ④ ⑤ ⑥ ⑦ ⑧ ⑨
	⓪ ① ② ③ ④ ⑤ ⑥ ⑦ ⑧ ⑨
	⓪ ① ② ③ ④ ⑤ ⑥ ⑦ ⑧ ⑨

주민등록번호 앞자리							고 유 번 호						
⓪	⓪	⓪	⓪	⓪	⓪		⓪	⓪	⓪	⓪	⓪	⓪	⓪
①	①	①	①	①	①		①	①	①	①	①	①	①
②	②	②	②	②	②		②	②	②	②	②	②	②
③	③	③	③	③	③		③	③	③	③	③	③	③
④	④	④	④	④	④	–	④	④	④	④	④	④	④
⑤	⑤	⑤	⑤	⑤	⑤		⑤	⑤	⑤	⑤	⑤	⑤	⑤
⑥	⑥	⑥	⑥	⑥	⑥		⑥	⑥	⑥	⑥	⑥	⑥	⑥
⑦	⑦	⑦	⑦	⑦	⑦		⑦	⑦	⑦	⑦	⑦	⑦	⑦
⑧	⑧	⑧	⑧	⑧	⑧		⑧	⑧	⑧	⑧	⑧	⑧	⑧
⑨	⑨	⑨	⑨	⑨	⑨		⑨	⑨	⑨	⑨	⑨	⑨	⑨

문항	답 란	문항	답 란	문항	답 란	문항	답 란	문항	답 란
1	ⓐ ⓑ ⓒ ⓓ	21	ⓐ ⓑ ⓒ ⓓ	41	ⓐ ⓑ ⓒ ⓓ	61	ⓐ ⓑ ⓒ ⓓ	81	ⓐ ⓑ ⓒ ⓓ
2	ⓐ ⓑ ⓒ ⓓ	22	ⓐ ⓑ ⓒ ⓓ	42	ⓐ ⓑ ⓒ ⓓ	62	ⓐ ⓑ ⓒ ⓓ	82	ⓐ ⓑ ⓒ ⓓ
3	ⓐ ⓑ ⓒ ⓓ	23	ⓐ ⓑ ⓒ ⓓ	43	ⓐ ⓑ ⓒ ⓓ	63	ⓐ ⓑ ⓒ ⓓ	83	ⓐ ⓑ ⓒ ⓓ
4	ⓐ ⓑ ⓒ ⓓ	24	ⓐ ⓑ ⓒ ⓓ	44	ⓐ ⓑ ⓒ ⓓ	64	ⓐ ⓑ ⓒ ⓓ	84	ⓐ ⓑ ⓒ ⓓ
5	ⓐ ⓑ ⓒ ⓓ	25	ⓐ ⓑ ⓒ ⓓ	45	ⓐ ⓑ ⓒ ⓓ	65	ⓐ ⓑ ⓒ ⓓ	85	ⓐ ⓑ ⓒ ⓓ
6	ⓐ ⓑ ⓒ ⓓ	26	ⓐ ⓑ ⓒ ⓓ	46	ⓐ ⓑ ⓒ ⓓ	66	ⓐ ⓑ ⓒ ⓓ	86	ⓐ ⓑ ⓒ ⓓ
7	ⓐ ⓑ ⓒ ⓓ	27	ⓐ ⓑ ⓒ ⓓ	47	ⓐ ⓑ ⓒ ⓓ	67	ⓐ ⓑ ⓒ ⓓ	87	ⓐ ⓑ ⓒ ⓓ
8	ⓐ ⓑ ⓒ ⓓ	28	ⓐ ⓑ ⓒ ⓓ	48	ⓐ ⓑ ⓒ ⓓ	68	ⓐ ⓑ ⓒ ⓓ	88	ⓐ ⓑ ⓒ ⓓ
9	ⓐ ⓑ ⓒ ⓓ	29	ⓐ ⓑ ⓒ ⓓ	49	ⓐ ⓑ ⓒ ⓓ	69	ⓐ ⓑ ⓒ ⓓ	89	ⓐ ⓑ ⓒ ⓓ
10	ⓐ ⓑ ⓒ ⓓ	30	ⓐ ⓑ ⓒ ⓓ	50	ⓐ ⓑ ⓒ ⓓ	70	ⓐ ⓑ ⓒ ⓓ	90	ⓐ ⓑ ⓒ ⓓ
11	ⓐ ⓑ ⓒ ⓓ	31	ⓐ ⓑ ⓒ ⓓ	51	ⓐ ⓑ ⓒ ⓓ	71	ⓐ ⓑ ⓒ ⓓ		
12	ⓐ ⓑ ⓒ ⓓ	32	ⓐ ⓑ ⓒ ⓓ	52	ⓐ ⓑ ⓒ ⓓ	72	ⓐ ⓑ ⓒ ⓓ		
13	ⓐ ⓑ ⓒ ⓓ	33	ⓐ ⓑ ⓒ ⓓ	53	ⓐ ⓑ ⓒ ⓓ	73	ⓐ ⓑ ⓒ ⓓ		
14	ⓐ ⓑ ⓒ ⓓ	34	ⓐ ⓑ ⓒ ⓓ	54	ⓐ ⓑ ⓒ ⓓ	74	ⓐ ⓑ ⓒ ⓓ		
15	ⓐ ⓑ ⓒ ⓓ	35	ⓐ ⓑ ⓒ ⓓ	55	ⓐ ⓑ ⓒ ⓓ	75	ⓐ ⓑ ⓒ ⓓ		
16	ⓐ ⓑ ⓒ ⓓ	36	ⓐ ⓑ ⓒ ⓓ	56	ⓐ ⓑ ⓒ ⓓ	76	ⓐ ⓑ ⓒ ⓓ		
17	ⓐ ⓑ ⓒ ⓓ	37	ⓐ ⓑ ⓒ ⓓ	57	ⓐ ⓑ ⓒ ⓓ	77	ⓐ ⓑ ⓒ ⓓ		
18	ⓐ ⓑ ⓒ ⓓ	38	ⓐ ⓑ ⓒ ⓓ	58	ⓐ ⓑ ⓒ ⓓ	78	ⓐ ⓑ ⓒ ⓓ		
19	ⓐ ⓑ ⓒ ⓓ	39	ⓐ ⓑ ⓒ ⓓ	59	ⓐ ⓑ ⓒ ⓓ	79	ⓐ ⓑ ⓒ ⓓ		
20	ⓐ ⓑ ⓒ ⓓ	40	ⓐ ⓑ ⓒ ⓓ	60	ⓐ ⓑ ⓒ ⓓ	80	ⓐ ⓑ ⓒ ⓓ		

password

⓪	⓪	⓪	⓪
①	①	①	①
②	②	②	②
③	③	③	③
④	④	④	④
⑤	⑤	⑤	⑤
⑥	⑥	⑥	⑥
⑦	⑦	⑦	⑦
⑧	⑧	⑧	⑧
⑨	⑨	⑨	⑨

ANSWER SHEET

※ TEST DATE	MO.	DAY	YEAR

감독 확인	

성 명		등급	① ② ③ ④ ⑤

성명란		
성	초 성	㉠ ㉡ ㉢ ㉣ ㉤ ㉥ ㉦ ㉧ ㉨ ㉩ ㉪ ㉫ ㉬ ㉭
	중 성	ㅏ ㅑ ㅓ ㅕ ㅗ ㅛ ㅜ ㅠ ㅡ ㅣ ㅐ ㅒ ㅔ ㅖ ㅘ ㅚ ㅢ ㅝ ㅟ ㅙ
	종 성	㉠ ㉡ ㉢ ㉣ ㉤ ㉥ ㉦ ㉧ ㉨ ㉩ ㉪ ㉫ ㉬ ㉭ ㄲ ㄸ ㅃ ㅆ ㅉ
명	초 성	㉠ ㉡ ㉢ ㉣ ㉤ ㉥ ㉦ ㉧ ㉨ ㉩ ㉪ ㉫ ㉬ ㉭
	중 성	ㅏ ㅑ ㅓ ㅕ ㅗ ㅛ ㅜ ㅠ ㅡ ㅣ ㅐ ㅒ ㅔ ㅖ ㅘ ㅚ ㅢ ㅝ ㅟ ㅙ
	종 성	㉠ ㉡ ㉢ ㉣ ㉤ ㉥ ㉦ ㉧ ㉨ ㉩ ㉪ ㉫ ㉬ ㉭ ㄲ ㄸ ㅃ ㅆ ㅉ
	초 성	㉠ ㉡ ㉢ ㉣ ㉤ ㉥ ㉦ ㉧ ㉨ ㉩ ㉪ ㉫ ㉬ ㉭
	중 성	ㅏ ㅑ ㅓ ㅕ ㅗ ㅛ ㅜ ㅠ ㅡ ㅣ ㅐ ㅒ ㅔ ㅖ ㅘ ㅚ ㅢ ㅝ ㅟ ㅙ
	종 성	㉠ ㉡ ㉢ ㉣ ㉤ ㉥ ㉦ ㉧ ㉨ ㉩ ㉪ ㉫ ㉬ ㉭ ㄲ ㄸ ㅃ ㅆ ㅉ
란	초 성	㉠ ㉡ ㉢ ㉣ ㉤ ㉥ ㉦ ㉧ ㉨ ㉩ ㉪ ㉫ ㉬ ㉭
	중 성	ㅏ ㅑ ㅓ ㅕ ㅗ ㅛ ㅜ ㅠ ㅡ ㅣ ㅐ ㅒ ㅔ ㅖ ㅘ ㅚ ㅢ ㅝ ㅟ ㅙ
	종 성	㉠ ㉡ ㉢ ㉣ ㉤ ㉥ ㉦ ㉧ ㉨ ㉩ ㉪ ㉫ ㉬ ㉭ ㄲ ㄸ ㅃ ㅆ ㅉ

수 험 번 호														
		–					–							
⓪	⓪		⓪	⓪	⓪	⓪		⓪	⓪	⓪	⓪	⓪	⓪	⓪
①	①		①	①	①	①		①	①	①	①	①	①	①
②	②		②	②	②	②		②	②	②	②	②	②	②
③	③		③	③	③	③		③	③	③	③	③	③	③
④	④	–	④	④	④	④	–	④	④	④	④	④	④	④
⑤	⑤		⑤	⑤	⑤	⑤		⑤	⑤	⑤	⑤	⑤	⑤	⑤
⑥	⑥		⑥	⑥	⑥	⑥		⑥	⑥	⑥	⑥	⑥	⑥	⑥
⑦	⑦		⑦	⑦	⑦	⑦		⑦	⑦	⑦	⑦	⑦	⑦	⑦
⑧	⑧		⑧	⑧	⑧	⑧		⑧	⑧	⑧	⑧	⑧	⑧	⑧
⑨	⑨		⑨	⑨	⑨	⑨		⑨	⑨	⑨	⑨	⑨	⑨	⑨

1) Code 1.

	⓪ ① ② ③ ④ ⑤ ⑥ ⑦ ⑧ ⑨
	⓪ ① ② ③ ④ ⑤ ⑥ ⑦ ⑧ ⑨
	⓪ ① ② ③ ④ ⑤ ⑥ ⑦ ⑧ ⑨

2) Code 2.

	⓪ ① ② ③ ④ ⑤ ⑥ ⑦ ⑧ ⑨
	⓪ ① ② ③ ④ ⑤ ⑥ ⑦ ⑧ ⑨
	⓪ ① ② ③ ④ ⑤ ⑥ ⑦ ⑧ ⑨

3) Code 3.

	⓪ ① ② ③ ④ ⑤ ⑥ ⑦ ⑧ ⑨
	⓪ ① ② ③ ④ ⑤ ⑥ ⑦ ⑧ ⑨
	⓪ ① ② ③ ④ ⑤ ⑥ ⑦ ⑧ ⑨

주민등록번호 앞자리							고 유 번 호						
⓪	⓪	⓪	⓪	⓪	⓪		⓪	⓪	⓪	⓪	⓪	⓪	⓪
①	①	①	①	①	①		①	①	①	①	①	①	①
②	②	②	②	②	②		②	②	②	②	②	②	②
③	③	③	③	③	③		③	③	③	③	③	③	③
④	④	④	④	④	④	–	④	④	④	④	④	④	④
⑤	⑤	⑤	⑤	⑤	⑤		⑤	⑤	⑤	⑤	⑤	⑤	⑤
⑥	⑥	⑥	⑥	⑥	⑥		⑥	⑥	⑥	⑥	⑥	⑥	⑥
⑦	⑦	⑦	⑦	⑦	⑦		⑦	⑦	⑦	⑦	⑦	⑦	⑦
⑧	⑧	⑧	⑧	⑧	⑧		⑧	⑧	⑧	⑧	⑧	⑧	⑧
⑨	⑨	⑨	⑨	⑨	⑨		⑨	⑨	⑨	⑨	⑨	⑨	⑨

문항	답 란	문항	답 란	문항	답 란	문항	답 란	문항	답 란
1	ⓐ ⓑ ⓒ ⓓ	21	ⓐ ⓑ ⓒ ⓓ	41	ⓐ ⓑ ⓒ ⓓ	61	ⓐ ⓑ ⓒ ⓓ	81	ⓐ ⓑ ⓒ ⓓ
2	ⓐ ⓑ ⓒ ⓓ	22	ⓐ ⓑ ⓒ ⓓ	42	ⓐ ⓑ ⓒ ⓓ	62	ⓐ ⓑ ⓒ ⓓ	82	ⓐ ⓑ ⓒ ⓓ
3	ⓐ ⓑ ⓒ ⓓ	23	ⓐ ⓑ ⓒ ⓓ	43	ⓐ ⓑ ⓒ ⓓ	63	ⓐ ⓑ ⓒ ⓓ	83	ⓐ ⓑ ⓒ ⓓ
4	ⓐ ⓑ ⓒ ⓓ	24	ⓐ ⓑ ⓒ ⓓ	44	ⓐ ⓑ ⓒ ⓓ	64	ⓐ ⓑ ⓒ ⓓ	84	ⓐ ⓑ ⓒ ⓓ
5	ⓐ ⓑ ⓒ ⓓ	25	ⓐ ⓑ ⓒ ⓓ	45	ⓐ ⓑ ⓒ ⓓ	65	ⓐ ⓑ ⓒ ⓓ	85	ⓐ ⓑ ⓒ ⓓ
6	ⓐ ⓑ ⓒ ⓓ	26	ⓐ ⓑ ⓒ ⓓ	46	ⓐ ⓑ ⓒ ⓓ	66	ⓐ ⓑ ⓒ ⓓ	86	ⓐ ⓑ ⓒ ⓓ
7	ⓐ ⓑ ⓒ ⓓ	27	ⓐ ⓑ ⓒ ⓓ	47	ⓐ ⓑ ⓒ ⓓ	67	ⓐ ⓑ ⓒ ⓓ	87	ⓐ ⓑ ⓒ ⓓ
8	ⓐ ⓑ ⓒ ⓓ	28	ⓐ ⓑ ⓒ ⓓ	48	ⓐ ⓑ ⓒ ⓓ	68	ⓐ ⓑ ⓒ ⓓ	88	ⓐ ⓑ ⓒ ⓓ
9	ⓐ ⓑ ⓒ ⓓ	29	ⓐ ⓑ ⓒ ⓓ	49	ⓐ ⓑ ⓒ ⓓ	69	ⓐ ⓑ ⓒ ⓓ	89	ⓐ ⓑ ⓒ ⓓ
10	ⓐ ⓑ ⓒ ⓓ	30	ⓐ ⓑ ⓒ ⓓ	50	ⓐ ⓑ ⓒ ⓓ	70	ⓐ ⓑ ⓒ ⓓ	90	ⓐ ⓑ ⓒ ⓓ
11	ⓐ ⓑ ⓒ ⓓ	31	ⓐ ⓑ ⓒ ⓓ	51	ⓐ ⓑ ⓒ ⓓ	71	ⓐ ⓑ ⓒ ⓓ		
12	ⓐ ⓑ ⓒ ⓓ	32	ⓐ ⓑ ⓒ ⓓ	52	ⓐ ⓑ ⓒ ⓓ	72	ⓐ ⓑ ⓒ ⓓ		
13	ⓐ ⓑ ⓒ ⓓ	33	ⓐ ⓑ ⓒ ⓓ	53	ⓐ ⓑ ⓒ ⓓ	73	ⓐ ⓑ ⓒ ⓓ		
14	ⓐ ⓑ ⓒ ⓓ	34	ⓐ ⓑ ⓒ ⓓ	54	ⓐ ⓑ ⓒ ⓓ	74	ⓐ ⓑ ⓒ ⓓ		
15	ⓐ ⓑ ⓒ ⓓ	35	ⓐ ⓑ ⓒ ⓓ	55	ⓐ ⓑ ⓒ ⓓ	75	ⓐ ⓑ ⓒ ⓓ		
16	ⓐ ⓑ ⓒ ⓓ	36	ⓐ ⓑ ⓒ ⓓ	56	ⓐ ⓑ ⓒ ⓓ	76	ⓐ ⓑ ⓒ ⓓ		
17	ⓐ ⓑ ⓒ ⓓ	37	ⓐ ⓑ ⓒ ⓓ	57	ⓐ ⓑ ⓒ ⓓ	77	ⓐ ⓑ ⓒ ⓓ		
18	ⓐ ⓑ ⓒ ⓓ	38	ⓐ ⓑ ⓒ ⓓ	58	ⓐ ⓑ ⓒ ⓓ	78	ⓐ ⓑ ⓒ ⓓ		
19	ⓐ ⓑ ⓒ ⓓ	39	ⓐ ⓑ ⓒ ⓓ	59	ⓐ ⓑ ⓒ ⓓ	79	ⓐ ⓑ ⓒ ⓓ		
20	ⓐ ⓑ ⓒ ⓓ	40	ⓐ ⓑ ⓒ ⓓ	60	ⓐ ⓑ ⓒ ⓓ	80	ⓐ ⓑ ⓒ ⓓ		

password

⓪	⓪	⓪	⓪
①	①	①	①
②	②	②	②
③	③	③	③
④	④	④	④
⑤	⑤	⑤	⑤
⑥	⑥	⑥	⑥
⑦	⑦	⑦	⑦
⑧	⑧	⑧	⑧
⑨	⑨	⑨	⑨

ANSWER SHEET

※ TEST DATE	MO.		DAY		YEAR			

감독관 확인	

성 명		등급	① ② ③ ④ ⑤

성명란		
	초성	ㄱ ㄴ ㄷ ㄹ ㅁ ㅂ ㅅ ㅇ ㅈ ㅊ ㅋ ㅌ ㅍ ㅎ
	중성	ㅏ ㅑ ㅓ ㅕ ㅗ ㅛ ㅜ ㅠ ㅡ ㅣ ㅔ ㅐ ㅖ ㅒ ㅘ ㅚ ㅢ ㅝ ㅟ ㅙ
	종성	ㄱ ㄴ ㄷ ㄹ ㅁ ㅂ ㅅ ㅇ ㅈ ㅊ ㅋ ㅌ ㅍ ㅎ ㄲ ㄸ ㅃ ㅆ ㅉ
	초성	ㄱ ㄴ ㄷ ㄹ ㅁ ㅂ ㅅ ㅇ ㅈ ㅊ ㅋ ㅌ ㅍ ㅎ
	중성	ㅏ ㅑ ㅓ ㅕ ㅗ ㅛ ㅜ ㅠ ㅡ ㅣ ㅔ ㅐ ㅖ ㅒ ㅘ ㅚ ㅢ ㅝ ㅟ ㅙ
	종성	ㄱ ㄴ ㄷ ㄹ ㅁ ㅂ ㅅ ㅇ ㅈ ㅊ ㅋ ㅌ ㅍ ㅎ ㄲ ㄸ ㅃ ㅆ ㅉ
	초성	ㄱ ㄴ ㄷ ㄹ ㅁ ㅂ ㅅ ㅇ ㅈ ㅊ ㅋ ㅌ ㅍ ㅎ
	중성	ㅏ ㅑ ㅓ ㅕ ㅗ ㅛ ㅜ ㅠ ㅡ ㅣ ㅔ ㅐ ㅖ ㅒ ㅘ ㅚ ㅢ ㅝ ㅟ ㅙ
	종성	ㄱ ㄴ ㄷ ㄹ ㅁ ㅂ ㅅ ㅇ ㅈ ㅊ ㅋ ㅌ ㅍ ㅎ ㄲ ㄸ ㅃ ㅆ ㅉ
	초성	ㄱ ㄴ ㄷ ㄹ ㅁ ㅂ ㅅ ㅇ ㅈ ㅊ ㅋ ㅌ ㅍ ㅎ
	중성	ㅏ ㅑ ㅓ ㅕ ㅗ ㅛ ㅜ ㅠ ㅡ ㅣ ㅔ ㅐ ㅖ ㅒ ㅘ ㅚ ㅢ ㅝ ㅟ ㅙ
	종성	ㄱ ㄴ ㄷ ㄹ ㅁ ㅂ ㅅ ㅇ ㅈ ㅊ ㅋ ㅌ ㅍ ㅎ ㄲ ㄸ ㅃ ㅆ ㅉ

수험번호														
		–					–							
⓪	⓪		⓪	⓪	⓪	⓪		⓪	⓪	⓪	⓪	⓪	⓪	⓪
①	①		①	①	①	①		①	①	①	①	①	①	①
②	②		②	②	②	②		②	②	②	②	②	②	②
③	③		③	③	③	③		③	③	③	③	③	③	③
④	④	–	④	④	④	④	–	④	④	④	④	④	④	④
⑤	⑤		⑤	⑤	⑤	⑤		⑤	⑤	⑤	⑤	⑤	⑤	⑤
⑥	⑥		⑥	⑥	⑥	⑥		⑥	⑥	⑥	⑥	⑥	⑥	⑥
⑦	⑦		⑦	⑦	⑦	⑦		⑦	⑦	⑦	⑦	⑦	⑦	⑦
⑧	⑧		⑧	⑧	⑧	⑧		⑧	⑧	⑧	⑧	⑧	⑧	⑧
⑨	⑨		⑨	⑨	⑨	⑨		⑨	⑨	⑨	⑨	⑨	⑨	⑨

1) Code 1.

	⓪ ① ② ③ ④ ⑤ ⑥ ⑦ ⑧ ⑨
	⓪ ① ② ③ ④ ⑤ ⑥ ⑦ ⑧ ⑨
	⓪ ① ② ③ ④ ⑤ ⑥ ⑦ ⑧ ⑨

2) Code 2.

	⓪ ① ② ③ ④ ⑤ ⑥ ⑦ ⑧ ⑨
	⓪ ① ② ③ ④ ⑤ ⑥ ⑦ ⑧ ⑨
	⓪ ① ② ③ ④ ⑤ ⑥ ⑦ ⑧ ⑨

3) Code 3.

	⓪ ① ② ③ ④ ⑤ ⑥ ⑦ ⑧ ⑨
	⓪ ① ② ③ ④ ⑤ ⑥ ⑦ ⑧ ⑨
	⓪ ① ② ③ ④ ⑤ ⑥ ⑦ ⑧ ⑨

주민등록번호 앞자리							고유번호						
⓪	⓪	⓪	⓪	⓪	⓪		⓪	⓪	⓪	⓪	⓪	⓪	⓪
①	①	①	①	①	①		①	①	①	①	①	①	①
②	②	②	②	②	②		②	②	②	②	②	②	②
③	③	③	③	③	③		③	③	③	③	③	③	③
④	④	④	④	④	④	–	④	④	④	④	④	④	④
⑤	⑤	⑤	⑤	⑤	⑤		⑤	⑤	⑤	⑤	⑤	⑤	⑤
⑥	⑥	⑥	⑥	⑥	⑥		⑥	⑥	⑥	⑥	⑥	⑥	⑥
⑦	⑦	⑦	⑦	⑦	⑦		⑦	⑦	⑦	⑦	⑦	⑦	⑦
⑧	⑧	⑧	⑧	⑧	⑧		⑧	⑧	⑧	⑧	⑧	⑧	⑧
⑨	⑨	⑨	⑨	⑨	⑨		⑨	⑨	⑨	⑨	⑨	⑨	⑨

문항	답 란	문항	답 란	문항	답 란	문항	답 란	문항	답 란
1	ⓐ ⓑ ⓒ ⓓ	21	ⓐ ⓑ ⓒ ⓓ	41	ⓐ ⓑ ⓒ ⓓ	61	ⓐ ⓑ ⓒ ⓓ	81	ⓐ ⓑ ⓒ ⓓ
2	ⓐ ⓑ ⓒ ⓓ	22	ⓐ ⓑ ⓒ ⓓ	42	ⓐ ⓑ ⓒ ⓓ	62	ⓐ ⓑ ⓒ ⓓ	82	ⓐ ⓑ ⓒ ⓓ
3	ⓐ ⓑ ⓒ ⓓ	23	ⓐ ⓑ ⓒ ⓓ	43	ⓐ ⓑ ⓒ ⓓ	63	ⓐ ⓑ ⓒ ⓓ	83	ⓐ ⓑ ⓒ ⓓ
4	ⓐ ⓑ ⓒ ⓓ	24	ⓐ ⓑ ⓒ ⓓ	44	ⓐ ⓑ ⓒ ⓓ	64	ⓐ ⓑ ⓒ ⓓ	84	ⓐ ⓑ ⓒ ⓓ
5	ⓐ ⓑ ⓒ ⓓ	25	ⓐ ⓑ ⓒ ⓓ	45	ⓐ ⓑ ⓒ ⓓ	65	ⓐ ⓑ ⓒ ⓓ	85	ⓐ ⓑ ⓒ ⓓ
6	ⓐ ⓑ ⓒ ⓓ	26	ⓐ ⓑ ⓒ ⓓ	46	ⓐ ⓑ ⓒ ⓓ	66	ⓐ ⓑ ⓒ ⓓ	86	ⓐ ⓑ ⓒ ⓓ
7	ⓐ ⓑ ⓒ ⓓ	27	ⓐ ⓑ ⓒ ⓓ	47	ⓐ ⓑ ⓒ ⓓ	67	ⓐ ⓑ ⓒ ⓓ	87	ⓐ ⓑ ⓒ ⓓ
8	ⓐ ⓑ ⓒ ⓓ	28	ⓐ ⓑ ⓒ ⓓ	48	ⓐ ⓑ ⓒ ⓓ	68	ⓐ ⓑ ⓒ ⓓ	88	ⓐ ⓑ ⓒ ⓓ
9	ⓐ ⓑ ⓒ ⓓ	29	ⓐ ⓑ ⓒ ⓓ	49	ⓐ ⓑ ⓒ ⓓ	69	ⓐ ⓑ ⓒ ⓓ	89	ⓐ ⓑ ⓒ ⓓ
10	ⓐ ⓑ ⓒ ⓓ	30	ⓐ ⓑ ⓒ ⓓ	50	ⓐ ⓑ ⓒ ⓓ	70	ⓐ ⓑ ⓒ ⓓ	90	ⓐ ⓑ ⓒ ⓓ
11	ⓐ ⓑ ⓒ ⓓ	31	ⓐ ⓑ ⓒ ⓓ	51	ⓐ ⓑ ⓒ ⓓ	71	ⓐ ⓑ ⓒ ⓓ		
12	ⓐ ⓑ ⓒ ⓓ	32	ⓐ ⓑ ⓒ ⓓ	52	ⓐ ⓑ ⓒ ⓓ	72	ⓐ ⓑ ⓒ ⓓ		
13	ⓐ ⓑ ⓒ ⓓ	33	ⓐ ⓑ ⓒ ⓓ	53	ⓐ ⓑ ⓒ ⓓ	73	ⓐ ⓑ ⓒ ⓓ		
14	ⓐ ⓑ ⓒ ⓓ	34	ⓐ ⓑ ⓒ ⓓ	54	ⓐ ⓑ ⓒ ⓓ	74	ⓐ ⓑ ⓒ ⓓ		
15	ⓐ ⓑ ⓒ ⓓ	35	ⓐ ⓑ ⓒ ⓓ	55	ⓐ ⓑ ⓒ ⓓ	75	ⓐ ⓑ ⓒ ⓓ		
16	ⓐ ⓑ ⓒ ⓓ	36	ⓐ ⓑ ⓒ ⓓ	56	ⓐ ⓑ ⓒ ⓓ	76	ⓐ ⓑ ⓒ ⓓ		
17	ⓐ ⓑ ⓒ ⓓ	37	ⓐ ⓑ ⓒ ⓓ	57	ⓐ ⓑ ⓒ ⓓ	77	ⓐ ⓑ ⓒ ⓓ		
18	ⓐ ⓑ ⓒ ⓓ	38	ⓐ ⓑ ⓒ ⓓ	58	ⓐ ⓑ ⓒ ⓓ	78	ⓐ ⓑ ⓒ ⓓ		
19	ⓐ ⓑ ⓒ ⓓ	39	ⓐ ⓑ ⓒ ⓓ	59	ⓐ ⓑ ⓒ ⓓ	79	ⓐ ⓑ ⓒ ⓓ		
20	ⓐ ⓑ ⓒ ⓓ	40	ⓐ ⓑ ⓒ ⓓ	60	ⓐ ⓑ ⓒ ⓓ	80	ⓐ ⓑ ⓒ ⓓ		

password

⓪	⓪	⓪	⓪
①	①	①	①
②	②	②	②
③	③	③	③
④	④	④	④
⑤	⑤	⑤	⑤
⑥	⑥	⑥	⑥
⑦	⑦	⑦	⑦
⑧	⑧	⑧	⑧
⑨	⑨	⑨	⑨

ANSWER SHEET

※ TEST DATE	MO.	DAY	YEAR

감독 확인	

성 명		등급	① ② ③ ④ ⑤

성	초 성	㉠ ㉡ ㉢ ㉣ ㉤ ㉥ ㉦ ㉧ ㉨ ㉩ ㉪ ㉫ ㉬ ㉭
	중 성	ㅏ ㅑ ㅓ ㅕ ㅗ ㅛ ㅜ ㅠ ㅡ ㅣ ㅔ ㅐ ㅖ ㅒ ㅘ ㅚ ㅢ ㅝ ㅟ ㅙ
	종 성	㉠ ㉡ ㉢ ㉣ ㉤ ㉥ ㉦ ㉧ ㉨ ㉩ ㉪ ㉫ ㉬ ㉭ ㄲ ㄸ ㅃ ㅆ ㅉ
명	초 성	㉠ ㉡ ㉢ ㉣ ㉤ ㉥ ㉦ ㉧ ㉨ ㉩ ㉪ ㉫ ㉬ ㉭
	중 성	ㅏ ㅑ ㅓ ㅕ ㅗ ㅛ ㅜ ㅠ ㅡ ㅣ ㅔ ㅐ ㅖ ㅒ ㅘ ㅚ ㅢ ㅝ ㅟ ㅙ
	종 성	㉠ ㉡ ㉢ ㉣ ㉤ ㉥ ㉦ ㉧ ㉨ ㉩ ㉪ ㉫ ㉬ ㉭ ㄲ ㄸ ㅃ ㅆ ㅉ
	초 성	㉠ ㉡ ㉢ ㉣ ㉤ ㉥ ㉦ ㉧ ㉨ ㉩ ㉪ ㉫ ㉬ ㉭
	중 성	ㅏ ㅑ ㅓ ㅕ ㅗ ㅛ ㅜ ㅠ ㅡ ㅣ ㅔ ㅐ ㅖ ㅒ ㅘ ㅚ ㅢ ㅝ ㅟ ㅙ
	종 성	㉠ ㉡ ㉢ ㉣ ㉤ ㉥ ㉦ ㉧ ㉨ ㉩ ㉪ ㉫ ㉬ ㉭ ㄲ ㄸ ㅃ ㅆ ㅉ
란	초 성	㉠ ㉡ ㉢ ㉣ ㉤ ㉥ ㉦ ㉧ ㉨ ㉩ ㉪ ㉫ ㉬ ㉭
	중 성	ㅏ ㅑ ㅓ ㅕ ㅗ ㅛ ㅜ ㅠ ㅡ ㅣ ㅔ ㅐ ㅖ ㅒ ㅘ ㅚ ㅢ ㅝ ㅟ ㅙ
	종 성	㉠ ㉡ ㉢ ㉣ ㉤ ㉥ ㉦ ㉧ ㉨ ㉩ ㉪ ㉫ ㉬ ㉭ ㄲ ㄸ ㅃ ㅆ ㅉ

수 험 번 호														
		–					–							
⓪	⓪		⓪	⓪	⓪	⓪		⓪	⓪	⓪	⓪	⓪	⓪	⓪
①	①		①	①	①	①		①	①	①	①	①	①	①
②	②		②	②	②	②		②	②	②	②	②	②	②
③	③		③	③	③	③		③	③	③	③	③	③	③
④	④	–	④	④	④	④	–	④	④	④	④	④	④	④
⑤	⑤		⑤	⑤	⑤	⑤		⑤	⑤	⑤	⑤	⑤	⑤	⑤
⑥	⑥		⑥	⑥	⑥	⑥		⑥	⑥	⑥	⑥	⑥	⑥	⑥
⑦	⑦		⑦	⑦	⑦	⑦		⑦	⑦	⑦	⑦	⑦	⑦	⑦
⑧	⑧		⑧	⑧	⑧	⑧		⑧	⑧	⑧	⑧	⑧	⑧	⑧
⑨	⑨		⑨	⑨	⑨	⑨		⑨	⑨	⑨	⑨	⑨	⑨	⑨

1) Code 1.

	⓪ ① ② ③ ④ ⑤ ⑥ ⑦ ⑧ ⑨
	⓪ ① ② ③ ④ ⑤ ⑥ ⑦ ⑧ ⑨
	⓪ ① ② ③ ④ ⑤ ⑥ ⑦ ⑧ ⑨

2) Code 2.

	⓪ ① ② ③ ④ ⑤ ⑥ ⑦ ⑧ ⑨
	⓪ ① ② ③ ④ ⑤ ⑥ ⑦ ⑧ ⑨
	⓪ ① ② ③ ④ ⑤ ⑥ ⑦ ⑧ ⑨

3) Code 3.

	⓪ ① ② ③ ④ ⑤ ⑥ ⑦ ⑧ ⑨
	⓪ ① ② ③ ④ ⑤ ⑥ ⑦ ⑧ ⑨
	⓪ ① ② ③ ④ ⑤ ⑥ ⑦ ⑧ ⑨

주민등록번호 앞자리							고 유 번 호						
⓪	⓪	⓪	⓪	⓪	⓪		⓪	⓪	⓪	⓪	⓪	⓪	⓪
①	①	①	①	①	①		①	①	①	①	①	①	①
②	②	②	②	②	②		②	②	②	②	②	②	②
③	③	③	③	③	③		③	③	③	③	③	③	③
④	④	④	④	④	④	–	④	④	④	④	④	④	④
⑤	⑤	⑤	⑤	⑤	⑤		⑤	⑤	⑤	⑤	⑤	⑤	⑤
⑥	⑥	⑥	⑥	⑥	⑥		⑥	⑥	⑥	⑥	⑥	⑥	⑥
⑦	⑦	⑦	⑦	⑦	⑦		⑦	⑦	⑦	⑦	⑦	⑦	⑦
⑧	⑧	⑧	⑧	⑧	⑧		⑧	⑧	⑧	⑧	⑧	⑧	⑧
⑨	⑨	⑨	⑨	⑨	⑨		⑨	⑨	⑨	⑨	⑨	⑨	⑨

문항	답 란	문항	답 란	문항	답 란	문항	답 란	문항	답 란
1	ⓐ ⓑ ⓒ ⓓ	21	ⓐ ⓑ ⓒ ⓓ	41	ⓐ ⓑ ⓒ ⓓ	61	ⓐ ⓑ ⓒ ⓓ	81	ⓐ ⓑ ⓒ ⓓ
2	ⓐ ⓑ ⓒ ⓓ	22	ⓐ ⓑ ⓒ ⓓ	42	ⓐ ⓑ ⓒ ⓓ	62	ⓐ ⓑ ⓒ ⓓ	82	ⓐ ⓑ ⓒ ⓓ
3	ⓐ ⓑ ⓒ ⓓ	23	ⓐ ⓑ ⓒ ⓓ	43	ⓐ ⓑ ⓒ ⓓ	63	ⓐ ⓑ ⓒ ⓓ	83	ⓐ ⓑ ⓒ ⓓ
4	ⓐ ⓑ ⓒ ⓓ	24	ⓐ ⓑ ⓒ ⓓ	44	ⓐ ⓑ ⓒ ⓓ	64	ⓐ ⓑ ⓒ ⓓ	84	ⓐ ⓑ ⓒ ⓓ
5	ⓐ ⓑ ⓒ ⓓ	25	ⓐ ⓑ ⓒ ⓓ	45	ⓐ ⓑ ⓒ ⓓ	65	ⓐ ⓑ ⓒ ⓓ	85	ⓐ ⓑ ⓒ ⓓ
6	ⓐ ⓑ ⓒ ⓓ	26	ⓐ ⓑ ⓒ ⓓ	46	ⓐ ⓑ ⓒ ⓓ	66	ⓐ ⓑ ⓒ ⓓ	86	ⓐ ⓑ ⓒ ⓓ
7	ⓐ ⓑ ⓒ ⓓ	27	ⓐ ⓑ ⓒ ⓓ	47	ⓐ ⓑ ⓒ ⓓ	67	ⓐ ⓑ ⓒ ⓓ	87	ⓐ ⓑ ⓒ ⓓ
8	ⓐ ⓑ ⓒ ⓓ	28	ⓐ ⓑ ⓒ ⓓ	48	ⓐ ⓑ ⓒ ⓓ	68	ⓐ ⓑ ⓒ ⓓ	88	ⓐ ⓑ ⓒ ⓓ
9	ⓐ ⓑ ⓒ ⓓ	29	ⓐ ⓑ ⓒ ⓓ	49	ⓐ ⓑ ⓒ ⓓ	69	ⓐ ⓑ ⓒ ⓓ	89	ⓐ ⓑ ⓒ ⓓ
10	ⓐ ⓑ ⓒ ⓓ	30	ⓐ ⓑ ⓒ ⓓ	50	ⓐ ⓑ ⓒ ⓓ	70	ⓐ ⓑ ⓒ ⓓ	90	ⓐ ⓑ ⓒ ⓓ
11	ⓐ ⓑ ⓒ ⓓ	31	ⓐ ⓑ ⓒ ⓓ	51	ⓐ ⓑ ⓒ ⓓ	71	ⓐ ⓑ ⓒ ⓓ		
12	ⓐ ⓑ ⓒ ⓓ	32	ⓐ ⓑ ⓒ ⓓ	52	ⓐ ⓑ ⓒ ⓓ	72	ⓐ ⓑ ⓒ ⓓ		
13	ⓐ ⓑ ⓒ ⓓ	33	ⓐ ⓑ ⓒ ⓓ	53	ⓐ ⓑ ⓒ ⓓ	73	ⓐ ⓑ ⓒ ⓓ		
14	ⓐ ⓑ ⓒ ⓓ	34	ⓐ ⓑ ⓒ ⓓ	54	ⓐ ⓑ ⓒ ⓓ	74	ⓐ ⓑ ⓒ ⓓ		
15	ⓐ ⓑ ⓒ ⓓ	35	ⓐ ⓑ ⓒ ⓓ	55	ⓐ ⓑ ⓒ ⓓ	75	ⓐ ⓑ ⓒ ⓓ		
16	ⓐ ⓑ ⓒ ⓓ	36	ⓐ ⓑ ⓒ ⓓ	56	ⓐ ⓑ ⓒ ⓓ	76	ⓐ ⓑ ⓒ ⓓ		
17	ⓐ ⓑ ⓒ ⓓ	37	ⓐ ⓑ ⓒ ⓓ	57	ⓐ ⓑ ⓒ ⓓ	77	ⓐ ⓑ ⓒ ⓓ		
18	ⓐ ⓑ ⓒ ⓓ	38	ⓐ ⓑ ⓒ ⓓ	58	ⓐ ⓑ ⓒ ⓓ	78	ⓐ ⓑ ⓒ ⓓ		
19	ⓐ ⓑ ⓒ ⓓ	39	ⓐ ⓑ ⓒ ⓓ	59	ⓐ ⓑ ⓒ ⓓ	79	ⓐ ⓑ ⓒ ⓓ		
20	ⓐ ⓑ ⓒ ⓓ	40	ⓐ ⓑ ⓒ ⓓ	60	ⓐ ⓑ ⓒ ⓓ	80	ⓐ ⓑ ⓒ ⓓ		

password

⓪	⓪	⓪	⓪
①	①	①	①
②	②	②	②
③	③	③	③
④	④	④	④
⑤	⑤	⑤	⑤
⑥	⑥	⑥	⑥
⑦	⑦	⑦	⑦
⑧	⑧	⑧	⑧
⑨	⑨	⑨	⑨

ANSWER SHEET

※ TEST DATE

MO.		DAY		YEAR			

감독 확인	

성 명		등급	① ② ③ ④ ⑤

성	초 성	㉠ ㉡ ㉢ ㉣ ㉤ ㉥ ㉦ ㉧ ㉨ ㉩ ㉪ ㉫ ㉬ ㉭
	중 성	ㅏ ㅑ ㅓ ㅕ ㅗ ㅛ ㅜ ㅠ ㅡ ㅣ ㅔ ㅐ ㅖ ㅒ ㅘ ㅚ ㅢ ㅝ ㅟ ㅙ
	종 성	㉠ ㉡ ㉢ ㉣ ㉤ ㉥ ㉦ ㉧ ㉨ ㉩ ㉪ ㉫ ㉬ ㉭ ㄲ ㄸ ㅃ ㅆ ㅉ
명	초 성	㉠ ㉡ ㉢ ㉣ ㉤ ㉥ ㉦ ㉧ ㉨ ㉩ ㉪ ㉫ ㉬ ㉭
	중 성	ㅏ ㅑ ㅓ ㅕ ㅗ ㅛ ㅜ ㅠ ㅡ ㅣ ㅔ ㅐ ㅖ ㅒ ㅘ ㅚ ㅢ ㅝ ㅟ ㅙ
	종 성	㉠ ㉡ ㉢ ㉣ ㉤ ㉥ ㉦ ㉧ ㉨ ㉩ ㉪ ㉫ ㉬ ㉭ ㄲ ㄸ ㅃ ㅆ ㅉ
	초 성	㉠ ㉡ ㉢ ㉣ ㉤ ㉥ ㉦ ㉧ ㉨ ㉩ ㉪ ㉫ ㉬ ㉭
	중 성	ㅏ ㅑ ㅓ ㅕ ㅗ ㅛ ㅜ ㅠ ㅡ ㅣ ㅔ ㅐ ㅖ ㅒ ㅘ ㅚ ㅢ ㅝ ㅟ ㅙ
	종 성	㉠ ㉡ ㉢ ㉣ ㉤ ㉥ ㉦ ㉧ ㉨ ㉩ ㉪ ㉫ ㉬ ㉭ ㄲ ㄸ ㅃ ㅆ ㅉ
란	초 성	㉠ ㉡ ㉢ ㉣ ㉤ ㉥ ㉦ ㉧ ㉨ ㉩ ㉪ ㉫ ㉬ ㉭
	중 성	ㅏ ㅑ ㅓ ㅕ ㅗ ㅛ ㅜ ㅠ ㅡ ㅣ ㅔ ㅐ ㅖ ㅒ ㅘ ㅚ ㅢ ㅝ ㅟ ㅙ
	종 성	㉠ ㉡ ㉢ ㉣ ㉤ ㉥ ㉦ ㉧ ㉨ ㉩ ㉪ ㉫ ㉬ ㉭ ㄲ ㄸ ㅃ ㅆ ㅉ

수 험 번 호														
		–					–							
⓪	⓪		⓪	⓪	⓪	⓪		⓪	⓪	⓪	⓪	⓪	⓪	⓪
①	①		①	①	①	①		①	①	①	①	①	①	①
②	②		②	②	②	②		②	②	②	②	②	②	②
③	③		③	③	③	③		③	③	③	③	③	③	③
④	④	–	④	④	④	④	–	④	④	④	④	④	④	④
⑤	⑤		⑤	⑤	⑤	⑤		⑤	⑤	⑤	⑤	⑤	⑤	⑤
⑥	⑥		⑥	⑥	⑥	⑥		⑥	⑥	⑥	⑥	⑥	⑥	⑥
⑦	⑦		⑦	⑦	⑦	⑦		⑦	⑦	⑦	⑦	⑦	⑦	⑦
⑧	⑧		⑧	⑧	⑧	⑧		⑧	⑧	⑧	⑧	⑧	⑧	⑧
⑨	⑨		⑨	⑨	⑨	⑨		⑨	⑨	⑨	⑨	⑨	⑨	⑨

1) Code 1.

	⓪ ① ② ③ ④ ⑤ ⑥ ⑦ ⑧ ⑨
	⓪ ① ② ③ ④ ⑤ ⑥ ⑦ ⑧ ⑨
	⓪ ① ② ③ ④ ⑤ ⑥ ⑦ ⑧ ⑨

2) Code 2.

	⓪ ① ② ③ ④ ⑤ ⑥ ⑦ ⑧ ⑨
	⓪ ① ② ③ ④ ⑤ ⑥ ⑦ ⑧ ⑨
	⓪ ① ② ③ ④ ⑤ ⑥ ⑦ ⑧ ⑨

3) Code 3.

	⓪ ① ② ③ ④ ⑤ ⑥ ⑦ ⑧ ⑨
	⓪ ① ② ③ ④ ⑤ ⑥ ⑦ ⑧ ⑨
	⓪ ① ② ③ ④ ⑤ ⑥ ⑦ ⑧ ⑨

주민등록번호앞자리							고 유 번 호						
⓪	⓪	⓪	⓪	⓪	⓪		⓪	⓪	⓪	⓪	⓪	⓪	⓪
①	①	①	①	①	①		①	①	①	①	①	①	①
②	②	②	②	②	②		②	②	②	②	②	②	②
③	③	③	③	③	③		③	③	③	③	③	③	③
④	④	④	④	④	④	–	④	④	④	④	④	④	④
⑤	⑤	⑤	⑤	⑤	⑤		⑤	⑤	⑤	⑤	⑤	⑤	⑤
⑥	⑥	⑥	⑥	⑥	⑥		⑥	⑥	⑥	⑥	⑥	⑥	⑥
⑦	⑦	⑦	⑦	⑦	⑦		⑦	⑦	⑦	⑦	⑦	⑦	⑦
⑧	⑧	⑧	⑧	⑧	⑧		⑧	⑧	⑧	⑧	⑧	⑧	⑧
⑨	⑨	⑨	⑨	⑨	⑨		⑨	⑨	⑨	⑨	⑨	⑨	⑨

문항	답 란	문항	답 란	문항	답 란	문항	답 란	문항	답 란
1	ⓐ ⓑ ⓒ ⓓ	21	ⓐ ⓑ ⓒ ⓓ	41	ⓐ ⓑ ⓒ ⓓ	61	ⓐ ⓑ ⓒ ⓓ	81	ⓐ ⓑ ⓒ ⓓ
2	ⓐ ⓑ ⓒ ⓓ	22	ⓐ ⓑ ⓒ ⓓ	42	ⓐ ⓑ ⓒ ⓓ	62	ⓐ ⓑ ⓒ ⓓ	82	ⓐ ⓑ ⓒ ⓓ
3	ⓐ ⓑ ⓒ ⓓ	23	ⓐ ⓑ ⓒ ⓓ	43	ⓐ ⓑ ⓒ ⓓ	63	ⓐ ⓑ ⓒ ⓓ	83	ⓐ ⓑ ⓒ ⓓ
4	ⓐ ⓑ ⓒ ⓓ	24	ⓐ ⓑ ⓒ ⓓ	44	ⓐ ⓑ ⓒ ⓓ	64	ⓐ ⓑ ⓒ ⓓ	84	ⓐ ⓑ ⓒ ⓓ
5	ⓐ ⓑ ⓒ ⓓ	25	ⓐ ⓑ ⓒ ⓓ	45	ⓐ ⓑ ⓒ ⓓ	65	ⓐ ⓑ ⓒ ⓓ	85	ⓐ ⓑ ⓒ ⓓ
6	ⓐ ⓑ ⓒ ⓓ	26	ⓐ ⓑ ⓒ ⓓ	46	ⓐ ⓑ ⓒ ⓓ	66	ⓐ ⓑ ⓒ ⓓ	86	ⓐ ⓑ ⓒ ⓓ
7	ⓐ ⓑ ⓒ ⓓ	27	ⓐ ⓑ ⓒ ⓓ	47	ⓐ ⓑ ⓒ ⓓ	67	ⓐ ⓑ ⓒ ⓓ	87	ⓐ ⓑ ⓒ ⓓ
8	ⓐ ⓑ ⓒ ⓓ	28	ⓐ ⓑ ⓒ ⓓ	48	ⓐ ⓑ ⓒ ⓓ	68	ⓐ ⓑ ⓒ ⓓ	88	ⓐ ⓑ ⓒ ⓓ
9	ⓐ ⓑ ⓒ ⓓ	29	ⓐ ⓑ ⓒ ⓓ	49	ⓐ ⓑ ⓒ ⓓ	69	ⓐ ⓑ ⓒ ⓓ	89	ⓐ ⓑ ⓒ ⓓ
10	ⓐ ⓑ ⓒ ⓓ	30	ⓐ ⓑ ⓒ ⓓ	50	ⓐ ⓑ ⓒ ⓓ	70	ⓐ ⓑ ⓒ ⓓ	90	ⓐ ⓑ ⓒ ⓓ
11	ⓐ ⓑ ⓒ ⓓ	31	ⓐ ⓑ ⓒ ⓓ	51	ⓐ ⓑ ⓒ ⓓ	71	ⓐ ⓑ ⓒ ⓓ		
12	ⓐ ⓑ ⓒ ⓓ	32	ⓐ ⓑ ⓒ ⓓ	52	ⓐ ⓑ ⓒ ⓓ	72	ⓐ ⓑ ⓒ ⓓ		
13	ⓐ ⓑ ⓒ ⓓ	33	ⓐ ⓑ ⓒ ⓓ	53	ⓐ ⓑ ⓒ ⓓ	73	ⓐ ⓑ ⓒ ⓓ		
14	ⓐ ⓑ ⓒ ⓓ	34	ⓐ ⓑ ⓒ ⓓ	54	ⓐ ⓑ ⓒ ⓓ	74	ⓐ ⓑ ⓒ ⓓ		
15	ⓐ ⓑ ⓒ ⓓ	35	ⓐ ⓑ ⓒ ⓓ	55	ⓐ ⓑ ⓒ ⓓ	75	ⓐ ⓑ ⓒ ⓓ		
16	ⓐ ⓑ ⓒ ⓓ	36	ⓐ ⓑ ⓒ ⓓ	56	ⓐ ⓑ ⓒ ⓓ	76	ⓐ ⓑ ⓒ ⓓ		
17	ⓐ ⓑ ⓒ ⓓ	37	ⓐ ⓑ ⓒ ⓓ	57	ⓐ ⓑ ⓒ ⓓ	77	ⓐ ⓑ ⓒ ⓓ		
18	ⓐ ⓑ ⓒ ⓓ	38	ⓐ ⓑ ⓒ ⓓ	58	ⓐ ⓑ ⓒ ⓓ	78	ⓐ ⓑ ⓒ ⓓ		
19	ⓐ ⓑ ⓒ ⓓ	39	ⓐ ⓑ ⓒ ⓓ	59	ⓐ ⓑ ⓒ ⓓ	79	ⓐ ⓑ ⓒ ⓓ		
20	ⓐ ⓑ ⓒ ⓓ	40	ⓐ ⓑ ⓒ ⓓ	60	ⓐ ⓑ ⓒ ⓓ	80	ⓐ ⓑ ⓒ ⓓ		

password

⓪	⓪	⓪	⓪
①	①	①	①
②	②	②	②
③	③	③	③
④	④	④	④
⑤	⑤	⑤	⑤
⑥	⑥	⑥	⑥
⑦	⑦	⑦	⑦
⑧	⑧	⑧	⑧
⑨	⑨	⑨	⑨

ANSWER SHEET

※ TEST DATE

MO.	DAY	YEAR

감독 확인

성 명		등급 ① ② ③ ④ ⑤

성	초 성	㉠ ㉡ ㉢ ㉣ ㉤ ㉥ ㉦ ㉧ ㉨ ㉩ ㉪ ㉫ ㉬ ㉭
	중 성	ㅏ ㅑ ㅓ ㅕ ㅗ ㅛ ㅜ ㅠ ㅡ ㅣ ㅔ ㅐ ㅖ ㅒ ㅘ ㅚ ㅢ ㅝ ㅟ ㅙ
	종 성	㉠ ㉡ ㉢ ㉣ ㉤ ㉥ ㉦ ㉧ ㉨ ㉩ ㉪ ㉫ ㉬ ㉭ ㄲ ㄸ ㅃ ㅆ ㅉ
명	초 성	㉠ ㉡ ㉢ ㉣ ㉤ ㉥ ㉦ ㉧ ㉨ ㉩ ㉪ ㉫ ㉬ ㉭
	중 성	ㅏ ㅑ ㅓ ㅕ ㅗ ㅛ ㅜ ㅠ ㅡ ㅣ ㅔ ㅐ ㅖ ㅒ ㅘ ㅚ ㅢ ㅝ ㅟ ㅙ
	종 성	㉠ ㉡ ㉢ ㉣ ㉤ ㉥ ㉦ ㉧ ㉨ ㉩ ㉪ ㉫ ㉬ ㉭ ㄲ ㄸ ㅃ ㅆ ㅉ
란	초 성	㉠ ㉡ ㉢ ㉣ ㉤ ㉥ ㉦ ㉧ ㉨ ㉩ ㉪ ㉫ ㉬ ㉭
	중 성	ㅏ ㅑ ㅓ ㅕ ㅗ ㅛ ㅜ ㅠ ㅡ ㅣ ㅔ ㅐ ㅖ ㅒ ㅘ ㅚ ㅢ ㅝ ㅟ ㅙ
	종 성	㉠ ㉡ ㉢ ㉣ ㉤ ㉥ ㉦ ㉧ ㉨ ㉩ ㉪ ㉫ ㉬ ㉭ ㄲ ㄸ ㅃ ㅆ ㅉ
	초 성	㉠ ㉡ ㉢ ㉣ ㉤ ㉥ ㉦ ㉧ ㉨ ㉩ ㉪ ㉫ ㉬ ㉭
	중 성	ㅏ ㅑ ㅓ ㅕ ㅗ ㅛ ㅜ ㅠ ㅡ ㅣ ㅔ ㅐ ㅖ ㅒ ㅘ ㅚ ㅢ ㅝ ㅟ ㅙ
	종 성	㉠ ㉡ ㉢ ㉣ ㉤ ㉥ ㉦ ㉧ ㉨ ㉩ ㉪ ㉫ ㉬ ㉭ ㄲ ㄸ ㅃ ㅆ ㅉ

수 험 번 호

		–					–							
⓪	⓪		⓪	⓪	⓪	⓪		⓪	⓪	⓪	⓪	⓪	⓪	⓪
①	①		①	①	①	①		①	①	①	①	①	①	①
②	②		②	②	②	②		②	②	②	②	②	②	②
③	③		③	③	③	③		③	③	③	③	③	③	③
④	④	–	④	④	④	④	–	④	④	④	④	④	④	④
⑤	⑤		⑤	⑤	⑤	⑤		⑤	⑤	⑤	⑤	⑤	⑤	⑤
⑥	⑥		⑥	⑥	⑥	⑥		⑥	⑥	⑥	⑥	⑥	⑥	⑥
⑦	⑦		⑦	⑦	⑦	⑦		⑦	⑦	⑦	⑦	⑦	⑦	⑦
⑧	⑧		⑧	⑧	⑧	⑧		⑧	⑧	⑧	⑧	⑧	⑧	⑧
⑨	⑨		⑨	⑨	⑨	⑨		⑨	⑨	⑨	⑨	⑨	⑨	⑨

1) Code 1.

	⓪ ① ② ③ ④ ⑤ ⑥ ⑦ ⑧ ⑨
	⓪ ① ② ③ ④ ⑤ ⑥ ⑦ ⑧ ⑨
	⓪ ① ② ③ ④ ⑤ ⑥ ⑦ ⑧ ⑨

2) Code 2.

	⓪ ① ② ③ ④ ⑤ ⑥ ⑦ ⑧ ⑨
	⓪ ① ② ③ ④ ⑤ ⑥ ⑦ ⑧ ⑨
	⓪ ① ② ③ ④ ⑤ ⑥ ⑦ ⑧ ⑨

3) Code 3.

	⓪ ① ② ③ ④ ⑤ ⑥ ⑦ ⑧ ⑨
	⓪ ① ② ③ ④ ⑤ ⑥ ⑦ ⑧ ⑨
	⓪ ① ② ③ ④ ⑤ ⑥ ⑦ ⑧ ⑨

주민등록번호 앞자리							고 유 번 호						
⓪	⓪	⓪	⓪	⓪	⓪		⓪	⓪	⓪	⓪	⓪	⓪	⓪
①	①	①	①	①	①		①	①	①	①	①	①	①
②	②	②	②	②	②		②	②	②	②	②	②	②
③	③	③	③	③	③		③	③	③	③	③	③	③
④	④	④	④	④	④	–	④	④	④	④	④	④	④
⑤	⑤	⑤	⑤	⑤	⑤		⑤	⑤	⑤	⑤	⑤	⑤	⑤
⑥	⑥	⑥	⑥	⑥	⑥		⑥	⑥	⑥	⑥	⑥	⑥	⑥
⑦	⑦	⑦	⑦	⑦	⑦		⑦	⑦	⑦	⑦	⑦	⑦	⑦
⑧	⑧	⑧	⑧	⑧	⑧		⑧	⑧	⑧	⑧	⑧	⑧	⑧
⑨	⑨	⑨	⑨	⑨	⑨		⑨	⑨	⑨	⑨	⑨	⑨	⑨

문항	답 란	문항	답 란	문항	답 란	문항	답 란	문항	답 란
1	ⓐ ⓑ ⓒ ⓓ	21	ⓐ ⓑ ⓒ ⓓ	41	ⓐ ⓑ ⓒ ⓓ	61	ⓐ ⓑ ⓒ ⓓ	81	ⓐ ⓑ ⓒ ⓓ
2	ⓐ ⓑ ⓒ ⓓ	22	ⓐ ⓑ ⓒ ⓓ	42	ⓐ ⓑ ⓒ ⓓ	62	ⓐ ⓑ ⓒ ⓓ	82	ⓐ ⓑ ⓒ ⓓ
3	ⓐ ⓑ ⓒ ⓓ	23	ⓐ ⓑ ⓒ ⓓ	43	ⓐ ⓑ ⓒ ⓓ	63	ⓐ ⓑ ⓒ ⓓ	83	ⓐ ⓑ ⓒ ⓓ
4	ⓐ ⓑ ⓒ ⓓ	24	ⓐ ⓑ ⓒ ⓓ	44	ⓐ ⓑ ⓒ ⓓ	64	ⓐ ⓑ ⓒ ⓓ	84	ⓐ ⓑ ⓒ ⓓ
5	ⓐ ⓑ ⓒ ⓓ	25	ⓐ ⓑ ⓒ ⓓ	45	ⓐ ⓑ ⓒ ⓓ	65	ⓐ ⓑ ⓒ ⓓ	85	ⓐ ⓑ ⓒ ⓓ
6	ⓐ ⓑ ⓒ ⓓ	26	ⓐ ⓑ ⓒ ⓓ	46	ⓐ ⓑ ⓒ ⓓ	66	ⓐ ⓑ ⓒ ⓓ	86	ⓐ ⓑ ⓒ ⓓ
7	ⓐ ⓑ ⓒ ⓓ	27	ⓐ ⓑ ⓒ ⓓ	47	ⓐ ⓑ ⓒ ⓓ	67	ⓐ ⓑ ⓒ ⓓ	87	ⓐ ⓑ ⓒ ⓓ
8	ⓐ ⓑ ⓒ ⓓ	28	ⓐ ⓑ ⓒ ⓓ	48	ⓐ ⓑ ⓒ ⓓ	68	ⓐ ⓑ ⓒ ⓓ	88	ⓐ ⓑ ⓒ ⓓ
9	ⓐ ⓑ ⓒ ⓓ	29	ⓐ ⓑ ⓒ ⓓ	49	ⓐ ⓑ ⓒ ⓓ	69	ⓐ ⓑ ⓒ ⓓ	89	ⓐ ⓑ ⓒ ⓓ
10	ⓐ ⓑ ⓒ ⓓ	30	ⓐ ⓑ ⓒ ⓓ	50	ⓐ ⓑ ⓒ ⓓ	70	ⓐ ⓑ ⓒ ⓓ	90	ⓐ ⓑ ⓒ ⓓ
11	ⓐ ⓑ ⓒ ⓓ	31	ⓐ ⓑ ⓒ ⓓ	51	ⓐ ⓑ ⓒ ⓓ	71	ⓐ ⓑ ⓒ ⓓ		
12	ⓐ ⓑ ⓒ ⓓ	32	ⓐ ⓑ ⓒ ⓓ	52	ⓐ ⓑ ⓒ ⓓ	72	ⓐ ⓑ ⓒ ⓓ		
13	ⓐ ⓑ ⓒ ⓓ	33	ⓐ ⓑ ⓒ ⓓ	53	ⓐ ⓑ ⓒ ⓓ	73	ⓐ ⓑ ⓒ ⓓ		
14	ⓐ ⓑ ⓒ ⓓ	34	ⓐ ⓑ ⓒ ⓓ	54	ⓐ ⓑ ⓒ ⓓ	74	ⓐ ⓑ ⓒ ⓓ		
15	ⓐ ⓑ ⓒ ⓓ	35	ⓐ ⓑ ⓒ ⓓ	55	ⓐ ⓑ ⓒ ⓓ	75	ⓐ ⓑ ⓒ ⓓ		
16	ⓐ ⓑ ⓒ ⓓ	36	ⓐ ⓑ ⓒ ⓓ	56	ⓐ ⓑ ⓒ ⓓ	76	ⓐ ⓑ ⓒ ⓓ		
17	ⓐ ⓑ ⓒ ⓓ	37	ⓐ ⓑ ⓒ ⓓ	57	ⓐ ⓑ ⓒ ⓓ	77	ⓐ ⓑ ⓒ ⓓ		
18	ⓐ ⓑ ⓒ ⓓ	38	ⓐ ⓑ ⓒ ⓓ	58	ⓐ ⓑ ⓒ ⓓ	78	ⓐ ⓑ ⓒ ⓓ		
19	ⓐ ⓑ ⓒ ⓓ	39	ⓐ ⓑ ⓒ ⓓ	59	ⓐ ⓑ ⓒ ⓓ	79	ⓐ ⓑ ⓒ ⓓ		
20	ⓐ ⓑ ⓒ ⓓ	40	ⓐ ⓑ ⓒ ⓓ	60	ⓐ ⓑ ⓒ ⓓ	80	ⓐ ⓑ ⓒ ⓓ		

password

⓪	⓪	⓪	⓪
①	①	①	①
②	②	②	②
③	③	③	③
④	④	④	④
⑤	⑤	⑤	⑤
⑥	⑥	⑥	⑥
⑦	⑦	⑦	⑦
⑧	⑧	⑧	⑧
⑨	⑨	⑨	⑨

ANSWER SHEET

※ TEST DATE

MO.	DAY	YEAR

감독 확인	

성 명	

등급	① ② ③ ④ ⑤

성명란		
	초 성	ㄱ ㄴ ㄷ ㄹ ㅁ ㅂ ㅅ ㅇ ㅈ ㅊ ㅋ ㅌ ㅍ ㅎ
	중 성	ㅏ ㅑ ㅓ ㅕ ㅗ ㅛ ㅜ ㅠ ㅡ ㅣ ㅔ ㅐ ㅖ ㅒ ㅘ ㅚ ㅢ ㅝ ㅟ ㅙ
	종 성	ㄱ ㄴ ㄷ ㄹ ㅁ ㅂ ㅅ ㅇ ㅈ ㅊ ㅋ ㅌ ㅍ ㅎ ㄲ ㄸ ㅃ ㅆ ㅉ
	초 성	ㄱ ㄴ ㄷ ㄹ ㅁ ㅂ ㅅ ㅇ ㅈ ㅊ ㅋ ㅌ ㅍ ㅎ
	중 성	ㅏ ㅑ ㅓ ㅕ ㅗ ㅛ ㅜ ㅠ ㅡ ㅣ ㅔ ㅐ ㅖ ㅒ ㅘ ㅚ ㅢ ㅝ ㅟ ㅙ
	종 성	ㄱ ㄴ ㄷ ㄹ ㅁ ㅂ ㅅ ㅇ ㅈ ㅊ ㅋ ㅌ ㅍ ㅎ ㄲ ㄸ ㅃ ㅆ ㅉ
	초 성	ㄱ ㄴ ㄷ ㄹ ㅁ ㅂ ㅅ ㅇ ㅈ ㅊ ㅋ ㅌ ㅍ ㅎ
	중 성	ㅏ ㅑ ㅓ ㅕ ㅗ ㅛ ㅜ ㅠ ㅡ ㅣ ㅔ ㅐ ㅖ ㅒ ㅘ ㅚ ㅢ ㅝ ㅟ ㅙ
	종 성	ㄱ ㄴ ㄷ ㄹ ㅁ ㅂ ㅅ ㅇ ㅈ ㅊ ㅋ ㅌ ㅍ ㅎ ㄲ ㄸ ㅃ ㅆ ㅉ
	초 성	ㄱ ㄴ ㄷ ㄹ ㅁ ㅂ ㅅ ㅇ ㅈ ㅊ ㅋ ㅌ ㅍ ㅎ
	중 성	ㅏ ㅑ ㅓ ㅕ ㅗ ㅛ ㅜ ㅠ ㅡ ㅣ ㅔ ㅐ ㅖ ㅒ ㅘ ㅚ ㅢ ㅝ ㅟ ㅙ
	종 성	ㄱ ㄴ ㄷ ㄹ ㅁ ㅂ ㅅ ㅇ ㅈ ㅊ ㅋ ㅌ ㅍ ㅎ ㄲ ㄸ ㅃ ㅆ ㅉ

수험번호														
		–					–							
0~9	0~9	–	0~9	0~9	0~9	0~9	–	0~9	0~9	0~9	0~9	0~9	0~9	0~9

1) Code 1.

	⓪ ① ② ③ ④ ⑤ ⑥ ⑦ ⑧ ⑨
	⓪ ① ② ③ ④ ⑤ ⑥ ⑦ ⑧ ⑨
	⓪ ① ② ③ ④ ⑤ ⑥ ⑦ ⑧ ⑨

2) Code 2.

	⓪ ① ② ③ ④ ⑤ ⑥ ⑦ ⑧ ⑨
	⓪ ① ② ③ ④ ⑤ ⑥ ⑦ ⑧ ⑨
	⓪ ① ② ③ ④ ⑤ ⑥ ⑦ ⑧ ⑨

3) Code 3.

	⓪ ① ② ③ ④ ⑤ ⑥ ⑦ ⑧ ⑨
	⓪ ① ② ③ ④ ⑤ ⑥ ⑦ ⑧ ⑨
	⓪ ① ② ③ ④ ⑤ ⑥ ⑦ ⑧ ⑨

주민등록번호 앞자리							고 유 번 호						
						–							
0~9	0~9	0~9	0~9	0~9	0~9	–	0~9	0~9	0~9	0~9	0~9	0~9	0~9

문항	답 란	문항	답 란	문항	답 란	문항	답 란	문항	답 란
1	ⓐ ⓑ ⓒ ⓓ	21	ⓐ ⓑ ⓒ ⓓ	41	ⓐ ⓑ ⓒ ⓓ	61	ⓐ ⓑ ⓒ ⓓ	81	ⓐ ⓑ ⓒ ⓓ
2	ⓐ ⓑ ⓒ ⓓ	22	ⓐ ⓑ ⓒ ⓓ	42	ⓐ ⓑ ⓒ ⓓ	62	ⓐ ⓑ ⓒ ⓓ	82	ⓐ ⓑ ⓒ ⓓ
3	ⓐ ⓑ ⓒ ⓓ	23	ⓐ ⓑ ⓒ ⓓ	43	ⓐ ⓑ ⓒ ⓓ	63	ⓐ ⓑ ⓒ ⓓ	83	ⓐ ⓑ ⓒ ⓓ
4	ⓐ ⓑ ⓒ ⓓ	24	ⓐ ⓑ ⓒ ⓓ	44	ⓐ ⓑ ⓒ ⓓ	64	ⓐ ⓑ ⓒ ⓓ	84	ⓐ ⓑ ⓒ ⓓ
5	ⓐ ⓑ ⓒ ⓓ	25	ⓐ ⓑ ⓒ ⓓ	45	ⓐ ⓑ ⓒ ⓓ	65	ⓐ ⓑ ⓒ ⓓ	85	ⓐ ⓑ ⓒ ⓓ
6	ⓐ ⓑ ⓒ ⓓ	26	ⓐ ⓑ ⓒ ⓓ	46	ⓐ ⓑ ⓒ ⓓ	66	ⓐ ⓑ ⓒ ⓓ	86	ⓐ ⓑ ⓒ ⓓ
7	ⓐ ⓑ ⓒ ⓓ	27	ⓐ ⓑ ⓒ ⓓ	47	ⓐ ⓑ ⓒ ⓓ	67	ⓐ ⓑ ⓒ ⓓ	87	ⓐ ⓑ ⓒ ⓓ
8	ⓐ ⓑ ⓒ ⓓ	28	ⓐ ⓑ ⓒ ⓓ	48	ⓐ ⓑ ⓒ ⓓ	68	ⓐ ⓑ ⓒ ⓓ	88	ⓐ ⓑ ⓒ ⓓ
9	ⓐ ⓑ ⓒ ⓓ	29	ⓐ ⓑ ⓒ ⓓ	49	ⓐ ⓑ ⓒ ⓓ	69	ⓐ ⓑ ⓒ ⓓ	89	ⓐ ⓑ ⓒ ⓓ
10	ⓐ ⓑ ⓒ ⓓ	30	ⓐ ⓑ ⓒ ⓓ	50	ⓐ ⓑ ⓒ ⓓ	70	ⓐ ⓑ ⓒ ⓓ	90	ⓐ ⓑ ⓒ ⓓ
11	ⓐ ⓑ ⓒ ⓓ	31	ⓐ ⓑ ⓒ ⓓ	51	ⓐ ⓑ ⓒ ⓓ	71	ⓐ ⓑ ⓒ ⓓ		
12	ⓐ ⓑ ⓒ ⓓ	32	ⓐ ⓑ ⓒ ⓓ	52	ⓐ ⓑ ⓒ ⓓ	72	ⓐ ⓑ ⓒ ⓓ		
13	ⓐ ⓑ ⓒ ⓓ	33	ⓐ ⓑ ⓒ ⓓ	53	ⓐ ⓑ ⓒ ⓓ	73	ⓐ ⓑ ⓒ ⓓ		
14	ⓐ ⓑ ⓒ ⓓ	34	ⓐ ⓑ ⓒ ⓓ	54	ⓐ ⓑ ⓒ ⓓ	74	ⓐ ⓑ ⓒ ⓓ		
15	ⓐ ⓑ ⓒ ⓓ	35	ⓐ ⓑ ⓒ ⓓ	55	ⓐ ⓑ ⓒ ⓓ	75	ⓐ ⓑ ⓒ ⓓ		
16	ⓐ ⓑ ⓒ ⓓ	36	ⓐ ⓑ ⓒ ⓓ	56	ⓐ ⓑ ⓒ ⓓ	76	ⓐ ⓑ ⓒ ⓓ		
17	ⓐ ⓑ ⓒ ⓓ	37	ⓐ ⓑ ⓒ ⓓ	57	ⓐ ⓑ ⓒ ⓓ	77	ⓐ ⓑ ⓒ ⓓ		
18	ⓐ ⓑ ⓒ ⓓ	38	ⓐ ⓑ ⓒ ⓓ	58	ⓐ ⓑ ⓒ ⓓ	78	ⓐ ⓑ ⓒ ⓓ		
19	ⓐ ⓑ ⓒ ⓓ	39	ⓐ ⓑ ⓒ ⓓ	59	ⓐ ⓑ ⓒ ⓓ	79	ⓐ ⓑ ⓒ ⓓ		
20	ⓐ ⓑ ⓒ ⓓ	40	ⓐ ⓑ ⓒ ⓓ	60	ⓐ ⓑ ⓒ ⓓ	80	ⓐ ⓑ ⓒ ⓓ		

password

0~9	0~9	0~9	0~9

MEMO

MEMO

해커스 지텔프 LEVEL 2 실전모의고사 독해 10회

해커스 어학연구소

지텔프 독해 한 번에 끝낼 수 있을까요?

맘만치 않은 시험 응시료에,
다른 할 일도 산더미처럼 많고...

[해커스 지텔프 실전모의고사 독해 10회 (Level 2)]는 자신 있게 말합니다.

지텔프 독해, 한 번에 끝낼 수 있습니다.

실전에 최적화된 문제 유형별 핵심 전략으로,
최신 출제경향을 완벽 반영한 실전모의고사 10회분으로,
그리고 목표 달성을 돕는 무료 강의와 지텔프 기출 단어암기장으로,

[해커스 지텔프 실전모의고사 독해 10회 (Level 2)]와 함께한다면

단기간에 확실하게 목표 점수를 달성할 수 있습니다.

**"이미 수많은 사람들이 안전하게 지나간 길,
가장 확실한 길,
가장 빠른 길로 가면 돼요."**

얼마 남지 않은 지텔프 시험,
해커스와 함께라면 한 번에 끝낼 수 있습니다!

: 목차

최신 출제경향 완벽 반영! 실전완성 **문제집** [책 속의 책]

명쾌한 해설로 점수 상승! 약점보완 **해설집**

<지텔프 기출 단어암기장> PDF

각 회차별로 암기하면 도움이 되는 지텔프 필수 어휘를 수록한 <지텔프 기출 단어암기장> PDF를 해커스인강(HackersIngang.com) 사이트에서 무료로 다운받을 수 있습니다. 단어암기장을 통해 언제 어디서든 지텔프 필수 어휘를 암기하세요!

책의 구성과 특징

최신 출제경향을 완벽 반영한 10회분으로 실전 감각 완성!

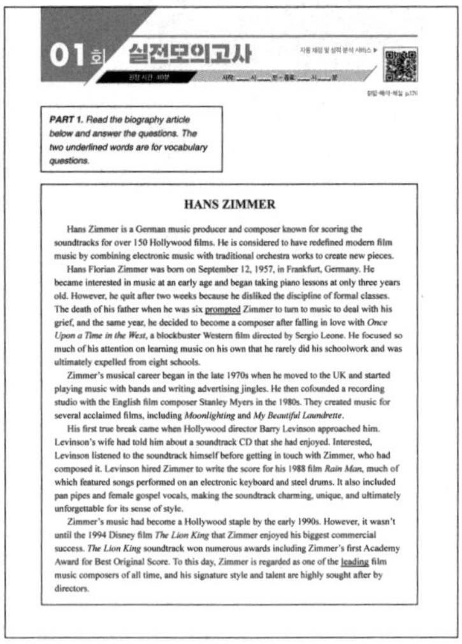
01회 실전모의고사

자동 채점 및 성적 분석 서비스 ▶

PART 1. Read the biography article below and answer the questions. The two underlined words are for vocabulary questions.

HANS ZIMMER

Hans Zimmer is a German music producer and composer known for scoring the soundtracks for over 150 Hollywood films. He is considered to have redefined modern film music by combining electronic music with traditional orchestra works to create new pieces.

Hans Florian Zimmer was born on September 12, 1957, in Frankfurt, Germany. He became interested in music at an early age and began taking piano lessons at only three years old. However, he quit after two weeks because he disliked the discipline of formal classes. The death of his father when he was six prompted Zimmer to turn to music to deal with his grief, and the same year, he decided to become a composer after falling in love with *Once Upon a Time in the West*, a blockbuster Western film directed by Sergio Leone. He focused so much of his attention on learning music on his own that he rarely did his schoolwork and was ultimately expelled from eight schools.

Zimmer's musical career began in the late 1970s when he moved to the UK and started playing music with bands and writing advertising jingles. He then cofounded a recording studio with the English film composer Stanley Myers in the 1980s. They created music for several acclaimed films, including *Moonlighting* and *My Beautiful Laundrette*.

His first true break came when Hollywood director Barry Levinson approached him. Levinson's wife had told him about a soundtrack CD that she had enjoyed. Interested, Levinson listened to the soundtrack himself before getting in touch with Zimmer, who had composed it. Levinson hired Zimmer to write the score for his 1988 film *Rain Man*, much of which featured songs performed on an electronic keyboard and steel drums. It also included pan pipes and female gospel vocals, making the soundtrack charming, unique, and ultimately unforgettable for its sense of style.

Zimmer's music had become a Hollywood staple by the early 1990s. However, it wasn't until the 1994 Disney film *The Lion King* that Zimmer enjoyed his biggest commercial success. *The Lion King* soundtrack won numerous awards including Zimmer's first Academy Award for Best Original Score. To this day, Zimmer is regarded as one of the leading film music composers of all time, and his signature style and talent are highly sought after by directors.

최신 지텔프 출제경향 완벽 반영

실제 지텔프 시험과 가장 비슷한 난이도와 문제 유형으로 구성된 실전모의고사 10회분을 제공하였습니다.

자동 채점 및 성적 분석 서비스

타이머, 모바일 OMR, 자동 채점, 정답률 및 취약 유형 분석까지 제공하는 자동 채점 및 성적 분석 서비스를 통해 실전 감각을 키울 수 있습니다.

문제 유형별 핵심 문제 풀이 전략으로 빠른 실력 향상!

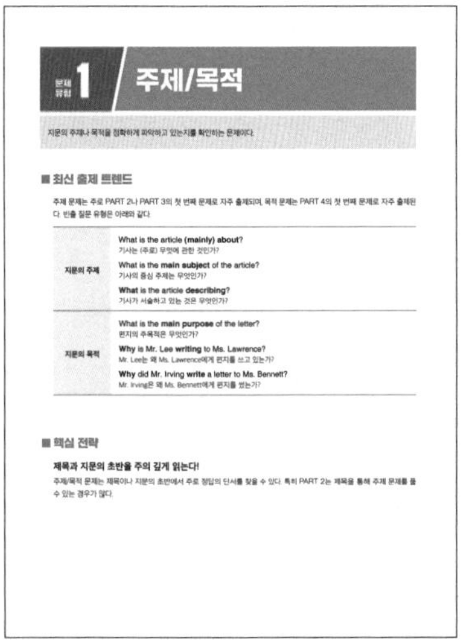
문제 유형 1 주제/목적

지문의 주제나 목적을 정확하게 파악하고 있는지를 확인하는 문제이다.

■ 최신 출제 트렌드

주제 문제는 주로 PART 2나 PART 3의 첫 번째 문제로 자주 출제되며, 목적 문제는 PART 4의 첫 번째 문제로 자주 출제된다. 빈출 질문 유형은 아래와 같다.

지문의 주제	What is the article **(mainly) about**? 기사는 (주로) 무엇에 관한 것인가? What is the **main subject** of the article? 기사의 중심 주제는 무엇인가? **What is the article describing?** 기사가 서술하고 있는 것은 무엇인가?
지문의 목적	What is the **main purpose** of the letter? 편지의 주목적은 무엇인가? **Why is Mr. Lee writing** to Ms. Lawrence? Mr. Lee는 왜 Ms. Lawrence에게 편지를 쓰고 있는가? **Why** did Mr. Irving **write** a letter to Ms. Bennett? Mr. Irving은 왜 Ms. Bennett에게 편지를 썼는가?

■ 핵심 전략

제목과 지문의 초반을 주의 깊게 읽는다!

주제/목적 문제는 제목이나 지문의 초반에서 주로 정답의 단서를 찾을 수 있다. 특히 PART 2는 제목을 통해 주제 문제를 풀 수 있는 경우가 많다.

핵심 전략

지텔프 독해에서 출제되는 문제 유형별 핵심 전략을 제공하여 목표 점수 달성을 위해 필요한 부분만 빠르고 효과적으로 학습할 수 있게 하였습니다.

문제 풀이 전략

시간을 단축시켜주는 문제 풀이 전략을 예제와 함께 제공하여 효율적인 문제 접근 방식을 단계별로 한눈에 확인할 수 있게 하였습니다.

취약 유형 분석과 명쾌한 해설로 확실한 점수 상승!

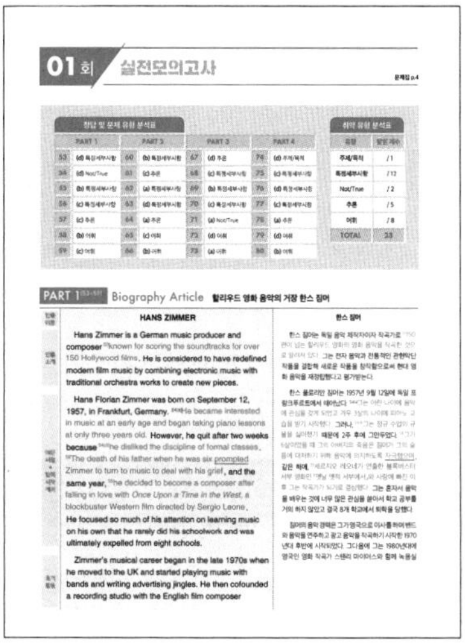

취약 유형 분석표

취약 유형 분석표를 통해 자신의 취약 유형을 스스로 확인할 수 있게 하였습니다.

지텔프 치트키

문제 풀이의 핵심이 되는 지텔프 치트키를 통해 문제를 쉽고 빠르게 푸는 전략을 제공하였습니다.

해설 & 오답분석

모든 문제에 대한 정확한 해석, 명쾌하고 상세한 해설과 필수 학습 어휘를 제공하였습니다. 해설과 오답분석을 통해 정답이 되는 이유와 오답이 되는 이유를 확실히 파악할 수 있습니다.

풍부한 추가 학습자료로 목표 점수 달성!

지텔프 기출 단어암기장

지텔프 시험에 등장하는 빈출 어휘만 모은 단어암기장을 무료로 다운받아 이용할 수 있습니다.

* 지텔프 기출 단어암기장은 해커스인강(HackersIngang.com) 사이트에서 무료로 제공됩니다.

무료 동영상 강의

해커스영어(Hackers.co.kr)에서 제공되는 지텔프 단기 고득점 비법 강의를 통해 학습 효과를 극대화하여 목표 점수를 달성할 수 있습니다.

지텔프 소개

지텔프 시험은?

지텔프(G-TELP)란 General Tests of English Language Proficiency의 약자로 국제테스트 연구원(ITSC, International Testing Services Center)에서 주관하는 국제적 공인영어시험이며, 한국에서는 1986년에 지텔프 코리아가 설립되어 지텔프 시험을 운영 및 주관하고 있습니다. 현재 공무원, 군무원 등 각종 국가고시 영어대체시험, 기업체의 신입사원 및 인사 · 승진 평가시험, 대학교 · 대학원 졸업자격 영어대체시험 등으로 널리 활용되고 있습니다.

지텔프 시험의 종류

지텔프는 Level 1부터 5까지 다섯 가지 Level의 시험으로 구분됩니다. 한국에서는 다섯 가지 Level 중 Level 2 정기시험 점수가 활용되고 있습니다. 그 외 Level은 현재 수시시험 접수만 가능하며, 공인 영어 성적으로 거의 활용되지 않습니다.

구분	출제 방식 및 시간	평가 기준	합격자의 영어 구사 능력	응시 자격
Level 1	청취 30문항(약 30분) 독해 및 어휘 60문항(70분) **총 90문항(약 100분)**	Native Speaker에 준하는 영어 능력: 상담, 토론 가능	외국인과 의사소통, 통역이 가능한 수준	Level 2 영역별 75점 이상 획득 시
Level 2	문법 26문항(20분) 청취 26문항(약 30분) 독해 및 어휘 28문항(40분) **총 80문항(약 90분)**	다양한 상황에서 대화 가능: 업무 상담 및 해외 연수 등 가능	일상 생활 및 업무 상담, 세미나, 해외 연수 등이 가능한 수준	제한 없음
Level 3	문법 22문항(20분) 청취 24문항(약 20분) 독해 및 어휘 24문항(40분) **총 70문항(약 80분)**	간단한 의사소통과 친숙한 상태에서의 단순 대화 가능	간단한 의사소통과 해외 여행, 단순 업무 출장이 가능한 수준	제한 없음
Level 4	문법 20문항(20분) 청취 20문항(약 15분) 독해 및 어휘 20문항(25분) **총 60문항(약 60분)**	기본적인 문장을 통해 최소한의 의사소통 가능	기본적인 어휘의 짧은 문장을 통한 최소한의 의사소통이 가능한 수준	제한 없음
Level 5	문법 16문항(15분) 청취 16문항(약 15분) 독해 및 어휘 18문항(25분) **총 50문항(약 55분)**	극히 초보적인 수준의 의사소통 가능	영어 초보자로 일상의 인사, 소개 등만 가능한 수준	제한 없음

지텔프 Level 2의 구성

영역	내용	문항 수	시간	배점
문법	시제, 가정법, 조동사, 준동사, 연결어, 관계사	26문항 (1~26번)	영역별 시험 시간 제한 규정 폐지됨	100점
청취	PART 1 개인적인 이야기나 경험담 PART 2 특정 주제에 대한 정보를 제공하는 공식적인 담화 PART 3 어떤 결정에 이르고자 하는 비공식적인 협상 등의 대화 PART 4 일반적인 어떤 일의 진행이나 과정에 대한 설명	7문항 (27~33번) 6문항 (34~39번) 6문항 (40~45번)* 7문항 (46~52번)*		100점
독해 및 어휘	PART 1 과거 역사 속의 인물이나 현시대 인물의 일대기 PART 2 최근의 사회적이고 기술적인 묘사에 초점을 맞춘 기사 PART 3 전문적인 것이 아닌 일반적인 내용의 백과사전 PART 4 어떤 것을 설명하거나 설득하는 상업 서신	7문항 (53~59번) 7문항 (60~66번) 7문항 (67~73번) 7문항 (74~80번)		100점
		80문항	**약 90분**	**300점**

* 간혹 청취 PART 3에서 7문항, PART 4에서 6문항이 출제되는 경우도 있습니다.

지텔프 시험 접수부터 성적 확인까지

■ 시험 접수 방법

- **접수 방법 :** 지텔프 홈페이지(www.g-telp.co.kr)에서 회원가입 후 접수할 수 있습니다.
  * 응시료는 정기접수 66,300원, 추가접수 71,100원입니다.
- **시험 일정 :** 매월 2~3회 일요일 오후 3시에 응시할 수 있습니다.
  * 정확한 날짜는 지텔프 홈페이지를 통해 확인할 수 있습니다.

■ 시험 당일 준비물

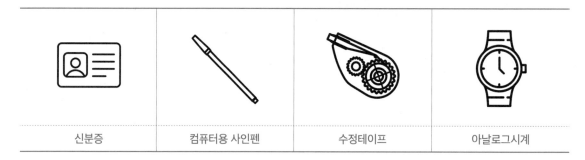

신분증	컴퓨터용 사인펜	수정테이프	아날로그시계

- 신분증은 주민등록증, 운전면허증, 기간 만료 전의 여권, 장애인등록증, 군신분증(군인), 학생증 · 청소년증 · 재학증명서(중고생), 외국인등록증(외국인)이 인정됩니다.
- 컴퓨터용 사인펜으로 마킹해야 하며 연필은 사용할 수 없습니다. 연필이나 볼펜으로 먼저 마킹한 후 사인펜으로 마킹하면 OMR 판독에 오류가 날 수 있으니 주의합니다.
- 마킹 수정 시, 수정테이프를 사용해야 하며 수정액은 사용할 수 없습니다. 다른 수험자의 수정테이프를 빌려 사용할 수 없으며, 본인의 것만 사용이 가능합니다.
- 대부분의 고사장에 시계가 준비되어 있지만, 자리에서 시계가 잘 보이지 않을 수도 있으니 개인 아날로그시계를 준비하면 좋습니다.
- 수험표는 별도로 준비하지 않아도 됩니다.

■ 시험 당일 유의 사항

① 고사장 가기 전

- 시험 장소를 미리 확인해 두고, 규정된 입실 시간에 늦지 않도록 유의합니다. 오후 2시 20분까지 입실해야 하며, 오후 2시 50분 이후에는 입실이 불가합니다.

② 고사장에서

- 1층 입구에 붙어 있는 고사실 배치표를 확인하여 자신이 배정된 고사실을 확인합니다.
- 고사실에는 각 응시자의 이름이 적힌 좌석표가 자리마다 놓여 있으므로, 자신이 배정된 자리에 앉으면 됩니다.

③ 시험 보기 직전

- 시험 도중에는 화장실에 다녀올 수 없고, 만약 화장실에 가면 다시 입실할 수 없으므로 미리 다녀오는 것이 좋습니다.
- 시험 시작 전에 OMR 카드의 정보 기입란에 올바른 정보를 기입해 둡니다.

④ 시험 시

- 답안을 따로 마킹할 시간이 없으므로 풀면서 바로 마킹하는 것이 좋습니다.
- 영역별 시험 시간 제한 규정이 폐지되었으므로, 본인이 취약한 영역과 강한 영역에 적절히 시간을 배분하여 자유롭게 풀 수 있습니다. 단, 청취 시간에는 다른 응시자에게 방해가 되지 않도록 주의해야 합니다.
- 시험지에 낙서를 하거나 다른 응시자들이 알아볼 수 있도록 큰 표시를 하는 것은 부정행위로 간주되므로 주의해야 합니다. 수험자 본인만 인지할 수 있는 작은 표기만 인정됩니다.
- OMR 카드의 정답 마킹란은 90번까지 제공되지만, 지텔프 Level 2의 문제는 80번까지만 있으므로 81~90번까지의 마킹란은 공란으로 비워두면 됩니다.

〈OMR 카드와 좌석표 미리보기〉

OMR

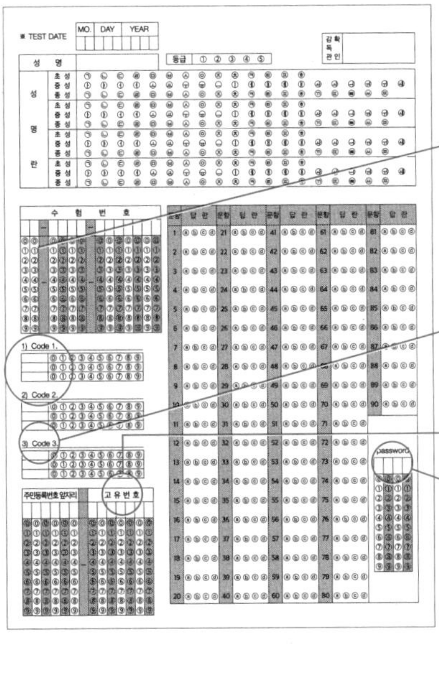

좌석표

수험번호: 06-0002-0021234	홍길동	고유번호: 7411234

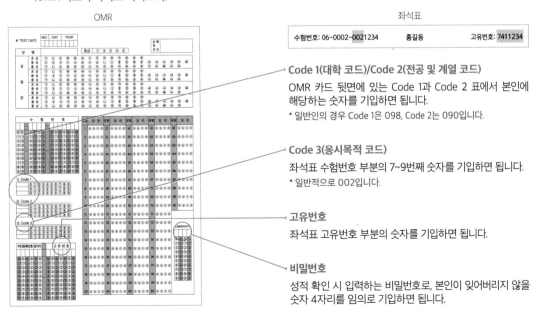

Code 1(대학 코드)/Code 2(전공 및 계열 코드)

OMR 카드 뒷면에 있는 Code 1과 Code 2 표에서 본인에 해당하는 숫자를 기입하면 됩니다.

* 일반인의 경우 Code 1은 098, Code 2는 090입니다.

Code 3(응시목적 코드)

좌석표 수험번호 부분의 7~9번째 숫자를 기입하면 됩니다.

* 일반적으로 002입니다.

고유번호

좌석표 고유번호 부분의 숫자를 기입하면 됩니다.

비밀번호

성적 확인 시 입력하는 비밀번호로, 본인이 잊어버리지 않을 숫자 4자리를 임의로 기입하면 됩니다.

지텔프 시험 접수부터 성적 확인까지

■ 지텔프 성적 확인 방법

- **성적 발표일 :** 시험 후 5일 이내에, 지텔프 홈페이지에서 확인이 가능합니다.
- **성적표 수령 방법 :** 온라인으로 출력(1회 무료)하거나 우편으로 수령할 수 있으며, 수령 방법은 접수 시 선택 가능합니다.

〈성적표 미리보기〉

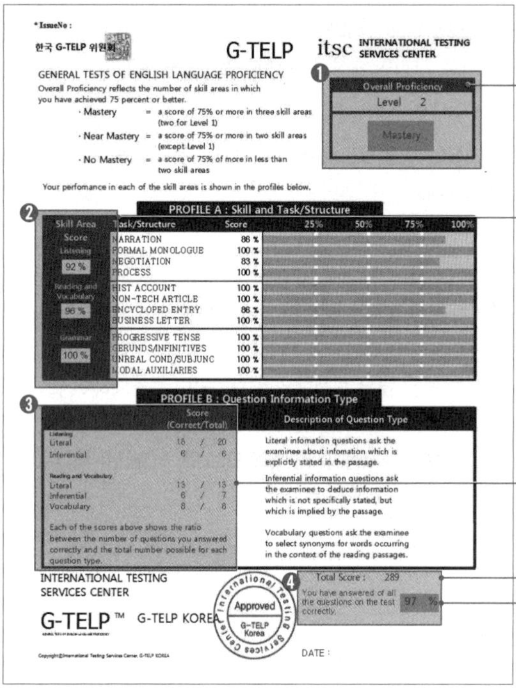

* 출처: 지텔프 홈페이지(www.g-telp.co.kr)

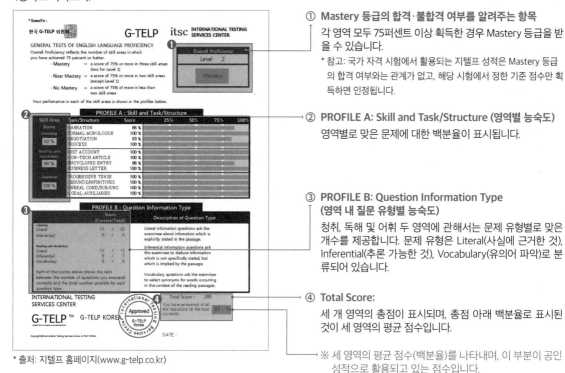

① **Mastery 등급의 합격·불합격 여부를 알려주는 항목**
각 영역 모두 75퍼센트 이상 획득한 경우 Mastery 등급을 받을 수 있습니다.
* 참고: 국가 자격 시험에서 활용되는 지텔프 성적은 Mastery 등급의 합격 여부와는 관계가 없고, 해당 시험에서 정한 기준 점수만 획득하면 인정됩니다.

② **PROFILE A: Skill and Task/Structure (영역별 능숙도)**
영역별로 맞은 문제에 대한 백분율이 표시됩니다.

③ **PROFILE B: Question Information Type (영역 내 질문 유형별 능숙도)**
청취, 독해 및 어휘 두 영역에 관해서는 문제 유형별로 맞은 개수를 제공합니다. 문제 유형은 Literal(사실에 근거한 것), Inferential(추론 가능한 것), Vocabulary(유의어 파악)로 분류되어 있습니다.

④ **Total Score:**
세 개 영역의 총점이 표시되며, 총점 아래 백분율로 표시된 것이 세 영역의 평균 점수입니다.

※ 세 영역의 평균 점수(백분율)를 나타내며, 이 부분이 공인 성적으로 활용되고 있는 점수입니다.

지텔프 점수 계산법

점수는 아래의 공식으로 산출할 수 있습니다. 총점과 평균 점수의 경우, 소수점 이하 점수는 올림 처리합니다.

각 영역 점수 : 맞은 개수 × 3.75

평균 점수 : 각 영역 점수 합계 ÷ 3

예) 문법 12개, 청취 5개, 독해 및 어휘 10개 맞혔을 시,

문법 12 × 3.75 = 45점 **청취** 5 × 3.75 = 18.75점 **독해 및 어휘** 10 × 3.75 = 37.5점

→ **평균 점수** (45+ 18.75 +37.5) ÷ 3 = 34점

지텔프 Level 2 성적 활용처

국가 자격 시험	기준 점수
경찰공무원(경사, 경장, 순경)	43점
경찰간부 후보생	50점
소방공무원(소방장, 소방교, 소방사)	43점
소방간부 후보생	50점
군무원 9급	32점
군무원 7급	47점
호텔서비스사	39점
군무원 5급	65점
국가공무원 5급	65점
외교관후보자	88점
국가공무원 7급	65점
국가공무원 7급 외무영사직렬	77점
입법고시	65점
법원행정고시	65점
카투사	73점
기상직 7급	65점
국가정보원	공인어학성적 제출 필수
변리사	77점
세무사	65점
공인노무사	65점
관광통역안내사	74점
호텔경영사	79점
호텔관리사	66점
감정평가사	65점
공인회계사	65점
보험계리사	65점
손해사정사	65점

* 그 외 공공기관 및 기업체에서도 지텔프 성적을 활용하고 있으며 지텔프 홈페이지에서 모든 활용처를 확인할 수 있습니다.

실전형 맞춤 학습 플랜

5일 완성 플랜

01. 1일 차에는 최신 출제 트렌드 및 문제 유형별 핵심 전략을 학습하고, 실전모의고사 2회분을 풀어보며 학습한 전략을 적용해 봅니다.

02. 2일 차부터 5일 차까지는 매일 실전모의고사를 2회분씩 풀어보며 실전 감각을 익힙니다.

03. 매일 실전모의고사 풀이 후, <지텔프 기출 단어암기장>에 수록된 단어를 암기하면 학습 효과를 극대화할 수 있습니다.

1일	2일	3일	4일	5일
□ 최신 출제 트렌드 및 문제 유형별 핵심 전략 학습 □ **01**회 실전모의고사 □ **02**회 실전모의고사	□ **03**회 실전모의고사 □ **04**회 실전모의고사	□ **05**회 실전모의고사 □ **06**회 실전모의고사	□ **07**회 실전모의고사 □ **08**회 실전모의고사	□ **09**회 실전모의고사 □ **10**회 실전모의고사

10일 완성 플랜

01. 1일 차에는 최신 출제 트렌드 및 문제 유형별 핵심 전략을 학습하고, 실전모의고사 1회분을 풀어보며 학습한 전략을 적용해 봅니다.

02. 2일 차부터 10일 차까지는 매일 실전모의고사를 1회분씩 풀어보며 실전 감각을 익힙니다.

03. 매일 실전모의고사 풀이 후, <지텔프 기출 단어암기장>에 수록된 단어를 암기하면 학습 효과를 극대화할 수 있습니다.

1일	2일	3일	4일	5일
□ 최신 출제 트렌드 및 문제 유형별 핵심 전략 학습 □ **01**회 실전모의고사	□ **02**회 실전모의고사	□ **03**회 실전모의고사	□ **04**회 실전모의고사	□ **05**회 실전모의고사
6일	**7일**	**8일**	**9일**	**10일**
□ **06**회 실전모의고사	□ **07**회 실전모의고사	□ **08**회 실전모의고사	□ **09**회 실전모의고사	□ **10**회 실전모의고사

최신 출제 트렌드 및 문제 유형별 핵심 전략

문제 유형 1	주제/목적
문제 유형 2	특정세부사항
문제 유형 3	Not/True
문제 유형 4	추론
문제 유형 5	어휘

문제 유형별 출제 비율

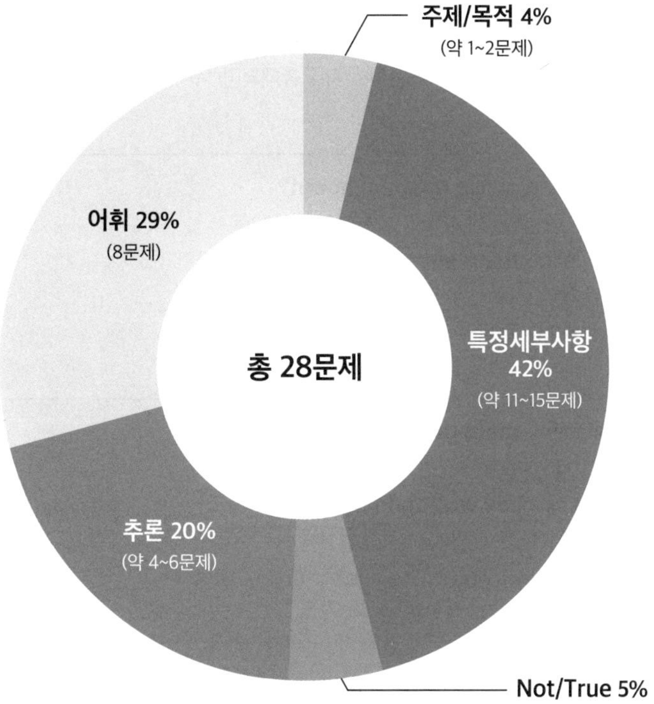

▲ 최신 5개년 평균 출제 비율

출제 1순위 **특정세부사항 문제 (42%)**
지문의 세부사항을 묻는 문제가 가장 많이 출제된다.

출제 2순위 **어휘 문제 (29%)**
지문 내 밑줄 친 어휘의 유의어를 고르는 문제가 많이 출제된다.

출제 3순위 **추론 문제 (20%)**
지문의 내용에서 추론할 수 있는 것을 묻는 문제가 출제된다.

* 주제/목적 문제, Not/True 문제는 간혹 출제된다.

문제 유형 1 주제/목적

지문의 주제나 목적을 정확하게 파악하고 있는지를 확인하는 문제이다.

■ 최신 출제 트렌드

주제 문제는 주로 PART 2나 PART 3의 첫 번째 문제로 자주 출제되며, 목적 문제는 PART 4의 첫 번째 문제로 자주 출제된다. 빈출 질문 유형은 아래와 같다.

지문의 주제	What is the article **(mainly) about**? 기사는 (주로) 무엇에 관한 것인가? What is the **main subject** of the article? 기사의 중심 주제는 무엇인가? **What** is the article **describing**? 기사가 서술하고 있는 것은 무엇인가?
지문의 목적	What is the **main purpose** of the letter? 편지의 주목적은 무엇인가? **Why** is Mr. Lee **writing** to Ms. Lawrence? Mr. Lee는 왜 Ms. Lawrence에게 편지를 쓰고 있는가? **Why** did Mr. Irving **write** a letter to Ms. Bennett? Mr. Irving은 왜 Ms. Bennett에게 편지를 썼는가?

■ 핵심 전략

제목과 지문의 초반을 주의 깊게 읽는다!

주제/목적 문제는 제목이나 지문의 초반에서 주로 정답의 단서를 찾을 수 있다. 특히 PART 2는 제목을 통해 주제 문제를 풀 수 있는 경우가 많다.

■ 문제 풀이 전략

STEP 1 질문을 읽고 주제/목적 문제임을 파악한다.

STEP 2 제목과 지문의 초반을 주의 깊게 읽고 정답의 단서를 찾는다.

STEP 3 지문에서 언급된 정답 단서를 올바르게 paraphrasing한 보기를 정답으로 선택한다.

예제

STUDY FINDS INTERESTING
REMEDY FOR DRY EYES

Recent research from the University of Waterloo has found that exercise can successfully treat dry, itchy eyes. It was observed that people who exercised regularly have greater tear secretion, which prevents dryness by coating the eyes with moisture.

What is the article **mainly about**?

(a) how dry eyes impact tear secretion
(b) how exercise relieves an eye condition
(c) how exercise affects our ability to see
(d) how regular treatments ease eye pain

STEP 1
질문을 읽고 **주제 문제**임을 파악한다.

STEP 2
제목과 지문의 초반을 주의 깊게 읽고 정답의 단서를 찾는다.

STEP 3
지문에서 언급된 treat dry, itchy eyes를 relieves an eye condition으로 **올바르게 paraphrasing한 보기 (b)**를 정답으로 선택한다.

해석

연구가 안구 건조증을 위한
흥미로운 치료법을 발견하다

워털루 대학의 최근 연구는 운동이 건조하고 가려운 눈을 성공적으로 치료할 수 있다는 것을 발견했다. 규칙적으로 운동한 사람들은 눈물 분비가 더 많은데, 이는 눈을 수분으로 덮어 건조함을 예방하는 것으로 관찰되었다.

기사는 주로 무엇에 관한 것인가?

(a) 어떻게 안구 건조증이 눈물 분비에 영향을 미치는지
(b) 어떻게 운동이 눈 질환을 완화하는지
(c) 어떻게 운동이 우리의 시력에 영향을 주는지
(d) 어떻게 정기적인 치료가 눈의 통증을 완화하는지

문제 유형 2 특정세부사항

지문의 세부 내용을 정확하게 파악하고 있는지를 확인하는 문제이다.

■ 최신 출제 트렌드

최빈출 문제 유형이며, 각 의문사별 질문 유형은 아래와 같다.

What	**What** is Tom Brady best known for? 톰 브래디는 무엇으로 가장 잘 알려져 있는가?
Why	**Why** did dinosaurs require less food to maintain their size? 왜 공룡들은 그것들의 크기를 유지하기 위해 더 적은 음식을 필요로 했는가?
How	**How** did the researchers collect data for the study? 어떻게 연구원들은 그 연구에 대한 자료를 수집했는가?
When	**When** did Murray begin to perform shows for celebrities and dignitaries? 언제 머레이는 유명 인사들과 고위 관리들을 위한 공연을 하기 시작했는가?
Where	**Where** did the name "Santa Claus" come from? 어디에서 '산타클로스'라는 이름이 유래되었는가?
Who	**Who** can drive the children home after the party this weekend? 누가 이번 주말 파티 후에 아이들을 집까지 태워 줄 수 있는가?

■ 핵심 전략

지문에서 질문의 키워드를 찾는다!

특정세부사항 문제는 질문의 키워드를 파악한 후, 지문에서 이를 찾아내는 것이 핵심이다. 세부적인 내용을 묻기 때문에 키워드의 주변 내용을 주의 깊게 읽으면 쉽게 정답을 찾을 수 있다. 정답은 일반적으로 지문의 내용이 그대로 언급되어 있거나 paraphrasing된 형태이다.

■ 문제 풀이 전략

STEP 1 특정세부사항 문제임을 확인한 후, 질문의 키워드를 파악한다.

STEP 2 질문의 키워드가 언급된 주변 내용을 주의 깊게 읽고 정답의 단서를 찾는다.

STEP 3 지문에서 언급된 정답 단서를 올바르게 paraphrasing한 보기를 정답으로 선택한다.

예제

F. SCOTT FITZGERALD

While stationed in Alabama, F. Scott Fitzgerald met a young socialite named Zelda Sayre and fell in love. Sadly, when Fitzgerald proposed marriage, the woman rejected him, citing his lack of financial means. However, when he published his first novel, *This Side of Paradise*, she reconsidered.

Why did Zelda Sayre initially turn down Fitzgerald's proposal?

(a) because he was not from the same local area

(b) because she was busy preparing for a book publication

(c) because he did not have enough wealth

(d) because she worried their relationship would not last

STEP 1
특정세부사항 문제임을 확인한 후, **질문의 키워드인 turn down**을 파악한다.

STEP 2
질문의 키워드 turn down이 rejected로 paraphrasing되어 **언급된 주변 내용**을 주의 깊게 읽는다.

STEP 3
지문에서 언급된 lack of financial means를 not have enough wealth로 **올바르게 paraphrasing한 보기 (c)**를 정답으로 선택한다.

해석

F. 스콧 피츠제럴드

앨라배마주에 머무르는 동안, F. 스콧 피츠제럴드는 젤다 세이어라는 이름의 젊은 사교계 명사를 만나 사랑에 빠졌다. 안타깝게도, 피츠제럴드가 청혼했을 때, 그 여성은 그의 경제적 능력 부족을 이유로 그를 거절했다. 하지만, 그가 그의 첫 번째 소설인 『낙원의 이편』을 출간했을 때, 그녀는 다시 생각했다.

왜 젤다 세이어는 처음에 피츠제럴드의 청혼을 거절했는가?

(a) 그가 같은 지역 출신이 아니었기 때문에

(b) 그녀가 책 출간을 준비하느라 바빴기 때문에

(c) 그가 충분한 재산을 가지고 있지 않았기 때문에

(d) 그녀가 그들의 관계가 지속되지 않을 것을 걱정했기 때문에

문제 유형 3 Not/True

지문의 내용을 바탕으로 보기 중 틀린 것 또는 옳은 것을 골라낼 수 있는지를 확인하는 문제이다.

■ 최신 출제 트렌드

보통 1~2문제가 출제되지만, 출제되지 않는 경우도 있으며 빈출 질문 유형은 아래와 같다.

Not 문제	Which is **not** true about the hyena's social behavior? 하이에나의 사회적 행동에 관해 사실이 아닌 것은 무엇인가? What is **not** included in the Golden Hills Trip itinerary? Golden Hills 여행 일정표에 포함되지 않은 것은 무엇인가? Which of the following is **not** part of the proposal? 다음 중 제안의 일부가 아닌 것은 무엇인가?
True 문제	Which is **true** about the Greenpoint Crew? Greenpoint 선원에 관해 사실인 것은 무엇인가? Which statement is **true** about dolphins? 돌고래에 관해 사실인 진술은 무엇인가?

■ 핵심 전략

각 보기의 키워드와 지문의 내용을 하나씩 대조하며 읽는다!

Not/True 문제는 각 보기의 키워드와 지문의 내용을 하나씩 대조하여 정답을 선택해야 한다. 질문에서 묻는 것이 무엇인지를 확인한 뒤, 해당 내용이 언급되는 주변에서 각 보기의 키워드와 관련된 내용을 주의 깊게 읽어야 한다. Not 문제는 지문의 내용과 일치하지 않거나 아예 지문에 언급되지 않은 것이 정답이며, True 문제는 지문의 내용이 그대로 언급되거나 paraphrasing 되어 언급된 것이 정답이다.

■ 문제 풀이 전략

STEP 1 질문을 읽고 Not/True 문제임을 파악한다.

STEP 2 보기의 키워드를 찾아 지문의 내용과 대조하며 읽는다.

STEP 3 지문의 내용과 일치하거나 일치하지 않는 보기를 정답으로 선택한다.

예제

NIAGARA FALLS

Niagara Falls is a series of three waterfalls on the US-Canada border. The structures were formed through glacial action during the last ice age, and today the Niagara River runs over them as it drains water from Lake Erie.

Which is true about the Niagara Falls?

(a) It is made up of multiple waterfalls.
(b) It is partly frozen from the last ice age.
(c) It floods Lake Erie every year.
(d) It is located only in Canada.

STEP 1
질문을 읽고 **True 문제**임을 파악한다.

STEP 2
보기 (a)의 키워드 multiple waterfalls가 지문에서 a series of three waterfalls로 **paraphrasing되어 언급된 주변 내용을 보기와 대조**하며 읽는다.

STEP 3
지문의 내용과 **일치하는 보기 (a)**를 정답으로 선택한다.

해석

나이아가라 폭포

나이아가라 폭포는 미국과 캐나다 국경에 있는 일련의 세 개의 폭포이다. 그 구조는 마지막 빙하기 동안의 빙하 작용을 통해 형성되었고, 오늘날 나이아가라강은 이리호에서 물을 빼내면서 그 위로 흐른다.

나이아가라 폭포에 관해 사실인 것은 무엇인가?

(a) 여러 개의 폭포로 이루어져 있다.
(b) 마지막 빙하기 때부터 부분적으로 얼어 있다.
(c) 매년 이리호를 범람시킨다.
(d) 캐나다에만 위치해 있다.

문제 유형 4 추론

지문의 내용을 근거로 명시적으로 언급되지 않은 사실을 추론할 수 있는지를 확인하는 문제이다.

■ 최신 출제 트렌드

보통 4~6문제가 출제되며, 특정사실이나 묘사에 관한 추론 문제가 자주 출제된다. 주로 질문에 probably, most likely 등이 포함되며, 빈출 질문 유형은 아래와 같다.

Why **probably** did Barnes include a business card with his letter?
왜 Barnes가 그의 편지에 명함을 넣은 것 같은가?

How **most likely** was Shakespeare able to start a theater company?
어떻게 셰익스피어가 극단을 시작할 수 있었던 것 같은가?

What **could be** said about the nature documentaries?
자연 다큐멘터리에 대해 무엇이 말해질 수 있는가?

■ 핵심 전략

지문의 내용을 토대로 가장 적절히 추론한 보기를 찾는다!

추론 문제는 지문에 직접적인 정답의 단서가 없으므로 까다로운 문제로 여겨질 수 있다. 하지만 지문에서 질문의 키워드가 언급된 주변 내용을 읽고 그 내용을 정확히 파악한 뒤, 이를 토대로 보기 중 가장 적절히 추론한 보기를 찾으면 어렵지 않게 정답을 찾을 수 있다. 단, 지문에서 언급되지 않은 일반 상식을 통해 추론할 수 있는 내용을 정답으로 선택하지 않도록 주의해야 한다.

■ 문제 풀이 전략

STEP 1 추론 문제임을 확인한 후, 질문의 키워드를 파악한다.

STEP 2 질문의 키워드가 언급된 주변 내용을 주의 깊게 읽고 정답의 단서를 찾는다.

STEP 3 정답의 단서를 토대로 올바르게 추론한 보기를 정답으로 선택한다.

예제

Dear Ms. Dent:

The rescue hook that your employee delivered this morning was not the one we originally ordered. Please send the proper one when your employee comes to clean our pool on Friday. We will need it before opening the pool to the public on Saturday.

Based on the letter, what will **most likely** happen on Friday?

(a) An employee will be fired.
(b) A pool will be expanded.
(c) An order will be corrected.
(d) A facility will accept guests.

STEP 1
추론 문제임을 확인한 후, **질문의 키워드 on Friday**를 파악한다.

STEP 2
질문의 키워드 on Friday가 그대로 **언급된 주변 내용**을 주의 깊게 읽고 정답의 단서를 찾는다.

STEP 3
정답의 단서를 토대로 직원이 금요일에 올 때 제대로 된 것을 가져옴으로써 주문이 바로잡힐 것이라고 **올바르게 추론한 보기 (c)**를 정답으로 선택한다.

해석
Ms. Dent께:

당신의 직원이 오늘 아침에 배달한 구조용 고리는 우리가 원래 주문했던 것이 아닙니다. 금요일에 당신의 직원이 우리 수영장을 청소하러 올 때 제대로 된 것을 보내 주시기 바랍니다. 우리는 토요일에 수영장을 대중에게 개장하기 전에 그것이 필요할 것입니다.

편지에 따르면, 금요일에 무슨 일이 일어날 것 같은가?
(a) 종업원이 해고될 것이다.
(b) 수영장이 확장될 것이다.
(c) 주문이 바로잡힐 것이다.
(d) 시설이 손님들을 수용할 것이다.

문제 유형 5 어휘

지문의 밑줄 친 어휘의 문맥상 유의어를 고르는 문제이다.

■ 최신 출제 트렌드

한 파트당 2문제씩 총 8문제가 고정적으로 출제되므로 중요도가 높으며, 최근에는 보기에 2개 이상의 유의어가 주어지는 경우와 정확한 사전적 유의어가 아니어도 지문의 문맥에서 의미하는 뜻을 가진 어휘가 정답인 경우가 많아지고 있다. 질문은 아래와 같이 출제된다.

In the context of the passage, calm means __________.
지문의 문맥에서, 'calm'은 -을 의미한다.

■ 핵심 전략

밑줄 친 어휘가 사용된 문맥을 파악한다!

밑줄 친 어휘가 사용된 문맥의 내용을 정확히 파악하고 어휘가 무슨 뜻으로 사용되었는지를 파악하는 것이 중요하다. 사전적 유의어라고 해도 문맥에서 사용된 의미와 다를 수 있기 때문에 사전적 유의어를 무조건 정답으로 선택하지 않도록 주의한다.

보기에 2개 이상의 유의어가 주어지는 경우

Users can only dismiss the warning after clicking the box indicating that they have read the software's terms and conditions.

(a) remove (b) fire (c) disagree (d) maintain

➡ dismiss의 유의어인 remove와 fire가 모두 보기에 주어졌다. 위 문장은 사용자들이 소프트웨어 약관을 읽었음을 나타내는 상자를 클릭한 후에만 경고문을 지울 수 있다는 뜻이므로, 문맥에서 dismiss가 '지우다'라는 의미로 사용되는 것이 더 자연스럽다. 따라서 (a) remove가 정답이다. 'fire the warning'은 '경고문을 해고하다'라는 어색한 의미가 되므로 오답이다.

정확한 사전적 유의어가 아니어도 지문의 문맥에서 의미하는 뜻을 가진 어휘가 정답인 경우

Brad wanted to prepare his apartment for the upcoming dinner party. So, he spent hours cleaning and putting up decorations.

(a) shape (b) equip (c) compare (d) admire

➡ prepare의 사전적 의미는 '준비하다'이며 동의어로는 arrange, ready 등이 있다. 하지만 위 문장은 다가오는 만찬회를 위해 자신의 아파트를 적합하게 만든다는 뜻이므로, prepare가 '적합하게 만들다'라는 의미로 사용된 것을 알 수 있다. 따라서 (a) shape가 prepare의 정확한 사전적 유의어가 아니어도 정답이 된다.

■ 문제 풀이 전략

STEP 1 밑줄 친 어휘가 포함된 구절을 읽고 문맥을 파악한다.

STEP 2 보기 중 문맥에 맞는 유의어를 찾는다.

STEP 3 밑줄 친 자리에 보기의 단어가 들어가도 말이 되는지 확인 후 정답으로 선택한다.

예제

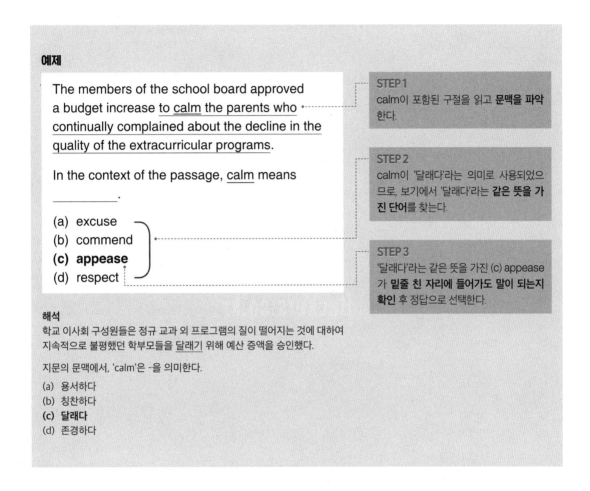

The members of the school board approved a budget increase to calm the parents who continually complained about the decline in the quality of the extracurricular programs.

In the context of the passage, calm means ___________.

(a) excuse
(b) commend
(c) appease
(d) respect

STEP 1
calm이 포함된 구절을 읽고 **문맥을 파악**한다.

STEP 2
calm이 '달래다'라는 의미로 사용되었으므로, 보기에서 '달래다'라는 **같은 뜻을 가진 단어**를 찾는다.

STEP 3
'달래다'라는 같은 뜻을 가진 (c) appease가 **밑줄 친 자리에 들어가도 말이 되는지 확인** 후 정답으로 선택한다.

해석

학교 이사회 구성원들은 정규 교과 외 프로그램의 질이 떨어지는 것에 대하여 지속적으로 불평했던 학부모들을 달래기 위해 예산 증액을 승인했다.

지문의 문맥에서, 'calm'은 -을 의미한다.

(a) 용서하다
(b) 칭찬하다
(c) 달래다
(d) 존경하다

약점보완
해설집

01회 실전모의고사

문제집 p.4

정답 및 문제 유형 분석표							
PART 1		PART 2		PART 3		PART 4	
53	(d) 특정세부사항	60	(b) 특정세부사항	67	(d) 추론	74	(d) 주제/목적
54	(d) Not/True	61	(c) 추론	68	(c) 특정세부사항	75	(c) 특정세부사항
55	(b) 특정세부사항	62	(a) 특정세부사항	69	(b) 특정세부사항	76	(d) 특정세부사항
56	(c) 특정세부사항	63	(d) 특정세부사항	70	(c) 특정세부사항	77	(c) 특정세부사항
57	(c) 추론	64	(a) 추론	71	(a) Not/True	78	(a) 추론
58	(b) 어휘	65	(c) 어휘	72	(d) 어휘	79	(d) 어휘
59	(c) 어휘	66	(b) 어휘	73	(a) 어휘	80	(b) 어휘

취약 유형 분석표	
유형	맞힌 개수
주제/목적	/ 1
특정세부사항	/ 12
Not/True	/ 2
추론	/ 5
어휘	/ 8
TOTAL	28

PART 1(53~59) Biography Article 할리우드 영화 음악의 거장 한스 짐머

인물 이름

HANS ZIMMER

인물 소개

Hans Zimmer is a German music producer and composer 53known for scoring the soundtracks for over 150 Hollywood films. He is considered to have redefined modern film music by combining electronic music with traditional orchestra works to create new pieces.

어린 시절 + 업적 시작 계기

Hans Florian Zimmer was born on September 12, 1957, in Frankfurt, Germany. 54(a)He became interested in music at an early age and began taking piano lessons at only three years old. However, he quit after two weeks because 54(d)he disliked the discipline of formal classes. 58The death of his father when he was six prompted Zimmer to turn to music to deal with his grief, and the same year, 55he decided to become a composer after falling in love with *Once Upon a Time in the West*, a blockbuster Western film directed by Sergio Leone. He focused so much of his attention on learning music on his own that he rarely did his schoolwork and was ultimately expelled from eight schools.

초기 활동

Zimmer's musical career began in the late 1970s when he moved to the UK and started playing music with bands and writing advertising jingles. He then cofounded a recording studio with the English film composer

한스 짐머

한스 짐머는 독일 음악 제작자이자 작곡가로 53150편이 넘는 할리우드 영화의 영화 음악을 작곡한 것으로 알려져 있다. 그는 전자 음악과 전통적인 관현악단 작품을 결합해 새로운 작품을 창작함으로써 현대 영화 음악을 재정립했다고 평가받는다.

한스 플로리안 짐머는 1957년 9월 12일에 독일 프랑크푸르트에서 태어났다. 54(a)그는 어린 나이에 음악에 관심을 갖게 되었고 겨우 3살의 나이에 피아노 교습을 받기 시작했다. 그러나, 54(d)그는 정규 수업의 규율을 싫어했기 때문에 2주 후에 그만두었다. 58그가 6살이었을 때 그의 아버지의 죽음은 짐머가 그의 슬픔에 대처하기 위해 음악에 의지하도록 자극했으며, 같은 해에, 55세르지오 레오네가 연출한 블록버스터 서부 영화인 「옛날 옛적 서부에서」와 사랑에 빠진 이후 그는 작곡가가 되기로 결심했다. 그는 혼자서 음악을 배우는 것에 너무 많은 관심을 쏟아서 학교 공부를 거의 하지 않았고 결국 8개 학교에서 퇴학을 당했다.

짐머의 음악 경력은 그가 영국으로 이사를 하며 밴드와 음악을 연주하고 광고 음악을 작곡하기 시작한 1970년대 후반에 시작되었다. 그다음에 그는 1980년대에 영국인 영화 작곡가 스탠리 마이어스와 함께 녹음실

	Stanley Myers in the 1980s. They created music for several acclaimed films, including *Moonlighting* and *My Beautiful Laundrette*.	을 공동 창립하였다. 「문라이팅」과 「나의 아름다운 세탁소」를 포함하여, 그들은 여러 칭송받는 영화의 음악을 창작했다.
경력의 변환점	His first true break came when Hollywood director Barry Levinson approached him. [56]Levinson's wife had told him about a soundtrack CD that she had enjoyed. Interested, Levinson listened to the soundtrack himself before getting in touch with Zimmer, who had composed it. Levinson hired Zimmer to write the score for his 1988 film *Rain Man*, much of which featured songs performed on an electronic keyboard and steel drums. It also included pan pipes and female gospel vocals, making the soundtrack charming, unique, and ultimately unforgettable for its sense of style.	그의 첫 번째 진정한 변환점은 할리우드 감독 배리 레빈슨이 그에게 다가왔을 때였다. [56]레빈슨의 아내는 그녀가 즐겨 들었던 영화 음악 CD에 대해 그(레빈슨)에게 말했다. 흥미로웠기 때문에, 레빈슨은 그것을 작곡한 짐머에게 연락하기 전에 직접 그 영화 음악을 들어 보았다. 레빈슨은 그의 1988년 영화인 「레인 맨」의 음악을 작곡하기 위해 짐머를 고용했는데, 음악 대부분은 전자 키보드와 스틸 드럼으로 연주된 노래를 특색으로 했다. 그것은 또한 팬파이프와 여성 복음 성악을 포함했는데, 이는 그 영화 음악을 매력적이고, 독특하며, 궁극적으로 그것의 스타일 감각 때문에 잊을 수 없는 것으로 만들었다.
주요 업적 + 근황	Zimmer's music had become a Hollywood staple by the early 1990s. However, [57]it wasn't until the 1994 Disney film *The Lion King* that Zimmer enjoyed his biggest commercial success. *The Lion King* soundtrack won numerous awards including Zimmer's first Academy Award for Best Original Score. To this day, [59]Zimmer is regarded as one of the leading film music composers of all time, and his signature style and talent are highly sought after by directors.	짐머의 음악은 1990년대 초반에 할리우드의 주요소가 되었다. 그러나, [57]1994년의 디즈니 영화 「라이온 킹」 이후에야 짐머는 그의 가장 큰 상업적 성공을 누렸다. 「라이온킹」 영화 음악은 짐머의 첫 번째 아카데미 최고 영화 음악상을 포함하여 많은 상을 받았다. 지금까지도 [59]짐머는 역대 최고의 영화 음악 작곡가 중 한 명으로 여겨지며, 그의 특유의 스타일과 재능은 감독들에게 매우 인기 있다.

어휘 | composer n. 작곡가 score v. 작곡하다; n. 음악, 작품 soundtrack n. 영화 음악 consider v. 여기다 redefine v. 재정립하다 combine v. 결합하다 electronic adj. 전자의 piece n. 작품 discipline n. 규율 formal adj. 정규의 turn to phr. ~에 의지하다 deal with phr. ~에 대처하다 grief n. 슬픔 ultimately adv. 결국, 궁극적으로 expel v. 퇴학시키다 career n. 경력, 직업 advertising n. 광고 jingle n. 광고 음악, 딸랑거리는 소리 cofound v. 공동 창립하다 acclaim v. 칭송하다; n. 찬사, 칭찬 break n. 변환점 approach v. 다가오다, 접근하다 get in touch with phr. ~와 연락하다 feature v. ~을 특색으로 하다 gospel n. 복음 charming adj. 매력적인 unique adj. 독특한 unforgettable adj. 잊을 수 없는 staple n. 주요소; adj. 주된 commercial adj. 상업적인 numerous adj. 많은 of all time phr. 역대 sought after phr. 인기 있는, 수요가 많은

53 특정세부사항 유명한 이유

난이도 ●○○

What is Hans Zimmer famous for?

(a) being a producer of popular Hollywood films
(b) hosting an electronic music festival
(c) conducting the Hollywood Orchestra
(d) creating a large amount of film music

한스 짐머는 무엇으로 유명한가?

(a) 인기 있는 할리우드 영화의 제작자인 것으로
(b) 전자 음악 축제를 주최하는 것으로
(c) 할리우드 관현악단을 지휘하는 것으로
(d) 많은 양의 영화 음악을 창작하는 것으로

지텔프 치트키

질문의 키워드 famous for가 known for로 paraphrasing되어 언급된 주변 내용을 주의 깊게 읽는다.

해설 | 1단락의 'known for scoring the soundtracks for over 150 Hollywood films'에서 한스 짐머는 150편이 넘는 할리우드 영화의 영화 음악을 작곡한 것으로 알려져 있다고 했다. 따라서 (d)가 정답이다.

Paraphrasing
scoring the soundtracks 영화 음악을 작곡한 것 → creating ~ film music 영화 음악을 창작하는 것
over 150 150편이 넘는 → a large amount 많은 양

어휘 | host v. 주최하다, 진행하다 conduct v. 지휘하다, (특정한 활동을) 하다

54 Not/True True 문제

난이도 ●●○

Which is true about Hans Zimmer's childhood?

(a) He could not afford piano lessons.
(b) He received high grades in music classes.
(c) He could play multiple musical instruments.
(d) He was not suited to formal education.

한스 짐머의 어린 시절에 대해 사실인 것은?

(a) 피아노 교습을 받을 여유가 되지 않았다.
(b) 음악 수업에서 높은 점수를 받았다.
(c) 많은 악기를 연주할 수 있었다.
(d) 정규 교육에 적합하지 않았다.

지텔프 치트키

질문의 키워드 childhood와 관련된 주변 내용을 주의 깊게 읽고, 보기의 키워드와 지문 내용을 대조하며 읽는다.

해설 | (d)의 키워드인 formal education이 formal classes로 paraphrasing되어 언급된 2단락의 'he disliked the discipline of formal classes'에서 한스 짐머는 정규 수업의 규율을 싫어했다고 했다. 따라서 (d)가 정답이다.

오답분석

(a) 보기의 키워드 piano lessons가 그대로 언급된 2단락에서 한스 짐머가 3살의 나이에 피아노 교습을 받기 시작했다고 했으므로 지문의 내용과 일치하지 않는다.
(b) 2단락에서 한스 짐머가 어린 나이에 음악에 관심을 갖게 되었으며 3살의 나이에 피아노 교습을 받기 시작했다고는 했지만, 음악 수업에서 높은 점수를 받았는지는 언급되지 않았다.
(c) 2단락에서 한스 짐머가 3살의 나이에 피아노 교습을 받기 시작했다고는 했지만, 많은 악기를 연주할 수 있었는지는 언급되지 않았다.

어휘 | afford v. 여유가 되다, 형편이 되다 suit v. 적합하다, 알맞다

55 특정세부사항 When

난이도 ●●○

When did Zimmer first become interested in being a composer?

(a) after being expelled from a number of schools
(b) after watching a popular movie
(c) when he was studying with Sergio Leone
(d) when he was taking care of his father

짐머는 언제 처음으로 작곡가가 되는 것에 흥미를 가지게 되었는가?

(a) 많은 학교에서 퇴학을 당한 후에
(b) 인기 있는 영화를 본 후에
(c) 세르지오 레오네 밑에서 공부하고 있었을 때
(d) 그의 아버지를 돌보고 있었을 때

지텔프 치트키

질문의 키워드 being a composer가 become a composer로 paraphrasing되어 언급된 주변 내용을 주의 깊게 읽는다.

해설 | 2단락의 'he decided to become a composer after falling in love with ~ a blockbuster ~ directed by Sergio Leone'에서 한스 짐머는 세르지오 레오네가 연출한 블록버스터와 사랑에 빠진 이후 작곡가가 되기로 결심했다고 했다. 따라서 (b)가 정답이다.

Paraphrasing
a blockbuster 블록버스터(상업적으로 성공한 영화) → a popular movie 인기 있는 영화

56 특정세부사항 What

난이도 ●●○

According to the article, what made Barry Levinson contact Zimmer?

(a) a prior working relationship with Stanley Myers
(b) a success of Zimmer's collaboration with Hollywood filmmakers
(c) a recommendation made by his spouse
(d) a soundtrack in his favorite film

기사에 따르면, 무엇이 배리 레빈슨이 짐머에게 연락하게 만들었는가?

(a) 스탠리 마이어스와의 이전의 작업 관계
(b) 할리우드 영화 제작사와 짐머의 협업 성공
(c) 그의 배우자로부터 받은 추천
(d) 그가 가장 좋아하는 영화의 영화 음악

지텔프 치트키

질문의 키워드 Barry Levinson이 그대로 언급된 주변 내용을 주의 깊게 읽는다.

해설 | 4단락의 'Levinson's wife had told him about a soundtrack CD that she had enjoyed.'에서 레빈슨의 아내가 자신이 즐겨 들었던 영화 음악 CD에 대해 레빈슨에게 말했다고 한 뒤, 'Interested, Levinson listened ~ before getting in touch with Zimmer, who had composed it.'에서 흥미로웠기 때문에 레빈슨은 그것을 작곡한 짐머에게 연락하기 전에 들어 보았다고 했다. 따라서 (c)가 정답이다.

Paraphrasing
contact 연락하다 → getting in touch 연락하기
Levinson's wife 레빈슨의 아내 → his spouse 그의 배우자

어휘 | collaboration n. 협업, 협동 filmmaker n. 영화 제작사 recommendation n. 추천, 권고 spouse n. 배우자

57 추론 특정사실

난이도 ●●●

What can most likely be said about *The Lion King*?

(a) It became the first animated film to win musical honors.
(b) It is the only Disney film that Zimmer has worked on.
(c) It brought Zimmer recognition from the public.
(d) It was nominated for more awards than it won.

「라이온킹」에 대해 무엇이 말해질 수 있는 것 같은가?

(a) 음악적인 영예를 얻은 첫 애니메이션 영화가 되었다.
(b) 짐머가 작업했던 유일한 디즈니 영화이다.
(c) 짐머에게 대중의 인정을 가져다주었다.
(d) 받은 것보다 더 많은 상의 후보에 올랐다.

지텔프 치트키

질문의 키워드 *The Lion King*이 그대로 언급된 주변 내용을 주의 깊게 읽는다.

해설 | 5단락의 'it wasn't until the 1994 Disney film *The Lion King* that Zimmer enjoyed his biggest commercial success'에서 1994년의 디즈니 영화 「라이온킹」 이후에야 짐머가 그의 가장 큰 상업적 성공을 누렸다고 했으므로, 「라이온킹」이 짐머에게 대중의 인정을 가져다주었을 것임을 추론할 수 있다. 따라서 (c)가 정답이다.

오답분석

(a) 5단락에서 「라이온킹」 영화 음악을 통해 짐머가 그의 첫 번째 아카데미 최고 영화 음악상을 받았다고는 했지만, 「라이온킹」이 음악적인 영예를 얻은 첫 애니메이션 영화였는지는 언급되지 않았으므로 오답이다.
(d) 5단락에서 「라이온킹」 영화 음악이 많은 상을 받았다고는 했지만, 받은 것보다 더 많은 상의 후보에 올랐는지는 언급되지 않았으므로 오답이다.

어휘 | honor n. 영예, 명예 recognition n. 인정 nominate v. 후보에 올리다, 지명하다

58 어휘 유의어

난이도 ●●●

In the context of the passage, prompted means ________.

(a) assisted
(b) motivated
(c) reminded
(d) persuaded

지문의 문맥에서 'prompted'는 -을 의미한다.

(a) 도왔다
(b) 동기를 부여했다
(c) 상기시켰다
(d) 설득했다

지텔프 치트키

밑줄 친 어휘의 유의어를 찾는 문제이므로, prompted가 포함된 구절을 읽고 문맥을 파악한다.

해설 | 2단락의 'The death of his father ~ prompted Zimmer to turn to music to deal with his grief'는 짐머의 아버지의 죽음이 짐머가 그의 슬픔에 대처하기 위해 음악에 의지하도록 자극했다는 뜻이므로, prompted가 '자극했다'라는 의미로 사용된 것을 알 수 있다. 따라서 '동기를 부여했다'라는 비슷한 의미의 (b) motivated가 정답이다.

59 어휘 유의어

난이도 ●○○

In the context of the passage, leading means ________.

(a) original
(b) famous
(c) best
(d) latest

지문의 문맥에서 'leading'은 -을 의미한다.

(a) 최초의
(b) 유명한
(c) 최고의
(d) 최신의

지텔프 치트키

밑줄 친 어휘의 유의어를 찾는 문제이므로, leading이 포함된 구절을 읽고 문맥을 파악한다.

해설 | 5단락의 'Zimmer is regarded as one of the leading film music composers of all time'은 짐머가 역대 최고의 영화 음악 작곡가 중 한 명으로 여겨진다는 뜻이므로, leading이 '최고의'라는 의미로 사용된 것을 알 수 있다. 따라서 '최고의'라는 같은 의미의 (c) best가 정답이다.

PART 2(60~66) Magazine Article 지속 가능성을 중시하는 MZ세대

연구 결과

[60]MILLENNIALS AND GENERATION Z EMBRACE SUSTAINABILITY

연구 소개

[60]Studies have found that the younger generations—Millennials and Generation Z—are more socially and environmentally conscious than their older counterparts. This is particularly true when it comes to consumer behavior, with many actively forcing corporations to adopt sustainable practices.

[60]밀레니얼 세대와 Z세대는 지속 가능성을 포용한다

[60]연구들은 젊은 세대들인 밀레니얼 세대와 Z세대가 구세대보다 사회적으로 그리고 환경적으로 더 의식적이라는 것을 발견했다. 이는 소비자 행태에 관해서라면 특히 사실인데, 많은 이들이 기업들로 하여금 지속 가능한 관행을 채택하도록 적극적으로 강요하고 있다.

밀레니얼 세대 특징

Just like previous generations, the attitudes of Millennials and Generation Z have been profoundly influenced by major events occurring during their lifetime. [61]For Millennials, it was the Great Recession of 2008. This event resulted from financial institutions engaging in high-risk, socially irresponsible lending practices. [61]It made many people question whether the procedures of banks and lending institutions were ethical, especially since taking out high-interest student loans became necessary for a large number of Millennials.

Z세대 특징

For Generation Z, who not only grew up in the aftermath of the recession but watched as the pandemic shut down world economies, [65]just how fragile the planet is was made very clear. As factories ceased production, and the smog lifted over the world's most polluted cities, people began to realize the extent to which the planet is being damaged. This inspired more intense environmental awareness.

의식 확산 과정

This consciousness has been spread across the Internet. [62]Social media influencers who support sustainability have shared their values with the digitally connected generations. This encouraged young people to pay closer attention to issues like plastic and deforestation as well as to the brands they buy and the foods they eat. Given that influencers are today's trendsetters and many have millions of followers, being like them has become fashionable.

압력 행사 사례

Platforms like Twitter also give regular people the power to publicly support companies that make an effort to be sustainable and [66]condemn those that fail in this regard. When companies neglect sustainability, the news spreads quickly on social media, and [63]young people work together to boycott the brand until changes are made. For example, thousands of students are currently boycotting the financial institution Barclays to pressure it into ceasing its funding of fossil fuels. If this trend continues, then [64]Millennials and Generation Z, who make up the largest share of the global population, will continue to dictate corporate practices and make the world a more sustainable place.

이전 세대들과 마찬가지로, 밀레니얼 세대와 Z세대의 사고방식은 그들의 일생 동안 일어나는 주요 사건들에 의해 영향을 깊이 받았다. [61]밀레니얼 세대에게, 그것은 2008년의 경기 대침체였다. 이 사건은 금융 기관들이 고위험의 사회적으로 무책임한 대출 관행에 관여한 것에서 비롯되었다. [61]이것은 많은 사람들이 은행과 대출 기관의 절차가 윤리적이었는지 의문을 품게 했는데, 이는 특히 다수의 밀레니얼 세대가 고금리 학자금 대출을 받는 것이 불가피해졌기 때문이다.

불황의 여파 속에서 성장했을 뿐만 아니라 전 세계적인 유행병이 세계 경제를 정지시키는 것을 본 Z세대에게는, [65]지구가 그저 얼마나 취약한 곳인지가 매우 분명해졌다. 공장들이 생산을 중단하고, 스모그가 세계의 가장 오염된 도시들 위로 걷히면서, 사람들은 지구가 어느 정도로 손상되고 있는지를 깨닫기 시작했다. 이것은 더욱 열정적인 환경적 인식을 불러일으켰다.

이러한 의식은 인터넷 전반에 걸쳐 확산되었다. [62]지속 가능성을 지지하는 소셜 미디어 인플루언서들은 디지털로 연결된 세대들에게 자신들의 가치관을 공유해 왔다. 이것은 젊은이들로 하여금 그들이 구입하는 브랜드와 그들이 먹는 음식뿐만 아니라 플라스틱과 삼림 벌채와 같은 문제들에 더 세심한 관심을 기울이도록 장려했다. 인플루언서가 오늘날 유행의 선도자이고 많은 이들이 수백만 명의 팔로워를 가지고 있다는 점에서, 그들과 같이 되는 것은 유행하게 되었다.

트위터 같은 플랫폼들은 일반 사람들이 지속 가능하도록 노력하는 기업들을 공개적으로 지지하고 이것과 관련하여 [66]기대에 어긋나는 것들을 비난할 권한을 준다. 기업들이 지속 가능성을 등한시할 때, 그 뉴스가 소셜 미디어에서 빠르게 퍼지고, [63]젊은이들은 변화가 만들어질 때까지 그 브랜드의 구매를 거부하기 위해 협력한다. 예를 들어, 수천 명의 학생들은 현재 화석 연료에 대한 재정 지원을 중단하도록 그것에 압력을 가하기 위해서 금융 기관인 바클리즈를 배척하고 있다. 만약 이러한 추세가 계속된다면, [64]세계 인구의 가장 큰 비중을 차지하고 있는 밀레니얼 세대와 Z세대가 계속 기업의 관행을 좌우하여 세상을 더욱 지속 가능한 곳으로 만들 것이다.

어휘 | embrace v. 포용하다 sustainability n. 지속 가능성 conscious adj. 의식적인 counterpart n. 대응 관계에 있는 것 when it comes to phr. ~에 관해서라면 force v. 강요하다 corporation n. 기업 adopt v. 채택하다 practice n. 관행; v. 실천하다 attitude n. 사고방식 profoundly adv. 깊이 Great Recession phr. 경기 대침체 financial institution phr. 금융 기관 engage in phr. ~에 관여하다 high-risk adj. 고위험의 irresponsible adj. 무책임한 lending n. 대출 question v. 의문을 품다 procedure n. 절차 ethical adj. 윤리적인 take out phr. ~을 받다 high-interest adj. 고금리의 loan n. 대출 aftermath n. 여파 pandemic n. 전 세계적인 유행병 cease v. 중단하다 intense adj. 열정적인 awareness n. 인식 deforestation n. 삼림 벌채 trendsetter n. 유행의 선도자 neglect v. 등한시하다 boycott v. 구매를 거부하다, 배척하다 funding n. 재정 지원 dictate v. 좌우하다

60 특정세부사항 연구의 결과

난이도 ●○○

What did researchers find out about the younger generations?

(a) that they are more aware of their consumerism
(b) that they pay more attention to sustainability
(c) that they care more about their social status
(d) that they are more influenced by corporations

연구원들은 젊은 세대들에 대해 무엇을 알아냈는가?

(a) 소비지상주의에 대해 더 많이 알고 있다는 것
(b) 지속 가능성에 더 많은 관심을 기울인다는 것
(c) 사회적 지위에 신경을 더 많이 쓴다는 것
(d) 기업들에 의해 영향을 더 많이 받는다는 것

지텔프 치트키

연구의 결과를 언급하는 제목과 지문의 초반을 주의 깊게 읽는다.

해설 | 기사의 제목 'Millennials and Generation Z embrace sustainability'에서 밀레니얼 세대와 Z세대가 지속 가능성을 포용한다고 했고, 1단락의 'Studies have found that the younger generations ~ are more socially and environmentally conscious than their older counterparts.'에서 연구들은 젊은 세대들이 사회적으로 그리고 환경적으로 더 의식적이라는 것을 발견했다고 했다. 따라서 (b)가 정답이다.

Paraphrasing
more ~ conscious 더 의식적인 → pay more attention 더 많은 관심을 기울인다

어휘 | consumerism n. 소비지상주의(소비에 가치의 중심을 두는 사고방식) status n. 지위

61 추론 묘사

난이도 ●●●

According to the article, which best describes Millennials?

(a) They are able to borrow money at better rates than their parents.
(b) They do not make high-risk investments.
(c) They do not trust banking institutions.
(d) They have similar attitudes to previous generations.

기사에 따르면, 밀레니얼 세대를 가장 잘 묘사하는 것은 무엇인가?

(a) 부모보다 더 나은 금리로 돈을 빌릴 수 있다.
(b) 고위험 투자를 하지 않는다.
(c) 금융 기관을 신뢰하지 않는다.
(d) 이전 세대와 비슷한 사고방식을 가지고 있다.

지텔프 치트키

질문의 키워드 Millennials와 관련된 주변 내용을 주의 깊게 읽는다.

해설 | 2단락의 'For Millennials, it was the Great Recession of 2008.'에서 밀레니얼 세대에게 그것(깊이 영향받은 사건)은 2008년의 경기 대침체였다고 한 뒤, 'It made many people question whether the procedures of banks and lending institutions were ethical'에서 이것(경기 대침체가 금융 기관들이 무책임한 대출 관행에 관여한 것에서 비롯된 것)은 많은 사람들이 은행과 대출 기관의 절차가 윤리적이었는지 의문을 품게 했다고 한 것을 통해, 밀레니얼 세대는 금융 기관을 신뢰하지 않을 것임을 추론할 수 있다. 따라서 (c)가 정답이다.

Paraphrasing
banks and lending institutions 은행과 대출 기관 → banking institutions 금융 기관

오답분석

(b) 2단락에서 밀레니얼 세대가 고위험의 대출 관행에 관여한 금융 기관의 절차가 윤리적이었는지에 의문을 품었다고는 했지만, 밀레니얼 세대가 고위험 투자를 하는지의 여부는 언급되지 않았으므로 오답이다.

어휘 | rate n. 금리, (금융상의) 교환 비율 investment n. 투자

62 특정세부사항 How

난이도 ●●●

How did ideas about sustainability become widespread online?

(a) by popular figures spreading their beliefs
(b) by influencers sharing posts amongst themselves
(c) by media outlets publishing more news on the Internet
(d) by social media users creating sustainable products

어떻게 지속 가능성에 대한 생각이 온라인상에서 널리 퍼지게 되었는가?

(a) 자신들의 신념을 퍼뜨리는 인기 있는 인물들에 의해서
(b) 자기들끼리 게시물을 공유하는 인플루언서들에 의해서
(c) 인터넷상에 더 많은 뉴스를 게재하는 언론 매체들에 의해서
(d) 지속 가능한 제품을 만드는 소셜 미디어 사용자들에 의해서

지텔프 치트키

질문의 키워드 widespread online이 spread across the Internet으로 paraphrasing되어 언급된 주변 내용을 주의 깊게 읽는다.

해설 | 4단락의 'Social media influencers who support sustainability have shared their values with the digitally connected generations.'에서 지속 가능성을 지지하는 소셜 미디어 인플루언서들이 디지털로 연결된 세대들에게 자신들의 가치관을 공유해 왔다고 했다. 따라서 (a)가 정답이다.

Paraphrasing
influencers 인플루언서들 → popular figures 인기 있는 인물들
have shared their values 자신들의 가치관을 공유해 왔다 → spreading their beliefs 자신들의 신념을 퍼뜨리는

오답분석

(b) 4단락에서 소셜 미디어 인플루언서들이 디지털로 연결된 세대들에게 자신들의 가치관을 공유해 왔다고 언급했는데, 이는 인터넷 전반에 공유한 것이지 자기들끼리만 게시물을 공유한다고 한 것은 아니므로 오답이다.

어휘 | widespread adj. 널리 퍼진 media outlet phr. 언론 매체 publish v. 게재하다

63 특정세부사항 What

난이도 ●●○

What do young people do when a company does not practice sustainability?

(a) petition for an investigation into the brand
(b) protest outside of the company's physical location
(c) make frequent posts complaining about its customers
(d) unite to withdraw their support for the company

기업이 지속 가능성을 실천하지 않을 때 젊은 사람들은 무엇을 하는가?

(a) 그 브랜드에 대한 조사를 청원한다
(b) 그 기업의 물리적 장소 밖에서 항의한다
(c) 그것의 고객들에 대해 불평하는 게시글을 자주 올린다
(d) 그 기업에 대한 자신들의 지지를 중단하기 위해 연합한다

지텔프 치트키

질문의 키워드 not practice sustainability가 neglect sustainability로 paraphrasing되어 언급된 주변 내용을 주의 깊게 읽는다.

해설 | 5단락의 'young people work together to boycott the brand until changes are made'에서 젊은이들은 변화가 만들어질 때까지 그 브랜드의 구매를 거부하기 위해 협력한다고 했다. 따라서 (d)가 정답이다.

Paraphrasing
work together 협력하다 → unite 연합하다
boycott the brand 그 브랜드의 구매를 거부하다 → withdraw ~ support for the company 그 기업에 대한 지지를 중단하다

어휘 | petition v. 청원하다 investigation n. 조사 protest v. 항의하다 unite v. 연합하다 withdraw v. 중단하다, 철회하다

64 추론 특정사실

난이도 ●●○

According to the passage, what will most likely result from the younger generations' vast population?

(a) Businesses will be forced to change for the better.
(b) The number of products sold globally will increase.
(c) The purchasing power of future generations will suffer.
(d) Businesses will have to improve their online presence.

지문에 따르면, 젊은 세대의 방대한 인구로 인해 어떤 결과가 나올 것 같은가?

(a) 기업들이 더 나은 방향으로 변화하도록 강요받을 것이다.
(b) 전 세계적으로 판매되는 제품의 수가 증가할 것이다.
(c) 미래 세대의 구매력이 타격을 입을 것이다.
(d) 기업들은 자신들의 온라인상에서의 입지를 강화해야 할 것이다.

지텔프 치트키

질문의 키워드 vast population이 largest ~ population으로 paraphrasing되어 언급된 주변 내용을 주의 깊게 읽는다.

해설 | 5단락의 'Millennials and Generation Z, who make up the largest share of the global population, will continue to dictate corporate practices and make the world a more sustainable place'에서 세계 인구의 가장 큰 비중을 차지하고 있는 밀레니얼 세대와 Z세대가 계속 기업의 관행을 좌우하여 세상을 더욱 지속 가능한 곳으로 만들 것이라고 한 것을 통해, 젊은 세대의 방대한 인구로 인해 기업들이 더 나은 방향으로 변화하도록 강요받을 것임을 추론할 수 있다. 따라서 (a)가 정답이다.

어휘 | vast adj. 방대한 suffer v. 타격을 입다 improve v. 강화하다 presence n. 입지

65 어휘 유의어

난이도 ●●●

In the context of the passage, fragile means ______.

(a) breakable
(b) light
(c) delicate
(d) subtle

지문의 문맥에서, 'fragile'은 -을 의미한다.

(a) 깨지기 쉬운
(b) 가벼운
(c) 취약한
(d) 미묘한

지텔프 치트키

밑줄 친 어휘의 유의어를 찾는 문제이므로, fragile이 포함된 구절을 읽고 문맥을 파악한다.

해설 | 3단락의 'just how fragile the planet is was made very clear'는 지구가 그저 얼마나 취약한 곳인지가 매우 분명해졌다는 뜻이므로, fragile이 '취약한'이라는 의미로 사용된 것을 알 수 있다. 따라서 '취약한'이라는 같은 의미의 (c) delicate가 정답이다.

오답분석

(a) fragile이 '깨지기 쉬운'이라는 의미를 가지고 있으므로 breakable도 fragile의 사전적 유의어가 될 수 있다. 하지만, breakable은 물리적으로 물건 등이 깨지기 쉽다는 의미로 사용되므로 문맥에 어울리지 않아 오답이다.

66 어휘 유의어

난이도 ●●○

In the context of the passage, condemn means ______.

(a) punish

지문의 문맥에서, 'condemn'은 -을 의미한다.

(a) 처벌하다

(b) criticize
(c) convict
(d) restrain

(b) 비난하다
(c) 유죄를 선고하다
(d) 제한하다

지텔프 치트키

밑줄 친 어휘의 유의어를 찾는 문제이므로, condemn이 포함된 구절을 읽고 문맥을 파악한다.

해설 | 5단락의 'condemn those that fail'은 기대에 어긋나는 것들을 비난한다는 뜻이므로, condemn이 '비난하다'라는 의미로 사용된 것을 알 수 있다. 따라서 '비난하다'라는 같은 의미의 (b) criticize가 정답이다.

오답분석

(b) '처벌하다'라는 의미의 punish도 condemn의 사전적 유의어 중 하나이지만, 문맥상 사람들이 트위터와 같은 플랫폼을 통해 기대에 어긋나는 기업들을 말이나 글로써 비난한다는 의미가 되어야 적절하므로 문맥에 어울리지 않아 오답이다.

PART 3[67~73] Encyclopedia Article 나무늘보의 특징과 생존 기술

표제어

SLOTHS

정의

Sloths are tree-dwelling mammals that are native to Central and South America. Until about 11,000 years ago, several species of sloths existed in North America, but [67]these became extinct shortly after human hunters migrated to the continent.

어원 + 특징1: 느린 이동 속도

The word *sloth* means "laziness" in English, and sloths were given this name for their inactivity. [72]Sloths spend about 90 percent of each day absolutely motionless, using their sharp claws to hang from tree branches. When they do move through the trees, they go very slowly from branch to branch, averaging no more than four meters per minute. If they descend to the ground, their speed drops to less than two meters per minute. This is because their legs are so weak that [68]they have to drag their bodies with their powerful arms.

특징2: 느린 신진 대사

Scientists speculate that one reason for their slow movement is the food they eat. [69]Sloths primarily consume leaves that do not provide many nutrients. Fortunately, their sedentary lifestyle results in little energy expenditure on physical activity. In addition, sloths have an extremely slow metabolic rate, so they do not use much energy for basic bodily functions like breathing and body temperature regulation.

The sluggishness of sloths is an advantage when it comes to surviving in an environment with many

나무늘보

나무늘보는 나무에서 사는 중앙아메리카와 남아메리카 토종의 포유동물이다. 약 11,000년 전까지만 해도, 여러 종의 나무늘보가 북아메리카에 존재했지만, [67]이것들은 인간 사냥꾼들이 그 대륙으로 이주한 직후 멸종되었다.

'sloth'라는 단어는 영어로 '게으름'을 의미하며, 나무늘보는 그것들의 게으름 때문에 이 이름이 붙여졌다. [72]나무늘보는 하루 중 약 90퍼센트를 전혀 움직이지 않고 보내는데, 나뭇가지에 매달리기 위해 그것의 날카로운 발톱을 사용한다. 나무 사이를 이동할 때, 그것들은 이 가지에서 저 가지로 매우 천천히 가며, 분당 단지 평균 4미터밖에 안 된다. 그것들이 땅으로 내려오면, 그것들의 속도는 분당 2미터 아래로 떨어진다. 이는 그것들의 다리가 너무 약해서 [68]그것들은 자신들의 힘센 팔로 몸을 끌고 가야 하기 때문이다.

과학자들은 그것들의 느린 움직임의 한 가지 이유가 그것들이 먹는 음식이라고 추측한다. [69]나무늘보는 많은 영양분을 제공하지 않는 잎을 주로 먹는다. 다행히도, 그것들의 주로 앉아서 지내는 생활 방식은 신체 활동에 에너지를 거의 소비하지 않는 결과를 낳는다. 게다가, 나무늘보는 신진대사 속도가 매우 느리기 때문에, 호흡과 체온 조절 같은 기본적인 신체 기능에 많은 에너지를 사용하지 않는다.

나무늘보의 느릿느릿함은 포식자가 많은 환경에서 살아남는 데 있어 유리한 점이다. 머리를 돌리는 것부

생존 기술1: 느릿함	predators. As every movement sloths make—from turning their heads to blinking their eyes—is incredibly slow, other animals have difficulty in spotting them. Furthermore, because sloths need very little energy to survive, [70]they are able to wait a long time before getting something to eat if predators are nearby.	터 눈을 깜박이는 것까지 나무늘보가 만드는 모든 움직임이 매우 느리기 때문에, 다른 동물들은 그것들을 발견하는 데 어려움을 겪는다. 그뿐만 아니라, 나무늘보는 생존하기 위해 매우 적은 에너지를 필요로 하기 때문에, [70]만약 포식자들이 근처에 있다면 먹을 것을 얻기 전까지 오랜 시간을 기다릴 수 있다.
생존 기술2: 은신 능력	[71(a)]Another survival skill is the sloths' ability to hide due to the algae and fungi on their bodies. [71(b)]The sloths' hairs are the perfect habitat for these microorganisms to grow. [71(c)]These turn the sloths' fur green so that they can blend in with the surrounding trees. As an added bonus, [71(d)]they also mask the sloths' scent, making them harder for predators to detect.	[71(a)]또 다른 생존 기술은 그것들의 몸에 있는 조류와 균류로 인한 나무늘보의 숨기 능력이다. [71(b)]나무늘보의 털은 이러한 미생물들이 자라기에 완벽한 서식지이다. [71(c)]이것들은 나무늘보의 털을 초록색으로 바꿔서 그것들이 주변 나무들과 어우러질 수 있게 한다. 덤으로, [71(d)]그것들은 또한 나무늘보의 냄새를 가려서 그것들을 포식자들이 발견하기 더 어렵게 만든다.
전망	Overall, [73]sloths are resilient creatures that are well adapted to their environment. If the rainforests they inhabit are protected, sloths will continue to thrive long into the future.	전반적으로, [73]나무늘보는 그것들의 환경에 상당히 적합한 회복력이 좋은 동물이다. 만약 그것들이 사는 열대 우림이 보호된다면, 나무늘보는 앞으로도 오랫동안 계속 번성할 것이다.

어휘 | sloth n. 나무늘보 mammal n. 포유동물 extinct adj. 멸종된 migrate v. 이주하다 continent n. 대륙 inactivity n. 게으름 absolutely adv. 전혀, 완전히 sharp adj. 날카로운 claw n. 발톱 hang v. 매달리다 branch n. 나뭇가지 average v. 평균 ~이 되다 descend v. 내려오다 drop v. 떨어지다 drag v. 끌고 가다 speculate v. 추측하다 primarily adv. 주로 consume v. 먹다 nutrient n. 영양분 sedentary adj. 주로 앉아서 지내는 expenditure n. 소비 metabolic adj. 신진대사의 regulation n. 조절 sluggishness n. 느릿느릿함, 나태 predator n. 포식자 blink v. 눈을 깜박이다 spot v. 발견하다 algae n. 조류 fungus n. 균류 habitat n. 서식지 microorganism n. 미생물 fur n. 털 blend v. 어우러지다 mask v. 가리다 scent n. 냄새 detect v. 발견하다 resilient adj. 회복력이 좋은 inhabit v. 살다, 서식하다 rainforest n. 열대 우림 thrive v. 번성하다

67 추론 특정사실

난이도 ●●○

Why most likely are sloths no longer present in North America?

(a) because they migrated to another continent
(b) because they were replaced by invasive animals
(c) because they experienced a lack of food
(d) because they were wiped out by people

왜 나무늘보가 북아메리카에 더 이상 존재하지 않는 것 같은가?

(a) 다른 대륙으로 이주했기 때문에
(b) 침입 동물들에 의해 대체되었기 때문에
(c) 식량 부족을 경험했기 때문에
(d) 사람들에 의해 전멸당했기 때문에

지텔프 치트키

질문의 키워드 North America가 그대로 언급된 주변 내용을 주의 깊게 읽는다.

해설 | 1단락의 'these became extinct shortly after human hunters migrated to the continent'에서 나무늘보는 인간 사냥꾼들이 북아메리카 대륙으로 이주한 직후 멸종되었다고 한 것을 통해, 북아메리카에 살던 나무늘보가 사람들에 의해 전멸당했을 것임을 추론할 수 있다. 따라서 (d)가 정답이다.

어휘 | replace v. 대체하다 invasive adj. 침입하는 wipe out phr. ~을 전멸시키다, 몰살하다

68 특정세부사항 How

난이도 ●●○

How do sloths travel along the ground?

(a) by swinging from the lower branches
(b) by supporting their weight with their claws
(c) by using their arms to pull their bodies
(d) by grasping tree trunks to remain upright

나무늘보는 어떻게 땅 위를 이동하는가?

(a) 더 낮은 나뭇가지에 매달림으로써
(b) 발톱으로 무게를 지탱함으로써
(c) 몸을 끌어당기기 위해 팔을 이용함으로써
(d) 똑바로 서 있기 위해 나무줄기를 움켜쥠으로써

지텔프 치트키

질문의 키워드 the ground가 그대로 언급된 주변 내용을 주의 깊게 읽는다.

해설 | 2단락의 'they have to drag their bodies with their powerful arms'에서 나무늘보는 자신들의 힘센 팔로 몸을 끌고 가야 한다고 했다. 따라서 (c)가 정답이다.

Paraphrasing

drag their bodies with their powerful arms 힘센 팔로 몸을 끌고 가다 → using their arms to pull their bodies 몸을 끌어당기기 위해 팔을 이용함

어휘 | swing v. 매달리다 pull v. 끌어당기다 grasp v. 움켜쥐다 trunk n. 줄기 upright adj. 똑바로 선

69 특정세부사항 What

난이도 ●●○

What is a reason sloths can live on nutrient-deficient food?

(a) They maintain a low body temperature.
(b) They spend little energy on their movements.
(c) They consume extremely large quantities of food.
(d) They slow their metabolism while sleeping.

나무늘보가 영양분이 부족한 음식으로 먹고 살 수 있는 이유는 무엇인가?

(a) 낮은 체온을 유지한다.
(b) 움직임에 에너지를 거의 쓰지 않는다.
(c) 엄청나게 많은 양의 음식을 먹는다.
(d) 잠을 자는 동안 신진대사를 늦춘다.

지텔프 치트키

질문의 키워드 nutrient-deficient가 not ~ many nutrients로 paraphrasing되어 언급된 주변 내용을 주의 깊게 읽는다.

해설 | 3단락의 'Sloths primarily consume leaves that do not provide many nutrients.'에서 나무늘보는 많은 영양분을 제공하지 않는 잎을 주로 먹는다고 한 뒤, 'Fortunately, their sedentary lifestyle results in little energy expenditure on physical activity.'에서 다행히 그것들의 주로 앉아서 지내는 생활 방식이 신체 활동에 에너지를 거의 소비하지 않는 결과를 낳는다고 했다. 따라서 (b)가 정답이다.

Paraphrasing

little energy expenditure on physical activity 신체 활동에 에너지를 거의 소비하지 않음 → spend little energy on their movements 움직임에 에너지를 거의 쓰지 않는다

오답분석

(d) 3단락에서 나무늘보의 신진대사 속도가 매우 느리다고는 했지만, 그것들이 잠을 자는 동안 신진대사를 늦추는지는 언급되지 않았으므로 오답이다.

어휘 | live on phr. ~으로 먹고 살다 quantity n. 양 slow v. 늦추다

70 특정세부사항 How

난이도 ●○○

According to the passage, how are sloths able to avoid predators?

(a) by staying away from predators' territory
(b) by spotting dangerous animals from a distance
(c) by waiting an extended period to eat
(d) by going a long time without blinking

지문에 따르면, 나무늘보는 어떻게 포식자를 피할 수 있는가?

(a) 포식자의 영역에 접근하지 않음으로써
(b) 멀리서 위험한 동물들을 발견함으로써
(c) 먹기 위해 장시간을 기다림으로써
(d) 눈을 깜박이지 않고 오랜 시간을 보냄으로써

지텔프 치트키

질문의 키워드 predators가 그대로 언급된 주변 내용을 주의 깊게 읽는다.

해설 | 4단락의 'they are able to wait a long time before getting something to eat if predators are nearby'에서 나무늘보는 만약 포식자들이 근처에 있다면 먹을 것을 얻기 전까지 오랜 시간을 기다릴 수 있다고 했다. 따라서 (c)가 정답이다.

Paraphrasing
a long time 오랜 시간 → an extended period 장시간

어휘 | stay away from phr. ~에 접근하지 않다 territory n. 영역, 영토

71 Not/True Not 문제

난이도 ●●○

Which is not true about the algae and fungi on sloths?

(a) They expose the sloths' bodies.
(b) They grow on the sloths' fur.
(c) They change the sloths' color.
(d) They disguise the sloths' smells.

나무늘보에 있는 조류와 균류에 대해 사실이 아닌 것은 무엇인가?

(a) 나무늘보의 몸을 노출시킨다.
(b) 나무늘보의 털에서 자란다.
(c) 나무늘보의 색을 바꾼다.
(d) 나무늘보의 냄새를 숨긴다.

지텔프 치트키

질문의 키워드 algae and fungi와 관련된 주변 내용을 주의 깊게 읽고, 보기의 키워드와 지문 내용을 대조하며 언급되는 것을 하나씩 소거한다.

해설 | (a)는 5단락의 'Another survival skill is the sloths' ability to hide due to the algae and fungi on their bodies.'에서 또 다른 생존 기술이 나무늘보의 몸에 있는 조류와 균류로 인한 나무늘보의 숨기 능력이라고 했으므로, 조류와 균류가 나무늘보의 몸을 노출시킨다는 것은 지문의 내용과 일치하지 않는다. 따라서 (a)가 정답이다.

오답분석

(b) 보기의 키워드 sloths' fur가 sloths' hairs로 paraphrasing되어 언급된 5단락에서 나무늘보의 털은 조류와 균류 같은 미생물들이 자라기에 완벽한 서식지라고 언급되었다.
(c) 보기의 키워드 change the sloths' color가 turn the sloths' fur green으로 paraphrasing되어 언급된 5단락에서 조류와 균류가 나무늘보의 털을 초록색으로 바꾼다고 언급되었다.
(d) 보기의 키워드 sloths' smells가 sloths' scent로 paraphrasing되어 언급된 5단락에서 조류와 균류가 나무늘보의 냄새를 가린다고 언급되었다.

어휘 | expose v. 노출시키다 disguise v. 숨기다

72 어휘 유의어

난이도 ●●○

In the context of the passage, motionless means ________.

(a) mindless
(b) restless
(c) silent
(d) stationary

지문의 문맥에서, 'motionless'는 -을 의미한다.

(a) 아무 생각이 없는
(b) 가만히 있지 못하는
(c) 조용한
(d) 움직이지 않는

지텔프 치트키

밑줄 친 어휘의 유의어를 찾는 문제이므로, motionless가 포함된 구절을 읽고 문맥을 파악한다.

해설 | 2단락의 'Sloths spend about 90 percent of each day absolutely motionless'는 나무늘보가 하루 중 약 90퍼센트를 전혀 움직이지 않고 보낸다는 뜻이므로, motionless가 '움직이지 않는'이라는 의미로 사용된 것을 알 수 있다. 따라서 '움직이지 않는'이라는 같은 의미의 (d) stationary가 정답이다.

73 어휘 유의어

난이도 ●●○

In the context of the passage, adapted means ________.

(a) suited
(b) adopted
(c) tamed
(d) established

지문의 문맥에서, 'adapted'는 -을 의미한다.

(a) 적합한
(b) 채택된
(c) 길든
(d) 확립된

지텔프 치트키

밑줄 친 어휘의 유의어를 찾는 문제이므로, adapted가 포함된 구절을 읽고 문맥을 파악한다.

해설 | 6단락의 'sloths are ~ creatures that are well adapted to their environment'는 나무늘보가 그것들의 환경에 상당히 적합한 동물이라는 뜻이므로, adapted가 '적합한'이라는 의미로 사용된 것을 알 수 있다. 따라서 '적합한'이라는 같은 의미의 (a) suited가 정답이다.

PART 4 (74~80) Business Letter 식당에 불만을 제기하기 위한 편지

수신인 정보

Martin Giles
Manager
Flavor City

Dear Mr. Giles:

편지의 목적: 불만 제기

[74]I am writing to inform you about the inferior food and service my family received at your restaurant on Christmas Eve.

Martin Giles
지배인
Flavor City

Mr. Giles께:

크리스마스이브에 [74]당신의 레스토랑에서 우리 가족이 받은 형편없는 음식과 서비스에 대해 알려 드리기 위해 편지를 씁니다.

불만1: 바뀐 메뉴	We've been eating at Flavor City for years and were excited to spend this special occasion there. [75]One of the main reasons we come back so often is because of the kids' menu, which has long featured healthy, gourmet food. So imagine our surprise when we found that [76]the children's spaghetti Bolognese had been switched out for unhealthy, frozen chicken tenders.	우리는 몇 년 동안 Flavor City에서 음식을 먹어 왔고 그곳에서 이 특별한 날을 보내게 되어 신이 났었습니다. [75]우리가 이렇게 자주 재방문하는 주된 이유 중 하나는 어린이 메뉴 때문인데, 그것은 오랫동안 건강에 좋은 고급 요리를 특색으로 삼아 왔습니다. 그러니 [76]아이들의 볼로네즈 스파게티가 건강에 좋지 않은 냉동 치킨텐더로 교체되었다는 것을 알았을 때 우리가 얼마나 놀랐을지 상상해 보십시오.
불만2: 상한 재료 + 직원의 태도	I was relieved to see that [79]the beloved starter was still available: the crab cakes. But that joy was short-lived. As I bit into one, I noticed that it tasted off. [77]I asked the waiter if the dish was fresh, and he replied impolitely, "I don't know. The crab comes from a can." Besides being disappointed with the lack of fresh ingredients used in the appetizer, I also believe the response from the waiter—I didn't catch his name—to be unprofessional.	[79]인기 많은 전채 요리인 게살 튀김이 아직 남아 있는 것을 보고 우리는 안심했습니다. 하지만 그 기쁨은 오래가지 못했습니다. 하나를 깨물어 보았을 때, 저는 그것이 상한 맛이 난다는 것을 인지했습니다. [77]제가 종업원에게 음식이 신선한지 물었더니, 그는 "모르겠는데요. 그 게는 통조림에서 가져온 겁니다."라며 [77]무례하게 대답했습니다. 전채 요리에 사용된 신선한 재료의 부족에 실망했을 뿐만 아니라, 그의 이름을 확인하지는 못했지만 그 종업원의 대응도 미숙하다고 생각합니다.
재방문 의사	Considering the menu changes and the overall diminished quality, my partner and I, as well as several other acquaintances I've spoken to about this matter, are [80]skeptical about visiting Flavor City again.	메뉴의 변화와 전반적으로 떨어진 품질을 고려하면, 제가 이 문제에 관해 이야기했던 몇몇 다른 지인들뿐만 아니라, 저와 제 남편은 [80]다시 Flavor City를 방문하는 것에 대해 회의적입니다.
끝인사	I understand that [78]Flavor City was recently sold and is now under new management, but I had hoped that it would retain some of the same charms that made it not only a personal favorite but one of the best eateries in town.	[78]Flavor City가 최근에 매도되어 현재 새로운 경영진 하에 있다는 것은 이해하지만, 저는 Flavor City가 그것을 개인적으로 가장 좋아하는 식당으로 만들었을 뿐만 아니라 동네에서 최고의 맛집 중 하나로 만들었던 동일한 매력을 어느 정도 유지하기를 바랐었습니다.
발신인 정보	Respectfully, Alice Reed	Alice Reed 드림

어휘 | inferior adj. 형편없는 occasion n. 특별한 날, 행사 feature v. ~을 특색으로 삼다 gourmet food phr. 고급 요리 switch out phr. ~을 교체하다 frozen adj. 냉동된 relieved adj. 안심한 beloved adj. 인기 많은 starter n. 전채 요리 crab cake phr. 게살 튀김 short-lived adj. 오래가지 못하는 bite v. 깨물다 notice v. 인지하다 off adj. 상한 impolitely adv. 무례하게 besides prep. ~뿐만 아니라 disappointed adj. 실망한 ingredient n. 재료 appetizer n. 전채 요리 response n. 대응 unprofessional adj. 미숙한 overall adv. 전반적으로 diminished adj. (위신이) 떨어진 acquaintance n. 지인 management n. 경영진 retain v. 유지하다 charm n. 매력 eatery n. 식당

74 주제/목적 편지의 목적

난이도 ●●○

Why did Alice Reed write a letter to Martin Giles?

(a) to place an order for Christmas Eve
(b) to explain the changes in a restaurant's service
(c) to protest the opening of a business
(d) to complain about a dining experience

왜 Alice Reed는 Martin Giles에게 편지를 썼는가?

(a) 크리스마스이브를 위한 주문을 하기 위해서
(b) 식당 서비스의 변화를 설명하기 위해서
(c) 개업에 반대하기 위해서
(d) 식사 경험에 대한 불만을 말하기 위해서

지텔프 치트키

지문의 초반을 주의 깊게 읽고 전체 맥락을 파악한다.

해설 | 1단락의 'I am writing to inform you about the inferior food and service ~ received at your restaurant'에서 Alice Reed는 Martin Giles가 지배인으로 있는 식당에서 받은 형편없는 음식과 서비스에 대해 알려 주기 위해 편지를 쓴다고 한 뒤, 그 식당의 음식과 종업원의 태도에 대해 불만을 제기하는 내용이 이어지고 있다. 따라서 (d)가 정답이다.

어휘 | place an order phr. 주문을 하다 protest v. 반대하다 complain v. 불만을 말하다, 항의하다 dining n. 식사

75 특정세부사항 Why

난이도 ●●○

Based on the letter, why did Reed visit Flavor City regularly?

(a) because of the frequent updates to the kid's menu
(b) because they had large portions of spaghetti Bolognese
(c) because they provided nutritious meal options for kids
(d) because of the available seating on special occasions

편지에 따르면, Reed는 왜 자주 Flavor City를 방문했는가?

(a) 어린이 메뉴의 잦은 업데이트 때문에
(b) 볼로네즈 스파게티의 양이 많았기 때문에
(c) 아이들을 위한 영양가 있는 식사 선택지를 제공했기 때문에
(d) 특별한 날에 이용 가능한 자리 때문에

지텔프 치트키

질문의 키워드 visit ~ regularly가 come back so often으로 paraphrasing되어 언급된 주변 내용을 주의 깊게 읽는다.

해설 | 2단락의 'One of the main reasons ~ is because of the kids' menu, which has long featured healthy, gourmet food.'에서 주된 이유 중 하나는 건강에 좋은 고급 요리를 특색으로 삼아 온 어린이 메뉴 때문이라고 했다. 따라서 (c)가 정답이다.

Paraphrasing
the kids' menu 어린이 메뉴 → meal options for kids 아이들을 위한 식사 선택지
healthy 건강에 좋은 → nutritious 영양가 있는

76 특정세부사항 What

난이도 ●●○

What happened to the spaghetti Bolognese on the children's menu?

(a) It seemed to include the wrong ingredients.
(b) It was served after the other courses.
(c) It cost more than the frozen chicken strips.
(d) It was replaced by a less healthy alternative.

어린이 메뉴에 있는 볼로네즈 스파게티에 무슨 일이 일어났는가?

(a) 잘못된 재료가 포함된 것 같았다.
(b) 다른 코스들 뒤에 제공되었다.
(c) 냉동 치킨 조각보다 더 비쌌다.
(d) 건강에 덜 좋은 대체품으로 교체되었다.

지텔프 치트키

질문의 키워드 spaghetti Bolognese가 그대로 언급된 주변 내용을 주의 깊게 읽는다.

해설 | 2단락의 'the children's spaghetti Bolognese had been switched out for unhealthy, frozen chicken tenders'에서 아이들의 볼로네즈 스파게티가 건강에 좋지 않은 냉동 치킨텐더로 교체되었다고 했다. 따라서 (d)가 정답이다.

Paraphrasing
had been switched out for ~으로 교체되었다 → was replaced by ~으로 교체되었다
unhealthy 건강에 좋지 않은 → less healthy 건강에 덜 좋은

어휘 | serve v. 제공하다 strip n. (작은) 조각 replace v. 교체하다 alternative n. 대체품

77 특정세부사항 How

난이도 ●●○

How did a staff member react to Reed's question about a dish?

(a) by offering complimentary crab cakes
(b) by apologizing for the slow service
(c) by answering in a rude manner
(d) by saying that the customer was incorrect

요리에 대한 Reed의 질문에 직원은 어떻게 반응했는가?

(a) 무료 게살 튀김을 제공함으로써
(b) 느린 서비스에 대해 사과함으로써
(c) 무례한 태도로 대답함으로써
(d) 고객이 틀렸다고 말함으로써

지텔프 치트키

질문의 키워드 staff member가 waiter로 paraphrasing되어 언급된 주변 내용을 주의 깊게 읽는다.

해설 | 3단락의 'I asked the waiter if the dish was fresh, and he replied impolitely'에서 Reed가 종업원에게 음식이 신선한지 물었더니 그가 무례하게 대답했다고 했다. 따라서 (c)가 정답이다.

Paraphrasing
impolitely 무례하게 → in a rude manner 무례한 태도로

어휘 | react v. 반응하다 complimentary adj. 무료의 rude adj. 무례한

78 추론 특정사실

난이도 ●●○

What probably occurred at Flavor City recently?

(a) It changed its previous operation policy.
(b) It was named as the best place in town.
(c) It diminished the managers at the restaurant.
(d) It moved to a new location in the city.

최근에 Flavor City에 무슨 일이 있었던 것 같은가?

(a) 기존의 운영 방침을 변경했다.
(b) 동네에서 가장 좋은 곳으로 선정되었다.
(c) 레스토랑에 있는 지배인들을 줄였다.
(d) 그 도시에서 새로운 위치로 이동했다.

지텔프 치트키

질문의 키워드 recently가 그대로 언급된 주변 내용을 주의 깊게 읽는다.

해설 | 5단락의 'Flavor City was recently sold and is now under new management'에서 Flavor City가 최근에 매도되어 현재 새로운 경영진 하에 있다고 한 것을 통해, Flavor City가 최근에 기존의 운영 방침을 변경했을 것임을 추론할 수 있다. 따라서 (a)가 정답이다.

Paraphrasing
management 경영진 → operation policy 운영 방침

오답분석
(b) Flavor City가 현재의 새로운 경영진 하에 있기 전에 동네에서 최고의 맛집 중 하나였던 것이므로 오답이다.

어휘 | operation policy phr. 운영 방침 diminish v. 줄이다

79 어휘 유의어

난이도 ●●●

In the context of the passage, <u>beloved</u> means _______.

(a) lovable
(b) familiar
(c) precious
(d) popular

지문의 문맥에서, 'beloved'는 -을 의미한다.

(a) 사랑스러운
(b) 친숙한
(c) 소중한
(d) 인기 있는

지텔프 치트키

밑줄 친 어휘의 유의어를 찾는 문제이므로, beloved가 포함된 구절을 읽고 문맥을 파악한다.

해설 | 3단락의 'the beloved starter was still available: the crab cakes'는 인기 많은 전채 요리인 게살 튀김이 아직 남아 있었다는 뜻이므로, beloved가 '인기 많은'이라는 의미로 사용된 것을 알 수 있다. 따라서 '인기 있는'이라는 비슷한 의미의 (d) popular가 정답이다.

오답분석

(a) '사랑스러운'이라는 의미의 lovable은 사람이나 사물의 사랑스럽거나 매력적인 특성을 묘사할 때 사용되는데, 사랑스러운 것이 항상 인기 있는 것은 아니므로 문맥에 어울리지 않아 오답이다.

80 어휘 유의어

난이도 ●●○

In the context of the passage, <u>skeptical</u> means _______.

(a) pessimistic
(b) doubtful
(c) indecisive
(d) afraid

지문의 문맥에서, 'skeptical'은 -을 의미한다.

(a) 비관적인
(b) 불확실한
(c) 우유부단한
(d) 두려워하는

지텔프 치트키

밑줄 친 어휘의 유의어를 찾는 문제이므로, skeptical이 포함된 구절을 읽고 문맥을 파악한다.

해설 | 4단락의 'skeptical about visiting Flavor City again'은 다시 Flavor City를 방문하는 것에 대해 회의적이라는 뜻이므로, skeptical이 '회의적인'이라는 의미로 사용된 것을 알 수 있다. 따라서 '불확실한'이라는 비슷한 의미의 (b) doubtful이 정답이다.

02회 실전모의고사

문제집 p.12

정답 및 문제 유형 분석표

PART 1		PART 2		PART 3		PART 4	
53	(b) 특정세부사항	60	(d) 주제/목적	67	(c) 특정세부사항	74	(c) 주제/목적
54	(a) 특정세부사항	61	(b) 특정세부사항	68	(b) 특정세부사항	75	(d) 특정세부사항
55	(d) 특정세부사항	62	(b) 추론	69	(a) 추론	76	(c) 특정세부사항
56	(c) 특정세부사항	63	(c) 특정세부사항	70	(d) 특정세부사항	77	(b) 특정세부사항
57	(b) 추론	64	(c) 특정세부사항	71	(b) 특정세부사항	78	(b) 추론
58	(a) 어휘	65	(a) 어휘	72	(d) 어휘	79	(a) 어휘
59	(c) 어휘	66	(d) 어휘	73	(c) 어휘	80	(c) 어휘

취약 유형 분석표

유형	맞힌 개수
주제/목적	/2
특정세부사항	/14
Not/True	0
추론	/4
어휘	/8
TOTAL	28

PART 1 (53~59) Biography Article 유치원의 창조자 프리드리히 프뢰벨

인물 이름

FRIEDRICH FRÖBEL

인물 소개

Friedrich Fröbel was a German educator and reformer best remembered for creating the concept of kindergarten. It was an educational approach recognizing that [53]young children learn most effectively while interacting with their peers as they play, sing, and explore.

어린 시절

Friedrich Fröbel was born on April 21, 1782, in Oberweissbach, Germany to Johann Fröbel and Jacobine Friederike. He was raised by his father and a stepmother after his mother died when he was nine months old. [54]They were inattentive to his needs, so he moved in with his maternal uncle in Stadtilm at 10 years old. In school, his primary areas of interest were plants and nature, and he became a forestry apprentice at 15.

업적 시작 계기

After his apprenticeship, Fröbel attended university and later found work as a land surveyor. It wasn't until he accepted a teaching position at a school in Frankfurt that he realized his true calling. The school was run by Anton Gruener and modeled on the philosophies of Swiss educator Johann Pestalozzi, who was an advocate for the poor and believed that everyone had a right to an education. In 1808, [55]Fröbel went to Switzerland to study under Pestalozzi, who taught him that early childhood was crucial to human development.

프리드리히 프뢰벨

프리드리히 프뢰벨은 유치원이라는 개념을 창안한 것으로 가장 잘 기억되는 독일의 교육자이자 개혁가였다. 그것은 [53]어린아이들이 놀고, 노래하고, 탐험하며 그들의 또래와 상호 작용하는 동안에 가장 효과적으로 학습한다는 것을 인정하는 교육적 접근법이었다.

프리드리히 프뢰벨은, 요한 프뢰벨과 야코비네 프리데리케의 사이에서, 1782년 4월 21일에 독일의 오버바이스바흐에서 태어났다. 그가 9개월일 때 그의 어머니가 돌아가신 후 그는 아버지와 새어머니 손에서 길러졌다. [54]그들은 그가 필요한 것에 무관심했고, 그래서 그는 10살 때 슈타트일름에 있는 그의 외삼촌 집으로 이사했다. 학교에서, 그의 주요 관심 분야는 식물과 자연이었으며, 15살 때 그는 임학 수습생이 되었다.

그의 수습 기간이 끝나고, 프뢰벨은 대학을 다녔으며 후에 토지 측량사로 취업했다. 프랑크푸르트에 있는 한 학교의 교직을 수락하고 나서야 그는 자신의 천직을 깨달았다. 그 학교는 안톤 그루너에 의해 운영되었고 스위스의 교육자 요한 페스탈로치의 철학을 본떠서 만들어졌는데, 페스탈로치는 영세민들의 지지자였으며 모든 사람들에게 교육받을 권리가 있다고 믿었다. 1808년에, [55]프뢰벨은 페스탈로치의 가르침을 받기 위해 스위스로 갔고, 페스탈로치는 그에게 유아기가 인적 발달에 중대하다는 것을 가르쳤다.

초기 활동 + 주요 업적

With his new knowledge in hand, Fröbel returned to Germany in 1816 and founded the Universal German Educational Institute. [58]This school flourished and became a large community. He also wrote about early childhood education, asserting that every child is born with a God-given force and that externalizing this force is necessary for growth. In 1837, he opened an institute for young children that he named Kindergarten, which means "garden of children." [56]It was here that he developed the educational toys he called "Fröbel Gifts." These were objects such as cubes, spheres, and rings designed to encourage children's exploration of the world through play.

위기 + 죽음

Fröbel's philosophy for teaching young learners led more kindergartens to open throughout Germany. However, in 1851, the minister of education Karl von Raumer banned all kindergartens because he believed [59]they undermined the traditional notion that play was a form of idleness. [57]Kindergartens were eventually allowed to reopen in 1860, eight years after Fröbel's death. Once the kindergartens opened again, they quickly spread throughout Europe, and today, they are a standard part of children's education globally.

새로운 지식을 손안에 넣고, 프뢰벨은 1816년에 독일로 돌아와 독일 교육연구소를 설립했다. [58]이 학교는 번성하여 큰 공동체가 되었다. 그는 또한 유아 교육에 관해 글을 썼는데, 모든 아이가 천부적인 힘을 가지고 태어나며 그 힘을 구체화하는 것이 성장에 필수적이라고 주장했다. 1837년에, 그는 어린아이들을 위한 기관을 열어 '아이들의 정원'이라는 뜻의 유치원이라는 이름을 지었다. [56]그가 '프뢰벨 은물'이라고 부르는 교육용 완구를 개발한 곳이 바로 여기였다. 이것들은 놀이를 통한 아이들의 세상 탐험을 장려하기 위해 고안된 정육면체, 구, 고리와 같은 물건들이었다.

어린 학습자들을 가르치는 것에 대한 프뢰벨의 철학은 더 많은 유치원이 독일 전역에 걸쳐 개원하도록 이끌었다. 하지만, 1851년에, 교육부 장관이었던 카를 폰 라우머가 모든 유치원을 금지했는데 이는 놀이가 게으름의 형태라는 [59]전통적인 개념을 그것들이 약화시켰다고 생각했기 때문이다. [57]프뢰벨의 사후 8년 만인 1860년에 유치원은 결국 다시 문을 열도록 허용되었다. 유치원이 다시 개원하자마자, 빠르게 유럽 전역으로 퍼졌고, 오늘날, 그것들은 전 세계적으로 유아 교육의 표준적인 부분이 되었다.

어휘 | educator n. 교육자 reformer n. 개혁가 kindergarten n. 유치원 educational adj. 교육적인 approach n. 접근법 recognize v. 인정하다 effectively adv. 효과적으로 interact v. 상호 작용하다 peer n. 또래, 동배 raise v. 기르다, 키우다 stepmother n. 새어머니 inattentive adj. 무관심한, 신경을 쓰지 않는 needs n. 필요한 것, 요구 maternal adj. 외가의 primary adj. 주요한 forestry n. 임학 apprentice n. 수습생, 견습생 apprenticeship n. 수습 기간 land surveyor phr. 토지 측량사 teaching position phr. 교직 true calling phr. 천직 model on phr. ~을 본떠서 만들다 advocate n. 지지자 crucial adj. 중대한 development n. 발달, 개발 found v. 설립하다 institute n. (연구) 기관 assert v. 주장하다 God-given adj. 천부적인 externalize v. 구체화하다, 표면화하다 cube n. 정육면체 sphere n. 구 ban v. 금지하다 undermine v. 약화시키다 idleness n. 게으름 spread v. 퍼지다, 퍼뜨리다 standard adj. 표준적인

53 특정세부사항 How

난이도 ●●○

How did Fröbel think children learn best?

(a) by working independently of a teacher
(b) by participating in various activities with friends
(c) by being involved in the creation of artistic works
(d) by observing peers in an academic setting

프뢰벨은 아이들이 어떻게 가장 잘 학습한다고 생각했는가?

(a) 선생님으로부터 독립적으로 공부함으로써
(b) 친구들과 다양한 활동에 참여함으로써
(c) 예술적인 작품들의 창작에 몰두함으로써
(d) 학업 환경에서 또래들을 관찰함으로써

지텔프 치트키

질문의 키워드 learn best가 learn most effectively로 paraphrasing되어 언급된 주변 내용을 주의 깊게 읽는다.

해설 | 프뢰벨이 창안한 유치원이라는 개념을 설명하는 1단락의 'young children learn most effectively while interacting with their peers as they play, sing, and explore'에서 어린아이들이 놀고, 노래하고, 탐험하며 그들의 또래와 상호 작용하는 동안에 가장 효과

적으로 학습한다고 했다. 따라서 (b)가 정답이다.

Paraphrasing
interacting with their peers as they play, sing, and explore 놀고, 노래하고, 탐험하며 그들의 또래와 상호 작용하는 → participating in various activities with friends 친구들과 다양한 활동에 참여하는

어휘 | independently adv. 독립적으로 observe v. 관찰하다

54 특정세부사항 Why

난이도 ●○○

Why did Fröbel go to live with his maternal uncle?

(a) because he was neglected by his parents
(b) so he could attend a school in Stadtilm
(c) so he could accept a position as a forester
(d) because he wanted to find out more about his mother

왜 프뢰벨은 그의 외삼촌과 살기 위해 떠났는가?

(a) 부모에 의해 등한시되었기 때문에
(b) 슈타트일름에 있는 학교에 다니기 위해서
(c) 산림 공무원직을 맡기 위해서
(d) 자신의 어머니에 대해 더 알아내고 싶어 했기 때문에

지텔프 치트키

질문의 키워드 maternal uncle이 그대로 언급된 주변 내용을 주의 깊게 읽는다.

해설 | 2단락의 'They were inattentive ~, so he moved in with his maternal uncle in Stadtilm at 10 years old.'에서 아버지와 새어머니가 프뢰벨이 필요한 것에 무관심해서 프뢰벨이 슈타트일름에 있는 외삼촌 집으로 이사했다고 했다. 따라서 (a)가 정답이다.

Paraphrasing
They were inattentive to his needs 그들은 그가 필요한 것에 무관심했다 → he was neglected by his parents 그는 부모에 의해 등한시되었다

어휘 | neglect v. 등한시하다, 무시하다 forester n. 산림 공무원, 수목 관리원

55 특정세부사항 What

난이도 ●●○

Based on the article, what did Fröbel do when he was in Switzerland?

(a) He studied education under Gruener at a local university.
(b) He advocated for the rights of people living in poverty.
(c) He developed new teaching methods with Pestalozzi.
(d) He learned about the importance of childhood in development.

기사에 따르면, 프뢰벨은 스위스에 있었을 때 무엇을 했는가?

(a) 지방 대학에서 그루너의 지도하에 교육학 공부를 했다.
(b) 가난한 생활을 하는 사람들의 권리를 지지했다.
(c) 페스탈로치와 함께 새로운 교수법을 개발했다.
(d) 발달에 있어 유년기의 중요성에 대해 배웠다.

지텔프 치트키

질문의 키워드 Switzerland가 그대로 언급된 주변 내용을 주의 깊게 읽는다.

해설 | 3단락의 'Fröbel went to Switzerland to study ~ that early childhood was crucial to human development'에서 프뢰벨은 페스탈로치의 가르침을 받기 위해 스위스로 갔고, 페스탈로치는 그에게 유아기가 인적 발달에 중대하다는 것을 가르쳤다고 했다. 따라서 (d)가 정답이다.

Paraphrasing

early childhood was crucial to human development 유아기가 인적 발달에 중대하다 → the importance of childhood in development 발달에 있어 유년기의 중요성

오답분석

(a) 3단락에서 프뢰벨이 스위스로 떠나기 전에 프랑크푸르트에서 안톤 그루너가 운영하는 학교의 교직을 수락했다고 했으므로 오답이다.

(b) 3단락에서 페스탈로치가 영세민들의 지지자였다고 했으므로 오답이다.

어휘 | teaching method phr. 교수법

56 특정세부사항 What

난이도 ●●○

What did Fröbel contribute to early childhood education in Germany?

(a) kindergartens modeled after institutes in other countries
(b) books about the importance of religion in schools
(c) playthings to aid in the education of young learners
(d) language classes for a complete education

프뢰벨이 독일의 유아 교육에 이바지한 것은 무엇이었는가?

(a) 다른 나라의 기관을 본떠 만든 유치원
(b) 학교에서 종교의 중요성에 관한 책
(c) 어린 학습자들의 교육에 도움이 되는 장난감
(d) 완벽한 교육을 위한 어학 수업

지텔프 치트키

질문의 키워드 early childhood education in Germany와 관련된 주변 내용을 주의 깊게 읽는다.

해설 | 프뢰벨이 독일로 돌아와 한 일들을 설명하는 4단락의 'It was here that he developed the educational toys he called "Fröbel Gifts."'에서 프뢰벨 은물이라고 부르는 교육용 완구를 개발한 곳이 독일이었다고 한 뒤, 'These were ~ designed to encourage children's exploration of the world through play.'에서 이것들은 놀이를 통한 아이들의 세상 탐험을 장려하기 위해 고안된 물건들이었다고 했다. 따라서 (c)가 정답이다.

Paraphrasing

educational toys 교육용 완구 → playthings to aid in the education 교육에 도움이 되는 장난감

오답분석

(a) 4단락에서 프뢰벨이 독일에서 유치원을 열었다고는 했지만, 다른 나라의 기관을 본떠서 만든 것은 아니므로 오답이다.

57 추론 특정사실

난이도 ●●●

What can probably be said about Fröbel's later life?

(a) He failed to get his books published because of Karl von Raumer.
(b) He never got to see the reestablishment of kindergartens.
(c) He used kindergartens to spread unconventional theories.
(d) He personally helped establish kindergartens in Europe.

프뢰벨의 노년에 대해 무엇이 말해질 수 있는 것 같은가?

(a) 카를 폰 라우머 때문에 그의 책이 출간되게 하는 데 실패했다.
(b) 유치원의 재건을 다시는 보지 못했다.
(c) 유치원을 이용해 관습에 얽매이지 않는 이론을 퍼트렸다.
(d) 유럽에서 유치원을 설립하는 것을 직접 도왔다.

지텔프 치트키

질문의 키워드 later life와 관련된 지문의 후반을 주의 깊게 읽는다.

해설 | 5단락의 'Kindergartens were eventually allowed to reopen in 1860, eight years after Fröebel's death.'에서 프뢰벨의 사후 8년 만인 1860년에 유치원이 다시 문을 열도록 허용되었다고 한 것을 통해, 노년에 프뢰벨은 유치원의 재건을 다시는 보지 못했을 것임을 추론할 수 있다. 따라서 (b)가 정답이다.

어휘 | reestablishment n. 재건 unconventional adj. 관습에 얽매이지 않는, 자유로운

58 어휘 유의어

난이도 ●●○

In the context of the passage, flourished means ______.	지문의 문맥에서, 'flourished'는 -을 의미한다.
(a) thrived	**(a) 번성했다**
(b) swelled	(b) 증가되었다
(c) glowed	(c) 빛을 냈다
(d) resurrected	(d) 되살아났다

지텔프 치트키

밑줄 친 어휘의 유의어를 찾는 문제이므로, flourished가 포함된 구절을 읽고 문맥을 파악한다.

해설 | 4단락의 'This school flourished'는 학교가 번성했다는 뜻이므로, flourished가 '번성했다'라는 의미로 사용된 것을 알 수 있다. 따라서 '번성했다'라는 같은 의미의 (a) thrived가 정답이다.

59 어휘 유의어

난이도 ●○○

In the context of the passage, notion means ______.	지문의 문맥에서, 'notion'은 -을 의미한다.
(a) principle	(a) 원칙
(b) fact	(b) 사실
(c) idea	**(c) 개념**
(d) faith	(d) 신뢰

지텔프 치트키

밑줄 친 어휘의 유의어를 찾는 문제이므로, notion이 포함된 구절을 읽고 문맥을 파악한다.

해설 | 5단락의 'they undermined the traditional notion'은 유치원들이 전통적인 개념을 약화시켰다는 뜻이므로, notion이 '개념'이라는 의미로 사용된 것을 알 수 있다. 따라서 '개념'이라는 같은 의미의 (c) idea가 정답이다.

PART 2(60~66) Magazine Article 화물선 에버 기븐호 좌초 사고

기사 제목	[60]*EVER GIVEN* **BLOCKAGE DISRUPTS GLOBAL SUPPLY CHAIN**	[60]**에버 기븐호 봉쇄 상태가 세계 공급망에 지장을 주다**
	In March 2021, the 400-meter-long, 200,000-ton	2021년 3월에, 400미터 길이의 20만 톤 화물선인

사건 소개

container ship *Ever Given* became wedged in the Suez Canal, [60]blocking all traffic and causing a global supply chain crisis. The vessel was stuck for six days and is estimated to have prevented $9.6 billion in trade.

사건 발생 장소

Located in Egypt, [65]the Suez Canal is vital to trade between Europe and Asia. It is 193 kilometers long and, despite an expansion having been completed in 2015, it is less than 300 meters wide. This means that it is a single-lane waterway in many parts, and convoys of ships must take turns traveling through the canal.

사건 발생 원인

On the day of the incident, March 23, [61]*Ever Given* was caught in a sandstorm, and strong winds caused it to turn sideways and go aground in the banks of the canal. As a consequence, three hundred sixty-nine ships were blocked on either side. Since up to $3 billion in cargo passes through the canal daily, there were immediate concerns about the effect the obstruction would have on global trade. While many ships docked in nearby areas or remained in place, [62]some shipping companies opted to divert their ships around the Cape of Good Hope in South Africa, a route that can set shipping schedules back by two weeks or longer.

해결 과정

In the immediate wake of *Ever Given* getting stuck, Egyptian, Dutch, and Italian rescue teams worked to free the ship. [63]The first step was to lighten the vessel, so fuel and nine tons of ballast water were drained from the tanks. At the time, *Ever Given* was carrying 18,000 shipping containers, but removing them would have been time-consuming and could have damaged the ship. Meanwhile, approximately 20,000 tons of sand and silt were dug out, and tugboats worked to pull the ship free. Finally, in the early hours of March 29, it was dislodged. [66]Cargo traffic resumed a few hours later.

시사점 + 향후 과제

The incident exposed just how fragile the global supply chain actually is and how much of an effect a single accident could have. It also revealed how necessary it is to improve existing infrastructure. [64]The Egyptian government has since announced plans to widen the narrowest parts of the canal by a further 40 meters.

에버 기븐호가 수에즈 운하에 박혀서 꼼짝하지 못했으며, [60]모든 운항을 막아 세계 공급망의 위기를 야기했다. 그 선박은 6일 동안 갇혀 있었고 96억 달러의 무역을 막았던 것으로 추정된다.

이집트에 있는 [65]수에즈 운하는 유럽과 아시아의 교역에 매우 중요하다. 이것의 길이는 193킬로미터이며, 2015년에 완료된 확장에도 불구하고, 너비는 300미터가 되지 않는다. 이는 그것이 대부분 편도 수로이며, 선박의 호송대들이 반드시 교대로 그 운하를 통과해야 함을 의미한다.

사고 당일인 3월 23일에, [61]에버 기븐호는 모래 폭풍을 만났고, 강한 바람은 그것이 옆으로 돌아 그 운하의 제방에 좌초하도록 야기했다. 결과적으로, 369개의 선박들이 양쪽에서 막혔다. 최대 30억 달러 규모의 화물이 그 운하를 매일 통과하기 때문에, 그 장애물이 세계 무역에 끼칠 영향에 대한 당면한 염려가 있었다. 대부분의 선박들은 인근 지역의 부두에 대거나 제자리에 남아 있었지만, [62]일부 운송 회사들은 남아프리카의 희망봉 주변으로 그들의 선박을 우회시키기로 선택했는데, 이는 해운 일정을 2주 혹은 그 이상 지연시킬 수 있는 노선이었다.

에버 기븐호가 갇히게 된 직후, 이집트, 네덜란드, 그리고 이탈리아의 구조대가 그 선박을 빼내기 위해 작업했다. [63]첫 번째 조치는 그 선박을 가볍게 하는 것이었으며, 따라서 탱크에서 연료와 9톤의 선박평형수가 배출되었다. 그 당시에, 에버 기븐호가 만 8천 개의 선적 컨테이너를 운반하고 있기는 했지만, 그것들을 제거하는 것은 시간 소모가 컸고 그 선박을 손상할 수 있었다. 그동안에, 대략 2만 톤의 모래와 토사가 파내어졌고, 예인선들이 그 선박을 끌어당겨 빼내기 위해 작동했다. 마침내, 3월 29일 이른 시간에, 그것은 제거되었다. [66]화물 수송은 몇 시간 후에 재개되었다.

그 사고는 세계 공급망이 실제로 얼마나 허술한지 그리고 단 하나의 사고가 얼마나 큰 영향을 줄 수 있는지를 그대로 드러냈다. 이것은 기존의 기반 시설을 향상시키는 것이 얼마나 필요한지도 드러냈다. [64]이집트 정부는 그 후 그 운하의 가장 좁은 부분을 추가적인 40미터만큼 확장할 계획을 발표했다.

어휘 | blockage n. 봉쇄, 방해 disrupt v. 지장을 주다, 방해하다 supply chain phr. 공급망 wedged adj. 박혀서 꼼짝하지 못하는 canal n. 운하 block v. 막다 crisis n. 위기 vessel n. 선박 estimate v. 추정하다 prevent v. 막다 expansion n. 확장 convoy n. 호송대 incident n. 사고 be caught in phr. ~을 만나다 sandstorm n. 모래 폭풍 sideways adv. 옆으로 go aground phr. 좌초하다 bank n. 제방, 둑 cargo n. 화물 immediate adj. 당면한, 즉각적인 obstruction n. 장애물, 방해 dock v. 부두에 대다 in place phr. 제자리에 opt v. 선택하다 divert v. 우회시키다 set back phr. 지연시키다 in the wake of phr. ~의 후에, ~에 뒤이어 stuck adj. 갇힌 rescue n. 구조 free v. 빼내다 lighten v. 가볍게 하다 ballast water phr. 선박평형수 drain v. 배출하다 time-consuming adj. 시간 소모가 큰 silt n. 토사 dig out phr. ~을 파내다 tugboat n. 예인선 dislodge v. 제거하다, 제자리에서 벗어나다 fragile adj. 허술한 infrastructure n. 기반 시설 widen v. 확장하다

60 주제/목적 기사의 주제

난이도 ●●○

What is the article all about?

(a) a shipping disaster that caused long-term environmental disruption
(b) a method of handling an emergency involving the supply chain
(c) a construction failure of the world's largest supply chain
(d) an incident that temporarily impacted global trade

기사의 주제는 무엇인가?

(a) 장기적인 환경 파괴를 야기했던 선박 참사
(b) 공급망과 관련된 위기 상황을 다루는 방법
(c) 세계의 가장 큰 공급망 구축의 실패
(d) 일시적으로 세계 무역에 영향을 준 사고

지텔프 치트키

제목과 지문의 초반을 주의 깊게 읽고 전체 맥락을 파악한다.

해설 | 기사의 제목 '*Ever Given* blockage disrupts global supply chain'에서 에버 기븐호의 봉쇄 상태가 세계 공급망에 지장을 준다고 언급하였다. 그다음에, 1단락의 'blocking all traffic and causing a global supply chain crisis'에서 에버 기븐호가 모든 운항을 막아 세계 공급망의 위기를 야기했다고 설명하고, 'The vessel was stuck for six days'에서 선박이 6일 동안 갇혀 있었다고 한 뒤, 사고에 관한 세부 내용이 이어지고 있다. 따라서 (d)가 정답이다.

Paraphrasing
crisis 위기 → incident 사고
for six days 6일 동안 → temporarily 일시적으로

오답분석
(a) 지문에 환경 파괴에 관한 내용은 언급되지 않았으므로 오답이다.
(b) 지문 전반에 걸쳐 공급망과 관련된 위기 상황에 관해 이야기하고 있으나, 그러한 상황을 다루는 방법에 대해서는 언급되어 있지 않으므로 오답이다.

어휘 | environmental disruption phr. 환경 파괴 handle v. 다루다, 처리하다 construction n. 구축 temporarily adv. 일시적으로 impact v. 영향을 주다

61 특정세부사항 Why

난이도 ●●○

Based on the article, why did *Ever Given* run aground in the Suez Canal?

(a) because it exceeded weight limits for ships on the canal
(b) because it went off course due to extreme weather conditions
(c) because it was obstructed by hundreds of other ships
(d) because it was accidentally steered sideways by the ship's crew

기사에 따르면, 에버 기븐호는 수에즈 운하에서 왜 좌초하였는가?

(a) 운하에서의 선박 중량 제한을 초과했기 때문에
(b) 극한의 기상 조건으로 인해 항로를 이탈했기 때문에
(c) 수백 개의 다른 선박들에 의해 가로막혔기 때문에
(d) 그 선박의 선원에 의해 잘못하여 옆으로 조종되었기 때문에

지텔프 치트키

질문의 키워드 run aground가 go aground로 paraphrasing되어 언급된 주변 내용을 주의 깊게 읽는다.

해설 | 3단락의 '*Ever Given* was caught in a sandstorm, and strong winds caused it to turn sideways and go aground in the banks of the canal'에서 에버 기븐호가 만난 모래 폭풍의 강한 바람이 에버 기븐호가 옆으로 돌아 수에즈 운하의 제방에 좌초하도록 야기했다고 했다. 따라서 (b)가 정답이다.

Paraphrasing

a sandstorm, and strong winds 모래 폭풍과 강한 바람 → extreme weather conditions 극한의 기상 조건
turn sideways 옆으로 돌다 → went off course 항로를 이탈했다

오답분석

(c) 3단락에서 369개의 선박들이 양쪽에서 막혔다고는 했지만, 이것은 에버 기븐호 좌초의 원인이 아니라 결과이므로 오답이다.
(d) 3단락에서 에버 기븐호가 모래 폭풍과 강한 바람 때문에 옆으로 돌았다고 했으며, 선원이 잘못 조종한 것이 원인은 아니므로 오답이다.

어휘 | exceed v. 초과하다 go off course phr. 항로를 이탈하다 extreme adj. 극한의, 극도의 obstruct v. 가로막다
accidentally adv. 잘못하여, 우연히 steer v. 조종하다, 움직이다

62 추론 특정사실

난이도 ●●●

Why most likely did some shipping companies send their ships on a different route?

(a) They were directed to deliver goods to South Africa.
(b) They expected the canal to be closed for more than two weeks.
(c) They hoped to make their deliveries ahead of schedule.
(d) They were given extra time to transport their goods.

일부 운송 회사들은 그들의 선박을 왜 다른 노선으로 보낸 것 같은가?

(a) 남아프리카에 화물을 운반하라는 지시를 받았다.
(b) 그 운하가 2주 넘게 닫혀 있을 것이라고 예상했다.
(c) 예정보다 빨리 배달하기를 희망했다.
(d) 화물을 운송할 추가적인 시간이 주어졌다.

지텔프 치트키

질문의 키워드 some shipping companies가 그대로 언급된 주변 내용을 주의 깊게 읽는다.

해설 | 3단락의 'some shipping companies opted to divert their ships around ~ a route that can set shipping schedules back by two weeks or longer'에서 해운 일정을 2주 혹은 그 이상 지연시킬 수 있는 노선이었음에도 일부 운송 회사들은 남아프리카의 희망봉 주변으로 그들의 선박을 우회시키기로 선택했다고 한 것을 통해, 그 회사들은 운하가 2주 넘게 닫혀 있을 것이라고 예상했던 것임을 추론할 수 있다. 따라서 (b)가 정답이다.

63 특정세부사항 How

난이도 ●●○

How was weight removed from *Ever Given*?

(a) through unloading all the cargo
(b) through damaging a section of the ship
(c) through emptying a significant amount of liquid
(d) through evacuating the on-board personnel

에버 기븐호에서 무게가 어떻게 제거되었는가?

(a) 모든 화물을 내림으로써
(b) 그 선박의 일부분을 손상시킴으로써
(c) 상당한 양의 액체를 비움으로써
(d) 선상의 직원들을 대피시킴으로써

지텔프 치트키

질문의 키워드 weight removed가 lighten으로 paraphrasing되어 언급된 주변 내용을 주의 깊게 읽는다.

해설 | 4단락의 'The first step was to lighten the vessel, so fuel and nine tons of ballast water were drained from the tanks.'에서 에버 기븐호를 가볍게 하기 위해 탱크에서 연료와 9톤의 선박평형수가 배출되었다고 했다. 따라서 (c)가 정답이다.

Paraphrasing

fuel and nine tons of ballast water were drained 연료와 9톤의 선박평형수가 배출되었다 → emptying a significant amount of liquid 상당한 양의 액체를 비우는

어휘 | unload v. 내리다 empty v. 비우다 significant adj. 상당한 evacuate v. 대피시키다 on-board adj. 선상의 personnel n. 직원들

64 특정세부사항 What

난이도 ●●○

What is the government of Egypt expected to do in the near future?

(a) It will restrict the size of cargo ships allowed on the canal.
(b) It will launch an investigation into the steering mechanism error.
(c) It will expand the waterway in several specific locations.
(d) It will decrease the overall amount of traffic in the canal.

이집트 정부는 가까운 미래에 무엇을 할 것으로 예상되는가?

(a) 운하에 허용되는 화물선의 크기를 제한할 것이다.
(b) 조종 장치 오류에 관한 조사를 시작할 것이다.
(c) 몇몇 특정한 곳의 수로를 확장할 것이다.
(d) 운하의 전반적인 교통량을 감소시킬 것이다.

지텔프 치트키

질문의 키워드 government of Egypt가 Egyptian government로 paraphrasing되어 언급된 주변 내용을 주의 깊게 읽는다.

해설 | 5단락의 'The Egyptian government ~ widen the narrowest parts of the canal by a further 40 meters.'에서 이집트 정부가 수에즈 운하의 가장 좁은 부분을 추가적인 40미터만큼 확장할 것이라고 했다. 따라서 (c)가 정답이다.

Paraphrasing
widen ~ the canal 운하를 확장하다 → expand the waterway 수로를 확장하다

어휘 | restrict v. 제한하다 investigation n. 조사 steering mechanism phr. 조종 장치 expand v. 확장하다

65 어휘 유의어

난이도 ●●○

In the context of the passage, vital means _______.

(a) essential
(b) standard
(c) decisive
(d) public

지문의 문맥에서, 'vital'은 -을 의미한다.

(a) 매우 중요한
(b) 일반적인
(c) 결정적인
(d) 공공의

지텔프 치트키

밑줄 친 어휘의 유의어를 찾는 문제이므로, vital이 포함된 구절을 읽고 문맥을 파악한다.

해설 | 2단락의 'the Suez Canal is vital to trade between Europe and Asia'는 수에즈 운하가 유럽과 아시아의 교역에 매우 중요하다는 뜻이므로, vital이 '매우 중요한'이라는 의미로 사용된 것을 알 수 있다. 따라서 '매우 중요한'이라는 같은 의미의 (a) essential이 정답이다.

66 어휘 유의어 난이도 ●○○

In the context of the passage, resumed means _______.

(a) arrived
(b) attained
(c) reunited
(d) continued

지문의 문맥에서, 'resumed'는 -을 의미한다.

(a) 배달되었다
(b) 도달했다
(c) 재결합했다
(d) 재개되었다

지텔프 치트키

밑줄 친 어휘의 유의어를 찾는 문제이므로, resumed가 포함된 구절을 읽고 문맥을 파악한다.

해설 | 4단락의 'Cargo traffic resumed a few hours later.'는 화물 수송이 몇 시간 후에 재개되었다는 뜻이므로, resumed가 '재개되었다'라는 의미로 사용된 것을 알 수 있다. 따라서 '재개되었다'라는 같은 의미의 (d) continued가 정답이다.

PART 3[67~73] Encyclopedia Article 마인크래프트의 기원 및 특징

표제어

MINECRAFT

정의

[67]*Minecraft* is a critically acclaimed video game developed by the Swedish company Mojang Studios. With over 238 million copies sold, *Minecraft* currently holds the record of being the best-selling computer game of all time.

게임 제작 과정

The programmer who created *Minecraft*, Markus Persson, worked on the prototype in his spare time while employed at a software company. In 2009, he released the initial version of *Minecraft*. The game attracted so much attention that [68]Persson quit his job the following year to form his own business, Mojang Studios. Over the next five years, *Minecraft* achieved great success due to its innovative gameplay.

게임의 독특한 특징

Minecraft is a sandbox game, meaning that there are no set goals or victory conditions. In addition, [69/72]starting a new game triggers the creation of a generated 3D world—one that is randomized based on a computer algorithm unlike any other. This gives players a great deal of freedom. There is no right way to play *Minecraft*, which encourages the use of imagination and creativity.

게임의 스토리 요소

As the name suggests, one of *Minecraft*'s core gameplay elements is the need to "mine" materials, such as stones, wood, and plants, to "craft" items like tools, clothing, and buildings. Another key aspect is exploration. Scattered throughout each world are

마인크래프트

[67]마인크래프트는 스웨덴 회사인 모장 스튜디오에 의해 개발된 비평가들의 극찬을 받은 비디오 게임이다. 2억 3,800만 장 이상이 팔리면서, 현재 마인크래프트는 역대 가장 많이 팔린 컴퓨터 게임이라는 기록을 보유하고 있다.

마인크래프트를 만든 프로그래머 마르쿠스 페르손은 한 소프트웨어 회사에 고용되어 있었을 때 짬짬이 그 원형 작업을 했다. 2009년에, 그는 마인크래프트의 첫 버전을 출시했다. 그 게임이 정말 많은 관심을 끌어서 [68]페르손은 자신의 회사 모장 스튜디오를 창립하기 위해 그 다음해 직장을 그만두었다. 이후 5년 동안, 마인크래프트는 혁신적인 게임 방식으로 엄청난 성공을 거두었다.

마인크래프트는 샌드박스 게임인데, 이는 정해진 목표나 승리 상황이 없다는 것을 의미한다. 게다가, [69/72]새로운 게임을 시작하는 것은 생성된 3D 세계의 발생을 촉발하는데, 그것은 다른 어떤 것과도 다른 컴퓨터 알고리즘을 기반으로 하여 무작위로 추출된 것이다. 이것은 게임 참가자들에게 많은 자유를 제공한다. 마인크래프트를 하는 데 옳은 방법은 없으며, 이는 상상력과 창의력의 사용을 부추긴다.

이름이 암시하듯이, 마인크래프트의 핵심적인 스토리 요소 중 하나는 공구, 옷, 그리고 건물과 같은 아이템을 '만들기' 위해, 돌, 나무, 그리고 식물과 같은 재료를 '채굴해야' 할 필요성이다. 또 다른 중요한 측면은 탐험이다. 마을, 절, 그리고 다른 주요 지형지물들이 각

	villages, temples, and other landmarks, many of which contain rare items that are difficult to locate elsewhere. Players can also fight monsters, such as zombies and giant spiders, although [70]this option can be turned off by parents to make the game suitable for young children.	세계의 방방곡곡에 흩어져 있으며, 그것들의 대부분이 다른 곳에서는 발견하기 어려운 희귀 아이템들을 포함하고 있다. 게임 참가자들은 좀비와 거대 거미와 같은 괴물과도 싸울 수 있지만, [70]그 게임을 어린아이들에게 적절하게 만들기 위해 이 옵션은 부모에 의해 꺼질 수 있다.
게임의 교육적 이점	The flexibility of *Minecraft* has led many experts to consider it a valuable educational tool. It is commonly used by teachers to provide students with simulated experiences that they might otherwise miss out on. In addition, [71]the British Museum is now recruiting volunteers to construct its entire building in a *Minecraft* world so that students everywhere can explore its exhibits.	마인크래프트의 유연성은 많은 전문가들이 그것을 가치 있는 교육적인 도구로 고려하도록 이끌었다. 학생들에게 다른 상황 아래에서라면 놓칠 수 있는 모의 경험을 제공하기 위해 이것은 교사들에 의해 흔히 사용된다. 게다가, [71]현재 대영 박물관은 모든 곳에 있는 학생들이 그것의 전시회를 답사할 수 있도록 마인크래프트 세계에 그 건물 전체를 건설하기 위해 자원봉사자들을 모집하고 있다.
현황	*Minecraft* will likely continue to attract new users because it is constantly being released on new platforms. [73]It is now available on computers, smartphones, and consoles, and a version of the game for virtual-reality devices is currently in development.	마인크래프트는 계속해서 새로운 이용자들을 끌어들일 가능성이 큰데 이는 그것이 꾸준히 새로운 플랫폼에서 출시되고 있기 때문이다. [73]이것은 지금 컴퓨터, 스마트폰, 그리고 전용 게임 기기에서 이용 가능하며, 가상 현실 기기를 위한 게임 버전도 현재 개발 중이다.

어휘 | critically acclaimed phr. 비평가들의 극찬을 받은 hold a record phr. 기록을 보유하다 prototype n. 원형, 견본
spare adj. 짬이 있는, 여가의 release v. 출시하다 innovative adj. 혁신적인 gameplay n. 게임 방식, 스토리 set adj. 정해진
generate v. 생성하다 randomize v. 무작위로 추출하다 suggest v. 암시하다 core adj. 핵심적인 need n. 필요성
mine v. 채굴하다; n. 광물 material n. 재료 craft v. 만들다; n. 공예 aspect n. 측면 exploration n. 탐험 scatter v. 흩어지게 만들다
landmark n. 주요 지형지물 locate v. 발견하다, 찾아내다 turn off phr. ~을 끄다 suitable adj. 적절한, 알맞은 flexibility n. 유연성
simulated adj. 모의의 miss out on phr. ~을 놓치다 recruit v. 모집하다, 설득하다 construct v. 건설하다 exhibit n. 전시(회)
console n. 전용 게임 기기

67 특정세부사항 What

난이도 ●○○

What is *Minecraft*?	마인크래프트는 무엇인가?
(a) an effective computer sales strategy	(a) 효과적인 컴퓨터 판매 전략
(b) a record-breaking electronic device	(b) 기록을 경신한 전자기기
(c) a digital entertainment product	**(c) 디지털 오락 상품**
(d) a successful video game developer	(d) 성공적인 비디오 게임 개발자

지텔프 치트키

표제어 *Minecraft*의 정의를 설명하는 1단락을 주의 깊게 읽는다.

해설 | 1단락의 '*Minecraft* is a ~ video game developed by the Swedish company Mojang Studios.'에서 마인크래프트는 스웨덴 회사인 모장 스튜디오에 의해 개발된 비디오 게임이라고 했다. 따라서 (c)가 정답이다.

Paraphrasing

a ~ video game 비디오 게임 → a digital entertainment product 디지털 오락 상품

오답분석

(b) 비디오 게임은 전자기기의 범주에 속하지 않으므로 오답이다.

어휘 | strategy n. 전략 record-breaking adj. 기록을 경신한

68 특정세부사항 Why

난이도 ●●○

Why did Markus Persson leave his position in 2010?

(a) He wanted to study programming at university.
(b) He started to run his own software company.
(c) He planned to create a popular video game.
(d) He managed to join an established game studio.

마르쿠스 페르손은 2010년에 왜 그의 직위를 떠났는가?

(a) 대학에서 프로그래밍을 공부하기를 원했다.
(b) 자신의 소프트웨어 회사를 운영하기 시작했다.
(c) 유명한 비디오 게임을 만들 계획이었다.
(d) 인정받는 게임 스튜디오에 간신히 합류했다.

지텔프 치트키

질문의 키워드 leave his position이 quit his job으로 paraphrasing되어 언급된 주변 내용을 주의 깊게 읽는다.

해설 | 2단락의 'Persson quit his job ~ to form his own business, Mojang Studios'에서 페르손이 자신의 회사를 창립하기 위해 직장을 그만두었다고 했다. 따라서 (b)가 정답이다.

Paraphrasing

2010 2010년 → In 2009 ~ the following year 2009년의 그 다음해
form his own business 자신의 회사를 창립하다 → started to run his own ~ company 자신의 회사를 운영하기 시작했다

오답분석

(c) 2단락에서 직장을 그만두기 전에 이미 페르손은 마인크래프트의 첫 버전을 출시했고, 그 게임이 정말 많은 관심을 끌었다고 했으므로 오답이다.

어휘 | established adj. 인정받는, 저명한

69 추론 특정사실

난이도 ●●●

What is probably a benefit of generating a *Minecraft* world?

(a) experiencing a unique playing environment
(b) keeping gameplay exciting with randomized goals
(c) sharing common locations with other users
(d) meeting players from all around the planet

마인크래프트 세계를 생성하는 것의 이점은 무엇일 것 같은가?

(a) 독특한 게임 환경을 경험하는 것
(b) 무작위로 추출된 목표로 스토리를 계속 흥미롭게 하는 것
(c) 다른 이용자들과 공동의 장소를 공유하는 것
(d) 전 세계로부터의 게임 참가자들을 만나는 것

지텔프 치트키

질문의 키워드 generating a *Minecraft* world가 a generated 3D world로 paraphrasing되어 언급된 주변 내용을 주의 깊게 읽는다.

해설 | 3단락의 'starting a new game triggers the creation of a generated 3D world ~ based on a computer algorithm unlike any other'에서 새로운 게임을 시작하는 것이 다른 어떤 것과도 다른 컴퓨터 알고리즘을 기반으로 하여 무작위로 추출된 3D 세계의 발생을 촉발한다고 한 것을 통해, 마인크래프트의 게임 환경이 독특할 것임을 추론할 수 있고, 'This gives players ~ freedom.'에서 이것이 게임 참가자들에게 자유를 제공한다고 한 것을 통해, 독특한 게임 환경이 게임 참가자들에게 이점으로 작용할 것임을 추론할 수 있다. 따라서 (a)가 정답이다.

Paraphrasing

unlike any other 다른 어떤 것과도 다른 → unique 독특한

70 특정세부사항 How

난이도 ●●○

Based on the article, how can parents make *Minecraft* appropriate for younger kids?

(a) by increasing the crafting speed
(b) by reducing the exploration area
(c) by changing an item's rarity
(d) by disabling a game feature

기사에 따르면, 부모들은 어떻게 마인크래프트를 어린아이에게 적절하게 만들 수 있는가?

(a) 공예 속도를 증가시킴으로써
(b) 탐험 지역을 줄임으로써
(c) 아이템의 희귀성을 변경함으로써
(d) 한 게임 기능을 억제함으로써

지텔프 치트키

질문의 키워드 younger kids가 young children으로 paraphrasing되어 언급된 주변 내용을 주의 깊게 읽는다.

해설 | 4단락의 'this option can be turned off by parents to make the game suitable for young children'에서 마인크래프트를 어린아이들에게 적절하게 만들기 위해 부모가 이 옵션(좀비와 거대 거미와 같은 괴물과 싸울 수 있는 옵션)을 끌 수 있다고 했다. 따라서 (d)가 정답이다.

Paraphrasing
appropriate 적절한 → suitable 적절한
this option can be turned off 이 옵션은 꺼질 수 있다 → disabling a game feature 한 게임 기능을 억제하는

어휘 | appropriate adj. 적절한 rarity n. 희귀성 disable v. (기능을) 억제하다, 무력하게 만들다 feature n. 기능, 특징

71 특정세부사항 What

난이도 ●●●

What is the British Museum planning to do for students?

(a) develop an educational version of a program
(b) have a copy of a facility built for virtual tours
(c) include *Minecraft* items in a physical exhibit
(d) hire teachers to show them around a building

대영 박물관이 학생들을 위해 무엇을 계획하고 있는가?

(a) 프로그램의 교육 버전을 개발한다
(b) 가상 투어를 위해 지어진 시설의 복제본을 갖춘다
(c) 실제 전시회에 마인크래프트 아이템을 포함시킨다
(d) 건물을 둘러보도록 안내할 교사들을 고용한다

지텔프 치트키

질문의 키워드 British Museum이 그대로 언급된 주변 내용을 주의 깊게 읽는다.

해설 | 5단락의 'the British Museum ~ construct its entire building in a *Minecraft* world so that students everywhere can explore its exhibits'에서 현재 대영 박물관은 모든 곳에 있는 학생들이 그것의 전시회를 답사할 수 있도록 마인크래프트 세계에 그 건물 전체를 건설하려고 한다고 했다. 따라서 (b)가 정답이다.

어휘 | virtual adj. (컴퓨터를 이용한) 가상의 physical adj. 실제의, 물리적인

72 어휘 유의어

난이도 ●●○

In the context of the passage, triggers means ________.

(a) frightens
(b) admits

지문의 문맥에서, 'triggers'는 -을 의미한다.

(a) 겁먹게 한다
(b) 인정한다

(c) shoots
(d) provokes

(c) 발사한다
(d) 유발한다

지텔프 치트키

밑줄 친 어휘의 유의어를 찾는 문제이므로, triggers가 포함된 구절을 읽고 문맥을 파악한다.

해설 | 3단락의 'starting a new game triggers the creation of a generated 3D world'는 새로운 게임을 시작하는 것이 생성된 3D 세계의 발생을 촉발한다는 뜻이므로, triggers가 '촉발한다'라는 의미로 사용된 것을 알 수 있다. 따라서 '유발한다'라는 비슷한 의미의 (d) provokes가 정답이다.

73 어휘 유의어

난이도 ●●○

In the context of the passage, available means ______.

(a) affordable
(b) exchangeable
(c) accessible
(d) traceable

지문의 문맥에서, 'available'은 -을 의미한다.

(a) 가격이 알맞은
(b) 교환 가능한
(c) 이용 가능한
(d) 추적 가능한

지텔프 치트키

밑줄 친 어휘의 유의어를 찾는 문제이므로, available이 포함된 구절을 읽고 문맥을 파악한다.

해설 | 6단락의 'It is now available on computers, smartphones, and consoles'는 마인크래프트가 지금 컴퓨터, 스마트폰, 그리고 전용 게임 기기에서 이용 가능하다는 뜻이므로, available이 '이용 가능한'이라는 의미로 사용된 것을 알 수 있다. 따라서 '이용 가능한'이라는 같은 의미의 (c) accessible이 정답이다.

PART 4(74~80) Business Letter 주차 문제 해결을 요구하는 편지

수신인 정보

Dave Berry
Lead Contractor
Peak Construction

Dear Mr. Berry:

편지의 목적: 불만 제기

[74]I am writing in regards to the inconvenience caused by the ongoing construction in front of the Pelican Apartments. [75]I received your contact information from an on-site worker named Robert Walsh. He suggested I get in touch with you so that my concerns could be addressed properly.

The issue I would like to bring to your attention is the parking obstruction. [79]It occurs outside regular working

Dave Berry
주 시공사
Peak 건설사

Mr. Berry께:

[74]저는 펠리컨 아파트 앞에서 진행 중인 공사에 의해 야기되는 불편과 관련하여 편지를 씁니다. Robert Walsh라는 이름의 [75]현장 직원에게 당신의 연락처를 받았습니다. 그는 제 걱정이 제대로 해결될 수 있도록 하기 위해서는 당신과 연락해야 한다고 제안했습니다.

제가 당신이 주목했으면 하는 문제는 주차 방해입니다. 이것은 현장에 게시되어 있는 표지판들에 명시된 [79]정규 작업 시간 외에 발생하고 있습니다. 표지판에

불만: 주차 문제

hours, as defined by the signs posted at the site. They say that construction will only last from 8 a.m. to 6 p.m., Monday through Friday.

불만의 원인

For the last week, I've had to park several blocks away when I get home from work at 6:30 p.m. because all the parking spots on my apartment's street are taken up by Peak Construction work vehicles. Not only is parking far away bothersome, but also it is perilous. [76]My fellow neighbors and I are concerned that our cars may be damaged or stolen if left overnight in dark, unfamiliar areas.

해결책 제시

I believe it would be more appropriate if your crew finished their work and vacated the premises by the agreed time. Of course, I understand that the work will sometimes run late. Therefore, [77]I am asking that all work vehicles be moved to another street by 6 p.m. so that residents can park in front of the apartment building.

끝인사 + 요청

[78/80]If this issue is not resolved promptly, I will have no other choice but to inform the Building Department of this violation. You can contact me with your desired course of action by e-mail at sjackson@fastmail.com or by phone at 354-555-0172.

발신인 정보

Respectfully,
Sophia Jackson
Unit 903

는 공사가 월요일에서 금요일까지, 오전 8시에서 오후 6시 사이에만 지속될 것이라고 쓰여 있습니다.

지난주 동안, 오후 6시 30분에 퇴근해서 집에 올 때면 아파트 거리에 있는 모든 주차 공간이 Peak 건설사의 작업 차들로 차지되어 있기 때문에 저는 여러 블록 떨어진 곳에 주차해야 했습니다. 멀리 떨어진 곳에 주차하는 것이 성가실 뿐만 아니라, 아주 위험하기도 합니다. [76]같은 처지에 있는 이웃들과 저는 어둡고, 낯선 지역에 저희 차를 밤새 그대로 둔다면 손상되거나 도난당할 수 있다는 걱정을 하고 있습니다.

당신의 팀이 일을 끝마치고 합의된 시간까지 그 부지를 비우는 것이 더 타당할 것이라고 생각합니다. 물론, 공사가 가끔 늦어질 수 있다는 것은 이해합니다. 그래서, 주민들이 아파트 건물 앞에 주차할 수 있도록 [77]모든 작업 차들은 오후 6시까지 다른 거리로 옮겨져야 한다고 요청하고 있는 것입니다.

[78/80]이 문제가 신속하게 해결되지 않는 경우에, 전 이 위반에 대해 건축 부서에 알릴 수밖에 없습니다. 이메일 sjackson@fastmail.com이나 전화 354-555-0172로 당신이 원하는 행동 방침과 함께 저에게 연락하실 수 있습니다.

Sophia Jackson 드림
903호

어휘 | contractor n. 시공사, 도급업자 construction n. 건설, 공사 in regards to prep. ~에 관해서 inconvenience n. 불편
ongoing adj. 진행 중인 on-site adj. 현장의 get in touch with phr. ~와 연락하다 address v. 해결하다, 다루다
properly adv. 제대로, 적절히 obstruction n. 방해, 가로막음 take up phr. 차지하다 vehicle n. 차(량) bothersome adj. 성가신
perilous adj. 아주 위험한 fellow adj. 같은 처지에 있는, 동료의 appropriate adj. 타당한 vacate v. 비우다, 떠나다
premises n. 부지, 구내 run late phr. 늦어지다 promptly adv. 신속히, 즉시 inform v. 알리다, 통지하다 violation n. 위반, 방해

74 주제/목적 편지의 목적

난이도 ●●○

What is the main purpose of the letter?

(a) to file a lawsuit against an on-site worker
(b) to notify neighbors of the ongoing construction
(c) to raise a complaint about a local disturbance
(d) to ask for the parking lot's contact information

이 편지의 주된 목적은 무엇인가?

(a) 현장 직원을 상대로 소송을 제기하기 위해서
(b) 진행 중인 공사에 대해 이웃들에게 알리기 위해서
(c) 장소에 관한 방해에 대해 불만을 제기하기 위해서
(d) 주차장의 연락 정보를 요청하기 위해서

지텔프 치트키

지문의 초반을 주의 깊게 읽고 전체 맥락을 파악한다.

해설 | 1단락의 'I am writing in regards to the inconvenience ~ in front of the Pelican Apartments.'에서 펠리컨 아파트 앞 공사에 의해 야기된 불편과 관련하여 편지를 쓴다고 한 뒤, 공사 작업 차들로 인한 아파트 주차 공간 문제에 관해 불만을 제기하는 내용이 이어지고 있다. 따라서 (c)가 정답이다.

어휘 | file a lawsuit against phr. ~를 상대로 소송을 제기하다 notify v. 알리다 local adj. 장소에 관한, 지역의 disturbance n. 방해

75 특정세부사항 How

난이도 ●○○

How was Ms. Jackson able to obtain Mr. Berry's contact details?

(a) by asking a neighbor at the Pelican Apartments
(b) by writing to the construction company
(c) by visiting the contractor's office
(d) by talking with a member of his staff

Ms. Jackson은 Mr. Berry의 연락처를 어떻게 얻을 수 있었는가?

(a) 펠리컨 아파트 이웃에게 물어봄으로써
(b) 건설 회사에 편지를 보냄으로써
(c) 시공사 사무소에 방문함으로써
(d) 그의 직원 중 한 명과 이야기함으로써

지텔프 치트키

질문의 키워드 contact details가 contact information으로 paraphrasing되어 언급된 주변 내용을 주의 깊게 읽는다.

해설 | 1단락의 'I received your contact information from an on-site worker'에서 Ms. Jackson은 현장 직원에게 Mr. Berry의 연락처를 받았다고 했다. 따라서 (d)가 정답이다.

Paraphrasing
worker 직원 → staff 직원

76 특정세부사항 What

난이도 ●●○

What is Ms. Jackson's concern about parking far from the apartment?

(a) Resident automobiles are not allowed to park there.
(b) The area might be too congested to park cars.
(c) Resident automobiles may not be safe.
(d) The area is known for criminal activity.

아파트에서 멀리 떨어진 곳에 주차하는 것에 대한 Ms. Jackson의 걱정은 무엇인가?

(a) 거주민 자동차가 그곳에 주차하도록 허용되지 않는다.
(b) 그 지역이 주차하기에 너무 혼잡할 수 있다.
(c) 거주민 자동차가 안전하지 않을 수 있다.
(d) 그 지역이 범죄 활동으로 알려져 있다.

지텔프 치트키

질문의 키워드 far from이 far away로 paraphrasing되어 언급된 주변 내용을 주의 깊게 읽는다.

해설 | 3단락의 'My fellow neighbors and I are concerned that our cars may be damaged or stolen ~ in dark, unfamiliar areas.'에서 같은 처지에 있는 이웃들과 Ms. Jackson은 어둡고 낯선 지역에 그들의 차를 밤새 그대로 둔다면 손상되거나 도난당할 수 있다는 걱정을 하고 있다고 했다. 따라서 (c)가 정답이다.

Paraphrasing
cars 차 → automobiles 자동차
may be damaged or stolen 손상되거나 도난당할 수 있다 → may not be safe 안전하지 않을 수 있다

어휘 | congested adj. 혼잡한 automobile n. 자동차 criminal adj. 범죄의

77 특정세부사항 What

난이도 ●●○

What is Ms. Jackson asking Mr. Berry to do about the parking obstruction?

(a) prohibit the workers from parking on the apartment's street
(b) have the construction team leave by the appointed time
(c) report to the residents currently on the premises
(d) finish the project near the apartment building

Ms. Jackson이 Mr. Berry에게 주차 방해에 관해 요청하고 있는 것은 무엇인가?

(a) 작업자들이 아파트 거리에 주차하는 것을 금지한다
(b) 정해진 시간까지 공사팀이 떠나게 한다
(c) 현재 구내에 있는 주민들에게 보고한다
(d) 아파트 건물 근처의 프로젝트를 끝마친다

지텔프 치트키

질문의 키워드 asking이 그대로 언급된 주변 내용을 주의 깊게 읽는다.

해설 | 4단락의 'I am asking that all work vehicles be moved to another street by 6 p.m.'에서 Ms. Jackson은 Mr. Berry에게 모든 작업 차들이 오후 6시까지 다른 거리로 옮겨져야 한다고 요청하고 있다고 했다. 따라서 (b)가 정답이다.

오답분석

(a) 4단락에서 작업 차들이 공사 시간 동안에는 주차를 하더라도 정해진 시간까지 다른 거리로 옮겨져야 한다고는 했지만, 아파트 거리에 주차하는 것 자체를 금지할 것을 요청한다는 내용은 언급되지 않았으므로 오답이다.

어휘 | prohibit v. 금지하다 appointed adj. 정해진, 약속된

78 추론 특정사실

난이도 ●●○

What will most likely happen if the parking problem is not solved soon?

(a) Ms. Jackson will start coming home at an earlier time.
(b) Ms. Jackson will no longer directly deal with the company.
(c) The work vehicles will be moved to undesirable areas.
(d) The Building Department will contact Ms. Jackson in person.

만약 주차 문제가 곧 해결되지 않는다면 무슨 일이 일어날 것 같은가?

(a) Ms. Jackson이 더 이른 시간에 집에 돌아오기 시작할 것이다.
(b) Ms. Jackson이 더는 그 회사를 직접 상대하지 않을 것이다.
(c) 작업 차들이 원하지 않은 구역으로 이동될 것이다.
(d) 건축 부서가 Ms. Jackson에게 직접 연락할 것이다.

지텔프 치트키

질문의 키워드 solved가 resolved로 paraphrasing되어 언급된 주변 내용을 주의 깊게 읽는다.

해설 | 5단락의 'If this issue is not resolved promptly, I will ~ inform the Building Department of this violation.'에서 주차 문제가 신속하게 해결되지 않는 경우에 Ms. Jackson은 이 위반에 대해 건축 부서에 알릴 수밖에 없다고 한 것을 통해, 주차 문제가 곧 해결되지 않는다면 그녀가 더는 그 건설 회사를 직접 상대하지 않고 건축 부서와 이야기할 것임을 추론할 수 있다. 따라서 (b)가 정답이다.

Paraphrasing

soon 곧 → promptly 신속하게

어휘 | directly adv. 직접 undesirable adj. 원하지 않은, 바람직하지 않은

79 어휘 유의어

난이도 ●●○

In the context of the passage, regular means _______.

(a) normal
(b) rational
(c) exact
(d) steady

지문의 문맥에서, 'regular'는 -을 의미한다.

(a) 정규의
(b) 합리적인
(c) 정확한
(d) 꾸준한

지텔프 치트키

밑줄 친 어휘의 유의어를 찾는 문제이므로, regular가 포함된 구절을 읽고 문맥을 파악한다.

해설 | 2단락의 'It occurs outside regular working hours'는 주차 방해가 정규 작업 시간 외에 발생하고 있다는 뜻이므로, regular가 '정규의'라는 의미로 사용된 것을 알 수 있다. 따라서 '정규의'라는 같은 의미의 (a) normal이 정답이다.

80 어휘 유의어

난이도 ●●○

In the context of the passage, resolved means _______.

(a) promised
(b) approved
(c) settled
(d) received

지문의 문맥에서, 'resolved'는 -을 의미한다.

(a) 약속된
(b) 승인된
(c) 해결된
(d) 받아들여진

지텔프 치트키

밑줄 친 어휘의 유의어를 찾는 문제이므로, resolved가 포함된 구절을 읽고 문맥을 파악한다.

해설 | 5단락의 'If this issue is not resolved promptly'는 문제가 신속하게 해결되지 않는 경우라는 뜻이므로, resolved가 '해결된'이라는 의미로 사용된 것을 알 수 있다. 따라서 '해결된'이라는 같은 의미의 (c) settled가 정답이다.

03회 실전모의고사

문제집 p.20

정답 및 문제 유형 분석표

PART 1		PART 2		PART 3		PART 4	
53	(d) 특정세부사항	60	(b) 추론	67	(a) 특정세부사항	74	(b) 주제/목적
54	(c) 추론	61	(c) 특정세부사항	68	(c) 특정세부사항	75	(a) 특정세부사항
55	(d) 특정세부사항	62	(d) 추론	69	(c) 특정세부사항	76	(c) 특정세부사항
56	(b) Not/True	63	(b) 특정세부사항	70	(b) 추론	77	(d) 특정세부사항
57	(a) 특정세부사항	64	(d) 특정세부사항	71	(d) 특정세부사항	78	(c) 추론
58	(c) 어휘	65	(c) 어휘	72	(c) 어휘	79	(b) 어휘
59	(c) 어휘	66	(b) 어휘	73	(d) 어휘	80	(a) 어휘

취약 유형 분석표

유형	맞힌 개수
주제/목적	/1
특정세부사항	/13
Not/True	/1
추론	/5
어휘	/8
TOTAL	28

PART 1(53~59) Biography Article 석유 거물이라 불리는 존 데이비슨 록펠러

JOHN DAVISON ROCKEFELLER

인물 이름 / 인물 소개

[53]John Davison Rockefeller was an oil tycoon famous for being the wealthiest person in modern history. His net worth in 1937 was over 1.5 percent of the total GDP of the United States at the time.

어린 시절

Rockefeller was born on July 8, 1839, in New York. His father was a salesman who was often away from home due to his involvement in dishonest get-rich-quick schemes. By contrast, his mother had strong moral principles and believed in saving money. At 16, following her lead, Rockefeller began working long hours as a bookkeeper. It was at this job that he first learned how to run a business and negotiate. [54]As he grew into a hard worker and became more disciplined, he began distancing himself from his father.

초기 활동

After learning all he could from the bookkeeping job, [55]Rockefeller founded his first business, a food company called Clark & Rockefeller, with his partner Maurice B. Clark in 1859. It was extremely successful and only prospered more when the Civil War broke out [58]as the demand for food soared. Although Rockefeller did not join the army, he donated money to the Union, supporting Abraham Lincoln and his anti-slavery platform. [55]At the end of the war, he got out of the food business and set his sights on what was then a rising commercial industry: oil.

존 데이비슨 록펠러

[53]존 데이비슨 록펠러는 현대 역사에서 가장 부유한 사람으로 유명한 석유 거물이었다. 1937년에 그의 순자산은 당시 미국 총 GDP의 1.5퍼센트 이상이었다.

록펠러는 1839년 7월 8일에 뉴욕에서 태어났다. 그의 아버지는 부정한 일확천금의 계획에 몰두함으로 인하여 자주 집을 떠나 있던 판매원이었다. 그에 반해, 그의 어머니는 강한 도덕적 원칙을 가지고 있었고 돈을 저축하는 것이 옳다고 생각했다. 16살 때, 그녀의 선례에 따라, 록펠러는 경리 사원으로 오랜 시간 일하기 시작했다. 그가 어떻게 사업을 운영하고 협상해야 하는지를 처음 알게 된 것은 이 직장에서였다. [54]열심히 일하는 사람으로 성장하고 규율을 더 따르게 되면서, 그는 아버지와 거리를 두기 시작했다.

경리 일을 통해 그가 할 수 있는 모든 것을 배운 후, 록펠러는 1859년에 그의 동업자 모리스 B. 클라크와 함께 클라크 앤 록펠러라는 이름의 [55]식품 회사인 그의 첫 사업체를 설립하였다. 그것은 매우 성공적이었고 남북전쟁이 발발했을 때 [58]식량 수요가 급증하면서 비로소 더욱 번창했다. 비록 록펠러가 군대에 입대하지는 않았지만, 그는 에이브러햄 링컨과 그의 노예제 반대 공약을 지지하며 북군에 돈을 기부했다. [55]그 전쟁이 끝났을 때, 그는 식품 사업에서 손을 떼고 당시 부상하고 있던 상업적 산업인 석유를 목표로 삼았다.

주요 활동	Shortly thereafter, Rockefeller and Clark built an oil refinery. 56(a)With the help of several other partners and Rockefeller's shrewd business sense, it thrived. Over the next several years, Rockefeller expanded the business, which later became Standard Oil in 1870. Through Standard Oil, Rockefeller was able to buy out competing companies, and by 1882, 56(d)he had gained control of nearly 90 percent of the US oil market. However, 56(c)Standard Oil engaged in monopolistic practices and was eventually broken up into 34 smaller companies. As Rockefeller remained the primary shareholder of all these companies, 56(b)the dissolution of Standard Oil was to his benefit since the profits from the multiple enterprises were much greater than those of Standard Oil alone.	얼마 지나지 않아, 록펠러와 클라크는 정유 공장을 세웠다. 56(a)여러 다른 동료들의 도움과 록펠러의 통찰력 있는 사업 감각 덕분에, 그것은 번창했다. 향후 몇 년 동안, 록펠러는 사업을 확장했고, 이것은 이후 1870년에 스탠더드 오일이 되었다. 스탠더드 오일을 통해, 록펠러는 경쟁사들을 매수할 수 있었고, 1882년까지, 56(d)그는 미국 석유 시장의 거의 90퍼센트를 장악했다. 하지만, 56(c)스탠더드 오일은 독점적인 관행에 관여했고 결국 34개의 소규모 회사들로 쪼개졌다. 록펠러가 이 모든 회사의 대주주로 남아 있었기 때문에, 56(b)스탠더드 오일의 해체는 그에게 이익이 되었는데 이는 다수의 기업으로부터 얻은 이익이 스탠더드 오일만으로 얻은 이익보다 훨씬 더 컸기 때문이다.
말년 + 죽음	57Rockefeller retired from Standard Oil in 1897 and devoted his attention to charity. Through the Rockefeller Foundation, 59he donated more than $550 million to educational, religious, and scientific establishments with exceeding generosity. He died on May 23, 1937, at the age of 97, and to this day, he is viewed both as a charitable man and as an insatiable enterpriser.	57록펠러는 1897년에 스탠더드 오일에서 은퇴했고 자선 사업에 그의 관심을 쏟았다. 록펠러 재단을 통해, 59그는 대단한 너그러움으로 교육, 종교, 그리고 과학 시설들에 5억 5천만 달러 넘게 기부했다. 그는 1937년 5월 23일에 97세의 나이로 세상을 떠났고, 오늘날까지 그는 자비로운 사람뿐만 아니라 만족할 줄 모르는 사업가로도 평가받고 있다.

어휘 | tycoon n. 거물 net worth phr. 순자산 salesman n. 판매원 involvement n. 몰두, 관여 dishonest adj. 부정한 get-rich-quick adj. 일확천금의 scheme n. 계획, 책략 moral adj. 도덕적인 principle n. 원칙 believe in phr. ~이 옳다고 생각하다 lead n. 선례, 본보기 bookkeeper n. 경리 사원 negotiate v. 협상하다 disciplined adj. 규율을 따르는 distance v. 거리를 두다 prosper v. 번창하다 break out phr. 발발하다 donate v. 기부하다 the Union phr. (남북전쟁 당시의) 북군 platform n. 공약, 정견 set one's sights on phr. ~을 목표로 삼다 oil refinery phr. 정유 공장 shrewd adj. 통찰력 있는 thrive v. 번창하다 expand v. 확장하다 buy out phr. 매수하다 gain control of phr. ~을 장악하다 engage in phr. ~에 관여하다 monopolistic adj. 독점적인 break up phr. 쪼개다, 나누다 shareholder n. 주주 dissolution n. 해체 enterprise n. 기업 retire v. 은퇴하다 devote v. 쏟다 charity n. 자선 사업 establishment n. 시설, 기관 generosity n. 너그러움 charitable adj. 자비로운 insatiable adj. 만족할 줄 모르는

53 특정세부사항 유명한 이유

난이도 ●●○

What is John Davison Rockefeller mostly known for?

(a) establishing the first successful US oil company
(b) creating laws for the modern American oil industry
(c) being the first tycoon in the state of New York
(d) having the largest fortune in recent history

존 데이비슨 록펠러는 무엇으로 주로 알려져 있는가?

(a) 최초의 성공적인 미국 석유 회사를 설립한 것
(b) 현대 미국 석유 산업을 위한 법률을 제정한 것
(c) 뉴욕주의 최초의 거물인 것
(d) 최근 역사에서 가장 많은 재산을 가진 것

지텔프 치트키

질문의 키워드 mostly known for가 famous for로 paraphrasing되어 언급된 주변 내용을 주의 깊게 읽는다.

해설 | 1단락의 'John Davison Rockefeller was ~ famous for being the wealthiest person in modern history.'에서 존 데이비슨 록펠러는 현대 역사에서 가장 부유한 사람으로 유명한 석유 거물이었다고 했다. 따라서 (d)가 정답이다.

Paraphrasing

being the wealthiest 가장 부유한 → having the largest fortune 가장 많은 재산을 가진
in modern history 현대 역사에서 → in recent history 최근 역사에서

오답분석

(c) 1단락에서 록펠러가 석유 거물이었다고는 했지만, 뉴욕주의 최초의 거물인지는 지문에 언급되지 않았으므로 오답이다.

어휘 | fortune n. 재산

54 추론 특정사실 난이도 ●●●

What most likely caused Rockefeller to grow apart from his father?

(a) his book reading habit during his teenage years
(b) his mother's advice to be an honest person
(c) his developing appreciation for working hard
(d) his father's frequent absences due to his unstable job

무엇이 록펠러가 그의 아버지와 사이가 멀어지도록 야기한 것 같은가?

(a) 십대 시절의 독서 습관
(b) 정직한 사람이 되라는 어머니의 충고
(c) 열심히 일하는 것에 대한 발전하는 올바른 인식
(d) 불안정한 직업으로 인한 아버지의 잦은 부재

지텔프 치트키

질문의 키워드 grow apart가 distancing으로 paraphrasing되어 언급된 주변 내용을 주의 깊게 읽는다.

해설 | 2단락의 'As he grew into a hard worker and became more disciplined, he began distancing himself from his father.'에서 록펠러가 열심히 일하는 사람으로 성장하고 규율을 더 따르게 되면서 부정한 일확천금의 계획에 몰두했던 그의 아버지와 거리를 두기 시작했다고 한 것을 통해, 열심히 일하는 것에 대한 록펠러의 발전하는 올바른 인식이 록펠러가 그의 아버지와 사이가 멀어지도록 야기했을 것임을 추론할 수 있다. 따라서 (c)가 정답이다.

오답분석

(b) 2단락에서 록펠러가 강한 도덕적 원칙을 가지고 돈을 저축하는 것이 옳다고 생각했던 그의 어머니의 선례를 따랐다고는 했지만, 어머니가 그에게 정직한 사람이 되라는 충고를 했는지는 지문에 언급되지 않았으므로 오답이다.
(d) 2단락에서 록펠러의 아버지가 자주 집을 떠나 있었다고는 했지만, 아버지의 직업이 불안정했는지는 지문에 언급되지 않았고 아버지의 잦은 부재가 록펠러가 아버지와 거리를 두기 시작한 이유도 아니므로 오답이다.

어휘 | grow apart from phr. ~와 사이가 멀어지다 appreciation n. 올바른 인식 absence n. 부재 unstable adj. 불안정한

55 특정세부사항 When 난이도 ●●○

When did Rockefeller leave his first business?

(a) when Maurice B. Clark came to him with a business idea
(b) before he gave a financial contribution to the Union Army
(c) while he served in the army on the side of Abraham Lincoln
(d) when the Civil War eventually came to a conclusion

록펠러는 언제 그의 첫 번째 사업을 그만두었는가?

(a) 모리스 B. 클라크가 사업 아이디어를 가지고 그에게 왔을 때
(b) 북군에 재정적인 도움을 주기 전에
(c) 에이브러햄 링컨의 편에서 군 복무를 하던 중에
(d) 남북전쟁이 마침내 종결되었을 때

지텔프 치트키

질문의 키워드 leave ~ business가 got out of ~ business로 paraphrasing되어 언급된 주변 내용을 주의 깊게 읽는다.

해설 | 3단락의 'Rockefeller founded his first business, a food company'에서 록펠러가 식품 회사인 그의 첫 사업체를 설립하였다고 한 뒤, 'At the end of the war, he got out of the food business'에서 (남북)전쟁이 끝났을 때 록펠러가 그 식품 사업에서 손을 뗐다고 했다. 따라서 (d)가 정답이다.

Paraphrasing

At the end of the war 그 전쟁이 끝났을 때 → when the Civil War ~ came to a conclusion 남북전쟁이 종결되었을 때

오답분석

(b) 3단락에서 록펠러가 북군에 돈을 기부한 후에 그의 식품 사업에서 손을 뗐다고 했으므로 오답이다.

어휘 | contribution n. 도움, 기여 serve v. 복무하다 come to a conclusion phr. 종결되다

56 Not/True Not 문제

난이도 ●●○

According to the article, which is not true about Rockefeller's oil business?

(a) It flourished with the assistance of a number of associates.
(b) It caused Rockefeller financial distress when it was dissolved.
(c) It pursued anticompetitive business activities.
(d) It controlled the majority of the American oil industry.

기사에 따르면, 록펠러의 석유 사업에 대해 사실이 아닌 것은?

(a) 많은 동료들의 도움으로 번창하였다.
(b) 그것이 해체되었을 때 록펠러에게 재정적인 어려움을 야기했다.
(c) 공정 경쟁을 막는 영업 행위를 추구했다.
(d) 미국 석유 산업의 대부분을 지배했다.

지텔프 치트키

질문의 키워드 oil business가 oil refinery로 paraphrasing되어 언급된 주변 내용을 주의 깊게 읽고, 보기의 키워드와 지문 내용을 대조하며 언급되는 것을 하나씩 소거한다.

해설 | (b)는 4단락의 'the dissolution of Standard Oil was to his benefit'에서 록펠러의 석유 사업인 스탠더드 오일의 해체가 록펠러에게 이익이 되었다고 언급되었으므로 지문의 내용과 일치하지 않는다. 따라서 (b)가 정답이다.

Paraphrasing

the dissolution of Standard Oil 스탠더드 오일의 해체 → it was dissolved 그것이 해체되었다

오답분석

(a) 보기의 키워드 associates가 partners로 paraphrasing되어 언급된 4단락에서 여러 다른 동료들의 도움 덕분에 록펠러의 정유 공장이 번창했다고 언급되었다.
(c) 보기의 키워드 anticompetitive business activities가 monopolistic practices로 paraphrasing되어 언급된 4단락에서 스탠더드 오일이 독점적인 관행에 관여했다고 언급되었다.
(d) 보기의 키워드 controlled the majority가 gained control of nearly 90 percent로 paraphrasing되어 언급된 4단락에서 록펠러가 미국 석유 시장의 거의 90퍼센트를 장악했다고 언급되었다.

어휘 | flourish v. 번창하다 associate n. 동료, 조합원 distress n. 어려움 pursue v. 추구하다
anticompetitive adj. 공정 경쟁을 막는, 경쟁 억제적인 majority n. 대부분

57 특정세부사항 How

난이도 ●○○

How did Rockefeller spend the time during his retirement?

(a) by donating money to certain organizations
(b) by boosting the size of his wealth through oil investments
(c) by returning to school to further his education
(d) by sharing his business methods with other establishments

록펠러는 은퇴 생활 동안의 시간을 어떻게 보냈는가?

(a) 특정 단체들에 돈을 기부함으로써
(b) 석유 투자를 통해 재산 규모를 늘림으로써
(c) 그의 소양을 발전시키기 위해 복학함으로써
(d) 자신의 사업 방식을 다른 기관들과 공유함으로써

지텔프 치트키

질문의 키워드 retirement가 retired로 언급된 주변 내용을 주의 깊게 읽는다.

해설 | 5단락의 'Rockefeller retired ~ and devoted his attention to charity.'에서 록펠러가 은퇴 후 자선 사업에 관심을 쏟았다고 한 뒤, 'Through the Rockefeller Foundation, he donated ~ to educational, religious, and scientific establishments'에서 그가 록펠러 재단을 통해 교육, 종교, 그리고 과학 시설들에 5억 5천만 달러 넘게 기부했다고 했다. 따라서 (a)가 정답이다.

Paraphrasing
educational, religious, and scientific establishments 교육, 종교, 그리고 과학 시설들 → certain organizations 특정 단체들

어휘 | retirement n. 은퇴 생활 boost v. 늘리다, 신장시키다 investment n. 투자 further v. 발전시키다

58 어휘 유의어

난이도 ●●○

In the context of the passage, soared means ______.

(a) changed
(b) soaked
(c) increased
(d) spread

지문의 문맥에서, 'soared'는 -을 의미한다.

(a) 변했다
(b) 잠겼다
(c) 증가했다
(d) 퍼졌다

지텔프 치트키

밑줄 친 어휘의 유의어를 찾는 문제이므로, soared가 포함된 구절을 읽고 문맥을 파악한다.

해설 | 3단락의 'as the demand for food soared'는 식량 수요가 급증했다는 뜻이므로, soared가 '급증했다'라는 의미로 사용된 것을 알 수 있다. 따라서 '증가했다'라는 비슷한 의미의 (c) increased가 정답이다.

59 어휘 유의어

난이도 ●●○

In the context of the passage, exceeding means ______.

(a) touching
(b) admiring
(c) surpassing
(d) stunning

지문의 문맥에서, 'exceeding'은 -을 의미한다.

(a) 감동적인
(b) 감탄하는
(c) 뛰어난
(d) 깜짝 놀랄

지텔프 치트키

밑줄 친 어휘의 유의어를 찾는 문제이므로, exceeding이 포함된 구절을 읽고 문맥을 파악한다.

해설 | 5단락의 'he donated more than $550 million ~ with exceeding generosity'는 록펠러가 대단한 너그러움으로 5억 5천만 달러 넘게 기부했다는 뜻이므로, exceeding이 '대단한'이라는 의미로 사용된 것을 알 수 있다. 따라서 '뛰어난'이라는 비슷한 의미의 (c) surpassing이 정답이다.

PART 2[60~66] Magazine Article 벽화 예술의 특징 및 변천

기사 제목

THE CHANGING FACE OF MURAL ART

기원 + 초기 벽화의 특징

Murals are large-scale paintings made directly on walls or other flat surfaces. They are found all over the world and are considered the earliest type of art. [60]The most ancient murals were discovered inside caves and date back at least 40,000 years to the Upper Paleolithic era, when [65]the most common scenes to be depicted were inspired by everyday activities such as hunting and gathering.

다양한 벽화의 목적

Throughout history, the purpose of murals has varied depending on the culture and the period. Murals portraying the deceased have been found in ancient Egyptian tombs, while murals from the Baroque Period in Europe usually illustrated scenes from the Bible and mythology. These were most often painted on the ceilings of churches or in the homes of affluent patrons. Frequently, the work of artists of this period was not only required to be beautiful but also to symbolize the status and wealth of their clients. [61]Artists sometimes accomplished this by painting their patrons as characters in the mural.

현대 미국 벽화의 특징

In the late 1960s, inspired by [66]the earlier Mexican Mural movement led by Diego Rivera, David Alfaro Siqueiros, and José Clemente Orozco, [62]murals began making their way to the exterior of buildings in America. These artworks were often used to make political or cultural statements about inner-city life. Commissioned murals of the period were usually painted using the fresco method, which involves applying water-soluble paints to wet plaster carefully prepared in advance of the artwork. However, most of the art that ended up on public buildings at the time was done without permission and was carried out quickly, causing some to see murals in cities as a form of gang-related vandalism, now

벽화 예술의 변화하는 모습

벽화는 벽이나 다른 평평한 표면에 직접 그려지는 큰 규모의 그림이다. 그것들은 전 세계에서 발견되며 가장 초기의 예술 유형으로 여겨진다. [60]가장 오래된 벽화는 동굴 안에서 발견되었으며 적어도 4만 년 전 후기 구석기 시대까지 거슬러 올라가는데, 그때는 [65]묘사되는 가장 흔한 장면이 사냥과 채집과 같은 일상적인 활동으로부터 영감을 받았던 때였다.

역사를 통틀어, 벽화의 목적은 문화와 시대에 따라 달라져 왔다. 고인을 묘사한 벽화가 고대 이집트 무덤에서 발견되어 온 반면, 유럽의 바로크 시대 벽화는 성경과 신화의 장면을 주로 묘사했다. 이것들은 대부분 교회의 천장이나 부유한 후원자들의 집에 그려졌다. 흔히, 이 시기 예술가들의 작품은 아름다워야 했을 뿐만 아니라 의뢰인의 신분과 부를 상징해야 했다. [61]화가들은 때때로 벽화에 그들의 후원자들을 등장인물로 그림으로써 이것을 달성했다.

1960년대 후반에, [66]디에고 리베라, 다비드 알파로 시케이로스, 호세 클레멘테 오로스코에 의해 주도된 초기 멕시코 벽화 운동에 영감을 받아, [62]벽화가 미국 건물의 외부로 진출하기 시작했다. 이 예술품들은 종종 도심지의 삶에 대한 정치적 또는 문화적 성명을 하는 데 사용되었다. 이 시기의 의뢰된 벽화는 보통 프레스코 방식을 사용하여 그려졌는데, 이 방식은 예술품 제작에 앞서 정성껏 준비된 아직 마르지 않은 회반죽에 수용성 페인트를 칠하는 것을 수반한다. 그러나, 그 당시 결국 공공건물에 그려진 회화 대부분은 허가 없이 그려졌으며 빠르게 완료되었는데, 이는 일부 사람들이 도시의 벽화를 범죄 조직과 관련된 반달리즘의 한 형태로 보도록 야기했으며, 이것은 현재 '그라피티'라고 불린다.

	referred to as "graffiti."	
발전 + 현황	[63]As time progressed and street art evolved, people began to view it not just as the damaging of public property, but as a cultural representation of modern life. Consequently, programs gradually emerged that gave urban muralists opportunities to showcase their art legally, and today, mural art is part of mainstream culture. [64]Many major cities are seeking out gifted muralists to create unique work that engages residents and visitors and beautifies formerly run-down neighborhoods. In addition, numerous top brands are also employing them to work on promotional campaigns that command attention and leave a mark.	[63]시간이 흐르고 거리 예술이 진화하면서, 사람들은 그것을 단순히 공공건물의 훼손으로서가 아니라, 현대 생활의 문화적 표현으로서 보기 시작했다. 그 결과, 도시 벽화가들이 합법적으로 그들의 예술을 선보일 기회를 주는 프로그램들이 점차 생겨났고, 오늘날, 벽화 예술은 주류 문화의 일부이다. [64]많은 주요 도시들은 주민들과 방문객들을 사로잡고 이전에 황폐했던 동네들을 아름답게 하는 독특한 작품을 만들기 위해 재능 있는 벽화가들을 찾고 있다. 게다가, 수많은 일류 브랜드들도 주의를 끌고 강한 영향을 미치는 홍보 활동을 펼치기 위해 그들을 고용하고 있다.

어휘 | mural adj. 벽화의; n. 벽화 flat adj. 평평한 surface n. 표면 ancient adj. 오래된, 고대의 date back to phr. ~까지 거슬러 올라가다 Upper Paleolithic era phr. 후기 구석기 시대 depict v. 묘사하다 inspire v. 영감을 주다, 고취시키다 gathering n. 채집, 수집 vary v. 달라지다 portray v. 묘사하다, 그리다 the deceased phr. 고인 tomb n. 무덤 illustrate v. 묘사하다 mythology n. 신화 ceiling n. 천장 affluent adj. 부유한 patron n. 후원자, 고객 symbolize v. 상징하다 status n. 신분 wealth n. 부 accomplish v. 달성하다 exterior n. 외부 artwork n. 예술품 statement n. 성명, 진술 inner-city adj. 도심지의 commissioned adj. 의뢰된 water-soluble adj. 수용성의 wet adj. 아직 마르지 않은 plaster n. 회반죽, 석고 반죽 permission n. 허가, 허락 carry out phr. 완료하다, 실행하다 vandalism n. 반달리즘(문화나 예술을 파괴하려는 경향) evolve v. 진화하다 representation n. 표현 muralist n. 벽화가 showcase v. 선보이다 legally adv. 합법적으로 mainstream culture phr. 주류 문화 gifted adj. 재능 있는 engage v. 사로잡다 beautify v. 아름답게 하다 formerly adv. 이전에 run-down adj. 황폐한 employ v. 고용하다 command attention phr. 주의를 끌다, 관심을 받다 leave a mark phr. 강한 영향을 미치다

60 추론 특정사실

난이도 ●●○

What is probably true about individuals during the Upper Paleolithic era?

(a) They migrated all over the world while hunting and gathering.
(b) They painted the earliest known cave murals.
(c) They created murals mostly based on their imaginations.
(d) They lived in caves covered in art for 40,000 years.

후기 구석기 시대 사람들에 대해 사실인 것은 무엇인 것 같은가?

(a) 사냥과 채집을 하면서 전 세계로 이주했다.
(b) 가장 오래된 것으로 알려진 동굴 벽화를 그렸다.
(c) 주로 그들의 상상력을 바탕으로 벽화를 만들었다.
(d) 회화로 뒤덮인 동굴에서 4만 년간 살았다.

지텔프 치트키

질문의 키워드 Upper Paleolithic era가 그대로 언급된 주변 내용을 주의 깊게 읽는다.

해설 | 1단락의 'The most ancient murals were discovered inside caves and date back ~ to the Upper Paleolithic era'에서 가장 오래된 벽화는 동굴 안에서 발견되었으며 후기 구석기 시대까지 거슬러 올라간다고 한 것을 통해, 후기 구석기 시대 사람들이 가장 오래된 것으로 알려진 동굴 벽화를 그렸을 것임을 추론할 수 있다. 따라서 (b)가 정답이다.

Paraphrasing

The most ancient murals 가장 오래된 벽화 → the earliest ~ murals 가장 오래된 벽화

오답분석

(c) 1단락에서 후기 구석기 시대 때 묘사되는 가장 흔한 장면이 사냥과 채집과 같은 일상적인 활동으로부터 영감을 받았다고 했으므로, 오답이다.

어휘 | migrate v. 이주하다 imagination n. 상상력

61 특정세부사항 How

난이도 ●●○

How did Baroque era muralists signify the prominence of their clients?

(a) by painting on ceilings to suggest their elevated status
(b) by artistically depicting the most influential biblical stories
(c) by using their patrons as models for their work
(d) by creating some of the most expensive work to date

바로크 시대의 벽화가들은 어떻게 의뢰인의 명성을 나타냈는가?

(a) 그들의 높은 신분을 시사하기 위해 천장에 그림을 그림으로써
(b) 가장 영향력 있는 성경 이야기를 예술적으로 묘사함으로써
(c) 그들의 작품에 후원자들을 모델로 활용함으로써
(d) 지금까지 가장 비싼 작품 중 일부를 창작함으로써

지텔프 치트키

질문의 키워드 prominence of ~ clients가 status ~ of ~ clients로 paraphrasing되어 언급된 주변 내용을 주의 깊게 읽는다.

해설 | 2단락의 'Artists ~ accomplished this by painting their patrons as characters in the mural.'에서 바로크 시대 예술가들은 벽화에 그들의 후원자들을 등장인물로 그림으로써 이것(의뢰인의 신분과 부를 상징해야 하는 것)을 달성했다고 했다. 따라서 (c)가 정답이다.

Paraphrasing

by painting their patrons as characters in the mural 벽화에 그들의 후원자들을 등장인물로 그림으로써 → by using their patrons as models for their work 그들의 작품에 그들의 후원자들을 모델로 활용함으로써

어휘 | signify v. 나타내다 prominence n. 명성 elevated adj. 높은 influential adj. 영향력 있는 to date phr. 지금까지

62 추론 특정사실

난이도 ●○○

What can probably be said about the majority of late 1960s murals in America?

(a) They paid respects to figures involved in Mexican Muralism.
(b) They were always created by artists using the fresco method.
(c) They often had to be covered with commissioned murals.
(d) They were usually painted on the outside walls of buildings.

1960년대 후반 미국 벽화의 대다수에 대해 무엇이 말해질 수 있는가?

(a) 멕시코 벽화주의와 관련된 인물들에게 경의를 표했다.
(b) 항상 프레스코 기법을 사용하는 예술가들에 의해 만들어졌다.
(c) 종종 의뢰된 벽화로 덮여야 했다.
(d) 보통 건물의 외벽에 그려졌다.

지텔프 치트키

질문의 키워드 late 1960s가 그대로 언급된 주변 내용을 주의 깊게 읽는다.

해설 | 3단락의 'murals began making their way to the exterior of buildings in America'에서 벽화가 미국 건물의 외부로 진출하기 시작했다고 한 것을 통해, 1960년대 후반 미국 벽화의 대다수는 보통 건물의 외벽에 그려졌을 것임을 추론할 수 있다. 따라서 (d)가 정답이다.

오답분석

(a) 3단락에서 1960년대 후반 초기 멕시코 벽화 운동에 영감을 받아 벽화가 미국 건물의 외부로 진출하기 시작했다고는 했지만, 그 당시 미

국 벽화의 대다수가 멕시코 벽화주의와 관련된 인물들에게 경의를 표했다는 내용은 언급되지 않았으므로 오답이다.

어휘 | pay respect to phr. ~에게 경의를 표하다 figure n. 인물

63 특정세부사항 Why

난이도 ●●●

Why were some graffiti artists given a chance to paint legally?

(a) because they volunteered to paint over acts of vandalism
(b) because there was a shift in how their artwork was interpreted
(c) because they began to change their style to showcase their talent
(d) because there were changes made to property laws

왜 몇몇 그라피티 화가들은 합법적으로 그림을 그릴 기회를 받았는가?

(a) 반달리즘의 소행에 덧칠하기를 자원했기 때문에
(b) 그들의 예술품이 해석되는 방식에 변화가 있었기 때문에
(c) 그들의 재능을 선보이기 위해 스타일을 바꾸기 시작했기 때문에
(d) 재산법에 생긴 변화가 있었기 때문에

지텔프 치트키

질문의 키워드 paint legally가 showcase ~ art legally로 paraphrasing되어 언급된 주변 내용을 주의 깊게 읽는다.

해설 | 4단락의 'As time progressed and street art evolved, people began to view it ~ as a cultural representation of modern life.'에서 시간이 흐르고 거리 예술이 진화하면서 사람들은 벽화를 현대 생활의 문화적 표현으로서 보기 시작했다고 했고, 'Consequently, programs gradually ~ gave urban muralists opportunities to showcase their art legally'에서 그 결과 도시 벽화가들이 합법적으로 예술을 선보일 기회를 주는 프로그램들이 점차 생겨났다고 했다. 따라서 (b)가 정답이다.

Paraphrasing
some graffiti artists given a chance 몇몇 그라피티 화가들이 기회를 받은 → gave urban muralists opportunities 도시 벽화가들에게 기회를 주었다

어휘 | paint over phr. ~에 덧칠하다 shift n. 변화 interpret v. 해석하다 property law phr. 재산법

64 특정세부사항 Why

난이도 ●●○

According to the article, why are major cities looking for talented muralists?

(a) to create unique artwork for private residences
(b) to inspire creativity in residents
(c) to attract sponsorship deals from big brands
(d) to improve the look of once-neglected areas

기사에 따르면, 주요 도시들은 왜 재능 있는 벽화가들을 찾고 있는가?

(a) 개인 주거지를 위한 독특한 예술품을 제작하기 위해서
(b) 거주민들의 창의력을 고취시키기 위해서
(c) 대형 브랜드로부터 후원 계약을 유치하기 위해서
(d) 한때 방치된 지역들의 외관을 개선하기 위해서

지텔프 치트키

질문의 키워드 looking for talented muralists가 seeking out gifted muralists로 paraphrasing되어 언급된 주변 내용을 주의 깊게 읽는다.

해설 | 4단락의 'Many major cities are seeking out gifted muralists to create unique work that ~ beautifies formerly run-down neighborhoods.'에서 많은 주요 도시들이 이전에 황폐했던 동네들을 아름답게 하는 독특한 작품을 만들기 위해 재능 있는 벽화가

들을 찾고 있다고 했다. 따라서 (d)가 정답이다.

Paraphrasing

beautifies formerly run-down neighborhoods 이전에 황폐했던 동네들을 아름답게 하다 → improve the look of once-neglected areas 한때 방치된 지역들의 외관을 개선하다

어휘 | private residence phr. 개인 주거지, 관저 sponsorship n. 후원 deal n. 계약, 거래 neglected adj. 방치된

65 어휘 유의어

난이도 ●●○

In the context of the passage, <u>common</u> means _______.

(a) banal
(b) shared
(c) ordinary
(d) exemplary

지문의 문맥에서, 'common'은 -을 의미한다.

(a) 지극히 평범한
(b) 공유되는
(c) 흔한
(d) 모범적인

지텔프 치트키

밑줄 친 어휘의 유의어를 찾는 문제이므로, common이 포함된 구절을 읽고 문맥을 파악한다.

해설 | 1단락의 'the most common scenes to be depicted'는 묘사되는 가장 흔한 장면이라는 뜻이므로, common이 '흔한'이라는 의미로 사용된 것을 알 수 있다. 따라서 '흔한'이라는 같은 의미의 (c) ordinary가 정답이다.

오답분석

(b) '공유되는'이라는 의미의 shared도 common의 사전적 유의어 중 하나이다. 하지만 문맥상 '후기 구석기 시대에 그려진 벽화에서 묘사되는 가장 흔한 장면'이라는 의미가 되어야 적절하므로 common이 '공유되는'이라는 의미가 아닌 '흔한'이라는 의미로 사용된 것을 알 수 있다. 따라서 문맥과 어울리지 않아 오답이다.

66 어휘 유의어

난이도 ●●○

In the context of the passage, <u>led</u> means _______.

(a) planned
(b) headed
(c) begun
(d) spurred

지문의 문맥에서, 'led'는 -을 의미한다.

(a) 계획된
(b) 이끌어진
(c) 시작된
(d) 자극된

지텔프 치트키

밑줄 친 어휘의 유의어를 찾는 문제이므로, led가 포함된 구절을 읽고 문맥을 파악한다.

해설 | 3단락의 'the earlier Mexican Mural movement led by Diego Rivera, David Alfaro Siqueiros, and José Clemente Orozco'는 디에고 리베라, 다비드 알파로 시케이로스, 호세 클레멘테 오로스코에 의해 주도된 초기 멕시코 벽화 운동이라는 뜻이므로, led가 '주도된'이라는 의미로 사용된 것을 알 수 있다. 따라서 '이끌어진'이라는 비슷한 의미의 (b) headed가 정답이다.

표제어	**ALCATRAZ PRISON**	**앨커트래즈 감옥**
정의 + 어원	Alcatraz prison was a maximum-security facility located on Alcatraz Island. [67]This island is a remote rocky outcrop near the mouth of San Francisco Bay in California, which earned it the nickname "The Rock." The name of the island is derived from the word *alcatraces*, which is the Spanish name for the gannet birds that reside on its shores.	앨커트래즈 감옥은 앨커트래즈 섬에 위치한 경비가 가장 삼엄한 시설이었다. [67]이 섬은 캘리포니아의 샌프란시스코만 어귀 근처에 있는 외딴 암석 노두이며, 이는 그것이 '더 록'이라는 별명을 얻게 했다. 섬의 이름은 그 해안가에 서식하는 북양가마우지 새의 스페인어 이름인 '앨커트래즈'에서 유래되었다.
초기 용도	Alcatraz was first acquired by the US government during the Mexican-American War, which lasted from 1846 to 1848. [68]It was originally envisioned as a defensive outpost to guard against future invasions, and it was further fortified to meet that purpose. However, by 1865, it had found use as a temporary detention center for rebellious soldiers. In 1907, it was officially designated as a military prison.	앨커트래즈는 1846년부터 1848년까지 지속된 멕시코-미국 전쟁 동안 미국 정부에 의해 처음으로 획득되었다. [68]그것은 원래 미래의 침략을 막기 위한 방어 전초 기지로 계획되었고, 그 목적에 부합하기 위해 더욱 요새화되었다. 그러나, 1865년까지, 그것은 반란군들을 위한 임시 수용소로 사용되었다. 1907년에, 그것은 공식적으로 군사 감옥으로 지정되었다.
용도 변화	In 1933, the US Department of Justice acquired the facility and modernized it to serve as a federal prison for civilians. It was believed that the island's isolation made the prison inescapable, so it was used for the new wave of criminals that had arisen during Prohibition—the period from 1920 to 1933 when alcohol was illegal in the US. [69]Alcatraz gained a reputation for being a prison of last resort, where those who had caused problems at other penal institutions could be sent.	1933년에, 미국 사법부가 이 시설을 취득하여 민간인을 위한 연방 교도소로 사용되도록 현대화했다. 섬의 고립이 그 감옥을 달아날 수 없는 것으로 만든다고 믿어졌고, 따라서 그것은 1920년부터 1933년까지 미국에서 술이 불법이었던 금주법 시행 동안에 생겨난 범죄자들의 새로운 유입을 위해 사용되었다. [69]앨커트래즈는 다른 교정 시설에서 문제를 일으켰던 사람들이 보내질 수 있는 최후 수단의 감옥이라는 평판을 얻었다.
특징	Although Alcatraz had the capacity to hold 450 convicts in total, [72]fewer than 250 inhabited it at one time, most of them living in sparsely furnished cells. Some of its most notorious inmates included the Chicago mobster Al Capone and convicted murderer Robert Stroud, also known as the "Birdman of Alcatraz."	앨커트래즈는 통틀어 450명의 죄수를 수용할 능력이 있었지만, [72]동시에 250명도 안 되는 죄수들이 이곳에 거주했으며, 그들 대부분은 듬성듬성 가구가 비치된 감방에 살았다. 가장 악명 높은 수감자들 중에는 시카고의 조직폭력배 알 카포네와 '앨커트래즈의 조류학자'로도 알려진 유죄 판결을 받은 살인범 로버트 스트라우드가 포함되어 있었다.
유명 사건	While several of its inmates attempted to escape, none are known to have been successful. In [73]one famous incident in 1962, [70]three escapees managed to get past the prison walls and, using a simple raft, set off from the island's shores. [70]However, what happened next remains a mystery. Their story is popularized in the Clint Eastwood film, *Escape from Alcatraz*.	수감자 중 몇 명이 탈옥을 시도했지만, 성공한 사람은 없는 것으로 알려져 있다. [73]1962년에 있었던 한 유명한 사건에서, [70]세 명의 탈옥자들이 간신히 감옥의 벽을 넘어, 단순한 뗏목을 이용하여 그 섬의 해안에서 출발했다. [70]하지만, 다음에 무슨 일이 일어났는지는 수수께끼로 남아있다. 그들의 이야기는 클린트 이스트우드의 영화 「앨커트래즈 탈출」에서 대중화되었다.
현황	Eventually, [71]with the upkeep proving to be too expensive, Alcatraz was shut down in 1963. The prison and its grounds became part of the newly formed Golden Gate National Recreation Area in 1972, and today Alcatraz is one of San Francisco's most popular tourist destinations.	결국, [71]유지비가 너무 비싸다는 것이 밝혀지면서, 앨커트래즈는 1963년에 폐쇄되었다. 그 감옥과 그것의 구내는 1972년에 새롭게 형성된 골든게이트 국립 휴양지의 일부가 되었고, 오늘날 앨커트래즈는 샌프란시스코의 가장 인기 있는 관광지 중 하나이다.

어휘 | maximum-security adj. 경비가 가장 삼엄한 facility n. 시설 remote adj. 외딴 rocky outcrop phr. 암석 노두 mouth n. 어귀 earn v. 얻게 하다 reside v. 서식하다 shore n. 해안(가) envision v. 계획하다 defensive adj. 방어의, 방어용의 outpost n. 전초 기지 invasion n. 침략 fortify v. 요새화하다 meet v. 부합하다, 충족시키다 temporary adj. 임시의 detention center phr. 수용소 rebellious adj. 반란의, 반역하는 designate v. 지정하다 modernize v. 현대화하다 civilian n. 민간인 isolation n. 고립 inescapable adj. 달아날 수 없는 criminal n. 범죄자 Prohibition n. 금주법 (시대) reputation n. 평판 last resort phr. 최후의 수단 penal institution phr. 교정 시설 capacity n. 능력, 수용력 hold v. 수용하다 convict n. 죄수; v. 유죄 판결을 내리다 sparsely adv. 듬성듬성 furnish v. 가구를 비치하다 notorious adj. 악명 높은 inmate n. 수감자 mobster n. 조직폭력배 murderer n. 살인범 raft n. 뗏목 set off phr. 출발하다 popularize v. 대중화하다 upkeep n. 유지비 shut down phr. 폐쇄하다 tourist destination phr. 관광지

67 특정세부사항 Where

난이도 ●●○

Where did Alcatraz Island get the nickname "The Rock"?

(a) from its geographic features
(b) from its security system
(c) from the dense population of its prison
(d) from its location near a rocky shore

앨커트래즈 섬은 어디에서 '더 록'이라는 별명을 얻었는가?

(a) 지리적 특징으로부터
(b) 보안 시스템으로부터
(c) 그것의 감옥의 밀집된 인구로부터
(d) 암초 해안 근처에 있는 그것의 위치로부터

지텔프 치트키

질문의 키워드 "The Rock"이 그대로 언급된 주변 내용을 주의 깊게 읽는다.

해설 | 1단락의 'This island is a remote rocky outcrop ~, which earned it the nickname "The Rock."'에서 앨커트래즈 섬이 외딴 암석 노두인 것이 그 섬이 '더 록'이라는 별명을 얻게 했다고 했다. 따라서 (a)가 정답이다.

Paraphrasing
rocky outcrop 암석 노두 → geographic features 지리적 특징

오답분석

(d) 1단락에서 앨커트래즈 섬이 캘리포니아의 샌프란시스코만 어귀 근처에 있다고는 했지만, 그곳이 암초 해안인지는 언급되지 않았고 그것의 위치로부터 별명을 얻은 것도 아니므로 오답이다.

어휘 | geographic adj. 지리적인 dense adj. 밀집된

68 특정세부사항 Why

난이도 ●●○

According to the passage, why was Alcatraz initially built?

(a) to keep the country's worst criminals
(b) to detain soldiers who rebelled
(c) to protect against hostile forces
(d) to train new military personnel

지문에 따르면, 앨커트래즈는 당초에 왜 지어졌는가?

(a) 그 나라의 최악의 범죄자들을 가두기 위해서
(b) 반란을 일으킨 군인들을 구금하기 위해서
(c) 적대 세력에 대항하여 보호하기 위해서
(d) 새로운 군 인력을 양성하기 위해서

지텔프 치트키

질문의 키워드 initially built가 originally envisioned로 paraphrasing되어 언급된 주변 내용을 주의 깊게 읽는다.

해설 | 2단락의 'It was originally envisioned as a defensive outpost to guard against future invasions'에서 앨커트래즈는 원래 미래의 침략을 막기 위한 방어 전초 기지로 계획되었다고 했다. 따라서 (c)가 정답이다.

01회 02회 03회 04회 05회 06회 07회 08회 09회 10회

Paraphrasing
to guard against ~ invasions 침략을 막기 위한 → to protect against hostile forces 적대 세력에 대항하여 보호하기 위해서

오답분석
(b) 2단락에서 앨커트래즈가 반란군들을 위한 임시 수용소로 사용되었다고는 했지만, 그것이 원래 앨커트래즈가 지어진 목적은 아니므로 오답이다.

어휘 | detain v. 구금하다, 억류하다 hostile adj. 적대적인 personnel n. 인력

69 특정세부사항 How

난이도 ●●○

How did Alcatraz gain its reputation as one of the ultimate prisons?

(a) by keeping prisoners isolated from each other
(b) by successfully rehabilitating some criminals
(c) by housing difficult inmates from other prisons
(d) by including many modern security features

어떻게 앨커트래즈가 최후의 감옥 중 하나라는 평판을 얻게 되었는가?

(a) 수감자들을 서로로부터 격리시킴으로써
(b) 성공적으로 몇몇 범죄자들을 갱생시킴으로써
(c) 다른 교도소에서 온 다루기 힘든 수감자들을 수용함으로써
(d) 많은 현대적인 보안 기능을 포함함으로써

지텔프 치트키

질문의 키워드 gain ~ reputation이 gained ~ reputation으로 언급된 주변 내용을 주의 깊게 읽는다.

해설 | 3단락의 'Alcatraz gained a reputation for being a prison of last resort, where those who had caused problems at other penal institutions could be sent.'에서 앨커트래즈는 다른 교정 시설에서 문제를 일으켰던 사람들이 보내질 수 있는 최후 수단의 감옥이라는 평판을 얻었다고 했다. 따라서 (c)가 정답이다.

Paraphrasing
one of the ultimate prisons 최후의 감옥 중 하나 → a prison of last resort 최후 수단의 감옥
other penal institutions 다른 교정 시설 → other prisons 다른 교도소

어휘 | rehabilitate v. 갱생시키다, 사회 복귀를 돕다 house v. 수용하다

70 추론 특정사실

난이도 ●●○

What can be inferred about the prisoners depicted in *Escape from Alcatraz*?

(a) They managed to board a passing sea vessel.
(b) They were not recaptured by the authorities.
(c) They returned to the prison due to rough waters.
(d) They were not able to scale the prison's walls.

「앨커트래즈 탈출」에서 묘사된 죄수들에 대해 추론될 수 있는 것은 무엇인가?

(a) 지나가는 해선에 가까스로 승선했다.
(b) 당국에 의해 다시 체포되지 않았다.
(c) 거친 파도로 인해 감옥으로 돌아왔다.
(d) 감옥의 벽을 오를 수 없었다.

지텔프 치트키

질문의 키워드 *Escape from Alcatraz*가 그대로 언급된 주변 내용을 주의 깊게 읽는다.

해설 | 5단락의 'three escapees managed to get past the prison walls'에서 세 명의 탈옥자들이 간신히 감옥의 벽을 넘었다고 한 뒤, 'However, what happened next remains a mystery.'에서 다음에 무슨 일이 일어났는지는 수수께끼로 남아있다고 한 것을 통해, 죄

수들이 탈옥하여 섬을 떠난 이후 당국에 의해 다시 체포되지 않았기 때문에 그들의 행방이 수수께끼일 것임을 추론할 수 있다. 따라서 (b)가 정답이다.

오답분석

(d) 5단락에서 탈옥자들이 감옥의 벽을 넘었다고 했으므로 오답이다.

어휘 | board v. 승선하다 vessel n. 선박 recapture v. 다시 체포하다 authorities n. 당국 rough adj. 거친 scale v. 오르다

71 특정세부사항 What

난이도 ●○○

What led to the closure of Alcatraz?

(a) a national crime reduction
(b) a recreation facility opening
(c) excessive tourist complaints
(d) high maintenance costs

무엇이 앨커트래즈의 폐쇄를 초래했는가?

(a) 국가 범죄 감소
(b) 휴양 시설의 개장
(c) 지나치게 많은 관광객 불평
(d) 높은 유지 비용

지텔프 치트키

질문의 키워드 closure가 shut down으로 paraphrasing되어 언급된 주변 내용을 주의 깊게 읽는다.

해설 | 6단락의 'with the upkeep proving to be too expensive, Alcatraz was shut down in 1963'에서 유지비가 너무 비싸다는 것이 밝혀지면서 앨커트래즈가 폐쇄되었다고 했다. 따라서 (d)가 정답이다.

Paraphrasing

upkeep 유지비 → maintenance costs 유지 비용
expensive 비싼 → high (가격이) 높은

오답분석

(b) 6단락에서 앨커트래즈가 먼저 폐쇄된 후에 그것이 국립 휴양지의 일부가 되었다고 했으므로 오답이다.

어휘 | reduction n. 감소 excessive adj. 지나치게 많은 complaint n. 불평 maintenance n. 유지

72 어휘 유의어

난이도 ●●○

In the context of the passage, inhabited means ______.

(a) inhibited
(b) relocated
(c) occupied
(d) entered

지문의 문맥에서, 'inhabited'는 -을 의미한다.

(a) 억제했다
(b) 재배치했다
(c) 거주했다
(d) 들어갔다

지텔프 치트키

밑줄 친 어휘의 유의어를 찾는 문제이므로, inhabited가 포함된 구절을 읽고 문맥을 파악한다.

해설 | 4단락의 'fewer than 250 inhabited it at one time'은 동시에 250명도 안 되는 죄수들이 앨커트래즈에 거주했다는 뜻이므로, inhabited가 '거주했다'라는 의미로 사용된 것을 알 수 있다. 따라서 '거주했다'라는 같은 의미의 (c) occupied가 정답이다.

73 어휘 유의어

난이도 ●○○

In the context of the passage, incident means ______.

(a) disorder
(b) crisis
(c) example
(d) occasion

지문의 문맥에서, 'incident'는 -을 의미한다.

(a) 무질서
(b) 위기
(c) 예시
(d) 경우

지텔프 치트키

밑줄 친 어휘의 유의어를 찾는 문제이므로, incident가 포함된 구절을 읽고 문맥을 파악한다.

해설 | 5단락의 'one famous incident in 1962'는 1962년에 있었던 한 유명한 사건이라는 뜻이므로, incident가 '사건'이라는 의미로 사용된 것을 알 수 있다. 따라서 '경우'라는 비슷한 의미의 (d) occasion이 정답이다.

PART 4(74~80) Business Letter 요리사로서 입사를 지원하는 편지

수신인 정보

Ms. Alyssa Benoit
Recruitment Manager
Alimentary Concepts
701 Whitelock Boulevard
Tallahassee, FL 21217

Dear Ms. Benoit,

편지의 목적: 입사 지원

[74]I am writing to express an interest in the position of development chef. Alimentary Concepts is a company I have long admired for its leadership in the industry and the many restaurants that it operates.

지원 동기

I am confident that I can make valuable contributions to your firm. Throughout my career, I have maintained a passion for food. [79]I have a particular interest in finding creative ways to combine ingredients, which is why I was selected to be a judge on the hit TV show *Cooking with Fire*.

관련 이력

I have had many opportunities to broaden my skills and experience. After earning a degree in food science from Bayfront University, I worked in the kitchens of various notable chefs, including Alton Flynn, learning to make food to the highest standards. In addition, I was with Celadon Cruises for 12 years. [75]While on board, we had to produce food on a large scale and simultaneously [80]cater to different tastes and food safety guidelines. Most recently, I was a partner in a food truck business called Nourishing Fusion but [76]gave up my stake to move with my family here to Florida.

Ms. Alyssa Benoit
채용 관리자
Alimentary Concepts사
701 화이트록 대로
탤러해시, 플로리다주 21217

Ms. Benoit께,

[74]개발 요리사라는 직책에 관심을 표하고자 편지를 씁니다. Alimentary Concepts사는 업계에서의 리더십과 그것이 운영하는 많은 레스토랑에 대해 제가 오랫동안 존경해 온 회사입니다.

저는 귀사에 가치 있는 기여를 할 수 있다는 것에 자신이 있습니다. 저의 경력 내내, 저는 음식에 대한 열정을 유지해 왔습니다. [79]저는 재료를 조합하는 창의적인 방법을 찾아내는 것에 특별한 관심이 있는데, 이것이 제가 인기 TV 프로그램인 「Cooking with Fire」의 심사위원으로 선발되었던 이유입니다.

저에게는 기술과 경험을 넓힐 수 있는 많은 기회들이 있었습니다. Bayfront 대학에서 식품학 학위를 받은 후, 저는 Alton Flynn을 비롯한 여러 유명 요리사들의 주방에서 일하며 최고 수준의 음식을 만드는 법을 배웠습니다. 덧붙여, 저는 12년 동안 Celadon 크루즈와 함께했습니다. [75]선상에 있으면서 대규모로 음식을 만들어야 함과 동시에 [80]각양각색의 취향과 식품 안전 지침을 충족시켜야 했습니다. 가장 최근에, 저는 Nourishing Fusion이라고 불리는 푸드 트럭 사업의 공동 경영자였지만 [76]이곳 플로리다주로 가족과 함께 이사하기 위해 제 지분을 포기했습니다.

포부	Now, I am seeking employment with Alimentary Concepts, where I want to devote the rest of my career. I am certain [77]I can meet the job's demands for designing cost-effective recipes and menus, staying aware of the latest food and restaurant trends, and adhering to precise specifications.	현재, 저는 Alimentary Concepts사의 일자리를 구하고 있으며, 이곳에서 제 남은 경력을 바치고 싶습니다. [77]비용 효율적인 조리법과 메뉴를 고안하고, 최신의 음식 및 식당 트렌드를 계속 파악하며, 꼼꼼한 내역을 준수하는 것에 대한 직업의 요구를 충족시킬 수 있다고 저는 확신합니다.
끝인사	My résumé is enclosed for your review. [78]I look forward to interviewing online as per the instructions in your advertisement in *Restaurant Outlook* magazine.	귀하의 검토를 위해 제 이력서가 동봉되어 있습니다. [78]「Restaurant Outlook」 잡지에 실린 귀하의 광고에 있는 설명에 따라 온라인으로 면접을 볼 수 있길 기대하고 있겠습니다.
발신인 정보	Sincerely, Kenneth Chen	Kenneth Chen 드림

어휘 | position n. 직책, 직위 admire v. 존경하다 operate v. 운영하다 confident adj. 자신이 있는 contribution n. 기여 maintain v. 유지하다 passion n. 열정 combine v. 조합하다 judge n. 심사위원 broaden v. 넓히다 notable adj. 유명한 standard n. 수준, 기준 on board phr. 선상에서 simultaneously adv. 동시에 cater to phr. ~을 충족시키다 guideline n. 지침 stake n. 지분 seek v. 구하다, 찾다 employment n. 일자리, 고용 devote v. 바치다, 헌신하다 cost-effective adj. 비용 효율적인 recipe n. 조리법 adhere to phr. ~을 준수하다 precise adj. 꼼꼼한 specification n. 내역, 명세 사항 résumé n. 이력서 enclose v. 동봉하다 look forward to phr. ~을 기대하다 instruction n. 설명

74 주제/목적 편지의 목적

난이도 ●○○

Why did Kenneth Chen write to Alyssa Benoit? (a) to voice appreciation for a local chef's food **(b) to apply for employment in the culinary field** (c) to get in touch with the leader of a business (d) to offer restaurant operations consultant services	왜 Kenneth Chen이 Alyssa Benoit에게 편지를 썼는가? (a) 현지 요리사의 음식에 대해 감탄을 표하기 위해서 **(b) 요리 분야에 취업 지원을 하기 위해서** (c) 사업체의 대표와 연락을 취하기 위해서 (d) 레스토랑 운영 상담 서비스를 제안하기 위해서

지텔프 치트키

지문의 초반을 주의 깊게 읽고 전체 맥락을 파악한다.

해설 | 1단락의 'I am writing to express an interest in the position of development chef.'에서 Kenneth Chen이 개발 요리사라는 직책에 관심을 표하고자 편지를 쓴다고 한 뒤, 취업을 지원하는 내용이 이어지고 있다. 따라서 (b)가 정답이다.

어휘 | voice v. 표하다, 나타내다 appreciation n. 감탄 culinary adj. 요리의

75 특정세부사항 What

난이도 ●●○

What did Chen learn when he worked on a cruise? **(a) the skill of producing food in large volumes** (b) the safety measures of ocean liners (c) the business strategies of famous restaurants (d) the value of an educational food background	Chen은 크루즈에서 일했을 때 무엇을 배웠는가? **(a) 대량으로 음식을 만드는 기술** (b) 원양 여객선의 안전 조치 (c) 유명한 레스토랑들의 영업 전략 (d) 교육적인 식품 기초 지식의 가치

지텔프 치트키

질문의 키워드 cruise가 Cruises로 언급된 주변 내용을 주의 깊게 읽는다.

해설 | 3단락의 'While on board, we had to produce food on a large scale'에서 Chen은 Celadon 크루즈 선상에 있으면서 대규모로 음식을 만들어야 했다고 했다. 따라서 (a)가 정답이다.

Paraphrasing
on a large scale 대규모로 → in large volume 대량으로

어휘 | measures n. 조치 ocean liner phr. 원양 여객선 background n. 기초 지식

76 특정세부사항 Why

난이도 ●○○

Why did Chen surrender his share in the food truck business?

(a) because he got into an argument with his partner
(b) because he failed to popularize fusion food in Florida
(c) because he recently moved to a new location
(d) because he wanted to start a solo business

왜 Chen은 푸드 트럭 사업에서의 그의 지분을 포기했는가?

(a) 그의 동업자와 말다툼을 했기 때문에
(b) 플로리다주에서 퓨전 음식을 대중화하는 데 실패했기 때문에
(c) 최근에 새로운 장소로 이사했기 때문에
(d) 단독 사업을 시작하기를 원했기 때문에

지텔프 치트키

질문의 키워드 food truck business가 그대로 언급된 주변 내용을 주의 깊게 읽는다.

해설 | 3단락의 'gave up my stake to move with my family here to Florida'에서 Chen은 플로리다주로 가족과 함께 이사하기 위해 푸드 트럭 사업에서의 자신의 지분을 포기했다고 했다. 따라서 (c)가 정답이다.

Paraphrasing
surrender ~ share 지분을 포기하다 → gave up ~ stake 지분을 포기했다

어휘 | surrender v. 포기하다 argument n. 말다툼 popularize v. 대중화하다 solo adj. 단독의

77 특정세부사항 What

난이도 ●●○

What is one of the requirements for the development chef?

(a) creating a list of unique recipes
(b) interviewing chefs at competing restaurants
(c) meeting arbitrary regulations
(d) developing affordable food items

개발 요리사의 자격 요건 중 하나는 무엇인가?

(a) 유일무이한 조리법 목록을 만드는 것
(b) 경쟁 레스토랑의 요리사들을 인터뷰하는 것
(c) 임의적인 규정을 충족시키는 것
(d) 가격이 알맞은 식품을 개발하는 것

지텔프 치트키

질문의 키워드 requirements가 demands로 paraphrasing되어 언급된 주변 내용을 주의 깊게 읽는다.

해설 | 4단락의 'I can meet the job's demands for designing cost-effective recipes and menus, ~ and adhering to precise specifications'에서 Chen은 비용 효율적인 조리법과 메뉴를 고안하는 것에 대한 직업의 요구를 충족시킬 수 있다고 했다. 따라서 (d)가 정답이다.

Paraphrasing

cost-effective ~ menus 비용 효율적인 메뉴 → affordable food items 가격이 알맞은 식품

오답분석

(c) 4단락에서 개발 요리사는 꼼꼼한 내역을 준수해야 한다고 했으므로 오답이다.

어휘 | arbitrary adj. 임의적인 affordable adj. 가격이 알맞은, 저렴한

78 추론 특정사실

난이도 ●●○

According to the letter, how did Chen probably become aware of the job opening?

(a) He read through a colleague's referral.
(b) He checked an online job board.
(c) He found it in an industry publication.
(d) He was informed at a culinary job fair.

편지에 따르면, Chen은 구인 공고를 어떻게 알게 된 것 같은가?

(a) 동료의 추천서를 통독했다.
(b) 온라인 취업 게시판을 확인했다.
(c) 업계 간행물에서 그것을 발견했다.
(d) 요리 채용 박람회에서 알게 되었다.

지텔프 치트키

질문의 키워드 job opening이 advertisement로 paraphrasing되어 언급된 주변 내용을 주의 깊게 읽는다.

해설 | 5단락의 'I look forward to interviewing online as per the instructions in your advertisement in *Restaurant Outlook* magazine.'에서 「Restaurant Outlook」 잡지에 실린 광고에 있는 설명에 따라 온라인으로 면접을 볼 수 있기를 기대하고 있겠다고 한 것을 통해, Chen이 업계 간행물인 해당 잡지에서 구인 공고를 알게 되었을 것임을 추론할 수 있다. 따라서 (c)가 정답이다.

Paraphrasing

Restaurant Outlook magazine 「Restaurant Outlook」 잡지 → an industry publication 업계 간행물

어휘 | colleague n. 동료 referral n. 추천서 publication n. 간행물 job fair phr. 채용 박람회

79 어휘 유의어

난이도 ●●○

In the context of the passage, particular means ________.

(a) great
(b) specific
(c) profound
(d) relevant

지문의 문맥에서, 'particular'는 -을 의미한다.

(a) 많은
(b) 특별한
(c) 깊은
(d) 적절한

지텔프 치트키

밑줄 친 어휘의 유의어를 찾는 문제이므로, particular가 포함된 구절을 읽고 문맥을 파악한다.

해설 | 2단락의 'I have a particular interest in finding creative ways to combine ingredients'는 재료를 조합하는 창의적인 방법을 찾아내는 것에 특별한 관심이 있다는 뜻이므로, particular가 '특별한'이라는 의미로 사용된 것을 알 수 있다. 따라서 '특별한'이라는 같은 의미의 (b) specific이 정답이다.

80 어휘 유의어

난이도 ●●○

In the context of the passage, tastes means ________.

(a) likings
(b) cravings
(c) savors
(d) traits

지문의 문맥에서, 'tastes'는 -을 의미한다.

(a) 취향
(b) 갈망
(c) 맛
(d) 특성

지텔프 치트키

밑줄 친 어휘의 유의어를 찾는 문제이므로, tastes가 포함된 구절을 읽고 문맥을 파악한다.

해설 | 3단락의 'cater to different tastes and food safety guidelines'는 각양각색의 취향과 식품 안전 지침을 충족시킨다는 뜻이므로, tastes가 '취향'이라는 의미로 사용된 것을 알 수 있다. 따라서 '취향'이라는 같은 의미의 (a) likings가 정답이다.

오답분석

(c) '맛'이라는 의미의 savor도 taste의 사전적 유의어 중 하나이다. 하지만 문맥상 '각양각색의 취향을 충족시킨다'라는 의미가 되어야 적절하므로 taste가 '맛'이 아닌 '취향'이라는 의미로 사용된 것을 알 수 있다. 따라서 문맥상 적절하지 않아 오답이다.

04회 실전모의고사

문제집 p.28

정답 및 문제 유형 분석표

PART 1		PART 2		PART 3		PART 4	
53	(c) 특정세부사항	60	(b) 특정세부사항	67	(d) 추론	74	(c) 주제/목적
54	(b) 특정세부사항	61	(c) Not/True	68	(d) 특정세부사항	75	(d) 특정세부사항
55	(d) 추론	62	(a) 특정세부사항	69	(b) Not/True	76	(a) 특정세부사항
56	(a) 추론	63	(c) 특정세부사항	70	(c) 특정세부사항	77	(a) 추론
57	(c) 특정세부사항	64	(b) 특정세부사항	71	(c) 특정세부사항	78	(b) 특정세부사항
58	(b) 어휘	65	(d) 어휘	72	(a) 어휘	79	(d) 어휘
59	(d) 어휘	66	(a) 어휘	73	(b) 어휘	80	(c) 어휘

취약 유형 분석표

유형	맞힌 개수
주제/목적	/1
특정세부사항	/13
Not/True	/2
추론	/4
어휘	/8
TOTAL	28

PART 1(53~59) Biography Article 유명한 만화 캐릭터 대피 덕

표제어

DAFFY DUCK

캐릭터 소개

Daffy Duck is one of the main characters of two animated series, *Looney Tunes* and *Merrie Melodies*. Produced by Warner Bros., both series had half-hour-long episodes and involved talking cartoon animals in comedic situations. [53]On account of the significant impact both shows had on American pop culture, Daffy Duck has been called one of the greatest cartoon characters of all time.

첫 등장 + 인기 요인

Daffy Duck was created by animators Bob Clampett and Tex Avery. The character was first introduced to audiences in 1937's *Porky's Duck Hunt* as a black-feathered duck with a ring of white feathers around his neck. [54]He was intended to be a secondary character hunted by the main character Porky Pig, but he quickly became a fan favorite due to his assertive, combative, and unrestrained personality. Hopping around wildly as he yelled "Woo-hoo," Daffy Duck [58]left an impression on juvenile viewers, who were unused to seeing characters behave this way.

One of Daffy Duck's most characteristic features is his lisp—a speech defect resulting in the letters "s" and "z" being pronounced like "th"—but [55]this was hardly apparent in the early cartoons he appeared in. There

대피 덕

대피 덕은 두 개의 만화 영화 시리즈 「루니 툰」과 「메리 멜로디즈」의 주요 등장인물들 중 하나이다. 워너 브라더스사에 의해 제작된 두 시리즈 모두 30분 길이의 에피소드를 가지고 있었고 희극적인 상황에서의 말하는 만화 동물들을 포함했다. [53]두 프로그램이 미국 대중문화에 미쳤던 상당한 영향력 때문에, 대피 덕은 역대 가장 유명한 만화 캐릭터들 중 하나로 일컬어져 왔다.

대피 덕은 만화 영화 제작자인 밥 크램펫과 텍스 에이버리에 의해 만들어졌다. 이 캐릭터는 1937년 「포키의 오리 사냥」에서 목 주위에 고리 모양의 흰 깃털을 두른 검은 깃털 오리로 시청자들에게 처음 소개되었다. [54]그것은 주인공인 포키 피그에 의해 사냥당하는 보조 캐릭터가 될 계획이었으나, 그것의 자신감이 넘치고, 투지가 왕성하며, 제멋대로인 성격 덕분에 빠르게 팬들이 가장 좋아하는 캐릭터가 되었다. 미친 듯이 '야호'라고 소리 지르며 이리저리 돌아다니는 대피 덕은 이런 방식으로 행동하는 캐릭터를 보는 것에 익숙하지 않은 [58]어린 시청자들에게 인상을 남겼다.

대피 덕의 가장 독특한 특징 중 하나는 알파벳 's'와 'z'가 'th'처럼 발음되게 하는 언어 능력 결함인 혀짤배기소리인데, [55]이것은 그것이 출연했던 초기의 만화 영화에서는 거의 뚜렷하지 않았다. 그 혀짤배기소리의 기원에 관해 약간의 논쟁이 있다. 가장 흔하게 전

독특한 특징

is some debate about the origin of the lisp. The most commonly told story is that it was based on the voice of the studio's founder, Leon Schlesinger, who actually had a lisp. However, [56]Mel Blanc, who portrayed Daffy Duck for 52 years, said the lisp was simply something he thought a long-billed duck would have. In any case, as Daffy Duck's personality became more defined, [59]the lisp would become markedly pronounced and used for comedic effect.

출연 작품 + 근황

Daffy Duck starred in about 130 short films, [57]with his popularity peaking in the 1950s and 1960s when he was paired with his friend and occasional rival Bugs Bunny. Following the end of *Looney Tunes* in 1969, Daffy Duck would make appearances in various cartoon compilations released by Warner Bros., and was used in major films such as the 1988 Disney movie *Who Framed Roger Rabbit*. More recently, in 2021, he appeared in *Space Jam: A New Legacy* and was voiced by Eric Bauza. Although Daffy Duck appears far less frequently than in the past, he lives on in the memories of generations of children who grew up watching his antics.

해지는 이야기는 이것이 그 영화사의 창립자 리온 슐레진저의 목소리에 바탕을 두고 있다는 것인데, 그는 실제로 혀짤배기소리가 있었다. 하지만, [56]대피 덕을 52년 동안 그린 멜 블랭크가 말하길 혀짤배기소리는 그가 생각했을 때 부리가 긴 오리가 가지고 있을 수 있는 것일 뿐이었다. 어쨌든, 대피 덕의 성격이 더욱 분명해지면서, [59]혀짤배기소리는 두드러지게 발음되며 희극적인 효과로 사용되었다.

[57]대피 덕이 그것의 친구이자 때때로 경쟁자였던 벅스 버니와 짝을 이뤘던 1950년대와 1960년대에 인기가 절정에 다다르면서, 약 130편의 단편 영화에 주연을 맡았다. 1969년 「루니 툰」의 종영에 이어, 대피 덕은 워너 브라더스사에 의해 공개된 다양한 만화 영화 모음집에 모습을 드러내곤 했으며, 1988년 디즈니 영화 「누가 로저 래빗을 모함했나」와 같은 주요 영화에 사용되었다. 더 최근인 2021년에는, 「스페이스 잼: 새로운 시대」에 등장했고 목소리 연기는 에릭 바우사가 맡았다. 대피 덕이 과거에 비해 훨씬 덜 자주 등장하지만, 그것의 익살스러운 행동을 보며 성장했던 아이들 세대의 기억 속에서 계속 존재한다.

어휘 | animated adj. 만화 영화의 comedic adj. 희극적인 on account of phr. ~ 때문에 significant adj. 상당한, 중요한 impact n. 영향력 pop culture phr. 대중문화 audience n. 시청자, 청중 feathered adj. ~한 깃털을 가진 secondary adj. 보조의 assertive adj. 자신감이 넘치는 combative adj. 투지가 왕성한 unrestrained adj. 제멋대로의, 거리낌이 없는 personality n. 성격, 인물 hop v. 돌아다니다 wildly adv. 미친 듯이 yell v. 소리 지르다 impression n. 인상 unused adj. 익숙하지 않은 behave v. 행동하다 characteristic adj. 독특한; n. 특징 feature n. 특징 lisp n. 혀짤배기소리 defect n. 결함, 장애 pronounce v. 발음하다 hardly adv. 거의 ~않다 apparent adj. 뚜렷한 debate n. 논쟁 origin n. 기원 portray v. 그리다 long-billed adj. 부리가 긴 in any case phr. 어쨌든 defined adj. 분명한, 정의된 effect n. 효과 star v. 주연을 맡다 popularity n. 인기 peak v. 절정에 다다르다 pair v. 짝을 이루다 occasional adj. 때때로의 compilation n. 모음집, 편집 live on phr. 계속 존재하다 generation n. 세대 antics n. 익살스러운 행동

53 특정세부사항 유명한 이유

난이도 ●●○

Why is Daffy Duck such a celebrated animated personality?

(a) He is credited with being the first talking cartoon character.
(b) He influenced the development of half-hour-long TV shows.
(c) He was part of culturally important TV programs.
(d) He helped Warner Bros. become a successful company.

왜 대피 덕은 아주 유명한 만화 영화 인물인가?

(a) 최초의 말하는 만화 캐릭터로 인정받는다.
(b) 30분짜리 텔레비전 프로그램의 발전에 영향을 미쳤다.
(c) 문화적으로 중요한 텔레비전 프로그램의 일부였다.
(d) 워너 브라더스사가 성공적인 회사가 되는 것을 도왔다.

지텔프 치트키

질문의 키워드 celebrated가 greatest로 paraphrasing되어 언급된 주변 내용을 주의 깊게 읽는다.

해설 | 1단락의 'On account of the significant impact ~ on American pop culture, Daffy Duck has been called one of the greatest cartoon characters of all time.'에서 대피 덕이 주요 등장인물로 등장한 두 프로그램이 미국 대중문화에 미쳤던 상당한 영향력 때문에 그것이 역대 가장 유명한 만화 캐릭터들 중 하나로 일컬어져 왔다고 했다. 따라서 (c)가 정답이다.

Paraphrasing
significant impact ~ on ~ pop culture 대중문화에 미친 상당한 영향력 → culturally important 문화적으로 중요한
shows 프로그램 → TV programs 텔레비전 프로그램

어휘 | celebrated adj. 유명한 credit v. 인정하다 influence v. 영향을 미치다 development n. 발전

54 특정세부사항 What

난이도 ●●○

What made Daffy Duck more beloved than originally anticipated?

(a) his strange manner of speaking
(b) his out-of-control behavior
(c) his funny catchphrase
(d) his startling appearance

무엇이 대피 덕을 원래 예상했던 것보다 더 사랑받게 했는가?

(a) 독특하게 말하는 방식
(b) 통제 불능의 행동
(c) 재미있는 캐치프레이즈
(d) 특이한 외모

지텔프 치트키

질문의 키워드 beloved가 fan favorite로 paraphrasing되어 언급된 주변 내용을 주의 깊게 읽는다.

해설 | 2단락의 'He was intended to be a secondary character ~, but he quickly became a fan favorite due to his ~ unrestrained personality.'에서 대피 덕은 보조 캐릭터가 될 계획이었으나 그것의 제멋대로인 성격 덕분에 팬들이 가장 좋아하는 캐릭터가 되었다고 했다. 따라서 (b)가 정답이다.

Paraphrasing
unrestrained personality 제멋대로인 성격 → out-of-control behavior 통제 불능의 행동

오답분석

(a) 3단락에서 대피 덕이 혀짧배기소리를 내는 독특한 말하기 방식을 가지고 있다고는 언급했지만, 이것 때문에 그것이 원래 예상했던 것보다 더 사랑받았다고 한 것은 아니므로 오답이다.

어휘 | beloved adj. 사랑받는, 인기 많은 originally adv. 원래 anticipate v. 예상하다 out-of-control adj. 통제 불능의 catchphrase n. 캐치프레이즈(타인의 주의를 끌기 위해 내세우는 기발한 문구) startling adj. 특이한, 깜짝 놀랄 appearance n. 외모

55 추론 특정사실

난이도 ●●●

What can probably be said about Daffy Duck's characteristics?

(a) His appearance evolved a lot over the years.
(b) His pronunciation was meant to mimic Porky Pig's.
(c) He was initially unpopular with viewers.
(d) He did not have a distinct lisp in *Porky's Duck Hunt.*

대피 덕의 특징에 대해 무엇이 말해질 수 있는 것 같은가?

(a) 그것의 외모는 시간이 지나면서 많이 발전했다.
(b) 그것의 발음은 포키 피그의 발음을 흉내 내려고 의도된 것이었다.
(c) 처음에는 시청자들에게 인기가 없었다.
(d) 「포키의 오리 사냥」에서 뚜렷한 혀짧배기소리를 내지 않았다.

지텔프 치트키

질문의 키워드 characteristics가 characteristic features로 paraphrasing되어 언급된 주변 내용을 주의 깊게 읽는다.

해설 | 3단락의 'this was hardly apparent in the early cartoons he appeared in'에서 혀짤배기소리는 대피 덕이 출연했던 초기의 만화 영화에서는 거의 뚜렷하지 않았다고 한 것을 통해, 대피 덕이 시청자들에게 처음 소개되었던 「포키의 오리 사냥」에서는 뚜렷한 혀짤배기소리를 내지 않았을 것임을 추론할 수 있다. 따라서 (d)가 정답이다.

어휘 | evolve v. 발전하다 mimic v. 흉내 내다 initially adv. 처음에 distinct adj. 뚜렷한, 분명한

56 추론 특정사실

난이도 ●●○

According to Mel Blanc, why most likely did Daffy Duck speak with a lisp?

(a) because a long bill would cause the speech impediment
(b) because he used his natural voice when playing Daffy Duck
(c) because the animators wanted to make Daffy Duck hard to understand
(d) because the size of Daffy Duck's bill increased over time

멜 블랭크에 따르면, 왜 대피 덕은 혀짤배기소리를 냈을 것 같은가?

(a) 긴 부리가 그 언어 장애를 초래했을 것이기 때문에
(b) 대피 덕을 연기할 때 자기 본연의 목소리를 사용했기 때문에
(c) 만화 영화 제작자들이 대피 덕을 이해하기 어렵게 만들기를 원했기 때문에
(d) 대피 덕의 부리 크기가 시간이 지나면서 커졌기 때문에

지텔프 치트키

질문의 키워드 Mel Blanc가 그대로 언급된 주변 내용을 주의 깊게 읽는다.

해설 | 3단락의 'Mel Blanc ~ said the lisp was simply something ~ a long-billed duck would have'에서 언어 사용 결함인 혀짤배기소리는 멜 블랭크가 생각했을 때 부리가 긴 오리가 가지고 있을 수 있는 것일 뿐이라고 한 것을 통해, 멜 블랭크는 대피 덕의 긴 부리가 언어 장애를 초래한다고 생각했을 것임을 추론할 수 있다. 따라서 (a)가 정답이다.

어휘 | speech impediment phr. 언어 장애

57 특정세부사항 When

난이도 ●○○

When did Daffy Duck reach the height of his popularity?

(a) when he began appearing in full-length films
(b) when *Looney Tunes* was taken off the air
(c) when he appeared with Bugs Bunny
(d) when Eric Bauza began providing his voice

대피 덕은 언제 인기의 절정에 도달했는가?

(a) 장편 영화에 등장하기 시작했을 때
(b) 「루니 툰」이 방송되지 않았을 때
(c) 벅스 버니와 함께 나타났을 때
(d) 에릭 바우사가 목소리를 제공하기 시작했을 때

지텔프 치트키

질문의 키워드 height of ~ popularity가 popularity peaking으로 paraphrasing되어 언급된 주변 내용을 주의 깊게 읽는다.

해설 | 4단락의 'with his popularity peaking ~ when he was paired with his friend and occasional rival Bugs Bunny'에서 대피 덕은 벅스 버니와 짝을 이뤘던 1950년대와 1960년대에 인기가 절정에 다다랐다고 했다. 따라서 (c)가 정답이다.

Paraphrasing
he was paired with ~ Bugs Bunny 벅스 버니와 짝을 이뤘다 → he appeared with Bugs Bunny 벅스 버니와 함께 나타났다

어휘 | height n. 절정, 높이 full-length adj. 장편의 off the air phr. 방송되지 않는

58 어휘 유의어

난이도 ●●○

In the context of the passage, juvenile means ______.

(a) mature
(b) young
(c) chief
(d) childish

지문의 문맥에서, 'juvenile'은 -을 의미한다.

(a) 어른스러운
(b) 어린
(c) 주요한
(d) 유치한

지텔프 치트키

밑줄 친 어휘의 유의어를 찾는 문제이므로, juvenile이 포함된 구절을 읽고 문맥을 파악한다.

해설 | 2단락의 'left an impression on juvenile viewers'는 어린 시청자들에게 인상을 남겼다는 뜻이므로, juvenile이 '어린'이라는 의미로 사용된 것을 알 수 있다. 따라서 '어린'이라는 같은 의미의 (b) young이 정답이다.

오답분석

(d) '유치한'이라는 의미의 childish도 juvenile의 사전적 유의어 중 하나이지만, '유치한 시청자들'은 문맥에 어울리지 않으므로 오답이다.

59 어휘 유의어

난이도 ●●○

In the context of the passage, markedly means ______.

(a) delicately
(b) unbelievably
(c) discreetly
(d) noticeably

지문의 문맥에서, 'markedly'는 을 의미한다.

(a) 우아하게
(b) 믿기 힘들 정도로
(c) 사려 깊게
(d) 두드러지게

지텔프 치트키

밑줄 친 어휘의 유의어를 찾는 문제이므로, markedly가 포함된 구절을 읽고 문맥을 파악한다.

해설 | 3단락의 'the lisp would become markedly pronounced'는 혀짤배기소리가 두드러지게 발음된다는 뜻이므로, markedly가 '두드러지게'라는 의미로 사용된 것을 알 수 있다. 따라서 '두드러지게'라는 같은 의미의 (d) noticeably가 정답이다.

연구 결과

[60]HAVING SOMEONE TO LISTEN TO MAY PREVENT COGNITIVE DECLINE

연구 소개

A recent study published in *JAMA Network Open* suggests that [60]having a strong social support system composed of people who listen to us helps keep the brain in good condition and protect it against age-related cognitive decline.

연구 대상 + 연구 방식

The study, led by Dr. Joel Salinas, involved more than 2,000 participants with an average age of 63, all of whom were surveyed on how they viewed the availability of emotional support in their life. [65]This included factors such as whether [61(b)]they had love and affection, [61(a)]contact with friends and family, [61(d)]good listeners around them, and [61(c)]access to advice.

실험 결과

Following the survey, the participants underwent MRI scans to gauge their total brain volume. [62]This was done to determine their cognitive resilience, which is the ability of the brain to act as a buffer against disease and remain healthy with age. It was found that participants with fewer people in their lives who listened to them when they needed to talk had a lower brain volume and lower cognitive capabilities. In fact, the brains of these individuals appeared to be four years older than those of individuals with friends or relatives who listened to them.

시사점

This ultimately suggests that feeling acknowledged as we get older can improve our cognitive resilience and help slow down or prevent Alzheimer's disease and other types of cognitive impairment. The researchers theorize that this could be because it is stimulating to talk to another person and that stimulation boosts neuroplasticity. [63]A boost to neuroplasticity establishes new pathways among the nerve cells in the brain, making it easier for the brain to continue functioning well as time passes.

의의

Given that cognitive decline associated with aging lowers the quality of all aspects of life, the findings of the study are important because [64]they imply that [66]people can address their cognitive resilience before it is too late. By finding someone to listen to us, we may be able to provide our brain with the protection needed to live a fulfilling life into old age.

[60]들어줄 누군가가 있는 것은 인지력 저하를 막을 수 있다

「자마 네트워크 오픈」에 게재된 최근의 연구는 [60]우리의 말을 들어주는 사람들로 이루어진 강력한 사회적 지원 체계를 가지는 것이 뇌를 좋은 상태로 유지하고 뇌를 나이에 따른 인지력 저하로부터 지키는 것을 도와준다고 제시한다.

조엘 살리나스 박사에 의해 진행된 이 연구는 평균 나이가 63세인 2,000명이 넘는 참가자들을 포함했으며, 이들은 모두 그들의 삶에서 정서적 지지의 효용을 어떻게 바라보는지에 대한 설문 조사에 참여했다. 이것은 [61(b)]그들이 사랑과 보살핌을 받고 있는지, [61(a)]친구 및 가족들과 연락하고 지내는지, [61(d)]주변에 좋은 청자들이 있는지, 그리고 [61(c)]조언에 접근할 기회가 있는지와 같은 [65]요소들을 포함했다.

설문 조사 이후, 참가자들은 뇌의 총 용량을 측정하는 MRI 검사를 받았다. [62]이것은 그들의 인지적 회복력을 알아내기 위해 행해졌는데, 이는 질병에 대해 완충 역할을 하고 나이가 들어도 건강을 유지하는 뇌의 능력이다. 자신이 이야기하고 싶을 때 들어주는 사람이 삶에서 더 적은 참가자들은 더 작은 뇌 용량과 더 낮은 인지 능력을 가진 것으로 밝혀졌다. 사실, 이러한 사람들의 뇌는 그들의 말을 들어준 친구나 친척이 있었던 사람들의 뇌에 비해 4년 더 노화한 것으로 나타났다.

이것은 궁극적으로 우리가 늙어감에 따라 인정받는 감정이 인지적 회복력을 향상시킬 수 있고 알츠하이머병이나 다른 종류의 인지 장애들을 늦추거나 막는 데 도움을 줄 수 있다는 것을 시사한다. 연구원들은 다른 사람에게 이야기를 하는 것이 자극이 되고 그 자극이 신경 가소성을 높이기 때문일 수 있다고 이론화한다. [63]신경 가소성의 증가는 뇌 신경 세포들 사이의 새로운 경로를 확립하고, 시간이 지남에 따라 뇌가 계속해서 잘 기능하기 쉽게 만든다.

노화와 관련된 인지력 저하가 삶의 모든 측면에서 질을 낮추는 것을 고려하면, 이 연구 결과들은 중요한데 이는 [64]그것들이 [66]사람들이 너무 늦기 전에 자신의 인지적 회복력을 다룰 수 있음을 의미하기 때문이다. 우리의 이야기를 들어주는 누군가를 찾음으로써, 우리가 노후에 성취감을 주는 삶을 사는 데 필요한 보호를 뇌에 제공할 수 있을 것이다.

어휘 | prevent v. 막다 cognitive adj. 인지력의, 인지의 decline n. 저하, 감퇴 support n. 지원, 지지 condition n. 상태 age-related adj. 나이에 따른, 나이와 관련된 participant n. 참가자 survey v. 설문 조사하다; n. 설문 조사 availability n. 효용, 유용성 emotional adj. 정서적인 affection n. 보살핌, 애정 access n. 접근 advice n. 조언, 충고 undergo v. 받다, 겪다

gauge v. 측정하다 volume n. 용량 determine v. 알아내다 resilience n. 회복력 buffer n. 완충 capability n. 능력
relative n. 친척 ultimately adv. 궁극적으로 acknowledged adj. 인정받는 slow down phr. 늦추다 impairment n. 장애
theorize v. 이론화하다 stimulating adj. 자극이 되는 stimulation n. 자극 boost v. 높이다; n. 증가
neuroplasticity n. 신경 가소성(뇌의 적응 및 재구성 능력) establish v. 확립하다, 규명하다 pathway n. 경로 nerve cell phr. 신경 세포
function v. 기능하다 aspect n. 측면 finding n. 결과 imply v. 의미하다, 암시하다 protection n. 보호 fulfilling adj. 성취감을 주는

60 특정세부사항 연구의 결과

난이도 ●●○

What did the study find out about cognitive decline?

(a) that it damages a person's ability to hear
(b) that it can be averted with social ties
(c) that it normally inflicts sociable individuals
(d) that it can be slowed by listening more to others

연구는 인지력 저하에 대해 무엇을 알아냈는가?

(a) 사람의 청력을 손상한다는 것
(b) 사회적 유대 관계로 방지될 수 있다는 것
(c) 보통 사교적인 사람들에게 고통을 준다는 것
(d) 다른 사람들에게 더 귀를 기울이면서 늦춰질 수 있다는 것

지텔프 치트키

연구의 결과를 언급하는 제목과 지문의 초반을 주의 깊게 읽는다.

해설 | 기사의 제목 'Having someone to listen to may prevent cognitive decline'에서 들어줄 누군가가 있는 것이 인지력 저하를 막을 수 있다고 한 뒤, 1단락의 'having a strong social support system ~ protect it against age-related cognitive decline'에서 우리의 말을 들어주는 사람들로 이루어진 강력한 사회적 지원 체계를 가지고 있는 것이 뇌를 나이에 따른 인지력 저하로부터 지킨다고 했다. 따라서 (b)가 정답이다.

Paraphrasing
social support system 사회적 지원 체계 → social ties 사회적 유대 관계

어휘 | avert v. 방지하다 ties n. 유대 관계 inflict v. 고통을 주다 sociable adj. 사교적인

61 Not/True Not 문제

난이도 ●●●

What were the participants in the study not asked about?

(a) whether they had communication with loved ones
(b) whether there were people who cared about them
(c) whether they were willing to take advice from others
(d) whether there were people who listened to them

연구의 참가자들이 질문받은 것이 아닌 것은?

(a) 가족과 의사소통을 했는지
(b) 그들에게 관심을 가지는 사람이 있었는지
(c) 다른 사람들의 조언을 기꺼이 받아들였는지
(d) 그들의 말을 들어주는 사람이 있었는지

지텔프 치트키

질문의 키워드 asked가 surveyed로 paraphrasing되어 언급된 주변 내용을 주의 깊게 읽고, 보기의 키워드와 지문 내용을 대조하며 언급되는 것을 하나씩 소거한다.

해설 | (c)는 보기의 키워드 advice가 그대로 언급된 2단락의 'access to advice'에서 조언에 접근할 기회가 있는지를 묻는 내용이 설문 조사에 포함되었다고 했지만, 참가자들이 다른 사람들의 조언을 기꺼이 받아들였는지를 물은 것은 아니므로 지문의 내용과 일치하지 않는다. 따라서 (c)가 정답이다.

오답분석

(a) 보기의 키워드 communication이 contact로 paraphrasing되어 언급된 2단락에서 가족들과 연락하고 지내는지를 물어봤다고 언급되었다.

01회 02회 03회 04회 05회 06회 07회 08회 09회 10회

(b) 보기의 키워드 cared가 had love and affection으로 paraphrasing되어 언급된 2단락에서 사랑과 보살핌을 받고 있는지를 물어봤다고 언급되었다.
(d) 보기의 키워드 people who listened to them이 listeners로 paraphrasing되어 언급된 2단락에서 주변에 좋은 청자들이 있는지를 물어봤다고 언급되었다.

어휘 | loved one phr. 가족, 연인 care about phr. ~에 관심을 가지다, 마음을 쓰다 be willing to phr. 기꺼이 ~하다

62 특정세부사항 Why

난이도 ●●○

Why did the researchers measure the brain volume of the participants?

(a) to determine the ability of their brains to resist disease
(b) to identify the condition of their memories
(c) to see the impact of brain volume on the aging process
(d) to correlate the size of the brain to an individual's intelligence

왜 연구원들은 참가자들의 뇌 용량을 측정했는가?

(a) 질병에 저항하는 뇌의 능력을 알아내기 위해서
(b) 그들의 기억 상태를 알아보기 위해서
(c) 노화 과정에 미치는 뇌 용량의 영향을 파악하기 위해서
(d) 사람의 지능과 뇌 크기의 연관성을 보여주기 위해서

지텔프 치트키

질문의 키워드 brain volume이 그대로 언급된 주변 내용을 주의 깊게 읽는다.

해설 | 3단락의 'This was done to determine ~ the ability ~ to act as a buffer against disease ~ with age.'에서 참가자들의 뇌 용량 측정은 질병에 대해 완충 역할을 하는 뇌의 능력인 인지적 회복력을 알아내기 위해 행해졌다고 했다. 따라서 (a)가 정답이다.

Paraphrasing
measure 측정하다 → gauge 측정하다
act as a buffer against disease 질병에 대해 완충 역할을 하다 → resist disease 질병에 저항하다

어휘 | identify v. 알아보다 aging n. 노화 process n. 과정, 작용 correlate v. 연관성을 보여주다 intelligence n. 지능

63 특정세부사항 What

난이도 ●●●

In what way does an increase in neuroplasticity benefit the brain?

(a) by stimulating the brain to have a deeper level of thought
(b) by increasing the speed of responses to nerve stimulation
(c) by creating additional nerve paths in the brain
(d) by allowing the brain to follow nerve pathways faster

신경 가소성의 증가가 어떤 방식으로 뇌에 도움이 되는가?

(a) 더 깊은 수준의 생각을 하도록 뇌를 자극함으로써
(b) 신경 자극에의 반응 속도를 증가시킴으로써
(c) 뇌에 추가적인 신경 경로를 만듦으로써
(d) 뇌가 신경 경로를 더 빠르게 따르도록 함으로써

지텔프 치트키

질문의 키워드 neuroplasticity가 그대로 언급된 주변 내용을 주의 깊게 읽는다.

해설 | 4단락의 'A boost to neuroplasticity establishes new pathways among the nerve cells in the brain ~ as time passes.'에

서 신경 가소성의 증가는 뇌 신경 세포들 사이의 새로운 경로를 확립하고 시간이 지남에 따라 뇌가 계속해서 잘 기능하기 쉽게 만든다고 했다. 따라서 (c)가 정답이다.

Paraphrasing

an increase 증가 → a boost 증가

establishes new pathways among the nerve cells 뇌 신경 세포들 사이의 새로운 경로를 확립한다 → creating additional nerve paths 추가적인 신경 연결을 만듦

오답분석

(a) 4단락에서 신경 가소성의 증가는 뇌가 계속해서 잘 기능하기 쉽게 만든다고는 했지만, 더 깊은 수준의 생각을 하도록 뇌를 자극하는지는 언급되지 않았으므로 오답이다.

(d) 4단락에서 신경 가소성의 증가는 뇌 신경 세포들 사이의 새로운 경로를 확립한다고는 했지만, 뇌가 신경 경로를 더 빠르게 따르도록 하는지는 언급되지 않았으므로 오답이다.

어휘 | additional adj. 추가적인

64 특정세부사항 Which

난이도 ●●○

Which of the following do the findings of the study ultimately reveal?

(a) People should pursue a fulfilling life.
(b) People can take action to help themselves.
(c) Cognitive decline cannot be significantly slowed.
(d) Cognitive decline does not necessarily mean a low quality of life.

다음 중 연구 결과가 궁극적으로 드러내는 것은 무엇인가?

(a) 사람들은 성취감을 주는 삶을 추구해야 한다.
(b) 사람들은 자신을 돕기 위해 조치를 취할 수 있다.
(c) 인지력 저하가 현저하게 늦춰질 수는 없다.
(d) 인지력 저하가 반드시 낮은 삶의 질을 의미하지는 않는다.

지텔프 치트키

질문의 키워드 findings of the study가 그대로 언급된 주변 내용을 주의 깊게 읽는다.

해설 | 5단락의 'they imply that people can address their cognitive resilience before it is too late'에서 연구 결과는 사람들이 너무 늦기 전에 자신의 인지적 회복력을 다룰 수 있음을 의미한다고 했다. 따라서 (b)가 정답이다.

Paraphrasing

address 다루다 → take action 조치를 취하다

오답분석

(d) 5단락에서 노화와 관련된 인지력 저하가 삶의 모든 측면에서 질을 낮춘다고 언급되었으므로 오답이다.

어휘 | pursue v. 추구하다 significantly adv. 현저하게, 상당히 necessarily adv. 반드시, 필연적으로

65 어휘 유의어

난이도 ●●○

In the context of the passage, included means _______.

(a) affected
(b) added
(c) integrated
(d) comprised

지문의 문맥에서, 'included'는 -을 의미한다.

(a) 영향을 주었다
(b) 추가했다
(c) 통합시켰다
(d) 포함했다

지텔프 치트키

밑줄 친 어휘의 유의어를 찾는 문제이므로, included가 포함된 구절을 읽고 문맥을 파악한다.

해설 | 2단락의 'This included factors'는 이것(설문 조사)이 요소들을 포함했다는 뜻이므로, included가 '포함했다'라는 의미로 사용된 것을 알 수 있다. 따라서 '포함했다'라는 같은 의미의 (d) comprised가 정답이다.

66 어휘 유의어

난이도 ●○○

In the context of the passage, address means ________.

(a) handle
(b) enhance
(c) identify
(d) cure

지문의 문맥에서, 'address'는 -을 의미한다.

(a) 다루다
(b) 높이다
(c) 확인하다
(d) 치유하다

지텔프 치트키

밑줄 친 어휘의 유의어를 찾는 문제이므로, address가 포함된 구절을 읽고 문맥을 파악한다.

해설 | 5단락의 'people can address their cognitive resilience'는 사람들이 자신의 인지적 회복력을 다룰 수 있다는 뜻이므로, address가 '다루다'라는 의미로 사용된 것을 알 수 있다. 따라서 '다루다'라는 같은 의미의 (a) handle이 정답이다.

PART 3 (67~73) Encyclopedia Article 퐁뒤의 특징 및 요리법

표제어

FONDUE

정의

[67]Fondue, the national dish of Switzerland, is made by heating up cheese, oil, or chocolate in a particular type of pot used specifically to prepare the dish. It is a communal comfort food that provides a relaxed dining experience for friends and family members. People choose what foods they want—usually bread, fruit, vegetables, or cured meats—and dip them in the melted sauce.

어원 + 기원

The dish takes its name from the French word *fondre*, meaning "to melt," as it originated in the French-speaking region of Switzerland. This name was initially used for a combination of scrambled eggs and cheese, but [72]it was applied exclusively to the modern dish featuring cheese and bread by the end of the 19th century. Although there are many theories about fondue's origin, [68]the most probable explanation is that the Swiss had to make old bread soft enough to eat.

퐁뒤

[67]스위스의 국민 요리인 퐁뒤는 이 요리를 준비하기 위해 특별하게 사용되는 특정한 종류의 냄비에 치즈, 오일, 혹은 초콜릿을 데움으로써 만들어진다. 이것은 친구와 가족 구성원들에게 편안한 식사 경험을 제공하는 공동체적인 힐링 음식이다. 사람들은 빵, 과일, 채소, 혹은 소금에 절인 고기와 같이 그들이 원하는 음식을 선택하고 녹인 소스에 그것들을 살짝 적신다.

이 요리는 스위스의 프랑스어권 지역에서 유래했기 때문에, '녹이다'라는 의미의 프랑스 단어 'fondre'에서 이름을 따온 것이다. 처음에 이 이름은 계란 스크램블과 치즈의 조합에 사용되었으나, 19세기 말 즈음에 치즈와 빵을 포함하는 [72]현대 요리에만 오로지 사용되었다. 퐁뒤의 기원에 관한 여러 학설들이 있지만, [68]스위스인들이 오래된 빵을 먹을 수 있을 정도로 충분히 부드럽게 만들어야 했다는 것이 가장 그럴듯한 설명이다.

최초의 요리법

[69(d)]The earliest fondue recipe was published in 1875, and [69(a)]the preparation process has not changed significantly since then. [69(b)]A combination of cheese, wine, and garlic is heated over a portable stove at the center of the dining table. [69(c)]The temperature has to be managed carefully to ensure that the cheese does not burn. Once the ingredients are blended, the sauce must be stirred continuously to prevent it from sticking to the pan. Bread is then dipped into the sauce before being eaten.

다양한 요리법

There are many different types of fondue. The most notable is chocolate fondue, created in the 1960s by the Swiss chef, Konrad Egli. He operated a popular restaurant Chalet Suisse in Manhattan and was [70]approached by the company that produces Toblerone chocolate to develop a dessert featuring its product. Egli's response was to serve heated chocolate with fruit and nuts, and he finally debuted his chocolate fondue to his customers on July 4th, 1964.

현황

Although fondue remains associated with the Swiss, it is now popular around the world. [71]As [73]the simple dish is very versatile in terms of what it can be made with, it is likely to remain an international favorite for years to come.

[69(d)]최초의 퐁뒤 요리법은 1875년에 발표되었고, [69(a)]조리 과정은 그때 이후로 크게 바뀌지 않았다. [69(b)]치즈, 와인, 그리고 마늘의 조합은 식탁 중앙에 있는 휴대용 화로에서 데워진다. 치즈가 타지 않는 것을 확실히 하기 위해서 [69(c)]온도는 주의 깊게 관리되어야 한다. 그 재료들이 섞이면, 소스가 냄비에 들러붙는 것을 막기 위해 계속해서 저어져야 한다. 그런 다음 먹기 전에 빵이 그 소스에 살짝 적셔진다.

많은 다양한 종류의 퐁뒤 요리법이 있다. 가장 주목할 만한 것은 스위스 요리사 콘라트 에글리가 1960년대에 만든 초콜릿 퐁뒤이다. 그는 맨해튼에서 샬레 스위스라는 유명한 식당을 운영했는데 [70]토블론 초콜릿을 생산하는 회사가 자사 제품을 포함하는 디저트를 개발하기 위해 접근해 왔다. 에글리의 답변은 가열된 초콜릿을 과일 및 견과류와 함께 제공하는 것이었으며, 그는 1964년 7월 4일에 마침내 그의 손님들에게 초콜릿 퐁뒤를 신상품으로 소개했다.

퐁뒤가 여전히 스위스와 관련지어 생각되기는 하지만, 현재 이것은 전 세계적으로 인기 있다. [71/73]이 간소한 요리는 그것이 무엇으로 만들어지는지에 관하여 매우 융통성 있기 때문에, 앞으로도 오랫동안 국제적으로 사랑받는 음식으로 남을 것 같다.

어휘 | national adj. 국민의, 국가의 heat up phr. 데우다 particular adj. 특정한 pot n. 냄비, 솥 specifically adv. 특별하게 communal adj. 공동체적인, 공동의 comfort food phr. 힐링 음식, 그리운 음식 relaxed adj. 편안한 dining n. 식사 cured adj. 소금에 절인 dip v. 살짝 적시다 melt v. 녹이다 originate v. 유래하다 region n. 지역 initially adv. 처음에 combination n. 조합 apply v. 사용하다 feature v. 포함하다 theory n. 학설 origin n. 기원 probable adj. 그럴듯한, 개연성 있는 explanation n. 설명, 원인 Swiss n. 스위스인; adj. 스위스의 publish v. 발표하다 preparation n. 조리, 준비 significantly adv. 크게, 상당히 portable adj. 휴대용의 stove n. 화로 temperature n. 온도 manage v. 관리하다 blend v. 섞다 stir v. 젓다 continuously adv. 계속해서 stick v. 들러붙다 notable adj. 주목할 만한 operate v. 운영하다 approach v. 접근하다, 다가가다 debut v. 신상품으로 소개하다 associate v. 관련지어 생각하다, 연상하다 versatile adj. 융통성 있는, 다용도적인 in terms of phr. ~에 관하여, ~의 측면에서

67 추론 특정사실

난이도 ●●●

According to the article, what will Swiss people probably avoid doing?

(a) sharing a meal from a common dish
(b) eating fondue with family members
(c) offering many different food options
(d) using a random pan to warm up fondue

기사에 따르면, 스위스 사람들이 하지 않을 것 같은 것은 무엇인가?

(a) 공동의 접시로 식사를 공유하는 것
(b) 가족 구성원들과 퐁뒤를 먹는 것
(c) 많은 다양한 음식 선택지를 제공하는 것
(d) 퐁뒤를 데우는 데 아무 냄비나 사용하는 것

지텔프 치트키

질문의 키워드 Swiss people과 관련된 주변 내용을 주의 깊게 읽는다.

해설 | 1단락의 'Fondue ~ is made ~ in a particular type of pot used specifically to prepare the dish.'에서 퐁뒤는 이 요리를 준비하기 위해 특별하게 사용되는 특정한 종류의 냄비에 치즈, 오일, 혹은 초콜릿을 데움으로써 만들어진다고 한 것을 통해, 스위스 사람들이 퐁뒤를 데우는 데 아무 냄비나 사용하지 않을 것임을 추론할 수 있다. 따라서 (d)가 정답이다.

Paraphrasing

heating up 데움 → warm up 데우다
pot 냄비 → pan 냄비

어휘 | avoid v. ~하지 않도록 하다, 피하다 meal n. 식사 offer v. 제공하다 option n. 선택지 random adj. 아무, 임의의

68 특정세부사항 What

난이도 ●●○

What was likely the origin of fondue?

(a) the demand to make more varieties of bread
(b) the preference of the Swiss for French cooking
(c) the increase in the supply of cheese
(d) the need to consume stale food

퐁뒤의 그럴듯한 기원은 무엇인가?

(a) 더 다양한 빵을 만드는 것에 대한 요구
(b) 프랑스 요리에 대한 스위스 사람들의 선호
(c) 치즈 공급의 증가
(d) 오래된 음식을 소비할 필요성

지텔프 치트키

질문의 키워드 origin이 그대로 언급된 주변 내용을 주의 깊게 읽는다.

해설 | 2단락의 'the most probable explanation is ~ to make old bread soft enough to eat'에서 스위스 사람들이 오래된 빵을 먹을 수 있을 정도로 충분히 부드럽게 만들어야 했다는 것이 퐁뒤의 가장 그럴듯한 설명이라고 했다. 따라서 (d)가 정답이다.

Paraphrasing

likely 그럴듯한 → probable 그럴듯한
old bread 오래된 빵 → stale food 오래된 음식

어휘 | demand n. 요구 varieties of phr. 다양한, 각종의 preference n. 선호 supply n. 공급 stale adj. 오래된, 신선하지 않은

69 Not/True Not 문제

난이도 ●●○

Which is not true about the process of making fondue?

(a) It has been essentially unchanged over time.
(b) The ingredients are heated separately.
(c) The temperature must be regulated.
(d) It was first recorded in 1875.

퐁뒤를 만드는 과정에 관해 사실이 아닌 것은?

(a) 시간이 지나면서 본질적으로는 변함이 없었다.
(b) 재료가 따로따로 데워진다.
(c) 온도가 조절되어야 한다.
(d) 1875년에 최초로 기록되었다.

지텔프 치트키

질문의 키워드 process of making이 recipe로 paraphrasing되어 언급된 주변 내용을 주의 깊게 읽고, 보기의 키워드와 지문 내용을 대조하며 언급되는 것을 하나씩 소거한다.

해설 | (b)는 3단락의 'A combination of cheese, wine, and garlic is heated ~ at the center of the dining table.'에서 치즈, 와인,

그리고 마늘의 조합이 휴대용 화로에서 데워진다고 언급되었으므로, 퐁뒤를 만드는 재료가 따로따로 데워진다는 것은 지문의 내용과 일치하지 않는다. 따라서 (b)가 정답이다.

오답분석

(a) 보기의 키워드 unchanged가 not changed로 paraphrasing되어 언급된 3단락에서 퐁뒤의 조리 과정은 크게 바뀌지 않았다고 언급되었다.

(c) 보기의 키워드 temperature가 그대로 언급된 3단락에서 온도가 주의 깊게 관리되어야 한다고 언급되었다.

(d) 보기의 키워드 recorded가 published로 paraphrasing되어 언급된 3단락에서 최초의 퐁뒤 요리법이 1875년에 발표되었다고 언급되었다.

어휘 | essentially adv. 본질적으로 separately adv. 따로따로, 각기 regulate v. 조절하다 record v. 기록하다

70 특정세부사항 Why

난이도 ●●○

Why did Chef Konrad Egli decide to serve chocolate fondue?

(a) because he faced competition from a restaurant
(b) because he wanted to update an ancient dish
(c) because he received a request from a producer
(d) because he employed a new dessert maker

왜 요리사 콘라트 에글리는 초콜릿 퐁뒤를 제공하기로 결심했는가?

(a) 한 식당과의 경쟁에 직면했기 때문에
(b) 오래된 요리를 새롭게 하기를 원했기 때문에
(c) 한 생산자로부터 요청을 받았기 때문에
(d) 새로운 파티시에를 고용했기 때문에

지텔프 치트키

질문의 키워드 Konrad Egli가 그대로 언급된 주변 내용을 주의 깊게 읽는다.

해설 | 초콜릿 퐁뒤가 만들어진 배경에 관해 언급하는 4단락의 'approached by the company ~ to develop a dessert featuring its product'에서 토블론 초콜릿을 생산하는 회사가 자사 제품을 포함하는 디저트를 개발하기 위해 콘라트 에글리에게 접근해 왔다고 했다. 따라서 (c)가 정답이다.

Paraphrasing
the company that produces 생산하는 회사 → a producer 한 생산자

어휘 | face v. 직면하다 competition n. 경쟁 ancient adj. 오래된 request n. 요청 employ v. 고용하다

71 특정세부사항 Which

난이도 ●●○

Which has contributed to the global popularity of fondue?

(a) its long-term connection to Swiss culture
(b) its inclusion of high-quality food items
(c) its adaptability with regard to ingredients
(d) its promotion by international companies

퐁뒤의 국제적 인기에 이바지한 것은 어떤 것인가?

(a) 스위스 문화와의 장기적인 연관성
(b) 질 높은 식품의 포함
(c) 재료에 관한 융통성
(d) 국제 기업들의 홍보

지텔프 치트키

질문의 키워드 global popularity가 popular around the world로 paraphrasing되어 언급된 주변 내용을 주의 깊게 읽는다.

해설 | 5단락의 'As the simple dish is very versatile ~, it is likely to remain an international favorite for years to come.'에서 퐁뒤는 그것이 무엇으로 만들어지는지에 관하여 매우 융통성 있기 때문에 국제적으로 사랑받는 음식으로 남을 것 같다고 했다. 따라서 (c)가 정답이다.

Paraphrasing

versatile in terms of what it can be made with 그것이 무엇으로 만들어지는지에 관하여 융통성 있는 → adaptability with regard to ingredients 재료에 관한 융통성

어휘 connection n. 연관성 inclusion n. 포함 adaptability n. 융통성 with regard to phr. ~에 관한 promotion n. 홍보

72 어휘 유의어

난이도 ●●○

In the context of the passage, exclusively means _______.

(a) solely
(b) totally
(c) certainly
(d) readily

지문의 문맥에서, 'exclusively'는 -을 의미한다.

(a) 오로지
(b) 완전히
(c) 틀림없이
(d) 손쉽게

지텔프 치트키

밑줄 친 어휘의 유의어를 찾는 문제이므로, exclusively가 포함된 구절을 읽고 문맥을 파악한다.

해설 | 2단락의 'it was applied exclusively to the modern dish'는 그것(요리 이름)이 현대 요리에만 오로지 사용되었다는 뜻이므로, exclusively가 '오로지'라는 의미로 사용된 것을 알 수 있다. 따라서 '오로지'라는 같은 의미의 (a) solely가 정답이다.

73 어휘 유의어

난이도 ●○○

In the context of the passage, simple means _______.

(a) quick
(b) humble
(c) casual
(d) natural

지문의 문맥에서, 'simple'은 -을 의미한다.

(a) 신속한
(b) 소박한
(c) 격식을 차리지 않는
(d) 천연의

지텔프 치트키

밑줄 친 어휘의 유의어를 찾는 문제이므로, simple이 포함된 구절을 읽고 문맥을 파악한다.

해설 | 5단락의 'the simple dish is very versatile'은 이 간소한 요리가 매우 융통성 있다는 뜻이므로, simple이 '간소한'이라는 의미로 사용된 것을 알 수 있다. 따라서 '소박한'이라는 비슷한 의미의 (b) humble이 정답이다.

 Business Letter 고객에게 공급 부족을 알리는 편지

수신인 정보

Ms. Dana Murphy
Nature's Greenhouse
22 Main Street
Worcester, Massachusetts

Dear Ms. Murphy,

편지의 목적: 재고 부족

I'm contacting you about your request to order one of our products. I see that you are interested in our 1-liter orchid pots for your flower business. While we are very glad that you chose us as one of your suppliers, [74]I regret to inform you that this particular product is currently not available at our store here in Worcester.

대안

We will be talking to our warehouse in Maryland to restock this product as soon as possible. Usually, we can get nursery pots shipped to us in two to three business days. However, as you know, [75]spring is the most hectic time of year in our industry, and this time frame is not feasible at the moment. I estimate we can get them within a week. If this works for you, we will process your order and bill you when it is ready. I'll let you know [79]if it takes longer than I anticipated.

필요 정보 요청

Also, [76]please send us your retail certificate. As we are a wholesale distributor, we can only sell to those who are licensed for retail sales. Once [80]we verify this, we will enter your information into our database so that you do not have to provide it in the future. [77]If you are not a retailer, I do know a company that sells to wholesalers.

끝인사

Should you have any questions or concerns, or [78]if you need to make changes to your order, don't hesitate to contact me personally. You can reach me at 555-764-3115 or at Jwallace@nsupplies.com. Thank you for considering us, and we look forward to adding you as a customer!

발신인 정보

Sincerely,
Jimmy Wallace
Sales Representative
Nursery Supplies Inc.

Ms. Dana Murphy
Nature's Greenhouse사
메인가 22번지
우스터, 매사추세츠주

Ms. Murphy께,

귀사가 저희 상품들 중 하나를 주문하고자 요청하신 것과 관련하여 연락드립니다. 화훼 사업을 위해 저희의 1리터 용량의 난초 화분에 관심이 있으신 것 같습니다. 귀사의 공급사들 중 한 곳으로 저희를 선택해 주신 것에 매우 감사하지만, 여기 우스터에 있는 저희 매장에서 [74]그 특정 상품은 현재 구매하실 수 없다는 것을 알리게 되어 유감입니다.

저희는 이 상품을 가능한 한 빨리 다시 채우기 위해 메릴랜드주에 있는 창고에 말할 것입니다. 보통, 식물 재배용 화분은 영업일 기준으로 2일에서 3일 이내에 저희 쪽으로 수송받을 수 있습니다. 하지만, 아시다시피, [75]봄은 저희 업계에서 일 년 중 가장 정신없이 바쁜 시기이고, 위 기간은 현재 실현 가능하지 않습니다. 저는 우리가 일주일 이내에 그것들을 받을 수 있을 것이라고 예측합니다. 만약 이것이 괜찮으시다면, 저희는 귀사의 주문을 처리하고 준비되는 대로 청구서를 보내 드리겠습니다. [79]제가 예상했던 것보다 오래 걸리는 경우에는 귀사에 알려 드리겠습니다.

또한, [76]저희에게 소매업 증명서를 보내 주시기를 부탁드립니다. 저희가 도매 유통업체이기 때문에, 소매 판매 허가를 받은 업체에만 판매할 수 있습니다. 일단 [80]저희가 그것을 확인하면, 향후 귀사가 정보를 다시 제공하지 않아도 되도록 저희 데이터베이스에 입력해 두겠습니다. [77]만약 소매업체가 아니시라면, 저는 도매업체에 판매하는 회사를 알고 있습니다.

질문 혹은 걱정이 있으시거나, [78]귀사의 주문을 변경하셔야 한다면, 망설이지 마시고 저에게 개인적으로 연락해 주시기 바랍니다. 555-764-3115 혹은 Jwallace@nsupplies.com으로 저에게 연락하실 수 있습니다. 저희를 고려해 주셔서 감사하며, 귀사를 저희 고객으로 추가하기를 기대하고 있겠습니다!

Jimmy Wallace 드림
판매 담당자
Nursery Supplies 주식회사

어휘 | orchid n. 난초 pot n. 화분 supplier n. 공급사 regret v. 유감이다 inform v. 알리다 warehouse n. 창고 restock v. 다시 채우다 nursery pot phr. 식물 재배용 화분 ship v. 수송하다 hectic adj. 정신없이 바쁜 feasible adj. 실현 가능한 estimate v. 예측하다, 추정하다 process v. 처리하다 bill v. 청구서를 보내다; n. 청구서 retail n. 소매(업) certificate n. 증명(서) wholesale adj. 도매의 distributor n. 유통업체 license v. 허가하다 concern n. 걱정 hesitate v. 망설이다 personally adv. 개인적으로 reach v. 연락하다 look forward to phr. ~하기를 기대하다 representative n. 담당자, 대리인

74 주제/목적 편지의 목적

난이도 ●●○

Why did Jimmy Wallace write to Dana Murphy?

(a) to invite her to try one of their products
(b) to inform her of their new store location
(c) to let her know the status of a product
(d) to give her directions to their warehouse in Maryland

왜 Jimmy Wallace가 Dana Murphy에게 편지를 썼는가?

(a) 상품들 중 하나를 써 보도록 초대하기 위해서
(b) 새로운 매장의 위치에 대해 알리기 위해서
(c) 제품의 상황을 알리기 위해서
(d) 메릴랜드주에 있는 창고 위치를 제공하기 위해서

지텔프 치트키

지문의 초반을 주의 깊게 읽고 전체 맥락을 파악한다.

해설 | 1단락의 'I regret to inform you that this particular product is currently not available'에서 Jimmy Wallace는 Dana Murphy가 주문 요청한 특정 상품을 현재 구매할 수 없다는 것을 알리게 되어 유감이라고 한 뒤, 지문 전반에 걸쳐 이유와 대안을 제시하고 있다. 따라서 (c)가 정답이다.

어휘 | status n. 상황 direction n. 위치, 방향

75 특정세부사항 Why

난이도 ●●○

Why will a delivery not be possible in the usual time frame?

(a) because the company's warehouse is located in another state
(b) because the company's delivery truck is currently unavailable
(c) because the company's prices do not include fast shipping
(d) because the company's busy season is underway

왜 일반적인 기간 내에 배달이 가능하지 않을 것인가?

(a) 회사의 창고가 다른 주에 위치해 있기 때문에
(b) 회사의 배달 트럭을 현재 이용할 수 없기 때문에
(c) 회사의 가격이 빠른 배송을 포함하지 않기 때문에
(d) 회사의 성수기가 진행 중이기 때문에

지텔프 치트키

질문의 키워드 time frame이 그대로 언급된 주변 내용을 주의 깊게 읽는다.

해설 | 2단락의 'spring is the most hectic time of year ~ at the moment'에서 봄은 화훼 업계에서 일 년 중 가장 정신없이 바쁜 시기이고 보통의 수송 기간은 현재 실현 가능하지 않다고 했다. 따라서 (d)가 정답이다.

Paraphrasing
not ~ possible 가능하지 않은 → not feasible 실현 가능하지 않은
hectic time of year 일 년 중 정신없이 바쁜 시기 → busy season 성수기

어휘 | locate v. 위치시키다 busy season phr. 성수기 underway adj. 진행 중인

76 특정세부사항 What

난이도 ●○○

What does Mr. Wallace ask Ms. Murphy to provide?

(a) an authorization for conducting retail sales
(b) an updated billing address for her business
(c) the exact number of orchid pots she needs
(d) the notification she received for her order

Ms. Murphy가 제공하도록 Mr. Wallace가 요청한 것은 무엇인가?

(a) 소매 판매를 하는 것에 대한 허가증
(b) 그녀의 사업체의 최신 청구서 발송 주소
(c) 그녀가 필요한 난초 화분의 정확한 수
(d) 주문에 대해 그녀가 받은 통지서

지텔프 치트키

질문의 키워드 provide가 send로 paraphrasing되어 언급된 주변 내용을 주의 깊게 읽는다.

해설 | 3단락의 'please send us your retail certificate'에서 Mr. Wallace가 Ms. Murphy에게 소매업 증명서를 보내 달라고 부탁했다. 따라서 (a)가 정답이다.

Paraphrasing
your retail certificate 소매업 증명서 → an authorization for conducting retail sales 소매 판매를 하는 것에 대한 허가증

어휘 | authorization n. 허가증 conduct v. (특정 활동을) 하다 notification n. 통지서

77 추론 특정사실

난이도 ●●○

According to Mr. Wallace, what most likely will happen if Ms. Murphy is not a retailer?

(a) She will be recommended a different supplier.
(b) She will be put in a database for the record.
(c) She will lose the wholesale discount on her purchase.
(d) She will receive advice on setting up a retail business.

Mr. Wallace에 따르면, Ms. Murphy가 소매업자가 아니라면 어떤 일이 일어날 것 같은가?

(a) 다른 공급사를 추천받을 것이다.
(b) 기록을 위해 데이터베이스에 입력될 것이다.
(c) 구매에 대한 도매 할인을 받지 못할 것이다.
(d) 소매업을 시작하는 것에 관한 조언을 받을 것이다.

지텔프 치트키

질문의 키워드 not a retailer가 그대로 언급된 주변 내용을 주의 깊게 읽는다.

해설 | 3단락의 'If you are not a retailer, I do know a company that sells to wholesalers.'에서 만약 Ms. Murphy가 소매업체가 아니라면 도매업체에 판매하는 회사를 알고 있다는 Mr. Wallace의 언급을 통해, Ms. Murphy가 Mr. Wallace에게 다른 공급사를 추천받을 것임을 추론할 수 있다. 따라서 (a)가 정답이다.

어휘 | recommend v. 추천하다 discount n. 할인; v. 할인하다 set up phr. ~을 시작하다, 설립하다

78 특정세부사항 How

난이도 ●○○

How can Dana Murphy update her order?

(a) by emailing customer service
(b) by contacting Mr. Wallace directly
(c) by filling out an online form
(d) by calling the shipping representative personally

Dana Murphy는 어떻게 주문을 갱신할 수 있는가?

(a) 고객 서비스에 이메일을 보냄으로써
(b) Mr. Wallace에게 직접 연락함으로써
(c) 온라인 양식을 채움으로써
(d) 배송 담당자에게 개인적으로 전화함으로써

지텔프 치트키

질문의 키워드 update가 make changes로 paraphrasing되어 언급된 주변 내용을 주의 깊게 읽는다.

해설 | 4단락의 'if you need to make changes to your order, ~ contact me personally'에서 Mr. Wallace가 Dana Murphy에게 주문을 변경해야 한다면 자신에게 개인적으로 연락해 달라고 했다. 따라서 (b)가 정답이다.

Paraphrasing
personally 개인적으로 → directly 직접

어휘 | directly adv. 직접 fill out phr. ~을 채우다, 기입하다

79 어휘 유의어

난이도 ●●○

In the context of the passage, <u>anticipated</u> means ________.

(a) understood
(b) contemplated
(c) evaluated
(d) expected

지문의 문맥에서, 'anticipated'는 -을 의미한다.

(a) 이해했다
(b) 고려했다
(c) 평가했다
(d) 예상했다

지텔프 치트키

밑줄 친 어휘의 유의어를 찾는 문제이므로, anticipated가 포함된 구절을 읽고 문맥을 파악한다.

해설 | 2단락의 'if it takes longer than I anticipated'는 자신이 예상했던 것보다 오래 걸리는 경우라는 뜻이므로, anticipated가 '예상했다'라는 의미로 사용된 것을 알 수 있다. 따라서 '예상했다'라는 같은 의미의 (d) expected가 정답이다.

80 어휘 유의어

난이도 ●●○

In the context of the passage, <u>verify</u> means ________.

(a) acknowledge
(b) justify
(c) confirm
(d) arrange

지문의 문맥에서, 'verify'는 -을 의미한다.

(a) 인정한다
(b) 정당화한다
(c) 확인한다
(d) 마련한다

지텔프 치트키

밑줄 친 어휘의 유의어를 찾는 문제이므로, verify가 포함된 구절을 읽고 문맥을 파악한다.

해설 | 3단락의 'we verify this'는 Jimmy Wallace의 회사가 그것(소매업 증명서)을 확인한다는 뜻이므로, verify가 '확인한다'라는 의미로 사용된 것을 알 수 있다. 따라서 '확인한다'라는 같은 의미의 (c) confirm이 정답이다.

05회 실전모의고사

문제집 p.36

정답 및 문제 유형 분석표							
PART 1		PART 2		PART 3		PART 4	
53	(c) 특정세부사항	60	(b) 특정세부사항	67	(b) 특정세부사항	74	(b) 주제/목적
54	(a) 특정세부사항	61	(c) 추론	68	(d) 추론	75	(c) 특정세부사항
55	(c) Not/True	62	(c) 특정세부사항	69	(b) 특정세부사항	76	(c) 추론
56	(c) 추론	63	(c) 추론	70	(d) Not/True	77	(c) 특정세부사항
57	(d) 특정세부사항	64	(d) 특정세부사항	71	(d) 특정세부사항	78	(a) 특정세부사항
58	(d) 어휘	65	(c) 어휘	72	(c) 어휘	79	(b) 어휘
59	(c) 어휘	66	(a) 어휘	73	(a) 어휘	80	(d) 어휘

취약 유형 분석표

유형	맞힌 개수
주제/목적	/1
특정세부사항	/12
Not/True	/2
추론	/5
어휘	/8
TOTAL	28

PART 1(53~59) Biography Article 다게레오타입의 발명가 루이 다게르

인물 이름

LOUIS DAGUERRE

인물 소개

Louis Daguerre was an accomplished French artist, photographer, and theatre designer. [53]He is best remembered for his invention of the daguerreotype, a process used for mechanically producing an image that was more efficient than prior photographic innovations.

어린 시절

Daguerre was born on November 18, 1787, in Cormeilles-en-Parisis, France, to a middle-class family. [54]Due to the start of the French Revolution in 1789, a violent period of social and political change, Daguerre's formal education was frequently interrupted. However, his parents were committed to fostering his artistic talent, so they sent him to become an apprentice to Pierre Prévost, the first French panorama painter, when he was 13.

초기 업적 + 위기

He later moved to Paris in 1804, where he painted theatrical scenery and [58]gained distinction for his work. There, he partnered with painter Charles Marie Bouton to invent the diorama theatre, a three-dimensional visual spectacle that has been called the forerunner of cinema. While he initially saw success with diorama theatres, by the 1830s, Daguerre had begun to reconsider his involvement with them. [55(a)]The novelty was subsiding for audiences, and [55(b)]a cholera outbreak in the city was negatively affecting ticket sales. Furthermore, [55(d)]since dioramas were costly to produce, Daguerre faced

루이 다게르

루이 다게르는 뛰어난 프랑스 화가이자, 사진작가이자, 무대 디자이너였다. [53]그는 그의 다게레오타입 발명으로 가장 잘 기억되는데, 그것은 사진을 기계적으로 제작하기 위해 사용된 방법으로 이전의 사진술 혁신들보다 더 효율적이었다.

다게르는 1787년 11월 18일에, 프랑스의 코르메유앙 파리지의 중산층 가정에서 태어났다. [54]사회 및 정치적 변화의 격렬한 시기였던 1789년 프랑스 혁명의 시작으로 인해, 다게르의 정규 교육은 자주 중단되었다. 그러나, 그의 부모님은 그의 예술적인 재능을 발전시키는 것에 전념했기 때문에, 그가 13살이었을 때, 그들은 그를 최초의 프랑스인 파노라마 화가인 피에르 프레보의 도제가 되도록 보냈다.

이후 그는 1804년에 파리로 옮겨가, 그곳에서 극장의 배경을 그렸고 [58]그의 작품에 대한 명성을 얻었다. 그곳에서, 그는 영화관의 전신이라고 불려 온 3차원의 시각적 장관인 디오라마 극장을 발명하기 위해 화가 샤를 마리 부통과 협력했다. 그는 처음에 디오라마 극장으로 성공을 거뒀지만, 1830년대에 이르러, 다게르는 그것에 대한 자신의 관여를 재고하기 시작했다. [55(a)]참신함은 관중들에게서 사그라들고 있었고, [55(b)]도시의 콜레라 발병은 티켓 판매에 부정적으로 영향을 미치고 있었다. 게다가, [55(d)]디오라마는 만드는 데 많은 비용이 들었기 때문에, 다게르는 상당한 재정 문제에 직면했다.

considerable financial problems.

업적 시작 계기

Complicating matters was that Bouton, who had produced half the paintings for the dioramas, had abandoned the partnership. As each diorama featured two realistic paintings measuring 70 feet wide and 45 feet high, [56]Daguerre lacked time to do all the work himself. This prompted him to become interested in utilizing photography to replace his former partner.

최고 업적

Therefore, he got to know Joseph Nicéphore Niépce, who had produced the world's first photograph through a technique known as the heliographic process. With his help, [57]Daguerre achieved his principal goal of refining the photography technique in 1835, when he discovered that an image could be produced by exposing iodized silver plates to light and then developing it using mercury fumes. He called his process the daguerreotype and presented it to the Académie des Sciences in 1839 where [59]it found instantaneous success because [57]it was faster than other photographic processes and less expensive.

후기 업적 + 죽음

Daguerre agreed to make the daguerreotype public and received a pension from France in return. Throughout the decade that followed, millions of daguerreotypes were produced worldwide. Daguerre spent the remainder of his life painting dioramas and died in 1851.

디오라마를 위한 그림의 절반을 제작했던 부통이 동업 관계를 그만두었다는 것이 상황을 더 복잡하게 만들었다. 각각의 디오라마는 너비 70피트에 높이 45피트인 두 개의 사실적인 그림을 포함했기 때문에, [56]다게르는 혼자서 이 모든 작업을 할 시간이 부족했다. 이것이 그가 전 동업자를 대체할 사진술을 활용하는 것에 관심을 갖게 되도록 촉발했다.

그 까닭에, 그는 조제프 니세포르 니에프스를 알게 되었는데, 그는 헬리오그래피 공정으로 알려진 기술을 통하여 세계 최초의 사진을 제작했던 사람이다. 그의 도움으로, [57]다게르는 1835년에 사진 기술을 개선하려는 그의 주요한 목표를 달성했는데, 그때 그는 요오드로 처리된 은판을 빛에 노출시킨 다음 수은 가스를 이용하여 그것을 현상함으로써 사진이 만들어질 수 있다는 것을 발견했다. 그는 자신의 방법을 다게레오타입이라고 불렀고 1839년에 그것을 학술원에 제시했으며 그곳에서 [59]그것은 즉각적인 성공을 거두었는데 이는 [57]그것이 다른 사진술 공정들보다 더 빠르고 비용이 더 적게 들었기 때문이다.

다게르는 다게레오타입을 대중화하는 것에 동의하였고 그 대가로 프랑스로부터 연금을 받았다. 그 후 10년 동안, 수백만 개의 다게레오타입 사진이 전 세계적으로 제작되었다. 다게르는 그의 남은 생애를 디오라마를 그리며 보냈고 1851년에 사망하였다.

어휘 | accomplished adj. 뛰어난, 통달한 theatre n. 무대, 연극 invention n. 발명(품) daguerreotype n. 다게레오타입(은판 사진법 혹은 이 사진법으로 제작한 사진) mechanically adv. 기계적으로 efficient adj. 효율적인 prior adj. 이전의 photographic adj. 사진(술)의 innovation n. 혁신 middle-class adj. 중산층의 revolution n. 혁명 violent adj. 격렬한 interrupt v. 중단시키다 be committed to phr. ~에 전념하다 foster v. 발전시키다 apprentice n. 도제, 견습생 theatrical adj. 연극의 scenery n. 배경, 풍경 diorama n. 디오라마(이동식 극장 장치) dimensional adj. ~차원의 spectacle n. 장관 forerunner n. 전신, 선구자 cinema n. 영화(관) reconsider v. 재고하다 involvement n. 관여, 개입 novelty n. 참신함, 새로움 subside v. 사그라들다, 가라앉다 outbreak n. 발병, 발생 costly adj. 많은 비용이 드는 considerable adj. 상당한 complicating adj. (더) 복잡하게 만드는 abandon v. 그만두다 measure v. (치수가) ~이다 lack v. 부족하다 prompt v. 촉발하다 heliographic adj. 헬리오그래피(광선에 노출되면 굳어지는 물질을 사용한 사진 기법)의 principal adj. 주요한 replace v. 대체하다 refine v. 개선하다, 정제하다 expose v. 노출시키다 iodize v. 요오드로 처리하다 develop v. (사진을) 현상하다 mercury n. 수은 fumes n. 가스, 매연 pension n. 연금 in return phr. 그 대가로

53 특정세부사항 유명한 이유

난이도 ●○○

How is Louis Daguerre best remembered?

(a) as the first French photographer
(b) as an inventor of the mass-produced camera
(c) as a creator of a new photographic technique

루이 다게르는 어떻게 가장 잘 기억되는가?

(a) 최초의 프랑스인 사진작가로
(b) 대량 생산된 카메라의 발명가로
(c) 새로운 사진 기술의 창시자로

(d) as an interior designer with a long career	(d) 오랜 경력의 인테리어 디자이너로

지텔프 치트키

질문의 키워드 best remembered가 그대로 언급된 주변 내용을 주의 깊게 읽는다.

해설 | 1단락의 'He is best remembered for his invention of the daguerreotype, a process used for mechanically producing an image'에서 루이 다게르는 사진을 기계적으로 제작하기 위해 사용된 방법인 다게레오타입의 발명으로 가장 잘 기억된다고 했다. 따라서 (c)가 정답이다.

Paraphrasing
a process used for mechanically producing an image 사진을 기계적으로 제작하기 위해 사용된 방법 → a ~ photographic technique 사진 기술

어휘 | mass-produce v. 대량 생산하다

54 특정세부사항 How

난이도 ●●○

According to the article, how did the French Revolution affect Daguerre?	기사에 따르면, 프랑스 혁명은 어떻게 다게르에게 영향을 끼쳤는가?
(a) It prevented him from receiving a consistent education.	**(a) 그가 지속적인 교육을 받지 못하게 했다.**
(b) It forced him to leave home to work when he was 13.	(b) 그가 13살이었을 때 일을 하기 위해 강제로 집을 떠나게 했다.
(c) It spoiled his plans to formally study art at university.	(c) 대학교에서 정식으로 미술을 공부하려던 그의 계획을 망쳤다.
(d) It sparked his interest in the changes occurring in France.	(d) 프랑스에서 일어난 변화에 대한 그의 흥미를 유발했다.

지텔프 치트키

질문의 키워드 French Revolution이 그대로 언급된 주변 내용을 주의 깊게 읽는다.

해설 | 2단락의 'Due to the start of the French Revolution in 1789, ~ Daguerre's formal education was frequently interrupted.'에서 1789년 프랑스 혁명의 시작으로 인해 다게르의 정규 교육이 자주 중단되었다고 했다. 따라서 (a)가 정답이다.

Paraphrasing
education was frequently interrupted 교육이 자주 중단되었다 → prevented ~ from receiving a consistent education 지속적인 교육을 받지 못하게 했다

어휘 | consistent adj. 지속적인 spoil v. 망치다 formally adv. 정식으로 spark v. 유발하다

55 Not/True Not 문제

난이도 ●●○

Which was not a cause that made Daguerre rethink diorama theatres?	다게르가 디오라마 극장에 대해 재고하게 만들었던 원인이 아닌 것은?
(a) the decrease in public interest	(a) 대중의 관심 감소
(b) the spread of a disease	(b) 질병의 확산
(c) the invention of cinema	**(c) 영화관의 발명**
(d) the high production cost	(d) 높은 제작 비용

지텔프 치트키

질문의 키워드 rethink가 reconsider로 paraphrasing되어 언급된 주변 내용을 주의 깊게 읽고, 보기의 키워드와 지문 내용을 대조하며 언급된 것을 하나씩 소거한다.

해설 | (c)는 지문에 언급되지 않았으므로, (c)가 정답이다.

오답분석

(a) 보기의 키워드 decrease가 subsiding으로 paraphrasing되어 언급된 3단락에서 참신함이 관중들에게서 사그라들고 있었다고 언급되었다.

(b) 보기의 키워드 disease가 cholera로 paraphrasing되어 언급된 3단락에서 도시의 콜레라 발병은 티켓 판매에 부정적으로 영향을 미치고 있었다고 언급되었다.

(d) 보기의 키워드 high ~ cost가 costly로 paraphrasing되어 언급된 3단락에서 디오라마는 만드는 데 많은 비용이 들었다고 언급되었다.

어휘 | spread n. 확산, 전파

56 추론 특정사실

난이도 ●●○

Why most likely did Daguerre want to use photographs in the dioramas? (a) because they would attract larger audiences (b) because they looked far more realistic **(c) because they took much less time to produce** (d) because they were cheaper than paintings	다게르는 왜 디오라마에 사진을 이용하기를 원했던 것 같은가? (a) 더 많은 관중을 끌어모았을 것이기 때문에 (b) 훨씬 더 사실적으로 보였기 때문에 **(c) 제작하는 데 훨씬 더 적은 시간이 걸렸기 때문에** (d) 그림보다 더 저렴했기 때문에

지텔프 치트키

질문의 키워드 use photographs가 utilizing photography로 paraphrasing되어 언급된 주변 내용을 주의 깊게 읽는다.

해설 | 4단락의 'Daguerre lacked time to do all the work himself.'에서 다게르가 혼자서 모든 작업(디오라마를 위한 그림을 제작하는 작업)을 할 시간이 부족했다고 했고, 'This prompted ~ utilizing photography to replace his former partner.'에서 이것이 그가 전 동업자를 대체할 사진술을 활용하는 것에 관심을 갖게 되도록 촉발했다고 한 것을 통해, 사진은 제작하는 데 훨씬 더 적은 시간이 걸렸기 때문에 다게르가 디오라마에 사진을 이용하기를 원했던 것임을 추론할 수 있다. 따라서 (c)가 정답이다.

어휘 | attract v. 끌어모으다

57 특정세부사항 When

난이도 ●●○

When did Daguerre accomplish his main objective? (a) when he presented the daguerreotype to an academy (b) when he produced the first heliographic photograph (c) when he began working for the inventor Nicéphore Niépce **(d) when he found a quicker process for developing a picture**	다게르는 언제 그의 주된 목표를 달성했는가? (a) 학술원에 다게레오타입을 제시했을 때 (b) 최초의 헬리오그래피 사진을 만들었을 때 (c) 발명가 니세포르 니에프스를 위해 일하기 시작했을 때 **(d) 사진을 현상하는 더 빠른 방법을 발견했을 때**

지텔프 치트키

질문의 키워드 main objective가 principal goal로 paraphrasing되어 언급된 주변 내용을 주의 깊게 읽는다.

해설 | 5단락의 'Daguerre achieved his principal goal of refining the photography technique in 1835'에서 다게르가 1835년에 사진 기술을 개선하려는 그의 주요한 목표를 달성했다고 한 뒤, 'it was faster than other photographic processes'에서 그 방법은 다른 사진 공정들보다 더 빨랐다고 했다. 따라서 (d)가 정답이다.

Paraphrasing

faster 더 빠른 → quicker 더 빠른

오답분석

(c) 5단락에서 다게르가 니세포르 니에프스의 도움으로 그의 목표를 달성했다고는 했지만, 그(니세포르 니에프스)를 위해서 일했다고 언급한 것은 아니므로 오답이다.

58 어휘 유의어

난이도 ●●●

In the context of the passage, distinction means ______.

(a) attainment
(b) attention
(c) acceptance
(d) reputation

지문의 문맥에서, 'distinction'은 -을 의미한다.

(a) 성과
(b) 주목
(c) 수락
(d) 명성

지텔프 치트키

밑줄 친 어휘의 유의어를 찾는 문제이므로, distinction이 포함된 구절을 읽고 문맥을 파악한다.

해설 | 3단락의 'gained distinction for his work'는 다게르가 그의 작품에 대한 명성을 얻었다는 뜻이므로, distinction이 '명성'이라는 의미로 사용된 것을 알 수 있다. 따라서 '명성'이라는 같은 의미의 (d) reputation이 정답이다.

59 어휘 유의어

난이도 ●○○

In the context of the passage, instantaneous means ______.

(a) expeditious
(b) temporary
(c) immediate
(d) straight

지문의 문맥에서, 'instantaneous'는 -을 의미한다.

(a) 신속한
(b) 일시적인
(c) 즉각적인
(d) 연속적인

지텔프 치트키

밑줄 친 어휘의 유의어를 찾는 문제이므로, instantaneous가 포함된 구절을 읽고 문맥을 파악한다.

해설 | 5단락의 'it found instantaneous success'는 그것(다게레오타입)이 즉각적인 성공을 거두었다는 뜻이므로, instantaneous가 '즉각적인'이라는 의미로 사용된 것을 알 수 있다. 따라서 '즉각적인'이라는 같은 의미의 (c) immediate가 정답이다.

연구 결과

AN EXPERIMENT SHOWS PEOPLE FEEL LESS RESPONSIBLE AS PART OF A GROUP

연구 소개

The famous Smoky Room experiment of 1968 found that people are more likely to react to an emergency when they are alone than in a group. This phenomenon is known as "diffusion of responsibility" and suggests that [60]people's responses are influenced by those around them.

연구 배경

American social psychologists John M. Darley and Bibb Latané theorized that [65]people look to others in a potential emergency to determine whether the situation is critical. They were inspired by the highly publicized death of Kitty Genovese, who was murdered in front of her apartment building in March 1964 as 38 neighbors watched from their windows and did nothing to help. The researchers posited that the neighbors had been aware that a crime was taking place but [61]failed to act because each assumed that others in the crowd had already called for law enforcement.

실험 내용 + 실험 결과

To test their theory, [62]Darley and Latané had three different groups of participants fill out a personal survey in a room. They wanted to see how each group would react when the room began to fill with smoke. The participants were made up of volunteers who did not expect the room would be full of smoke and actors who were instructed to behave like nothing was wrong. The experiment found that the smoke was reported mostly when a volunteer was left in the room alone and that [66]volunteers grouped with actors usually tried to disregard the smoke since the actors did not react to it.

결과 분석

It is believed that there are several reasons why diffusion of responsibility occurs, including fear of rejection when offering one's help and simply being too self-conscious to assume a leadership position. The most prevalent cause, however, is the notion that taking action won't make a difference in a situation. For instance, [63]in a life-threatening emergency, some people do nothing because they are not doctors and do not wish to get in the way of any medical professional who might be present.

시사점

Ultimately, the results of the experiment suggest just how much of an effect social pressure has on people. [64]They offer an explanation for why information about criminal activity is sometimes not provided to authorities and serve as an important reminder that it is not always wise to simply follow the crowd.

한 실험은 사람들이 무리의 일부로서 책임감을 덜 느낀다는 것을 보여준다

유명한 1968년의 스모키 룸 실험은 사람들이 무리 안에 있을 때보다 혼자 있을 때 비상사태에 반응할 가능성이 더 크다는 것을 발견했다. 이 현상은 '책임의 분산'으로 알려져 있으며 [60]사람들의 반응은 그들 주변에 있는 사람들에 영향을 받는다는 것을 시사한다.

미국의 사회 심리학자인 존 M. 달리와 빕 라탄은 [65]사람들은 잠재적인 비상사태에서 그 상황이 위태로운지를 결정하기 위해 다른 사람들에게 의존한다는 이론을 제시했다. 그들은 널리 알려진 키티 제노비스의 죽음에 의해 영감을 받았는데, 그녀는 38명의 이웃들이 창문으로 지켜보고도 돕기 위해 아무것도 하지 않았기 때문에 1964년 3월에 그녀의 아파트 건물 앞에서 살해당했다. 연구원들은 이웃들이 범행이 일어나고 있다는 것을 인지하고 있었지만 [61]각자가 군중 속의 다른 사람들이 이미 사법 집행을 요청했다고 추측했기 때문에 행동하지 않았다는 것을 사실로 가정했다.

그들의 이론을 실험하기 위해, [62]달리와 라탄은 서로 다른 세 집단의 참가자들이 방 안에서 개인적인 설문 조사를 작성하게 했다. 그들은 방이 연기로 가득 차기 시작했을 때 각각의 집단이 어떻게 반응하는지 보기를 원했다. 참가자들은 방이 연기로 가득 찰 것을 예상하지 못한 지원자들과 아무것도 잘못되지 않은 것처럼 행동하도록 지시받은 연기자들로 구성되어 있었다. 실험은 지원자가 방에 혼자 남아 있었을 때 연기가 주로 보고되었다는 것과 [66]연기자들과 무리 지어진 지원자들은 연기자들이 그것에 반응하지 않았기 때문에 대개 연기를 무시하려고 노력했다는 것을 발견했다.

도움을 줄 때 거절당할 두려움과 그저 너무 남의 시선을 의식하여 주도적인 입장을 취하지 못하는 것을 포함하여, 책임의 분산이 발생하는 것에는 여러 가지 이유들이 있다고 여겨진다. 그러나, 가장 일반적인 원인은 조치를 취하는 것이 상황을 바꾸지 않을 것이라는 생각이다. 예를 들어, [63]생명을 위협하는 비상사태에서, 일부 사람들은 그들이 의사가 아니기도 하고 있을지도 모르는 어떠한 의료 전문가에게라도 방해되고 싶지 않기 때문에 아무것도 하지 않는다.

궁극적으로, 실험의 결과는 사회적 압력이 사람들에게 얼마나 많은 영향을 미치는지를 시사한다. [64]그것들은 범죄 활동에 관한 정보가 왜 때때로 당국에 제공되지 않는지를 설명해 주며 그저 대세를 따르는 것이 항상 현명한 것은 아니라는 점을 중요하게 상기시키는 역할을 한다.

어휘 | experiment n. 실험 smoky adj. 연기가 자욱한 react v. 반응하다 emergency n. 비상사태 phenomenon n. 현상
diffusion n. 분산 responsibility n. 책임 theorize v. 이론을 제시하다 look to phr. ~에게 의존하다 determine v. 결정하다
critical adj. 위태로운 inspire v. 영감을 주다 publicize v. 알리다 murder v. 살해하다 neighbor n. 이웃 posit v. 사실로 가정하다
crime n. 범행, 범죄 take place phr. 일어나다 assume v. 추측하다, (태도 등을) 취하다 call for phr. ~을 요청하다
law enforcement phr. 사법 집행 participant n. 참가자 fill out phr. (문서 등을) 작성하다 fill with phr. ~으로 가득 차다 smoke n. 연기
volunteer n. 지원자 be full of phr. ~으로 가득 차다 instruct v. 지시하다 behave v. 행동하다 report v. 보고하다; n. 보고서
rejection n. 거절 self-conscious adj. 남의 시선을 의식하는 prevalent adj. 일반적인 notion n. 생각 take action phr. 조치를 취하다
life-threatening adj. 생명을 위협하는 get in the way of phr. ~에게 방해되다 pressure n. 압력; v. 압박을 가하다
authorities n. 당국, 관계자 reminder n. 상기시키는 것 wise adj. 현명한 follow the crowd phr. 대세를 따르다

60 특정세부사항 연구의 결과

난이도 ●○○

What did the researchers find out about people in an emergency?

(a) that they take actions mostly to save themselves
(b) that the presence of others affects their reactions
(c) that they feel pressured to be socially responsible
(d) that the onlookers do not get involved without an incentive

연구원들은 비상사태에 있는 사람들에 관해 무엇을 알아냈는가?

(a) 주로 스스로를 구하기 위해 조치를 취한다는 것
(b) 다른 이들의 존재가 그들의 반응에 영향을 미친다는 것
(c) 사회적으로 책임을 지는 것에 압박을 느낀다는 것
(d) 방관자들은 보상 없이는 관여하지 않는다는 것

지텔프 치트키

연구의 결과를 언급하는 제목과 지문의 초반을 주의 깊게 읽는다.

해설 | 1단락의 'people's responses are influenced by those around them'에서 사람들의 반응이 그들 주변에 있는 사람들에 영향을 받는다고 했다. 따라서 (b)가 정답이다.

Paraphrasing

people's responses are influenced 사람들의 반응이 영향을 받는다 → affects their reactions 그들의 반응에 영향을 미친다
those around them 그들 주변에 있는 사람들 → the presence of others 다른 이들의 존재

어휘 | presence n. 존재 onlooker n. 방관자 incentive n. 보상

61 추론 묘사

난이도 ●●○

Which best describes Kitty Genovese's neighbors?

(a) They were uninterested in helping their neighbors.
(b) They did not perceive the illegal act.
(c) They expected police to come to stop the attack.
(d) They were careless with their own safety.

키티 제노비스의 이웃들을 가장 잘 묘사하는 것은 무엇인가?

(a) 이웃들을 돕는 것에 무관심했다.
(b) 위법 행위를 인지하지 않았다.
(c) 공격을 멈추기 위해 경찰이 올 것으로 예상했다.
(d) 그들 자신의 안전에 대해 부주의했다.

지텔프 치트키

질문의 키워드 neighbors가 그대로 언급된 주변 내용을 주의 깊게 읽는다.

해설 | 2단락의 'failed to act because each assumed that others in the crowd had already called for law enforcement'에서 키티 제노비스의 이웃들은 각자가 군중 속의 다른 사람들이 이미 사법 집행을 요청했다고 추측했기 때문에 행동하지 않았다고 한 것을 통해, 그들은 공격을 멈추기 위해 경찰이 올 것으로 예상했을 것임을 추론할 수 있다. 따라서 (c)가 정답이다.

Paraphrasing
law enforcement 사법 집행 → police ~ to stop the attack 공격을 멈추기 위한 경찰

어휘 | uninterested adj. 무관심한 perceive v. 인지하다 illegal adj. 위법의 careless adj. 부주의한

62 특정세부사항 What

난이도 ●●○

What were participants in the experiment required to do?

(a) write a report about any unusual occurrences
(b) discuss the reactions of other participants
(c) complete a questionnaire about themselves
(d) try to locate the source of smoke

실험의 참가자들은 무엇을 해야 했는가?

(a) 모든 특이한 사건에 대해 보고서를 작성한다
(b) 다른 참가자들의 반응을 논의한다
(c) 그들 자신에 관한 설문지를 완성한다
(d) 연기의 출처를 찾으려고 노력한다

지텔프 치트키

질문의 키워드 participants가 그대로 언급된 주변 내용을 주의 깊게 읽는다.

해설 | 3단락의 'Darley and Latané had three different groups of participants fill out a personal survey in a room'에서 달리와 라탄은 서로 다른 세 집단의 참가자들이 방 안에서 개인적인 설문 조사를 작성하게 했다고 했다. 따라서 (c)가 정답이다.

Paraphrasing
fill out a ~ survey 설문 조사를 작성하다 → complete a questionnaire 설문지를 완성하다
personal 개인적인 → about themselves 그들 자신에 관한

어휘 | occurrence n. 사건, 발생 questionnaire n. 설문지 locate v. 찾다 source n. 출처

63 추론 특정사실

난이도 ●●●

Why most likely would individuals not help someone facing a medical crisis?

(a) because they are afraid of contracting a deadly disease
(b) because their assistance could be overlooked
(c) because there may be more qualified people around
(d) because they lack the necessary leadership skills

사람들은 왜 의료적 위기에 처한 누군가를 돕지 않을 것 같은가?

(a) 치명적인 병에 걸리는 것이 두렵기 때문에
(b) 그들의 도움이 무시될 수 있기 때문에
(c) 주변에 더 자격이 있는 사람들이 있을 수도 있기 때문에
(d) 필수적인 리더십 능력이 부족하기 때문에

지텔프 치트키

질문의 키워드 medical crisis가 life-threatening emergency로 paraphrasing되어 언급된 주변 내용을 주의 깊게 읽는다.

해설 | 4단락의 'in a life-threatening emergency, some people do nothing because they ~ do not wish to get in the way of any medical professional who might be present'에서 생명을 위협하는 비상사태에서 일부 사람들은 있을지도 모르는 어떠한 의료 전문가에게라도 방해되고 싶지 않기 때문에 아무것도 하지 않는다고 한 것을 통해, 주변에 더 자격이 있는 사람들이 있을 수도 있기 때문에 사람들은 의료적 위기에 처한 누군가를 돕지 않을 것임을 추론할 수 있다. 따라서 (c)가 정답이다.

Paraphrasing
professional 전문가 → more qualified people 더 자격이 있는 사람들

어휘 | contract v. (병에) 걸리다 deadly adj. 치명적인 overlook v. 무시하다, 간과하다 qualified adj. 자격이 있는

64 특정세부사항 What

난이도 ●●○

Based on the article, what did the results of the study provide?

(a) suggestions on how to communicate in group settings
(b) reminders that the rate of crime is declining
(c) information on how authorities respond to illegal acts
(d) reasons crimes are not reported by witnesses

기사에 따르면, 연구 결과는 무엇을 제공했는가?

(a) 집단 환경에서 의사소통하는 방법에 대한 제안
(b) 범죄율이 감소하고 있음을 상기시킴
(c) 당국이 위법 행위에 대응하는 방법에 관한 정보
(d) 목격자들에 의해 범죄가 보고되지 않는 이유

지텔프 치트키

질문의 키워드 results of the study가 results of the experiment로 paraphrasing되어 언급된 주변 내용을 주의 깊게 읽는다.

해설 | 5단락의 'They offer an explanation for why information about criminal activity is ~ not provided to authorities'에서 그것들(실험의 결과)이 범죄 활동에 관한 정보가 왜 때때로 당국에 제공되지 않는지를 설명해 준다고 했다. 따라서 (d)가 정답이다.

Paraphrasing
provide 제공하다 → offer 제공하다
information about criminal activity is ~ not provided 범죄 활동에 관한 정보가 제공되지 않는다 → crimes are not reported 범죄가 보고되지 않는다

어휘 | setting n. 환경 decline v. 감소하다 witness n. 목격자

65 어휘 유의어

난이도 ●●○

In the context of the passage, potential means ________.

(a) capable
(b) promising
(c) possible
(d) plausible

지문의 문맥에서, 'potential'은 -을 의미한다.

(a) 할 수 있는
(b) 유망한
(c) 발생 가능성이 있는
(d) 타당한 것 같은

지텔프 치트키

밑줄 친 어휘의 유의어를 찾는 문제이므로, potential이 포함된 구절을 읽고 문맥을 파악한다.

해설 | 2단락의 'people look to others in a potential emergency to determine whether the situation is critical'은 사람들이 잠재적인 비상사태에서 그 상황이 위태로운지를 결정하기 위해 다른 사람들에게 의존한다는 뜻이므로, potential이 '잠재적인'이라는 의미로 사용된 것을 알 수 있다. 따라서 '발생 가능성이 있는'이라는 비슷한 의미의 (c) possible이 정답이다.

오답분석

(a) '할 수 있는'이라는 의미를 가진 capable은 주로 사람의 능력이나 자질을 나타낼 때 또는 사물의 성능을 나타낼 때 쓰이므로, 특정 상황의 발생 가능성을 설명하는 문맥에 어울리지 않아 오답이다.

66 어휘 유의어

난이도 ●●○

In the context of the passage, disregard means ________.

(a) ignore
(b) deny
(c) distract
(d) forget

지문의 문맥에서, 'disregard'는 -을 의미한다.

(a) 무시하다
(b) 부인하다
(c) 산만하게 하다
(d) 잊다

지텔프 치트키

밑줄 친 어휘의 유의어를 찾는 문제이므로, disregard가 포함된 구절을 읽고 문맥을 파악한다.

해설 | 3단락의 'volunteers grouped with actors usually tried to disregard the smoke since the actors did not react to it'은 연기자들과 무리 지어진 지원자들은 연기자들이 그것(연기)에 반응하지 않았기 때문에 대개 연기를 무시하려고 노력했다는 뜻이므로, disregard가 '무시하다'라는 의미로 사용된 것을 알 수 있다. 따라서 '무시하다'라는 같은 의미의 (a) ignore가 정답이다.

PART 3 [67~73] Encyclopedia Article 옥토버페스트의 유래 및 특징

표제어

OKTOBERFEST

정의

Oktoberfest, an event featuring beer and a traveling carnival, is the world's largest folk festival. It is held every autumn in Munich, Germany from mid-September to the first week of October, with millions of people attending to feast on beer and sausages.

유래 + 어원

[67]The festival began in October 1810, when Crown Prince Ludwig of Bavaria was married to Princess Theresa of Munich. To celebrate the wedding, the prince's subjects were invited to attend the festivities which were held on the fields in front of the city gates. The fields were named *Theresienwiese*, which means "Theresa's Meadow," in honor of the Crown Princess. A shortened version of this name, *d'Wiesn*, is what locals call Oktoberfest today.

변화 과정

In the following years, the event was repeated and games, plays, and rides were added, requiring large amounts of space and making the festival resemble a modern fair. However, by the late 1800s, [68]those responsible for Oktoberfest limited the area dedicated to other activities, devoting it instead to beer tents. Over time, [72]Oktoberfest evolved into a hybridized form of beer festival and carnival, known as a *Volksfest* in German.

Beer remains the focus of the modern version of the festival. Participants today consume roughly seven to eight million liters of specialty brews created by

옥토버페스트

맥주와 순회 축제를 특색으로 하는 행사인 옥토버페스트는 세계 최대의 민속 축제이다. 그것은 매년 가을에 독일 뮌헨에서 9월 중순부터 10월 첫째 주까지 열리는데, 수백만 명의 사람들이 맥주와 소시지를 마음껏 먹기 위해 참석한다.

[67]이 축제는 바이에른주의 루트비히 황태자와 뮌헨의 테레제 공주가 결혼한 1810년 10월에 시작되었다. 결혼을 축하하기 위해, 태자의 국민들은 축제 행사에 참석하도록 초대되었는데 이것은 성문 앞의 광장에서 개최되었다. 그 광장은 태자비에게 경의를 표하여 '테레제의 초원'이라는 뜻의 '테레지엔비제'라고 이름 지어졌다. 이 명칭의 축약형인 '비즌'은 오늘날 현지인들이 옥토버페스트를 부르는 명칭이다.

그 후 몇 년 동안, 행사가 반복되면서 게임, 놀이, 그리고 놀이기구가 추가되었는데, 이는 많은 공간을 필요로 했고 그 축제를 현대의 박람회와 비슷하게 만들었다. 하지만, 1800년대 후반에, [68]옥토버페스트를 책임지는 사람들은 다른 활동들에 제공되는 공간을 제한했으며, 대신에 그것을 맥주 천막으로 사용했다. 시간이 지나면서, [72]옥토버페스트는 맥주 축제와 카니발의 혼합된 형태로 발전하였으며, 독일어로 '폭스페스트'로 알려졌다.

맥주는 현대판 축제의 중심으로 남아 있다. 오늘날 참가자들은 뮌헨의 여섯 개 맥주 제조업체에 의해 만들어진 특제 양조 맥주를 대략 7백만에서 8백만 리

현대 축제 모습	six Munich beer-makers, [69]which have a higher alcohol content than typical German beers. The event doesn't kick off until the mayor taps the first keg of the festival and drinks one of these beers.	터 마시는데, [69]이것은 일반적인 독일 맥주보다 알코올 함유량이 더 높다. 행사는 시장이 축제의 첫 번째 맥주 통의 꼭지를 따고 이 맥주 중 하나를 마시고 나서야 시작된다.
문화적 측면의 의의	[70(a)]Oktoberfest also highlights other aspects of Bavarian culture, [70(b)]such as the traditional dress, called the *dirndl*, and traditional foods like the pretzel. Because of this, many German people view Oktoberfest as an important part of their national identity. Furthermore, [73]Oktoberfest reveals German culture to a significant number of outsiders, [70(c)]with international guests arriving from all over the world. As a result of this high turnout, the festival brings more than one billion euros to Munich in revenue annually.	[70(a)]옥토버페스트는 또한 바이에른 문화의 다른 측면들, [70(b)]예를 들어 '디른들'이라고 불리는 전통 의상과 프레첼과 같은 전통 음식을 강조한다. 이것 때문에, 많은 독일 사람들은 옥토버페스트를 그들의 국민 정체성의 중요한 부분으로 본다. 더욱이, [70(c)]옥토버페스트는 전 세계에서 찾아오는 국제 손님들을 포함하여, [73]상당히 많은 외부인들에게 독일 문화를 보여준다. 이 많은 참가자 수의 결과로, 축제는 뮌헨에 매년 10억 유로가 넘는 수익을 가져다준다.
현황	The Oktoberfest celebration has become one of the most well-known parts of German culture, and [71]countries around the world now take part by hosting their own versions of the festival.	옥토버페스트 기념행사는 독일 문화의 가장 유명한 부분 중 하나가 되었고, [71]전 세계 국가들은 이제 그들만의 방식으로 이 축제를 주최함으로써 참여한다.

어휘 | feature v. ~을 특색으로 하다; n. 특징 traveling adj. 순회하는, 여행의 carnival n. 축제, 카니발 folk adj. 민속의, 전통적인 feast on phr. ~을 마음껏 먹다, 대접하다 crown prince phr. 황태자 subject n. 국민, 신하 festivity n. 축제 행사 field n. 광장, 장 meadow n. 초원 in honor of phr. ~에게 경의를 표하여 local n. 현지인 require v. 필요로 하다 resemble v. 비슷하다, 닮다 modern adj. 현대의 fair n. 박람회 dedicate v. 제공하다, 바치다 devote v. 사용하다, 할애하다 hybridized adj. 혼합된 consume v. 마시다, 먹다 roughly adv. 대략 specialty n. 특제, 특산품 brew n. 양조 맥주; v. 양조하다 kick off phr. 시작되다 tap v. 꼭지를 따다, 두드리다 keg n. (맥주 등을 담는) 통 highlight v. 강조하다 national adj. 국민의, 국가의 identity n. 정체성 significant adj. 상당한, 중요한 outsider n. 외부인 turnout n. 참가자 수 revenue n. 수익 take part phr. 참여하다

67 특정세부사항 What

난이도 ●●○

Based on the article, what was the original purpose of Oktoberfest?

(a) celebrating the accession of Prince Ludwig
(b) commemorating the wedding of a royal couple
(c) promoting German beer-making innovations
(d) attracting visitors to the Kingdom of Bavaria

기사에 따르면, 옥토버페스트의 원래 목적은 무엇이었는가?

(a) 루트비히 태자의 즉위를 축하하는 것
(b) 왕실 부부의 결혼을 기념하는 것
(c) 독일의 맥주 주조 혁신을 촉진하는 것
(d) 바이에른 왕국에 방문객들을 끌어모으는 것

지텔프 치트키

질문의 키워드 original purpose와 관련된 주변 내용을 주의 깊게 읽는다.

해설 | 2단락의 'The festival began ~ when Crown Prince Ludwig of Bavaria was married to Princess Theresa of Munich.'에서 옥토버페스트가 황태자와 공주가 결혼했을 때 시작되었다고 한 뒤, 'To celebrate the wedding, ~ subjects ~ attend the festivities'에서 결혼을 축하하기 위해 태자의 국민들이 축제 행사에 참석하도록 초대되었다고 했다. 따라서 (b)가 정답이다.

Paraphrasing
To celebrate the wedding 결혼을 축하하기 위해 → commemorating the wedding 결혼을 기념하는 것

어휘 | accession n. 즉위, 취임 commemorate v. 기념하다 royal adj. 왕실의 innovation n. 혁신 attract v. 끌어모으다

68 추론 특정사실

난이도 ●●●

Why most likely did the Oktoberfest organizers reduce the number of activities?

(a) to limit injuries from drunken guests
(b) to allocate more of the budget to brewing beer
(c) to enable a longer period of celebration during the event
(d) to make more room for drinking venues

왜 옥토버페스트의 주최자들이 활동의 수를 줄인 것 같은가?

(a) 술에 취한 손님들의 부상을 막기 위해서
(b) 맥주를 양조하는 데 더 많은 예산을 할당하기 위해서
(c) 행사 중 더 긴 축하 기간을 가능하게 하기 위해서
(d) 술 마실 장소를 위한 공간을 더 만들기 위해서

지텔프 치트키

질문의 키워드 organizers가 those responsible로 paraphrasing되어 언급된 주변 내용을 주의 깊게 읽는다.

해설 | 3단락의 'those responsible for Oktoberfest limited the area dedicated to other activities, devoting it instead to beer tents'에서 옥토버페스트를 책임지는 사람들이 다른 활동들에 제공되는 공간을 제한하고 대신에 그것(그 공간)을 맥주 천막으로 사용했다고 한 것을 통해, 옥토버페스트 주최자들이 술 마실 장소를 위한 공간을 더 만들기 위해 활동의 수를 줄였을 것임을 추론할 수 있다. 따라서 (d)가 정답이다.

Paraphrasing
beer tents 맥주 천막 → drinking venues 술 마실 장소

어휘 | injury n. 부상 allocate v. 할당하다 venue n. 장소

69 특정세부사항 What

난이도 ●●○

According to the article, what can be said about the beers at Oktoberfest?

(a) They come with hybridized forms of modern beer.
(b) They contain more alcohol than ordinary beer.
(c) They are now the most common beers in Germany.
(d) They are all served from kegs tapped by the mayor.

기사에 따르면, 옥토버페스트의 맥주에 대해 무엇이 말해질 수 있는가?

(a) 혼합된 형태의 현대 맥주와 함께 제공된다.
(b) 일반 맥주보다 더 많은 알코올을 함유한다.
(c) 현재 독일에서 가장 흔한 맥주이다.
(d) 전부 시장이 꼭지를 딴 맥주 통에서 제공된다.

지텔프 치트키

질문의 키워드 beers at Oktoberfest가 specialty brews로 paraphrasing되어 언급된 주변 내용을 주의 깊게 읽는다.

해설 | 4단락의 'which have a higher alcohol content than typical German beers'에서 옥토버페스트의 특제 양조 맥주가 일반적인 독일 맥주보다 알코올 함유량이 더 높다고 했다. 따라서 (b)가 정답이다.

Paraphrasing
typical ~ beers 일반적인 맥주 → ordinary beer 일반 맥주

오답분석

(d) 4단락에서 시장이 축제의 첫 번째 맥주 통의 꼭지를 딴다고 했으므로, 옥토버페스트의 맥주가 전부 시장이 꼭지를 딴 맥주 통에서 제공된다는 것은 오답이다.

어휘 | contain v. 함유하다 ordinary adj. 일반적인

70 Not/True　Not 문제

난이도 ●●○

Which of the following statements is incorrect about Oktoberfest?

(a) It puts a spotlight on various aspects of Bavarian culture.
(b) It features traditional clothing and food items.
(c) It draws a large number of tourists from abroad.
(d) It costs Munich over one billion euros to put on.

다음 중 옥토버페스트에 대해 사실이 아닌 것은?

(a) 바이에른 문화의 다양한 측면들을 집중 조명한다.
(b) 전통 의복과 식품을 특색으로 한다.
(c) 해외에서 많은 관광객을 끌어들인다.
(d) 뮌헨이 개최하는 데 10억 유로 이상의 비용이 든다.

지텔프 치트키

보기의 키워드와 지문 내용을 대조하며 언급된 것을 하나씩 소거한다.

해설 | (d)는 지문에 언급되지 않았으므로, (d)가 정답이다.

오답분석

(a) 보기의 키워드 Barbarian culture가 그대로 언급된 5단락에서 옥토버페스트는 바이에른 문화의 다른 측면들을 강조한다고 언급되었다.
(b) 보기의 키워드 traditional이 그대로 언급된 5단락에서 옥토버페스트는 전통 의상과 전통 음식을 강조한다고 언급되었다.
(c) 보기의 키워드 tourists from abroad가 international guests로 paraphrasing되어 언급된 5단락에서 옥토버페스트는 전 세계에서 찾아오는 국제 손님들을 포함한다고 언급되었다.

어휘 | put a spotlight phr. 집중 조명하다, 이목을 집중시키다 various adj. 다양한 abroad adv. 해외에서 put on phr. 개최하다, 착용하다

71 특정세부사항　What

난이도 ●●○

Based on the article, what is a result of Oktoberfest getting more popular?

(a) an increase in Germany's expenditures
(b) the improvement of Munich's tourism facilities
(c) a decline in Germans traveling abroad
(d) the rise of similar events in other regions

기사에 따르면, 옥토버페스트가 더 많은 인기를 끌고 있는 것의 결과는 무엇인가?

(a) 독일의 지출 증가
(b) 뮌헨 관광 시설의 발전
(c) 독일인들의 해외여행 감소
(d) 다른 지역에서의 비슷한 행사 증가

지텔프 치트키

질문의 키워드 popular가 well-known으로 paraphrasing되어 언급된 주변 내용을 주의 깊게 읽는다.

해설 | 6단락의 'countries around the world now take part by hosting their own versions of the festival'에서 전 세계 국가들이 이제 그들만의 방식으로 이 축제(옥토버페스트)를 주최함으로써 참여한다고 했다. 따라서 (d)가 정답이다.

어휘 | expenditure n. 지출 facility n. 시설 decline n. 감소

72 어휘　유의어

난이도 ●○○

In the context of the passage, evolved means ________.

(a) extended

지문의 문맥에서, 'evolved'는 -을 의미한다.

(a) 확장했다

(b) stimulated **(c) developed** (d) moved	(b) 자극했다 **(c) 발전했다** (d) 이동했다

지텔프 치트키

밑줄 친 어휘의 유의어를 찾는 문제이므로, evolved가 포함된 구절을 읽고 문맥을 파악한다.

해설 | 3단락의 'Oktoberfest evolved into a hybridized form of beer festival and carnival'은 옥토버페스트가 맥주 축제와 카니발의 혼합된 형태로 발전했다는 뜻이므로, evolved가 '발전했다'라는 의미로 사용된 것을 알 수 있다. 따라서 '발전했다'라는 같은 의미의 (c) developed가 정답이다.

73 어휘 유의어

난이도 ●●○

In the context of the passage, reveals means _______. **(a) shows** (b) declares (c) uncovers (d) explains	지문의 문맥에서, 'reveals'는 -을 의미한다. **(a) 보여준다** (b) 선언한다 (c) 폭로한다 (d) 설명한다

지텔프 치트키

밑줄 친 어휘의 유의어를 찾는 문제이므로, reveals가 포함된 구절을 읽고 문맥을 파악한다.

해설 | 5단락의 'Oktoberfest reveals German culture to a significant number of outsiders'는 옥토버페스트가 상당히 많은 외부인들에게 독일 문화를 보여준다는 뜻이므로, reveals가 '보여준다'라는 의미로 사용된 것을 알 수 있다. 따라서 '보여준다'라는 같은 의미의 (a) shows가 정답이다.

오답분석

(c) '폭로하다'라는 의미의 uncover도 reveal의 사전적 유의어 중 하나이지만, uncover는 숨겨져 있거나 비밀이었던 것을 밝혀내거나 파헤친다는 것을 의미하므로 문맥에 어울리지 않아 오답이다.

PART 4 (74~80) Business Letter 연설을 요청하는 비즈니스 편지

수신인 정보	To: Pamburns@pearlliterary.com From: Hankdalton@brightonwriters.com Dear Pam Burns,	To: Pamburns@pearlliterary.com From: Hankdalton@brightonwriters.com Pam Burns님께,
편지의 목적: 워크숍 초대	[74]We, the Brighton Writers Club, are pleased to invite you to come and speak at our forthcoming Fiction and Publishing Workshop. This one-day event will be held at the Midtown Convention Center on August 20.	[74]저희 Brighton 작가 클럽은 귀하를 다가오는 소설 및 출판 워크숍에 오셔서 강연하시도록 초대하게 되어 기쁩니다. 이 하루 동안의 행사는 8월 20일 미드타운 컨벤션 센터에서 열릴 예정입니다.

기조 연설 제안	The workshop starts at 9 a.m., and we would like to offer you our keynote speaking slot at 11 a.m. [75]During our spring workshop, [79]you gave one of our most instrumental talks. Your story of how you transitioned from working as a chef to starting your career in the publishing world inspired many of our guests.	워크숍은 오전 9시에 시작되며, 저희는 오전 11시에 귀하에게 기조연설 시간을 제안드리고 싶습니다. [75]저희의 봄 워크숍 동안, [79]귀하는 저희에게 가장 중요한 강연들 중 하나를 해 주셨습니다. 요리사로 일하는 것으로부터 어떻게 출판업계에서 경력을 시작하는 것으로 이행했는지에 대한 귀하의 이야기는 많은 내빈들을 고무하였습니다.
요청 연설 내용	For this event, [76]we ask that you detail how you begin getting one of your clients a book deal with a major publishing house. We're sure [77]our attendees including aspiring writers, established authors, students, hobbyists, and other agents like yourself will be keenly interested to learn about the whole picture of this process.	이번 행사에서, [76]귀하가 어떻게 고객들 중 한 명에게 대형 출판사와의 도서 계약을 따주기 시작하셨는지를 상세히 설명해 주실 것을 요청드립니다. 저희는 [77]장차 저술가가 되려는 사람, 인정받는 작가, 학생, 취미 애호가, 그리고 귀하와 같은 다른 대행업자들을 포함한 참석자들이 이 과정의 전체적인 상황에 대해 알게 되는 것에 몹시 흥미를 느낄 것이라고 확신합니다.
세부 내용	Your prepared remarks need only to be 15 minutes long. You may notice that [80]the time allotment is five minutes shorter than previous engagements. We made this change in order to allow time for a question and answer session with the audience.	귀하가 준비하실 연설은 15분 분량이면 됩니다. [80]할당된 시간이 이전 계약보다 5분 더 짧다는 것을 인지하실 것입니다. 저희는 청중들과의 질의응답 시간을 가능하게 하기 위해 이렇게 변경하게 되었습니다.
끝인사	We very much hope you will be able to participate in our workshop and impart your knowledge and experience. To respond, please send me an email at Hankdalton@brightonwriters.com. [78]Once your attendance has been confirmed, I will be in contact in regards to taking care of transportation, accommodation, or any other logistical issues you may have.	저희는 귀하가 저희 워크숍에 참석하여 귀하의 지식과 경험을 전할 수 있기를 매우 희망합니다. 답장을 보내시려면, Hankdalton@brightonwriters.com으로 이메일을 보내 주시기 바랍니다. [78]귀하의 참석이 확정되면, 교통, 숙소, 또는 귀하에게 있을 수 있는 다른 어떤 실행 계획상의 사안들을 처리하는 것과 관련해 연락드리겠습니다.
발신인 정보	Sincerely, Hank Dalton	Hank Dalton 드림

어휘 | forthcoming adj. 다가오는, 곧 나올 publishing n. 출판 offer v. 제안하다 keynote speaking phr. 기조연설 slot n. 시간 transition v. 이행하다; n. 전환, 변천 inspire v. 고무하다 detail v. 상세히 설명하다 deal n. 계약, 거래 attendee n. 참석자 aspiring adj. 장차 ~이 되려는 established adj. 인정받는 hobbyist n. 취미 애호가 agent n. 대행업자 keenly adv. 몹시 remark n. 연설, 발언 allotment n. 할당, 할당량 engagement n. 계약, 약속 allow v. 가능하게 하다 impart v. 전하다 attendance n. 참석, 출석 confirm v. 확정하다, 확인하다 in regards to phr. ~과 관련하여 accommodation n. 숙소 logistical adj. 실행 계획상의

74 주제/목적 편지의 목적

난이도 ●○○

Why did Hank Dalton write an email to Pam Burns?

(a) to ask about her forthcoming work of fiction
(b) to invite her to appear at a seminar
(c) to send her a one-day pass to the convention
(d) to inform her about the benefits of the club

Hank Dalton은 왜 Pam Burns에게 이메일을 썼는가?

(a) 그녀의 곧 나올 소설 작품에 대해 물어보기 위해서
(b) 그녀를 세미나에 참석하도록 초대하기 위해서
(c) 그녀에게 전시회의 1일 이용권을 보내기 위해서
(d) 그녀에게 클럽의 혜택에 대해 알려주기 위해서

지텔프 치트키

지문의 초반을 주의 깊게 읽고 전체 맥락을 파악한다.

해설 | 1단락의 'We, the Brighton Writers Club, are pleased to invite you to come and speak at our forthcoming Fiction and Publishing Workshop.'에서 Hank Dalton이 Pam Burns를 다가오는 소설 및 출판 워크숍에 와서 강연하도록 초대하게 되어 기쁘다고 한 뒤, 기조연설을 제안하는 내용이 이어지고 있다. 따라서 (b)가 정답이다.

Paraphrasing
Workshop 워크숍 → seminar 세미나

어휘 | one-day pass phr. 1일 이용권 convention n. 전시회, 회의

75 특정세부사항 What

난이도 ●●○

What happened at the spring workshop?

(a) The opening speech lasted two hours.
(b) The keynote lecture started at 9 a.m.
(c) Pam Burns spoke about changing professions.
(d) Pam Burns talked about the world of food.

봄 워크숍에서는 무슨 일이 있었는가?

(a) 개회사가 두 시간 동안 지속되었다.
(b) 기조 강연이 오전 9시에 시작했다.
(c) Pam Burns가 직종을 바꾸는 것에 관해 이야기했다.
(d) Pam Burns가 식품계에 대해 이야기했다.

지텔프 치트키

질문의 키워드 spring workshop이 그대로 언급된 주변 내용을 주의 깊게 읽는다.

해설 | 2단락의 'During our spring workshop, you gave one of our most instrumental talks.'에서 Pam Burns가 봄 워크숍 동안 강연을 했다고 한 뒤, 'Your story of how you transitioned from working as a chef to starting your career in the publishing world'에서 그 강연은 요리사로 일하는 것으로부터 어떻게 출판업계에서 경력을 시작하는 것으로 이행했는지에 대한 이야기라고 했다. 따라서 (c)가 정답이다.

Paraphrasing
transitioned 이행했다 → changing 바꾸는

어휘 | profession n. 직종, 직업

76 추론 특정사실

난이도 ●●●

What is probably true about Burns's job?

(a) She is an established fiction writer.
(b) She still has a career as a chef.
(c) She helps authors publish books.
(d) She runs her own company.

Burns의 직업에 대해 사실인 것은 무엇일 것 같은가?

(a) 인정받는 소설 작가이다.
(b) 요리사로서의 직업을 여전히 가지고 있다.
(c) 작가들이 책을 출판하는 것을 돕는다.
(d) 그녀 자신의 회사를 경영한다.

지텔프 치트키

Burns가 하는 일에 대해 서술하는 3단락 내용을 주의 깊게 읽는다.

해설 | 3단락의 'we ask that you detail how you begin ~ a book deal with a major publishing house'에서 Burns가 어떻게 그녀

의 고객들 중 한 명에게 대형 출판사와의 도서 계약을 따주기 시작했는지를 상세히 설명해 줄 것을 요청한다고 한 것을 통해, Burns의 직업이 작가들이 책을 출판하는 것을 돕는 일일 것임을 추론할 수 있다. 따라서 (c)가 정답이다.

오답분석

(d) 3단락에서 Burns가 대행업자라고는 했지만, 그녀가 자신의 회사를 경영한다는 내용은 지문에 언급되지 않았으므로 오답이다.

어휘 | run v. 경영하다

77 특정세부사항 Who

난이도 ●●○

According to Hank Dalton, who will listen to Pam Burns's speech?

(a) those who manage a publishing company
(b) those who teach students in a literature department
(c) those who enjoy writing stories for fun
(d) those who specialize in the performing arts

Hank Dalton에 따르면, Pam Burns의 연설을 누가 들을 것인가?

(a) 출판사를 운영하는 사람들
(b) 문학 학과에서 학생들을 가르치는 사람들
(c) 취미 삼아 이야기 쓰기를 즐기는 사람들
(d) 공연 예술을 전공하는 사람들

지텔프 치트키

질문의 키워드인 who will listen이 attendees로 paraphrasing되어 언급된 주변 내용을 주의 깊게 읽는다.

해설 | 3단락의 'our attendees including ~ hobbyists, and other agents like yourself'에서 참석자들은 장차 저술가가 되려는 사람, 인정받는 작가, 학생, 취미 애호가, 그리고 다른 대행업자들을 포함한다고 했다. 따라서 (c)가 정답이다.

Paraphrasing
hobbyists 취미 애호가 → those who enjoy ~ for fun 취미 삼아 즐기는 사람들

오답분석

(a) 3단락에서 대행업자인 Burns는 고객에게 대형 출판사와의 도서 계약을 따준다고 한 것을 통해 대행업자와 출판사는 서로 다른 업종임을 알 수 있으므로 오답이다.

어휘 | literature n. 문학 department n. 학과 specialize in phr. ~을 전공하다 performing arts phr. 공연 예술

78 특정세부사항 What

난이도 ●●○

What will Hank Dalton do if Ms. Burns decides to come?

(a) make a lodging reservation
(b) share his experience about past workshop issues
(c) give her email address to a transportation service
(d) verify the attendance figures

만약 Ms. Burns가 오기로 결정한다면 Hank Dalton은 무슨 일을 할 것인가?

(a) 숙소 예약을 한다
(b) 지난 워크숍 문제에 대해 그의 경험을 공유한다
(c) 운송 회사에 그녀의 이메일 주소를 제공한다
(d) 참석자 수를 확인한다

지텔프 치트키

질문의 키워드인 decide to come이 attendance ~ confirmed로 paraphrasing되어 언급된 주변 내용을 주의 깊게 읽는다.

해설 | 5단락의 'Once your attendance has been confirmed, I will be in contact in regards to taking care of ~ accommodation, or any other logistical issues you may have.'에서 Burns의 참석이 확정되면 교통, 숙소, 또는 Burns에게 있을 수 있는 다른 어떤 실행 계획상의 사안들을 처리하는 것과 관련하여 연락하겠다고 했다. 따라서 (a)가 정답이다.

Paraphrasing
accommodation 숙소 → lodging 숙소

어휘 | lodging n. 숙소, 숙박 verify v. 확인하다 figure n. 수, 수치

79 어휘 유의어

난이도 ●●○

In the context of the passage, instrumental means _______.

(a) symbolic
(b) influential
(c) dominant
(d) agreeable

지문의 문맥에서, 'instrumental'은 -을 의미한다.

(a) 상징적인
(b) 영향력 있는
(c) 지배적인
(d) 기분 좋은

지텔프 치트키

밑줄 친 어휘의 유의어를 찾는 문제이므로, instrumental이 포함된 구절을 읽고 문맥을 파악한다.

해설 | 2단락의 'you gave one of our most instrumental talks'는 Pam Burns가 가장 중요한 연설들 중 하나를 해 주었다는 뜻이므로, instrumental이 '중요한'이라는 의미로 사용된 것을 알 수 있다. 따라서 '영향력 있는'이라는 비슷한 의미의 (b) influential이 정답이다.

80 어휘 유의어

난이도 ●○○

In the context of the passage, previous means _______.

(a) ensuing
(b) due
(c) following
(d) earlier

지문의 문맥에서, 'previous'는 -을 의미한다.

(a) 다음의
(b) 적절한
(c) 다음의
(d) 이전의

지텔프 치트키

밑줄 친 어휘의 유의어를 찾는 문제이므로, previous가 포함된 구절을 읽고 문맥을 파악한다.

해설 | 4단락의 'the time allotment is five minutes shorter than previous engagements'는 할당된 시간이 이전 계약보다 5분 더 짧다는 뜻이므로, previous가 '이전의'라는 의미로 사용된 것을 알 수 있다. 따라서 '이전의'라는 같은 의미의 (d) earlier가 정답이다.

문제집 p.44

정답 및 문제 유형 분석표

PART 1		PART 2		PART 3		PART 4	
53	(c) 특정세부사항	60	(a) 특정세부사항	67	(b) 특정세부사항	74	(a) 주제/목적
54	(b) 추론	61	(d) 특정세부사항	68	(d) 특정세부사항	75	(c) 추론
55	(d) 특정세부사항	62	(b) 추론	69	(d) Not/True	76	(d) 특정세부사항
56	(b) 추론	63	(a) 추론	70	(a) 특정세부사항	77	(b) Not/True
57	(b) 특정세부사항	64	(c) 특정세부사항	71	(c) 추론	78	(a) 특정세부사항
58	(a) 어휘	65	(b) 어휘	72	(c) 어휘	79	(c) 어휘
59	(d) 어휘	66	(d) 어휘	73	(b) 어휘	80	(b) 어휘

취약 유형 분석표

유형	맞힌 개수
주제/목적	/1
특정세부사항	/11
Not/True	/2
추론	/6
어휘	/8
TOTAL	28

PART 1 (53~59) Biography Article 미국 최초의 우주 탐험을 도운 수학자 캐서린 존슨

인물 이름

KATHERINE JOHNSON

인물 소개

Katherine Johnson was an American mathematician whose work played a vital role in America's first voyages into space. [53]She is best known for helping to break down racial and gender barriers as one of the first African-American women to work at NASA.

어린 시절

Katherine Johnson was born on August 26, 1918, in West Virginia as the youngest child of parents Joshua Coleman and Joylette Lowe. [58]She exhibited a strong aptitude for mathematics from a very young age. In fact, by the time she was 10, [54]she had completed the eighth grade, the highest level of education available to African Americans in her town. Not wanting to limit her potential, her family moved 120 miles away to another county, where she attended high school. Johnson completed high school at 14 and enrolled in West Virginia State College, graduating with degrees in Mathematics and French at the age of 18.

초기 활동

Johnson worked as a teacher until 1952 when she learned that the National Advisory Committee for Aeronautics (NACA) was hiring African-American women with math experience to serve as "computers" in [59]a segregated office. These human computers were required to complete time-consuming calculations for

캐서린 존슨

캐서린 존슨은 그녀의 활동이 미국의 첫 번째 우주 탐험에 중대한 역할을 했던 미국인 수학자였다. 그녀는 미국 항공 우주국(NASA)에서 일한 최초의 아프리카계 미국인 여성 중 한 명으로서 [53]인종과 성별 장벽을 허무는 것을 도운 것으로 가장 잘 알려져 있다.

캐서린 존슨은 1918년 8월 26일에, 웨스트버지니아주에서 조슈아 콜맨과 조일레트 로위 부부의 막내 아이로 태어났다. 매우 어린 나이부터 [58]그녀는 수학에 대한 큰 소질을 보였다. 사실, 그녀가 10살이 되었을 때, [54]그녀는 8학년을 끝냈는데, 이것은 그녀의 마을에서 아프리카계 미국인에게 가능한 가장 높은 수준의 교육이었다. 그녀의 잠재력을 제한하고 싶지 않았기 때문에, 그녀의 가족은 120마일 떨어진 다른 군으로 이사했고, 그곳에서 그녀는 고등학교에 다녔다. 존슨은 14살에 고등학교를 마치고 웨스트버지니아 주립 대학교에 입학했으며, 18살의 나이에 수학과 프랑스어 학위를 취득하며 졸업했다.

존슨은 미국 국가 항공자문위원회(NACA)가 [59]분리된 사무실에서 '컴퓨터'로 일할 수학 관련 경험이 있는 아프리카계 미국인 여성을 고용하고 있다는 것을 알게 된 1952년까지 교사로 일했다. 이러한 인간 컴퓨터들은 기술자들을 위해 시간 소모가 큰 계산들을 완료하도록 요구받았으며, 그 기술자들은 그것들을

	engineers, who would use them to create aircraft for national defense. She began working in 1953 at the NACA with other African-American women. Unlike the other computers, Johnson was assertive and asked questions. After only two weeks on the job, [55]she conducted a review of an engineer's calculations and caught a mistake. Impressed with this display of knowledge in analytical geometry, Johnson's boss reassigned her to work closely with the engineers, all of whom were white men.	국방용 항공기를 만드는 데 이용했다. 1953년에 그녀는 NACA에서 다른 아프리카계 미국인 여성들과 일하기 시작했다. 다른 인간 컴퓨터들과 다르게, 존슨은 적극적이었고 의문점들을 질의했다. 근무를 한 지 2주 만에, [55]그녀는 한 기술자의 계산을 검토했는데 오류를 찾아냈다. 해석 기하학에 대해 그녀가 보인 지식에 깊은 인상을 받은 존슨의 상사는 그녀를 재배치하여 모두 백인 남성이었던 기술자들과 긴밀하게 일하도록 했다.
주요 업적	Johnson quickly gained the respect of the engineers and was entrusted with increasingly important tasks. She worked on calculating the path Alan Shepard took when he became the first American to travel to space. She also helped send John Glenn into orbit around Earth in 1962, and this was the first time an American astronaut accomplished this feat. At this point, [56]NACA had been renamed NASA and was using electronic computers for calculations, but Glenn refused to fly until Johnson checked the figures herself.	존슨은 곧 기술자들의 존경을 받았고 점점 더 중요한 임무를 맡았다. 그녀는 앨런 셰퍼드가 우주로 가는 최초의 미국인이 되었을 때 그가 가는 항로를 계산하는 일을 했다. 그녀는 또한 1962년에 존 글렌을 지구 궤도에 보내는 것을 도왔고, 이것은 미국인 우주 비행사가 최초로 이 업적을 달성한 것이었다. 이 시점에, [56]NACA는 NASA로 이름이 바뀌었고 계산을 위해 전자 컴퓨터를 사용하고 있었는데도, 글렌은 존슨이 직접 계산을 확인해주기 전까지 비행하는 것을 거절했다.
말년 + 죽음	Johnson retired from NASA in 1986, with numerous achievements to her name, including mapping the moon's surface and helping the Apollo 13 astronauts return to Earth. Johnson died on February 24, 2020, at age 101, [57]having devoted her twilight years to encouraging students to follow their dreams of studying science, technology, engineering, and mathematics.	존슨은 1986년에 NASA에서 은퇴했는데, 달 표면을 도식화하고 아폴로 13호의 우주 비행사들이 지구로 돌아오는 것을 돕는 것을 포함하여 그녀의 이름으로 많은 업적을 남겼다. 존슨은 101살의 나이로, 2020년 2월 24일에 별세했는데, [57]그녀는 학생들이 과학, 기술, 공학, 그리고 수학을 공부하는 자신들의 꿈을 좇도록 장려하는 데 그녀 인생의 황혼기를 바쳤다.

어휘 | vital adj. 중대한, 필수적인 voyage n. 탐험, 항해 racial adj. 인종의 gender n. 성별 barrier n. 장벽, 장애물
African-American adj. 아프리카계 미국인의 exhibit v. 보이다, 전시하다 mathematics n. 수학 potential n. 잠재력
enroll v. 입학하다, 등록하다 degree n. 학위 advisory adj. 자문의 aeronautics n. 항공학 time-consuming adj. 시간 소모가 큰
calculation n. 계산 assertive adj. 적극적인 review n. 검토 impress v. 깊은 인상을 주다 analytical geometry phr. 해석 기하학
reassign v. (다른 임무·직책 등에) 재배치하다 entrust v. 맡기다 increasingly adv. 점점 더 path n. 항로, 길 orbit n. 궤도
astronaut n. 우주 비행사 accomplish v. 달성하다 feat n. 업적, 위업 rename v. 이름을 바꾸다 refuse v. 거절하다
figure n. 계산, 산수 retire v. 은퇴하다 achievement n. 업적 map v. 도식화하다 devote v. (노력·시간 등을) 바치다 twilight n. 황혼기

53 특정세부사항 유명한 이유

난이도 ●●○

What is Katherine Johnson most famous for?

(a) being the first African-American woman astronaut
(b) demanding the employment of women at NASA
(c) aiding in eliminating discrimination at NASA
(d) using a computer on the first space voyage

캐서린 존슨은 무엇으로 가장 유명한가?

(a) 최초의 아프리카계 미국인 여성 우주 비행사로
(b) NASA에 여성 고용을 요구한 것으로
(c) NASA에서의 차별 철폐를 도운 것으로
(d) 최초의 우주 탐험에서 컴퓨터를 사용한 것으로

지텔프 치트키

질문의 키워드 most famous for가 best known for로 paraphrasing되어 언급된 주변 내용을 주의 깊게 읽는다.

해설 | 1단락의 'She is best known for helping to break down racial and gender barriers'에서 캐서린 존슨은 인종과 성별 장벽을 허무는 것을 도운 것으로 가장 잘 알려져 있다고 했다. 따라서 (c)가 정답이다.

Paraphrasing

helping 도운 것 → aiding 도운 것

break down racial and gender barriers 인종과 성별 장벽을 허물다 → eliminating discrimination 차별 철폐

오답분석

(a) 1단락에서 캐서린 존슨이 NASA에서 일한 최초의 아프리카계 미국인 여성 중 한 명이라고는 했지만, 그녀가 우주 비행사였다고 한 것은 아니므로 오답이다.

어휘 | demand v. 요구하다 employment n. 고용 aid v. 돕다 eliminate v. 철폐하다, 없애다 discrimination n. 차별

54 추론 특정사실

난이도 ●●●

What could have prevented Johnson from getting an education?

(a) the family's move to an out-of-state town
(b) the lack of higher education for African Americans
(c) the high cost of receiving a university education
(d) the discrimination against female students

무엇이 존슨이 교육을 받는 것을 방해할 수도 있었던 것 같은가?

(a) 다른 주에 있는 마을로의 가족 이사
(b) 아프리카계 미국인들을 위한 고등 교육의 부족
(c) 대학 교육을 받는 것에 대한 높은 비용
(d) 여학생들에 대한 차별

지텔프 치트키

질문의 키워드 prevented가 limit으로 paraphrasing되어 언급된 주변 내용을 주의 깊게 읽는다.

해설 | 2단락의 'she had completed the eighth grade, the highest level of education available to African Americans in her town'에서 존슨의 마을에서 8학년이 아프리카계 미국인에게 가능한 가장 높은 수준의 교육이었다고 한 뒤, 'Not wanting to limit her potential, her family moved ~ where she attended high school.'에서 존슨의 잠재력을 제한하고 싶지 않았기 때문에 그녀의 가족은 이사했고 그곳에서 그녀가 고등학교에 다녔다고 한 것을 통해, 존슨이 교육을 받는 것을 방해할 수도 있었던 것은 아프리카계 미국인들을 위한 고등 교육의 부족이었을 것임을 추론할 수 있다. 따라서 (b)가 정답이다.

오답분석

(d) 2단락에서 존슨이 원래 살고 있던 마을에서는 아프리카계 미국인에게 가능한 교육 수준에 한계가 있었다고는 했지만, 여학생들에 대한 차별이 존재했다는 내용은 언급되지 않았으므로 오답이다.

어휘 | out-of-state adj. 다른 주의

55 특정세부사항 Why

난이도 ●●○

Why did Johnson's boss give her a new job?

(a) because the office became integrated
(b) because she earned an engineering degree

왜 존슨의 상사는 그녀에게 새로운 일을 주었는가?

(a) 사무실이 통합되었기 때문에
(b) 그녀가 공학 학위를 받았기 때문에

(c) because NACA stopped using human computers
(d) because she pointed out a mathematical error

(c) NACA가 인간 컴퓨터들의 사용을 중단했기 때문에
(d) 그녀가 수학적 오류를 잡아냈기 때문에

지텔프 치트키

질문의 키워드 Johnson's boss가 그대로 언급된 주변 내용을 주의 깊게 읽는다.

해설 | 3단락의 'she conducted a review of an engineer's calculations and caught a mistake'에서 존슨이 한 기술자의 계산을 검토하여 오류를 찾아냈다고 한 뒤, 'Impressed with this display of knowledge ~, Johnson's boss reassigned her'에서 그녀가 보인 지식에 깊은 인상을 받은 존슨의 상사가 그녀를 재배치하였다고 했다. 따라서 (d)가 정답이다.

Paraphrasing
give ~ a new job 새로운 일을 주다 → reassigned 재배치했다
caught a mistake 오류를 찾아냈다 → pointed out a ~ error 오류를 잡아냈다

어휘 | integrate v. 통합하다 earn v. 받다, (돈을) 벌다 point out phr. 잡아내다, 지적하다

56 추론 특정사실

난이도 ●●○

Why most likely did Glenn need Johnson's confirmation for his flight?

(a) He had no experience using electronic computers.
(b) He trusted her more than electronic computers.
(c) The electronic computers could not calculate the orbit.
(d) The computers made a dangerous miscalculation before.

왜 글렌은 그의 비행을 위해 존슨의 확인이 필요했을 것 같은가?

(a) 그는 전자 컴퓨터를 사용한 경험이 없었다.
(b) 그는 전자 컴퓨터보다 그녀를 더 믿었다.
(c) 전자 컴퓨터가 궤도를 계산할 수 없었다.
(d) 컴퓨터가 이전에 위험한 오산을 했다.

지텔프 치트키

질문의 키워드 Johnson's confirmation이 Johnson checked로 paraphrasing되어 언급된 주변 내용을 주의 깊게 읽는다.

해설 | 4단락의 'NACA had been renamed NASA and was using electronic computers for calculations, but Glenn refused to fly until Johnson checked the figures herself'에서 NASA가 계산을 위해 전자 컴퓨터를 사용하고 있었는데도 글렌은 존슨이 직접 계산을 확인해주기 전까지 비행하는 것을 거절했다고 한 것을 통해, 글렌은 전자 컴퓨터보다 존슨의 계산을 더 믿었기 때문에 그의 비행을 위해 존슨의 확인이 필요했을 것임을 추론할 수 있다. 따라서 (b)가 정답이다.

어휘 | confirmation n. 확인 miscalculation n. 오산

57 특정세부사항 How

난이도 ●●○

How did Johnson spend the final years of her life?

(a) by studying the moon's surface
(b) by inspiring students to pursue their ambitions
(c) by teaching technology at a college
(d) by completing calculations for Apollo 13 engineers

존슨은 그녀의 말년을 어떻게 보냈는가?

(a) 달의 표면을 연구하면서
(b) 학생들이 자신들의 포부를 추구하도록 고무하면서
(c) 대학에서 기술을 가르치면서
(d) 아폴로 13호의 기술자들을 위한 계산을 완료하면서

지텔프 치트키

질문의 키워드 final years가 twilight years로 paraphrasing되어 언급된 주변 내용을 주의 깊게 읽는다.

해설 | 5단락의 'having devoted her twilight years to encouraging students to follow their dreams of studying ~ mathematics'에서 존슨은 학생들이 수학 등을 공부하는 자신들의 꿈을 좇도록 장려하는 데 그녀 인생의 황혼기를 바쳤다고 했다. 따라서 (b)가 정답이다.

Paraphrasing

encouraging ~ to follow ~ dreams 꿈을 좇도록 장려하는 → inspiring ~ to pursue ~ ambitions 포부를 추구하도록 고무하는

어휘 | inspire v. 고무하다, 영감을 주다 pursue v. 추구하다 ambition n. 포부, 야망

58 어휘 유의어

난이도 ●●○

In the context of the passage, aptitude means _______.

(a) **talent**
(b) vigor
(c) passion
(d) attitude

지문의 문맥에서, 'aptitude'는 -을 의미한다.

(a) **재능**
(b) 활기
(c) 열정
(d) 태도

지텔프 치트키

밑줄 친 어휘의 유의어를 찾는 문제이므로, aptitude가 포함된 구절을 읽고 문맥을 파악한다.

해설 | 2단락의 'She exhibited a strong aptitude for mathematics'는 캐서린 존슨이 수학에 대한 큰 소질을 보였다는 뜻이므로, aptitude가 '소질'이라는 의미로 사용된 것을 알 수 있다. 따라서 '재능'이라는 비슷한 의미의 (a) talent가 정답이다.

59 어휘 유의어

난이도 ●●○

In the context of the passage, segregated means _______.

(a) confined
(b) classified
(c) dedicated
(d) **differentiated**

지문의 문맥에서, 'segregated'는 -을 의미한다.

(a) 좁고 사방이 막힌
(b) 분류된
(c) 전용의
(d) **구분된**

지텔프 치트키

밑줄 친 어휘의 유의어를 찾는 문제이므로, segregated가 포함된 구절을 읽고 문맥을 파악한다.

해설 | 3단락의 'a segregated office'는 분리된 사무실이라는 뜻이므로, segregated가 '분리된'이라는 의미로 사용된 것을 알 수 있다. 따라서 '구분된'이라는 비슷한 의미의 (d) differentiated가 정답이다.

오답분석

(b) '분류하다'라는 의미의 classify는 사람이나 사물을 유사성에 근거해 여러 집단으로 나누는 경우에 사용되는데, 문맥상 인종과 성별이라는 차별적 이유에 근거하여 분리된 사무실이라는 의미가 되어야 적절하므로 사람들을 특정한 인종이나 종교 등에 따라 차별하여 분리한다는 의미의 segregate의 유의어로 적절하지 않다.

연구 결과

RESEARCH FINDS A CLOSE LINK BETWEEN FACIAL EXPRESSIONS AND EMOTION

가설 소개

Numerous studies have led many scientists to theorize that facial expressions do more than represent emotions. Known as the facial feedback hypothesis, [60]this concept suggests the physical act of making a facial expression can provide feedback to the brain and influence our state of mind.

가설 유래

The facial feedback hypothesis stems from Charles Darwin's observation that [61]the experience of emotions is more intense when emotions are expressed freely and less intense when repressed. This idea was later developed by William James, who suggested that if we did not make facial expressions, we would not have emotions. Since then, [65]extensive research has been done on the facial feedback hypothesis, with the most notable study being conducted by researchers Fritz Strack, Leonard Martin, and Sabine Stepper in 1988.

연구1: 만화 시청 실험

In this study, participants were asked to observe humorous cartoons, either while holding a pen between their lips or teeth. The participants who held a pen between their teeth reported that the cartoons were funny more often than those who held a pen between their lips. [62]The researchers concluded this was because holding something between one's teeth forces the mouth into a smile. The physical act of smiling, therefore, can convince people that they are experiencing happiness.

연구2: 보톡스 치료 실험

A 2009 study involving Botox, a drug used to prevent sagging skin, also supports the hypothesis. Using fMRI, a technique that measures brain activity, [63]researcher Andreas Hennenlotter had participants react to [66]situations meant to induce anger before and after receiving a Botox treatment. Following the Botox treatments, participants were unable to frown naturally due to the facial paralysis resulting from the drug. He found the areas of their brains involved in processing emotions were no longer being activated with as much intensity as before. This shows the inability to physically express emotions changes how the brain responds to stimuli.

시사점

The most discussed implication of the facial feedback hypothesis is that, since the brain responds to smiling by releasing chemicals that actually make a person feel happier, even fake smiling may help elevate mood.

연구가 얼굴 표정과 감정 사이의 밀접한 연관성을 발견하다

여러 연구들은 많은 과학자가 얼굴 표정이 감정을 드러내는 것 이상으로 더 많은 것을 한다는 이론을 제시하도록 이끌었다. 안면 피드백 가설로 알려진 [60]이 개념은 얼굴 표정을 짓는 신체적 행위가 뇌에 피드백을 제공하여 우리의 정신 상태에 영향을 줄 수 있다는 것을 암시한다.

안면 피드백 가설은 [61]감정에 대한 경험이 감정이 자유롭게 표현될 때 더 강하고 억눌릴 때 덜 강하다는 찰스 다윈의 관찰에서 유래한다. 이 개념은 훗날 윌리엄 제임스에 의해 발전되었는데, 그는 우리가 얼굴 표정을 짓지 못하면, 감정을 가지지 못할 것이라고 말했다. 그 이후로, 안면 피드백 가설에 대한 [65]광범위한 연구가 이루어져 왔는데, 1988년에 연구원 프리츠 슈트라크, 레너드 마틴, 그리고 자비네 스테퍼에 의해 수행된 가장 주목할 만한 연구를 포함한다.

이 연구에서, 참가자들은 입술 사이나 치아 사이에 펜을 물고 재미있는 만화를 보라고 요청받았다. 치아 사이에 펜을 물고 있던 참가자들은 입술 사이에 펜을 물고 있던 참가자들보다 더 자주 만화가 재미있다고 보고했다. [62]연구원들은 이것이 치아 사이에 무언가를 물고 있는 것이 강제로 입을 웃게 만들었기 때문이었다는 결론을 내렸다. 따라서, 미소를 짓는 신체적 행위는 사람들에게 그들이 행복을 경험하고 있다는 것을 납득시킬 수 있다.

늘어지는 피부를 방지하는 데 사용되는 약물인 보톡스와 관련한 2009년의 연구도 이 가설을 뒷받침한다. 두뇌 활동을 측정하는 fMRI 기술을 사용하여, [63]연구원 안드레아스 헤넨로터는 보톡스 치료를 받기 전후로 [66]화를 유발하도록 의도된 상황에 참가자들이 반응하게 했다. 보톡스 치료 이후에, 참가자들은 그 약물로 인한 안면 마비 때문에 자연스럽게 얼굴을 찌푸릴 수 없었다. 그는 감정을 처리하는 데 관여하는 그들의 뇌 영역이 더 이상 예전만큼 강렬하게 활성화되지 않는다는 것을 발견했다. 이것은 신체적으로 감정을 표현하지 못하는 것이 뇌가 자극에 얼마나 반응하는지를 바꾼다는 것을 보여준다.

가장 많이 논의된 안면 피드백 가설의 시사점은, 뇌가 사람을 실제로 더 행복하게 만드는 화학 물질을 방출함으로써 미소 짓는 것에 반응하기 때문에, 심지어 가짜 웃음도 기분을 좋게 하는 데 도움을 줄 수 있다

Another suggestion is that cognitive processes are influenced by smiling because [64]physically altering one's facial expressions can affect the volume and temperature of blood flow to the brain.	는 것이다. 또 다른 시사점은 인지 과정이 미소 짓는 것에 의해 영향을 받는다는 것인데 이는 [64]신체적으로 얼굴 표정을 바꾸는 것이 뇌로 가는 혈류의 양과 온도에 영향을 미칠 수 있기 때문이다.

어휘 | facial adj. 얼굴의, 안면의 expression n. 표정, 표현 theorize v. 이론을 제시하다 represent v. 드러내다, 표현하다 hypothesis n. 가설 concept n. 개념 suggest v. 암시하다, 시사하다 physical adj. 신체적인 stem from phr. ~에서 유래하다 observation n. 관찰 intense adj. 강한, 강렬한 repress v. 억누르다 notable adj. 주목할 만한 conduct v. 수행하다 humorous adj. 재미있는 report v. 보고하다, 알리다 conclude v. 결론을 내리다 convince v. 납득시키다 sag v. 늘어지다 react v. 반응하다 treatment n. 치료, 치료제 frown v. 얼굴을 찌푸리다 paralysis n. 마비 activate v. 활성화하다 intensity n. 강렬함, 강도 stimulus n. 자극 implication n. 시사점, 암시 release v. 방출하다 chemical n. 화학 물질 fake adj. 가짜의, 거짓된 elevate v. 기분을 좋게 하다, 높이다 cognitive adj. 인지의, 인식의 alter v. 바꾸다, 고치다 volume n. 양, 부피 blood flow phr. 혈류

60 특정세부사항 연구의 결과

난이도 ●●○

What does the article say about the facial feedback hypothesis?

(a) that physically expressing an emotion generates that emotion
(b) that expressions do not always indicate feelings
(c) that we can understand others through their facial expressions
(d) that different brain regions are responsible for different emotions

기사는 안면 피드백 가설에 관해 무엇이라고 말하는가?

(a) 신체적으로 감정을 표현하는 것이 그 감정을 일으킨다는 것
(b) 표정이 항상 감정을 나타내지는 않는다는 것
(c) 우리가 다른 사람들의 얼굴 표정을 통해 그들을 이해할 수 있다는 것
(d) 각기 다른 대뇌 영역이 서로 다른 감정을 담당한다는 것

지텔프 치트키

연구의 결과를 언급하는 지문의 초반을 주의 깊게 읽는다.

해설 | 1단락의 'this concept suggests the physical act of making a facial expression can ~ influence our state of mind'에서 안면 피드백 가설 개념은 얼굴 표정을 짓는 신체적 행위가 우리의 정신 상태에 영향을 줄 수 있다는 것을 암시한다고 했다. 따라서 (a)가 정답이다.

Paraphrasing
physical act of making ~ expression 표정을 짓는 신체적 행위 → physically expressing 신체적으로 표현하는 것
state of mind 정신 상태 → emotion 감정

어휘 | generate v. 일으키다, 발생시키다 indicate v. 나타내다 brain region phr. 대뇌 영역 responsible for phr. ~을 담당하는

61 특정세부사항 What

난이도 ●●○

What did Charles Darwin discover about emotional experiences?

(a) People cannot feel any emotions without them.
(b) They force people to feel more positive emotions.

찰스 다윈은 감정적인 경험들에 관해 무엇을 발견했는가?

(a) 사람들은 그것들 없이는 어떠한 감정도 느낄 수 없다.
(b) 그것들은 더 긍정적인 감정을 느끼도록 사람들을 강제한다.

(c) People are inclined to suppress intense negative feelings.
(d) They are enhanced when emotions are not inhibited.

(c) 사람들은 강렬한 부정적 감정을 억누르려는 경향이 있다.
(d) 그것들은 감정이 억제되지 않을 때 강화된다.

지텔프 치트키

질문의 키워드 Charles Darwin이 그대로 언급된 주변 내용을 주의 깊게 읽는다.

해설 | 2단락의 'the experience of emotions is more intense when emotions are expressed freely'에서 감정에 대한 경험은 감정이 자유롭게 표현될 때 더 강하다고 했다. 따라서 (d)가 정답이다.

Paraphrasing
more intense when ~ expressed freely 자유롭게 표현될 때 더 강한 → enhanced when ~ not inhibited 억제되지 않을 때 강화되는

오답분석

(c) 2단락에서 감정이 억눌릴 때 감정에 대한 경험이 덜 강하다고는 했지만, 사람들이 감정을 억누르는 경향이 있는지는 언급되지 않았으므로 오답이다.

어휘 | be inclined to phr. ~하는 경향이 있다 suppress v. 억누르다, 숨기다 enhance v. 강화하다 inhibit v. 억제하다, 저해하다

62 추론 특정사실

난이도 ●●○

Why most likely were some participants not able to enjoy the cartoons as much?

(a) because they were unfamiliar with watching cartoons
(b) because they were incapable of making a happy face
(c) because they reported feeling unhappier than usual
(d) because they could not see their facial expression

왜 일부 참가자들은 만화를 그만큼 즐길 수 없었던 것 같은가?

(a) 만화를 보는 것이 익숙하지 않았기 때문에
(b) 행복한 얼굴을 만들 수 없었기 때문에
(c) 평소보다 더 불행하게 느낀다고 보고했기 때문에
(d) 자신들의 얼굴 표정을 볼 수 없었기 때문에

지텔프 치트키

질문의 키워드 cartoons가 그대로 언급된 주변 내용을 주의 깊게 읽는다.

해설 | 3단락의 'The researchers concluded this was because holding something between one's teeth forces the mouth into a smile.'에서 연구원들은 이것(치아 사이에 펜을 물고 있던 참가자들이 입술 사이에 펜을 물고 있던 참가자들보다 더 자주 만화가 재미있다고 보고한 것)이 치아 사이에 무언가를 물고 있는 것이 강제로 입을 웃게 만들었기 때문이었다는 결론을 내렸다고 했다. 이를 통해 일부 참가자들은 행복한 얼굴을 만들 수 없었기 때문에 만화를 그만큼 즐길 수 없었을 것임을 추론할 수 있다. 따라서 (b)가 정답이다.

어휘 | unfamiliar adj. 익숙하지 않은 incapable of phr. ~을 할 수 없는

63 추론 특정사실

난이도 ●●●

Which can be said about Hennenlotter's research?

(a) It involved situations prompting the same emotion.
(b) Participants were able to move their faces normally.

헤넨로터의 연구에 대해 무엇이 말해질 수 있는가?

(a) 같은 감정을 촉발하는 상황을 수반했다.
(b) 참가자들이 정상적으로 자신들의 얼굴을 움직일 수 있었다.

(c) Participants' brain activity remained consistent. (d) It relied on the use of a mental health treatment.	(c) 참가자들의 두뇌 활동이 일관성을 유지했다. (d) 정신 건강 치료제의 사용에 의존했다.

지텔프 치트키

질문의 키워드 Hennenlotter가 그대로 언급된 주변 내용을 주의 깊게 읽는다.

해설 | 4단락의 'researcher ~ Hennenlotter had participants react to situations meant to induce anger before and after receiving a Botox treatment'에서 연구원 헤넨로터는 보톡스 치료를 받기 전후로 화를 유발하도록 의도된 상황에 참가자들이 반응하게 했다고 한 것을 통해, 헤넨로터의 연구는 '화'라는 같은 감정을 촉발하는 상황을 수반했을 것임을 추론할 수 있다. 따라서 (a)가 정답이다.

오답분석

(b) 4단락에서 참가자들은 보톡스로 인한 안면 마비 때문에 자연스럽게 얼굴을 찌푸릴 수 없었다고 했으므로 오답이다.

(c) 4단락에서 헤넨로터는 참가자들의 뇌 영역이 더 이상 예전만큼 강렬하게 활성화되지 않는다는 것을 발견했다고 했으므로 오답이다.

어휘 | prompt v. 촉발하다, 유도하다 remain v. 계속 ~이다 consistent adj. 일관성 있는, 변함없는 rely on phr. ~에 의존하다, 기대다

64 특정세부사항 How

난이도 ●●○

According to the facial feedback hypothesis, how does the act of smiling have an effect on the brain? (a) by adding more intellectual processes (b) by altering its total volume **(c) by changing features of blood flow** (d) by reducing the intensity of chemicals	안면 피드백 가설에 따르면, 미소를 짓는 행위는 어떻게 뇌에 영향을 미치는가? (a) 더 지능을 요하는 과정을 추가함으로써 (b) 그것의 총 부피를 바꿈으로써 **(c) 혈류의 특징을 바꿈으로써** (d) 화학 물질의 강도를 줄임으로써

지텔프 치트키

질문의 키워드 the act of smiling have an effect가 influenced by smiling으로 paraphrasing되어 언급된 주변 내용을 주의 깊게 읽는다.

해설 | 5단락의 'physically altering one's facial expressions can affect the volume and temperature of blood flow to the brain'에서 신체적으로 얼굴 표정을 바꾸는 것이 뇌로 가는 혈류의 양과 온도에 영향을 미칠 수 있다고 했다. 따라서 (c)가 정답이다.

Paraphrasing

volume and temperature of blood flow 혈류의 양과 온도 → features of blood flow 혈류의 특징

어휘 | intellectual adj. 지능을 요하는, 지적인 feature n. 특징, 특색

65 어휘 유의어

난이도 ●●●

In the context of the passage, extensive means _______. (a) contemplative **(b) comprehensive** (c) consequential (d) experimental	지문의 문맥에서, 'extensive'는 -을 의미한다. (a) 사색하는 **(b) 광범위한** (c) 중대한 (d) 실험적인

지텔프 치트키

밑줄 친 어휘의 유의어를 찾는 문제이므로, extensive가 포함된 구절을 읽고 문맥을 파악한다.

해설 | 2단락의 'extensive research has been done'은 광범위한 연구가 이루어져 왔다는 뜻이므로, extensive가 '광범위한'이라는 의미로 사용된 것을 알 수 있다. 따라서 '광범위한'이라는 같은 의미의 (b) comprehensive가 정답이다.

66 어휘 유의어

난이도 ●●○

In the context of the passage, induce means ______.

(a) deepen
(b) influence
(c) guide
(d) cause

지문의 문맥에서, 'induce'는 -을 의미한다.

(a) 깊게 하다
(b) 영향을 주다
(c) 인도하다
(d) 야기하다

지텔프 치트키

밑줄 친 어휘의 유의어를 찾는 문제이므로, induce가 포함된 구절을 읽고 문맥을 파악한다.

해설 | 4단락의 'situations meant to induce anger'는 화를 유발하도록 의도된 상황이라는 뜻이므로, induce가 '유발하다'라는 의미로 사용된 것을 알 수 있다. 따라서 '야기하다'라는 비슷한 의미의 (d) cause가 정답이다.

PART 3(67~73) Encyclopedia Article 3차원의 가상 세계인 메타버스의 정의 및 한계

표제어

METAVERSE

정의

The metaverse is a highly immersive virtual world in which cutting-edge technologies enable people to interact whenever and however they like.

유래

The term comes from *meta*, meaning "beyond", and universe, and was introduced by science-fiction author Neal Stephenson in his 1992 novel, *Snow Crash*. [67]In Stephenson's fictional metaverse, human avatars interact inside a 3D virtual world that is clearly distinct from the physical one. As envisioned today, however, the metaverse will link the virtual and physical worlds through the Internet so that they are closely intertwined.

목표 + 의의

[72]The metaverse is considered to be the next step in the Internet's natural evolution. Whereas the Internet's current social and mobile innovations provide rich content and functionality, [68]the metaverse aims to utilize the newest technologies like artificial intelligence and

메타버스

메타버스는 최첨단 기술이 사람들이 원할 때 언제든지 그리고 원하는 어떤 방식으로도 상호 작용할 수 있게 하는 고도의 몰입형 가상 세계이다.

이 용어는 '넘어서'라는 의미의 'meta', 그리고 universe(우주)에서 비롯되었으며, 공상 과학 작가 닐 스티븐슨의 1992년 소설 『스노 크래시』에서 소개되었다. [67]스티븐슨의 소설 속 메타버스에서, 인간의 아바타들은 물리적 세계와는 뚜렷이 구별되는 3차원의 가상 세계 안에서 상호 작용한다. 하지만, 오늘날 상상되는 것처럼, 메타버스는 인터넷을 통해 가상 세계와 물리적 세계를 연결하여 그것들이 밀접하게 관련되도록 할 것이다.

[72]메타버스는 인터넷의 자연스러운 진화의 다음 단계로 여겨진다. 인터넷의 현재의 사회적 혁신과 모바일 혁신이 풍부한 콘텐츠와 기능성을 제공하긴 하지만, [68]오늘날 인터넷의 더 깊이 몰두하게 하는 버전을 만들기 위해 메타버스는 인공 지능과 가상 현실 헤드폰과

virtual-reality headsets to create a more deeply engaging version of today's Internet. This will allow people to seamlessly interact across different virtual platforms for work, entertainment, and more, giving people the ability to perform Internet-enabled activities in a more cohesive way.

예시

[69(b)]Some have compared metaverse to living within the Internet rather than viewing it from the outside. And [69(d)]while the metaverse as a whole does not presently exist, many parts of it already do. Examples include [69(a)]streaming technologies that permit large groups of people to hold live chats online, video games with complex rule-based systems and virtual economies, and [69(c)]software-based robots that help people do their jobs in finance, medicine, customer service, and more.

한계

For the metaverse to become widespread, however, three key challenges must be overcome. First, Internet access will have to be persistent, or available everywhere at all times, requiring wider adoption of wireless network technologies. Second, [70]the metaverse must allow users to work across multiple platforms and devices with minimal trouble. Finally, issues like security and privacy should be solved.

현황 + 과제

Because of these and other obstacles, the metaverse is unlikely to be monopolized by a single company. Rather, it will demand that [73]competing firms combine their efforts. And [71]if these firms should succeed, together they will create a powerful platform that will integrate people's digital and physical worlds.

같이 최신의 기술을 활용하는 것을 목표로 한다. 이것은 사람들이 노동, 오락 등을 위한 서로 다른 가상의 플랫폼들 전반에 걸쳐 매끄럽게 상호 작용할 수 있게 할 것이며, 사람들에게 인터넷 기반 활동들을 더욱 결합력 있는 방식으로 수행할 수 있는 능력을 줄 것이다.

[69(b)]일부 사람들은 메타버스를 외부에서 바라보는 것보다는 인터넷 속에서 사는 것에 비유했다. 그리고 [69(d)]전체로서의 메타버스는 현재 존재하지 않지만, 그것의 많은 부분들은 이미 존재한다. 사례들은 [69(a)]큰 무리의 사람들이 온라인으로 실시간 채팅을 여는 것을 허용하는 스트리밍 기술, 복잡한 규칙 기반 체제와 가상 경제를 갖춘 비디오 게임, 그리고 [69(c)]사람들이 금융, 의료, 고객 서비스 등의 업무를 하는 것을 돕는 소프트웨어 기반의 로봇을 포함한다.

하지만, 메타버스가 널리 확산되게 하기 위해서는, 세 가지 주요 문제가 극복되어야만 한다. 첫째, 인터넷 접속은 끊임없거나, 항상 어디에서나 이용 가능해야 할 것이며, 이는 무선 네트워크 기술의 더욱 광범위한 채택을 필요로 한다. 둘째, [70]메타버스는 이용자들이 최소한의 수고로 다양한 플랫폼과 장치들을 오가며 작업할 수 있게 해야 한다. 마지막으로, 보안과 사생활 같은 문제들이 해결되어야 한다.

이것들과 다른 방해물들 때문에, 메타버스가 단 하나의 회사에 의해 독점될 가능성은 거의 없다. 오히려, 이것은 [73]경쟁하는 회사들이 그것들의 노력을 결합하는 것을 요구할 것이다. 그리고 [71]이러한 회사들이 성공하려면, 그것들은 함께 사람들의 디지털 세계와 물리적 세계를 통합할 강력한 플랫폼을 만들어야 할 것이다.

어휘 | immersive adj. 몰입형의 virtual adj. 가상의 cutting-edge adj. 최첨단의 interact v. 상호 작용을 하다 come from phr. ~에서 비롯되다 beyond prep. ~을 넘어서 science-fiction adj. 공상 과학의 distinct adj. 구별되는 envision v. 상상하다 intertwine v. 관련짓다, 엮다 evolution n. 진화 current adj. 현재의 innovation n. 혁신 functionality n. 기능성 artificial adj. 인공적인 intelligence n. 지능 virtual-reality adj. 가상 현실의 engaging adj. 몰두하게 하는 seamlessly adv. 매끄럽게 cohesive adj. 결합력 있는 presently adv. 현재, 곧 exist v. 존재하다 streaming n. 스트리밍(인터넷에 연결된 상태에서 실시간으로 재생하는 행위) complex adj. 복잡한 rule-based adj. 규칙 기반의 finance n. 금융, 재정 overcome v. 극복하다 access n. 접속 persistent adj. 끊임없는 adoption n. 채택, 선정 wireless adj. 무선의 minimal adj. 최소한의 security n. 보안 privacy n. 사생활 obstacle n. 방해물 monopolize v. 독점하다 compete v. 경쟁하다 firm n. 회사 integrate v. 통합하다

67 특정세부사항 What

난이도 ●●○

What was Stephenson's idea of a metaverse?

(a) a video game where people choose their avatars
(b) a digital world separate from the real one

스티븐슨의 메타버스에 대한 생각은 무엇이었는가?

(a) 사람들이 자신들의 아바타를 고르는 비디오 게임
(b) 실제 세계와 분리된 디지털 세계

(c) an online space where money can be exchanged
(d) an electronic device installed in a laboratory

(c) 화폐가 교환될 수 있는 온라인 공간
(d) 실험실에 설치된 전자 장치

지텔프 치트키

질문의 키워드 Stephenson이 그대로 언급된 주변 내용을 주의 깊게 읽는다.

해설 | 2단락의 'In Stephenson's fictional metaverse, human avatars interact inside a 3D virtual world that is clearly distinct from the physical one.'에서 스티븐슨의 소설 속 메타버스에서 인간의 아바타들은 물리적 세계와는 뚜렷이 구별되는 3차원의 가상 세계 안에서 상호 작용한다고 했다. 따라서 (b)가 정답이다.

Paraphrasing
distinct from the physical one 물리적인 것과는 구별되는 → separate from the real one 실제의 것과 분리된

오답분석
(a) 2단락에서 스티븐슨의 소설 속 메타버스에서 인간의 아바타들이 3차원의 가상 세계 안에서 상호 작용한다고는 했지만, 이것은 비디오 게임이 아니므로 오답이다.

어휘 | separate adj. 분리된, 독립된 exchange v. 교환하다 install v. 설치하다 laboratory n. 실험실

68 특정세부사항 How

난이도 ●●○

How can the existing Internet be converted into the metaverse?

(a) by exploiting current mobile networks
(b) by taking advantage of social media
(c) by centralizing the processing of data
(d) by using the latest tech advancements

어떻게 기존 인터넷이 메타버스로 전환될 수 있는가?

(a) 현재의 모바일 네트워크를 이용함으로써
(b) 소셜 미디어를 이용함으로써
(c) 정보 처리를 집중시킴으로써
(d) 최신 기술 발전을 이용함으로써

지텔프 치트키

질문의 키워드 existing Internet이 today's Internet으로 paraphrasing되어 언급된 주변 내용을 주의 깊게 읽는다.

해설 | 3단락의 'the metaverse aims to utilize the newest technologies ~ to create a more deeply engaging version of today's Internet'에서 오늘날 인터넷의 더 깊이 몰두하게 하는 버전을 만들기 위해 메타버스는 최신의 기술을 활용하는 것을 목표로 한다고 했다. 따라서 (d)가 정답이다.

Paraphrasing
utilize the newest technologies 최신의 기술을 활용하다 → using the latest tech advancements 최신 기술 발전을 이용함

어휘 | convert v. 전환하다 exploit v. 이용하다 take advantage of phr. ~을 이용하다 centralize v. 집중시키다 processing n. 처리, 가공

69 Not/True True 문제

난이도 ●●○

Based on the passage, which of the following is true about the metaverse today?

(a) It requires robots to monitor streaming technologies.

지문에 따르면, 다음 중 오늘날 메타버스에 관해 사실인 것은?

(a) 스트리밍 기술을 감시할 로봇을 필요로 한다.

(b) It draws people closer physically than before.
(c) It depends on technologies that are not yet available.
(d) It exists as smaller pieces of a whole.

(b) 사람들을 예전보다 물리적으로 더 가깝게 끌어모은다.
(c) 아직 이용할 수 없는 기술들에 의존한다.
(d) 전체의 더 작은 부분들로 존재한다.

지텔프 치트키

질문의 키워드 today가 presently로 paraphrasing되어 언급된 주변 내용을 주의 깊게 읽고, 보기의 키워드와 지문 내용을 대조하며 읽는다.

해설 | (d)의 키워드인 pieces가 parts로 paraphrasing되어 언급된 4단락의 'while the metaverse as a whole does not presently exist, many parts of it already do'에서 전체로서의 메타버스는 현재 존재하지 않지만, 그것의 많은 부분들은 이미 존재한다고 했으므로 지문의 내용과 일치한다. 따라서 (d)가 정답이다.

오답분석

(a) 보기의 키워드 streaming technologies가 그대로 언급된 4단락에서 스트리밍 기술이 사람들이 온라인으로 실시간 채팅을 여는 것을 허용한다고는 했지만, 스트리밍 기술을 감시할 로봇을 필요로 한다는 내용은 언급되지 않았다.
(b) 4단락에서 일부 사람들은 메타버스를 외부에서 바라보는 것보다는 인터넷 속에서 사는 것에 비유했다고 했으므로 지문의 내용과 반대된다.
(c) 4단락에서 메타버스는 사람들이 금융, 의료, 고객 서비스 등의 업무를 하는 것을 돕는 소프트웨어 기반의 로봇을 포함한다고 했으므로 지문의 내용과 일치하지 않는다.

어휘 | monitor v. 감시하다 draw v. 끌어모으다

70 특정세부사항 What

난이도 ●●●

What is one difficulty that the developers of the metaverse have to address?

(a) making it easier to use across various devices
(b) enabling persistent updates on Internet networks
(c) lowering the price of metaverse hardware products
(d) providing guidance to unfamiliar new users

메타버스의 개발자들이 해결해야 할 한 가지 어려움은 무엇인가?

(a) 다양한 장치에 걸쳐 사용하는 것을 더 쉽게 만드는 것
(b) 인터넷 네트워크의 끊임없는 업데이트를 가능하게 하는 것
(c) 메타버스 하드웨어 제품의 가격을 낮추는 것
(d) 익숙하지 않은 새로운 이용자들에게 지침을 제공하는 것

지텔프 치트키

질문의 키워드 difficulty가 challenges로 paraphrasing되어 언급된 주변 내용을 주의 깊게 읽는다.

해설 | 5단락의 'the metaverse must allow users to work across multiple platforms and devices with minimal trouble'에서 메타버스는 이용자들이 최소한의 수고로 다양한 플랫폼과 장치들을 오가며 작업할 수 있게 해야 한다고 했다. 따라서 (a)가 정답이다.

Paraphrasing
work across multiple ~ devices 다양한 장치들을 오가며 작업하다 → use across various devices 다양한 장치에 걸쳐 사용하다

오답분석

(b) 5단락에서 무선 네트워크 기술의 더욱 광범위한 채택을 필요로 한다고는 했지만, 이것이 인터넷 네트워크의 끊임없는 업데이트를 의미하는 것은 아니므로 오답이다.

어휘 | address v. 해결하다, 다루다 guidance n. 지침, 안내

71 추론 특정사실

난이도 ●●●

Why most likely will companies not hold monopolies in the metaverse?

(a) to relieve excessive competition
(b) to avoid the risks of the metaverse market failing
(c) to bring about a merged reality collectively
(d) to deploy marketing strategies for the metaverse

왜 회사들은 메타버스에 대한 독점권을 갖지 않을 것 같은가?

(a) 과도한 경쟁을 완화하기 위해서
(b) 메타버스 시장 실패의 위험을 피하기 위해서
(c) 단결하여 통합된 현실을 생기게 하기 위해서
(d) 메타버스를 위한 마케팅 전략을 알맞게 사용하기 위해서

지텔프 치트키

질문의 키워드 hold monopolies가 monopolized로 paraphrasing되어 언급된 주변 내용을 주의 깊게 읽는다.

해설 | 6단락의 'if these firms should succeed, together they will create a powerful platform that will integrate people's digital and physical worlds'에서 메타버스 관련 회사들이 성공하려면 그것들은 함께 사람들의 디지털 세계와 물리적 세계를 통합할 강력한 플랫폼을 만들어야 할 것이라고 한 것을 통해, 단결하여 통합된 현실을 생기게 하기 위해서 회사들이 메타버스에 대한 독점권을 갖지 않을 것임을 추론할 수 있다. 따라서 (c)가 정답이다.

Paraphrasing
integrate people's digital and physical worlds 사람들의 디지털 세계와 물리적 세계를 통합하다 → bring about a merged reality 통합된 현실을 생기게 하다

어휘 | relieve v. 완화하다, 경감시키다 excessive adj. 과도한, 지나친 failing n. 실패, 결함 bring about phr. 생기게 하다, 일으키다 merge v. 통합하다, 합치다 collectively adv. 단결하여 deploy v. 알맞게 사용하다 strategy n. 전략

72 어휘 유의어

난이도 ●●○

In the context of the passage, considered means ______.

(a) spotlighted
(b) assumed
(c) regarded
(d) valued

지문의 문맥에서, 'considered'는 -을 의미한다.

(a) 이목이 쏠리는
(b) 추정되는
(c) 여겨지는
(d) 평가되는

지텔프 치트키

밑줄 친 어휘의 유의어를 찾는 문제이므로, considered가 포함된 구절을 읽고 문맥을 파악한다.

해설 | 3단락의 'The metaverse is considered to be the next step in the Internet's natural evolution.'은 메타버스가 인터넷의 자연스러운 진화의 다음 단계로 여겨진다는 뜻이므로, considered가 '여겨지는'이라는 의미로 사용된 것을 알 수 있다. 따라서 '여겨지는'이라는 같은 의미의 (c) regarded가 정답이다.

오답분석
(b) '추정하다'라는 의미의 assume은 어떤 것을 사실이라고 믿거나 기정사실로 추정하는 경우에 사용하므로, 무엇을 특정하게 생각하거나 여긴다는 의미의 consider의 유의어로 적절하지 않아 오답이다.

73 어휘 유의어

난이도 ●○○

In the context of the passage, efforts means _______.

(a) purposes
(b) endeavors
(c) duties
(d) benefits

지문의 문맥에서, 'efforts'는 -을 의미한다.

(a) 목적
(b) 노력
(c) 임무
(d) 혜택

지텔프 치트키

밑줄 친 어휘의 유의어를 찾는 문제이므로, efforts가 포함된 구절을 읽고 문맥을 파악한다.

해설 | 6단락의 'competing firms combine their efforts'는 경쟁하는 회사들이 그것들의 노력을 결합한다는 뜻이므로, efforts가 '노력'이라는 의미로 사용된 것을 알 수 있다. 따라서 '노력'이라는 같은 의미의 (b) endeavors가 정답이다.

PART 4(74~80) Business Letter 사진 기자 일자리를 제안하는 편지

수신인 정보

Mr. Robert Meyers
849 Springer Drive
Rochester, NY 15074

Dear Mr. Meyers,

편지의 목적: 일자리 제안

[74]We are delighted to offer you the position of staff photographer at Moment Magazine.

수신인 칭찬

Out of all the candidates, you made the strongest impression during the interview process. [75]Our hiring managers were struck by your confidence, experience, and knowledge, all of which will be major assets going forward in this role.

회사의 사명

In addition, the photography project you shared with us as a required work sample not only [79]showcased your skill but also summed up the mission of our monthly magazine. As you know, [76]we aim to capture moments of extraordinary individuals accomplishing great feats despite difficult challenges.

계약 조건

For this position, Moment Magazine is providing a full-time, [77(a)]one-year contract starting on November 1 [77(d)]at our downtown office. [77(c)]Standard work hours of 9 a.m. to 6 p.m., Monday through Friday, will apply. [77(b)]The staff photographer works under the editor-in-chief, with whom you had your final interview.

급여 + 복지

As for compensation, you will be paid a yearly salary of 50,000 dollars, with payments made once every two weeks via direct deposit. Also, as an employee at Moment

Mr. Robert Meyers
스프링어가 849번지
15074 뉴욕주 로체스터

Mr. Meyers께,

[74]당신에게 Moment 잡지사의 사진 기자 자리를 제안하게 되어 아주 기쁩니다.

모든 지원자들 중, 당신이 면접 과정에서 가장 강한 인상을 남겼습니다. [75]당사의 인사 관리자들은 당신의 자신감, 경험, 그리고 지식에 감동 받았으며, 이것들은 모두 이 역할에 장차 주요한 자산이 될 것입니다.

게다가, 필수 작업 샘플로서 당신이 우리와 공유한 사진 촬영 프로젝트는 [79]당신의 기술을 돋보이게 했을 뿐만 아니라 우리 월간 잡지의 사명을 압축해서 보여주기도 했습니다. 아시다시피, [76]우리는 어려운 도전에도 불구하고 대단한 위업들을 달성한 뛰어난 개인들의 순간을 정확히 담아내는 것을 목표로 합니다.

이 직책에 대해, Moment 잡지사는 정규직의 [77(d)]시내 사무실에서 [77(a)]11월 1일부터 시작하는 1년 계약을 제공합니다. [77(c)]월요일부터 금요일, 오전 9시에서 오후 6시까지의 표준 근무 시간이 적용될 것입니다. [77(b)]당사의 사진 기자는 편집장 밑에서 일하며, 당신의 최종 면접을 진행했던 사람입니다.

보수에 있어서 당신은 연봉 5만 달러를 받게 될 것이며, 보수는 자동 이체를 통해 2주마다 한 번씩 지급될 것입니다. 또한, Moment 잡지사의 직원으로서 당신은 건강 보험과 치아 보험, 그리고 고용주와 사용자가 같은 비율로 적립하는 퇴직 연금을 받을 자격이 있습니다.

	Magazine, you will be eligible for health and dental insurance, and an employer-matching retirement plan.	
회신 요청	Should [80]you accept this offer, we would like to ask that you respond to this email as soon as possible. [78]We are intent on completing job training before October 17 at the latest. Please feel free to reach me by phone at 508-555-7122 with any questions you may have.	[80]당신이 이 제안을 수락하신다면, 가능한 한 빨리 이 이메일에 회신을 주시기를 요청합니다. [78]우리는 늦어도 10월 17일 전까지 실무 교육을 완료하는 데 열중하고 있습니다. 어떠한 질문이라도 있으시다면 전화 508-555-7122로 편하게 저에게 연락해 주시기 바랍니다.
끝인사	Congratulations! We are looking forward to having you join the team.	축하드립니다! 우리는 당신이 팀에 합류하기를 기대하고 있습니다.
발신인 정보	Sincerely, Mary Wilson Hiring Director Moment Magazine	Mary Wilson 드림 인사부장 Moment 잡지사

어휘 | delighted adj. 아주 기뻐하는 offer v. 제안하다; n. 제안, 제의 position n. 자리, 직책 candidate n. 지원자, 후보자 impression n. 인상 hiring n. 인사, 고용 strike v. 감동하게 하다, 치다 asset n. 자산 going forward phr. 장차, 앞으로 share v. 공유하다 sum up phr. 압축해서 보여주다 capture v. 정확히 담아내다 moment n. 순간, 시기 extraordinary adj. 뛰어난, 특별한 accomplish v. 달성하다 feat n. 위업, 공적 contract n. 계약 standard adj. 표준의 apply v. 적용되다 editor-in-chief n. 편집장 compensation n. 보수, 보상 direct deposit phr. 자동 이체 eligible adj. 자격이 있는 insurance n. 보험 employer-matching retirement plan phr. 고용주 매칭 퇴직 연금(고용주와 사용자가 같은 비율로 적립하는 퇴직 연금) be intent on phr. ~에 열중하다, 여념이 없다 at the latest phr. 늦어도 look forward to phr. ~을 기대하다, 고대하다

74 주제/목적 편지의 목적

난이도 ●○○

Why did Mary Wilson write a letter to Robert Meyers?

(a) to extend an employment opportunity at a magazine
(b) to list the qualities of a good photographer
(c) to inform him about an available writer position
(d) to explain the interview process in detail

왜 Mary Wilson은 Robert Meyers에게 편지를 썼는가?

(a) 잡지사에서의 취업 기회를 제공하기 위해서
(b) 좋은 사진 기자의 자질을 열거하기 위해서
(c) 그에게 가능한 작가 자리에 관해 알려주기 위해서
(d) 인터뷰 과정을 자세히 설명하기 위해서

지텔프 치트키

지문의 초반을 주의 깊게 읽고 전체 맥락을 파악한다.

해설 | 1단락의 'We are delighted to offer you the position of staff photographer at Moment Magazine.'에서 Robert Meyers에게 Moment 잡지사의 사진 기자 자리를 제안하게 되어 아주 기쁘다고 했다. 따라서 (a)가 정답이다.

Paraphrasing
offer ~ the position 자리를 제안하다 → extend an employment opportunity 취업 기회를 제공하다

어휘 | extend v. 제공하다, 주다 employment n. 취업, 고용 list v. 열거하다 quality n. 자질, 특성 in detail phr. 자세히

75 추론 묘사

난이도 ●●○

How can Robert Meyers most likely be described?

(a) He is the only applicant for the photographer role.
(b) He is not confident about getting the job.
(c) He is competent enough as a photographer.
(d) He is an experienced interviewer.

Robert Meyers는 어떻게 묘사될 수 있을 것 같은가?

(a) 사진 기자 역할의 유일한 지원자이다.
(b) 취직하는 것에 대해 자신감이 없다.
(c) 사진 기자로서 충분히 역량이 있다.
(d) 경험이 있는 면접관이다.

지텔프 치트키

수신인 Robert Meyers에 대해 평가한 지문의 초반을 주의 깊게 읽는다.

해설 | 2단락의 'Our hiring managers were struck by your confidence, experience, and knowledge, all of which will be major assets going forward in this role.'에서 Moment 잡지사의 인사 관리자들은 Robert Meyers의 자신감, 경험, 그리고 지식에 감동 받았으며, 이것들은 모두 이 역할(잡지사의 사진 기자)에 장차 주요한 자산이 될 것이라고 한 것을 통해, 그는 사진 기자로서 충분히 역량이 있을 것임을 추론할 수 있다. 따라서 (c)가 정답이다.

오답분석

(a) 2단락에서 Robert Meyers가 모든 지원자들 중 가장 강한 인상을 남겼다고 했으므로, 그가 사진 기자 역할의 유일한 지원자라는 것은 지문의 내용과 일치하지 않아 오답이다.

어휘 | applicant n. 지원자 competent adj. 역량이 있는, 유능한

76 특정세부사항 What

난이도 ●●○

According to Ms. Wilson, what is the goal of Moment Magazine?

(a) to give motivation to accomplished individuals
(b) to document people's everyday problems
(c) to capture readers going through difficult moments
(d) to share stories of remarkable achievements

Ms. Wilson에 따르면, Moment 잡지사의 목표는 무엇인가?

(a) 기량이 뛰어난 개인들에게 동기 부여를 하는 것
(b) 사람들의 일상 문제들을 기록하는 것
(c) 어려운 시기를 겪는 독자들을 정확히 담아내는 것
(d) 놀랄 만한 업적들의 이야기를 공유하는 것

지텔프 치트키

질문의 키워드 goal이 aim으로 paraphrasing되어 언급된 주변 내용을 주의 깊게 읽는다.

해설 | 3단락의 'we aim to capture moments of extraordinary individuals accomplishing great feats despite difficult challenges'에서 Moment 잡지사는 어려운 도전에도 불구하고 대단한 위업들을 달성한 뛰어난 개인들의 순간을 정확히 담아내는 것을 목표로 한다고 했다. 따라서 (d)가 정답이다.

Paraphrasing
great feats 대단한 위업들 → remarkable achievements 놀랄 만한 업적들

어휘 | accomplished adj. 기량이 뛰어난, 재주가 많은 document v. 기록하다 go through phr. ~을 겪다 remarkable adj. 놀랄 만한

77 Not/True Not 문제

난이도 ●●○

Which is not true about the photographer role at the company?

(a) It will last until October next year.
(b) It will oversee the editor-in-chief.
(c) Its schedule consists of normal weekday hours.
(d) Its duties will be performed at the downtown office.

그 회사의 사진 기자의 역할로 사실이 아닌 것은?

(a) 내년 10월까지 지속될 것이다.
(b) 편집장을 감독할 것이다.
(c) 일정은 표준 근무 시간으로 구성된다.
(d) 업무는 시내 사무실에서 수행될 것이다.

지텔프 치트키

질문의 키워드 role이 position으로 paraphrasing되어 언급된 주변 내용을 주의 깊게 읽고, 보기의 키워드와 지문 내용을 대조하며 언급되는 것을 하나씩 소거한다.

해설 | (b)는 4단락의 'The staff photographer works under the editor-in-chief'에서 당사의 사진 기자는 편집장 밑에서 일한다고 언급되었으므로 지문의 내용과 일치하지 않는다. 따라서 (b)가 정답이다.

오답분석

(a) 계약 기간이 언급된 4단락에서 11월 1일부터 시작하는 1년 계약을 제공한다고 언급되었다.
(c) 보기의 키워드 normal weekday hours가 standard work hours로 paraphrasing되어 언급된 4단락에서 표준 근무 시간이 적용될 것이라고 언급되었다.
(d) 보기의 키워드 downtown office가 그대로 언급된 4단락에서 시내 사무실에서의 계약을 제공한다고 언급되었다.

어휘 | oversee v. 감독하다 normal adj. 표준의, 정규의 duty n. 업무, 임무

78 특정세부사항 Why

난이도 ●●○

Why is Ms. Wilson asking Mr. Meyers for an immediate reply?

(a) because she wants to finish career training by a certain date
(b) because she will temporarily close the office at the month's end
(c) because she needs a photographer for the company's latest project
(d) because she will have to start contacting photography subjects

왜 Ms. Wilson은 Mr. Meyers에게 즉각적인 회신을 요청하고 있는가?

(a) 특정 날짜까지 직업 교육을 완료하기를 원하기 때문에
(b) 월말에 일시적으로 사무실을 닫을 것이기 때문에
(c) 회사의 최신 프로젝트를 위해 사진 기자가 필요하기 때문에
(d) 사진 촬영 대상들에게 연락하기 시작해야 할 것이기 때문에

지텔프 치트키

질문의 키워드 immediate가 as soon as possible로 paraphrasing되어 언급된 주변 내용을 주의 깊게 읽는다.

해설 | 6단락의 'We are intent on completing job training before October 17 at the latest.'에서 Moment 잡지사는 늦어도 10월 17일 전까지 실무 교육을 완료하는 데 열중하고 있다고 했다. 따라서 (a)가 정답이다.

Paraphrasing

completing job training 실무 교육을 완료하는 것 → finish career training 직업 교육을 완료하다
before October 17 10월 17일 전까지 → by a certain date 특정한 날짜까지

어휘 | temporarily adv. 일시적으로, 임시로 contact v. 연락하다 subject n. 대상, 소재

79 어휘 유의어

난이도 ●●○

In the context of the passage, <u>showcased</u> means _______.

(a) boasted
(b) assessed
(c) demonstrated
(d) guaranteed

지문의 문맥에서, 'showcased'는 -을 의미한다.

(a) 자랑했다
(b) 평가했다
(c) 명백히 나타냈다
(d) 보장했다

지텔프 치트키

밑줄 친 어휘의 유의어를 찾는 문제이므로, showcased가 포함된 구절을 읽고 문맥을 파악한다.

해설 | 3단락의 'showcased your skill'은 기술을 돋보이게 했다는 뜻이므로, showcased가 '돋보이게 했다'라는 의미로 사용된 것을 알 수 있다. 따라서 '명백히 나타냈다'라는 비슷한 의미의 (c) demonstrated가 정답이다.

80 어휘 유의어

난이도 ●○○

In the context of the passage, <u>offer</u> means _______.

(a) inquiry
(b) proposal
(c) decision
(d) deal

지문의 문맥에서 'offer'는 -을 의미한다.

(a) 조사
(b) 제안
(c) 결정
(d) 거래

지텔프 치트키

밑줄 친 어휘의 유의어를 찾는 문제이므로, offer가 포함된 구절을 읽고 문맥을 파악한다.

해설 | 6단락의 'you accept this offer'는 제안을 수락한다는 뜻이므로, offer가 '제안'이라는 의미로 사용된 것을 알 수 있다. 따라서 '제안'이라는 같은 의미의 (b) proposal이 정답이다.

07회 실전모의고사

문제집 p.52

정답 및 문제 유형 분석표							
PART 1		PART 2		PART 3		PART 4	
53	(d) 특정세부사항	60	(b) 주제/목적	67	(c) 특정세부사항	74	(b) 주제/목적
54	(a) 추론	61	(d) 특정세부사항	68	(b) 특정세부사항	75	(a) 특정세부사항
55	(c) 특정세부사항	62	(a) 특정세부사항	69	(b) Not/True	76	(d) 특정세부사항
56	(a) 특정세부사항	63	(c) 추론	70	(d) 추론	77	(d) 특정세부사항
57	(b) 특정세부사항	64	(c) 특정세부사항	71	(c) 특정세부사항	78	(c) 추론
58	(b) 어휘	65	(d) 어휘	72	(a) 어휘	79	(c) 어휘
59	(c) 어휘	66	(b) 어휘	73	(b) 어휘	80	(d) 어휘

취약 유형 분석표	
유형	맞힌 개수
주제/목적	/2
특정세부사항	/13
Not/True	/1
추론	/4
어휘	/8
TOTAL	28

PART 1 (53~59) Biography Article 세계적인 환경 운동가 그레타 툰베리

인물 이름

GRETA THUNBERG

인물 소개

Greta Thunberg is a Swedish environmental activist who is leading millions of young people to demand climate change action. [53]She is famous for publicly challenging world leaders even at a young age and she became the first teenager chosen to be *Time* magazine's Person of the Year since that tradition started in 1927.

어린 시절 + 업적 시작 계기

Greta Thunberg was born on January 3, 2003, in Stockholm, Sweden. Her father, Svante Thunberg, is an actor, and her mother, Malena Ernman, is an international opera singer. Greta Thunberg first learned about climate change when she was eight years old. She did not understand why so little was being done about it and fell into a deep depression. She began asking her family to reduce their environmental impact by becoming vegan and giving up air travel. [54]When they complied with her demands, her mother even sacrificing her career, Thunberg felt hopeful that she could make a real difference.

초기 활동

Greta Thunberg's climate change activism began in August 2018. That was when she started missing school to spend her days outside the Swedish Parliament holding up a sign reading "School Strike for Climate." [55]She was reportedly inspired by [58]teenagers in the United States who refused to go to school as a result of

그레타 툰베리

그레타 툰베리는 수백만 명의 젊은이들이 기후 변화 조치를 요구하도록 이끌고 있는 스웨덴의 환경 운동가이다. [53]그녀는 어린 나이에도 세계 지도자들에게 공개적으로 이의를 제기한 것으로 유명하며 1927년에 그 전통이 시작된 이래 타임지의 '올해의 인물'로 선정된 첫 번째 십 대가 되었다.

그레타 툰베리는 2003년 1월 3일에 스웨덴의 스톡홀름에서 태어났다. 그녀의 아버지 스반테 툰베리는 배우이고, 그녀의 어머니 말레나 에른만은 세계적인 오페라 가수이다. 그레타 툰베리는 그녀가 8살이었을 때 기후 변화에 대해 처음 알게 되었다. 그녀는 왜 그것에 대해 그렇게 아무것도 행해지고 있지 않았는지를 이해하지 못했고 깊은 침울감에 빠졌다. 그녀는 자신의 가족에게 엄격한 채식주의자가 되고 비행기 여행을 포기함으로써 그들이 환경에 미치는 영향을 줄이자고 요청하기 시작했다. [54]그녀의 어머니는 심지어 자신의 경력을 희생하기까지 하며 그들이 그녀의 요구를 받아들였을 때, 툰베리는 그녀가 실질적인 변화를 만들 수 있다는 희망을 느꼈다.

그레타 툰베리의 기후 변화 행동주의는 2018년 8월에 시작되었다. 그때 그녀는 스웨덴 의회 밖에서 '기후를 위한 학교 파업'이라고 쓰인 팻말을 들고 그녀의 나날들을 보내느라 학교에 빠지기 시작했다. [55]알려진 바에 따르면 그녀는 [58]증가하는 총기 폭력의 결과로 학교 가기를 거부했던 미국의 십 대들로부터 영감을 받았다. 소셜 미디어에 도움을 구하는 것은 툰베리가 그녀의 메시지를 전파하는 데 도움이 되었다.

	mounting gun violence. Turning to social media helped Thunberg spread her message. By October, she was participating in demonstrations across Europe. Two months later, an estimated 20,000 students in over 270 cities were skipping school on Fridays to join her campaign, which brought the world's attention to how strongly young people want to effect change.
주요 활동	Thunberg has gained considerable notice for her many speaking engagements, [56]with her appearance at the 2018 United Nations Climate Change Conference making her known around the world. Thunberg, who was 15 at the time, joined [59]iconic figures like the Dalai Lama, former US Vice President Al Gore, and British naturalist Sir David Attenborough in urging world leaders to reduce emissions.
평가	For her contributions to raising awareness of climate issues, Thunberg received three consecutive Nobel Peace Prize nominations from 2019 to 2021 and [57]she was named one of the 10 most valuable people of 2019 by *Nature*, a world-renowned scientific journal. The following year, a Nathan Grossman documentary about her life called *I Am Greta* was shown at the Venice Film Festival. Clearly, her activism has made her a global leader in the cause.

10월까지, 그녀는 유럽 전역에 걸쳐 시위에 참석하고 있었다. 두 달 후, 270개가 넘는 도시에서 추산 2만 명의 학생들이 그녀의 운동에 합류하기 위해 금요일마다 학교를 빼먹었으며, 이는 젊은이들이 얼마나 강경하게 변화를 가져오고 싶어하는지에 대한 세계의 관심을 불러왔다.

[56]2018년 유엔 기후변화협약에 출석하여 그녀가 전 세계에 알려지게 되고, 툰베리는 그녀의 많은 연설 참여로 상당한 주목을 받아 왔다. 그 당시 15살이었던 툰베리는 세계 지도자들에게 배기가스를 줄이라고 촉구하는 것에 있어 [59]달라이 라마, 전 미국 부통령 앨 고어, 그리고 영국의 동식물학자 데이비드 애튼버러경과 같은 유명한 인물들과 함께했다.

기후 문제에 대한 인식을 고취시키는 데 기여한 공로로, 툰베리는 2019년에서 2021년까지 3년 연속으로 노벨 평화상 후보에 올랐고 [57]세계적으로 유명한 과학 학술지인 「네이처」에 의해 2019년의 가장 중요한 인물 10인 중 한 명으로 선정되었다. 이듬해에, 그녀의 삶에 관한 나탄 그로스만의 「나는 그레타」라는 다큐멘터리가 베니스 국제영화제에서 상영되었다. 분명히, 그녀의 행동주의가 그 운동에 있어 그녀를 세계적인 지도자로 만들었다.

어휘 | environmental activist phr. 환경 운동가 publicly adv. 공개적으로 challenge v. ~에게 이의를 제기하다 depression n. 침울감 vegan n. 엄격한 채식주의자 comply v. 받아들이다, 따르다 sacrifice v. 희생하다 activism n. 행동주의 parliament n. 의회, 국회 hold up phr. ~을 들다 reportedly adv. 알려진 바에 따르면, 소문에 의하면 inspire v. 영감을 주다 violence n. 폭력, 폭행 turn to phr. ~에 도움을 구하다 demonstration n. 시위 effect v. (어떤 결과를) 가져오다 considerable adj. 상당한, 많은 notice n. 주목, 관심 engagement n. 참여, 약속 figure n. 인물 naturalist n. 동식물학자 urge v. 촉구하다 emission n. 배기가스 awareness n. 의식 consecutive adj. 연속적인 nomination n. 후보에 오름 name v. 선정하다, 지명하다 world-renowned adj. 세계적으로 유명한 cause n. 운동, 대의

53 특정세부사항 유명한 이유

난이도 ●●○

What is Greta Thunberg best known for?

(a) challenging conventional ideas about activists
(b) logging the effects of global warming
(c) being the youngest environmental leader in Sweden
(d) questioning influential people as a youth

그레타 툰베리는 무엇으로 가장 잘 알려져 있는가?

(a) 운동가에 대한 상투적인 생각에 도전한 것
(b) 지구 온난화의 영향을 기록한 것
(c) 스웨덴에서 최연소 환경 선도자가 된 것
(d) 어릴 때 영향력 있는 사람들에게 이의를 제기한 것

지텔프 치트키

질문의 키워드 best known for가 famous for로 paraphrasing되어 언급된 주변 내용을 주의 깊게 읽는다.

해설 | 1단락의 'She is famous for publicly challenging world leaders even at a young age'에서 그레타 툰베리가 어린 나이에도 세계 지도자들에게 공개적으로 이의를 제기한 것으로 유명하다고 했다. 따라서 (d)가 정답이다.

Paraphrasing

challenging world leaders even at a young age 어린 나이에도 세계 지도자들에게 이의를 제기한 것 → questioning influential people as a youth 어릴 때 영향력 있는 사람들에게 이의를 제기한 것

오답분석

(c) 1단락에서 그레타 툰베리가 스웨덴의 환경 운동가라고는 했지만, 최연소라는 내용은 언급되지 않았으므로 오답이다.

어휘 | conventional adj. 상투적인, 관례적인 log v. 기록하다 question v. 이의를 제기하다

54 추론 특정사실

난이도 ●○○

Why most likely did Greta Thunberg's mother give up her career?

(a) because she wanted to support her daughter
(b) because she decided to pursue her dream of acting
(c) because she found it hard to manage childcare
(d) because she chose to go on an international trip

그레타 툰베리의 어머니가 자신의 경력을 왜 포기했던 것 같은가?

(a) 그녀의 딸을 지원하기를 원했기 때문에
(b) 연기에 대한 그녀의 꿈을 좇기로 결심했기 때문에
(c) 육아를 감당하기 힘들다고 생각했기 때문에
(d) 해외여행을 가는 것을 택했기 때문에

지텔프 치트키

질문의 키워드 give up이 sacrificing으로 paraphrasing되어 언급된 주변 내용을 주의 깊게 읽는다.

해설 | 2단락의 'When they complied with her demands, her mother even sacrificing her career'에서 그레타 툰베리의 어머니는 심지어 자신의 경력을 희생하기까지 하며 그녀의 요구를 받아들였다고 한 것을 통해, 그레타 툰베리의 어머니가 딸을 지원하기를 원했기 때문에 자신의 경력을 포기했던 것임을 추론할 수 있다. 따라서 (a)가 정답이다.

어휘 | pursue v. 좇다, 추구하다 acting n. 연기 manage v. 감당하다, 관리하다 childcare n. 육아

55 특정세부사항 What

난이도 ●●○

What prompted Greta Thunberg to hold the "School Strike for Climate"?

(a) the school's lack of commitment to climate change action
(b) the demonstrations by young people throughout Europe
(c) a protest by other youths concerned about a social issue
(d) a post on social media about how students can be campaigners

그레타 툰베리가 '기후를 위한 학교 파업'을 하도록 촉발한 것은 무엇인가?

(a) 기후 변화 조치에 대한 학교의 책임 부족
(b) 유럽 전역에 걸친 젊은 사람들의 시위
(c) 사회적 이슈를 우려하는 다른 청소년들의 항의
(d) 학생들이 어떻게 운동가가 될 수 있는지에 관한 소셜 미디어의 게시글

지텔프 치트키

질문의 키워드 School Strike for Climate가 그대로 언급된 주변 내용을 주의 깊게 읽는다.

해설 | 3단락의 'She was ~ inspired by teenagers in the United States who refused to go to school as a result of mounting gun violence.'에서 그레타 툰베리는 증가하는 총기 폭력의 결과로 학교 가기를 거부했던 미국의 십 대들로부터 이것(기후를 위한 학교 파업)의 영감을 받았다고 했다. 따라서 (c)가 정답이다.

어휘 | lack n. 부족, 결핍 commitment n. 책임, 헌신 protest n. 항의, 이의

56 특정세부사항 How

난이도 ●●○

According to the article, how did Greta Thunberg gain widespread attention?

(a) by presenting at a conference on the environment
(b) by meeting the US President at the White House
(c) by engaging in an American publicity campaign
(d) by having a meeting with noted naturalists

기사에 따르면, 그레타 툰베리는 어떻게 광범위한 관심을 받았는가?

(a) 환경에 관한 회의에 참석함으로써
(b) 백악관에서 미국 대통령을 만남으로써
(c) 미국의 공보 활동에 참여함으로써
(d) 유명한 동식물학자들과 회의를 함으로써

지텔프 치트키

질문의 키워드 widespread attention이 known around the world로 paraphrasing되어 언급된 주변 내용을 주의 깊게 읽는다.

해설 | 4단락의 'with her appearance at the 2018 United Nations Climate Change Conference making her known around the world'에서 그레타 툰베리가 2018년 유엔 기후변화협약에 출석하여 전 세계에 알려지게 되었다고 했다. 따라서 (a)가 정답이다.

Paraphrasing
appearance at the ~ United Nations Climate Change Conference 유엔 기후변화협약에 출석 → presenting at a conference on the environment 환경에 관한 회의에 참석함

어휘 | engage in phr. ~에 참여하다, 관여하다 publicity n. 공보, 홍보 noted adj. 유명한

57 특정세부사항 What

난이도 ●●○

What did Greta Thunberg accomplish in 2019?

(a) She received her third Nobel Peace Prize nomination.
(b) She was honored by a publication for her achievements.
(c) She spoke about her activism at the Venice Film Festival.
(d) She won an award for making a film about her life.

그레타 툰베리는 2019년에 무엇을 성취했는가?

(a) 세 번째로 노벨 평화상 후보에 올랐다.
(b) 한 간행물에 의해 그녀의 업적에 대한 명예를 얻었다.
(c) 베니스 국제영화제에서 그녀의 행동주의에 관해 연설했다.
(d) 그녀의 삶에 대한 영화를 만든 것으로 상을 받았다.

지텔프 치트키

질문의 키워드 2019가 그대로 언급된 주변 내용을 주의 깊게 읽는다.

해설 | 5단락의 'she was named one of the 10 most valuable people of 2019 by *Nature*, a world-renowned scientific journal'에서 그레타 툰베리가 세계적으로 유명한 과학 학술지인 「네이처」에 의해 2019년의 가장 중요한 10인 중 한 명으로 선정되었다고 했다. 따라서 (b)가 정답이다.

Paraphrasing
a ~ journal 학술지 → a publication 간행물

오답분석
(a) 5단락에서 그레타 툰베리가 2019년부터 2021년까지 3년 연속으로 노벨 평화상 후보에 올랐다고 했다. 따라서 2019년은 그녀가 첫 번째로 노벨 평화상 후보에 오른 해일 것임을 알 수 있으므로 오답이다.

어휘 | honor v. 명예를 주다, 존경하다 publication n. 간행물, 출판물

58 어휘 유의어

난이도 ●●○

In the context of the passage, mounting means ________.

(a) alarming
(b) rising
(c) emerging
(d) loading

지문의 문맥에서, 'mounting'은 -을 의미한다.

(a) 걱정스러운
(b) 증가하는
(c) 떠오르는
(d) 적재하는

지텔프 치트키

밑줄 친 어휘의 유의어를 찾는 문제이므로, mounting이 포함된 구절을 읽고 문맥을 파악한다.

해설 | 3단락의 'teenagers ~ who refused to go to school as a result of mounting gun violence'는 증가하는 총기 폭력의 결과로 학교 가기를 거부했던 십 대들이라는 뜻이므로, mounting이 '증가하는'이라는 의미로 사용된 것을 알 수 있다. 따라서 '증가하는'이라는 같은 의미의 (b) rising이 정답이다.

59 어휘 유의어

난이도 ●●○

In the context of the passage, iconic means ________.

(a) heroic
(b) brand-new
(c) well-known
(d) photogenic

지문의 문맥에서, 'iconic'은 -을 의미한다.

(a) 영웅적인
(b) 신형의
(c) 유명한
(d) 사진이 잘 받는

지텔프 치트키

밑줄 친 어휘의 유의어를 찾는 문제이므로, iconic이 포함된 구절을 읽고 문맥을 파악한다.

해설 | 4단락의 'iconic figures like ~ Sir David Attenborough'는 데이비드 애튼버러경 등과 같은 유명한 인물들이라는 뜻이므로, iconic이 '유명한'이라는 의미로 사용된 것을 알 수 있다. 따라서 '유명한'이라는 같은 의미의 (c) well-known이 정답이다.

오답분석

(a) '영웅적인'이라는 의미의 heroic은 큰 용기를 지니고 영웅적인 행위를 한 사람을 묘사할 때 쓰이므로, 널리 알려진 유명한 사람들을 소개하는 문맥에 어울리지 않아 오답이다.

PART 2(60~66) Magazine Article 탄소나노튜브 섬유로 만들어진 스마트 셔츠의 개발

연구 결과

SCIENTISTS CREATE A SHIRT THAT MONITORS THE HEART

연구 소개

[60]Scientists at Rice University have developed [65]a "smart" shirt embedded with carbon nanotube fibers that can monitor a person's heart rate. Carbon nanotubes (CNTs) are carbon-based elements that have a diameter measured in nanometers, a unit equal to one billionth of

과학자들이 심장을 관찰하는 셔츠를 만들다

[60]라이스 대학의 과학자들은 사람의 심장 박동 수를 관찰할 수 있는 [65]탄소나노튜브 섬유가 내장된 '스마트' 셔츠를 개발했다. 탄소나노튜브(CNT)는 10억분의 1미터와 동일한 단위인 나노미터로 측정되는 지름을 갖는 탄소 기반 성분이다. 그것들로 만들어진 섬유

a meter. Fibers made from them are soft, flexible, and as conductive as metal wire. The research center Carbon Hub introduced them in 2013, and since then, their potential uses in various fields have been explored.

연구 방식

[61]One of the initial challenges of using CNT fibers as thread was that they are too fine for a sewing machine. To create a thread they could use, the researchers first wove together three bundles of seven fibers each and then put them together, [61]making them as thick as regular thread. They were unable to do this by hand, so [62]they had to specially order the construction of a machine to help them. The machine was similar to a larger version of a device used to make ropes for model ships.

실험 결과 + 시사점

The result was fibers that could be sewn into a shirt. As long as the shirt is worn very close to the chest, it is able to monitor the wearer's heart rate. At the same time, it provides a continual electrocardiogram (ECG), [66]a test that measures and records a person's heart rhythm and electrical activity. In fact, so far, [63]the shirt has given slightly more accurate ECGs than machines typically used for this purpose. According to researcher Lauren Taylor, [63]the team will use denser patches of the fibers in later versions of the shirt so that even more of them touch the skin directly.

현황 + 잠재력

The fibers in the smart shirt also serve as electrodes. They allow electronics such as Bluetooth transmitters to be connected so they can relay information to devices that help keep track of data. Fibers made of CNTs may be beneficial for other implementations as well. They have been found to be more effective at dispersing energy than Kevlar, the material used in bulletproof vests. This means that [64]they could be used to create more defensive military uniforms in the future.

는 부드럽고, 신축성이 있으며, 금속 철사만큼 전도력이 있다. 카본 허브 연구 센터는 그것들을 2013년에 도입했고, 그때부터, 다양한 분야에서의 그것들의 잠재적 용도가 탐구되어 왔다.

[61]CNT 섬유를 실로 사용하는 것의 초기 문제점들 중 하나는 그것들이 재봉틀에 사용하기에는 너무 가느다랗다는 것이었다. 그들이 사용할 수 있는 실을 만들어 내기 위해, 연구원들은 먼저 각각 7개의 섬유로 이루어진 3개의 묶음을 함께 엮었고 그런 다음 그것들을 합쳐서, [61]표준적인 실만큼 두껍게 만들었다. 그들은 이것을 손으로 할 수 없었고, 따라서 [62]그들을 도울 기계의 건설을 특별히 주문해야 했다. 그 기계는 모형선의 밧줄을 만드는 데 사용되는 장치의 더 큰 버전과 유사했다.

그 결과는 셔츠로 바느질될 수 있는 섬유였다. 셔츠가 가슴에 매우 가깝게 입혀지기만 하면, 그것이 착용자의 심장 박동 수를 관찰하는 것이 가능하다. 동시에, 이것은 [66]사람의 심장 박동과 전기적 활동을 측정하고 기록하는 검사인 심전도(ECG)를 계속 제공한다. 실제로, 지금까지, 이 목적을 위해 일반적으로 사용되는 기계들보다 [63]그 셔츠는 조금 더 정확한 심전도를 제공해 왔다. 연구원 로렌 테일러에 따르면, [63]그 팀은 그것(섬유)의 훨씬 더 많은 부분이 피부에 직접적으로 닿도록 셔츠의 최신 버전에 섬유의 더 조밀한 조각들을 사용할 것이다.

스마트 셔츠의 섬유들은 전극의 역할을 하기도 한다. 그것들은 블루투스 송신기와 같은 전자 장치가 연결되는 것을 허용하여 그것들이 데이터를 기록하는 데 도움을 주는 기기에 정보를 전달할 수 있도록 한다. CNT로 만들어진 섬유는 다른 수행에도 유용할 수 있다. 그것들은 방탄조끼에 사용되는 물질인 케블라보다 에너지를 분산시키는 데 더 효과적이라고 밝혀졌다. 이는 [64]그것들이 미래에 더 방어력 있는 군복을 만드는 데 사용될 수 있다는 것을 의미한다.

어휘 | monitor v. 관찰하다, 감시하다 fiber n. 섬유 element n. 성분, 요소 diameter n. 지름 measure v. 측정하다 billionth n. 10억분의 1 flexible adj. 신축성 있는 conductive adj. 전도력이 있는, 전도성의 wire n. 철사 thread n. 실 fine adj. 가느다란 sewing machine phr. 재봉틀 weave v. 엮다, 짜다 bundle n. 묶음 construction n. 건설 sew v. 바느질하다 chest n. 가슴 electrocardiogram n. 심전도 electrical activity phr. 전기적 활동 dense adj. 조밀한, 밀집한 patch n. 조각 electrode n. 전극 electronics n. 전자 장치 transmitter n. 송신기 relay v. 전달하다 keep track of phr. ~을 기록하다 implementation n. 수행, 이행 disperse v. 분산시키다 bulletproof adj. 방탄의 defensive adj. 방어력 있는 military uniform phr. 군복

60 주제/목적 기사의 주제

난이도 ●●○

What is the article mainly about?

(a) the development of versatile thread
(b) the invention of clothing containing CNTs
(c) the thermal properties of CNTs
(d) the establishment of a process for making clothes

기사의 주제는 무엇인가?

(a) 용도가 다양한 실의 개발
(b) CNT를 포함하는 옷의 발명
(c) CNT의 열적 물성
(d) 의류 제작 과정의 확립

지텔프 치트키

지문의 초반을 주의 깊게 읽고 전체 맥락을 파악한다.

해설 | 1단락의 'Scientists at Rice University have developed a "smart" shirt embedded with carbon nanotube fibers that can monitor a person's heart rate.'에서 라이스 대학의 과학자들이 사람의 심장 박동 수를 관찰할 수 있는 탄소나노튜브 섬유가 내장된 '스마트' 셔츠를 개발했다고 한 뒤, 그 스마트 셔츠에 관한 내용이 이어지고 있다. 따라서 (b)가 정답이다.

어휘 | versatile adj. 용도가 다양한 thermal adj. 열의 property n. 물성, 특성 establishment n. 확립, 수립

61 특정세부사항 What

난이도 ●●○

What was the early problem with utilizing CNT fibers?

(a) There was no perfect method for producing CNTs.
(b) There were not enough fibers available.
(c) They were too rigid to be woven.
(d) They were far thinner than typical fabric thread.

CNT 섬유를 활용하는 것의 초기 문제는 무엇이었는가?

(a) CNT를 생산하는 완벽한 방법이 없었다.
(b) 이용 가능한 섬유가 충분하지 않았다.
(c) 너무 뻣뻣해서 짜일 수 없었다.
(d) 일반적인 직물의 실보다 훨씬 더 가늘었다.

지텔프 치트키

질문의 키워드 early problem이 initial challenges로 paraphrasing되어 언급된 주변 내용을 주의 깊게 읽는다.

해설 | 2단락의 'One of the initial challenges ~ was that they are too fine for a sewing machine.'에서 초기 문제점들 중 하나는 그것들이 재봉틀에 사용하기에는 너무 가느다랗다는 것이었다고 한 뒤, 'making them as thick as regular thread'에서 문제의 해결을 위해 연구원들이 CNT 섬유를 표준적인 실만큼 두껍게 만들었다고 했다. 따라서 (d)가 정답이다.

Paraphrasing
too fine 너무 가느다란 → far thinner 훨씬 더 가는
regular thread 표준적인 실 → typical fabric thread 일반적인 직물의 실

어휘 | rigid adj. 뻣뻣한 typical adj. 일반적인, 전형적인 fabric n. 직물

62 특정세부사항 How

난이도 ●●○

How did the researchers obtain thread for their work?

(a) by employing a specially created device
(b) by putting regular thread into three bundles
(c) by stitching fibers together using a sewing machine

연구원들은 자신들의 작업을 위한 실을 어떻게 얻었는가?

(a) 특별히 제작된 장치를 이용함으로써
(b) 표준적인 실을 3개의 묶음으로 합침으로써
(c) 재봉틀을 이용해 섬유들을 함께 꿰맴으로써

(d) by having a model ship maker do the weaving work	(d) 모형선 제작자가 직조 작업을 하게 함으로써

지텔프 치트키

질문의 키워드 obtain thread가 create a thread로 paraphrasing되어 언급된 주변 내용을 주의 깊게 읽는다.

해설 | 2단락의 'they had to specially order the construction of a machine to help them'에서 연구원들은 (CNT 섬유를 두껍게 만들기 위해) 그들을 도울 기계의 건설을 특별히 주문해야 했다고 했다. 따라서 (a)가 정답이다.

Paraphrasing

specially order the construction of a machine 기계의 건설을 특별히 주문하다 → a specially created device 특별히 제작된 장치

오답분석

(b) 2단락에서 표준적인 실이 아닌 CNT 섬유로 이루어진 3개의 묶음을 함께 엮었다고 했으므로 오답이다.

어휘 | stitch v. 꿰매다, 깁다

63 추론 특정사실

난이도 ●●●

Why most likely will compact fibers be included in forthcoming shirts?	앞으로 나올 셔츠에 왜 조밀한 섬유가 포함될 것 같은가?
(a) to allow for the creation of larger garments	(a) 더 큰 의복의 제작을 고려하기 위해서
(b) to facilitate the use of electronic devices	(b) 전자 기기의 사용을 가능하게 하기 위해서
(c) to further improve future ECG results	**(c) 미래의 심전도 결과를 향상시키기 위해서**
(d) to make wireless connections possible	(d) 무선 연결을 가능하게 하기 위해서

지텔프 치트키

질문의 키워드 compact fibers가 denser ~ fibers로 paraphrasing되어 언급된 주변 내용을 주의 깊게 읽는다.

해설 | 3단락의 'the shirt has given slightly more accurate ECGs'에서 CNT 섬유로 바느질된 셔츠가 조금 더 정확한 심전도를 제공해 왔다고 한 뒤, 'the team will use denser patches ~ so that even more of them touch the skin directly'에서 섬유의 훨씬 더 많은 부분이 피부에 직접적으로 닿도록 연구팀은 더 조밀한 조각들을 사용할 것이라고 했다. 이를 통해, 셔츠를 피부에 더 직접적으로 닿게 하여 미래의 심전도 결과를 향상시키기 위해 앞으로 나올 셔츠에 조밀한 섬유가 포함될 것임을 추론할 수 있다. 따라서 (c)가 정답이다.

어휘 | compact adj. 조밀한 forthcoming adj. 앞으로 나올 allow for phr. ~을 고려하다 garment n. 의복 facilitate v. 가능하게 하다 further v. 향상시키다 wireless adj. 무선의

64 특정세부사항 Why

난이도 ●●○

Based on the article, why might future military uniforms be comprised of CNT fibers?	기사에 따르면, 미래의 군복은 왜 CNT 섬유로 구성될 수도 있는가?
(a) because they enable the military to track personnel	(a) 군대가 인원을 추적할 수 있게 하기 때문에
(b) because they afford intelligence information	(b) 기밀 정보를 제공하기 때문에
(c) because they provide soldiers with more protection	**(c) 군인들에게 더 많은 보호를 제공하기 때문에**
(d) because they result in clothing weighing less	(d) 무게가 덜 나가는 옷이 되기 때문에

지텔프 치트키

질문의 키워드 military uniforms가 그대로 언급된 주변 내용을 주의 깊게 읽는다.

해설 | 4단락의 'they could be used to create more defensive military uniforms in the future'에서 그것들(CNT 섬유)이 미래에 더 방어력 있는 군복을 만드는 데 사용될 수 있다고 했다. 따라서 (c)가 정답이다.

Paraphrasing
more defensive 더 방어력 있는 → provide ~ with more protection 더 많은 보호를 제공하다

어휘 | be comprised of phr. ~으로 구성되다 track v. 추적하다 afford v. 제공하다 intelligence n. 기밀, 지능 weigh v. 무게가 나가다

65 어휘 유의어

난이도 ●●○

In the context of the passage, embedded means ______.

(a) covered
(b) engraved
(c) fit
(d) set

지문의 문맥에서, 'embedded'는 -을 의미한다.

(a) 덮인
(b) 새겨진
(c) 알맞은
(d) 심어진

지텔프 치트키

밑줄 친 어휘의 유의어를 찾는 문제이므로, embedded가 포함된 구절을 읽고 문맥을 파악한다.

해설 | 1단락의 'a "smart" shirt embedded with carbon nanotube fibers'는 탄소나노튜브 섬유가 내장된 스마트 셔츠라는 뜻이므로, embedded가 '내장된'이라는 의미로 사용된 것을 알 수 있다. 따라서 '심어진'이라는 비슷한 의미의 (d) set이 정답이다.

오답분석

(b) '새기다'라는 의미의 engrave는 단단한 표면에 글자 등을 조각하여 새기는 경우에 사용하므로, 무언가를 다른 어떤 것에 단단히 박아 넣어 내장한다는 의미의 embed의 유의어로 적절하지 않아 오답이다.

66 어휘 유의어

난이도 ●○○

In the context of the passage, records means ______.

(a) depicts
(b) documents
(c) catalogs
(d) remembers

지문의 문맥에서, 'records'는 -을 의미한다.

(a) 묘사한다
(b) 기록한다
(c) 목록을 작성한다
(d) 기억한다

지텔프 치트키

밑줄 친 어휘의 유의어를 찾는 문제이므로, records가 포함된 구절을 읽고 문맥을 파악한다.

해설 | 3단락의 'a test that measures and records a person's heart rhythm and electrical activity'는 사람의 심장 박동과 전기적 활동을 측정하고 기록하는 검사라는 뜻이므로, records가 '기록한다'라는 의미로 사용된 것을 알 수 있다. 따라서 '기록한다'라는 같은 의미의 (b) documents가 정답이다.

표제어

JOHN HENRY EFFECT

정의

[67]The John Henry effect is a cognitive bias that can be exhibited by participants in an experiment. It occurs when the members of one group think that they need to outperform those of another group, thereby [67]invalidating the experiment.

기원 + 어원

This phenomenon takes its name from John Henry, an American steel driver who worked for a railway company building a tunnel. According to the legend, the company began using a steam-powered device to drill holes for explosives, [72]claiming that it could surpass human workers. [68]This hurt Henry's pride because he believed his abilities were being unfairly questioned, so he offered to race the machine using only his hammer and spike. Henry won, but in doing so, he exerted such a great effort that he died.

원리

A similar competitive instinct can affect an experiment that includes [69(a)]a control group, whose members do not receive the experimental treatment, and a treatment group. [69(b)]When people perceive that they are in the control group and feel other participants possess an unfair advantage, [69(c)]they may put in additional effort to prove their worth. [69(d)]This will distort the data and lead to inaccurate results.

예시

The John Henry Effect is particularly common in studies related to the workplace, as participants are naturally motivated to avoid being rated negatively. For example, when an accounting company considers [73]adopting a new software program to minimize errors, it may decide to test its effectiveness first. To do this, management would divide workers into one group that uses the current application and another that uses the new one. [70]In order for this experiment to succeed, the only variable should be the type of software used. However, if the members of the control group do their tasks twice as fast as usual to overcome the perceived disadvantage, it would be impossible for the company to accurately compare the two programs.

방지 방법

The most effective way to prevent the John Henry effect from occurring is to make certain that experiment participants do not know which group they belong to. If this is not possible, [71]ensuring that the groups cannot observe each other's progress can reduce the impact of this effect on the results of the study.

존 헨리 효과

[67]존 헨리 효과는 실험의 참가자들이 보일 수 있는 인지 편향이다. 이것은 한 그룹의 구성원들이 또 다른 그룹의 구성원들보다 더 나은 결과를 내야 한다고 생각할 때 발생하며, 그렇게 함으로써 [67]실험을 무효화한다.

이 현상은 터널을 뚫는 철도회사에서 일했던 미국의 철강 기사 존 헨리의 이름을 딴다. 전해 내려오는 이야기에 따르면, 그 회사는 화약을 위한 구멍을 뚫는 데 증기 동력 장치를 사용하기 시작했으며, [72]이것이 인간 노동자들을 뛰어넘을 수 있다고 주장했다. [68]그의 능력이 부당하게 의심받고 있다고 생각했기 때문에 이것은 헨리의 자존심을 상하게 했고, 그래서 그는 오직 자신의 망치와 못을 사용해 그 기계와 경쟁하겠다고 제안했다. 헨리가 이겼지만, 그렇게 하면서, 그는 너무 큰 노력을 가하였기 때문에 죽음에 이르렀다.

유사한 경쟁 본능은 [69(a)]구성원들이 실험 처리를 받지 않는 통제 집단 그리고 실험 집단을 포함하는 실험에 영향을 미칠 수 있다. [69(b)]사람들이 자신이 통제 집단에 속해 있다는 것을 인지하고 다른 참가자들이 부당한 이점을 가진다고 느낄 때, [69(c)]그들은 자신들의 가치를 증명하기 위해 추가적인 노력을 기울일 수도 있다. [69(d)]이것은 자료를 왜곡하여 부정확한 결과를 낳을 것이다.

존 헨리 효과는 작업장과 관련된 연구에서 특히 흔한데, 이는 참가자들이 부정적으로 평가받는 것을 피하도록 자연스럽게 동기를 부여받기 때문이다. 예를 들어, 한 회계 법인이 [73]오류를 최소화하기 위한 새로운 소프트웨어 프로그램을 채택하는 것을 고려할 때, 그것의 유효성을 먼저 시험해 보기로 결정할 수도 있다. 이것을 하기 위해, 경영진은 직원들을 현재의 응용 프로그램을 사용하는 집단과 새로운 것을 사용하는 또 다른 집단으로 나눌 것이다. [70]이 실험이 성공하기 위해, 유일한 변수는 사용되는 소프트웨어의 종류여야 한다. 하지만, 만약 통제 집단의 구성원들이 감지된 약점을 극복하기 위해 평소보다 두 배 빠르게 업무를 한다면, 회사가 그 두 프로그램을 정확하게 비교하는 것은 불가능할 것이다.

존 헨리 효과가 발생하는 것을 막는 가장 효과적인 방법은 실험 참가자들이 자신이 어떤 집단에 속해 있는지를 모르도록 확실히 해두는 것이다. 만약 이것이 가능하지 않다면, [71]반드시 집단들이 서로의 진행 상황을 알 수 없게 하는 것이 연구 결과에 미치는 이 효과의 영향을 줄일 수 있다.

어휘 | cognitive adj. 인지의 bias n. 편향, 편견 exhibit v. 보이다, 드러내다 outperform v. 더 나은 결과를 내다 invalidate v. 무효화하다 phenomenon n. 현상 explosive n. 화약, 폭발물 surpass v. 뛰어넘다, 능가하다 unfairly adv. 부당하게 question v. 의심하다 race v. 경쟁하다, 시합하다 spike n. 못, 뾰족한 것 exert v. 가하다, 행사하다 competitive adj. 경쟁의 instinct n. 본능 treatment n. 처리, 처치 treatment group phr. 실험 집단 perceive v. 인지하다, 감지하다 possess v. 가지다, 소유하다 distort v. 왜곡하다 motivate v. 동기를 부여하다, 자극하다 rate v. 평가하다 accounting company phr. 회계 법인 adopt v. 채택하다 effectiveness n. 유효성 variable n. 변수 overcome v. 극복하다 disadvantage n. 약점, 불리한 점 ensure v. 반드시 ~하게 하다, 보장하다 observe v. 알다, 보다 progress n. 진행 상황

67 특정세부사항 What

난이도 ●●○

What is the John Henry effect?

(a) a method of selecting group members
(b) a prejudiced view of experiment results
(c) a preconception that negatively affects a study
(d) a mental disorder that limits performance

존 헨리 효과는 무엇인가?

(a) 집단 구성원을 선발하는 방법
(b) 실험 결과에 대한 편파적인 시각
(c) 연구에 부정적으로 영향을 미치는 선입견
(d) 수행력을 제한하는 정신 장애

지텔프 치트키

질문의 키워드 John Henry effect가 그대로 언급된 주변 내용을 주의 깊게 읽는다.

해설 | 1단락의 'The John Henry effect is a cognitive bias that can be exhibited by participants in an experiment.'에서 존 헨리 효과는 실험의 참가자들이 보일 수 있는 인지 편향이라고 한 뒤, 'invalidating the experiment'에서 이것이 실험을 무효화한다고 했다. 따라서 (c)가 정답이다.

Paraphrasing

a ~ bias 편향 → a preconception 선입견
invalidating the experiment 실험을 무효화한다 → negatively affects a study 연구에 부정적으로 영향을 미친다

오답분석

(b) 존 헨리 효과는 실험 결과에 대한 편파적인 시각이 아닌, 실험 진행 과정에 작용하여 최종 결과를 부정확하게 만드는 선입견이므로 오답이다.

어휘 | prejudiced adj. 편파적인 preconception n. 선입견, 편견 disorder n. 장애, 질환

68 특정세부사항 Why

난이도 ●●○

Why did John Henry challenge the machine?

(a) because his company tried to motivate its staff
(b) because he felt an insult to his pride
(c) because his co-workers were being unfairly treated
(d) because he wanted to try new equipment

존 헨리는 왜 그 기계에 도전했는가?

(a) 회사가 직원들을 동기 부여하려 했기 때문에
(b) 자존심에 대한 모욕을 느꼈기 때문에
(c) 동료들이 부당하게 취급되고 있었기 때문에
(d) 새로운 장비를 써 보고 싶었기 때문에

지텔프 치트키

질문의 키워드 challenge the machine이 race the machine으로 paraphrasing되어 언급된 주변 내용을 주의 깊게 읽는다.

해설 | 2단락의 'This hurt Henry's pride ~, so he offered to race the machine using only his hammer and spike.'에서 회사의 주장이 헨리의 자존심을 상하게 했고, 그래서 그가 그 기계와 경쟁하겠냐고 제안했다고 했다. 따라서 (b)가 정답이다.

Paraphrasing

hurt ~ pride 자존심을 상하게 했다 → felt an insult to ~ pride 자존심에 대한 모욕을 느꼈다

어휘 | insult n. 모욕

69 Not/True Not 문제

난이도 ●●○

Based on the article, which of the following is not true about the members of a control group?

(a) They are unable to receive the treatment that is being tested.
(b) They have a significant advantage over other participants.
(c) They may purposely adjust their behavior during an experiment.
(d) They might cause the collection of erroneous information.

기사에 따르면, 다음 중 통제 집단 구성원들에 대해 사실이 아닌 것은?

(a) 실험되고 있는 처리를 받지 못한다.
(b) 다른 참가자들에 비해 상당한 이점을 가진다.
(c) 실험 중에 의도적으로 자신들의 행동을 조정할 수도 있다.
(d) 잘못된 정보의 수집을 유발할 수도 있다.

지텔프 치트키

질문의 키워드 control group이 그대로 언급된 주변 내용을 주의 깊게 읽고, 보기의 키워드와 지문 내용을 대조하며 언급되는 것을 하나씩 소거한다.

해설 | (b)는 보기의 키워드 advantage가 그대로 언급된 3단락의 'When people perceive that they are in the control group and feel other participants possess an unfair advantage'에서 사람들은 자신이 통제 집단에 속해 있다는 것을 인지하고 다른 참가자들이 부당한 이점을 가진다고 느낀다고 했으므로, 통제 집단 구성원들이 다른 참가자들에 비해 상당한 이점을 가진다는 것은 지문의 내용과 일치하지 않는다. 따라서 (b)가 정답이다.

오답분석

(a) 보기의 키워드 unable to receive가 do not receive로 paraphrasing되어 언급된 3단락에서 통제 집단의 구성원들은 실험 처리를 받지 않는다고 언급되었다.
(c) 보기의 키워드 adjust their behavior와 관련된 put in additional effort가 언급된 3단락에서 통제 집단의 구성원들은 자신들의 가치를 증명하기 위해 실험 중에 추가적인 노력을 기울일 수도 있다고 언급되었다.
(d) 보기의 키워드 cause ~ erroneous information이 distort the data로 paraphrasing되어 언급된 3단락에서 통제 집단의 구성원들이 추가적인 노력을 기울이는 것은 자료를 왜곡할 것이라고 언급되었다.

어휘 | purposely adv. 의도적으로, 특별히 adjust v. 조정하다 erroneous adj. 잘못된

70 추론 특정사실

난이도 ●●●

Which is probably a factor that could make the accounting company's experiment unreliable?

(a) The purpose of the tasks is unclear.
(b) The duration of the test is too long.
(c) The sizes of the groups are varied.
(d) The number of variables is too large.

회계 법인의 실험을 신뢰할 수 없게 만들 수 있는 요인은 무엇인 것 같은가?

(a) 작업의 목적이 불분명하다.
(b) 실험 기간이 너무 길다.
(c) 집단의 규모가 다양하다.
(d) 변수의 수가 너무 많다.

지텔프 치트키

질문의 키워드 accounting company가 그대로 언급된 주변 내용을 주의 깊게 읽는다.

해설 | 4단락의 'In order for this experiment to succeed, the only variable should be the type of software used.'에서 회계 법인의 실험이 성공하기 위해 유일한 변수는 사용되는 소프트웨어의 종류여야 한다고 한 뒤, 'However, if the members of the control group do their tasks twice as fast as usual ~, it would be impossible ~ to accurately compare the two programs.'에서 만약 통제 집단의 구성원들이 평소보다 두 배 빠르게 업무를 한다면 그 두 프로그램을 정확하게 비교하는 것은 불가능할 것이라고 한 것을 통해, 사용되는 소프트웨어의 종류 외에 변수의 수가 너무 많은 것이 회계 법인의 실험을 신뢰할 수 없게 만들 수 있는 요인일 것임을 추론할 수 있다. 따라서 (d)가 정답이다.

Paraphrasing
unreliable 신뢰할 수 없는 → impossible ~ to accurately compare 정확하게 비교하는 것이 불가능한

71 특정세부사항 What

난이도 ●●○

What can researchers do to avoid the occurrence of the John Henry effect?

(a) ensure that observers are impartial
(b) provide participants with more information
(c) ban communication between the groups
(d) limit the scope of the results

존 헨리 효과의 발생을 피하기 위해 연구원들은 무엇을 할 수 있는가?

(a) 관찰자들이 공정하다는 것을 보장한다
(b) 참가자들에게 더 많은 정보를 제공한다
(c) 집단들 간의 의사소통을 금지한다
(d) 결과의 범위를 제한한다

지텔프 치트키

질문의 키워드 avoid ~ occurrence가 prevent ~ from occurring으로 paraphrasing되어 언급된 주변 내용을 주의 깊게 읽는다.

해설 | 5단락의 'ensuring that the groups cannot observe each other's progress can reduce the impact of this effect on the results of the study'에서 반드시 집단들이 서로의 진행 상황을 알 수 없게 하는 것이 연구 결과에 미치는 존 헨리 효과의 영향을 줄일 수 있다고 했다. 따라서 (c)가 정답이다.

어휘 | observer n. 관찰자 impartial adj. 공정한 ban v. 금지하다 scope n. 범위

72 어휘 유의어

난이도 ●○○

In the context of the passage, claiming means _______.

(a) asserting
(b) complaining
(c) requesting
(d) opposing

지문의 문맥에서, 'claiming'은 -을 의미한다.

(a) 주장하는
(b) 불평하는
(c) 요청하는
(d) 반대하는

지텔프 치트키

밑줄 친 어휘의 유의어를 찾는 문제이므로, claiming이 포함된 구절을 읽고 문맥을 파악한다.

해설 | 2단락의 'claiming that it could surpass human workers'는 이것(증기 동력 장치)이 인간 노동자들을 뛰어넘을 수 있다고 주장했다는 뜻이므로, claiming이 '주장하는'이라는 의미로 사용된 것을 알 수 있다. 따라서 '주장하는'이라는 같은 의미의 (a) asserting이 정답이다.

73 어휘 유의어

난이도 ●○○

In the context of the passage, minimize means ________.

(a) demean
(b) lessen
(c) remove
(d) downsize

지문의 문맥에서, 'minimize'는 -을 의미한다.

(a) 위신을 떨어뜨리다
(b) 줄이다
(c) 제거하다
(d) 축소하다

지텔프 치트키

밑줄 친 어휘의 유의어를 찾는 문제이므로, minimize가 포함된 구절을 읽고 문맥을 파악한다.

해설 | 4단락의 'adopting a new software program to minimize errors'는 오류를 최소화하기 위한 새로운 소프트웨어 프로그램을 채택하는 것이라는 뜻이므로, minimize가 '최소화하다'라는 의미로 사용된 것을 알 수 있다. 따라서 '줄이다'라는 비슷한 의미의 (b) lessen이 정답이다.

오답분석

(d) '축소하다'라는 의미의 downsize는 자동차 등의 크기를 작게 만들거나 조직의 인원을 감축하는 경우에 사용하므로, 문맥에 어울리지 않아 오답이다.

PART 4 (74~80) Business Letter 출장 요리 서비스를 홍보하는 편지

수신인 정보

Natalie Holmes
Marketing Manager
Rasputin Technologies

편지의 목적: 서비스 홍보

Greetings! I'm reaching out in regard to the Technology Development Conference your company will host at the Civic Auditorium on October 17. We have successfully accommodated hundreds of events at this venue before, and [74]we would like to offer our unique catering services to you.

서비스 장점

Cool Catering provides the tastiest selection of finger foods in the state. [75]Each one of our bite-sized dishes is prepared by a professionally trained chef, so the quality is guaranteed. In addition to the outstanding flavor, [76]our style of cuisine is perfect for the vibe of a conference, as attendees can conveniently enjoy the finger foods while walking and without the need for special cutlery.

메뉴 옵션

Our three menu options make it easy [79]to choose the right variety of dishes that will appeal to all of your guests.

Basic: Preset cold dishes
Dish: 4 finger foods
Price: $10 per person

Natalie Holmes
마케팅 관리자
Rasputin Technologies사

안녕하세요! 귀사가 10월 17일에 시민 회관에서 주최하실 기술 개발 회의와 관련하여 연락드립니다. 저희는 이전에 이 장소에서 수백 개의 행사를 성공적으로 치러 왔으며, [74]귀사에 저희의 독특한 출장 요리 서비스를 제공하고 싶습니다.

Cool 출장 요리는 이 주에서 가장 맛있는 엄선된 핑거푸드를 제공합니다. [75]저희의 한입 크기 요리들 각각은 전문적으로 훈련받은 요리사에 의해 준비되기 때문에, 그 품질이 보장됩니다. 뛰어난 풍미에 더해, [76]저희의 요리 스타일은 회의 분위기에 안성맞춤인데, 이는 참석자들이 걸으면서 특별한 식기구 없이 핑거푸드를 편리하게 즐길 수 있기 때문입니다.

저희의 세 가지 메뉴 선택지는 귀사의 모든 손님들의 마음에 들 [79]적당한 종류의 요리들을 고르는 것을 쉽게 만듭니다.

기본: 미리 정해진 가열하지 않은 요리
요리: 4개의 핑거푸드
가격: 1인당 10달러

Standard: Select three hot options and three cold options Dish: 6 finger foods, 20 dishes to choose from Price: $17 per person [77]**Deluxe:** Full selection available Dish: 8 finger foods, 28 dishes* to choose from (**includes seasonal seafood options*) Price: $22 per person	**표준:** 세 가지 가열된 요리와 세 가지 가열하지 않은 요리 선택 요리: 6개의 핑거푸드, 20개의 요리 중에서 선택 가격: 1인당 17달러 [77]**고급:** 전체 선택지 이용 가능 요리: 8개의 핑거푸드, 28개의 요리* 중에서 선택 (**제철 해산물 선택지를 포함함*) 가격: 1인당 22달러
추천 + 추가 정보 Each menu serves one portion of each dish for the number of guests specified in the order. [78]To provide a meal's worth of food, we recommend six to eight servings per person. On the day of the event, our team will deliver the food on visually-pleasing plates and [80]arrange chafing dishes to keep hot items warm during service. If you have any questions, please feel free to contact me at 402-444-0508.	각각의 메뉴는 주문서에 명시된 손님들의 수만큼 각 요리의 1인분을 제공합니다. [78]한 끼 분량의 음식을 제공하려면, 한 사람당 6~8인분을 추천합니다. 행사 당일에, 저희 팀은 시각적으로 만족스러운 접시에 음식을 담아 배달하고 서비스 동안 [80]뜨거운 음식들을 따뜻하게 유지하기 위해 보온용 냄비를 마련할 것입니다. 어떤 문의 사항이라도 있으시다면, 언제든지 402-444-0508로 연락해 주시기 바랍니다.
발신인 정보 Best Regards, Ed Bowen Outreach Coordinator Cool Catering	Ed Bowen 드림 현장 출장 서비스 진행자 Cool 출장 요리

어휘 | reach out phr. 연락하다 host v. 주최하다 accommodate v. 치르다, 공간을 제공하다 venue n. 장소 unique adj. 독특한 catering n. 출장 요리, 음식 공급업 tasty adj. 맛있는 selection n. 엄선(품), 선택지 bite-sized adj. 한입 크기의 dish n. 요리, 음식 guarantee v. 보장하다 outstanding adj. 뛰어난 flavor n. 풍미, 맛 cuisine n. 요리 vibe n. 분위기 attendee n. 참석자 conveniently adv. 편리하게 cutlery n. 식기구 variety n. 종류, 품종 appeal v. 마음에 들다, 관심을 끌다 preset adj. 미리 정해진 seasonal adj. 제철의, 계절에 따라 다른 portion n. (음식의) 1인분, 양 specified adj. 명시된 meal n. 끼니, 식사 serving n. (음식의) 1인분 deliver v. 배달하다 chafing dish phr. 보온용 냄비, 신선로 outreach n. 현장 출장 서비스

74 주제/목적 편지의 목적

난이도 ●○○

Why did Ed Bowen write to Natalie Holmes?	왜 Ed Bowen은 Natalie Holmes에게 편지를 썼는가?
(a) to detail success stories from past events	(a) 지난 행사들의 성공담을 상세히 알리기 위해서
(b) to propose food services for a convention	**(b) 회의를 위한 음식 서비스를 제안하기 위해서**
(c) to invite a company to a tech conference	(c) 기술 회의에 기업을 초대하기 위해서
(d) to offer an upgrade to an event venue	(d) 행사 장소를 상위 등급으로 올려주기 위해서

지텔프 치트키

지문의 초반을 주의 깊게 읽고 전체 맥락을 파악한다.

해설 | 1단락의 'we would like to offer our unique catering services to you'에서 Ed Bowen이 Natalie Holmes의 회사에 독특한 출장 요리 서비스를 제공하고 싶다고 한 뒤, 출장 요리 서비스에 대해 홍보하는 내용이 이어지고 있다. 따라서 (b)가 정답이다.

Paraphrasing

catering services 출장 요리 서비스 → food services 음식 서비스

어휘 | detail v. 상세히 알리다, 열거하다 propose v. 제안하다 convention n. 회의, 협의회

75 특정세부사항 How

난이도 ●●○

How does Cool Catering ensure the quality of its food?

(a) by employing skilled culinary experts
(b) by getting feedback from food critics
(c) by using the freshest ingredients in the state
(d) by exclusively serving tasty finger foods

Cool 출장 요리는 어떻게 음식의 질을 보장하는가?

(a) 숙련된 요리 전문가들을 고용함으로써
(b) 요리 평론가들로부터 의견을 받음으로써
(c) 그 주에서 가장 신선한 재료를 사용함으로써
(d) 맛있는 핑거푸드를 독점적으로 제공함으로써

지텔프 치트키

질문의 키워드 ensure ~ quality가 quality is guaranteed로 paraphrasing되어 언급된 주변 내용을 주의 깊게 읽는다.

해설 | 2단락의 'Each one ~ is prepared by a professionally trained chef, so the quality is guaranteed.'에서 요리들 각각은 전문적으로 훈련받은 요리사에 의해 준비되기 때문에 그 품질이 보장된다고 했다. 따라서 (a)가 정답이다.

Paraphrasing
a professionally trained chef 전문적으로 훈련받은 요리사 → skilled culinary experts 숙련된 요리 전문가들

어휘 | culinary adj. 요리의 expert n. 전문가 critic n. 평론가, 비평가 ingredient n. 재료 exclusively adv. 독점적으로

76 특정세부사항 Why

난이도 ●●○

According to Mr. Bowen, why are Cool Catering's dishes suitable for conferences?

(a) because they vary depending on the needs of the event
(b) because they come with convenient cutlery
(c) because they help provide a professional vibe
(d) because they can be eaten on the move

Mr. Bowen에 따르면, Cool 출장 요리의 음식들이 왜 회의에 적합한가?

(a) 행사의 요구에 따라 다양하기 때문에
(b) 편리한 식기구가 딸려 있기 때문에
(c) 전문적인 분위기를 내도록 돕기 때문에
(d) 이동 중에 섭취될 수 있기 때문에

지텔프 치트키

질문의 키워드 suitable for conferences가 perfect for ~ conference로 paraphrasing되어 언급된 주변 내용을 주의 깊게 읽는다.

해설 | 2단락의 'our style of cuisine is perfect for the vibe of a conference, as attendees ~ enjoy the finger foods while walking and without the need for special cutlery'에서 참석자들이 걸으면서 핑거푸드를 즐길 수 있기 때문에 Cool 출장 요리의 요리 스타일은 회의 분위기에 안성맞춤이라고 했다. 따라서 (d)가 정답이다.

Paraphrasing
enjoy the finger foods while walking 걸으면서 핑거푸드를 즐기다 → can be eaten on the move 이동 중에 섭취될 수 있다

어휘 | vary v. 다양하다, 다르다 come with phr. ~이 딸려 있다

77 특정세부사항 What

난이도 ●○○

What can Ms. Holmes request if she orders the highest-priced menu option?

(a) seasonal desserts
(b) larger portions
(c) more beverage options
(d) seafood dishes

Ms. Holmes가 가장 비싼 메뉴 선택지를 주문한다면 무엇을 요청할 수 있는가?

(a) 제철 디저트
(b) 더 많은 양
(c) 더 많은 음료 선택지
(d) 해산물 요리

지텔프 치트키

질문의 키워드 highest-priced menu option과 관련된 Deluxe 주변 내용을 주의 깊게 읽는다.

해설 | 언급된 세 가지 메뉴 선택지 가운데 가장 비싼 Deluxe 선택지에 관한 설명 중 '*includes seasonal seafood options*'에서 선택 가능한 요리가 제철 해산물 선택지를 포함한다고 했다. 따라서 (d)가 정답이다.

Paraphrasing
seafood options 해산물 선택지 → seafood dishes 해산물 요리

78 추론 특정사실

난이도 ●●○

Why most likely would Ms. Holmes choose to order six to eight portions per guest?

(a) to get a discount on an order
(b) to qualify for free delivery
(c) to ensure everyone gets enough food
(d) to prepare for a number of unexpected guests

왜 Ms. Holmes는 손님당 6~8인분을 주문하는 것을 선택할 것 같은가?

(a) 주문에서 할인을 받기 위해서
(b) 무료 배달 권한을 얻기 위해서
(c) 모든 사람이 충분한 음식을 받도록 하기 위해서
(d) 예상치 못한 다수의 손님들에 대비하기 위해서

지텔프 치트키

질문의 키워드 portions가 portion으로 언급된 주변 내용을 주의 깊게 읽는다.

해설 | 마지막 단락의 'To provide a meal's worth of food, we recommend six to eight servings per person.'에서 한 끼 분량의 음식을 제공하려면 한 사람당 6~8인분을 추천한다고 한 것을 통해, 모든 사람이 핑거푸드로 한 끼를 해결할 수 있을 만큼 충분한 음식을 받도록 하기 위해서 Ms. Holmes가 손님당 6~8인분을 주문하는 것을 선택할 것임을 추론할 수 있다. 따라서 (c)가 정답이다.

Paraphrasing
six to eight portions per guest 손님당 6~8인분 → six to eight servings per person 한 사람당 6~8인분

어휘 | qualify v. 권한을 얻다 unexpected adj. 예상치 못한

79 어휘 유의어

난이도 ●●○

In the context of the passage, <u>right</u> means _______.

(a) genuine
(b) accurate
(c) proper
(d) pleasant

지문의 문맥에서, 'right'는 -을 의미한다.

(a) 진짜의
(b) 정확한
(c) 적절한
(d) 즐거운

지텔프 치트키

밑줄 친 어휘의 유의어를 찾는 문제이므로, right가 포함된 구절을 읽고 문맥을 파악한다.

해설 | 3단락의 'to choose the right variety of dishes'는 적당한 종류의 요리들을 고르는 것이라는 뜻이므로, right가 '적당한'이라는 의미로 사용된 것을 알 수 있다. 따라서 '적절한'이라는 비슷한 의미의 (c) proper가 정답이다.

오답분석

(b) '정확한'이라는 의미의 accurate도 right의 사전적 유의어 중 하나이다. 하지만 문맥상 손님들의 마음에 들 적당한 종류의 음식이라는 의미가 되어야 적절하므로, '실수나 오류가 없이 정확한'이라는 의미의 accurate는 문맥에 어울리지 않아 오답이다.

80 어휘 유의어

난이도 ●●○

In the context of the passage, <u>arrange</u> means _______.

(a) adjust
(b) give
(c) decorate
(d) organize

지문의 문맥에서, 'arrange'는 -을 의미한다.

(a) 조정하다
(b) 주다
(c) 장식하다
(d) 준비하다

지텔프 치트키

밑줄 친 어휘의 유의어를 찾는 문제이므로, arrange가 포함된 구절을 읽고 문맥을 파악한다.

해설 | 마지막 단락의 'arrange chafing dishes to keep hot items warm'은 뜨거운 음식들을 따뜻하게 유지하기 위해 보온용 냄비를 마련한다는 뜻이므로, arrange가 '마련하다'라는 의미로 사용된 것을 알 수 있다. 따라서 '준비하다'라는 비슷한 의미의 (d) organize가 정답이다.

08회 실전모의고사

문제집 p.60

정답 및 문제 유형 분석표

PART 1		PART 2		PART 3		PART 4	
53	(c) 특정세부사항	60	(b) 특정세부사항	67	(d) 특정세부사항	74	(b) 주제/목적
54	(b) 특정세부사항	61	(b) 특정세부사항	68	(a) Not/True	75	(d) 특정세부사항
55	(d) 추론	62	(c) 특정세부사항	69	(d) 특정세부사항	76	(c) 특정세부사항
56	(b) Not/True	63	(d) 추론	70	(b) 추론	77	(c) 특정세부사항
57	(d) 특정세부사항	64	(d) 추론	71	(a) 추론	78	(a) 추론
58	(c) 어휘	65	(c) 어휘	72	(b) 어휘	79	(b) 어휘
59	(a) 어휘	66	(a) 어휘	73	(c) 어휘	80	(a) 어휘

취약 유형 분석표

유형	맞힌 개수
주제/목적	/ 1
특정세부사항	/ 11
Not/True	/ 2
추론	/ 6
어휘	/ 8
TOTAL	28

PART 1 (53~59) Biography Article 그랜드 슬램에서 우승한 첫 아시아 테니스 선수 리나

인물 이름

LI NA

인물 소개

Li Na is a Chinese former professional tennis player known for being the first Asian to win a Grand Slam tournament. She is considered the driving force behind an explosion of the sport's popularity in China.

어린 시절 + 업적 시작 계기

Li Na was born on February 26, 1982, in Hubei, China. Her father, Li Shengpeng, was a professional badminton player. Inspired by her dad, Li began playing badminton at six years old. However, two years later, [53]Li accepted her coach's suggestion and started to play tennis. Li sharpened her tennis skills, and when her father died in 1996, she decided that playing the sport could be a means of supporting her mother. Li joined China's National Tennis Team and became a professional player at age 16. Although she saw tremendous success initially, [54]Li chose to take a break from tennis in 2002 to fulfill her dream of studying journalism at university.

복귀 + 소속 변경

When Li returned to the sport in 2004, [58]she managed to resurrect her career, climbing up the ranks and winning several cash prizes. Up until this point, she had remained part of the Chinese Tennis Association, which took 65 percent of her winnings. Li was critical of this practice and participated in a program called "Fly Solo" in 2008. Under "Fly Solo," Li only had to contribute

리나

리나는 그랜드 슬램 대회에서 우승한 최초의 아시아인으로 알려져 있는 중국의 전 프로 테니스 선수이다. 그녀는 중국에서 그 스포츠의 인기 폭발의 원인이 된 원동력으로 여겨진다.

리나는 1982년 2월 26일에 중국 후베이성에서 태어났다. 그녀의 아버지 리셩펑은 프로 배드민턴 선수였다. 아버지에게 영감을 받아, 리는 6살 때 배드민턴을 치기 시작했다. 하지만, 2년 후에, [53]리는 그녀의 코치의 제안을 받아들여 테니스를 치기 시작했다. 리는 자신의 테니스 기술을 연마했고, 1996년에 그녀의 아버지가 돌아가셨을 때, 그녀는 이 운동을 하는 것이 어머니를 부양할 수단이 될 수 있을 것이라는 결론을 내렸다. 리는 중국 테니스 국가 대표팀에 합류했고 16살의 나이에 프로 선수가 되었다. 비록 그녀가 초기에 엄청난 성공을 겪었을지라도, [54]리는 대학에서 신문학을 공부하고자 하는 자신의 꿈을 이루기 위해 2002년에 테니스를 쉬기로 결정했다.

2004년에 리가 이 운동에 복귀했을 때, 그녀는 순위권에 오르고 몇 번의 상금을 타며 [58]간신히 자신의 경력을 되살려냈다. 이때까지만 해도, 그녀는 중국 테니스 협회의 일원으로 남아 있었고, 그것(협회)은 그녀가 탄 상금의 65퍼센트를 가져갔다. 리는 이 관행에 비판적이었고 2008년에 '플라이 솔로'라고 불리는 프로그램에 참여했다. '플라이 솔로'에 따라서, 리는 그녀가

주요 업적

eight percent of her winnings to the Chinese Tennis Association. [55]However, she had to hire her own coaches and pay for all training and touring costs herself.

[56(a)]Her triumphant performance at the 2010 Australian Open marked a crucial moment for her, and more success followed [56(b)]in 2011 when her worldwide ranking leaped to No. 4 with her first Grand Slam singles win at the French Open. This win was historic since Li was the first Asian tennis player, either male or female, to win a Grand Slam singles event. [56(d)]This prompted her popularity to grow considerably throughout China, and people began to see her as an icon. [59]Her celebrity status was cemented [56(c)]when she won her second Grand Slam singles title in 2014.

은퇴 이후 활동

Li retired in September 2014 due to a knee injury but her legacy has no doubt lived on. [57]Li has plans to found her own tennis academy for young athletes, although she is still looking for the right location and wants to make sure she partners with a school that provides a comprehensive education.

탄 상금의 8퍼센트만 중국 테니스 협회에 기부하면 됐다. [55]하지만, 그녀는 자신의 코치를 고용해야 했고 모든 훈련 및 순회 비용을 직접 지불해야 했다.

[56(a)]2010년 호주 오픈에서 승리를 거둔 성과는 그녀에게 매우 중요한 순간으로 남았고, 프랑스 오픈에서의 첫 그랜드 슬램 단식 우승으로 [56(b)]그녀의 세계 랭킹이 4위로 급등했을 때인 2011년에 더 많은 성공이 뒤를 이었다. 이 승리는 역사적이었는데 이는 리가 남녀를 불문하고 그랜드 슬램 단식 경기에서 우승한 최초의 아시아 테니스 선수였기 때문이다. [56(d)]이것은 그녀의 인기가 중국 전역에서 상당히 증가하도록 촉발했고, 사람들은 그녀를 우상으로 보기 시작했다. [56(c)]2014년에 그녀가 두 번째 그랜드 슬램 단식 타이틀을 차지하면서 [59]그녀의 유명 인사 지위는 굳어졌다.

2014년 9월에 리는 무릎 부상으로 인해 은퇴했지만 그녀의 영향은 의심할 여지 없이 계속되고 있다. [57]리는 젊은 운동선수들을 위한 자신의 테니스 학교를 설립할 계획이 있기는 하지만, 그녀는 여전히 적절한 위치를 찾고 있으며 그녀가 종합적인 교육을 제공하는 학교와 협력하는 것을 확실히 하기를 원한다.

어휘 | former adj. 이전의, 과거의 driving force phr. 원동력 explosion n. 폭발 popularity n. 인기 sharpen v. 연마하다 decide v. 결론을 내리다, 결정하다 means n. 수단 support v. 부양하다, 지지하다 tremendous adj. 엄청난 initially adv. 초기에 take a break phr. 쉬다 fulfill v. 이루다, 달성하다 journalism n. 신문학, 신문 잡지 winning n. 상금 critical adj. 비판적인 triumphant adj. 승리를 거둔, 의기양양한 crucial adj. 매우 중요한 leap v. 급등하다 historic adj. 역사적인, 역사적으로 중요한 prompt v. 촉발하다 considerably adv. 상당히 icon n. 우상 status n. 지위 retire v. 은퇴하다 injury n. 부상 legacy n. 영향, 여파 athlete n. 운동선수 partner v. 협력하다 comprehensive adj. 종합적인

53 특정세부사항 When

난이도 ●○○

When did Li Na begin to play tennis?

(a) when her father introduced her to the sport
(b) when it started to get popular in China
(c) when her instructor suggested it to her
(d) when it became more lucrative

리나는 언제 테니스를 치기 시작했는가?

(a) 그녀의 아버지가 그녀에게 그 운동을 소개했을 때
(b) 그것이 중국에서 인기를 끌기 시작했을 때
(c) 그녀의 지도자가 그녀에게 그것을 제안했을 때
(d) 그것이 수익성이 더 좋아졌을 때

지텔프 치트키

질문의 키워드 begin이 started로 paraphrasing되어 언급된 주변 내용을 주의 깊게 읽는다.

해설 | 2단락의 'Li accepted her coach's suggestion and started to play tennis'에서 리는 그녀의 코치의 제안을 받아들여 테니스를 치기 시작했다고 했다. 따라서 (c)가 정답이다.

Paraphrasing

her coach's suggestion 그녀의 코치의 제안 → her instructor suggested 그녀의 지도자가 제안했다

오답분석

(a) 2단락에서 리나가 아버지에게 영감을 받아 시작했던 운동은 배드민턴이라고 했으므로 오답이다.
(b) 1단락에서 리나 덕분에 중국에서 테니스의 인기가 많아졌다고 했으므로 오답이다.

어휘 | instructor n. 지도자, 강사 lucrative adj. 수익성이 좋은

54 특정세부사항 Why

난이도 ●●○

Why did Li take a break from tennis at the beginning of her career?

(a) because she could not play professionally at the time
(b) because she wanted to receive higher education
(c) because she felt a need to get away from journalists
(d) because she was grieving the death of her father

리는 왜 경력 초반에 테니스를 쉬었는가?

(a) 그 당시에 프로 선수로 될 수 없었기 때문에
(b) 대학 교육을 받고 싶어 했기 때문에
(c) 언론인들에게서 벗어날 필요를 느꼈기 때문에
(d) 아버지의 죽음을 몹시 슬퍼하고 있었기 때문에

지텔프 치트키

질문의 키워드 take a break from tennis가 그대로 언급된 주변 내용을 주의 깊게 읽는다.

해설 | 2단락의 'Li chose to take a break from tennis ~ to fulfill her dream of studying journalism at university'에서 리는 대학에서 신문학을 공부하고자 하는 자신의 꿈을 이루기 위해 테니스를 쉬기로 결정했다고 했다. 따라서 (b)가 정답이다.

Paraphrasing
studying ~ at university 대학에서 공부하는 → receive higher education 대학 교육을 받다

어휘 | professionally adv. 프로 선수로, 직업적으로 higher education phr. 대학 교육 get away from phr. ~에게서 벗어나다
journalist n. 언론인 grieve v. 몹시 슬퍼하다

55 추론 특정사실

난이도 ●●●

Based on the passage, what is probably a benefit of the Chinese Tennis Association?

(a) protecting winnings from bad investments
(b) finding companies to offer athletes sponsorships
(c) creating events for players to participate in
(d) paying the training expenses for its players

지문에 따르면, 중국 테니스 협회의 혜택은 무엇인 것 같은가?

(a) 손해나는 투자로부터 상금을 보호하는 것
(b) 운동선수들에게 후원을 제공할 기업을 찾는 것
(c) 선수들이 참여할 경기가 생기게 하는 것
(d) 협회 선수들을 위한 훈련비를 지불하는 것

지텔프 치트키

질문의 키워드 Chinese Tennis Association이 그대로 언급된 주변 내용을 주의 깊게 읽는다.

해설 | 3단락의 'However, she had to ~ pay for all training and touring costs herself.'에서 '플라이 솔로'에 따라서 리가 모든 훈련 및 순회 비용을 직접 지불해야 했다고 한 것을 통해, 중국 테니스 협회의 혜택은 협회 선수들을 위한 훈련비를 지불하는 것일 것임을 추론할 수 있다. 따라서 (d)가 정답이다.

Paraphrasing
training ~ costs 훈련 비용 → training expenses 훈련비

어휘 | investment n. 투자 sponsorship n. 후원, 협찬 expense n. 비용

56 Not/True Not 문제

난이도 ●●○

Which of the following did not happen to Li from 2010 onward?

(a) She competed in the Australian Open.
(b) She was named the world's top tennis player.
(c) She won two Grand Slam singles titles.
(d) She grew increasingly famous in her home country.

다음 중 2010년부터 리에게 일어나지 않은 일은 무엇인가?

(a) 호주 오픈에 참가했다.
(b) 세계 1위의 테니스 선수로 이름이 올랐다.
(c) 두 개의 그랜드 슬램 단식 타이틀을 획득했다.
(d) 고국에서 점점 더 유명해졌다.

지텔프 치트키

질문의 키워드 2010이 그대로 언급된 주변 내용을 주의 깊게 읽고, 보기의 키워드와 지문 내용을 대조하며 언급되는 것을 하나씩 소거한다.

해설 | (b)는 4단락의 'in 2011 her worldwide ranking leaped to No. 4'에서 2011년에 리의 세계 랭킹이 4위로 급등했다고는 했지만, 세계 1위의 테니스 선수로 이름이 올랐는지는 언급되지 않았으므로 지문의 내용과 일치하지 않는다. 따라서 (b)가 정답이다.

오답분석

(a) 보기의 키워드 Australian Open이 그대로 언급된 4단락에서 리가 2010년 호주 오픈에서 승리를 거두었다고 언급되었다.
(c) 보기의 키워드 Grand Slam singles titles가 그대로 언급된 4단락에서 리가 2014년에 두 번째 그랜드 슬램 단식 타이틀을 차지했다고 언급되었다.
(d) 보기의 키워드 grew ~ famous가 popularity ~ grow로 paraphrasing되어 언급된 4단락에서 리의 인기가 중국 전역에서 상당히 증가했다고 언급되었다.

어휘 | onward adv. ~부터, ~ 이래 줄곧 compete v. 참가하다, 경쟁하다

57 특정세부사항 How

난이도 ●●○

How does Li plan to influence the next generation of tennis players?

(a) by partnering with former professional players
(b) by traveling to locations to discuss her career
(c) by developing sports injury prevention steps
(d) by opening a comprehensive tennis school

리는 차세대 테니스 선수들에게 어떻게 영향을 미치려고 계획하는가?

(a) 전 프로 선수들과 협력함으로써
(b) 자신의 경력을 이야기할 장소들을 다님으로써
(c) 스포츠 부상 예방 단계를 개발함으로써
(d) 종합 테니스 학교를 개교함으로써

지텔프 치트키

질문의 키워드 next generation of ~ players가 young athletes로 paraphrasing되어 언급된 주변 내용을 주의 깊게 읽는다.

해설 | 5단락의 'Li has plans to found her own tennis academy for young athletes ~ wants to make sure she partners with a school that provides a comprehensive education.'에서 리는 젊은 운동선수들을 위한 자신의 테니스 학교를 설립할 계획이 있으며 그녀가 종합적인 교육을 제공하는 학교와 협력하는 것을 확실히 하기를 원한다고 했다. 따라서 (d)가 정답이다.

Paraphrasing
found ~ tennis academy 테니스 학교를 설립하다 → opening a ~ tennis school 테니스 학교를 개교함

어휘 | discuss v. 이야기하다 prevention n. 예방

58 어휘 유의어

난이도 ●●○

In the context of the passage, resurrect means ______.

(a) retain
(b) save
(c) restore
(d) construct

지문의 문맥에서, 'resurrect'는 -을 의미한다.

(a) 보유하다
(b) 지키다
(c) 복구하다
(d) 구성하다

지텔프 치트키

밑줄 친 어휘의 유의어를 찾는 문제이므로, resurrect가 포함된 구절을 읽고 문맥을 파악한다.

해설 | 3단락의 'she managed to resurrect her career'는 리나가 간신히 자신의 경력을 되살려냈다는 뜻이므로, resurrect가 '되살리다'라는 의미로 사용된 것을 알 수 있다. 따라서 '복구하다'라는 비슷한 의미의 (c) restore가 정답이다.

59 어휘 유의어

난이도 ●●○

In the context of the passage, cemented means ______.

(a) established
(b) earned
(c) clarified
(d) defended

지문의 문맥에서, 'cemented'는 -을 의미한다.

(a) 확립된
(b) 얻어진
(c) 명확해진
(d) 방어된

지텔프 치트키

밑줄 친 어휘의 유의어를 찾는 문제이므로, cemented가 포함된 구절을 읽고 문맥을 파악한다.

해설 | 4단락의 'Her celebrity status was cemented'는 리나의 유명 인사 지위가 굳어졌다는 뜻이므로, cemented가 '굳어진'이라는 의미로 사용된 것을 알 수 있다. 따라서 '확립된'이라는 비슷한 의미의 (a) established가 정답이다.

PART 2(60~66) Magazine Article 많은 인구가 거주했음을 보여주는 아마존의 대지 예술

연구 결과

THE AMAZON WAS MORE INHABITED THAN BELIEVED

연구의 발견

Archaeologists have discovered numerous Pre-Columbian earthworks in the Amazon. [60]In the past, they believed that Pre-Columbian civilizations were concentrated only in rich floodplains. However, the new findings show that there were also significant populations in areas of mixed grassland and forest.

The earthworks cover a massive area in modern-day Bolivia and Brazil. Some have geometric patterns that

아마존에는 생각했던 것보다 더 많은 사람이 거주했었다

고고학자들은 아마존에서 수많은 콜럼버스 이전의 대지 예술을 발견했다. [60]과거에, 그들은 콜럼버스 이전의 문명은 비옥한 범람원에만 집중되어 있었다고 생각했다. 하지만, 새로운 발견은 혼합 목초지와 삼림 지역에도 상당한 인구가 있었다는 것을 보여준다.

그 대지 예술은 오늘날의 볼리비아와 브라질의 엄청나게 큰 지역에 걸쳐 있다. 몇몇은 정사각형, 원형, 또는 육각형의 기하학무늬를 가지고 있다. 지면 위 재료

발견1: 의식 중심지	are square, circular, or hexagonal. These patterned earthworks, which are formed by the careful arrangement of materials on the ground, are known as geoglyphs. [61]The researchers consider these to have been ceremonial centers because they have found evidence of ritualistic sacrifices but no objects suggesting actual human habitation. However, near the geoglyphs were villages located in rings on large mounds, [65]deliberately kept above the level of seasonal floods.
발견2: 큰 정착지	In some areas, there were large settlements connected by causeways—the equivalent of modern roadways. These communities were reinforced for protection and surrounded by one or more channels. In this sense, they were clearly constructed for long-term occupation and represent primitive, low-density urban populations. According to the researchers, these populations were not migratory and had hierarchical social classes. Furthermore, [62]they had frequent interactions both at the community and regional levels.
연구 방식	Researchers used satellite imagery and other remote sensing technology to spot potential settlements and sent out teams to investigate the sites. In total, they found 81 previously unrecorded sites, which helped fill in large gaps in the archaeological record. The areas they discovered span an interconnected space of 1,800 kilometers from east to west.
정보 분석 결과	[66]The researchers then entered data into a computer model to estimate the population size. After revising the results for differences in population density, they determined that there were 1,087,150 residents. This number dwarfs the census data recorded by the Jesuit missionaries who conducted population surveys after the arrival of Columbus. [63]This can probably be explained by the devastation European diseases, such as smallpox, brought to the native population.
의의	Although the distances covered by the settlements were enormous, they were found in similar terrains and climates. [64]The alternating wet and dry seasons produced sparse forests, which made it easier to clear existing trees. This sheds new light on the environmental impact of Pre-Columbian communities as scientists now believe that [64]it was far greater than was previously presumed.

들의 섬세한 배열에 의해 형성된, 이러한 무늬로 장식된 대지 예술은 지상화로 알려져 있다. [61]연구원들은 이것들이 의식의 중심지였을 것으로 생각하는데 이는 그들이 제사의 제물에 관한 증거는 찾았지만 실제 사람의 거주를 암시하는 물건은 찾지 못했기 때문이다. 하지만, 지상화 주변에는 큰 언덕 위에 원형으로 자리 잡은 마을이 있었으며, 이것은 [65]의도적으로 주기적인 홍수의 수위보다 높게 위치했다.

어떤 지역에는, 둑길로 연결된 큰 정착지가 있었는데, 그 둑길은 현대의 도로와 동등한 것이다. 이러한 지역 공동체들은 방호를 위해 강화되었고 한 개 혹은 그 이상의 수로에 의해 둘러싸여 있었다. 이러한 의미에서, 그것들은 분명히 장기적인 거주를 위해 건설되었으며 원시 사회의 저밀도 도시 인구를 보여준다. 연구원들에 따르면, 이 인구는 이주하지 않았고 계층에 따른 사회 계급을 가지고 있었다. 더욱이, [62]그들은 공동체와 지역적 차원 모두에서 잦은 교류를 했다.

연구원들은 잠재적인 정착지를 찾아내기 위해 인공위성 사진과 다른 원격 감지 기술을 사용했고 그 부지들을 조사하기 위해 팀을 파견했다. 통틀어, 그들은 이전에 기록되지 않았던 81개의 부지들을 찾아냈고, 이는 고고학적 기록의 큰 공백을 메우는 데 도움을 주었다. 그들이 발견한 지역은 동서로 1,800킬로미터에 이르는 상호 연결된 공간에 걸쳐 있다.

[66]연구원들은 그런 다음 인구의 규모를 추정하기 위해 컴퓨터 모델에 정보를 입력했다. 인구 밀도의 차이에 대한 결과를 수정한 후, 그들은 그곳에 1,087,150명의 주민들이 있었다는 것을 밝혀냈다. 이 숫자는 콜럼버스의 도착 이후에 인구 조사를 시행했던 예수회 선교사들에 의해 기록된 인구 조사 자료를 작아 보이게 한다. [63]이것은 아마도 천연두와 같은 유럽의 질병들이 원주민들에게 초래한 파괴로 설명될 수 있을 것이다.

정착지들이 걸쳐 있는 거리가 막대했음에도 불구하고, 그것들은 비슷한 지형과 기후에서 발견되었다. [64]번갈아 일어나는 건기와 우기는 드문드문한 숲을 만들었고, 이는 기존에 있던 나무들을 제거하는 것을 더 쉽게 만들었다. 이것은 콜럼버스 이전 공동체의 환경적 영향을 재조명하는데 이는 과학자들이 이제 [64]그것이 이전에 추정되었던 것보다 훨씬 더 컸다고 믿기 때문이다.

어휘 | inhabit v. ~에 거주하다 archaeologist n. 고고학자 earthwork n. 대지 예술, 토공 civilization n. 문명 floodplain n. 범람원 geometric adj. 기하학의 circular adj. 원형의 hexagonal adj. 육각형의 geoglyph n. 지상화 ceremonial adj. 의식의, 예식의

ritualistic adj. 제사의 sacrifice n. 제물, 희생물 seasonal adj. 주기적인, 계절적인 settlement n. 정착지, 개척지
causeway n. 둑길, 포장도로 equivalent n. 동등한 것 reinforce v. 강화하다 channel n. 수로 occupation n. 거주, 점령
primitive adj. 원시 사회의 low-density adj. 저밀도의 migratory adj. 이주하는 hierarchical adj. 계층에 따른 imagery n. 사진
send out phr. 파견하다 span v. 걸치다; n. 기간, 거리 dwarf v. 작아 보이게 하다; n. 난쟁이 census n. 인구 조사 Jesuit n. 예수회 (성원)
missionary n. 선교사 devastation n. 파괴, 황폐화 smallpox n. 천연두 terrain n. 지형 alternating adj. 번갈아 일어나는
sparse adj. 드문드문한 shed new light phr. 재조명하다 presume v. 추정하다

60 특정세부사항 연구의 결과

난이도 ●●○

What did the study find out about the Amazon before Columbus?

(a) that its floodplains were popular settlements
(b) that it was actually occupied quite extensively
(c) that its population density transformed the landscape
(d) that it had a major effect on future civilizations

연구는 콜럼버스 이전의 아마존에 대해 무엇을 알아냈는가?

(a) 범람원이 인기 있는 정착지였다는 것
(b) 사실 꽤 광범위하게 사람이 살고 있었다는 것
(c) 인구 밀도가 경관을 변형시켰다는 것
(d) 미래 문명에 주요한 영향을 미쳤다는 것

지텔프 치트키

연구의 결과를 언급하는 지문의 초반을 주의 깊게 읽는다.

해설 | 1단락의 'In the past, they believed ~ Pre-Columbian civilizations were concentrated only in rich floodplains.'에서 과거에 고고학자들은 콜럼버스 이전 문명이 비옥한 범람원에만 집중되어 있었다고 생각했다고 한 뒤, 'However, the new findings show ~ significant populations in areas of mixed grassland and forest.'에서 하지만 새로운 발견은 혼합 목초지와 삼림 지역에도 상당한 인구가 있었다는 것을 보여준다고 했다. 따라서 (b)가 정답이다.

Paraphrasing
there were ~ populations 인구가 있었다 → it was ~ occupied 사람이 살고 있었다

오답분석
(a) 1단락에서 과거에 고고학자들이 콜럼버스 이전의 문명은 범람원에만 집중되어 있었다고 생각했다고는 했지만, 범람원이 실제로 인기 있는 정착지였는지는 언급되지 않았으므로 오답이다.

어휘 | occupied adj. 사람이 살고 있는, 지배된 extensively adv. 광범위하게 transform v. 변형시키다 landscape n. 경관, 풍경

61 특정세부사항 Why

난이도 ●●○

Why do the researchers believe that the geoglyphs were used for rituals?

(a) The geoglyphs feature patterns that reflect worship.
(b) The researchers uncovered proof of ancient rites.
(c) The geoglyphs are located in the center of the civilization.
(d) The researchers found objects suggesting habitation.

연구원들은 왜 지상화가 제사에 사용되었다고 믿는가?

(a) 지상화가 숭배를 나타내는 무늬를 특징으로 한다.
(b) 연구원들이 고대 제식의 증거를 발견했다.
(c) 지상화가 문명의 중심지에 위치해 있다.
(d) 연구원들이 거주를 암시하는 물건을 찾았다.

지텔프 치트키

질문의 키워드 geoglyphs가 그대로 언급된 주변 내용을 주의 깊게 읽는다.

해설 | 2단락의 'The researchers consider these to have been ceremonial centers because they have found evidence of ritualistic sacrifices'에서 연구원들은 제사의 제물에 관한 증거를 찾았기 때문에 이것들(지상화)이 의식의 중심지였을 것으로 생각한다고 했다. 따라서 (b)가 정답이다.

Paraphrasing

believe 믿다 → consider 생각하다

found evidence of ritualistic sacrifices 제사의 제물에 관한 증거를 찾았다 → uncovered proof of ~ rites 제식의 증거를 발견했다

오답분석

(d) 2단락에서 연구원들이 실제 사람의 거주를 암시하는 물건은 찾지 못했다고 언급되었으므로 오답이다.

어휘 | reflect v. 나타내다, 반영하다 worship n. 숭배 uncover v. 발견하다 ancient adj. 고대의 rite n. 제식

62 특정세부사항 What

난이도 ●●○

According to the article, what was a characteristic of the people in large settlements?

(a) a habit of migrating to new locations with the seasons
(b) a common conflict between different social classes
(c) a tendency to mix with people from other communities
(d) a lack of knowledge about channel construction

기사에 따르면, 큰 정착지에 사는 사람들의 특징은 무엇이었는가?

(a) 계절에 따라 새로운 장소로 이주하는 습관
(b) 다른 사회 계층들 간의 흔한 갈등
(c) 다른 공동체의 사람들과 왕래하는 경향
(d) 수로 건설에 관한 지식의 부족

지텔프 치트키

질문의 키워드 large settlements가 그대로 언급된 주변 내용을 주의 깊게 읽는다.

해설 | 3단락의 'they had frequent interactions both at the community and regional levels'에서 그들(큰 정착지의 인구)은 공동체와 지역적 차원 모두에서 잦은 교류를 했다고 했다. 따라서 (c)가 정답이다.

Paraphrasing

interactions ~ at the community and regional levels 공동체와 지역적 차원에서의 교류 → mix with people from other communities 다른 공동체의 사람들과 왕래하다

오답분석

(a) 3단락에서 큰 정착지의 인구는 이주하지 않았다고 언급되었으므로 오답이다.
(b) 3단락에서 큰 정착지의 인구가 계층에 따른 사회 계급을 가지고 있었다고는 했지만, 그 계층들 간에 갈등이 있었는지는 언급되지 않았으므로 오답이다.

어휘 | conflict n. 갈등 mix v. 왕래하다, 어울리다

63 추론 특정사실

난이도 ●●●

Why most likely did the Jesuits document low population numbers?

(a) because the surveys were conducted in a limited area
(b) because the methods used in the census were flawed
(c) because most of the native people refused to participate
(d) because many natives had died from exotic diseases

예수회 성원들은 왜 적은 인구수를 문서에 기록했던 것 같은가?

(a) 조사가 제한된 지역에서 수행되었기 때문에
(b) 인구 조사에 사용된 방법에 결함이 있었기 때문에
(c) 대부분의 원주민들이 참여를 거절했기 때문에
(d) 많은 원주민들이 외래병들로 죽었었기 때문에

지텔프 치트키

질문의 키워드 Jesuits가 Jesuit missionaries로 paraphrasing되어 언급된 주변 내용을 주의 깊게 읽는다.

해설 | 5단락의 'This can ~ be explained by the devastation European diseases ~ brought to the native population.'에서 이것(연구원들이 추정한 인구수가 예수회 선교사들에 의해 기록된 인구 조사 자료를 작아 보이게 하는 것)은 유럽의 질병들이 원주민들에게 초래한 파괴로 설명될 수 있을 것이라고 한 것을 통해, 많은 원주민들이 유럽에서 온 외래병으로 죽었었기 때문에 예수회 성원들이 적은 인구수를 문서에 기록했던 것임을 추론할 수 있다. 따라서 (d)가 정답이다.

Paraphrasing
European diseases 유럽의 질병들 → exotic diseases 외래병들

어휘 | flawed adj. 결함이 있는 exotic adj. 외래(국)의, 이국적인

64 추론 특정사실

난이도 ●●●

What can be concluded about Pre-Columbian people based on the geographical feature?

(a) They had difficulty cutting down the forests.
(b) They adapted to life in dissimilar surroundings.
(c) They grew different crops depending on the season.
(d) They altered the environment more than thought.

지리적 특색에 근거하여 콜럼버스 이전의 사람들에 관해 결론지을 수 있는 것은 무엇인가?

(a) 삼림을 벌채하는 데 어려움이 있었다.
(b) 다른 환경에서의 생활에 적응했다.
(c) 계절에 따라 다른 곡식을 재배했다.
(d) 생각했던 것보다 더 많이 환경을 바꿨다.

지텔프 치트키

질문의 키워드 geographical feature가 terrains로 paraphrasing되어 언급된 주변 내용을 주의 깊게 읽는다.

해설 | 6단락의 'The alternating wet and dry seasons produced sparse forests, which made it easier to clear existing trees.'에서 번갈아 일어나는 건기와 우기는 드문드문한 숲을 만들었고 이는 기존에 있던 나무들을 제거하는 것을 더 쉽게 만들었다고 한 뒤, 'it was far greater than was previously presumed'에서 그것(콜럼버스 이전 공동체의 환경적 영향)이 이전에 추정되었던 것보다 훨씬 더 컸다고 한 것을 통해, 콜럼버스 이전의 사람들은 생각했던 것보다 더 많이 환경을 바꿨다고 결론지을 수 있음을 추론할 수 있다. 따라서 (d)가 정답이다.

어휘 | geographical adj. 지리적인 cut down phr. 벌채하다 adapt v. 적응하다 alter v. 바꾸다

65 어휘 유의어

난이도 ●○○

In the context of the passage, deliberately means ______.

(a) willingly
(b) systematically
(c) intentionally
(d) accidentally

지문의 문맥에서 'deliberately'는 -을 의미한다.

(a) 기꺼이
(b) 체계적으로
(c) 의도적으로
(d) 우연히

지텔프 치트키

밑줄 친 어휘의 유의어를 찾는 문제이므로, deliberately가 포함된 구절을 읽고 문맥을 파악한다.

해설 | 2단락의 'deliberately kept above the level of seasonal floods'는 의도적으로 주기적인 홍수의 수위보다 높게 위치했다는 뜻이므로, deliberately가 '의도적으로'라는 의미로 사용된 것을 알 수 있다. 따라서 '의도적으로'라는 같은 의미의 (c) intentionally가 정답이다.

66 어휘 유의어

난이도 ●●●

In the context of the passage, estimate means ______.

(a) calculate
(b) solve
(c) imagine
(d) assume

지문의 문맥에서 'estimate'는 -을 의미한다.

(a) 어림잡다
(b) 해결하다
(c) 상상하다
(d) 가정하다

지텔프 치트키

밑줄 친 어휘의 유의어를 찾는 문제이므로, estimate가 포함된 구절을 읽고 문맥을 파악한다.

해설 | 5단락의 'The researchers ~ entered data into a computer model to estimate the population size.'는 연구원들이 인구의 규모를 추정하기 위해 컴퓨터 모델에 정보를 입력했다는 뜻이므로, estimate가 '추정하다'라는 의미로 사용된 것을 알 수 있다. 따라서 '어림잡다'라는 비슷한 의미의 (a) calculate가 정답이다.

오답분석

(d) '가정하다'라는 의미의 assume은 객관성을 고려하지 않고 막연히 추측하여 사실이라고 가정하는 경우에 사용되므로, 객관적인 정보를 이용해 인구의 규모를 추정한다는 문맥에 어울리지 않아 오답이다.

PART 3 (67~73) Encyclopedia Article 건반 악기 하프시코드의 역사 및 특징

표제어

HARPSICHORD

정의

The harpsichord is a keyboard instrument that is closely associated with the Renaissance and Baroque periods. [67]Most music historians consider it to be a predecessor of the modern piano, which it strongly resembles.

하프시코드

하프시코드는 르네상스 및 바로크 시대와 밀접하게 관련된 건반 악기이다. [67]대부분의 음악 사학자들은 이것을 현대 피아노의 전신으로 여기는데, 이것(하프시코드)은 피아노를 매우 닮았다.

장점	The earliest known reference to the harpsichord was made in 1397, and this instrument was widely used throughout Europe from the early 16th century until the end of the 18th century. Many prominent composers, such as Bach and Vivaldi, [72]created musical pieces specifically for it. The design of the harpsichord played an important role in its early popularity. The other keyboard instrument commonly used during this period—[68(a)]the pipe organ—cannot be moved without great difficulty due to its size and complexity. In contrast, [68(b)]the harpsichord is convenient to transport. Furthermore, [68(c)]it is less expensive to make and [68(d)]easier to clean and repair.	하프시코드에 대해 최초로 알려진 참고 자료는 1397년에 만들어졌으며, 이 악기는 16세기 초부터 18세기 말까지 유럽 전역에서 널리 사용되었다. 바흐와 비발디와 같은 많은 유명한 작곡가들은 [72]특별히 이것을 위한 음악 작품을 창작했다. 하프시코드의 디자인은 이것의 초기 유명세에 중요한 역할을 했다. 이 시기에 흔하게 사용되었던 다른 건반 악기인 [68(a)]파이프 오르간은 그것의 크기와 복잡성 때문에 큰 어려움 없이는 옮겨질 수 없다. 반면에, [68(b)]하프시코드는 이동시키기에 편리하다. 게다가, [68(c)]그것은 제작하기에 덜 비싸고 [68(d)]닦고 수리하기가 더 쉽다.
작동원리	Harpsichords rely on a relatively simple mechanism to generate sound. A harpsichord key functions like a lever. When the musician presses down on the front of a key, the back of it rises. This motion pushes a narrow wooden board called a jack upwards as well. [69]As the jack ascends, it quickly pulls and releases a string, producing a musical note in a manner similar to that of a guitar string being plucked.	하프시코드는 소리를 만들어 내기 위해 비교적 간단한 기제에 의존한다. 하프시코드의 건반은 지렛대와 같은 기능을 한다. 연주자가 건반의 앞부분을 누르면, 그것(건반)의 뒷부분이 올라간다. 이 동작은 잭이라고 불리는 좁은 나무판을 밀어 올리기도 한다. [69]잭이 올라갈 때, 그것(잭)은 줄을 빠르게 당겼다가 놓아주며, 기타 줄이 튕겨지는 것과 비슷한 방식으로 음을 만든다.
단점	The primary disadvantage of the harpsichord is that [70]a musician cannot change the volume or length of a note. Regardless of how hard or how quickly a key is struck, the action of plucking a string results in a sound of the same volume and duration each time. [70]It was this limitation that eventually caused the harpsichord to be superseded by the piano. This newer instrument includes hammers that strike the strings with different speeds and intensities depending on how the musician presses the keys.	하프시코드의 주된 단점은 [70]연주자가 음량이나 음의 길이를 바꿀 수 없다는 것이다. 건반이 얼마나 세게 혹은 얼마나 빠르게 쳐지는가에 상관없이, 줄을 튕기는 행동은 매번 동일한 음량과 길이의 소리를 만들어 낸다. [70]하프시코드가 결국 피아노로 대체되도록 야기한 것은 바로 이 한계였다. 이 더 새로운 악기는 연주자가 건반을 어떻게 누르는지에 따라 상이한 속도와 강도로 줄을 치는 해머를 포함한다.
현황	Although the harpsichord had lost its popularity among musicians by the end of the 18th century, [71]it has experienced a limited revival in modern times. It was played by early pop groups, such as the Beatles, and featured in the celebrated 2015 musical *Hamilton*. However, [71/73]it remains a niche instrument used mainly in performances of historical pieces, rather than in popular modern compositions.	비록 하프시코드가 18세기 말 무렵에 음악가들 사이에서 인기가 떨어졌지만, [71]이것은 현대에 한정적인 부흥을 경험했다. 하프시코드는 비틀스와 같은 초기 팝 그룹에 의해 연주되었고, 2015년의 유명한 뮤지컬 「해밀턴」에 등장했다. 하지만, 그것은 대중적인 현대 작품보다는 [71/73]주로 역사와 관련된 작품의 공연에 사용되는 특수화된 악기로 남아 있다.

어휘 | instrument n. 악기 associate v. 관련시키다 predecessor n. 전신, 전임자 resemble v. 닮다 reference n. 참고 자료, 언급
prominent adj. 유명한, 중요한 piece n. 작품, 조각 complexity n. 복잡성 transport v. 이동시키다
rely on phr. ~에 의존하다, 필요로 하다 relatively adv. 비교적, 상대적으로 mechanism n. 기제, 방법 key n. 건반 lever n. 지렛대
press down phr. ~을 누르다 narrow adj. 좁은 jack n. 잭(하프시코드에서 건반과 지렛대로 연결된 판) ascend v. 올라가다
release v. 놓아주다 note n. 음, 음표 pluck v. (기타 등의 현을) 튕기다, 뜯다 volume n. 음량, 용량 length n. 길이
strike v. 치다, 때리다 duration n. 길이, 기간 limitation n. 한계, 제약 supersede v. 대체하다
hammer n. 해머(건반 악기에서 현을 때려 음을 내는 망치) intensity n. 강도 revival n. 부흥 feature v. 등장하다, 출연하다

67 특정세부사항 How

난이도 ●●○

Based on the article, how do academics view the harpsichord?

(a) as superior to modern instruments
(b) as being based on the designs of the first piano
(c) as better suited for Baroque than Renaissance music
(d) as the early form of a contemporary instrument

기사에 따르면, 학자들은 하프시코드를 어떻게 여기는가?

(a) 현대 악기보다 우수한 것으로
(b) 최초의 피아노 디자인에 기반을 둔 것으로
(c) 르네상스 음악보다 바로크 음악에 더 적합한 것으로
(d) 현대 악기의 초기 형태로

지텔프 치트키

질문의 키워드 academics view가 historians consider로 paraphrasing되어 언급된 주변 내용을 주의 깊게 읽는다.

해설 | 1단락의 'Most music historians consider it to be a predecessor of the modern piano'에서 대부분의 음악 사학자들은 하프시코드를 현대 피아노의 전신으로 여긴다고 했다. 따라서 (d)가 정답이다.

Paraphrasing
a predecessor of the modern piano 현대 피아노의 전신 → the early form of a contemporary instrument 현대 악기의 초기 형태

어휘 | academic n. 학자, 교수 superior adj. 우수한, 우세한 suited adj. 적합한, 어울리는 contemporary adj. 현대의, 당대의

68 Not/True Not 문제

난이도 ●○○

Which is not a benefit of the harpsichord over the pipe organ?

(a) its more complex design
(b) its greater mobility
(c) its cheaper production cost
(d) its simpler maintenance

파이프 오르간을 넘어서는 하프시코드의 장점이 아닌 것은 무엇인가?

(a) 더 복잡한 디자인
(b) 더 탁월한 이동성
(c) 더 저렴한 제작 비용
(d) 더 간단한 보수 관리

지텔프 치트키

질문의 키워드 pipe organ이 그대로 언급된 주변 내용을 주의 깊게 읽고, 보기의 키워드와 지문 내용을 대조하며 언급되는 것을 하나씩 소거한다.

해설 | (a)는 2단락의 'the pipe organ—cannot be moved without great difficulty due to its size and complexity'에서 파이프 오르간은 그것의 크기와 복잡성 때문에 큰 어려움 없이는 옮겨질 수 없다면서 복잡성을 파이프 오르간의 단점으로 언급하였으므로, 하프시코드의 장점이 아니다. 따라서 (a)가 정답이다.

오답분석
(b) 보기의 키워드 mobility와 관련된 transport가 언급된 2단락에서 하프시코드는 이동시키기에 편리하다고 언급되었다.
(c) 보기의 키워드 cheaper가 less expensive로 paraphrasing되어 언급된 2단락에서 하프시코드는 제작하기에 덜 비싸다고 언급되었다.
(d) 보기의 키워드 maintenance가 repair로 paraphrasing되어 언급된 2단락에서 하프시코드는 닦고 수리하기가 더 쉽다고 언급되었다.

어휘 | mobility n. 이동성, 유동성 production n. 제작, 제조 maintenance n. 보수 관리, 유지

69 특정세부사항 What

난이도 ●●●

What is the function of the jack?	잭의 기능은 무엇인가?
(a) to press a key	(a) 건반을 누르는 것
(b) to lift a board	(b) 판을 들어 올리는 것
(c) to activate a lever	(c) 지렛대를 작동시키는 것
(d) to pluck a string	**(d) 줄을 튕기는 것**

지텔프 치트키

질문의 키워드 jack이 그대로 언급된 주변 내용을 주의 깊게 읽는다.

해설 | 3단락의 'As the jack ascends, it quickly pulls and releases a string, producing a musical note in a manner similar to that of a guitar string being plucked.'에서 잭이 올라갈 때 그것은 줄을 빠르게 당겼다가 놓아주며 기타 줄이 튕겨지는 것과 비슷한 방식으로 음을 만든다고 했다. 따라서 (d)가 정답이다.

오답분석

(b) 3단락에서 연주자가 건반을 누르는 동작이 나무판, 즉 잭을 밀어 올린다고 했으므로 오답이다.

어휘 | lift v. 들어 올리다 activate v. 작동시키다

70 추론 특정사실

난이도 ●●○

Why most likely did musicians switch from the harpsichord to the piano?	왜 많은 음악가들이 하프시코드에서 피아노로 바꾼 것 같은가?
(a) because the harpsichord's music is produced at a very low volume	(a) 하프시코드의 음악은 매우 낮은 음량으로 만들어지기 때문에
(b) because the harpsichord's player cannot alter the qualities of notes	**(b) 하프시코드의 연주자가 음의 특성을 바꿀 수 없기 때문에**
(c) because the harpsichord's keyboard is difficult to operate	(c) 하프시코드의 건반이 작동시키기 어렵기 때문에
(d) because the harpsichord's hammers generate inconsistent sounds	(d) 하프시코드의 해머가 일관성 없는 소리를 만들어내기 때문에

지텔프 치트키

질문의 키워드 switch가 superseded로 paraphrasing되어 언급된 주변 내용을 주의 깊게 읽는다.

해설 | 4단락의 'a musician cannot change the volume or length of a note'에서 연주자가 하프시코드의 음량이나 음의 길이를 바꿀 수 없다고 한 뒤, 'It ~ caused the harpsichord to be superseded by the piano.'에서 이것이 하프시코드가 피아노로 대체되도록 야기했다고 한 것을 통해, 하프시코드의 경우 연주자가 음의 특성을 바꿀 수 없기 때문에 많은 음악가들이 하프시코드에서 피아노로 바꾼 것임을 추론할 수 있다. 따라서 (b)가 정답이다.

Paraphrasing

cannot change 바꿀 수 없다 → cannot alter 바꿀 수 없다
the volume or length of a note 음량이나 음의 길이 → the qualities of notes 음의 특성

어휘 | inconsistent adj. 일관성 없는, 모순되는

71 추론 특정사실

난이도 ●●●

What can be inferred about the recent renewal of interest in the harpsichord?

(a) It is unlikely to be widespread.
(b) It was revived by historical performances.
(c) It will probably be limited to pop music.
(d) It resulted from a famous musical.

최근 하프시코드에 대한 관심의 부활에 관해 추론될 수 있는 것은 무엇인가?

(a) 널리 퍼질 것 같지 않다.
(b) 역사와 관련된 공연에 의해 되살아났다.
(c) 아마도 팝 음악에 한정될 것이다.
(d) 유명 뮤지컬에서 비롯되었다.

지텔프 치트키

질문의 키워드 recent renewal of interest가 revival in modern times로 paraphrasing되어 언급된 주변 내용을 주의 깊게 읽는다.

해설 | 5단락의 'it has experienced a limited revival in modern times'에서 하프시코드가 현대에 한정적인 부흥을 경험했다고 한 뒤, 'it remains a niche instrument'에서 그것이 특수화된 악기로 남아 있다고 한 것을 통해, 최근 하프시코드에 대한 관심의 부활은 널리 퍼질 것 같지 않음을 추론할 수 있다. 따라서 (a)가 정답이다.

Paraphrasing
limited 한정적인 → unlikely to be widespread 널리 퍼질 것 같지 않은

어휘 | renewal n. 부활, 재개 unlikely adj. ~할 것 같지 않은 result from phr. ~에서 비롯되다

72 어휘 유의어

난이도 ●○○

In the context of the passage, specifically means ______.

(a) essentially
(b) particularly
(c) absolutely
(d) partially

지문의 문맥에서 'specifically'는 -을 의미한다.

(a) 본질적으로
(b) 특별히
(c) 절대적으로
(d) 부분적으로

지텔프 치트키

밑줄 친 어휘의 유의어를 찾는 문제이므로, specifically가 포함된 구절을 읽고 문맥을 파악한다.

해설 | 2단락의 'created musical pieces specifically for it'은 특별히 이것(하프시코드)을 위한 음악 작품을 창작했다는 뜻이므로, specifically가 '특별히'라는 의미로 사용된 것을 알 수 있다. 따라서 '특별히'라는 같은 의미의 (b) particularly가 정답이다.

73 어휘 유의어

난이도 ●●○

In the context of the passage, niche means ______.

(a) suitable
(b) sophisticated
(c) specialized
(d) marginal

지문의 문맥에서 'niche'는 -을 의미한다.

(a) 적합한
(b) 정교한
(c) 특수화된
(d) 주변부의

지텔프 치트키

밑줄 친 어휘의 유의어를 찾는 문제이므로, niche가 포함된 구절을 읽고 문맥을 파악한다.

해설 | 5단락의 'it remains a niche instrument used mainly in performances of historical pieces'는 하프시코드가 주로 역사와 관련된 작품의 공연에 사용되는 특수화된 악기로 남아있다는 뜻이므로, niche가 '특수화된'이라는 의미로 사용된 것을 알 수 있다. 따라서 '특수화된'이라는 같은 의미의 (c) specialized가 정답이다.

PART 4(74~80) Business Letter 회사의 새로운 관리 시스템을 소개하는 편지

수신인 정보

Mr. Ralph Henderson
Marketing Director
Corporate Headquarters

Dear Mr. Henderson,

편지의 목적: 새로운 시스템 소개

Welcome back! While you were on vacation, [74/79]we announced the implementation of the Total Management System (TMS), which will go into full effect on July 12. Not only will the TMS make the company more efficient but it will simplify many processes for managers and team members alike.

시스템 용도

The TMS is a paperless system that holds employee payroll information, attendance record, and emergency contact numbers in one convenient place. In addition, [75]this system can be used to easily request days off and schedule meetings, without the inconvenience of tracking down a coworker to choose a time or place.

시스템 사용 방법

To access the TMS, first set up your account and password with this link (www.startTMS.com). [76]Before the system is fully implemented, explore the system and get familiar with the attendance and vacation request features, which will be most frequently used.

시스템 안내 책자

To ease the transition, we will email a user manual to each team member. The manual will cover the system's basic functions, and will also detail how to handle [77]less common situations like bereavement leave, employee complaints, and resignations. Please note that while the TMS can be used on a mobile device, accounts must be set up on a PC.

Finally, we ask that you join the other department heads for an educational session this Friday at 10 a.m. in the main conference room. This training will last until lunchtime and [80]will equip you with the knowledge to

Mr. Ralph Henderson
마케팅 본부장
기업 본사

Mr. Henderson께,

돌아오신 것을 환영합니다! 당신이 휴가 중이었을 때, [74/79]우리는 종합 관리 시스템(TMS)의 시행을 발표했는데, 이것은 7월 12일에 완전히 실시될 예정입니다. TMS가 회사를 더욱 능률적으로 만들어 줄 뿐만 아니라 관리자들과 팀원들 모두에게 많은 절차를 간소화해 줄 것입니다.

TMS는 직원 급여 대상자 명단 정보, 출근 기록, 그리고 비상 연락망을 하나의 편리한 공간에 담고 있는 종이를 쓰지 않는 시스템입니다. 게다가, [75]이 시스템은 쉽게 휴일을 신청하고 회의 일정을 잡는 데 사용될 수 있어, 시간이나 장소를 고르기 위해 동료를 추적할 불편함이 없습니다.

TMS에 접속하기 위해서, 첫 번째로 이 링크(www.startTMS.com)에서 당신의 계정과 비밀번호를 설정하세요. [76]시스템이 완전히 시행되기 전에, 시스템을 탐색하며 가장 자주 사용될 출근과 휴가 신청 기능을 익혀보세요.

전환을 쉽게 하기 위해, 우리는 각 팀원에게 사용자 안내 책자를 이메일로 보낼 것입니다. 안내 책자는 시스템의 기본적인 기능들을 포함할 것이고, [77]장례 휴가, 사원 불만, 그리고 사임과 같이 덜 흔한 상황을 다루는 방법도 상세히 알려줄 것입니다. TMS가 모바일 기기에서 사용될 수 있지만, 계정은 컴퓨터에서 설정되어야 한다는 것을 주의해 주세요.

마지막으로, 우리는 당신께 이번 주 금요일 오전 10시에 대회의실에서 있을 다른 부서장들과의 교육 회의에 참여하실 것을 요청합니다. 이번 교육은 점심시간까지 이어질 예정이며, 당신이 받을 수도 있는 [80]어떠

끝인사 + 요청	cope with any TMS inquiry you may receive. If you can't attend the group session, [78]contact me by email at jstewartHR@littlefoot.org and we can arrange a private meeting, preferably before July 12. Thank you in advance for your cooperation.	한 TMS 질문에도 대처할 수 있는 지식을 갖추게 할 것입니다. 만약 이 단체 회의에 참석할 수 없으신 경우, [78]저의 이메일인 jstewartHR@littlefoot.org로 연락해 주시면 가급적 7월 12일 전에 개인적인 회의를 마련해 드릴 수 있습니다. 당신의 협조에 미리 감사드립니다.
발신인 정보	Sincerely, Julie Stewart HR General Manager Littlefoot Shoes	Julie Stewart 드림 인사 실장 Littlefoot 신발 회사

어휘 | implementation n. 시행, 실행 go into effect phr. 실시되다, 효력이 발생되다 efficient adj. 능률적인 simplify v. 간소화하다 alike adv. 똑같이 paperless adj. 종이를 쓰지 않는 employee n. 직원, 사원 payroll n. 급여 대상자 명단, 임금 대장 attendance n. 출근, 출석 emergency n. 비상 (사태) day off phr. 휴일, 쉬는 날 schedule v. 일정을 잡다; n. 일정 track down phr. ~를 추적하다 access v. 접속하다 set up phr. 설정하다 account n. 계정 explore v. 탐색하다, 살피다 get familiar with phr. ~을 익히다 feature n. 기능, 특징 transition n. 전환, 이동 manual n. 안내 책자 bereavement n. 장례, 상 complaint n. 불만, 불평 resignation n. 사임, 사퇴 note v. 주의하다, 주목하다 session n. 회의, 모임 cope with phr. ~에 대처하다 inquiry n. 질문 arrange v. 마련하다, 준비하다 preferably adv. 가급적(이면) cooperation n. 협조

74 주제/목적 편지의 목적

난이도 ●○○

What is the main purpose of Julie Stewart's letter?

(a) to celebrate the productivity of the company
(b) to introduce a new organizational tool
(c) to share employee contact information
(d) to launch a system to reduce paper waste

Julie Stewart의 편지의 주된 목적은 무엇인가?

(a) 회사의 생산성을 축하하기 위해서
(b) 새로운 조직적 도구를 소개하기 위해서
(c) 직원 연락처를 공유하기 위해서
(d) 종이 낭비를 줄이기 위한 시스템을 시작하기 위해서

지텔프 치트키

지문의 초반을 주의 깊게 읽고 전체 맥락을 파악한다.

해설 | 1단락의 'we announced the implementation of the Total Management System (TMS), which will go into full effect on July 12'에서 회사가 7월 12일에 완전히 실시될 예정인 종합 관리 시스템(TMS)의 시행을 발표했다고 한 뒤, 시스템 소개와 사용 방법 등에 관한 내용이 이어지고 있다. 따라서 (b)가 정답이다.

Paraphrasing
Total Management System 종합 관리 시스템 → a ~ organizational tool 조직적 도구

어휘 | productivity n. 생산성 launch v. 시작하다, 개시하다 waste n. 낭비

75 특정세부사항 How

난이도 ●●○

How does the new system assist workers at Littlefoot Shoes?

(a) It reports emergency situations automatically.
(b) It simplifies the ordering process.

새로운 시스템은 어떻게 Littlefoot 신발 회사의 직원들에게 도움이 될 수 있는가?

(a) 비상 상황을 자동으로 알려준다.
(b) 발주 절차를 간소화한다.

(c) It offers them more opportunities for days off.
(d) It allows them to organize meetings more simply.

(c) 휴일의 기회를 더 많이 제공한다.
(d) 회의를 더 간편하게 준비할 수 있게 한다.

지텔프 치트키

질문의 키워드 assist workers와 관련된 convenient 주변 내용을 주의 깊게 읽는다.

해설 | 2단락의 'this system can be used to easily ~ schedule meetings'에서 새로운 시스템은 쉽게 회의 일정을 잡는 데 사용될 수 있다고 했다. 따라서 (d)가 정답이다.

Paraphrasing
easily ~ schedule meetings 쉽게 회의 일정을 잡다 → organize meetings ~ simply 간편하게 회의를 준비하다

어휘 | report v. 알리다 automatically adv. 자동으로

76 특정세부사항 What

난이도 ●●○

What does Ms. Stewart suggest workers do prior to using the system?

(a) follow the TMS link to a manager's account
(b) monitor the time in the attendance function
(c) take a look at the common features
(d) delete the default password

Ms. Stewart가 시스템을 이용하기 전에 직원들에게 제안하는 것은 무엇인가?

(a) 관리자 계정으로 TMS 링크를 따라간다
(b) 출근 기능의 시간을 관찰한다
(c) 일반적인 기능을 살펴본다
(d) 초기 설정 비밀번호를 삭제한다

지텔프 치트키

질문의 키워드 prior to using이 Before ~ implemented로 paraphrasing되어 언급된 주변 내용을 주의 깊게 읽는다.

해설 | 3단락의 'Before the system is fully implemented, explore the system and get familiar with ~ features, which will be most frequently used.'에서 Ms. Stewart는 새로운 시스템이 완전히 시행되기 전에, 시스템을 탐색하며 가장 자주 사용될 기능을 익혀 보라고 했다. 따라서 (c)가 정답이다.

Paraphrasing
explore 탐색하다 → take a look 살펴보다
most frequently used 가장 자주 사용되는 → common 일반적인

어휘 | take a look at phr. ~을 살펴보다 default n. 초기 설정, 기본값

77 특정세부사항 Which

난이도 ●○○

Which TMS feature will be used less frequently?

(a) requesting holiday leave
(b) maintaining attendance records
(c) registering worker dissatisfaction
(d) tracking staff payroll hours

어떤 TMS 기능이 덜 자주 사용될 것인가?

(a) 명절 휴가를 신청하는 것
(b) 출근 기록을 보유하는 것
(c) 직원 불만족을 등록하는 것
(d) 직원의 근무 시간을 추적하는 것

지텔프 치트키

질문의 키워드 less frequently가 less common으로 paraphrasing되어 언급된 주변 내용을 주의 깊게 읽는다.

해설 | 4단락의 'less common situations like bereavement leave, employee complaints, and resignations'에서 장례 휴가, 사원 불만, 그리고 사임은 덜 흔한 상황이라고 했다. 따라서 (c)가 정답이다.

Paraphrasing
employee complaints 사원 불만 → worker dissatisfaction 직원 불만족

어휘 | maintain v. 보유하다, 유지하다 register v. 등록하다 dissatisfaction n. 불만족 payroll hours phr. 근무 시간

78 추론 특정사실

난이도 ●●○

Why most likely did Ms. Stewart mention her contact information in the letter?

(a) so Mr. Henderson can schedule a potential individual training
(b) so Mr. Henderson can ask department heads about the system
(c) to share the schedule for the group session
(d) to get the lunch orders of the training participants

편지에서 Ms. Stewart는 왜 그녀의 연락처 정보를 언급한 것 같은가?

(a) Mr. Henderson이 잠재적인 개인 교육 일정을 잡을 수 있게 하기 위해서
(b) Mr. Henderson이 그 시스템에 대해 부서장들에게 물어볼 수 있게 하기 위해서
(c) 단체 회의를 위한 일정을 공유하기 위해서
(d) 교육 참가자들의 점심 주문을 받기 위해서

지텔프 치트키

질문의 키워드 her contact information과 관련된 이메일 주소 주변 내용을 주의 깊게 읽는다.

해설 | 5단락의 'contact me by email ~ and we can arrange a private meeting, preferably before July 12'에서 Ms. Stewart가 자신의 이메일로 연락하면 가급적 7월 12일 전에 개인적인 회의를 마련해줄 수 있다고 한 것을 통해, Mr. Henderson이 잠재적인 개인 교육 일정을 잡을 수 있게 하기 위해서 편지에 그녀의 연락처 정보를 언급한 것임을 추론할 수 있다. 따라서 (a)가 정답이다.

Paraphrasing
a private meeting 개인적인 회의 → a ~ individual training 개인 교육

어휘 | potential adj. 잠재적인, 일어날 수 있는

79 어휘 유의어

난이도 ●●○

In the context of the passage, announced means _______.

(a) authorized
(b) declared
(c) discussed
(d) divulged

지문의 문맥에서 'announced'는 -을 의미한다.

(a) 승인했다
(b) 공표했다
(c) 논의했다
(d) 누설했다

지텔프 치트키

밑줄 친 어휘의 유의어를 찾는 문제이므로, announced가 포함된 구절을 읽고 문맥을 파악한다.

해설 | 1단락의 'we announced the implementation of the Total Management System (TMS)'은 종합 관리 시스템(TMS)의 시행을 발표했다는 뜻이므로, announced가 '발표했다'라는 의미로 사용된 것을 알 수 있다. 따라서 '공표했다'라는 비슷한 의미의 (b) declared가 정답이다.

오답분석

(d) '누설하다'라는 의미의 divulge는 사사로운 일이나 비밀 등을 남에게 폭로하는 경우에 사용하므로, 어떠한 정보를 공개적으로 발표한다는 문맥에 어울리지 않아 오답이다.

80 어휘 유의어

난이도 ●●○

In the context of the passage, <u>equip</u> means _______.

(a) provide
(b) position
(c) award
(d) entreat

지문의 문맥에서 'equip'은 -을 의미한다.

(a) 제공하다
(b) 배치하다
(c) 수여하다
(d) 간청하다

지텔프 치트키

밑줄 친 어휘의 유의어를 찾는 문제이므로, equip이 포함된 구절을 읽고 문맥을 파악한다.

해설 | 5단락의 'will equip you with the knowledge to cope with any TMS inquiry'는 어떠한 TMS 질문에도 대처할 수 있는 지식을 갖추게 할 것이라는 뜻이므로, equip이 '갖추게 하다'라는 의미로 사용된 것을 알 수 있다. 따라서 '제공하다'라는 비슷한 의미의 (a) provide가 정답이다.

09회 실전모의고사

문제집 p.68

정답 및 문제 유형 분석표

PART 1		PART 2		PART 3		PART 4	
53	(c) 특정세부사항	60	(d) 특정세부사항	67	(a) 특정세부사항	74	(b) 주제/목적
54	(b) 추론	61	(b) 특정세부사항	68	(d) 특정세부사항	75	(d) 특정세부사항
55	(a) 특정세부사항	62	(d) 특정세부사항	69	(d) 특정세부사항	76	(c) 특정세부사항
56	(b) 추론	63	(a) 특정세부사항	70	(b) 추론	77	(b) 특정세부사항
57	(c) 특정세부사항	64	(b) 추론	71	(c) 특정세부사항	78	(c) 특정세부사항
58	(b) 어휘	65	(d) 어휘	72	(c) 어휘	79	(b) 어휘
59	(a) 어휘	66	(a) 어휘	73	(a) 어휘	80	(d) 어휘

취약 유형 분석표

유형	맞힌 개수
주제/목적	/1
특정세부사항	/15
Not/True	0
추론	/4
어휘	/8
TOTAL	28

PART 1 (53~59) Biography Article 서스펜스 영화의 대가 앨프리드 히치콕

인물 이름

ALFRED HITCHCOCK

인물 소개

Alfred Hitchcock, known as the "Master of Suspense," was a prolific British movie director who became one of the most influential and widely studied filmmakers in cinema history.

어린 시절 + 업적 시작 계기

Alfred Joseph Hitchcock was born on August 13, 1899, in Leytonstone, England. He grew up in a strict household under the watchful eyes of a devoted mother and an oppressive father. As a youth, Hitchcock spent a lot of time alone and learned to entertain himself. He was creative, and [58]to satisfy his impulses, he later studied art at university. In 1920, [53]he found an entry-level job designing title cards for silent films, which introduced him to moviemaking.

데뷔 + 초기 업적

In 1925, Hitchcock made his directorial debut with *The Pleasure Garden*, a silent drama film. [54]However, as it was unlike the movies for which he is now admired, film enthusiasts acknowledge the 1927 thriller *The Lodger: A Story of the London Fog* as his first real work. By the time Hitchcock concluded his first talking film, *Blackmail*, in 1929, he had a wealth of experience in visual storytelling and every aspect of production.

Over the next decade, [59]Hitchcock developed his craft, producing mainly suspenseful thrillers. Following the

앨프리드 히치콕

'서스펜스의 대가'로 알려져 있는 앨프리드 히치콕은 영화 역사상 가장 영향력 있고 널리 연구된 영화 제작자 중 한 명이 된 다작하는 영국 영화감독이다.

앨프리드 조지프 히치콕은 1899년 8월 13일에 영국의 레이턴스톤에서 태어났다. 그는 헌신적인 어머니와 억압적인 아버지가 예의 주시하는 엄한 가정에서 자랐다. 어렸을 때, 히치콕은 많은 시간을 혼자 보냈고 스스로를 즐겁게 하는 법을 배웠다. 그는 창의적이었으며, [58]그의 욕구를 만족시키기 위해, 후에 대학에서 미술을 공부했다. 1920년에, [53]그는 무성 영화의 타이틀 카드를 디자인하는 말단의 일자리를 구했고, 이것은 그에게 영화 제작을 처음으로 접하게 했다.

1925년에, 히치콕은 무성 극영화인 「프리주어 가든」으로 감독 데뷔를 했다. [54]하지만, 이것은 그가 현재 그것들 덕분에 존경받고 있는 영화들과는 달랐기 때문에, 영화 애호가들은 1927년 스릴러물 「하숙인: 런던의 안개 이야기」를 그의 사실상의 첫 번째 작품으로 인정한다. 1929년에 히치콕이 그의 첫 번째 유성 영화 「협박」을 마무리했을 즈음에, 그는 시각적 스토리텔링과 제작의 모든 측면에서 풍부한 경험을 가지고 있었다.

그 후 10년 동안, [59]히치콕은 주로 긴장감 넘치는 스릴러를 제작하면서 자신의 기술을 발전시켰다. 「나는 비밀을 알고 있다」와 「39 계단」의 국제적인 개봉에 이

주요 업적1	international releases of *The Man Who Knew Too Much* and *The 39 Steps*, [55]he drew the attention of noted film producer David O. Selznick, who invited him to Hollywood.	어, [55]그는 유명한 영화 제작자 데이비드 O. 셀즈닉의 관심을 끌었고, 셀즈닉은 그를 할리우드에 초대했다.
주요 업적2 + 예시	During this time, [56]Hitchcock popularized a plot device known as the "MacGuffin," an element that is indispensable to the beginning of a film's plot and the motivation of the protagonist but meaningless to the overall story. A famous example of a MacGuffin is the money the character Marion Crane steals at the start of the movie *Psycho*, which is the reason she finds herself at the Bates Motel, the story's setting. However, this fortune soon becomes insignificant when Crane gets murdered and the money sinks to the bottom of a swamp.	이 시기 동안, [56]히치콕은 '맥거핀'으로 알려져 있는 구성 장치를 대중화시켰는데, 이것은 영화 줄거리의 시작 부분과 주인공의 동기 부여에는 필수적이지만 전반적인 이야기에 중요하지 않은 요소이다. 맥거핀의 한 유명한 예는 영화 「싸이코」의 도입 부분에서 등장인물인 마리온 크레인이 훔치는 돈으로, 이것은 그녀가 이야기의 배경인 베이츠 모텔에 있게 되는 이유이다. 그러나, 크레인이 살해되고 돈이 늪의 바닥으로 가라앉으면서 이 재산은 곧 무의미해진다.
말년 + 죽음	Hitchcock directed over 50 feature films in total. [57]He remains a familiar face to this day thanks to his enjoyment of making cameos in his films, a habit that endeared him to fans. Near the end of his life, Hitchcock was working on the script for a film called *The Short Night*, but it was never filmed. He died of kidney failure on April 29, 1980, at his home in Los Angeles.	히치콕은 총 50편이 넘는 장편 극영화를 감독했다. [57]그가 자신의 영화에 카메오로 출연하는 것을 즐긴 덕에 그는 오늘날까지 친숙한 얼굴로 남아 있는데, 이는 그가 팬들에게 사랑받게 하는 습관이었다. 그의 생애가 끝날 무렵, 히치콕은 「짧은 밤」이라는 이름의 영화 대본을 쓰고 있었지만, 조금도 촬영되지는 않았다. 그는 1980년 4월 29일에 로스앤젤레스의 자택에서 신장병으로 사망했다.

어휘 | suspense n. 서스펜스, 긴장감 prolific adj. 다작하는 strict adj. 엄한 household n. 가정 watchful adj. 예의 주시하는 devoted adj. 헌신적인 oppressive adj. 억압적인 impulse n. 욕구, 충동 entry-level adj. 말단인, 초보적인 title card phr. 타이틀 카드(영화 속에서 설명을 삽입한 화면) silent film phr. 무성 영화 introduce v. 처음으로 접하게 하다 directorial adj. 감독의 admire v. 존경하다 acknowledge v. 인정하다 talking film phr. 유성 영화 suspenseful adj. 긴장감 넘치는 popularize v. 대중화시키다, 보급하다 plot n. (소설·영화 등의) 구성, 줄거리 indispensable adj. 필수적인, 없어서는 안 될 motivation n. 동기 부여 protagonist n. 주인공 meaningless adj. 중요하지 않은 setting n. 배경, 설정 fortune n. 재산, 거금 insignificant adj. 무의미한, 하찮은 get murdered phr. 살해되다 sink v. 가라앉다 swamp n. 늪 feature film phr. 장편 극영화 make a cameo phr. 카메오로 출연하다 endear v. 사랑받게 하다 kidney failure phr. 신장병

53 특정세부사항 How

난이도 ●●○

How did Hitchcock first become exposed to moviemaking?

(a) by majoring in film studies in college
(b) by watching movies with his parents
(c) by taking a small job in the film industry
(d) by studying art with a well-known director

어떻게 히치콕은 처음으로 영화 제작을 접하게 되었는가?

(a) 대학에서 영화학을 전공함으로써
(b) 부모와 함께 영화를 봄으로써
(c) 영화 산업에서 작은 일거리를 맡음으로써
(d) 유명한 감독과 함께 미술을 공부함으로써

지텔프 치트키

질문의 키워드 exposed to moviemaking이 introduced ~ to moviemaking으로 paraphrasing되어 언급된 주변 내용을 주의 깊게 읽는다.

해설 | 2단락의 'he found an entry-level job designing title cards for silent films, which introduced him to moviemaking'에서

히치콕은 무성 영화의 타이틀 카드를 디자인하는 말단의 일자리를 구했고, 이것이 그에게 영화 제작을 처음으로 접하게 했다고 했다. 따라서 (c)가 정답이다.

Paraphrasing

found an entry-level job 말단의 일자리를 구했다 → taking a small job 작은 일거리를 맡음

어휘 | major in phr. ~을 전공하다 industry n. 산업 well-known adj. 유명한

54 추론 특정사실

난이도 ●●○

Why most likely is Hitchcock's 1927 thriller considered to be his first film?

(a) because it was his first talking film
(b) because it showed his esteemed style
(c) because it received much international praise
(d) because it garnered him a fan base

왜 히치콕의 1927년 스릴러물이 그의 첫 번째 영화로 여겨지는 것 같은가?

(a) 그의 첫 번째 유성 영화였기 때문에
(b) 그의 존경받는 스타일을 보여줬기 때문에
(c) 많은 국제적인 찬사를 받았기 때문에
(d) 그에게 팬층을 모아줬기 때문에

지텔프 치트키

질문의 키워드 1927 thriller가 그대로 언급된 주변 내용을 주의 깊게 읽는다.

해설 | 3단락의 'However, as it was unlike the movies for which he is now admired, film enthusiasts acknowledge the 1927 thriller ~ as his first real work.'에서 히치콕이 감독 데뷔를 한 영화인 「프리주어 가든」이 그가 현재 그것들 덕분에 존경받고 있는 영화들과는 달랐기 때문에 영화 애호가들은 히치콕의 1927년 스릴러물을 그의 사실상의 첫 번째 작품으로 인정한다고 한 것을 통해, 1927년 스릴러물은 히치콕의 존경받는 스타일을 보여줬기 때문에 그의 첫 번째 영화로 여겨지는 것임을 추론할 수 있다. 따라서 (b)가 정답이다.

Paraphrasing

admired 존경받는 → esteemed 존경받는

오답분석

(a) 3단락에서 히치콕의 첫 번째 유성 영화는 1929년에 마무리된 「협박」이라고 했으므로 오답이다.

어휘 | esteemed adj. 존경받는, 호평받는 praise n. 찬사, 칭찬 garner v. 모으다 fan base phr. 팬층

55 특정세부사항 What

난이도 ●●○

Based on the article, what made Hitchcock move to Hollywood?

(a) attention from an industry figure
(b) the release of American horror films
(c) the slow pace of the traditional film industry
(d) rejection from movie critics in England

기사에 따르면, 무엇이 히치콕을 할리우드로 진출하게 했는가?

(a) 업계 인사로부터의 관심
(b) 미국 공포 영화의 개봉
(c) 전통 영화 산업의 느린 속도
(d) 영국 영화 평론가들로부터의 거절

지텔프 치트키

질문의 키워드 Hollywood가 그대로 언급된 주변 내용을 주의 깊게 읽는다.

해설 | 4단락의 'he drew the attention of noted film producer ~ who invited him to Hollywood'에서 히치콕이 유명한 영화 제작자

의 관심을 끌었고, 그(데이비드 O. 셀즈닉)가 히치콕을 할리우드에 초대했다고 했다. 따라서 (a)가 정답이다.

Paraphrasing
the attention of noted film producer 유명한 영화 제작자의 관심 → attention from an industry figure 업계 인사로부터의 관심

어휘 | figure n. 인사, 인물 pace n. 속도 rejection n. 거절 critic n. 평론가, 비평가

56 추론 특정사실

난이도 ●●●

What can be said about the money stolen by a character in *Psycho*?

(a) It was Hitchcock's first known use of a MacGuffin.
(b) It had little to do with the actual plot of the film.
(c) It proved its importance at the end of the movie.
(d) It was mentioned often by characters throughout the film.

「싸이코」에서 한 등장인물에 의해 도난당한 돈에 대해 무엇이 말해질 수 있는가?

(a) 히치콕의 최초로 알려진 맥거핀의 사용이었다.
(b) 영화의 실제 줄거리와는 거의 관련이 없었다.
(c) 영화 말미에서 그것의 중요성을 증명했다.
(d) 영화 내내 등장인물들에 의해 자주 언급되었다.

지텔프 치트키

질문의 키워드 money가 그대로 언급된 주변 내용을 주의 깊게 읽는다.

해설 | 5단락의 'Hitchcock popularized a plot device known as the "MacGuffin," an element ~ meaningless to the overall story.'에서 히치콕이 대중화시킨 맥거핀은 영화의 전반적인 이야기에 중요하지 않은 요소라고 한 뒤, 'A famous example of a MacGuffin is the money the character ~ steals at the start of the movie *Psycho*'에서 맥거핀의 한 유명한 예는 영화 「싸이코」의 도입 부분에서 등장인물이 훔치는 돈이라고 했다. 따라서 (b)가 정답이다.

Paraphrasing
meaningless to the overall story 전반적인 이야기에 중요하지 않은 → had little to do with the actual plot 실제 줄거리와는 거의 관련이 없었다

오답분석
(a) 5단락에서 「싸이코」의 등장인물이 훔치는 돈이 맥거핀의 한 유명한 예라고는 했지만, 히치콕의 최초로 알려진 맥거핀의 사용이었는지는 언급되지 않았으므로 오답이다.
(c) 5단락에서 등장인물 마리온 크레인이 살해되고 돈이 늪의 바닥으로 가라앉으면서 이 재산이 무의미해졌다고 했으므로 오답이다.

어휘 | have little to do with phr. ~과 거의 관련이 없다 mention v. 언급하다

57 특정세부사항 What

난이도 ●●○

What has caused people to be familiar with Hitchcock's image?

(a) his work on the screenplay for *The Short Night*
(b) his many interactions with loyal fans
(c) his brief appearances in his own movies
(d) his habit of spending time out in Los Angeles

사람들이 히치콕의 모습에 친숙하도록 만든 것은 무엇인가?

(a) 「짧은 밤」의 영화 대본 작업
(b) 충성스러운 팬들과의 많은 교류
(c) 자신의 영화에서의 짧은 출연
(d) 로스앤젤레스에서 시간을 보내는 습관

지텔프 치트키

질문의 키워드 familiar ~ image가 familiar face로 paraphrasing되어 언급된 주변 내용을 주의 깊게 읽는다.

해설 | 6단락의 'He remains a familiar face to this day thanks to his enjoyment of making cameos in his films'에서 히치콕이 자신의 영화에 카메오로 출연하는 것을 즐긴 덕에 그는 오늘날까지 친숙한 얼굴로 남아 있다고 했다. 따라서 (c)가 정답이다.

Paraphrasing

making cameos in his films 자신의 영화에 카메오로 출연하는 → his brief appearances in his own movies 자신의 영화에서의 짧은 출연

어휘 | screenplay n. 영화 대본, 시나리오 loyal adj. 충성스러운 brief adj. 짧은, 잠시 동안의 appearance n. 출연, 등장

58 어휘 유의어

난이도 ●●○

In the context of the passage, satisfy means ________.

(a) amuse
(b) fulfill
(c) match
(d) verify

지문의 문맥에서, 'satisfy'는 -을 의미한다.

(a) 즐겁게 하다
(b) 충족시키다
(c) 맞추다
(d) 확인하다

지텔프 치트키

밑줄 친 어휘의 유의어를 찾는 문제이므로, satisfy가 포함된 구절을 읽고 문맥을 파악한다.

해설 | 2단락의 'to satisfy his impulses, he ~ studied art at university'는 히치콕이 자신의 욕구를 만족시키기 위해 대학에서 미술을 공부했다는 뜻이므로, satisfy가 '만족시키다'라는 의미로 사용된 것을 알 수 있다. 따라서 '충족시키다'라는 비슷한 의미의 (b) fulfill이 정답이다.

오답분석

(a) '즐겁게 하다'라는 의미의 amuse는 사람을 즐겁게 하거나 웃긴다는 것을 의미하므로, 욕구나 충동을 만족시킨다는 문맥에 어울리지 않아 오답이다.

59 어휘 유의어

난이도 ●○○

In the context of the passage, craft means ________.

(a) skill
(b) scheme
(c) enthusiasm
(d) bottom

지문의 문맥에서, 'craft'는 -을 의미한다.

(a) 기술
(b) 계획
(c) 열정
(d) 토대

지텔프 치트키

밑줄 친 어휘의 유의어를 찾는 문제이므로, craft가 포함된 구절을 읽고 문맥을 파악한다.

해설 | 4단락의 'Hitchcock developed his craft, producing mainly suspenseful thrillers'는 히치콕이 주로 긴장감 넘치는 스릴러를 제작하면서 자신의 기술을 발전시켰다는 뜻이므로, craft가 '기술'이라는 의미로 사용된 것을 알 수 있다. 따라서 '기술'이라는 같은 의미의 (a) skill이 정답이다.

연구 결과

ANIMALS ARE ADAPTING BECAUSE OF CLIMATE CHANGE

연구 소개

A new study in *Trends in Ecology & Evolution* suggests that [60]some animals are physically adapting in response to climate change. This makes it clear that global warming is not just a problem for humans to navigate.

근거

Just like humans, warm-blooded animals must maintain their body temperature within a specific range in order to survive. [61]In warm climates, they must disperse the heat to keep from overheating. Birds do this through their bare beaks and legs, while in mammals, this process occurs primarily through their ears or tails. These body parts are vital for thermoregulation, or the ability to regulate body temperature, because they tend not to be insulated with feathers or fur.

연구 내용

According to the study, these body parts are growing larger as climates are getting increasingly warmer. For instance, the beak size of some Australian parrots has increased as much as 10 percent since 1871, and a slight increase in the tail length of field mice has also been reported. While [65]the documented changes have been negligible so far, one of the researchers, Sara Ryding of Deakin University, says that [62]such growth is worrying because it is happening at a much faster rate than what would normally occur through evolution. [63]She believes that the size of the body parts regulating temperature could only continue to increase in correlation with the changing climate and that, in the future, many animals may look very different than they currently do.

향후 연구 과제

At this point, it is known that animals are adapting in an attempt to survive, but whether they actually will remains to be seen. Apart from [66]affecting how they look, these adaptations could alter them in ways that somehow endanger them or have ecological consequences. For example, it is possible that having a larger beak could change how and what birds are able to eat. [64]Further research is still needed to determine exactly which animals have faced repercussions so far, and the researchers intend to start this investigation by using a 3D scanner to examine various bird specimens from the past century.

동물들이 기후 변화 때문에 적응하고 있다

학술지 「생태와 진화의 경향」의 한 새로운 연구는 [60]일부 동물들이 기후 변화에 대응하여 신체적으로 적응하고 있다고 시사한다. 이것은 지구 온난화가 단지 인간이 다뤄야 할 문제만이 아니라는 것을 분명히 한다.

인간과 다를 바 없이, 온혈 동물들도 생존하기 위해서 특정 범위 내로 그것들의 체온을 유지해야 한다. [61]따뜻한 기후에서, 그것들은 너무 뜨거워지지 않도록 열을 분산시켜야 한다. 새들이 민숭민숭한 그것들의 부리와 다리를 통해 이것을 하는 반면, 포유류에서는, 이 과정이 주로 귀나 꼬리를 통해 일어난다. 이러한 몸통 부위들은 체온 조절, 즉 체온을 조절하는 능력에 필수적인데, 이는 그것들이 깃털이나 털로 단열되지 않는 경향이 있기 때문이다.

이 연구에 따르면, 기후가 점점 더 따뜻해짐에 따라 이러한 몸통 부위들이 더 커지고 있다. 예를 들어, 일부 호주 앵무새의 부리 크기는 1871년 이래로 10퍼센트만큼 증가했으며, 들쥐 꼬리 길이의 약간의 증가 또한 보고되었다. [65]기록된 변화들이 지금까지는 무시해도 될 정도였지만, 연구원들 중 한 명인 디킨 대학의 사라 라이딩은 [62]이와 같은 성장이 진화를 통해 정상적으로 발생하는 것보다 훨씬 더 빠른 속도로 일어나고 있기 때문에 걱정스럽다고 말한다. [63]그녀는 온도를 조절하는 몸통 부위의 크기가 변화하는 기후와의 상관관계 속에서 계속 증가할 수밖에 없으며, 미래에는 많은 동물들이 현재와 매우 다르게 보일지도 모른다고 생각한다.

현시점에서는, 동물들이 생존하기 위한 시도로 적응하고 있다는 것이 알려져 있지만, 그것들이 실제로 살아남을지는 두고 봐야 한다. [66]그것들이 어떻게 보이는지에 영향을 미치는 것 외에도, 이러한 적응은 어떻게 해서든지 그것들을 위험에 빠뜨리는 방식으로 그것들을 변화시키거나 생태학적 결과를 가져올 수 있다. 예를 들어, 더 큰 부리를 갖는 것은 새들이 어떻게 그리고 무엇을 먹을 수 있는지를 바꿀 수 있다. [64]지금까지 정확히 어떤 동물들이 영향에 직면해 왔는지 알아내기 위해서는 여전히 더 많은 연구가 필요하며, 연구원들은 지난 세기의 다양한 조류 표본을 검토하기 위해 3D 스캐너를 사용하여 이 조사를 시작하려고 한다.

어휘 | adapt v. 적응하다 physically adv. 신체적으로 navigate v. 다루다, 항해하다 warm-blooded adj. 온혈의 disperse v. 분산시키다 overheat v. 너무 뜨거워지다 bare adj. 민숭민숭한 beak n. (새의) 부리 mammal n. 포유류 tail n. 꼬리

thermoregulation n. 체온 조절 regulate v. 조절하다 insulate v. 단열하다 feather n. 깃털 fur n. 털 parrot n. 앵무새 rate n. 속도 evolution n. 진화 correlation n. 상관관계 attempt n. 시도 alter v. 변화시키다 endanger v. 위험에 빠뜨리다, 위태롭게 하다 ecological adj. 생태학적인 consequence n. 결과, 영향력 repercussion n. 영향 investigation n. 조사 examine v. 검토하다, 조사하다 specimen n. 표본

60 특정세부사항 How

난이도 ●●○

According to the article, how are some animals responding to climate change?

(a) by improving their natural navigational abilities
(b) by searching for new home environments
(c) by approaching areas where humans reside
(d) by undergoing changes to their bodies

기사에 따르면, 일부 동물들은 기후 변화에 어떻게 대응하고 있는가?

(a) 타고난 항해 능력을 향상시킴으로써
(b) 새로운 서식 환경을 탐색함으로써
(c) 인간이 거주하는 지역에 접근함으로써
(d) 그것들의 신체의 변화를 겪음으로써

지텔프 치트키

질문의 키워드 responding to가 in response to로 paraphrasing되어 언급된 주변 내용을 주의 깊게 읽는다.

해설 | 1단락의 'some animals are physically adapting in response to climate change'에서 일부 동물들이 기후 변화에 대응하여 신체적으로 적응하고 있다고 했다. 따라서 (d)가 정답이다.

Paraphrasing
physically adapting 신체적으로 적응하고 있는 → undergoing changes to ~ bodies 신체의 변화를 겪음

어휘 | natural adj. 타고난, 자연 발생적인 navigational adj. 항해의 approach v. 접근하다 reside v. 거주하다 undergo v. 겪다

61 특정세부사항 What

난이도 ●●○

What do birds do to control their body temperature?

(a) puff out their feathers regularly
(b) release heat through featherless parts
(c) travel to regions with cooler climates
(d) disperse excess warmth through their tails

새들은 체온을 조절하기 위해 무엇을 하는가?

(a) 정기적으로 깃털을 불룩하게 부풀린다
(b) 깃털이 없는 부분을 통해 열을 방출한다
(c) 더 시원한 기후의 지역으로 이동한다
(d) 꼬리를 통해 과잉의 온기를 분산시킨다

지텔프 치트키

질문의 키워드 body temperature가 그대로 언급된 주변 내용을 주의 깊게 읽는다.

해설 | 2단락의 'In warm climates, they must disperse the heat to keep from overheating.'에서 온혈 동물들은 따뜻한 기후에서 너무 뜨거워지지 않도록 열을 분산시켜야 한다고 한 뒤, 'Birds do this through their bare beaks and legs'에서 새들은 민숭민숭한 그것들의 부리와 다리를 통해 이것(열을 분산시키는 것)을 한다고 했다. 따라서 (b)가 정답이다.

Paraphrasing
disperse the heat 열을 분산시키다 → release heat 열을 방출하다
bare beaks and legs 민숭민숭한 부리와 다리 → featherless parts 깃털이 없는 부분

오답분석

(d) 2단락에서 새들은 부리와 다리를 통해 열을 분산시킨다고 했으므로 오답이다.

어휘 | puff out phr. 불룩하게 부풀리다 featherless adj. 깃털이 없는 excess adj. 과잉의, 초과된

62 특정세부사항 Why

난이도 ●●○

Why does Ryding suggest that the documented changes are a concern?

(a) because they have been considerable so far
(b) because they may create serious disadvantages for some species
(c) because they imply that climate change is inevitable
(d) because they are occurring more rapidly than what is natural

라이딩은 왜 기록된 변화들이 걱정거리라고 말하는가?

(a) 지금까지 무시 못 할 정도였기 때문에
(b) 몇몇 종들에게 심각한 불이익을 일으킬 수 있기 때문에
(c) 기후 변화가 불가피하다는 것을 암시하기 때문에
(d) 자연 발생적인 것보다 더 빠르게 일어나고 있기 때문에

지텔프 치트키

질문의 키워드 documented changes가 그대로 언급된 주변 내용을 주의 깊게 읽는다.

해설 | 3단락의 'such growth is worrying because it is happening at a much faster rate than what would normally occur through evolution'에서 이와 같은 동물들의 몸통 부위 성장이 진화를 통해 정상적으로 발생하는 것보다 훨씬 더 빠른 속도로 일어나고 있기 때문에 걱정스럽다고 했다. 따라서 (d)가 정답이다.

Paraphrasing

are a concern 걱정거리이다 → is worrying 걱정스럽다
happening at a much faster rate than what would normally occur through evolution 진화를 통해 정상적으로 발생하는 것보다 훨씬 더 빠른 속도로 일어나는 → occurring more rapidly than what is natural 자연 발생적인 것보다 더 빠르게 일어나는

오답분석

(a) 3단락에서 지금까지 기록된 변화들은 무시해도 될 정도였다고 했으므로 오답이다.

어휘 | considerable adj. 무시 못 할, 상당한 disadvantage n. 불이익 imply v. 암시하다 inevitable adj. 불가피한

63 특정세부사항 What

난이도 ●●○

What does Sara Ryding believe about the connection between climate and the size of certain body parts?

(a) that it will impact the appearance of animals
(b) that it will only be evident in bird species going forward
(c) that it will eventually shrink some body parts
(d) that it could be reversed with temperature drops

사라 라이딩은 기후와 특정한 몸통 부위의 크기 사이의 연관성에 대해 무엇이라고 생각하는가?

(a) 동물의 외형에 영향을 줄 것이라고
(b) 앞으로 조류 종에서만 분명할 것이라고
(c) 결국에 일부 몸통 부위를 작아지게 할 것이라고
(d) 온도 강하로 뒤바뀔 수 있을 것이라고

지텔프 치트키

질문의 키워드 connection이 correlation으로 paraphrasing되어 언급된 주변 내용을 주의 깊게 읽는다.

해설 | 3단락의 'She believes that the size of the body parts ~ increase in correlation with the changing climate and ~ in the future, many animals may look very different than they currently do.'에서 사라 라이딩은 온도를 조절하는 몸통 부위의 크기가 변화하는 기후와의 상관관계 속에서 계속 증가할 수밖에 없으며, 미래에는 많은 동물들이 현재와 매우 다르게 보일지도 모른다고 생각한다고 했다. 따라서 (a)가 정답이다.

Paraphrasing

many animals may look very different than they currently do 많은 동물들이 현재와 매우 다르게 보일지도 모른다 → impact the appearance of animals 동물의 외형에 영향을 주다

오답분석

(c) 3단락에서 사라 라이딩은 온도를 조절하는 신체 부위의 크기가 변화하는 기후와의 상관관계 속에서 계속 증가할 수밖에 없다고 생각한다고 했으므로 오답이다.

어휘 | evident adj. 분명한 shrink v. 작아지게 하다 reverse v. 뒤바꾸다, 반전시키다 drop n. 강하, 낙하

64 추론 특정사실

난이도 ●●○

Why most likely do researchers want to study old bird specimens?

(a) to determine what their eating habits were
(b) to see which birds have changed physically over time
(c) to discover the factors that resulted in their death
(d) to confirm some previous findings on bird physiology

왜 연구원들은 오래된 조류 표본을 연구하기를 원하는 것 같은가?

(a) 그것들의 식습관이 무엇이었는지를 알아내기 위해서
(b) 시간이 지남에 따라 어떤 새들이 신체적으로 변했는지를 알아보기 위해서
(c) 그것들의 죽음을 초래한 요인을 알아내기 위해서
(d) 조류 생리학에 관한 몇몇 이전 연구 결과들을 확증하기 위해서

지텔프 치트키

질문의 키워드 old ~ specimens가 specimens from the past century로 paraphrasing되어 언급된 주변 내용을 주의 깊게 읽는다.

해설 | 4단락의 'Further research is still needed to determine exactly which animals have faced repercussions so far, and the researchers intend to ~ examine various bird specimens from the past century.'에서 지금까지 정확히 어떤 동물들이 영향에 직면해 왔는지 알아내기 위해서는 여전히 더 많은 연구가 필요하며, 연구원들은 지난 세기의 다양한 조류 표본을 검토하기 위해 이 조사를 시작하려고 한다고 했다. 이를 통해, 시간이 지남에 따라 어떤 새들이 신체적으로 변했는지를 알아보기 위해 연구원들이 오래된 조류 표본을 연구하기를 원하는 것임을 추론할 수 있다. 따라서 (b)가 정답이다.

어휘 | confirm v. 확증하다, 확인하다 physiology n. 생리학

65 어휘 유의어

난이도 ●●○

In the context of the passage, negligible means _______.

(a) careless
(b) meager
(c) irresponsible
(d) unimportant

지문의 문맥에서, 'negligible'은 -을 의미한다.

(a) 부주의한
(b) 빈약한
(c) 무책임한
(d) 하찮은

지텔프 치트키

밑줄 친 어휘의 유의어를 찾는 문제이므로, negligible이 포함된 구절을 읽고 문맥을 파악한다.

해설 | 3단락의 'the documented changes have been negligible so far'는 기록된 변화들이 지금까지는 무시해도 될 정도였다는 뜻이므로, negligible이 '무시해도 될 정도의'라는 의미로 사용된 것을 알 수 있다. 따라서 '하찮은'이라는 비슷한 의미의 (d) unimportant가 정답이다.

66 어휘 유의어

난이도 ●○○

In the context of the passage, affecting means ________.

(a) influencing
(b) transferring
(c) simulating
(d) reforming

지문의 문맥에서, 'affecting'은 -을 의미한다.

(a) 영향을 미치는
(b) 옮기는
(c) 흉내 내는
(d) 쇄신하는

지텔프 치트키

밑줄 친 어휘의 유의어를 찾는 문제이므로, affecting이 포함된 구절을 읽고 문맥을 파악한다.

해설 | 4단락의 'affecting how they look'은 그것들(동물들)이 어떻게 보이는지에 영향을 미치는 것이라는 뜻이므로, affecting이 '영향을 미치는'이라는 의미로 사용된 것을 알 수 있다. 따라서 '영향을 미치는'이라는 같은 의미의 (a) influencing이 정답이다.

PART 3 (67~73) Encyclopedia Article 궁도의 기원 및 특징

표제어

ARCHERY

정의

Archery is the practice of shooting an arrow from a bow. [72]It was ubiquitous throughout much of human history and made its Olympic debut as a sport in 1900.

초기 용도

The earliest evidence of archery is a collection of bone and stone arrowheads discovered at Sibudu Cave in South Africa. [67]These artifacts are approximately 70,000 years old and depict that the bow and arrow was used for hunting over an extended time period. The first known instance of its employment as a weapon occurred at [68]a site in Kenya, where a human skull from around 10,000 years ago was found with the remains of a stone-tipped arrow in it.

[69]Archery came to play a vital role in medieval warfare because the bows of that era were capable of regularly punching through the metal protective gear soldiers wore. In much of Asia, the military preferred the

궁도

궁도는 활로 화살을 쏘는 행위이다. [72]그것은 인류 역사의 많은 부분에 걸쳐 어디에나 존재했고 1900년에 스포츠로 올림픽 데뷔를 했다.

궁도의 최초 증거물은 남아프리카의 시부두 동굴에서 발견된 뼈와 돌로 된 화살촉 더미이다. [67]이 인공 유물들은 약 7만 년 전의 것으로 활과 화살이 장기간에 걸친 시간 동안 사냥에 사용되었음을 보여준다. 그것이 무기로 사용된 최초의 사례로 알려진 것은 [68]케냐의 한 유적지에서 나왔는데, 그곳에서 약 1만 년 전의 인간 두개골과 그것에 박힌 돌화살의 잔해가 함께 발견되었다.

[69]궁도는 중세 전쟁에서 필수적인 역할을 하게 되었는데 이는 그 시대의 활이 군인들이 착용하는 금속 보호구를 어김없이 관통하여 구멍을 뚫을 수 있었기 때문이다. 아시아의 많은 지역에서, 군사들은 뼈와 나

중기 용도

composite bow, a short bow constructed using layers of bone and wood. The combination of materials gave it great strength despite its small size. In contrast, Western Europeans used a single piece of wood, usually yew or ash, to create a bow that was powerful because of its great length.

위기 + 부활

By the 16th century, however, the use of archery by the military declined dramatically due to the introduction of guns. Nevertheless, it continued to be practiced as a hobby by a small number of enthusiasts. [70]In the late 18th century, archery underwent a revival among the nobility. Many archery societies were formed, and [70]membership in these was viewed as an indicator of high social status because people from the middle and lower classes were generally excluded.

현황

In modern times, archery has been reborn as a competitive sport, and [73]it has been featured in every Summer Olympics since 1972. Olympic archery is performed exclusively with the compound bow. It utilizes mechanical parts such as a pulley to increase arrow velocity and a sophisticated sight to improve accuracy. However, the inclusion of these components can pose a problem, as [71]they cause it to weigh much more than other types of bow.

무를 수 겹으로 쌓아 만든 짧은 활인 합성 활을 선호했다. 재료들의 조합은 그것의 작은 크기에도 불구하고 큰 힘을 주었다. 대조적으로, 서유럽 사람들은 긴 길이로 인한 강력한 활을 만들기 위해 보통 주목나무나 물푸레나무의 단일 목재 조각을 사용했다.

그러나 16세기에 이르러, 총기의 도입으로 인해 군대에 의한 궁도의 사용이 급격히 줄어들었다. 그럼에도 불구하고, 그것은 소수의 열렬한 지지자들에 의해 취미로 계속 행해졌다. [70]18세기 후반에, 궁도는 귀족 사이에서 부활을 경험했다. 많은 궁도 협회가 형성되었고, [70]이것들에 가입하는 것이 높은 사회적 지위의 지표로 여겨졌는데 이는 중하위 계층의 사람들은 일반적으로 배제되었기 때문이다.

현대에, 궁도는 경기 종목으로 다시 인기를 얻었고, 1972년 이래로 [73]모든 하계 올림픽에 등장해 왔다. 올림픽 궁도는 오로지 콤파운드 활로만 진행된다. 이것은 화살 속도를 높이기 위한 활차와 정확도를 향상시키기 위한 정교한 조준기 같은 기계 부품들을 활용한다. 하지만, 이러한 부품들의 포함은 문제를 야기할 수 있는데, 이는 [71]그것들이 이것(콤파운드 활)을 다른 종류의 활보다 훨씬 더 무겁게 하기 때문이다.

어휘 | arrow n. 화살 bow n. 활 collection n. 더미, 모음 arrowhead n. 화살촉 artifact n. 인공 유물 depict v. 보여주다 extended adj. 장기간에 걸친 employment n. 사용 skull n. 두개골 remains n. 잔해, 유적 medieval adj. 중세의 warfare n. 전쟁 regularly adv. 어김없이 protective gear phr. 보호구 composite adj. 합성의 layer n. 겹, 층 combination n. 조합 decline v. 줄어들다 dramatically adv. 급격히 enthusiast n. 열렬한 지지자 undergo v. 경험하다 revival n. 부활 nobility n. 귀족 indicator n. 지표 status n. 지위 exclude v. 배제하다, 제외하다 reborn v. 다시 인기를 얻다 exclusively adv. 오로지 compound bow phr. 콤파운드 활(활의 양쪽 끝에 도르래 역할을 하는 도구인 활차를 달아 궁수가 적은 힘으로 당길 수 있게 한 활) mechanical adj. 기계의 pulley n. 활차 velocity n. 속도 sophisticated adj. 정교한 sight n. 조준기, 시각 accuracy n. 정확도 component n. 부품, 요소 pose v. 야기하다

67 특정세부사항 What

난이도 ●●○

What was the original use for archery?

(a) a tool for pursuing prey
(b) a way to defend against enemies
(c) a means to damage tough armor
(d) a symbol for displaying wealth

궁도의 원래 용도는 무엇이었는가?

(a) 사냥감 추격을 위한 도구
(b) 적들을 막아내는 방법
(c) 단단한 갑옷에 손상을 입히는 수단
(d) 부를 과시하기 위한 상징

지텔프 치트키

질문의 키워드 original이 earliest로 paraphrasing되어 언급된 주변 내용을 주의 깊게 읽는다.

해설 | 2단락의 'These artifacts ~ depict that the bow and arrow was used for hunting over an extended time period.'에서 이

인공 유물들(궁도의 최초 증거물)은 활과 화살이 장기간에 걸친 시간 동안 사냥에 사용되었음을 보여준다고 했다. 따라서 (a)가 정답이다.

Paraphrasing
hunting 사냥 → pursuing prey 사냥감 추격

오답분석

(b), (c) 궁도가 후에 무기로 사용된 것은 맞지만, 이것이 궁도의 원래 용도였던 것은 아니므로 오답이다.

어휘 | pursue v. 추격하다 prey n. 사냥감, 먹이 defend v. 막아내다, 방어하다 damage v. 손상을 입히다 tough adj. 단단한 armor n. 갑옷

68 특정세부사항 Why

난이도 ●●●

Why is the site in Kenya considered the place where archery was first used as a weapon?

(a) It was home to an ancient group of warriors.
(b) It had a large collection of bows and arrows.
(c) It was filled with the remains of many skulls.
(d) It had evidence of a human dying by an arrow.

왜 케냐의 유적지가 궁도가 무기로서 최초로 사용된 장소로 여겨지는가?

(a) 고대 전사 집단의 고향이었다.
(b) 활과 화살의 큰 더미가 있었다.
(c) 많은 두개골의 잔해로 가득 차 있었다.
(d) 인간이 화살에 맞아 죽은 증거가 있었다.

지텔프 치트키

질문의 키워드 site in Kenya가 그대로 언급된 주변 내용을 주의 깊게 읽는다.

해설 | 2단락의 'a site in Kenya, where a human skull ~ found with the remains of a stone-tipped arrow in it'에서 케냐의 한 유적지에서 인간 두개골과 그것(두개골)에 박힌 돌화살의 잔해가 함께 발견되었다고 했다. 따라서 (d)가 정답이다.

Paraphrasing
first used as a weapon 무기로서 최초로 사용된 → The first ~ instance of its employment as a weapon 무기로서 사용된 최초의 사례
a stone-tipped arrow in it 그것(두개골)에 박힌 돌화살 → evidence of a human dying by an arrow 인간이 화살에 맞아 죽은 증거

오답분석

(c) 2단락에서 케냐의 유적지에서 인간 두개골이 발견되었다고는 했지만, 그곳이 많은 두개골의 잔해로 가득 차 있었는지는 언급되지 않았으므로 오답이다.

어휘 | warrior n. 전사

69 특정세부사항 Why

난이도 ●●○

Based on the passage, why was archery commonly used in medieval military conflicts?

(a) because it had a greatly increased range
(b) because it was made from strong metals
(c) because it had a compact design
(d) because it was able to pierce armor

지문에 따르면, 왜 궁도는 중세의 군사 전투에서 흔히 사용되었는가?

(a) 크게 증가된 사거리를 가졌기 때문에
(b) 강한 금속으로 만들어졌기 때문에
(c) 소형 디자인을 가졌기 때문에
(d) 갑옷을 뚫을 수 있었기 때문에

지텔프 치트키

질문의 키워드 medieval military conflicts가 medieval warfare로 paraphrasing되어 언급된 주변 내용을 주의 깊게 읽는다.

해설 | 3단락의 'Archery came to play a vital role in medieval warfare because the bows ~ punching through the metal protective gear soldiers wore.'에서 궁도가 중세 전쟁에서 필수적인 역할을 하게 되었는데 이는 그 시대의 활이 군인들이 착용하는 금속 보호구를 어김없이 관통하여 구멍을 뚫을 수 있었기 때문이라고 했다. 따라서 (d)가 정답이다.

Paraphrasing

punching through the metal protective gear 금속 보호구를 관통하여 구멍을 뚫는 → pierce armor 갑옷을 뚫다

어휘 | conflict n. 전투, 충돌 compact adj. 소형의, 간편한 pierce v. 뚫다

70 추론 특정사실

난이도 ●●○

Which of the following is probably true about the 18th-century archery societies? (a) They were available to all classes. **(b) They had aristocratic members.** (c) They were restored by the military. (d) They held frequent public competitions.	다음 중 18세기 궁도 협회에 대해 사실인 것은 무엇일 것 같은가? (a) 모든 계층에 이용 가능했다. **(b) 귀족 구성원들이 있었다.** (c) 군대에 의해 복원되었다. (d) 자주 공공 대회를 개최했다.

지텔프 치트키

질문의 키워드 18th-century가 18th century로 언급된 주변 내용을 주의 깊게 읽는다.

해설 | 4단락의 'In the late 18th century, archery underwent a revival among the nobility.'에서 18세기 후반에 궁도가 귀족 사이에서 부활을 경험했다고 했고, 'membership in these was viewed as an indicator of high social status'에서 궁도 협회에 가입하는 것이 높은 사회적 지위의 지표로 여겨졌다고 한 것을 통해, 18세기 궁도 협회에는 귀족 구성원들이 속해 있었을 것임을 추론할 수 있다. 따라서 (b)가 정답이다.

Paraphrasing

the nobility 귀족 → aristocratic members 귀족 구성원들

오답분석

(a) 4단락에서 중하위 계층의 사람들은 일반적으로 궁도 협회 가입에서 배제되었다고 했으므로 오답이다.

(c) 4단락에서 궁도가 귀족 사이에서 부활을 경험했다고 했으므로 오답이다.

어휘 | aristocratic adj. 귀족의 restore v. 복원하다

71 특정세부사항 What

난이도 ●●○

What makes the bow for Olympic archery different from other types of bows? (a) its quick loading of arrows (b) its frequent need for repairs **(c) its relatively greater weight** (d) its expensive electric parts	올림픽 궁도의 활을 다른 종류의 활들과 다르게 만드는 것은 무엇인가? (a) 빠른 화살 장전 (b) 빈번한 수리의 필요성 **(c) 상대적으로 더 무거운 무게** (d) 비싼 전기 부품

지텔프 치트키

질문의 키워드 Olympic archery가 그대로 언급된 주변 내용을 주의 깊게 읽는다.

해설 | 5단락의 'they cause it to weigh much more than other types of bow'에서 그것들(활차와 조준기 같은 기계 부품들)이 올림픽 궁도에서 사용되는 콤파운드 활을 다른 종류의 활보다 훨씬 더 무겁게 한다고 했다. 따라서 (c)가 정답이다.

Paraphrasing
weigh much more 훨씬 더 무겁다 → greater weight 더 무거운 무게

오답분석
(a) 5단락에서 올림픽 궁도의 활이 화살 속도를 높이기 위해 활차를 활용한다고는 했지만, 화살을 빠르게 장전할 수 있는지는 언급되지 않았으므로 오답이다.
(d) 5단락에서 올림픽 궁도의 활이 기계 부품들을 활용한다고는 했지만, 비싼 전기 부품이라는 것은 언급되지 않았으므로 오답이다.

어휘 | relatively adv. 상대적으로

72 어휘 유의어

난이도 ●●○

In the context of the passage, ubiquitous means ________.

(a) existing
(b) continuous
(c) widespread
(d) fashionable

지문의 문맥에서, 'ubiquitous'는 -을 의미한다.

(a) 현존하는
(b) 지속적인
(c) 널리 퍼진
(d) 유행하는

지텔프 치트키

밑줄 친 어휘의 유의어를 찾는 문제이므로, ubiquitous가 포함된 구절을 읽고 문맥을 파악한다.

해설 | 1단락의 'It was ubiquitous throughout much of human history'는 궁도가 인류 역사의 많은 부분에 걸쳐 어디에나 존재했다는 뜻이므로, ubiquitous가 '어디에나 존재하는'이라는 의미로 사용된 것을 알 수 있다. 따라서 '널리 퍼진'이라는 비슷한 의미의 (c) widespread가 정답이다.

73 어휘 유의어

난이도 ●●○

In the context of the passage, featured means ________.

(a) presented
(b) treated
(c) favored
(d) described

지문의 문맥에서, 'featured'는 -을 의미한다.

(a) 등장한
(b) 취급된
(c) 선호된
(d) 묘사된

지텔프 치트키

밑줄 친 어휘의 유의어를 찾는 문제이므로, featured가 포함된 구절을 읽고 문맥을 파악한다.

해설 | 5단락의 'it has been featured in every Summer Olympics'는 궁도가 모든 하계 올림픽에 등장해 왔다는 뜻이므로, featured가 '등장한'이라는 의미로 사용된 것을 알 수 있다. 따라서 '등장한'이라는 같은 의미의 (a) presented가 정답이다.

수신인 정보

John White
Hiring Manager
Easy Learning

Dear Mr. White,

편지의 목적: 지원자 추천

[74]It is my immense pleasure to endorse Shawn Gardner for employment at Easy Learning. For the last 10 years, I have worked with him **as the education team manager at Tier Leap, an early childhood education company.** [75]In his position as senior content developer, Shawn was responsible for the creation of the company's curriculum, learning products, toys, and award-winning textbooks.

지원자 강점1

As long as I have known him, Shawn has always exhibited tremendous professionalism, routinely going above and beyond the scope of his duties. [79]His tasks were completed on time and to a high level without exception. **He also maintained strong relationships with his peers, who frequently turned to him for advice when they needed a fresh perspective on a project or idea.**

지원자 강점2

Ultimately, [76]his strengths lie in his creativity, attention to detail, and writing ability. Because of these skills, he was chosen as the lead scriptwriter for Tier Leap's TV series. **Thanks in part to Shawn's dedication and craftsmanship, the program currently airs in 10 countries across three continents.** [77]It continues to provide thousands of children around the world with access to entertaining and informative content.

끝인사 + 요청

I am confident Shawn will be a great asset to your company. [80]I sincerely hope that you give his candidacy favorable consideration. [78]If you need any further information, please do not hesitate to email me at nclark@Tierone.com or call me at 818-555-0172. My office hours are from 9 a.m. to 4:30 p.m.

발신인 정보

Sincerely,
Nicole Clark
Manager
Education Team
Tier Leap

John White
인사부장
Easy Learning사

Mr. White께,

[74]Easy Learning사의 채용에 Shawn Gardner를 추천하게 되어 대단히 기쁩니다. 지난 10년 동안, 저는 **유아 교육 회사인 Tier Leap사의 교육팀장으로서** [74]그와 함께 일해 왔습니다. [75]수석 콘텐츠 개발자라는 그의 직책에서, Shawn은 회사의 커리큘럼, 학습용 제품, 장난감, 그리고 상을 받은 교재들의 제작을 담당했습니다.

제가 그를 아는 한, Shawn은 항상 엄청난 전문성을 보여 왔고, 언제나 그의 직무 목표를 넘어섰습니다. [79]그의 업무는 예외 없이 제시간에 그리고 높은 수준으로 완성되었습니다. **그는 또한 그의 동료들과 끈끈한 관계를 유지했으며, 그들은 프로젝트나 아이디어에 대해 신선한 관점이 필요할 때 조언을 구하기 위해 그에게 자주 의지했습니다.**

궁극적으로, [76]그의 강점은 창의력, 세부사항에 대한 주의력, 그리고 글쓰기 능력에 있습니다. 이러한 능력들 때문에, 그는 Tier Leap사의 TV 시리즈를 위한 주요 각본가로 선정되었습니다. **Shawn의 헌신과 장인 정신도 한몫하면서, 그 프로그램은 현재 3개 대륙의 10개 국가에서 방영되고 있습니다.** [77]그것은 전 세계 수천 명의 아이들에게 재미있고 교육적인 콘텐츠에 대한 접근 기회를 계속해서 제공합니다.

저는 Shawn이 귀사에 큰 자산이 될 것이라고 확신합니다. [80]저는 귀사가 그의 지원에 대해 호의적인 고려를 해 주시기를 진심으로 바랍니다. [78]어떤 추가적인 정보라도 필요하시다면, 주저하지 마시고 nclark@Tierone.com으로 이메일을 보내시거나 818-555-0172로 전화해 주십시오. 제 근무 시간은 오전 9시부터 오후 4시 30분까지입니다.

Nicole Clark 드림
팀장
교육팀
Tier Leap사

어휘 | immense adj. 대단한, 엄청난 endorse v. 추천하다, 보증하다 employment n. 채용 position n. 직책, 일자리 award-winning adj. 상을 받은 exhibit v. 보이다 tremendous adj. 엄청난 professionalism n. 전문성 routinely adv. 언제나, 일상적으로 go above and beyond phr. ~을 넘어서다 scope n. 목표, 범위 exception n. 예외 peer n. 동료 turn to phr. ~에게 의지하다 perspective n. 관점 strength n. 강점 scriptwriter n. 각본가, 대본 작가 dedication n. 헌신 craftsmanship n. 장인 정신 air v. 방영되다 continent n. 대륙 access n. 접근 기회 informative adj. 교육적인, 지식을 주는 confident adj. 확신하는 asset n. 자산

74 주제/목적 편지의 목적

난이도 ●○○

What is the main purpose of Nicole Clark's letter?

(a) to publicize newly released children's books
(b) to recommend a colleague for a position
(c) to give an endorsement for learning tools
(d) to offer a work contract to a recent interviewee

Nicole Clark의 편지의 주된 목적은 무엇인가?

(a) 새로 출간된 아동 도서를 홍보하기 위해서
(b) 일자리에 동료를 추천하기 위해서
(c) 학습 도구에 대한 추천을 제공하기 위해서
(d) 최근 면접자에게 근로 계약을 제안하기 위해서

지텔프 치트키

지문의 초반을 주의 깊게 읽고 전체 맥락을 파악한다.

해설 | 1단락의 'It is my immense pleasure to endorse Shawn Gardner for employment at Easy Learning.'에서 Nicole Clark는 Easy Learning사의 채용에 Shawn Gardner를 추천하게 되어 대단히 기쁘다고 한 뒤, 'For the last 10 years, I have worked with him'에서 지난 10년 동안 그와 함께 일해 왔다고 했다. 따라서 (b)가 정답이다.

Paraphrasing
endorse ~ for employment 채용에 추천하다 → recommend ~ for a position 일자리에 추천하다

어휘 | publicize v. 홍보하다 colleague n. 동료 contract n. 계약

75 특정세부사항 What

난이도 ●●○

What did Shawn Gardner do as a content developer at Tier Leap?

(a) He was in charge of hiring education team members.
(b) He won content creator awards.
(c) He defined early childhood learning theories.
(d) He produced Tier Leap's syllabus.

Shawn Gardner는 Tier Leap사에서 콘텐츠 개발자로서 무엇을 했는가?

(a) 교육팀의 팀원들을 고용하는 일을 맡았다.
(b) 콘텐츠 제작자상을 받았다.
(c) 유아기 학습 이론을 정의했다.
(d) Tier Leap사의 강의 요강을 작성했다.

지텔프 치트키

질문의 키워드 content developer가 그대로 언급된 주변 내용을 주의 깊게 읽는다.

해설 | 1단락의 'In his position as senior content developer, Shawn was responsible for the creation of the company's curriculum, ~ and ~ textbooks.'에서 Shawn Gardner가 Tier Leap사의 수석 콘텐츠 개발자라는 직책에서 회사의 커리큘럼 등의 제작을 담당했다고 했다. 따라서 (d)가 정답이다.

Paraphrasing
the creation of the ~ curriculum 커리큘럼의 제작 → produced ~ syllabus 강의 요강을 작성했다

오답분석
(b) 1단락에서 Shawn이 만든 교재가 상을 받았다고는 했지만, 그가 콘텐츠 제작자상을 받았는지는 언급되지 않았으므로 오답이다.

어휘 | in charge of phr. ~을 맡은, 담당하는

76 특정세부사항 What

난이도 ●●○

What was one reason why Shawn was picked to write the TV series scripts?

(a) because he came up with the show's concept
(b) because of his acting experience
(c) because of his strong imagination
(d) because he knows television trends

Shawn이 TV 시리즈 각본을 쓰도록 선택되었던 이유 중 하나는 무엇이었는가?

(a) 그가 프로그램의 콘셉트를 생각해 냈기 때문에
(b) 그의 연기 경험 때문에
(c) 그의 풍부한 상상력 때문에
(d) 그가 텔레비전의 동향을 알고 있기 때문에

지텔프 치트키

질문의 키워드 write ~ scripts와 관련된 scriptwriter가 언급된 주변 내용을 주의 깊게 읽는다.

해설 | 3단락의 'his strengths lie in his creativity, attention to detail, and writing ability'에서 Shawn의 강점은 창의력, 세부사항에 대한 주의력, 그리고 글쓰기 능력에 있다고 한 뒤, 'Because of these skills, he was chosen as the lead scriptwriter for Tier Leap's TV series.'에서 이러한 능력들 때문에 그가 Tier Leap사의 TV 시리즈를 위한 주요 각본가로 선정되었다고 했다. 따라서 (c)가 정답이다.

Paraphrasing
creativity 창의력 → strong imagination 풍부한 상상력

어휘 | come up with phr. ~을 생각해 내다 imagination n. 상상력

77 특정세부사항 How

난이도 ●●○

How does Nicole Clark regard Tier Leap's TV series?

(a) as a program teaching children to write
(b) as an academic show for international viewers
(c) as an educational product for all ages
(d) as a talk show for the national audience

Nicole Clark는 Tier Leap사의 TV 시리즈를 어떻게 생각하는가?

(a) 아이들에게 글을 쓰는 것을 가르치는 프로그램으로
(b) 국제적인 시청자들을 위한 학구적인 프로그램으로
(c) 모든 연령대를 위한 교육적인 상품으로
(d) 국내 시청자를 위한 토크 쇼로

지텔프 치트키

질문의 키워드 Tier Leap's TV series가 그대로 언급된 주변 내용을 주의 깊게 읽는다.

해설 | 3단락의 'It continues to provide thousands of children around the world with access to entertaining and informative content.'에서 Tier Leap사의 TV 시리즈는 전 세계 수천 명의 아이들에게 재미있고 교육적인 콘텐츠에 대한 접근 기회를 계속해서 제공한다고 했다. 따라서 (b)가 정답이다.

Paraphrasing
around the world 전 세계의 → international 국제적인
informative content 교육적인 콘텐츠 → academic show 학구적인 프로그램

오답분석
(c) 3단락에서 Tier Leap사의 프로그램이 모든 연령대가 아니라 아이들을 위한 콘텐츠를 제공한다고 했으므로 오답이다.
(d) 3단락에서 Tier Leap사의 프로그램이 3개 대륙의 10개 국가에서 방영된다고 했으므로 국내 시청자를 위한 쇼가 아니고, 프로그램의 형식이 토크 쇼라는 것도 언급되지 않았으므로 오답이다.

어휘 | academic adj. 학구적인 audience n. 시청자

78 특정세부사항 How

난이도 ●○○

Based on the letter, how can Mr. White get more information about Shawn Gardner?

(a) by contacting educational TV broadcasts
(b) by writing an email to Shawn Gardner
(c) by calling Nicole Clark during work hours
(d) by stopping by the Tier Leap company

편지에 따르면, Mr. White는 Shawn Gardner에 대한 더 많은 정보를 어떻게 얻을 수 있는가?

(a) 교육 TV 방송에 연락함으로써
(b) Shawn Gardner에게 이메일을 보냄으로써
(c) 근무 시간에 Nicole Clark에게 전화함으로써
(d) Tier Leap사에 잠깐 방문함으로써

지텔프 치트키

질문의 키워드 more information이 further information으로 paraphrasing되어 언급된 주변 내용을 주의 깊게 읽는다.

해설 | 4단락의 'If you need any further information, ~ call me at 818-555-0172.'에서 Nicole Clark가 Mr. White에게 어떤 추가적인 정보라도 필요하다면 자신에게 전화해 달라고 한 뒤, 'My office hours are ~ to 4:30 p.m.'에서 자신의 근무 시간을 알려주었다. 따라서 (c)가 정답이다.

Paraphrasing
office hours 근무 시간 → work hours 근무 시간

어휘 | broadcast n. 방송 stop by phr. ~에 잠깐 방문하다

79 어휘 유의어

난이도 ●○○

In the context of the passage, completed means _______.

(a) performed
(b) finished
(c) submitted
(d) stopped

지문의 문맥에서, 'completed'는 -을 의미한다.

(a) 수행되었다
(b) 완성되었다
(c) 제출되었다
(d) 중단되었다

지텔프 치트키

밑줄 친 어휘의 유의어를 찾는 문제이므로, completed가 포함된 구절을 읽고 문맥을 파악한다.

해설 | 2단락의 'His tasks were completed on time and to a high level without exception.'은 Shawn Gardner의 업무가 예외 없이 제시간에 그리고 높은 수준으로 완성되었다는 뜻이므로, completed가 '완성되었다'라는 의미로 사용된 것을 알 수 있다. 따라서 '완성되었다'라는 같은 의미의 (b) finished가 정답이다.

80 어휘 유의어

난이도 ●●●

In the context of the passage, candidacy means _______.

(a) expertise
(b) election
(c) admission
(d) application

지문의 문맥에서, 'candidacy'는 -을 의미한다.

(a) 전문 지식
(b) 선출
(c) 입장
(d) 지원

지텔프 치트키

밑줄 친 어휘의 유의어를 찾는 문제이므로, candidacy가 포함된 구절을 읽고 문맥을 파악한다.

해설 | 4단락의 'I sincerely hope that you give his candidacy favorable consideration.'은 Shawn Gardner의 지원에 대해 호의적인 고려를 해 주기를 진심으로 바란다는 뜻이므로, candidacy가 '지원'이라는 의미로 사용된 것을 알 수 있다. 따라서 '지원'이라는 같은 의미의 (d) application이 정답이다.

10회 실전모의고사

문제집 p.76

정답 및 문제 유형 분석표

PART 1		PART 2		PART 3		PART 4	
53	(d) 특정세부사항	60	(b) 특정세부사항	67	(d) 특정세부사항	74	(d) 주제/목적
54	(c) 특정세부사항	61	(d) 특정세부사항	68	(b) 특정세부사항	75	(a) 특정세부사항
55	(c) 추론	62	(d) 특정세부사항	69	(a) 추론	76	(c) 특정세부사항
56	(b) 특정세부사항	63	(c) 추론	70	(c) 특정세부사항	77	(b) 추론
57	(b) 특정세부사항	64	(c) 특정세부사항	71	(c) Not/True	78	(b) 특정세부사항
58	(a) 어휘	65	(b) 어휘	72	(d) 어휘	79	(d) 어휘
59	(d) 어휘	66	(a) 어휘	73	(b) 어휘	80	(a) 어휘

취약 유형 분석표

유형	맞힌 개수
주제/목적	/1
특정세부사항	/14
Not/True	/1
추론	/4
어휘	/8
TOTAL	28

PART 1 (53~59) Biography Article 자신의 고통을 예술로 승화한 프리다 칼로

인물 이름

FRIDA KAHLO

인물 소개

53Frida Kahlo was a Mexican painter best known for her colorful and imaginative self-portraits. Her portraits explore themes of pain, identity, and gender while also incorporating Mexican history.

어린 시절

Frida Kahlo was born on July 6, 1907, in Coyoacán, Mexico. Her father Guillermo Kahlo, a photographer, was of German descent, and her mother Matilde Calderón y González was of mixed European and Indigenous heritage. 54Kahlo routinely assisted her father in his studio, where she developed an eye for detail. While she took drawing classes in her youth, 58her interest was in science. So in 1922, she enrolled in the National Preparatory School to study medicine.

전환점

Kahlo would have become a doctor had it not been for a near-fatal bus accident in 1925. Confined to bed for months, she turned to painting self-portraits to pass the time. After she recovered, she met Diego Rivera, a renowned muralist who encouraged her to keep painting, and they started a relationship.

결혼 생활

In August of 1929, they got married. As both of them were artists, they were often competitive with each other, with Kahlo sometimes feeling overshadowed by her husband. 55Rivera's numerous extramarital affairs and

프리다 칼로

53프리다 칼로는 그녀의 다채롭고 창의적인 자화상으로 가장 잘 알려져 있는 멕시코 화가였다. 그녀의 초상화는 고통, 정체성, 그리고 성별과 관련된 주제를 탐구하는 동시에 멕시코의 역사도 포함하고 있다.

프리다 칼로는 멕시코의 코요아칸주에서 1907년 7월 6일에 태어났다. 사진사였던 그녀의 아버지 기예르모 칼로는 독일 혈통이었고, 그녀의 어머니 마틸다 칼데론 이 곤살레스는 유럽과 멕시코 토착 혈통의 혼혈이었다. 54칼로는 일상적으로 아버지의 사진관에서 그를 도왔으며, 그곳에서 그녀는 세부 묘사에 대한 안목을 발달시켰다. 그녀가 어렸을 때 그림 수업을 듣기는 했지만, 58그녀의 관심은 과학에 있었다. 그래서 1922년에, 그녀는 의학을 공부하기 위해 국립 대학 예비 학교에 입학했다.

칼로는 1925년의 거의 죽을 뻔한 버스 사고가 없었더라면 의사가 되었을 것이다. 몇 달 동안 침대에 틀어박혀 있으면서, 그녀는 시간을 보내기 위해 자화상을 그리기 시작했다. 건강이 회복된 후에 그녀는 디에고 리베라를 만났는데, 그는 계속 그림을 그리도록 그녀를 부추겼던 유명한 벽화가였고, 그들은 교제를 시작했다.

1929년 8월, 그들은 결혼했다. 둘 다 예술가였기 때문에 그들은 자주 서로 경쟁했으며, 칼로는 때때로 남편의 그늘에 가려 빛을 보지 못한다고 느꼈다. 55리베라의 다수의 외도와 칼로의 여러 번의 유산이 상황을 더 복잡하게 만들었다.

	Kahlo's multiple miscarriages complicated matters further.
주요 작품	During their relationship, [59]Kahlo created many pieces that conveyed her grief. [56]Her 1932 painting *Henry Ford Hospital* represented her miscarriage, while *The Two Fridas*, finished in 1939 during their divorce, depicted two versions of Kahlo sitting hand in hand: the woman Rivera fell in love with and the one he left with a broken heart. The following year, she completed *Self-Portrait with Cropped Hair*. This piece showed her sitting on a chair in men's clothing, having cut off her long hair, which Rivera had loved. Soon after, in *Self-Portrait with Thorn Necklace and Hummingbird*, she painted herself with thorns around her neck to render her anguish.
말년 + 평가	[57]The final years of her life were dedicated to campaigning for peace and promoting political causes. Kahlo died on July 13, 1954, never having received recognition outside of Mexico. In fact, it was not until the 1970s, when academics commenced publishing books about her, that international interest in her began to develop.

그들의 결혼 관계 동안, [59]칼로는 그녀의 슬픔을 나타내는 많은 작품을 창작했다. [56]그녀의 1932년 작품 「헨리 포드 병원」은 그녀의 유산을 나타냈으며, 그들이 이혼 중이었던 1939년에 완성된 「두 명의 프리다」는 두 모습의 칼로가 서로 손을 잡고 앉아 있는 것을 묘사했는데, 그 두 모습은 리베라가 사랑에 빠진 여성과 그가 실연의 상처를 남기고 떠난 여성이었다. 이듬해에, 그녀는 「짧은 머리의 자화상」을 완성했다. 이 작품은 그녀가 리베라가 사랑했던 자신의 긴 머리를 잘라내고, 남자 옷을 입은 채로 의자에 앉아 있는 모습을 보여주었다. 곧이어, 「가시 목걸이와 벌새가 있는 자화상」에서 그녀는 괴로움을 표현하기 위해 목에 가시를 두른 자신의 모습을 그렸다.

[57]그녀의 말년은 평화를 위한 캠페인을 펼치는 것과 정치적 명분을 알리는 데 바쳐졌다. 칼로는 1954년 7월 13일 사망했으며, 멕시코 밖에서는 어떠한 인정도 받지 못했었다. 사실, 학자들이 그녀에 관한 책을 출판하기 시작한 1970년대가 되어서야 그녀에 대한 국제적인 관심이 커지기 시작했다.

어휘 | imaginative adj. 창의적인 self-portrait n. 자화상 portrait n. 초상화 theme n. 주제 identity n. 정체성 incorporate v. 포함하다 descent n. 혈통 indigenous adj. 토착의, 고유의 heritage n. 혈통, 유산 routinely adv. 일상적으로 eye for phr. ~에 대한 안목 enroll v. 입학하다 preparatory school phr. (대학 진학을 목적으로 한) 대학 예비 학교 fatal adj. 죽음을 초래하는, 치명적인 confine v. 틀어박히게 하다 turn to phr. ~하기 시작하다 recover v. (건강이) 회복되다 renowned adj. 유명한 muralist n. 벽화가 competitive adj. 경쟁하는, 경쟁적인 overshadow v. (~의 그늘에 가려) 빛을 잃게 만들다 extramarital affair phr. 외도 miscarriage n. 유산 complicate v. 복잡하게 만들다 grief n. 슬픔 represent v. 나타내다, 표현하다 divorce n. 이혼 depict v. 묘사하다 thorn n. 가시 render v. 표현하다 anguish n. 괴로움, 비통 dedicate v. 바치다 campaign v. 캠페인을 펼치다 promote v. 알리다, 홍보하다 political adj. 정치적인 recognition n. 인정, 인식 commence v. 시작하다

53 특정세부사항 유명한 이유

난이도 ●●○

What is Frida Kahlo most famous for?

(a) her use of natural materials
(b) her ideas about imagination
(c) her strong Mexican identity
(d) her artistic depictions of herself

프리다 칼로는 무엇으로 가장 유명한가?

(a) 천연 재료의 사용
(b) 상상력에 대한 견해
(c) 강한 멕시코인 정체성
(d) 그녀 자신에 대한 미술적 묘사

지텔프 치트키

질문의 키워드 most famous for가 best known for로 paraphrasing되어 언급된 주변 내용을 주의 깊게 읽는다.

해설 | 1단락의 'Frida Kahlo was ~ best known for her colorful and imaginative self-portraits.'에서 프리다 칼로는 다채롭고 창의적인 자화상으로 가장 잘 알려져 있다고 했다. 따라서 (d)가 정답이다.

Paraphrasing
her ~ self-portraits 그녀의 자화상 → artistic depictions of herself 그녀 자신에 대한 미술적 묘사

어휘 | material n. 재료, 자재 artistic adj. 미술적인, 예술적인

54 특정세부사항 When

난이도 ●○○

When did Kahlo develop her keen eye?

(a) when she attended university to study medicine
(b) when she studied different drawing techniques
(c) when she helped out at her father's workplace
(d) when she discovered her passion for science

칼로는 언제 예리한 관찰력을 발달시켰는가?

(a) 의학을 공부하기 위해 대학에 다녔을 때
(b) 다양한 그림 기법을 공부했을 때
(c) 아버지의 일터에서 일을 도왔을 때
(d) 과학에 대한 자신의 열정을 발견했을 때

지텔프 치트키

질문의 키워드 keen eye가 eye for detail로 paraphrasing되어 언급된 주변 내용을 주의 깊게 읽는다.

해설 | 2단락의 'Kahlo ~ assisted her father in his studio, where she developed an eye for detail.'에서 칼로는 아버지의 사진관에서 그를 도왔으며, 그곳에서 그녀는 세부 묘사에 대한 안목을 발달시켰다고 했다. 따라서 (c)가 정답이다.

Paraphrasing
assisted her father in his studio 아버지의 사진관에서 그를 도왔다 → helped out at her father's workplace 아버지의 일터에서 일을 도왔다

어휘 | keen adj. 예리한 discover v. 발견하다 passion n. 열정

55 추론 특정사실

난이도 ●●○

What can most likely be said about Kahlo and Rivera's marriage?

(a) It ended because of Kahlo's affair.
(b) It made them less competitive with one another.
(c) It faced many difficulties that made it hard to sustain.
(d) It complicated Rivera's artistic identity.

칼로와 리베라의 결혼에 대해 무엇이 말해질 수 있을 것 같은가?

(a) 칼로의 외도로 인해 끝이 났다.
(b) 그들이 서로에게 덜 경쟁적이게 만들었다.
(c) 그것을 지속하기 어렵게 만든 많은 어려움에 직면했다.
(d) 리베라의 예술적 정체성을 복잡하게 만들었다.

지텔프 치트키

질문의 키워드 marriage가 got married로 paraphrasing되어 언급된 주변 내용을 주의 깊게 읽는다.

해설 | 4단락의 'Rivera's numerous extramarital affairs and Kahlo's multiple miscarriages complicated matters further.'에서 리베라의 다수의 외도와 칼로의 여러 번의 유산이 상황을 더 복잡하게 만들었다고 한 것을 통해, 칼로와 리베라의 결혼이 그것(결혼)을 지속하기 어렵게 만든 많은 어려움에 직면했을 것임을 추론할 수 있다. 따라서 (c)가 정답이다.

어휘 | face v. 직면하다 sustain v. 지속하다, 유지하다

56 특정세부사항 Which

난이도 ●●●

Based on the passage, which characterizes Kahlo's artworks in the 1930s?

(a) They depict interpretations of her personality.
(b) They portray her feelings of emotional distress.
(c) They represent the slow passage of time.
(d) They show the changes in her appearance.

지문에 따르면, 무엇이 1930년대 칼로 작품들을 특징짓는가?

(a) 그녀의 성격에 관한 해석을 묘사한다.
(b) 그녀의 정서적 고통의 감정을 묘사한다.
(c) 느린 시간의 흐름을 표현한다.
(d) 그녀의 외모 변화를 보여준다.

지텔프 치트키

질문의 키워드 1930s와 관련된 주변 내용을 주의 깊게 읽는다.

해설 | 5단락의 'Her 1932 painting *Henry Ford Hospital* represented her miscarriage, while *The Two Fridas*, finished in 1939 during their divorce'에서 칼로의 1932년 작품 「헨리 포드 병원」과 1939년 작품 「두 명의 프리다」는 각각 그녀의 유산과 이혼에 관한 그림이라고 했다. 따라서 (b)가 정답이다.

오답분석

(d) 5단락에서 1939년의 바로 다음 해인 1940년에 완성된 「짧은 머리의 자화상」에서 칼로가 자신의 긴 머리를 잘라내고 남자 옷을 입은 변화된 모습을 보여줬다고 했으므로 오답이다.

어휘 | interpretation n. 해석 personality n. 성격 portray v. 묘사하다 distress n. (정신적) 고통 appearance n. 외모

57 특정세부사항 How

난이도 ●●○

How did Kahlo live out her final years?

(a) by releasing art books internationally
(b) by participating in political activism
(c) by developing other Mexican painters
(d) by devoting herself to medical care

칼로는 자신의 말년을 어떻게 보냈는가?

(a) 국제적으로 미술 서적을 발표함으로써
(b) 정치적 활동에 참여함으로써
(c) 다른 멕시코 화가들을 성장시킴으로써
(d) 의학적 치료에 전념함으로써

지텔프 치트키

질문의 키워드 final years가 그대로 언급된 주변 내용을 주의 깊게 읽는다.

해설 | 6단락의 'The final years of her life were dedicated to ~ promoting political causes.'에서 칼로의 말년이 정치적 명분을 알리는 데 바쳐졌다고 했다. 따라서 (b)가 정답이다.

Paraphrasing
promoting political causes 정치적 명분을 알리는 → participating in political activism 정치적 활동에 참여함

어휘 | release v. 발표하다 devote oneself to phr. ~에 전념하다

58 어휘 유의어

난이도 ●●○

In the context of the passage, interest means ________.

(a) curiosity

지문의 문맥에서, 'interest'는 -을 의미한다.

(a) 호기심

(b) novelty (c) preference (d) confidence	(b) 참신함 (c) 선호 (d) 자신감

지텔프 치트키

밑줄 친 어휘의 유의어를 찾는 문제이므로, interest가 포함된 구절을 읽고 문맥을 파악한다.

해설 | 2단락의 'her interest was in science'는 그녀의 관심은 과학에 있었다는 뜻이므로, 'interest'가 '관심'이라는 의미로 사용된 것을 알 수 있다. 따라서 '호기심'이라는 비슷한 의미의 (a) curiosity가 정답이다.

오답분석

(c) '선호'라는 의미를 가진 preference는 두 개 이상의 비교 대상 중 어떤 것을 더 좋아하거나 원하는 감정을 나타낼 때 쓰이므로, 칼로가 과학에 대해 더 배우거나 알고 싶은 관심이 있었다는 문맥에 어울리지 않아 오답이다.

59 어휘 유의어

난이도 ●●○

In the context of the passage, conveyed means ______. (a) transported (b) conquered (c) dispatched **(d) expressed**	지문의 문맥에서, 'conveyed'는 -을 의미한다. (a) 이동시켰다 (b) 정복했다 (c) 발송했다 **(d) 표현했다**

지텔프 치트키

밑줄 친 어휘의 유의어를 찾는 문제이므로, conveyed가 포함된 구절을 읽고 문맥을 파악한다.

해설 | 5단락의 'Kahlo created many pieces that conveyed her grief'는 칼로가 그녀의 슬픔을 나타내는 많은 작품을 창작했다는 뜻이므로, conveyed가 '나타냈다'라는 의미로 사용된 것을 알 수 있다. 따라서 '표현했다'라는 비슷한 의미의 (d) expressed가 정답이다.

PART 2 [60~66] Magazine Article 실수를 줄어들게 하는 명상의 효과

연구 결과	**60 MEDITATION MAY HELP SHARPEN YOUR FOCUS**	**60 명상이 당신의 집중력을 향상시키는 데 도움이 될 수 있다**
연구 소개	A recent study led by Jeff Lin, a psychologist at Michigan State University, has found that 60 meditation may reduce the number of mistakes that people make. The findings of the study suggest that this is because meditation enhances brain function, changing how we detect and respond to errors.	미시간 주립대학의 심리학자인 제프 린이 이끈 최근 연구는 60 명상이 사람들이 저지르는 실수의 수를 줄일 수 있다는 것을 발견했다. 연구의 결과는 이것은 명상이 우리가 오류를 발견하고 오류에 반응하는 방법을 바꾸면서, 뇌의 기능을 강화하기 때문이라는 것을 시사한다.
	The study focused on open monitoring meditation, also known as choiceless awareness meditation. Unlike other forms of meditation, which can center on a single	이 연구는 무 선택 자각 명상이라고도 알려진, 통찰 명상에 중점을 두었다. 호흡, 소리, 혹은 그냥 방 안에 있는 하나의 물체와 같이 어떤 한 가지에 집중할 수

연구 내용	thing, such as one's breathing, a sound, or simply an object in the room, [61]open monitoring meditation requires practitioners to sit quietly and pay careful attention to everything that is going on in their mind and body. The goal is to cultivate awareness of thoughts and physical sensations as they arise because it is believed that [65]acknowledging them helps people transform bad cognitive and emotional habits over time.
연구 방식	The researchers recruited more than 200 participants with no prior meditation experience for the study. They were connected to an electroencephalography (EEG) machine, which measures electrical activity in the brain, and guided through a 20-minute choiceless awareness meditation session. [62]They were then asked to complete a computerized test designed to distract them and assess their concentration.
실험 결과	Through the use of the EEG, the scientists discovered that [63]a specific neural signal linked to conscious error recognition was stronger in the meditators than in the participants of the control group. The meditators essentially demonstrated [66]a greater ability to identify the mistakes they made on the test shortly after making them. Although the group of meditators did not outperform the control group on the actual test, Lin believes their relatively fast awareness of slipups indicates meditation's influence on brain performance.
한계 + 과제	Though meditation and mindfulness have become increasingly popular in recent years, Lin's research team is one of the few to study the effect these practices have on the brain and its functions. They intend to conduct [64]further research to see if lasting behavioral changes can occur as a result of the influence of meditation on brain activity.

있는 다른 방식의 명상과 달리, [61]통찰 명상은 견습생들에게 조용히 앉아서 그들의 마음과 몸에서 일어나고 있는 모든 것에 세심한 주의를 기울이도록 요구한다. 생각과 신체적 감각이 일어나는 대로 그것들의 자각을 기르는 것이 목표인데, [65]그것들을 인정하는 것이 사람들이 시간이 지남에 따라 나쁜 인지적, 정서적 습관을 바꾸도록 돕는다고 여겨지기 때문이다.

연구원들은 이 연구를 위해 이전의 명상 경험이 없는 200명 이상의 참가자들을 모집했다. 그들은 뇌의 전기 활동을 측정하는 뇌파 검사(EEG) 기계에 연결되었고, 20분간의 무 선택 자각 명상 활동을 안내받았다. [62]그다음에 그들은 그들의 주의를 분산시켜 집중력을 평가하기 위해 설계된 전산화된 시험을 완료할 것을 요청받았다.

뇌파 검사의 사용을 통해, 과학자들은 [63]자각적 오류 인식과 관련된 특정한 신경 신호가 대조군의 참가자들보다 명상을 한 사람들에게서 더 강했다는 것을 발견했다. 명상가들은 기본적으로 그들이 시험에서 실수를 한 직후에 그들이 한 [66]실수를 식별하는 더 대단한 능력을 입증했다. 비록 명상가 집단이 실전 시험에서 대조군보다 더 나은 결과를 내지는 못했지만, 린은 실수에 대한 그들의 비교적 빠른 인식이 뇌의 수행 능력에 대한 명상의 영향력을 나타낸다고 생각한다.

명상과 마음 챙김이 최근 몇 년 동안 점점 더 인기를 얻고 있지만, 린의 연구팀은 이러한 실행이 뇌와 그것의 기능에 미치는 영향을 연구하는 몇 안 되는 연구팀 중 하나이다. 그들은 뇌 활동에 미치는 명상의 영향력에 대한 결과로서 [64]혹시 영구적인 행동의 변화가 일어날 수 있을지를 확인하기 위한 추가적인 연구를 수행할 예정이다.

어휘 | meditation n. 명상 sharpen v. 향상시키다 psychologist n. 심리학자 enhance v. 강화하다, 높이다 detect v. 발견하다 awareness n. 자각, 인식 breathing n. 호흡 practitioner n. 견습생 cultivate v. 기르다, 함양하다 sensation n. 감각, 느낌 arise v. 일어나다, 생기다 acknowledge v. 인정하다 cognitive adj. 인지적인 recruit v. 모집하다 electroencephalography(EEG) n. 뇌파 검사 electrical adj. 전기의 computerized adj. 전산화된 distract v. 주의를 분산시키다, 산만하게 하다 assess v. 평가하다 concentration n. 집중력 specific adj. 특정한 neural adj. 신경의 conscious adj. 자각적인, 의식적인 control group phr. 대조군(동일한 실험에서 실험 요건을 가하지 않는 집단) essentially adv. 기본적으로 demonstrate v. 입증하다 outperform v. 더 나은 결과를 내다, 능가하다 slipup n. 실수 indicate v. 나타내다 mindfulness n. 마음 챙김, 명상 lasting adj. 영구적인 behavioral adj. 행동의

60 특정세부사항 연구의 결과

난이도 ●●○

What did the study find out about meditation's effect?

(a) that it may boost the brain's information processing speed
(b) that it could improve people's accuracy
(c) that it might alter how a person's brain reacts to changes
(d) that it can release chemicals to enhance intelligence

연구는 명상의 효과에 관해 무엇을 알아냈는가?

(a) 뇌의 정보 처리 속도를 올릴 수 있다는 것
(b) 사람들의 정확도를 향상시킬 수 있다는 것
(c) 사람의 뇌가 변화에 반응하는 방법을 바꿀 수 있다는 것
(d) 지능을 높이기 위한 화학 물질을 방출할 수 있다는 것

지텔프 치트키

연구의 결과를 언급하는 제목과 지문의 초반을 주의 깊게 읽는다.

해설 | 기사의 제목 'Meditation may help sharpen your focus'에서 명상이 집중력을 향상시키는 데 도움이 될 수 있다고 했고, 1단락의 'meditation may reduce the number of mistakes that people make'에서 명상이 사람들이 저지르는 실수의 수를 줄일 수 있다고 했다. 따라서 (b)가 정답이다.

Paraphrasing
reduce the number of mistakes that people make 사람들이 저지르는 실수의 수를 줄이다 → improve people's accuracy 사람들의 정확도를 향상시키다

어휘 | boost v. 올리다 processing n. 처리 accuracy n. 정확도 alter v. 바꾸다 chemical n. 화학 물질 intelligence n. 지능

61 특정세부사항 How

난이도 ●●○

How does open monitoring meditation differ from other forms of meditation?

(a) It requires meditators to emit a soft noise.
(b) It makes people pay attention to a single activity.
(c) It includes acknowledging bad habits.
(d) It involves focusing on the full state of oneself.

통찰 명상은 다른 방식의 명상과 어떻게 다른가?

(a) 명상가들에게 은은한 소음을 내도록 요구한다.
(b) 사람들을 한 가지 활동에 집중하게 한다.
(c) 나쁜 습관들을 인정하는 것을 포함한다.
(d) 자신의 모든 상태에 집중하는 것을 수반한다.

지텔프 치트키

질문의 키워드 open monitoring meditation이 그대로 언급된 주변 내용을 주의 깊게 읽는다.

해설 | 2단락의 'open monitoring meditation requires practitioners to ~ pay careful attention to everything that is going on in their mind and body'에서 통찰 명상은 견습생들의 마음과 몸에서 일어나고 있는 모든 것에 세심한 주의를 기울이도록 요구한다고 했다. 따라서 (d)가 정답이다.

Paraphrasing
pay careful attention 세심한 주의를 기울이다 → focusing 집중하는 것
everything that is going on in ~ mind and body 마음과 몸에서 일어나고 있는 모든 것 → full state of oneself 자신의 모든 상태

오답분석
(b) 2단락에서 어떤 한 가지에 집중할 수 있는 명상은 통찰 명상이 아닌 다른 방식의 명상이라고 했으므로 오답이다.

어휘 | differ from phr. ~과 다르다 emit v. (소리를) 내다 noise n. 소음 state n. 상태

62 특정세부사항 How

난이도 ●●○

How did the researchers attempt to measure the participants' ability to concentrate?

(a) by checking them for cognitive disorders with an EEG
(b) by distracting them during the meditation session
(c) by asking them to engage in a test for 20 minutes
(d) by having them take a deliberately diverting exam

연구원들은 참가자들의 집중력을 어떻게 측정하려고 시도했는가?

(a) 뇌파 검사로 인지 장애를 확인함으로써
(b) 명상 시간 동안에 주의를 분산시킴으로써
(c) 20분 동안 시험에 참여하라고 요청함으로써
(d) 의도적으로 주의를 다른 데로 돌리는 시험을 치르게 함으로써

지텔프 치트키

질문의 키워드 ability to concentrate가 concentration으로 paraphrasing되어 언급된 주변 내용을 주의 깊게 읽는다.

해설 | 3단락의 'They were ~ asked to complete a computerized test designed to distract them and assess their concentration.'에서 참가자들이 그들의 주의를 분산시켜 집중력을 평가하기 위해 설계된 전산화된 시험을 완료할 것을 요청받았다고 했다. 따라서 (d)가 정답이다.

Paraphrasing

a ~ test designed to distract 주의를 분산시키도록 설계된 시험 → a deliberately diverting exam 의도적으로 주의를 다른 데로 돌리는 시험

오답분석

(b) 3단락에서 참가자들이 그들의 주의를 분산시키도록 설계된 시험을 완료할 것을 요청받은 것은 20분간의 명상 활동을 한 다음이라고 했으므로 오답이다.
(c) 3단락에서 참가자들이 20분 동안의 참여를 요청받은 것은 시험이 아닌 명상 활동이라고 했으므로 오답이다.

어휘 | disorder n. 장애 engage in phr. ~에 참여하다 deliberately adv. 의도적으로 divert v. (주의·관심을) 다른 데로 돌리다, 전환시키다

63 추론 특정사실

난이도 ●●●

Why most likely did the meditators in the study notice their mistakes promptly?

(a) They made a conscious effort to be as accurate as possible.
(b) They realized that they were being distracted.
(c) They benefited from a more intense cognitive function.
(d) They had higher test results than the other participants.

이 연구에서 명상가들은 왜 자신들의 실수를 즉시 알아챘을 것 같은가?

(a) 가능한 한 정확하기 위해 의식적인 노력을 했다.
(b) 자신들이 산만하다는 것을 알아차렸다.
(c) 더욱 강력한 인지 기능의 도움을 받았다.
(d) 다른 참가자들보다 더 높은 시험 결과를 받았다.

지텔프 치트키

질문의 키워드 notice ~ mistakes가 error recognition으로 paraphrasing되어 언급된 주변 내용을 주의 깊게 읽는다.

해설 | 4단락의 'a specific neural signal linked to conscious error recognition was stronger in the meditators than in the participants of the control group'에서 자각적 오류 인식과 관련된 특정한 신경 신호가 대조군의 참가자들보다 명상을 한 사람들에게서 더 강했다고 한 것을 통해, 더욱 강력한 인지 기능의 도움을 받아 명상가들이 자신들의 실수를 즉시 알아챘을 것임을 추론할 수 있다. 따라서 (c)가 정답이다.

오답분석

(d) 4단락에서 명상가 집단이 실전 시험에서 대조군보다 더 나은 결과를 내지 못했다고 했으므로 오답이다.

어휘 | promptly adv. 즉시 accurate adj. 정확한 benefit from phr. ~의 도움을 받다, ~으로부터 이익을 얻다 intense adj. 강력한

64 특정세부사항 What

난이도 ●●○

What is the goal of Lin's future research on meditation?

(a) to verify the influence of various meditation types
(b) to test the effectiveness of meditation as a therapy
(c) to determine the long-term observable impact of meditation
(d) to define meditation's connection with attentiveness

린의 명상에 관한 미래 연구의 목표는 무엇인가?

(a) 다양한 명상 유형의 영향력을 입증하는 것
(b) 치료법으로서 명상의 유효성을 검증하는 것
(c) 명상의 장기적인 관찰 가능한 영향을 밝히는 것
(d) 주의력과 명상의 연관성을 정의하는 것

지텔프 치트키

질문의 키워드 future research가 further research로 paraphrasing되어 언급된 주변 내용을 주의 깊게 읽는다.

해설 | 5단락의 'further research to see if lasting behavioral changes can occur'에서 명상에 관한 추가적인 연구는 혹시 영구적인 행동의 변화가 일어날 수 있을지를 확인하기 위한 것이라고 했다. 따라서 (c)가 정답이다.

Paraphrasing
lasting behavioral changes 영구적인 행동의 변화 → long-term observable impact 장기적인 관찰 가능한 영향

어휘 | verify v. 입증하다 effectiveness n. 유효성 therapy n. 치료법 determine v. 밝히다 observable adj. 관찰 가능한 impact n. 영향 define v. 정의하다 attentiveness n. 주의력, 조심성

65 어휘 유의어

난이도 ●○○

In the context of the passage, transform means ________.

(a) transmit
(b) change
(c) preserve
(d) transcribe

지문의 문맥에서, 'transform'은 -을 의미한다.

(a) 전송하다
(b) 바꾸다
(c) 지키다
(d) 옮기다

지텔프 치트키

밑줄 친 어휘의 유의어를 찾는 문제이므로, transform이 포함된 구절을 읽고 문맥을 파악한다.

해설 | 2단락의 'acknowledging them helps people transform bad cognitive and emotional habits over time'은 그것들(생각과 신체적 감각)을 인정하는 것이 사람들이 시간이 지남에 따라 나쁜 인지적, 정서적 습관을 바꾸도록 돕는다는 뜻이므로, transform이 '바꾸다'라는 의미로 사용된 것을 알 수 있다. 따라서 '바꾸다'라는 같은 의미의 (b) change가 정답이다.

66 어휘 유의어

난이도 ●●○

In the context of the passage, identify means ________.

(a) recognize
(b) analyze
(c) comprehend
(d) resolve

지문의 문맥에서, 'identify'는 -을 의미한다.

(a) 분간하다
(b) 분석하다
(c) 이해하다
(d) 해결하다

지텔프 치트키

밑줄 친 어휘의 유의어를 찾는 문제이므로, identify가 포함된 구절을 읽고 문맥을 파악한다.

해설 | 4단락의 'a greater ability to identify the mistakes'는 실수를 식별하는 더 대단한 능력이라는 뜻이므로, identify가 '식별하다'라는 의미로 사용된 것을 알 수 있다. 따라서 '분간하다'라는 비슷한 의미의 (a) recognize가 정답이다.

PART 3 (67~73) Encyclopedia Article 바오바브나무의 특징 및 위기

표제어	**BAOBABS**	**바오바브나무**
정의	Baobabs are a group of nine different species of trees native to Madagascar, mainland Africa, and Australia. Found in arid regions, baobabs play a vital ecological role in the ecosystems they inhabit. Studies have shown that [67]a baobab tree maintains soil humidity and prevents erosion, allowing nearby plants to grow more easily.	바오바브나무는 마다가스카르, 아프리카 본토, 그리고 호주 자생의 서로 다른 9가지 종의 나무들로 이루어진 하나의 분류군이다. 건조한 지대에서 발견되는 바오바브나무는 그것들이 서식하는 생태계에서 필수적인 생태학적 역할을 한다. 연구는 [67]바오바브나무가 토양의 습도를 유지하고 침식을 막아서, 주변 식물들이 더 쉽게 자랄 수 있게 한다는 것을 보여주었다.
특징1: 수명 + 크기	Baobabs have an extremely long life span, with the record-holding tree being 2,450 years old when it died in 2011. This makes baobabs some of the oldest-known flowering plants on the planet. Also, [68]baobabs can reach an immense size because they continue to grow throughout their life. One of the largest known individual trees is the Sunland Baobab, which is located in South Africa. It has a height of 22 meters and a trunk diameter of just over 10 meters.	바오바브나무는 매우 긴 수명을 가지고 있는데, 최장 기록을 세운 나무가 2011년에 죽었을 당시 2,450살이었다. 이것은 바오바브나무를 지구상에서 가장 오래된 것으로 알려진 꽃식물 중 일부로 만든다. 또한, [68]바오바브나무는 일생 동안 계속 자라기 때문에 엄청난 크기에 이를 수 있다. 가장 거대하다고 알려진 나무 개체 중 하나는 선랜드 바오바브나무인데, 남아프리카에 있다. 높이는 22미터이고 몸통의 지름은 10미터를 조금 넘는다.
특징2: 성장 방식	Baobabs utilize a unique method of growth. Similar to the way that other trees sprout new branches, baobabs grow additional stems. These stems join with one another, [72]merging into a ring around the center of the tree, [69]creating a chamber that enables the tree to hold large amounts of water. The baobab is capable of storing up to 120,000 liters of water, which is crucial to surviving periods of drought.	바오바브나무는 독특한 성장 방식을 이용한다. 다른 나무들이 새로운 나뭇가지를 자라게 하는 것과 유사한 방식으로, 바오바브나무는 추가적인 줄기들을 성장시킨다. 이 줄기들은 [72]나무의 중심을 빙 둘러 고리 모양으로 합쳐지면서 서로 결합하고, [69]나무가 많은 양의 물을 수용할 수 있는 공간을 만든다. 바오바브나무는 12만 리터의 물을 비축할 수 있는데, 이것은 가뭄 기간에 살아남기 위해 필수적이다.
특징3: 열매	The fruit produced by these trees is extremely dense in nutrients and can remain edible for up to three years after being harvested. [73]It is rich in fiber and vitamin C, and it contains the largest amount of antioxidants of any fruit. Additionally, the seeds can be a source of vegetable oil for many people, and [70]the oil they produce stimulates collagen growth, leading to it being frequently used in cosmetic products, particularly moisturizers.	이 나무들이 만드는 열매는 영양소가 매우 농후하고 수확된 후 최대 3년까지 먹을 수 있다. [73]이것은 섬유질과 비타민 C가 풍부하고, 모든 과일 중 가장 많은 양의 노화 방지 물질을 함유한다. 게다가, 그 씨앗은 많은 사람들에게 식물성 기름의 공급원이 될 수 있으며, [70]그것들이 생산하는 기름은 콜라겐의 증가를 활발하게 하여 특히 수분 크림과 같은 화장품에 그것이 자주 사용되게 한다.
	Unfortunately, baobab trees throughout the world have been dying off, with many of the largest and	불행히도, 세계 곳곳에 있는 바오바브나무들이 죽어 나가고 있으며, 2005년 이래로 가장 크고 [71(d)]가장

현황 + 위기	71(d)longest-lived trees expiring **since** 2005. 71(c)Scientists are currently unsure why this is happening **as** 71(a)the dead trees showed no signs of disease. **Researchers hypothesize that** 71(b)the mass death of these trees is related to the rise in global temperatures.	오래된 나무들 대부분이 죽고 있다. 71(c)과학자들은 현재 왜 이러한 일이 발생하고 있는지 확신하지 못하는데, **이는** 71(a)죽은 나무들이 질병의 징후를 보이지 않았기 **때문이다. 연구원들은** 71(b)이 나무들의 대규모 죽음이 지구 온도의 상승과 관련이 있다**고 가설을 제기한다.**

어휘 | native adj. 자생의, 토종의 arid adj. 건조한, 불모의 vital adj. 필수적인 ecological adj. 생태학적인 inhabit v. 서식하다 soil n. 토양 humidity n. 습도 erosion n. 침식 life span phr. 수명 flowering plant phr. 꽃식물 immense adj. 엄청난 trunk n. 몸통 diameter n. 지름 utilize v. 이용하다, 활용하다 sprout v. 자라게 하다, 싹이 나다 branch n. 나뭇가지 stem n. 줄기 chamber n. 공간, 방 store up phr. 비축하다 crucial adj. 필수적인, 중대한 drought n. 가뭄 dense adj. 농후한 nutrient n. 영양소 edible adj. 먹을 수 있는 harvest v. 수확하다 fiber n. 섬유질 antioxidant n. 노화 방지 물질 seed n. 씨앗 stimulate v. 활발하게 하다 collagen n. 콜라겐(피부나 뼈에서 발견되는 단백질 성분) cosmetic adj. 화장의 moisturizer n. 수분 크림 die off phr. 죽어 나가다 expire v. 죽다, 만료되다 hypothesize v. 가설을 제기하다 mass adj. 대규모의

67 특정세부사항 What

난이도 ●●○

What makes the baobab tree ecologically important?

(a) its tendency to provide extensive shade
(b) its effect on moisture removal
(c) its ability to replace eroded soil
(d) its benefit on other vegetation

무엇이 바오바브나무를 생태학적으로 중요하게 만드는가?

(a) 넓은 그늘을 제공하는 기질
(b) 수분 제거에 미치는 효과
(c) 침식된 토양을 대체하는 능력
(d) 다른 초목에 주는 이익

지텔프 치트키

질문의 키워드 ecologically important가 vital ecological role로 paraphrasing되어 언급된 주변 내용을 주의 깊게 읽는다.

해설 | 1단락의 'a baobab tree maintains soil humidity and prevents erosion, allowing nearby plants to grow more easily'에서 바오바브나무가 토양의 습도를 유지하고 침식을 막아서 주변 식물들이 더 쉽게 자랄 수 있게 한다고 했다. 따라서 (d)가 정답이다.

Paraphrasing
allowing nearby plants to grow more easily 주변 식물들이 더 쉽게 자랄 수 있게 하는 → benefit on other vegetation 다른 초목에 주는 이익

오답분석
(c) 1단락에서 바오바브나무가 토양의 침식을 막는다고는 했지만, 침식된 토양을 대체한다고는 언급되지 않았으므로 오답이다.

어휘 | tendency n. 기질, 경향 shade n. 그늘 moisture n. 수분 removal n. 제거 replace v. 대체하다 vegetation n. 초목, 식물

68 특정세부사항 How

난이도 ●●○

Based on the article, how do baobab trees become extremely large?

(a) by bearing numerous seasonal flowers
(b) by maintaining a lifelong pattern of growth
(c) by utilizing the nutrients in dead trees
(d) by growing rare blossoms at great heights

기사에 따르면, 바오바브나무는 어떻게 매우 커지는가?

(a) 다수의 계절에 따른 꽃을 피움으로써
(b) 평생 동안 성장 패턴을 유지함으로써
(c) 죽은 나무의 영양소를 활용함으로써
(d) 아주 높은 곳에 희귀한 꽃을 자라게 함으로써

지텔프 치트키

질문의 키워드 extremely large가 immense size로 paraphrasing되어 언급된 주변 내용을 주의 깊게 읽는다.

해설 | 2단락의 'baobabs can reach an immense size because they continue to grow throughout their life'에서 바오바브나무는 일생 동안 계속 자라기 때문에 엄청난 크기에 이를 수 있다고 했다. 따라서 (b)가 정답이다.

Paraphrasing
grow throughout ~ life 일생 동안 계속 자라다 → maintaining a lifelong pattern of growth 평생 동안 성장 패턴을 유지함

어휘 | bear v. (꽃을) 피우다 seasonal adj. 계절에 따른 lifelong adj. 평생 동안의 rare adj. 희귀한 blossom n. 꽃 height n. 높은 곳

69 추론 특정사실

난이도 ●●●

Why do baobab trees most likely produce extra stems?

(a) to cope with exceptionally dry periods
(b) to support the weight of the branches
(c) to protect the surrounding trees
(d) to survive infestation by pests

바오바브나무는 왜 추가적인 줄기들을 만들어 내는 것 같은가?

(a) 매우 건조한 기간에 대처하기 위해서
(b) 나뭇가지의 무게를 지탱하기 위해서
(c) 주변 나무들을 보호하기 위해서
(d) 해충의 습격을 견뎌 내기 위해서

지텔프 치트키

질문의 키워드 extra stems가 additional stems로 paraphrasing되어 언급된 주변 내용을 주의 깊게 읽는다.

해설 | 3단락의 'creating a chamber that enables the tree to hold large amounts of water'에서 추가적인 줄기들이 나무가 많은 양의 물을 수용할 수 있는 공간을 만든다고 한 뒤, 'The baobab is capable of storing up ~ water, which is crucial to surviving periods of drought.'에서 바오바브나무가 비축할 수 있는 물은 가뭄 기간에 살아남기 위해 필수적이라고 했다. 이를 통해, 바오바브나무가 매우 건조한 기간에 대처하기 위해서 추가적인 줄기들을 만들어 내는 것임을 추론할 수 있다. 따라서 (a)가 정답이다.

Paraphrasing
periods of drought 가뭄 기간 → exceptionally dry periods 매우 건조한 기간

어휘 | cope with phr. ~에 대처하다 exceptionally adv. 매우, 유난히 infestation n. 습격, 침입 pest n. 해충

70 특정세부사항 What

난이도 ●●○

What is the oil from baobab seeds used for?

(a) producing a range of vitamin C tablets
(b) creating fiber supplements for daily use
(c) making products to relieve dry skin
(d) developing various antioxidant pills

바오바브나무 씨앗의 기름은 무엇에 사용되는가?

(a) 다양한 비타민 C 정을 생산하는 것
(b) 일용의 섬유질 보충제를 만드는 것
(c) 건조한 피부를 완화하기 위한 제품을 만드는 것
(d) 다양한 노화 방지 물질 알약을 개발하는 것

지텔프 치트키

질문의 키워드 oil이 그대로 언급된 주변 내용을 주의 깊게 읽는다.

해설 | 4단락의 'the oil they produce ~ used in cosmetic products, particularly moisturizers'에서 바오바브나무가 생산하는 기름은 특히 수분 크림과 같은 화장품에 사용된다고 했다. 따라서 (c)가 정답이다.

Paraphrasing

moisturizers 수분 크림 → products to relieve dry skin 건조한 피부를 완화하기 위한 제품

어휘 | a range of phr. 다양한 tablet n. 정, 정제 supplement n. 보충제 relieve v. 완화하다 pill n. 알약

71 Not/True Not 문제

난이도 ●●○

Which is not true about the mass die-off of baobab trees?

(a) It involves trees that seemed to be healthy.
(b) It is possibly related to the global warming trend.
(c) It was restrained by scientific intervention.
(d) It also affected some of the oldest specimens.

바오바브나무의 대규모 소멸에 관한 내용으로 사실이 아닌 것은?

(a) 건강해 보였던 나무들을 포함한다.
(b) 아마도 지구 온난화 추세와 관련이 있다.
(c) 과학적 개입으로 인해 억제되었다.
(d) 가장 오래된 표본들 중 몇몇에도 영향을 미쳤다.

지텔프 치트키

질문의 키워드 mass die-off가 mass death로 paraphrasing되어 언급된 주변 내용을 주의 깊게 읽고, 보기의 키워드와 지문 내용을 대조하며 언급되는 것을 하나씩 소거한다.

해설 | (c)는 5단락의 'Scientists are currently unsure why this is happening'에서 과학자들은 현재 왜 이러한 일이 발생하고 있는지 확신하지 못한다고 했고, 바오바브나무의 대규모 소멸이 억제되었다는 내용도 언급되지 않았으므로 지문의 내용과 일치하지 않는다. 따라서 (c)가 정답이다.

오답분석

(a) 보기의 키워드 healthy와 관련된 내용이 언급된 5단락에서 죽은 나무들이 질병의 징후를 보이지 않았다고 언급되었다.
(b) 보기의 키워드 the global warming trend가 the rise in global temperatures로 paraphrasing되어 언급된 5단락에서 바오바브나무의 대규모 죽음이 지구 온도의 상승과 관련이 있다는 가설이 제기된다고 언급되었다.
(d) 보기의 키워드 oldest specimens가 longest-lived trees로 paraphrasing되어 언급된 5단락에서 가장 오래된 나무들 대부분이 죽고 있다고 언급되었다.

어휘 trend n. 추세 restrain v. 억제하다 intervention n. 개입 affect v. 영향을 미치다 specimen n. 표본, 견본

72 어휘 유의어

난이도 ●●○

In the context of the passage, merging means ________.

(a) turning
(b) twisting
(c) weaving
(d) blending

지문의 문맥에서, 'merging'은 -을 의미한다.

(a) 변하는
(b) 비틀리는
(c) 엮는
(d) 섞이는

지텔프 치트키

밑줄 친 어휘의 유의어를 찾는 문제이므로, merging이 포함된 구절을 읽고 문맥을 파악한다.

해설 | 3단락의 'merging into a ring around the center of the tree'는 나무의 중심을 빙 둘러 고리 모양으로 합쳐진다는 뜻이므로, merging이 '합쳐지는'이라는 의미로 사용된 것을 알 수 있다. 따라서 '섞이는'이라는 비슷한 의미의 (d) blending이 정답이다.

73 어휘 유의어 난이도 ●○○

In the context of the passage, rich means _______.

(a) valuable
(b) plentiful
(c) affluent
(d) greasy

지문의 문맥에서, 'rich'는 -을 의미한다.

(a) 귀중한
(b) 풍부한
(c) 부유한
(d) 기름진

지텔프 치트키

밑줄 친 어휘의 유의어를 찾는 문제이므로, rich가 포함된 구절을 읽고 문맥을 파악한다.

해설 | 4단락의 'It is rich in fiber and vitamin C'는 이것(바오바브나무의 열매)이 섬유질과 비타민 C가 풍부하다는 뜻이므로, rich가 '풍부한'이라는 의미로 사용된 것을 알 수 있다. 따라서 '풍부한'이라는 같은 의미의 (b) plentiful이 정답이다.

PART 4(74~80) Business Letter 식량 후원을 요청하는 편지

수신인 정보

Ryan Evans
Principal
Parkside High School

Dear Mr. Evans:

편지의 목적: 후원 요청

Thanks to your participation in our past events, we at The Giving Tree Food Bank could help feed those in need. With this year's holiday season approaching, [74/79]we are once again wholeheartedly asking for your further support in our Winter Food Drive.

후원 의의

As you already know, many of the families in our community often don't have enough to eat, especially at the end of the year. But with your help, the Winter Food Drive can ensure that everyone will have plenty of food to have a safe and happy holiday season. We're confident this event will be a success because [75]last year we received a record number of donations, in large part due to the generous contributions made by the parents, students, and faculty of Parkside High School.

후원 방법 + 주의 사항

As in past years, donations can be left at our facility located at 436 Pepper Avenue. [76]Perishable items must be delivered between our operating hours of 10 a.m. and 4 p.m. so that the food can be properly stored in our refrigerator. All other items can be donated at any time by simply [80]depositing them in the secure "Giving Boxes" located outside our facility. You can donate any nonperishable food, but please note that [77]dented cans

Ryan Evans
교장
Parkside 고등학교

Mr. Evans께:

귀하가 저희의 지난 행사에 참여해 주신 덕분에, 저희 The Giving Tree 식량 은행은 어려움에 처한 분들에게 음식을 제공하는 도움을 줄 수 있었습니다. 올해 연휴 기간이 다가오고 있으므로, [74/79]저희의 겨울 음식 기부 운동에 대한 귀하의 추가 지원을 다시 한번 진심으로 요청드립니다.

이미 알고 계시듯이, 우리 지역사회의 많은 가정은 특히 연말에 먹을 것이 충분하지 않은 경우가 많습니다. 하지만 귀하의 도움이 있다면, 겨울 음식 기부 운동은 모든 사람들이 안전하고 행복한 연휴 기간을 보내는 데 충분한 양의 음식을 먹도록 보장할 수 있습니다. 저희는 이 행사가 성공적일 것이라고 확신하는데, 이는 [75]작년에 Parkside 고등학교의 학부모님들, 학생들, 그리고 교직원분들이 주신 아낌없는 기증 덕분에, 많은 부분에서 기록적인 수의 기부를 받았기 때문입니다.

지난해와 마찬가지로, 기증품을 페퍼가 436번지에 있는 저희 시설에 두실 수 있습니다. 냉장고에 제대로 보관될 수 있도록 [76]상하기 쉬운 물품들은 저희의 운영 시간인 오전 10시에서 오후 4시 사이에 전달되어야 합니다. 기타 모든 물품들은 저희 시설 외부에 위치한 [80]안전한 '기부 상자' 안에 그것들을 놓기만 하면 언제든지 기부될 수 있습니다. 부패하지 않는 어떤 음식도 기부하실 수 있지만, [77]훼손된 통조림에는 해로운 세균이 있을 수 있으므로 받아들여질 수 없다는 것에 주의해 주십시오.

	cannot be accepted because they could contain harmful bacteria.	
끝인사	If you have any questions or need more information about the drive, [78]please do not hesitate to directly reach out to our operations director, Jack Thomas, by phone at (402) 555-1017 or by email at operations@givingtree.org. Once again, we thank you for your continued generosity.	어떠한 문의라도 있으시거나 이 기부 운동에 관해 더 많은 정보가 필요하시다면, [78]주저하지 마시고 운영 책임자인 Jack Thomas에게 전화 (402) 555-1017이나 이메일 operations@givingtree.org로 바로 연락해 주시길 바랍니다. 다시 한번, 귀하의 지속적인 아량에 감사드립니다.
발신인 정보	Respectfully, Elle Richards Outreach Manager The Giving Tree Food Bank	Elle Richards 드림 봉사 활동부장 The Giving Tree 식량 은행

어휘 | principal n. 교장 participation n. 참여 feed v. 음식을 제공하다, 먹이다 in need phr. 어려움에 처한, 궁핍한 approach v. 다가오다 food drive phr. 음식 기부 운동 especially adv. 특히 ensure v. 보장하다 confident adj. 확신하는, 자신감 있는 donation n. 기부, 기증품 generous adj. 아낌없는, 관대한 contribution n. 기증, 기부 faculty n. 교직원 facility n. 시설 perishable adj. 상하기 쉬운, 부패하는 deliver v. 전달하다 operate v. 운영하다 properly adv. 제대로 store v. 보관하다, 저장하다 refrigerator n. 냉장고 secure adj. 안전한 dent v. 훼손하다, 찌그러뜨리다 harmful adj. 해로운 bacteria n. 세균, 박테리아 hesitate v. 주저하다 reach out phr. 연락하다, 접근하다 director n. 책임자, 대표 outreach n. 봉사 활동

74 주제/목적 편지의 목적

난이도 ●○○

Why did Elle Richards write the principal a letter? (a) to send warm wishes for the holiday season (b) to offer food supplies for a school event (c) to explain how a charity program works **(d) to make a request for charitable contributions**	왜 Elle Richards가 교장에게 편지를 썼는가? (a) 연휴 기간을 맞아 훈훈한 안부를 전하기 위해서 (b) 학교 행사를 위한 식량 공급을 제안하기 위해서 (c) 자선 단체 프로그램이 운영되는 방식을 설명하기 위해서 **(d) 자선 기부를 요청하기 위해서**

지텔프 치트키

지문의 초반을 주의 깊게 읽고 전체 맥락을 파악한다.

해설 | 1단락의 'we are ~ asking for your further support in our Winter Food Drive'에서 겨울 음식 기부 운동에 대한 Parkside 고등학교의 추가 지원을 요청한다고 한 뒤, 후원 의의와 후원 방법에 관한 내용이 이어지고 있다. 따라서 (d)가 정답이다.

Paraphrasing

asking for ~ support in ~ Drive 기부 운동에 대한 지원을 요청하는 → make a request for charitable contributions 자선 기부를 요청하다

어휘 | wishes n. 안부 offer v. 제안하다 charity n. 자선 단체 charitable adj. 자선의

75 특정세부사항 What

난이도 ●●○

What happened during the previous Winter Food Drive? **(a) The school community gave an unprecedented amount of aid.**	이전 겨울 음식 기부 운동 동안 무슨 일이 있었는가? **(a) 학교 공동체가 전례 없는 양의 원조를 제공했다.**

(b) The school provided a place to hold the event.
(c) Parkside citizens were unable to claim food donations.
(d) Parkside High School teachers were ineligible to participate.

(b) 학교가 행사를 열기 위한 장소를 제공했다.
(c) Parkside 시민들은 식량 기부를 요구할 수 없었다.
(d) Parkside 고등학교 교사들은 참여할 자격이 없었다.

지텔프 치트키

질문의 키워드인 previous가 last year로 paraphrasing되어 언급된 주변 내용을 주의 깊게 읽는다.

해설 | 2단락의 'last year we received a record number of donations, ~ contributions made by the parents, students, and faculty of Parkside High School'에서 The Giving Tree 식량 은행은 작년에 Parkside 고등학교의 학부모, 학생, 그리고 교직원들이 준 기증 덕분에 기록적인 수의 기부를 받았다고 했다. 따라서 (a)가 정답이다.

Paraphrasing
a record number of donations 기록적인 수의 기부 → an unprecedented amount of aid 전례 없는 양의 원조

어휘 | unprecedented adj. 전례 없는 aid n. 원조 citizen n. 시민 claim v. 요구하다 ineligible adj. 자격이 없는

76 특정세부사항 When

난이도 ●○○

Based on the letter, when can perishable items be donated?

(a) before 10 a.m. on school days
(b) at night in the "Giving Boxes"
(c) during food bank business hours
(d) anytime during the food drive

편지에 따르면, 상하기 쉬운 물품들은 언제 기부될 수 있는가?

(a) 수업이 있는 날 오전 10시 전에
(b) '기부 상자' 안에 밤에
(c) 식량 은행의 업무 시간 동안에
(d) 음식 기부 운동 기간 동안 언제든지

지텔프 치트키

질문의 키워드 perishable items가 그대로 언급된 주변 내용을 주의 깊게 읽는다.

해설 | 3단락의 'Perishable items must be delivered between our operating hours of 10 a.m. and 4 p.m.'에서 상하기 쉬운 물품들은 The Giving Tree 식량 은행의 운영 시간인 오전 10시에서 오후 4시 사이에 전달되어야 한다고 했다. 따라서 (c)가 정답이다.

Paraphrasing
operating hours 운영 시간 → business hours 업무 시간

77 추론 특정사실

난이도 ●●●

What will most likely happen when the canned foods are donated?

(a) They will be disinfected to prevent the spread of bacteria.
(b) They will be closely inspected for any damage.
(c) They will gradually be transferred to the refrigerator.
(d) They will be distributed outside the cafeteria.

통조림 식품이 기부되었을 때 무슨 일이 있을 것 같은가?

(a) 세균의 확산을 막기 위해 소독될 것이다.
(b) 어떠한 손상도 면밀히 점검될 것이다.
(c) 순차적으로 냉장고에 옮겨질 것이다.
(d) 구내식당 밖에서 배급될 것이다.

지텔프 치트키

질문의 키워드 canned foods가 cans로 paraphrasing되어 언급된 주변 내용을 주의 깊게 읽는다.

해설 | 3단락의 'dented cans cannot be accepted because they could contain harmful bacteria'에서 훼손된 통조림에는 해로운 세균이 있을 수 있으므로 받아들여질 수 없다고 한 것을 통해, 통조림 식품이 기부되면 그것이 훼손되었는지 판단하기 위해 어떠한 손상도 면밀히 점검될 것임을 추론할 수 있다. 따라서 (b)가 정답이다.

어휘 | disinfect v. 소독하다 closely adv. 면밀히 inspect v. 점검하다, 검사하다 transfer v. 옮기다 distribute v. 배급하다, 분배하다

78 특정세부사항 What

난이도 ●●○

What does Ms. Richards recommend that Mr. Evans do to learn more about the campaign?

(a) send an email to the outreach manager
(b) get in touch with the head of operations
(c) sign up for an online mailing list
(d) visit the office of Jack Thomas

Ms. Richards는 Mr. Evans가 그 운동에 관해 더 많이 알기 위해 무엇을 할 것을 권장하는가?

(a) 봉사 활동부장에게 이메일을 보낸다
(b) 운영 책임자와 연락을 취한다
(c) 온라인 우편 수신자 명단에 등록한다
(d) Jack Thomas의 사무실에 방문한다

지텔프 치트키

질문의 키워드 learn more가 more information으로 paraphrasing되어 언급된 주변 내용을 주의 깊게 읽는다.

해설 | 4단락의 'please do not hesitate to ~ reach out to our operations director ~ by phone ~ or by email at operations@givingtree.org'에서 주저하지 말고 운영 책임자에게 전화나 이메일로 연락해 달라고 했다. 따라서 (b)가 정답이다.

Paraphrasing

reach out 연락하다 → get in touch 연락을 취하다
operations director 운영 책임자 → head of operations 운영 책임자

오답분석

(a) 4단락에서 봉사 활동부장이 아닌 운영 책임자에게 연락하라고 했으므로 오답이다.
(d) 4단락에서 운영 책임자인 Jack Thomas에게 전화나 이메일로 연락해 달라고는 했지만, 그의 사무실에 방문하라는 내용은 언급되지 않았으므로 오답이다.

79 어휘 유의어

난이도 ●●○

In the context of the passage, <u>wholeheartedly</u> means ________.

(a) gladly
(b) faithfully
(c) hopefully
(d) sincerely

지문의 문맥에서, 'wholeheartedly'는 -을 의미한다.

(a) 기꺼이
(b) 충실히
(c) 희망을 품고
(d) 진심으로

지텔프 치트키

밑줄 친 어휘의 유의어를 찾는 문제이므로, wholeheartedly가 포함된 구절을 읽고 문맥을 파악한다.

해설 | 1단락의 'we are once again wholeheartedly asking for your further support'는 추가 지원을 다시 한번 진심으로 요청한다는 뜻이므로, wholeheartedly가 '진심으로'라는 의미로 사용된 것을 알 수 있다. 따라서 '진심으로'라는 같은 의미의 (d) sincerely가 정답이다.

80 어휘 유의어

난이도 ●●○

In the context of the passage, depositing means _______.

(a) dropping
(b) collecting
(c) hoarding
(d) banking

지문의 문맥에서, 'depositing'은 -을 의미한다.

(a) 내려놓는
(b) 모으는
(c) 비축하는
(d) 예금하는

지텔프 치트키

밑줄 친 어휘의 유의어를 찾는 문제이므로, depositing이 포함된 구절을 읽고 문맥을 파악한다.

해설 | 3단락의 'depositing them in the secure "Giving Boxes"'는 안전한 '기부 상자' 안에 그것들을 놓는다는 뜻이므로, depositing이 '놓는'이라는 의미로 사용된 것을 알 수 있다. 따라서 '내려놓는'이라는 비슷한 의미의 (a) dropping이 정답이다.

MEMO

MEMO

MEMO

해커스 지텔프 LEVEL 2 실전모의고사 독해 10회

초판 3쇄 발행 2023년 5월 15일
초판 1쇄 발행 2022년 4월 29일

지은이	해커스 어학연구소
펴낸곳	㈜해커스 어학연구소
펴낸이	해커스 어학연구소 출판팀

주소	서울특별시 서초구 강남대로61길 23 ㈜해커스 어학연구소
고객센터	02-537-5000
교재 관련 문의	publishing@hackers.com
동영상강의	HackersIngang.com

ISBN	978-89-6542-475-8 (13740)
Serial Number	01-03-01